MeeksHeit Sexuality and Character Education K–12
Abstinence Edition

Linda Meeks
The Ohio State University

Philip Heit
The Ohio State University

Character in Relationships

Dating and Abstinence

Violent Relationships

Reproductive Health

STDs and HIV/AIDS

Marriage and Parenthood

Pregnancy and Childbirth

*Content for Teachers, a Curriculum Guide,
and Lesson Plans with Totally Awesome®
Teaching Strategies and Blackline Masters*

The Winning Combination ...

Meeks Heit Publishing Company and Everyday Learning Corporation

To increase our ability to produce quality product and at the same time provide excellent service to our colleagues and customers, we chose to be acquired by Everyday Learning Corporation, a division of Tribune Education. As a team, we are a winning combination—nationally recognized authors, research-based programs, state-of-the art technology, comprehensive teacher resources, totally awesome® teacher training, personal customer service, and dedicated sales representatives. Please contact Everyday Learning Corporation to place orders and to get our catalog of health education programs.

Linda Meeks and Philip Heit
Co-Authors and Emeritus Professors

Everyday Learning Development Staff

Vice President of Product Development: Anna Belluomini

Production Manager: Elizabeth Gabbard

Credits

Cover Design: Jim Brower

Illustration: Jim Brower, Deborah Rubenstein, Jennifer King

Graphic Design: Elizabeth S. Kim, Deborah Rubenstein, DanniElena Wolfe Hernández

Editors: Sally Meckling, Daniel J. Fawcett, Chad Painter

The authors wish to acknowledge Dr. John Burt for his contributions to previous works on sexuality education.

Teacher Responsibility
Stay Informed on Current Medical Research

The facts included in this Teacher Resource Book were based on information available at the time of publication. These facts are NOT intended to be a substitute for medical advice from a physician. Further, it is the teacher's responsibility to stay informed on the current medical research pertaining to the topics included in this book and to include up-to-date information in lessons (s)he presents to students.

Everyday Learning Corporation

P.O. Box 812960

Chicago, IL 60681

1 2 3 4 5 6 7 8 9 EB 05 04 03 02 01 00

Medical Consultants

Jacqueline Amico, M.D.
Internal Medicine
Westerville, Ohio

Albert Hart, Jr., M.D.
Mid-Ohio OB-GYN, Inc.
Westerville, Ohio

Ann Rogers, M.D.
Pediatrician, Clinical Associate Professor at
   The Ohio State University
Dublin, Ohio

Centers for Disease Control and Prevention Consultant

Brenda Garza
Deputy Chief
Technical Information and
   Communications Branch
Division of HIV/AIDS Prevention
Centers for Disease Control and Prevention
Atlanta, Georgia

National Curriculum Consultant

Susan Wooley, Ph.D., CHES
Executive Director
American School Health Association
Kent, Ohio

National Sexuality and Character Education Consultants

Bill T. Moser, M.S.
Program Specialist for Health and
   Character Education
Winston-Salem/Forsyth County Schools
Winston-Salem, North Carolina

Michael Schaffer, M.A.
Supervisor of Health Education and Wellness
Prince George's County Public Schools
Upper Marlboro, Maryland

Linda Wright, M.A.
Program Director
HIV/AIDS Education Program
District of Columbia Public Schools
Washington, D.C.

Reviewers

Jacqueline R. Benedik, M.S., CHES
Health Instructor
University of Louisiana at Lafayette
Lafayette, Louisiana

Kari L. Berg, M.S.
Assistant Professor of Health Education
Department of Health and Physical Education
Moorhead State University
Moorhead, Minnesota

Donna Breitenstein, Ed.D.
Professor and Coordinator
Director of North Carolina School Health
   Training Center
Boone, North Carolina

W.P. Buckner, H.S.D.
Professor, Department of Health
   and Human Performance
University of Houston
Houston, Texas

Karen Edwards, Ed.D.
Assistant Professor of Health Education
Department of Health Sciences
University of Delaware
Newark, Delaware

Mary Ann Waldrop Felger, M.A.T., M.S.
Health Educator
Fort Wayne Community Schools
Fort Wayne, Indiana

continued on page iv

Tommy Flemming, Ph.D.

Director of Health and Physical Education

Texas Education Agency

Austin, Texas

Elizabeth Gallun, M.A.

Specialist in Comprehensive School Health
    and Physical Education

Maryland State Department of Education

Baltimore, Maryland

Dawn Graff-Haight, Ph.D., CHES

Assistant Professor

Department of Health Studies

Portland State University

Portland, Oregon

Russ Henke, M.Ed.

Coordinator of Health Education

Montgomery County Public Schools

Rockville, Maryland

Dickie Hill, Ph.D.

Professor of Health Education

Department of Exercise Science and Health

Abilene Christian University

Abilene, Texas

Kathleen Hillman, Ph.D.

Professor, Chair of Health Department

East Stroudsberg University

East Stroudsberg, Pennsylvania

Patricia M. Legos, Ed.D., CHES

Professor and Chair of the Department
    of Health Studies

Temple University

Philadelphia, Pennsylvania

Deborah Miller, Ph.D., CHES

Professor and Health Coordinator

College/University of Charleston

Charleston, South Carolina

Terri Mitchell, M.S.

Instructor of Health Education

Appalachian State

Boone, North Carolina

Deborah Ogden, M.A.

Coordinator, Instructional Services

Collier County Public Schools

Naples, Florida

Maria Okeke, Ph.D.

Professor of Health Science

Department of Health and Physical Education

Florida A&M University

East Tallahassee, Florida

Fred Peterson, Ph.D.

Associate Professor

Health Education

University of Texas at Austin

Austin, Texas

John Ray, M.S.

Coordinator of Health and Physical Education

West Virginia Department of Education

Charleston, West Virginia

Michael Tenoshchok, Ed.D.

Supervisor, Health and Physical Education

Cobb County Schools

Marietta, Georgia

Phyliss Thornthwaite, M.S., CHES

Health Consultant

Charleston County School District

Charleston, South Carolina

Deitra Wengert, Ph.D.

Professor of Health Science Department

Towson University

Towson, Maryland

Shae Willis, Ph.D., A.B.D.

Assistant Professor

Northeastern State University

Tahlequah, Oklahoma

Table of Contents

Section 1   **Content for Teachers** *Only*

Chapter 3

Friendship, Dating, and Abstinence

Pages 47–66

Chapter 4

Male Reproductive Health

Pages 67–82

Chapter 5

Female Reproductive Health

Pages 83–106

Section 1 Continued

Chapter 6

Sexually Transmitted Diseases

Pages 107–124

Section 1 Continued

Chapter 7

HIV/AIDS

Pages 125–138

© 2001 Everyday Learning Corporation

Chapter 8

Marriage, Parenthood, and Family Living

Pages 139–170

Chapter 9

Pregnancy and Childbirth

Pages 171–206

Section 2 — The Meeks Heit K–12 Sexuality and Character Education Curriculum Guide

Section  **3** | **Grades K–2 Lesson Plans and Blackline Masters**

Section 4　Grades 3–4 Lesson Plans and Blackline Masters

Section 5 — Grades 5–6 Lesson Plans and Blackline Masters

Section 5 Continued

Section 6 — Grades 7–8 Lesson Plans and Blackline Masters

Section 6 Continued

| Section | **7** | **Grades 9–12 Lesson Plans and Blackline Masters** |

Section 7 Continued

How to Use This Book

Sexuality and Character Education K–12 is a comprehensive teacher resource book that can be used to write or revise and implement a sexuality and character education curriculum: Content for Teachers *Only*, The Meeks Heit K–12 Sexuality and Character Education Curriculum Guide, Grades K–2 Lesson Plans and Blackline Masters, Grades 3–4 Lesson Plans and Blackline Masters, Grades 5–6 Lesson Plans and Blackline Masters, Grades 7–8 Lesson Plans and Blackline Masters, and Grades 9–12 Lesson Plans and Blackline Masters.

Section 1   Content for Teachers *Only*

Section 1 includes ten chapters of Content for Teachers *Only*. Each chapter corresponds to one of the ten content areas in The Meeks Heit K–12 Sexuality and Character Education Curriculum Guide. The content includes up-to-date background information so that teachers will be well-informed and confident. However, the facts that are included are NOT intended to be a substitute for medical advice from a physician. Further, it is the teacher's responsibility to stay informed on the current medical research pertaining to the topics included in the content chapters. The header on every page of Section 1 reads "Section 1 Content for Teachers *Only*" to make it clear that the chapter content is intended to be read by teachers, not by students.

Section 2   The Meeks Heit K–12 Sexuality and Character Education Curriculum Guide

Section 2 includes The Meeks Heit K–12 Sexuality and Character Education Curriculum Guide. The Curriculum Guide is a state-of-the-art, organized, sequential curriculum that facilitates the teaching and evaluation of knowledge, behaviors, attitudes, and skills that promote committed family relationships, good character, and reproductive health. It is an absolute must for school districts that are writing or revising and implementing a sexuality and character education curriculum. The Guide provides a statement of goals and philosophy that includes information on health literacy and The National Health Education Standards. It also includes *The Meeks Heit Umbrella of Sexuality and Character Education* to illustrate and describe the purposes and outcomes of the sexuality and character education curriculum. The Guide includes the Meeks Heit Guidelines for Making Responsible Decisions™ and the Meeks Heit Models for Using Resistance Skills that are used to teach students how to make decisions and resist negative peer pressure. It also describes the format used in the Meeks Heit Lesson Plans with Totally Awesome® Teaching Strategies. The Guide presents Lesson Plans that promote good character as well as Lesson Plans that promote abstinence from sex. It showcases symbols used to indicate that a Lesson Plan might be infused into another area of the curriculum and the symbols used to indicate the kind of health literacy a Lesson Plan promotes. It also explains ways to assess and/or evaluate the life skills, objectives, and The National Health Education Standards for each Lesson Plan.

The Meeks Heit K–12 Sexuality and Character Education Curriculum Guide also includes a Scope and Sequence Chart. The Scope and Sequence Chart serves as a ready-made action plan for implementing the sexuality and character education curriculum. It identifies the life skills and objectives that are appropriate for Grades K–2, Grades 3–4, Grades 5–6, Grades 7–8, and Grades 9–12 and correlates them to The National Health Education Standards. The chart designates the Lesson Plan(s) in this teacher resource book that can be used to master the appropriate life skills, objectives, and The National Health Education Standards identified for the aforementioned grade level groupings.

How to Use This Book Continued

Section 3   Grades K–2 Lesson Plans and Blackline Masters

Section 3 includes Lesson Plans and Blackline Masters that cover the life skills, objectives, and The National Health Education Standards appropriate for Grades K–2. The Blackline Masters may be duplicated and used as student handouts or made into transparencies for classroom use only.

Section 4   Grades 3–4 Lesson Plans and Blackline Masters

Section 4 includes Lesson Plans and Blackline Masters that cover the life skills, objectives, and The National Health Education Standards appropriate for Grades 3–4. The Blackline Masters may be duplicated and used as student handouts or made into transparencies for classroom use only.

Section 5   Grades 5–6 Lesson Plans and Blackline Masters

Section 5 includes Lesson Plans and Blackline Masters that cover the life skills, objectives, and The National Health Education Standards appropriate for Grades 5–6. The Blackline Masters may be duplicated and used as student handouts or made into transparencies for classroom use only. The Lesson Plans and Blackline Masters may also be used with the following student books and videos that are described on the back cover of this teacher resource book.

Student Books for Grades 5–6

Your Body Book: What to Know About Puberty and Human Reproduction

Your Body Book: What to Know About Puberty and Human Reproduction (Abstinence Edition)

Videos for Grades 5–6

Your Body Video: All About Girls, All About Character

Your Body Video: All About Boys, All About Character

Section 6   Grades 7–8 Lesson Plans and Blackline Masters

Section 6 includes Lesson Plans and Blackline Masters that cover the life skills, objectives, and The National Health Education Standards appropriate for Grades 7–8. The Blackline Masters may be duplicated and used as student handouts or made into transparencies for classroom use only. The Lesson Plans and Blackline Masters may also be used with the following student book and multimedia programs that are described on the back cover of this teacher resource book.

Student Book for Grades 7–8

Your Relationships: Choosing Abstinence and Good Character

Multimedia Programs for Teens

Developing Good Character: Guidelines for Making Responsible Decisions™

Abstinence Only: Send a Clear Message

How to Use This Book Continued

Section 7 — Grades 9–12 Lesson Plans and Blackline Masters

Section 7 includes Lesson Plans and Blackline Masters that cover the life skills, objectives, and The National Health Education Standards appropriate for Grades 9–12. The Blackline Masters may be duplicated and used as student handouts or made into transparencies for classroom use only. The Lesson Plans and Blackline Masters may also be used with the following multimedia programs that are described on the back cover of this teacher resource book.

Multimedia Programs for Teens

Developing Good Character: Guidelines for Making Responsible Decisions™

Abstinence Only: Send a Clear Message

Content for Teachers *Only*

Table of Contents

Character in Relationships

Content for Teachers *Only*

A Word from the Authors

The **Sexuality and Character Education Curriculum** is a curriculum that teaches knowledge, behaviors, attitudes, and skills that promote committed family relationships, healthful relationships, good character, healthful sexuality, and reproductive health. Our concept and definition of sex education is more inclusive than other definitions. This is because we believe that healthful sexuality and human reproduction must be taught within a curriculum whose primary purpose is to strengthen family life and personal relationships and build good character. Chapter 1 examines the quality of relationships and discusses ten skills needed for healthful relationships. It highlights the ten responsible values that make up good character and examines how each affects the quality of a person's relationships.

The Quality of Relationships

Relationships are the connections that people have with each other. The quality of a person's relationships affects his or her well-being. **Inspiriting relationships** are relationships that lift the spirit and contribute to a sense of well-being. They are characterized by feelings of being worthy, connected, content, optimistic, energized, passionate, composed, focused, joyful, and a sense of well-being. **Dispiriting relationships** are relationships that depress the spirit and contribute to a lack of well-being. Dispiriting relationships are characterized by feelings of being worthless, alienated, frustrated, hopeless, depressed, bored, anxious, distracted, unhappy, and a lack of well-being. This section of the chapter includes the spirit-relationship continuum and contrasts inspiriting relationships with dispiriting relationships.

The Spirit-Relationship Continuum

Most relationships do not have the extreme effect of being dispiriting or inspiriting. Most relationships exist somewhere in between. The **spirit-relationship continuum** is a continuum that shows the range of relationships with dispiriting relationships at one end and inspiriting relationships at the other end (Table 1.1). The continuum is marked in units ranging from 0 (dispiriting relationships) to 100 (inspiriting relationships). After a careful evaluation, most people state that their relationships fall within the 30–60 range on the spirit-relationship continuum. This indicates that most people could improve the quality of their relationships. This, in turn, would improve their sense of well-being.

Research documents the association between the quality of a person's relationships and the

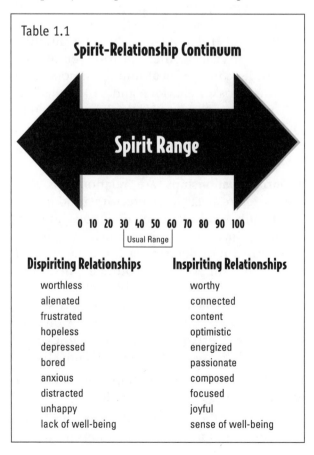

Table 1.1

Spirit-Relationship Continuum

Spirit Range

0 10 20 30 40 50 60 70 80 90 100

Usual Range

Dispiriting Relationships	Inspiriting Relationships
worthless	worthy
alienated	connected
frustrated	content
hopeless	optimistic
depressed	energized
bored	passionate
anxious	composed
distracted	focused
unhappy	joyful
lack of well-being	sense of well-being

person's well-being. For example, one study showed that people who were experiencing stressors were more likely to stay healthy if they had high-quality relationships. They were less likely to develop symptoms of emotional distress (NIMH, 1999).

Other studies showed that people who had high quality relationships were less likely to develop life-threatening illnesses, including heart disease, cancer, circulatory diseases, respiratory diseases, and gastrointestinal conditions. On the other hand, people who were socially isolated were at increased risk for developing illnesses that resulted in death from the aforementioned illnesses (NIH, 1997). It is no wonder that a recent public health campaign in California promoted the following message in the media: "Friends can be good medicine!"

Skills That Promote Healthful Relationships

Healthful relationships are relationships that promote self-respect, encourage productivity and health, and are free of addictions and violence. In healthful relationships, people identify strengths in each other, provide emotional support, encourage healthful behaviors, and discourage risk behaviors and risk situations such as drug abuse and sexual behavior that might result in violence, unintended pregnancy, and/or sexually transmitted diseases including HIV and AIDS.

Harmful relationships are relationships that destroy self-respect, interfere with productivity and health, and include addictions and/or violence. In harmful relationships, people might criticize or demean each other, withhold emotional support, discourage healthful behaviors, and encourage risk behaviors and risk situations such as drug abuse and sexual behavior that might result in violence, unintended pregnancy, and/or sexually transmitted diseases including HIV and AIDS.

A person's ability to develop and maintain healthful relationships is dependent on

- recognizing the difference between healthful relationships and harmful relationships,

- choosing healthful relationships and avoiding harmful relationships,

- developing and practicing skills that promote healthful relationships.

This section of the chapter examines ten skills that promote healthful relationships (Table 1.2).

Table 1.2	**Ten Skills That Promote Healthful Relationships**
Skill 1:	Make family life a priority.
Skill 2:	Show good character.
Skill 3:	Make responsible decisions.
Skill 4:	Resist pressure to do something wrong.
Skill 5:	Correct wrong actions.
Skill 6:	Communicate in healthful ways.
Skill 7:	Resolve conflict without violence.
Skill 8:	Cope without using drugs or other addictive substances or behaviors.
Skill 9:	Choose entertainment that promotes healthful relationships.
Skill 10:	Express affection in appropriate ways.

Skill 1: Make Family Life a Priority

The family offers the first opportunity for a person to learn and practice relationship skills. The effectiveness or ineffectiveness of family relationships often is a predictor of the success a person will have in other relationships. This is why family life must be a priority. A person's actions demonstrate whether or not family life is a priority to him or her.

Suppose a person receives an invitation to attend a favorite sports event that conflicts with an important family celebration, such as the parents' anniversary or a sibling's birthday. The person who chooses to forego the sports event in order to participate in the family celebration demonstrates that family life is a priority to him or her.

A person also might demonstrate that family life is a priority to him or her by participating in family traditions such as birthday and holiday celebrations. He or she might recognize the achievements of other family members. He or she might support the healthful behavior of other family members such as weight loss or adherence to an exercise regimen. Other ways a person might demonstrate that family life is a priority might include

- keeping an album of family photographs,
- attending reunions of extended family members,
- encouraging and maintaining communication with extended family members,
- expressing and showing affection among family members,
- introducing peers, friends, and neighbors to other family members,
- representing or participating with other family members in neighborhood activities,
- inviting family members to attend spectator events such as sports and recreational activities that include peers.

People who interact and discuss health, school, relationship, and employment issues with family members keep family members involved in their lives. They demonstrate an inclusive attitude by acknowledging the thoughts and opinions of other family members. These are ways to make family life a priority. There are other ways to make family life a priority. Family members might seek the advice of more experienced family members. Family members might be emotionally supportive of other family members when they are sensitive to issues that affect family life and practice consideration in family relationships.

The Family Round Table

A family might choose to have a Family Round Table. **The Family Round Table** is a special time when family members meet to discuss important topics of interest or concern, share feelings, discuss opinions and decisions, and encourage responsible behaviors that are associated with good character. A family can choose a regular time and place to have The Family Round Table. A family might sit around a table or in a circle. Then all family members have eye contact with one another.

Participation in The Family Round Table encourages healthful behaviors and the development of skills that promote healthful relationships. Family members who participate in The Family Round Table:

- spend quality time with their families;
- improve their communication skills;
- discuss sensitive topics and practice honest talk in a safe setting;
- keep family members aware of what they are doing and feeling;
- are reminded to show good character and follow family guidelines;
- get support from family members in order to resist peer pressure to choose wrong actions; and
- keep other family members informed about their health concerns.

Skill 2: Show Good Character

Good character is the use of self-control to act on responsible values. **Self-control** is the effort a person makes to regulate his or her behavior. Self-control might be needed to resist temptation, practice moderation, and/or delay gratification in order to act on responsible values. **Moderation** is placing limits to avoid excess. **Delayed gratification** is voluntarily postponing an immediate reward in order to complete a task before enjoying a reward. A **responsible value** is a belief that guides a person to act in responsible ways. There are ten responsible values that make up good character and promote healthful relationships (Table 1.3).

- **Honesty** is refusing to lie, steal, or deceive anyone. When a person is honest, other people trust him or her. Trust is a must in any relationship that has depth. It is a prerequisite for resolving difficulties and experiencing personal growth within a relationship. For

---

Table 1.3	**Ten Responsible Values That Make up Good Character and Promote Healthful Relationships**		
1.	Honesty	6.	Courage
2.	Self-Discipline	7.	Citizenship
3.	Fairness	8.	Responsibility
4.	Healthful behavior	9.	Respect
5.	Determination	10.	Integrity

example, suppose friends have a conflict. Each friend must be honest with the other in order to resolve the conflict.

• **Self-discipline** is the effort a person makes to follow through on what he or she says. When a person is self-disciplined, other people can depend on him or her. Self-discipline is a must in a committed relationship. People must be able to count on one another. For example, suppose a married person is attracted to a single person at the office. The single person is flirtatious and invites the married person for a drink after work. The married person uses self-discipline and declines the invitation. The married person upholds his or her marriage vows and protects the marriage relationship.

• **Fairness** is following the same rules so everyone has a fair chance. When a person is fair, other people know he or she will not change the rules. They know the person will not take advantage of them. For example, suppose two friends are trying to decide what movie to see. Each has chosen a different movie. One of the two friends agrees to the other friend's choice. However, the next time the two friends differ on their choice of what to do, the friend who chose the previous movie agrees to the other friend's choice. These friends are committed to keeping fairness in their relationship. Neither friend wants to dominate the other.

• **Healthful behaviors** are actions a person chooses that promote health; prevent injury, illness, and premature death; and improve the quality of the environment. When a person chooses healthful behaviors, other people know their well-being is not at risk when they are with this person. For example, suppose a family member chooses healthful behaviors and is tobacco-free. This family member protects other family members from breathing secondhand smoke. Suppose an adolescent chooses healthful behaviors including a healthful diet. A friend who is invited to lunch can count on having a healthful lunch.

• **Determination** is working hard to get what a person wants. When a person is determined, other people know he or she will not give up

easily. Determination is necessary to sustain relationships, especially during difficult times. Determination also helps people focus their energies to get something done. For example, suppose a parent gets a job that requires the family to move to a new location. Other family members show determination when they pitch in and work hard to prepare for the move. After the move, they continue to show determination by working hard to help each other adjust to the changes resulting from the move.

• **Courage** is showing strength when a person otherwise would be afraid. When a person shows courage, other people can lean on him or her during difficult times. For example, suppose a family lives in an area in which a hurricane has damaged property and caused flooding. Some of the family members might be very discouraged. However, if one family member shows courage and encourages other family members, the family can pull together and get through this natural disaster. This family member's courage strengthens other family members. The spirits of the other family members are elevated, and they begin to bounce back from their feelings of depression and fear.

• **Citizenship** is following the laws of a person's community and nation. When a person practices citizenship, other people know he or she will not break laws. Other people do not worry that they will get into trouble or be in danger if they are with the person. For example, suppose an adolescent abides by drug laws. The adolescent knows it is illegal to use marijuana. When an older teen offers him a joint, he says "NO." This adolescent also tells his parent or guardian right away if someone breaks laws. Other adolescents observe the adolescent who demonstrates good citizenship. They know this adolescent follows laws and expects others to follow laws. Other adolescents know they will not get into trouble if they are with the adolescent who demonstrates good citizenship.

• **Responsibility** is being accountable for what a person says or does. When a person is responsible, other people know he or she is accountable for his or her actions. Other people know the person will not blame others or hide wrong actions. For example, suppose a boy borrows his friend's jacket. The boy spills a soda pop on the jacket. He takes responsibility and does not blame anyone else. The boy gives thought to how he can make restitution for what he has done. He speaks with his parents and they agree to get the jacket cleaned before he returns it to the friend. The boy keeps a healthful relationship with his friend because he was accountable for his actions.

• **Respect** is liking that comes from having esteem for someone's admirable characteristics and responsible and caring actions. When a person is respectful, other people know he or she believes they are worthy of being treated in kind ways. They know the person will not abuse them. For example, suppose an elderly grandmother moves in with an adolescent's family. The elderly grandmother is hearing impaired and forgetful. The adolescent speaks loudly, clearly, and slowly so the elderly grandmother can understand conversations. He or she is patient when the elderly grandmother is confused and is respectful of the elderly grandmother.

• **Integrity** is acting on responsible values regardless of the consequences. When a person has integrity, other people know that he or she cannot be tempted or convinced to do something wrong. Other people know the person who has integrity will not give in to pressure. For example, suppose an adolescent promises his parents he will not drink alcohol. He attends a party where other adolescents are drinking. The adolescents who are drinking pressure him to drink. They tell him they do not want to be his friend unless he drinks. He demonstrates integrity and leaves the party knowing those adolescents might not invite him to a party again. He keeps his integrity regardless of the consequences.

Reasons to Demonstrate Good Character

The aforementioned examples illustrate each of the ten responsible values that make up good character and promote healthful relationships. There are other reasons for people to show good character.

• **To have self-respect. Self-respect** is a high regard for oneself because one behaves in responsible ways. It can be very difficult to demonstrate good character in some situations. However, people who use self-control and resist temptation maintain their self-respect.

• **To get along with one's family members.** Parents and guardians expect their children and adolescents to follow their guidelines. There are consequences and family discord if guidelines are broken. Adult family members also must demonstrate good character to get along with one another and prevent family discord.

• **To keep the respect of others.** Other people hold in high regard a person who demonstrates good character. It is a good feeling to have earned the respect of others. It helps promote self-respect.

• **To protect one's future.** When a person shows good character early, it can affect the direction his or her life will take. People who demonstrate good character do not limit their future opportunities. They do not have a blemish on their record that keeps them from getting what they want later in life.

• **To stay out of trouble. Reputation** is the quality of a person's life as judged by others. People who have a good reputation want to associate with other people who have a good reputation. They do not want to be "guilty by association" by associating with a person who chooses wrong actions.

• **To keep a clear conscience. Conscience** is a person's inner sense of right and wrong. Having a clear conscience promotes health. It keeps a person from experiencing the kind of stress that is associated with wrong actions.

Skill 3: Make Responsible Decisions

A **decision** is a choice that a person makes. Decision-making styles affect relationships. There are three decision-making styles. These are

• inactive decision-making style;
• reactive decision-making style; and
• proactive decision-making style.

An **inactive decision-making style** is a habit in which a person fails to make choices, and this failure determines the outcome. People who have an inactive decision-making style:

- often procrastinate (To **procrastinate** is to postpone something until a future time);
- have little control over the direction their lives take; and
- have difficulty gaining the self-confidence that would result if they took responsibility for making decisions when they should.

People who have an inactive decision-making style often cause others to become frustrated, resulting in conflict or confusion in their relationships.

A **reactive decision-making style** is a habit in which a person allows others to make his or her decisions. People who have a reactive decision-making style:

- are easily influenced by what others think, do, or suggest;
- lack self-confidence and have a great need to be liked by others; and
- give control of their lives over to others.

People who have a reactive decision-making style cave in to external pressure. As a result, they lose the respect of others.

A **proactive decision-making style** is a habit in which a person takes responsibility for his or her decisions and uses *The Responsible Decision-Making Model*™. ***The Responsible Decision-Making Model***™ (Table 1.4) is a series of steps to follow to assure that the decisions a person makes result in actions that

1. promote health,
2. protect safety,
3. follow laws,
4. show respect for self and others,
5. follow the guidelines of parents and of other responsible adults, and
6. demonstrate good character.

People who have a proactive decision-making style:

- are not driven by circumstances and conditions;
- are not easily influenced by peers;

- have principles, such as integrity, honesty, and dignity that guide their decisions and behavior; and
- are empowered. To be **empowered** is to be energized because a person has some control over his or her decisions and behavior.

People who have a proactive decision-making style earn the respect of others. Other people can count on them to make responsible decisions. Other people value their opinions and have confidence in them. Other people choose them as confidants when they want help sorting out their own decisions.

Skill 4: Resist Pressure to Do Something Wrong

A **peer** is a person of similar age or status. **Peer pressure** is the influence that people of similar age or status apply to effect certain behaviors. **Positive peer pressure** is influence from peers to behave in a responsible way. People who apply positive peer pressure influence others to form healthful relationships. They discourage behaviors such as racial or gender stereotyping that

---

Table 1.4

The Responsible Decision-Making Model™

STEP 1   Describe the situation that requires a decision.

STEP 2   List possible decisions you might make.

STEP 3   Share the list of possible decisions with a parent, guardian, or other responsible adult.

STEP 4   Use six questions to evaluate the possible consequences of each decision.

Will this decision result in actions that:

1. promote health?
2. protect safety?
3. follow laws?
4. show respect for myself and others?
5. follow the guidelines of my parents and of other responsible adults?
6. demonstrate good character?

STEP 5   Decide which decision is most responsible and appropriate.

STEP 6   Act on your decision and evaluate the results.

---

interfere with relationships. They influence others to choose healthful behaviors and healthful situations. Their influence contributes to the well-being of others. Positive peer pressure is a part of all healthful relationships.

Negative peer pressure is influence from peers to behave in a way that is not responsible. People who apply negative peer pressure might influence others to choose risk behaviors and risk situations. They might influence others to choose behaviors such as stereotyping and discrimination that harm relationships.

Their influence does not have the effect of contributing to the well-being of others. People should avoid having relationships with those who apply negative peer pressure, because they often want support for wrong actions. People who apply negative peer pressure usually are not concerned about the consequences others might experience as a result of actions that are wrong.

Resistance skills are skills that help a person say NO to an action or to leave a situation. Resistance skills are sometimes called refusal skills and can be used to resist negative peer pressure. *The Model for Using Resistance Skills* is a list of suggested ways to resist negative peer pressure (Table 1.5).

Skill 5: Correct Wrong Actions

A wrong action that is not based on responsible values disturbs a person's conscience. The effect of a wrong decision that caused a wrong action is associated with lack of inner peace or disturbed conscience. A person who has good character does not ignore his or her conscience especially when the wrong action affects a relationship. There are five steps a person can take to correct wrong actions.

Step 1: Take responsibility for the wrong action. A person should not try to cover up wrong actions or make excuses. He or she should not blame someone else. Other people have more respect for a person who is honest and takes responsibility for his or her actions.

Step 2: Apologize and pledge not to do the wrong action again. A person should show remorse for wrongful behavior. **Remorse** is the expression

Table 1.5
The Model for Using Resistance Skills

1. Say NO with self-confidence.

2. Give reasons for saying NO.

NO. I want to promote my health.

NO. I want to protect my safety.

NO. I want to follow laws.

NO. I want to show respect for myself and others.

NO. I want to follow the guidelines of my parents and other responsible adults.

NO. I want to demonstrate good character.

3. Use the broken-record technique.

4. Use nonverbal behavior to match verbal behavior.

5. Avoid being in situations in which there will be pressure to make wrong decisions.

6. Avoid being with people who make wrong decisions.

7. Resist pressure to engage in illegal behavior.

8. Influence others to make responsible decisions.

of regret for having caused harm. A person who shows remorse deals with the feelings of the wronged person. This helps diffuse the wronged person's anger and avoids higher levels of anger that are associated with disease. A person who shows remorse also sets the stage for the wronged person to practice forgiveness. The release of hurt that accompanies forgiveness has a healthful effect on the wronged person (Viscott, 1996). The emotional release that accompanies forgiveness fosters resiliency in the wronged person (AMA, 1999). **Resiliency** is the ability to adjust, recover, bounce back, and learn from difficult times.

Step 3: Discuss the wrong action with a trusted adult. When a pattern of wrongful behavior exists, a person needs to change. A person might seek the counsel of an adult family member, another trusted adult, and/or a health care provider. A health care provider might assist in determining effective sources of treatment.

Step 4: Accept appropriate punishment. **Punishment** is a penalty for wrongdoing. Forgiveness does not exclude making amends for wrong actions. The person who commits a wrong action might have to accept appropriate punishment in order to restore a relationship.

Step 5: Make restitution. Restitution is making good for loss or damage. To **pay back** is to make restitution for harm to a person. To **pay forward** is to make restitution to society.

Examples of paying back and paying forward might help clarify these forms of restitution. Suppose an adolescent is playing baseball and hits a ball through a neighbor's window. The adolescent wants to correct wrong actions so he tells the neighbor, apologizes, shows remorse, and discusses the wrong action with his parents or guardian. His parents assign him extra chores to earn the money to pay for the window. The payback is the money he pays for the window.

Suppose an adult drinks and drives. She runs a red light and strikes another car killing its driver. She takes responsibility for her wrong actions, apologizes to the family of the driver who was killed, shows remorse, and gets counseling for her wrong actions. But, she still might have to accept punishment and make restitution. She might have to pay forward or make restitution to society. She might be charged with vehicular manslaughter and have to serve time in a correctional facility. She also might have to undergo treatment for the abuse of alcohol. Restitution does not bring back the person who is killed but the guilty driver is accountable to society. And when the guilty driver shows remorse it helps the family members of the deceased person begin the process of healing.

To have healthful relationships, people always must stand accountable for the effects their actions have on others. And, people who desire healthful relationships must always correct wrong actions.

Skill 6: Communicate in Healthful Ways

Communication is the sharing of emotions, thoughts, and information with another person. Learning to communicate in healthful ways is one of the legacies of growing up in a family that communicates in healthful ways. Some of the skills that are practiced include expressing emotions in healthful ways, using I-messages,

being an effective listener, and avoiding mixed messages.

How to express emotions in healthful ways

People experience a wide range of emotions, such as depression, anger, sadness, jealousy, love, and many others. It is healthful to recognize, accept, and express these emotions. Failure to express emotions such as anger and depression might affect a person's health. However, it is important for people to be

---

Table 1.6 **Five Guidelines for Expressing Emotions in Healthful Ways**

1. **Identify the emotion.**
   - What emotion am I experiencing?

2. **Identify the source of the emotion.**
   - Why do I feel this way?

3. **Decide whether or not you need to respond right away.**
   - Should I talk to a parent, guardian, or other responsible adult about the emotions I am experiencing?
   - Should I try to sort out my emotions by myself?
   - Do I need more information before I respond?
   - Do I need to rehearse what I will say before I respond?

4. **Choose a responsible and healthful response.**
   - What I-message might I use? (I-messages are explained in the next part of this chapter.)
   - Would it be helpful to express my emotions by writing in a journal?
   - Could I write a poem, sculpt clay, or draw a picture to express emotions?

5. **Protect your health.**
   - Do I need extra sleep?
   - Do I need to work off my strong emotions with vigorous exercise?
   - Am I aware of any physical disorders that might be connected to the emotional response I am experiencing? If so, I might need to see a physician.
   - Am I able to function in daily activities? If not, I might need to speak with a trusted adult or obtain counseling from a health care provider.

---

accountable for the ways in which they express emotions. Table 1.6 includes Five Guidelines for Expressing Emotions in Healthful Ways.

How to use I-messages

In healthful relationships, people use I-messages to express their feelings. An **I-message** is a statement describing a specific behavior or event, the effect that behavior or event has on a person, and the feelings that result.

Knowing how to express I-messages is helpful in relationships because a person learns to express emotions such as anger, sadness, disappointment, frustration, or depression in a non-threatening way. Table 1.7 illustrates how an I-message is used to communicate angry feelings. Suppose two friends have made last-minute plans to attend a concert. Since only lawn seating is available, the friends decide to meet early and get seats close to the front. However, one friend does not organize her time well and arrives late. The friend who has been waiting might use an I-message to express her angry feelings: "Because we are late getting our seats, we will not be able to sit close to the front and I am angry." This friend shares her anger without attacking the friend who was late and also opens the dialogue for getting the situation resolved. The friend who was late might apologize or give a valid reason for being late.

Suppose the friend who had been waiting used a you-message to share her angry feelings. A **you-message** is a statement that blames or shames another person. The friend who had been waiting might say "You are so thoughtless and selfish to arrive late." The friend who arrived late would feel attacked and defensive. The communication might break down, and it would be more difficult to resolve the situation. I-messages always are better than you-messages for the expression of feelings. Their use opens the dialogue for honest communication, which, in turn, promotes closeness in a relationship.

How to be an effective listener

Listening is an ingredient in all relationships. It is an important ingredient because listening is an expression of interest and respect. People who do not listen often tune out others for one or more of the following reasons:

- They were thinking of something or someone else.
- They could not hear the person who was speaking.
- They were tired and dozing off.
- They were thinking about what they were going to say next.
- They were distracted by noise.
- They thought they already knew what the other person was going to say.

Unfortunately, when people tune out others, they make others feel unimportant. They risk harming their relationships.

This is why people who desire healthful relationships must take listening skills seriously. Listening skills are first practiced in family relationships. People who have not developed adequate listening skills must make a conscious effort to develop them. Active listening is a skill worth developing. **Active listening** is a way of responding to show that a person hears and understands. A person who uses active listening might respond in four different ways to let the other person know that he or she is hearing and understanding. The listener might:

- ask for more information (clarifying response);
- repeat what was said (restating response);
- summarize the main ideas (summarizing response); and
- acknowledge and show appreciation for the feelings expressed (confirming response).

Table 1.7	**I-Messages**

An **I-message** is a statement that describes:

1. a specific behavior or event;
2. the effect that behavior or event has on a person; and
3. the feelings that result.

Example:

1. Because we are late getting our seats,
2. we will not be able to sit close to the front,
3. and I am angry.

How to avoid sending mixed messages

Actions also are used to communicate in relationships. **Nonverbal communication** is the use of actions instead of words to express a person's thoughts and feelings. Examples might include nodding the head, hugging, and smiling. Nonverbal communication is a powerful way to reinforce what is being said or felt.

To communicate effectively, a person must avoid sending mixed messages. A **mixed message** is a message that conveys two different or double meanings. A mixed message occurs in two ways. It occurs when words and the tone of voice convey two different meanings, such as when a person expresses words of affection in an insincere or dutiful tone. A mixed message also might occur when words and nonverbal communication convey two different meanings, such as when a person gives a friend a compliment but has an insincere facial expression or does not make eye contact. Healthful communication in a relationship includes clear messages in which words, tone of voice, and actions reinforce one another.

Skill 7: Resolve Conflict Without Violence

A **conflict** is a disagreement between people or between choices. A **conflict response style** is a pattern of behavior that a person demonstrates when a conflict arises. A person might demonstrate one or a combination of conflict response styles including conflict avoidance, conflict confrontation, and conflict resolution.

Conflict avoidance is a conflict response style in which a person avoids disagreements at all costs. A person who practices this style does not admit that there is a disagreement because he or she might fear the loss of others' approval. He or she relinquishes control and allows others to make decisions. Practicing conflict avoidance interferes with healthful relationships. It prevents honest talk about what is disturbing in a relationship. As a result, issues continue to be unresolved. For example, suppose a father has

a drinking problem. If a family member says something to him, he gets angry and denies his problem. As a result, family members might practice conflict avoidance because they do not want to deal with his anger. Their use of conflict avoidance backfires because he continues to drink and family communication worsens. Conflict avoidance is characteristic of people who are enablers. An **enabler** is a person who supports the harmful behavior of others.

Conflict confrontation is a conflict response style that attempts to settle a disagreement in a hostile, defiant, and aggressive way. The person who practices this response style enjoys confrontation. Conflict is viewed as a win-lose situation, and the person desires victory at all costs. Practicing conflict confrontation interferes with healthful relationships. People who use conflict confrontation often make other people angry and defensive. Other people do not want to be put into the position of defeat. This conflict response style is associated with violence. For example, suppose students from opposing schools call each other names. As the name-calling continues, tempers flare, which might lead to pushing and punching. A fight might break out and some students might be harmed. Suppose a child on a playground is a bully. A child who is a bully demonstrates that he or she has learned conflict confrontation. This child picks on other children and is likely to start fights.

Conflict resolution is a conflict response style in which a person uses conflict resolution skills to resolve disagreements. **Conflict resolution skills** are steps that can be taken to settle a disagreement in a responsible way. Although the opposing view is acknowledged, the potential for a win-win solution in situations and relationships in which conflict exists is recognized. People who work to resolve conflict show respect for others. They do not need to win at all costs. They demonstrate that they respect others and want to work things out in a fair and responsible way. This, in turn, promotes healthful relationships. Table 1.8 lists Guidelines for the Use of Conflict Resolution Skills.

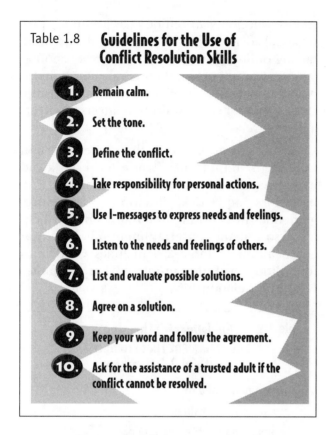

Table 1.8 **Guidelines for the Use of Conflict Resolution Skills**

1. Remain calm.
2. Set the tone.
3. Define the conflict.
4. Take responsibility for personal actions.
5. Use I-messages to express needs and feelings.
6. Listen to the needs and feelings of others.
7. List and evaluate possible solutions.
8. Agree on a solution.
9. Keep your word and follow the agreement.
10. Ask for the assistance of a trusted adult if the conflict cannot be resolved.

Skill 8: Cope Without Using Drugs or Other Addictive Substances or Behaviors

Difficult times can happen, and they do happen to everyone—even to people who have good character and who have done nothing to bring upon themselves misfortune or difficult times. How a person copes at these times can affect the quality of a person's relationships. This is why coping skills are important.

In her classic study On Death and Dying, Dr. Elisabeth Kübler-Ross described stages that a person goes through when he or she is dealing with his or her own death or the death of a loved one. The five stages are denial, anger, bargaining, depression, and acceptance (Kübler-Ross, 1975).

Interestingly, these fives stages are identical to the five stages a person goes through when he or she experiences misfortune, difficult times, adversity, or other life crises:

1. denying or refusing to believe what is happening,
2. being angry about what is happening,
3. bargaining or making promises hoping it will change what is happening,
4. being depressed after recognizing that the outcome is unlikely to change,
5. accepting what is happening, adjusting, and bouncing back.

Willingness to experience the five stages of emotional response associated with a life crisis is important because it produces resiliency in a person. **Resiliency** is the ability to adjust, recover, bounce back, and learn from difficult times.

People who do not want to work through the five stages of emotional response might not be willing to delay gratification. To **delay gratification** is to postpone satisfaction until an issue has been confronted and resolved. People who do not want to delay gratification choose instant gratification to avoid waiting for a benefit until a more appropriate time. **Instant gratification** is choosing an immediate reward regardless of potentially harmful effects. People who choose instant gratification might choose harmful behavior to avoid the struggle associated with coping. For example, they might drink alcohol to numb the pain associated with a struggle. They might turn to promiscuous sexual relationships rather than resolving issues within a marital relationship. Being unwilling to struggle and to delay gratification during times when a person must cope undermines healthful relationships.

Skill 9: Choose Entertainment That Promotes Healthful Relationships

Entertainment is something that is designed to hold the interest of people. Messages from entertainment influence a person's thoughts and actions, and might influence relationships.

Some entertainment is wholesome and encourages positive thoughts and actions. This type of entertainment often produces a healthful response such as laughter or tears. A "tear-jerker" movie might be cathartic, relieving the stresses of people in the audience. The good feelings that result from healthful entertainment might promote healthful behavior in people and in their relationships.

Entertainment also might have harmful effects. These might include

- faulty thinking;
- desensitization; and
- the neglect of relationships.

Faulty thinking is a thought process in which a person denies facts or believes erroneous facts. Entertainment often presents people and relationships in fictitious settings and situations that differ from real outcomes in life. A popular television sitcom in which one or more characters do not practice self-control resulting in harmful behaviors that include alcohol abuse might lead some viewers to associate chronic drinking with pleasure. Some people might mistake such behaviors as coping skills.

Some musical entertainment presents songs and raps with violent themes. People who listen to this entertainment might not practice discernment. It might influence them to participate in risk behaviors and risk situations that show a lack of respect for authority and/or to break laws.

Desensitization is the effect of reacting less and less to the exposure to something. Frequent exposure to acts of violence presented as entertainment might cause desensitization to harmful behaviors. The prevalence of movies or television programs that contain violent themes or that promote violence as a universal theme of life might result in a harmful perspective. People who watch entertainment that has a violent theme might conclude that participation in violence is a way of life.

Entertainment addiction might cause neglect in relationships. An **addiction** is the compelling need to take a drug or engage in a specific behavior. **Television addiction** is the compelling need to watch television. The long-running popularity of television soap operas might be associated with the compelling need to watch television. **Computer addiction** is the compelling need to use the computer beyond required use, such as for work. The widening use of the Internet might result in further isolation of people who are already experiencing loss of connectedness in relationships. For example, a spouse who joins an online chat group for professional advice might begin to spend more time talking online than talking to his or her spouse. Since communication between spouses helps maintain the health of a marital relationship, lack of spousal communication adversely effects a marital relationship (APA, 1998).

Choosing entertainment that meets certain criteria is important. These criteria avoid exposure to entertainment that promotes risk behaviors and risk situations. Therefore, guidelines in choosing entertainment can help a person make entertainment choices that are healthful. Table 1.9 includes Guidelines for Choosing Entertainment That Promotes Healthful Relationships.

Table 1.9 Guidelines for Choosing Entertainment That Promotes Healthful Relationships

Entertainment should:

- promote family values.
- be approved for the age group.
- portray healthful behaviors and situations.
- portray respectful relationships.
- not show promiscuous sexual activity, illicit drug use, or violence.

The **V-Chip** is a small electronic device that can be installed in a television set to block transmission of television programs. Parents or other responsible adults might choose to install a V-Chip in order to block television programs that are inappropriate for family viewing.

Entertainment rating systems are ratings to assist people in determining the suitability of content for certain age groups. In 1997, additional content definitions were included in the television rating system to assist parents in choosing television entertainment for their children. Table 1.10 includes the Television Rating System. There also are rating systems for movies (Table 1.11) and entertainment software (Table 1.12).

Table 1.10	**Television Rating System**
TV-Y	Suitable for all children and specifically designed for very young children, including ages 2 to 6
TV-7	Suitable for ages 7 and up, especially children who can distinguish between make-believe and reality
TV-G	Suitable for all ages, not specifically designed for children
TV-PG	Parental Guidance Suggested
TV-14	Unsuitable for children ages 14 and under
TV-M	Adults Only

V=Violence, S=Sex, L=Offensive language, D=Dialogue with sexual innuendo, FV=Fantasy or cartoon violence

Table 1.11	**Movie Rating System**
G:	General Audiences, all ages admitted
PG:	Parental Guidance Suggested. Some material may not be suitable for children.
PG-13:	Parents Strongly Cautioned. Some material may be inappropriate for pre-adolescents under 13.
R:	Restricted. Adolescent under 17 requires accompanying parent or adult guardian.
NC-17:	No one 17 and under admitted
X:	Adults Only

Table 1.12

Entertainment Software Rating System

For Computer Games and Internet Game Software

EC-I	Early Childhood, suitable for ages 3 and up
K-A-I	Kids to Adults, suitable for ages 6 and up
T-I	Teen, suitable for 13 and up
M-I	Mature, suitable for 17 and up
AO-I	Adults Only, suitable for ages 18 and up
RP-I	Rating Pending, content currently under review

Skill 10: Express Affection in Appropriate Ways

Affection is a fond or tender feeling that a person has toward another person. Expressions of affection include verbal and nonverbal behavior such as hugging, kissing good night or good-bye, and holding hands.

Verbal and nonverbal expressions of affection in a family establish behaviors in children and adolescents. Family guidelines encourage the practice of healthful behaviors including appropriate expressions of affection. As a result, children and adolescents develop self-respect and do not participate in sexual activity that might destroy self-respect and the respect of others. Family guidelines teach that expressions of sexual affection belong within loving, committed relationships that are monogamous. Family guidelines teach adolescents that abstinence from sex is the expected standard for teens.

Setting boundaries in relationships helps promote healthful behaviors and situations. Since a person first experiences the setting of boundaries in family life, family relationships influence how a person establishes social boundaries. Consider a person who experienced a lack of love during his or her childhood years. He or she might develop weakened boundaries, resulting in indiscriminate attachments and harmful relationships. If a person experienced love during his or her childhood years, strong boundaries associated with self-respect and the respect of others would develop, promoting healthful relationships.

The practice of responsible values in all relationships protects a person's boundaries. This helps maintain the person's integrity and sense of well-being (Viscott, 1996).

References

American Medical Association. 1999. "Emotional Expression and Disease Outcome." *Journal of the American Medical Association*. 281 (April): 1328–1329. Accessed 7/1999. http://www.4journals.com.

American Psychological Association. 1998. "Isolation Increases with Internet Use." Article Online (September). Accessed 8/1999. http://www.apa.org.

Kübler-Ross, Elisabeth. 1975. *Death: The Final Stage of Growth.* Englewood Cliffs, New Jersey: Prentice-Hall.

National Institute of Health. 1997. "Risk
    Factors Cluster to Harm Health." Article
    Online. Accessed 10/1999. http://www.
    1.nih.gov/obssr/riskclu.htm.

National Institute of Mental Health. 1999.
    "Family Processes and Social Networks."
    Government Publication. Accessed
    10/1999. http://www.nimh.nih.gov/
    publicat/baschap6.htm.

Viscott, David. 1996. *Emotional Resilience.*
    New York: Harmony Books.

2 Harmful and Violent Relationships

Content for Teachers *Only*

A Word from the Authors

Chapter 1 examined the quality of relationships and discussed the ten skills needed for healthful relationships. Healthful relationships are inspiriting and contribute to a person's well-being. Unfortunately, some relationships are harmful and/or violent. Harmful and/or violent relationships are dispiriting and contribute to a person's lack of well-being. This chapter examines risk factors for being involved in harmful and/or violent relationships. It includes a discussion of profiles of people who relate in harmful ways. It examines why people get into harmful relationships and how to get out of them. It examines violent relationships and strategies to recover, heal, and protect oneself from being harmed by violent relationships. This chapter also addresses sexual behaviors that interfere with relationships.

Risk Factors for Being Involved in Harmful and/or Violent Relationships

Harmful relationships are relationships that destroy self-respect, interfere with productivity and health, and include addictions and/or violence. A **violent relationship** is a relationship that harms another person physically, mentally, and/or emotionally. The following definitions clarify the role some people have in a violent relationship. A **perpetrator of violence** is a person who commits a violent act. A **victim of violence** is a person who has been harmed by violence. A **survivor of violence** is a person who was harmed by violence, has participated in recovery to heal from its emotional effects, and has adopted self-protection strategies. **Self-protection strategies** are strategies that can be practiced to protect oneself and others from harm.

This section of the chapter discusses risk factors for being involved in harmful and/or violent relationships (Table 2.1). A **risk factor** is something that increases the likelihood of a negative outcome. Some risk factors describe a person's behavior while others describe the characteristics of the environment in which a person might live. The risk factors listed in Table 2.1 refer only to the statistical probability that a person will be involved in harmful and/or violent relationships.

Table 2.1

Risk Factors for Being Involved in Harmful and/or Violent Relationships

1. Lacking self-respect
2. Being raised in a dysfunctional family
3. Living in an adverse environment
4. Lacking social skills
5. Being unable to manage anger
6. Resolving conflict in harmful ways
7. Practicing discriminatory behavior
8. Misusing or abusing alcohol and/or other drugs
9. Being a consumer of entertainment that portrays harmful and violent relationships
10. Being a victim of violence

1. Lacking Self-Respect

Self-respect is a high regard for oneself because one behaves in responsible ways. It is a product of the beliefs a person has about himself or herself. The members of a person's family have the most influence over a person's beliefs about himself or herself. If a person received messages that he or she was worthy, then he or she began to believe these messages. A person who has self-respect expects others to treat him or her with respect. He or she expects others to demonstrate the ten responsible values that make up good character. For example, a person who has self-respect expects others to be honest, fair, and respectful. People who lack self-respect send a message to others that it is OK for them to be treated in a disrespectful manner.

People who lack self-respect often compensate by being self-centered and self-destructive. **Self-centered behavior** is actions that fulfill personal needs with little regard for the needs of others. In other words, self-centered people "want what they want when they want it." They often talk only about themselves. This stems from their feelings of inadequacy. They might brag or dominate the conversation as a way of getting attention and affirmation. They might be aggressive or violent in order to get what they want. Other people resent self-centered behavior. Other people also might be fearful of people who are self-centered. They question what these people might do to get their way.

Self-destructive behavior is behavior in which a person harms himself or herself. People who lack self-respect do not feel they are worthy. These people might have so little regard for themselves that they choose relationships that reinforce their lack of self-worth. For example, suppose a female lacks self-respect. She might choose friends who put her down. She might choose a boyfriend who is dishonest and cheats on her. Her self-destructive behavior reinforces her belief that she is not worthy. Suppose a young boy is bullied by his peers. Because he lacks self-respect, he does not stand up for himself or tell an adult about the bullying. His behavior is self-destructive because he accepts their insults.

2. Being Raised in a Dysfunctional Family

A **dysfunctional family** is a family that lacks the skills to be successful and to function in healthful ways. The term *dysfunctional family* was first used to describe families in which one or more members were alcoholic. Family members who are alcoholic have a compelling need to drink alcohol. They exhibit other harmful behaviors that keep them from relating well with other family members. As a result, family life is dispiriting for all family members. The term *dysfunctional family* is now applied to families in which members relate to one another in destructive and irresponsible ways. Some of the causes of dysfunctional families include chemical dependence, other addictions, perfectionism, violence, physical abuse, emotional abuse, neglect, sexual abuse, abandonment, and mental disorders.

People who are raised in a dysfunctional family are at increased risk for interacting in harmful and violent ways. Consider young children and adolescents raised in dysfunctional families. As they observe family members acting in harmful ways, they might believe that this is the norm. They might not be able to discern the difference between healthful relationships and harmful relationships (one of the very good reasons to include relationship skills in the K–12 curriculum). As a result, these young children and adolescents model the harmful and/or violent behaviors they experience at home. And they select friends who behave in the same ways. Their "comfort zone" is continuing the kinds of relationships and behaviors they have at home.

Children and adolescents who are raised in dysfunctional families might develop codependence. **Codependence** is a mental disorder in which a person denies feelings and begins to cope in harmful ways. A **codependent** is a person who wants to rescue and control another person. People who are codependent exhibit behaviors that interfere with relationships. They hide anger, are people pleasers, try to fix other people's problems, fear abandonment, are very controlling, withdraw for protection, resist authority figures, lack self-respect, are overly responsible, and deny their feelings. Consider how these behaviors might affect relationships. Suppose an adolescent is overly responsible. The teacher assigns a group project. Other members in her group are unwilling to do their fair share. She does the project by herself but resents them. She has a harmful relationship with the group. Suppose an adolescent resists authority figures. He tries out and makes the soccer team but he disobeys his coach. He develops a harmful relationship with his coach because of his codependence.

3. Living in an Adverse Environment

The **environment** is everything that is around a person and the place in which a person lives. An **adverse environment** is a set of conditions and surroundings that interferes with a person's growth, development, and success. People who live in an adverse environment might describe the living conditions in their neighborhood as follows:

- Many people live in poverty. **Poverty** is a condition in which a person does not have the financial resources or other assistance to sustain a healthful life.

- Many people are unemployed and have few job skills.

- Many people do not have enough food or clothing.

- Many people have difficulty getting medical and dental care.

- Many people experience discriminatory behavior. **Discriminatory behavior** is to make distinctions in treatment or to show behavior in favor of or prejudiced against an individual or group of people.

- Many people live in overcrowded conditions.

- Some people use or sell illegal drugs.

- Some people purchase illegal guns and carry them.

- Many people engage in criminal activity or are victims of crime.

- Many adolescents drop out of school.

- Most children and adolescents are being raised in a single-parent family.

Unfortunately, many young people live in adverse environments. Four million young people live in deeply troubled neighborhoods in which there is poverty and unemployment. One-third of the children in this nation experience at least one year of poverty before age 17. Poverty is associated with overcrowding and lack of adult supervision. These conditions increase the risk that young people will be involved in harmful and violent relationships.

For example, suppose an adolescent lives with one parent and many younger siblings in a small apartment. If the parent is employed and requires the adolescent to supervise the younger children, the adolescent might experience frustration. The adolescent might be abusive toward the younger siblings. In turn, the younger siblings might be abusive with peers. The younger siblings might have difficulty in social relationships and become vulnerable to gang participation. Studies have associated the experience of living in poverty in childhood with aggression and delinquency during adolescence and young adulthood (NIH, 1999).

Research also suggests that the experience of living in an adverse environment is associated with excessive and rigid control. People who were raised with rigid control are less likely to develop adequate social skills. People who were raised with rigid control might practice certain social skills only to avoid punishment. When the risk of punishment is removed, they often develop antisocial behavior. And, having been raised with excessive and rigid control, they become rigid and controlling in their relationships.

4. Lacking Social Skills

Social skills are the abilities that a person uses to interact effectively with other people. A person who is lacking social skills does not have the ability to interact appropriately and establish healthful relationships. Children who do not learn and practice social skills are more likely to lack self-respect, fail at school, and misbehave (NIMH, 1994). As a result, they are more likely to experience alienation from peers. **Alienation** is the feeling that one is apart from others. People can feel alienated even when they are around other people. For example, adolescents who feel alienated might attend a school function but not feel like they are a part of what is happening. They do not feel included even though they are physically present with others.

Feelings of alienation are associated with loneliness. **Loneliness** is an anxious, unpleasant, and painful feeling that results from having few friends or from being alienated. Most young people feel lonely some of the time. However, some young people feel lonely most of the time. Young people who are lonely are likely to be shy and lack self-confidence. When they are unable to gain acceptance by peers, they feel even more lonely and alienated. This contributes to a negative cycle, the outcome of which is difficult to change. They have fewer chances to develop adequate social skills, further limiting their opportunities to form healthful relationships. As a result, they sometimes connect with peers who also lack social skills. This often is how juvenile delinquents band together and how gangs form. A **juvenile delinquent** is a young person who has antisocial behavior or refuses to follow the law.

5. Being Unable to Manage Anger

Anger is the feeling of being irritated, annoyed, and/or furious. Anger is usually a response to being hurt or frustrated. The hurt might be emotional, psychological, social, and/or physical. **Anger triggers** are thoughts or events that cause a person to become angry. For example, if someone physically harms a person, the person who was harmed is likely to become angry. Other causes of anger might be frustration, rejection by peers, constant criticism, failing at something important, and life changes.

A **life change** is an event or situation that requires a person to make a readjustment. **Coping** is a person's ability to confront negative feelings such as hurt or anger that can result from life changes and to make appropriate readjustments. Chapter 1 identified five emotional stages people must work through when they experience life changes (Kübler-Ross, 1975):

1. Denying or refusing to believe what is happening

2. Being angry about what is happening

3. Bargaining or making promises hoping it will change what is happening

4. Being depressed after recognizing that the outcome is unlikely to change

5. Accepting what is happening, adjusting, and bouncing back

People who are unable to manage anger might stay angry rather than moving through all five emotional stages to acceptance.

Hidden anger is anger that is not recognized or is expressed in a harmful way and might result in inappropriate behavior and poor health. The following types of behavior might be signs of hidden anger:

- being negative;
- making cruel remarks to others;
- being flippant;
- procrastinating;
- blowing up easily;
- having very little interest in anything;
- being bored;
- sighing frequently; and
- being depressed.

Hidden anger often is the underlying cause of harmful and violent behavior. People might not express the anger they feel because they were abused, rejected, or mistreated. They might not express the anger they feel because a group to which they belong has been treated unfairly. They might be angry due to discrimination. People might have hidden anger because of a life change. When angry feelings are not recognized and expressed, they usually build up and become hidden anger. Eventually, people cannot keep hidden anger inside and they act out in inappropriate ways. They might have an outburst, temper tantrum, start a fight, say something inappropriate, harm themselves, or harm others.

The ways people express hidden anger often are inappropriate for the situation. Inappropriate expressions of anger can lead to harmful and/or violent relationships. **Projection** is blaming others for actions or events for which they are not responsible. Projection can lead to harmful and/or violent relationships. For example, there have been situations in which students who felt rejected by their peers blamed peers for their feelings of alienation and harmed their peers.

Displacement is the releasing of anger on someone or something other than the cause of the anger. For example, an adolescent who is angry about his parent's divorce might release his anger on his girlfriend.

6. Resolving Conflict in Harmful Ways

Chapter 1 discussed conflict resolution. **Conflict resolution** is a conflict response style in which a person uses conflict resolution skills to resolve disagreements. Some people are not skilled in conflict resolution. They might choose conflict avoidance or conflict confrontation when they disagree with others.

Conflict avoidance is a conflict response style in which a person avoids disagreements at all cost. A person might bury his or her head in the sand to avoid acknowledging that conflict exists. Or a person might allow those people with whom he or she is in conflict to solve a conflict in a manner of their choosing.

Conflict confrontation is a conflict response style that attempts to settle a disagreement in a hostile, defiant, and aggressive way. People who adopt conflict confrontation as their primary conflict response style usually view conflict as a win-lose proposition. When conflict occurs, they choose a position and disagree with the opposition. A confronter wants to win or be right at all costs. The conflict often increases because the confronter refuses to consider any other viewpoint or side to the issue.

People who practice conflict avoidance and conflict confrontation have difficulty forming inspiriting relationships. **Inspiriting relationships** are relationships that lift the spirit and contribute to a sense of well-being. These people are at increased risk for having dispiriting relationships. **Dispiriting relationships** are relationships that depress the spirit and contribute to a lack of well-being.

People who practice conflict avoidance usually are dishonest with others. They do not share their true feelings about events and situations.

There are at least two reasons why practicing conflict avoidance harms relationships. First, other people are unable to respond to the needs and feelings of those who practice conflict avoidance—their needs and feelings are not known. Second, people who practice conflict avoidance often harbor resentment. Although they accommodate other people through outward behavior, they have hidden anger.

Relationships also are hampered when people practice conflict confrontation. People engaging in relationships with confronters lack the psychological safety that is needed to develop closeness. It is difficult to have this sense of safety when people are hostile and aggressive. Instead, the people feel uneasy and lack the comfort that intimacy might otherwise provide.

Both conflict avoidance and conflict confrontation are associated with increased risks of violence. As mentioned previously, people who demonstrate conflict avoidance often experience inner hostility and hidden anger. They are often passive-aggressive. This means that much of the time they behave in a passive and pleasing way yet they continue to be irritated, annoyed, and furious on the inside. Suddenly they reach a boiling point and harm others.

Conflict avoiders also might be harmed by others. Because they are people pleasers and attempt to keep the peace, they might not stand up for themselves. They might be abused and not take steps to get help. They are the people who keep family secrets such as rape, incest, and use of addictive substances including alcohol and other drugs.

It is more obvious why people who demonstrate conflict confrontation are likely to be involved in harmful and/or violent relationships. Their defiant, hostile, and aggressive behavior might cause others to be angry and respond. When their behavior is challenged by others, they are more likely to act out and to harm others. They are more likely to rely on coercion to manage interpersonal relationships.

7. Practicing Discriminatory Behavior

Discriminatory behavior is to make distinctions in treatment or to show behavior in favor of or prejudiced against an individual or group of people. **Prejudice** is suspicion, intolerance, or irrational hatred directed at an individual or group of people. Discriminatory behavior and prejudice divide people. People who discriminate against others might try to harm them. And, people who are the targets of discriminatory behavior and prejudice might become very angry because they are treated unfairly. They might express their anger in harmful and/or violent ways. They might begin to believe they are inferior and allow themselves to be treated in disrespectful and abusive ways.

Gender Discrimination

Sex discrimination based on gender differences is one kind of discrimination. The Equal Employment Opportunity Commission (EEOC) has guidelines prohibiting gender discrimination including sex discrimination. Sexual harassment is a form of sex discrimination. **Sexual harassment** is unwanted sexual behavior that ranges from making sexual comments to forcing another person into unwanted sexual acts. Federal law prohibits the practice of sexual harassment.

8. Misusing or Abusing Alcohol and/or Other Drugs

Drugs are substances that change the way the body and/or mind work. **Drug misuse** is the incorrect use of a prescription or over-the-counter (OTC) drug. **Drug abuse** is the use of drugs that lessen the user's ability to function normally or that are harmful to the user or others. For example, young people who drink alcohol are involved in drug abuse. Not only is it illegal for them to drink alcohol, but also they do not function normally when drinking alcohol. They are at special risk for harming themselves and others when they have been drinking alcohol.

Certain drugs might be used in a healthful way or their use might be drug abuse. For example, a doctor might prescribe a painkiller when a person is injured. In this case, the painkiller is used for medical reasons. However, another person might obtain the painkiller illegally and use it for reasons other than pain.

The misuse or abuse of alcohol and/or other drugs is a risk factor for being involved in harmful and/or violent relationships. The following drugs can influence behavior and relationships: alcohol, sedative-hypnotic drugs, PCP, cocaine, crack, amphetamines, heroin, anabolic steroids, and marijuana.

Alcohol

Alcohol is a drug that depresses the central nervous system and often changes behavior. Alcohol is the most widely used and abused drug. Alcohol use is known to interfere with clear thinking and decision-making. When people are under the influence of alcohol, they are more likely to harm themselves and others because alcohol strengthens the intensity of feelings. People who are angry or aggressive get stronger feelings when they drink alcohol. They might act on their feelings and harm themselves or others. Many young people who attempt suicide have been drinking. Many adults who harm young people are under the influence of alcohol. Most cases of domestic violence involve drinking. **Domestic violence** is violence that occurs within a family. Murder is often the result of a fight that occurred when someone was drinking. People who commit sexual assault or rape often are under the influence of alcohol. **Rape** is the threatened or actual use of physical force to get someone to have sex without giving consent. **Sexual assault** is a violent sexual attack on another person.

People who are under the influence of alcohol are more likely to be harmed. They are less likely to make responsible decisions about relationships. They are less likely to make responsible decisions about their safety. For example, an adolescent female under the influence of alcohol might not be able to maintain her decision to practice abstinence from sex. As a result, she might become infected with HIV and develop AIDS.

Sedative-Hypnotic Drugs

Sedative-hypnotic drugs are drugs that depress the central nervous system and are called "downers." Barbiturates and tranquilizers are examples. These drugs can be prescribed by a physician to help people relax. But, often they are used illegally. Downers are second to alcohol in contributing to harmful and violent behavior. Because downers dull the way people think, people who use them are not as likely to think about the consequences of their harmful and violent behavior.

PCP

PCP, or **angel dust**, is a drug that changes the way people see things. People who use PCP might have memory and speech problems. They might have hallucinations and depression. PCP can cause very violent behavior. People who use this drug become more and more angry over time. They are more likely to commit rape, sexual assault, murder, and suicide.

Cocaine

Cocaine is a drug that stimulates the central nervous system and its use frequently results in drug dependence. **Drug dependence** is the continued use of a drug even though it harms the body, mind, and relationships. Cocaine use changes personality in different ways. Some people become very hostile toward others. Other people get very depressed. Cocaine use might result in harming others or in suicide. There are other ways in which cocaine use threatens relationships. People who share needles to inject cocaine into their veins are at risk for HIV infection and AIDS.

Crack

Crack is a drug that is pure cocaine and produces rapid ups and downs. People who use crack get a very quick "high" that is followed by a rapid drop to "low." People can become dependent on crack immediately. They then will have an urge to get more. They might harm others in order to get the money to pay for the drug.

Amphetamines

Amphetamines are drugs that "speed up" the central nervous system. This is why they are called "speed." People who use amphetamines might become overactive, impulsive, and out of control. They might provoke fights. When people stop using amphetamines, they might get very depressed.

Heroin

Heroin is a drug that slows body functions such as heart rate and breathing and produces drowsiness and mood swings. Because heroin is injected into a vein, users who share needles are at risk for HIV infection. People who use heroin can become dependent on the drug. Heroin use increases violent behavior.

Anabolic Steroids

Anabolic steroids are drugs produced from male sex hormones. People who use them can experience "roid rages." These are outbursts of very angry behavior. During roid rages, users might harm others. After using these powerful drugs for some time, depression might occur. Users are at risk for suicide.

Marijuana

Marijuana is a drug containing THC that impairs short term memory and causes mood changes. In the past, marijuana usually had about one to five percent THC in it. Today, it might have as much as eight to fifteen percent THC in it. This increase is why marijuana use has become increasingly more dangerous. People under the influence of THC have mood swings. They might have hallucinations, become extremely worried, and feel threatened and paranoid around others.

9. Being a Consumer of Entertainment That Portrays Harmful and Violent Relationships

A **consumer** is a person who chooses sources of information and buys or uses products and services. The **media** are the means of communication including television, radio, the movies, and newspapers that influence a consumer's information and decisions. **Entertainment** is something that is designed to hold the interest of people.

Entertainment rating systems are ratings to assist people in determining suitability of content for certain age groups. Chapter 1 identified the following:

• Guidelines for Choosing Entertainment that Promotes Healthful Relationships;

- a Television Rating System;
- a Movie Rating System; and
- an Entertainment Software Rating System.

Being a consumer of entertainment that portrays harmful and/or violent relationships increases the risk of becoming involved in harmful and/or violent relationships. The National Television Violence Study conducted by media scholars at the University of California at Santa Barbara, the University of Texas at Austin, the University of Wisconsin, and the University of North Carolina examined the content of approximately 2,500 hours of television. Research focused on three components: the amount and nature of violence on television; the response of children to media ratings; and the promotion of anti-violence through public service messages. The study established these findings about television depiction of violence:

- an association between the context in which television violence is presented and harmful risks to viewers for developing violent behavior, experiencing desensitization to the harmful effects of violence, and becoming fearful of attack;
- a pattern of unpunished violence;
- infrequent portrayal of the harmful consequences of violence;
- use of a handgun in one-fourth of the violent events presented; and
- a lack of anti-violent themes (Mediascope, 1998).

Patterns of violence in children's television programs are associated with aggressive behavior in children who view these programs. Young viewers might identify with characters who commit violent actions. Young viewers also might develop anxiety and fear if they identify with persons who are victims of violence (Mediascope, 1998).

There are other reasons why children who view television programs that portray harmful and violent relationships are at risk. By completion of elementary school, the average child in the United States has viewed approximately 8,000 murders and 100,000 acts of violence on television (Mediascope, 1998). Studies of the

viewing habits and behavior patterns of eight-year-old males established violent television programs as a major factor in the development of aggressive and delinquent behavior during adolescence and criminal behavior in adulthood (AMA, 1996).

Studies have established a relationship between the television viewing habits of adolescents and the use of interactive video games that might contribute to aggressive behavior and desensitization to violence. **Desensitization** is the effect of reacting less and less to the exposure of something. More than 1000 studies affirm that substantial exposure to media violence desensitizes young viewers to effects of violence on relationships. In one study of adolescents who played video games, researchers determined the most popular game category to be fantasy violence (Mediascope, 1996).

Research suggests a link between the preference of some adolescents for heavy metal music and the risk for suicide. However, a causal relationship has not been established (APA, 1996). A study of the effect of televised music videos, especially rock and rap videos, containing positive portrayals of violent behavior suggested the influence of these portrayals on the practice of aggression by adolescents (AMA, 1996).

The occurrence of violence as a result of Internet access has not been established because of the rapid growth of technology. However, the availability of sexually explicit materials and pornography on the Internet has increased public concern about children's access to information that is not monitored by a government or private agency. **Pornography** is sexually explicit material that is sexually arousing and obscene. Incidents of child molestation resulting from on-line communication between sexual molesters and children have been reported by the National Center for Missing and Exploited Children (AMA, 1996).

10. Being a Victim of Violence

Earlier in this chapter, a distinction was made between being a survivor of violence and being a victim of violence. A survivor of violence has been harmed by violence, has participated in recovery to heal from its emotional effects, and has adopted self-protection strategies. Being a survivor of violence is not a risk factor for being involved in harmful and/or violent relationships. On the other hand, a victim of violence has not recovered from the emotional effects of violence and/or has not become skilled in self-protection strategies. Victims of violence are at risk for being involved in harmful and violent relationships. This is especially true when violence occurred within the family. Victims of violence who were abused by parents, grow up and might become parents themselves. They have learned how to parent from their parents. Without outside help, they might parent in the same ways and abuse their own children. The **cycle of abuse** is the repeating of abuse from one generation to the next. People who were victims of child abuse are six times more likely to abuse their own children.

Victims of violence often lack self-respect. They might have been abused for so long that they actually begin to believe they deserve to be abused. They lack self-worth, one of the other risk factors for being involved in harmful and/or violent relationships. Without counseling, victims of violence are likely to allow others to harm them if they do not regain self-respect and self-worth.

Some victims of violence need to become skilled at self-protection strategies. This helps them feel empowered. Unfortunately, less than one in five gets help within the first year. There are different reasons for this. They might not want to spend money for professional services. They might not want to spend time in counseling. They might find that the effort needed to fully recover is exhausting. As a result, they decide to let time pass believing they will recover without effort over time. The saying, "Time alone will not heal wounds," is true. Usually, the emotional effects of violence do not go away without participating in recovery. Victims of violence continue to suffer and be at risk for being involved in harmful and/or violent relationships.

Harmful Relationships

Harmful relationships are relationships that destroy self-respect, interfere with productivity and health, and include addictions and/or violence. This section of the chapter includes profiles of people who relate in harmful ways, kinds of harmful relationships, and what to do about harmful relationships.

Ten Profiles of People Who Relate in Harmful Ways

1. The People Pleaser

A **people pleaser** is a person who constantly seeks the approval of others. A people pleaser might choose a harmful behavior, such as alcohol or drug abuse just to please others. His or her choice is not based on responsible values. The result would be a harmful relationship. Consider a male who is in college and joins a fraternity. Although he does not like the taste of alcohol, he drinks alcohol when a fraternity brother offers it to him to gain the approval of his fraternity brothers. His fraternity brothers view him as a "doormat," because they can "walk over" him. He seeks to please his fraternity brothers at his own expense. He loses his self-respect and sabotages his potential for developing healthful relationships.

2. The Enabler

An **enabler** is a person who supports the harmful behavior of others. The enabler might deny or refuse to acknowledge that another person is participating in behavior that might result in negative consequences for the relationship. The enabler might rationalize and seek to camouflage the harmful behavior of another person, thus appearing to approve of the behavior. An example is a wife who agrees to accompany her husband to a gambling casino. The husband has been unemployed for several weeks and has chosen to gamble their savings in an attempt to restore his lost earnings rather than begin a job search. Although the wife might experience feelings of anxiety about the risk behavior of gambling, her decision to participate suggests an attitude of support, causing her to become an enabler. The opportunity for her to establish expectations based on the practice of responsible values has been undermined because as an enabler she has made a decision that adversely affects their needs.

3. The Clinger

A **clinger** is a person who is needy and dependent. The clinger is characterized by a feeling of emptiness. The clinger might seek fulfillment by demanding the constant attention of another person. The clinger often establishes a pattern of unrealistic demands that eventually "suffocates" a relationship by attempting to monopolize the time and attention of the other person. Consider a female who wants to spend every weekend with one of her friends. When the friend explains she needs to spend time with others, the clinger becomes upset and tries to make her friend feel guilty. Such a pattern of insistence that does not provide "breathing space" in a relationship might result in the friend trying to distance himself or herself from the clinger.

4. The Fixer

A **fixer** is a person who tries to fix other people's problems. The fixer establishes a position of authority in a person's life and assumes responsibility for solving his or her difficulties. The fixer offers constant advice and might try to choose solutions for the person with the problem. For example, a high school student is having difficulty in his science courses. His father wants him to be accepted into a prestigious medical college and is unhappy with his son's grades. He calls his son's teachers and tells them to go "easy" on his son. He offers to do his son's homework for him. He tries to "fix" his son's grades without allowing his son to take responsibility. Such interference sabotages any potential for a healthful relationship because most people do not want others to make decisions for them. Healthy people seek advice and counsel with the expectation of support, not control.

5. The Distancer

A **distancer** is a person who is emotionally unavailable to others. This behavior might be expressed in several ways including extreme busyness that precludes the possibility of having a relationship and ensures the avoidance of sharing feelings that might lead to intimacy. For example, if a male has recently experienced a breakup, he might establish a demanding study or work schedule so he doesn't have much time for future girlfriends. Although this practice might reduce the risk of emotional hurt, the potential for healthful relationships also is reduced because the person is unwilling to risk emotional involvement.

6. The Controller

A **controller** is a person who is possessive, jealous, and domineering. The controller seeks to have power over other people by demanding certain behaviors or activities or by practicing indoctrination of certain beliefs. The controller does not like to share the object of attention. For example, an adolescent female experiences jealousy when her boyfriend becomes the focus of attention after becoming his football team's star player. The female refuses to participate in the team's celebrations and insists that the boyfriend spend the time with her instead. It is important to recognize the characteristics of a controller since attempts to control a person might result in physical harm. Signs of jealousy and possessiveness might have preceded the harmful behavior; however, the issues were not confronted and resolved. As a result, the controller has sabotaged the possibility of a healthful relationship.

7. The Center

A **center** is a person who is self-centered. The center's beliefs, attitudes, and ideas are related to his or her own best interests and rarely reflect the interests of other people. The center prefers to participate in activities that he or she chooses and reflect personal interests. For example, a female calls her friend on the phone every day to discuss her own problems. She never asks questions about her friend but only talks about herself. A healthful relationship is not possible because the center is the established focus of attention, and the needs of the other person are ignored.

8. The Abuser

An **abuser** is a person who is abusive. Abusive behavior might be expressed in demeaning remarks, threats, or violent behavior. The abuser might force a person to engage in sexual activity. An act or expression of gentleness might follow the act of aggression. For example, if a male expresses rage toward a female and beats her repeatedly, then later demonstrates affection to her, the female might experience confused feelings. The female might think that the male is experiencing remorse and has chosen to change. However, the male is an abuser, and the cycle of abuse including aggression and apology is predictable. A person who suspects the potential for abuse in a relationship resulting in physical or emotional harm should not associate with the abuser.

9. The Liar

A **liar** is a person who does not tell the truth. A liar will lie to appear more acceptable or more skilled than he or she actually is. Since honesty is a foundation in any healthful relationship, the practice of honesty in conversations and actions is important. When a person does not tell the truth, other people respond and behave based on false information. If the truth had been expressed, the responses and behaviors might have been different. For example, a college female begins dating a college male. She tells him their relationship is exclusive. However, when she goes home for vacation, she goes out on dates with her high school boyfriend. She doesn't tell her college boyfriend about the continuing relationship. Their relationship is based on a lie and is harmful.

10. The Promise Breaker

A **promise breaker** is a person who is not reliable. The promise breaker might arrange to participate in an activity with another person but does not honor the promise. Perhaps the promise breaker decided to accept a later invitation instead. The promise breaker might even promise to change this annoying behavior but does not do so. Consider the person who plans a camping trip with a friend. The promise is made to pick up a friend and drive together to the camp ground. However, the promise breaker does not arrive. The friend later discovers that the promise breaker has gone shopping with a different friend. The promise breaker's behavior is associated with insincerity and lack of commitment, causing other people to doubt his or her actions. This undermines the chance for healthful relationships.

Kinds of Harmful Relationships

People who relate in harmful ways often are attracted to each other. They tend to "match-up" to form a harmful relationship in which each of them can act out a specific role. The discussion that follows explains what might happen when the following types of people have a relationship:

- a promise breaker and a people pleaser;
- a controller and an enabler;
- a clinger and a distancer.

A Promise Breaker and a People Pleaser

Suppose a promise broker and a people pleaser match up. The promise breaker agrees to attend a movie with a people pleaser. However, the promise breaker receives an invitation to attend a concert the same evening and cancels plans to go to the movie. The people pleaser feels angry and hurt but does not express the anger. Instead, the people pleaser accommodates the promise breaker by agreeing to attend the movie at a later date.

The people pleaser will resent the promise breaker's behavior but will not express his or her true feelings. The promise breaker will continue letting him or her down and the harmful relationship will continue. The people pleaser must learn to express feelings healthfully. The promise breaker must recognize that his or her behavior is harmful and learn to keep commitments.

A Controller and an Enabler

Suppose a controller and an enabler match up. The controller is a jealous male who demands the undivided attention of a female. The jealousy is expressed in objections to her relationships with females and in outbursts about interactions with other males. The controller is suspicious and uses accusations to control the female's behavior and relationships. The female is an enabler and misinterprets the behavior of the male as an expression of love. As a result, the female breaks off other friendships and supports the male's harmful behavior.

The male must respect the right of the female to find friendship with others and to practice healthful behaviors based on responsible values. The female must take responsibility for her behavior and practice self-respect by not denying feelings and needs.

A Clinger and a Distancer

Suppose a clinger and a distancer match up. The clinger is a female who was raised in a family separated by divorce. The female experienced abandonment at age 10 when her father deserted her family. Although she rarely speaks of the event, her hurt feelings are evident. The depth of the hurt is expressed in her fear of abandonment, resulting in fears of vulnerability and intimacy. The female becomes attracted to a distancer, who is emotionally unavailable.

The clinger and the distancer share the same fears but use different methods to protect themselves against negative consequences.

The clinger is attracted to a person who avoids intimacy. The distancer seeks to escape relationships and avoids emotional involvement with the clinger. The distancer might spend some time with the clinger, then leaves. This causes the clinger to chase harder. The establishment of a healthful relationship between the clinger and the distancer is associated with changes of behavior. The clinger must address the issue of emptiness and develop greater self-confidence. The distancer must address fears of intimacy.

Changing Profiles in Different Relationships

There are many match-ups of people who relate in harmful ways, such as a center and a fixer or a people pleaser and an abuser. However, a person might reflect different behaviors in some relationships depending on the profile or the other person. Suppose a female has several close friendships. However, she practices the behavior of being an enabler only with one certain male friend. She should examine the factors in this relationship that promote her harmful behavior.

What to Do About Harmful Relationships

Suppose a person is involved in a harmful relationship. There are steps he or she can take to end or improve the harmful relationship.

1. Evaluate Relationships with Regularity.

It is important to evaluate relationships. Suppose there is harmful behavior in the relationship. Then a person must identify

- the behaviors of the other person that cause concern; and
- the reactions or responses he or she has to the harmful behaviors of the other person.

Suppose a female shares an apartment with a roommate. The roommate does not pay her share of the rent and refuses to clean up after herself. The female must be aware of her roommate's wrong actions. Then she must be aware of her response—anger.

2. Recognize the Necessity to End a Harmful Relationship Rather Than Work Toward Change.

Sometimes harmful behaviors in a person cannot be changed without professional help. Being able to recognize the necessity to end a harmful relationship is important to health. A person should end a relationship

- when the other person chooses illegal behaviors;
- when the other person's actions threaten his or her health or safety; and
- on the advice of parents or guardian.

Suppose a female is dating a male who abuses drugs. The male continues abusing drugs even though the female expresses resistance and disapproval. The female should end the relationship.

3. Identify Changes in Behavior That Must Occur in the Harmful Relationship to Promote Healthful Interaction.

Certain changes in behavior must occur in harmful relationships in order to promote healthful interaction. After the harmful behaviors are identified, a person should prepare lists of ways to encourage necessary changes in the relationship. These should include

- changes that a person expects in himself or herself; and
- changes that a person expects in other people.

For example, a person might determine not to be a people pleaser by expressing resentment and hurt feelings in a healthful way. A person also might enlist the expectation of others to respect his or her feelings.

4. Seek the Advice of a Respected Adult or a Skilled Professional About Expected Changes in the Relationship.

Expectations about changes in behavior in a relationship should be discussed with an experienced adult who might provide assistance. The issues a person might share include the following:

- concerns about the relationship;
- behaviors that a person expects to change;
- behaviors that a person expects the other person to change;
- realistic assessment of expectations;
- the wisdom of continuing the relationship;
- the nature and similarities of other relationships; and
- the ways to improve relationship skills.

Decisions based on the discussion with the adult should be implemented. The person might arrange to discuss the results of changes in

behavior with the adult at a later time to evaluate the progress toward a healthful relationship.

5. Have a Frank Discussion with the Other Person About Concerns and Expectations of the Relationship.

Honest communication about issues in a relationship promotes healthful behaviors. When a person has concerns about harmful behaviors in a relationship, communication with the other person is essential and should include

- identification of a person's concerns and expectations;
- request for the identification of concerns and expectations of the other person;
- discussion about continuing the relationship; and
- strategies for maintaining the relationship, if mutually agreed.

Consider the relationship of two college students. A female student expresses concern that her male friend has increased his study time, thus reducing the amount of time they spend together. The male student expresses his expectation of her understanding since course demands require more preparation. The two might establish a strategy for maintaining their relationship by agreeing to meet on a regular basis, although with less frequency. The two also might choose to separate until the male has achieved certain academic goals. The communication of needs in a relationship and a willingness to practice a change in behaviors help promote a healthful relationship.

6. Set a Future Date to Reevaluate the Relationship.

Since changes in behaviors must be practiced in order to develop healthy patterns of interaction, a person should establish a future time to discuss the relationship again. Reevaluating the relationship should include

- a realistic time frame for the establishment and practice of changes in behavior; and
- the expectation that further evaluation will determine the progress of changes in behavior.

For example, a spouse expresses concern that the other spouse repeatedly breaks the promise to attend their daughter's basketball games. The promise breaker might agree to attend the next game in which the daughter participates. However, the daughter injures herself and will not be able to play basketball for two weeks. Therefore, the change in behavior must not be expected until the daughter resumes participation in the game.

Violent Relationships

Violent relationships are relationships that harm another person physically, mentally, and/or emotionally. This section of the chapter discusses kinds of violent relationships and focuses on physical abuse, emotional abuse, neglect, sexual abuse, rape, sexual harassment, and stalking.

Physical Abuse

Physical abuse is harmful treatment that results in physical injury to the victim. Examples include hitting, slapping, kicking, choking, shoving, and other physically harming behaviors. Physical abuse should not be confused with the practice of discipline, since discipline is associated with corrective actions that develop self-control and do not cause harm to a person.

Suppose a parent or guardian hits a child and says, "I'll teach you to follow my rules." Although the parent's remark associates the harmful behavior with the practice of discipline, hitting is not an appropriate form of discipline because it is an act of violence. Other expressions of physical abuse against children and adolescents include the use of a belt buckle, rope, or other object to inflict harm. Physical abuse also is associated with intentional acts of burning, bruising, cutting, or breaking bones. In 1995, physical abuse was reported as the second most frequent type of mistreatment of children and adolescents ages 18 and under (USDOJ, 1995a).

Domestic violence can result in physical abuse. **Domestic violence** is violence that occurs within a family. Although males might experience physical abuse by females or other males, females are more likely to experience physical abuse by males. Females at high risk for physical abuse are usually unmarried, separated or divorced, between the ages of 17 and 28, alcohol or drug abusers, pregnant, and/or jealous or possessive in an intimate relationship (AMA, 1999a).

Certain characteristics are associated with people who experience domestic violence. Often, these people observed the practice of abuse within family relationships during childhood. About 20 percent of adult females who are physically abused by adult males experienced child abuse (AMA, 1999a).

The effects of domestic violence might range from self-neglect or self-injury to various psychological symptoms including depression, alcohol and drug abuse, aggressiveness, eating disorders, sexual dysfunction, and attempts to commit suicide (AMA, 1999a).

A person who experiences domestic violence should separate from the abuser. However, some people feel unable to make this decision because of fear of retaliation or loss of self-esteem. Any observations of domestic violence should be reported immediately by calling the local emergency telephone number.

Emotional Abuse

Emotional abuse is "putting down" another person and making the person feel worthless. This includes the harmful treatment of a person that is expressed through threats, intimidation, humiliation, blame, or disparagement. Emotional abuse also might be associated with deprivation. Suppose a mother makes comments to her children such as, "You are small because you are worth nothing." The comment is demeaning and might result in feelings of inadequacy that harm the children's self-respect. The practice of emotional abuse might be experienced in less obvious ways that are difficult to recognize. An example of more subtle emotional abuse would be teasing that might seem to be humorous but actually is ridicule.

A distinction should be made between emotional abuse and constructive criticism. Consider the instructor who suggests that a student carefully apply the use of logic in developing the next term paper about the language of philosophy. In this case, the suggestion is constructive criticism. If the instructor said to the student, "Your last term paper was stupid," the comment would be abusive.

People who seek to practice responsible behaviors that do not cause harm should consider some values that might lead instead to emotional abuse. These values might include excessive emphasis on participation in activities, such as beauty pageants and athletics, that do not allow a child or an adolescent to experience a healthful, normal childhood, thus resulting in a form of child abuse.

The experience of abuse in childhood has been established as a factor in subsequent violent criminal activity. Therefore, it is important to be aware of certain behaviors that suggest emotional abuse in a child. The warning signs of emotional abuse in a child include the following:

- difficulty in establishing friendships;
- avoidance of activities with peers;
- anxiety or depression;
- demanding behavior or extreme obedience;
- adult behavior;
- age-inappropriate behavior, such as thumb-sucking;
- bedwetting;
- delayed physical and emotional development; and
- suicide attempts (AMA, 1999a).

Neglect

Neglect is failure to provide proper care and guidance. It includes harmful treatment that results in deprivation including access to nutritious food, shelter, clothing, medical and dental care, and emotional support. Child neglect also is associated with lack of education. Child neglect might result in serious health consequences associated with physical injuries and mental and behavioral difficulties leading to delinquency and adult criminal activity. Child neglect also might affect normal social and cognitive development and social relationships (NIH, 1999).

Child protection laws govern cases of maltreatment including neglect. Young children require adult supervision. If their parents or guardians are employed, an alternative arrangement must be made to provide supervision by a responsible adult. The absence of the proper supervision of children is associated with neglect.

Sexual Abuse

Sexual abuse is sexual contact that is forced on a person. A survey of more than 6,000 college students enrolled at 32 institutions in the United States established that 54 percent of the females had experienced sexual abuse. Among adolescent females, at least 12 percent have experienced sexual abuse (AMA, 1999b). Males also might experience sexual abuse. The practice of sexual abuse might occur within family relationships. It is possible that the family might ignore the issue and practice secrecy. Sexual abuse might be expressed in different forms including

- incest;
- inappropriate touching of private body parts; and
- the display or production of pornographic pictures.

Incest is the practice of sexual intercourse with a family member. A person who experienced incest in childhood might try to ignore the feelings of anger associated with the behavior. If a person does not obtain treatment, he or she might continue to feel guilt, shame, and depression. Therefore, it is important for the person who experienced incest to accept the truth of the event that produced a harmful relationship.

Sexual abuse might be expressed in other harmful behaviors including inappropriate touching of body parts. Sexual abuse also is associated with the practice of pornography. **Pornography** is sexually explicit material that is sexually arousing and obscene. Pornography might be in the form of printed, visual, or audio material. Usually, pornography includes a graphic portrayal of sexual acts and/or sexual organs. Showing pornographic pictures to and taking pornographic pictures of children and adolescents is a form of sexual abuse.

Concerns regarding family values, sexual behavior and society, and the sexual attitudes of adolescents have prompted examination of pornography and its effects from the community level to the Supreme Court. The courts have held that obscene materials are not protected by the First Amendment (United States Supreme Court, 1998).

The case of *Roth v. United States* attempted to clarify what material could be defined as obscene according to the Constitution. Three criteria help clarify the classification of materials as being obscene:

1. The dominant theme of the material taken as a whole appeals to a prurient interest in sex.

2. The material is patently offensive because it affronts contemporary community standards relating to the description or representation of sexual matters.

3. The material is utterly without redeeming social value.

Additional criteria might be used to determine if material is obscene and should be avoided:

1. The material interferes with the development of loving and responsible relationships.

2. The material is degrading to females and/or males.

3. The material promotes violent sexual behaviors.

4. The material encourages harmful paraphilias including sadomasochism and necrophilia.

The issue of child pornography activities is an important source of concern among medical societies working in cooperation with various national organizations and federal and local agencies (AMA, 1998).

Rape

Rape is the threatened or actual use of physical force to get someone to have sex without giving consent. A common perception of rape is that it is a sudden, violent attack perpetrated by a male against a female. The reality, however, is that rape occurs in a variety of situations that might differ widely from the common perception. The disparity is such that the perpetrator and/or the victim might not even recognize the behavior as rape.

The incidence of rape affects more than 700,000 females each year (AMA, 1999b). No one is immune from becoming a rape victim. Rape victims range in age from infants to elderly. About 61 percent of females who experienced rape are under the age of 18 (AMA, 1999b). Although rape most commonly is perpetrated by males against females, males might be the rape victims of other males and/or females.

It is difficult to obtain accurate statistics because many victims of rape are reluctant to make reports. In fact, rape is one of the least reported of all violent crimes in our society. Females are more likely to report a rape when a stranger is involved, when a significant amount of personal property is stolen, when serious injury occurs, or when married. Reasons females choose not to report rape include the following:

• fear of retaliation;

• sense of futility (the perpetrator is unlikely to be caught or convicted);

• fear of publicity and embarrassment;

• fear of mistreatment by the judicial system;

• pressure from family members; and

• fear of ruining a relationship with a significant other.

Rape is exploitative sexual behavior that appears to be motivated by a combination of power, anger, and the desire for sexual gratification. When rape is committed by a person unknown to the victim, power and anger are likely to be the dominant motivating factors. This type of rape often is interpreted as an act of violence and domination that is expressed in a sexual manner rather than as an attempt to seek sexual gratification.

People who commit rape are frequently socially inept and have difficulty establishing meaningful relationships. Often a person who is a rapist is a victim of sexual abuse. In nearly three-fourths of the cases, rape is associated with drinking alcohol (AMA, 1999b).

Many males who are rapists express negative attitudes and displaced anger toward females. These males often will attempt to justify the behavior claiming that "females want to be raped" or "they were asking for it." These males fail to realize or do not care that rape is devastating to a female. The sexual acts performed are often humiliating and degrading. Females who have been raped might suffer vaginal tears, contract an infection such as an STD including HIV, or become impregnated. In addition, the family and friends of the victim might blame or reject the female.

Rape-Related Post-Traumatic Stress Disorder (RR-PTSD) often results from sexual assault. In the past, the emotional symptoms experienced by survivors of rape were identified as rape trauma syndrome. There are four common symptoms of RR-PTSD. The first symptom produces repeated recollection of the trauma in thoughts, nightmares, and dreams. The second symptom is social withdrawal and loss of interest in relationships and daily activities. The third symptom produces avoidance behaviors and actions, resulting in avoidance of the place or activities associated with the event. The fourth symptom is characterized by physiological arousal to sights and sounds in the environment that might result in sleep disorders (National Center for Victims of Crime, 1992).

There are many precautions that a female can take to reduce the risk of being raped (Table 2.2).

Acquaintance or Date Rape

The preceding discussion of rape focused on an unknown person raping someone in an act of violence. However, the majority of cases of rape involve a form of rape known as acquaintance rape. **Acquaintance rape** is rape in which the rapist is known to the person who is raped. Acquaintance rapes often occur in dating situations.

Table 2.2

Guidelines to Follow to Reduce the Risk of Rape

1. Do not indicate that you will be home alone.

2. Do not give your name, address, or telephone number to strangers or people who seem untrustworthy.

3. Use dead-bolt locks on outside doors and keep windows locked.

4. Change door locks when a house key is lost.

5. Use a peephole in the door before opening the door. Do not open the door for a stranger.

6. Keep outside entrances to the house brightly lighted.

7. Have car keys in your hand when planning to drive a car.

8. Check the back seat and floor of the car before entering.

9. Drive with the car doors locked.

10. Learn self-defense techniques to gain confidence and to defend against a possible assailant.

11. Carry a device for making a loud noise such as a whistle and use it at the first sign of danger.

12. Do not hitchhike.

13. Do not leave a party, shopping mall, or other place with a stranger.

The myth that characterizes a person who has been raped as "sexually loose" and evidence that depends on the words of the rapist against the words of person who was raped hinder the prosecution of acquaintance rape cases (National Center for Victims of Crime, 1997a).

A disparity often exists as to how a rape situation is perceived. For example, a male might believe a female who goes into a hotel room with a male is "asking for it." A male might believe a female's actions indicate her consent even as she says "no" to his sexual advances. It is therefore important to teach males that sex without consent is rape and that circumstances do not change this definition of an unlawful behavior. A male must understand that "no" means "no." It is prudent for a female to avoid being in a compromising situation that sends a mixed message. The discussion that follows clarifies further some important points regarding acquaintance rape.

Inappropriate sexual attitudes and failure to communicate appear to be important in the incidence of acquaintance rape. Some males regard sexual relationships as adversarial. Some males believe they are expected to initiate sexual intercourse and that females are expected to resist. Some males view the dating situation as a sexual "game" in which females want to be coerced into sexual intercourse and often feel that the use of force is justified in some circumstances. To these males, forceful sexual behavior is considered a normal part of courtship and is not considered rape. Consequently, they have no associated sense of guilt.

Some males misinterpret actions such as cuddling and kissing as indicating a desire to engage in intercourse. These males believe that females offer token resistance so as not to appear too easy. In addition, some males believe that when a female says "no" she really means "maybe," and when she says "maybe" she really means "yes." As a result, these males ignore messages of nonconsent and proceed to engage in sexual activity especially if little physical resistance is encountered.

Such communication problems are exacerbated and perpetuated by the fact that alcohol abuse often is a factor. Some females who have been victimized are not even sure that a crime has been committed. Perhaps as a consequence of ambiguities in the dating situation, victims of acquaintance rape are sometimes reluctant to report the crime to the authorities. Although a report is not mandatory, the following is facilitated:

- participation in crime victim compensation programs that require immediate reporting;
- higher arrest rates; and
- access to other assistance (National Center for Victims of Crime, 1997a).

Table 2.3 identifies measures that might be taken to reduce the risk of being a victim of acquaintance rape.

Table 2.3

Guidelines to Follow to Avoid Acquaintance Rape

1. Establish clear limits for sexual behavior.

2. Communicate these limits to the person with whom you have a date.

3. Avoid sending mixed messages that confuse a verbal "no" with actions that encourage sexual advances.

4. Firmly tell the person to stop when unwanted sexual advances are experienced.

5. Respond by making loud noises and resisting if the person does not stop.

6. Avoid dating or being in the company of a person who is very controlling and demanding.

7. Avoid drinking alcohol and using other drugs that interfere with judgment and response.

8. Avoid being in places where calls for help will not be heard should unwanted sexual advances occur.

In addition, a change in the sexual attitudes of many young males is necessary in order to reduce the incidence of acquaintance rape. Education programs have been developed to educate young males about the difference between healthful sexual behavior and sexual violence. The following guidelines might be used to educate young males:

- express feelings;
- practice ways to describe comfort levels;
- evaluate the effect of behavior on females;
- practice respect;
- confront aggressive attitudes toward females;
- seek to build healthful relationships with males and females; and
- accept "no" as a response to sexual advances.

It is important to remember that an intoxicated person does not have the capacity to give consent to sexual intercourse. A person who has sex with a person who is too intoxicated to give consent can be charged with rape. And the voluntary intoxication of a rapist cannot be used as a legal defense.

A victim of acquaintance rape should report the incident to the police. Prompt medical attention must be obtained.

Date Rape Drugs

Flunitrazepam, or **Rohypnol**, is an odorless, colorless sedative drug. On the street, the drug is known as "roofies," "rope," "the forget pill," and "roach." This drug is ten times stronger than valium, which is a tranquilizer (USDOJ, 1999a). Like alcohol, it can cause faulty thinking in some users. It is referred to as "the date-rape drug" because it can cause blackouts, with complete or partial loss of memory. A male can slip a "roofie" into a female's drink and commit date rape after she blacks out. Other effects include aggressiveness and fearlessness. It can cause breathing irregularities and can be fatal.

Although the use of "roofies" is associated with incidents of rape, a new study suggests voluntary use of the drug by females between the ages of 14 and 26. When the drug is combined with alcohol or other drugs, euphoria is heightened (AAP, 1999). Other date rape drugs include Gamma hydroxybutyric acid (GHB), Ketamine, and Burundanga. Methylenedioxymethamphetamine (MDMA), known on the street as "ecstasy," also might be used to heighten aggression, mood, and sexual activity (NIDA, 1999). The use of MDMA among college students and young adults rose sharply during the past decade. GHB, a colorless, odorless liquid drug with a slightly salty taste, acts as a depressant on the central nervous system causing dizziness, drowsiness, or unconsciousness. In 1997, the FDA re-issued a warning about the serious health consequences that might result from the use of GHB for body building and recreational purposes. GHB cannot be legally marketed in the United States. Ketamine is an anesthetic used in veterinary medicine that produces hallucinations and feelings of separation from the body in a person. An overdose of Ketamine can cause cardiac arrest. Burundanga, a highly soluble and tasteless drug, causes a person to become disoriented and enter a trance-like state, resulting in amnesia.

The Drug-Induced Rape Prevention and Punishment Act of 1996 established that giving a controlled substance, such as flunitrazepam, GHB, Ketamine, Burundanga, or MDMA, to a person with intent to commit a sexual assault or other crime of violence is a federal felony and might result in incarceration.

A victim of rape requires confidentiality and services that include the following:

- immediate medical care;
- information about the transmission of STDs including HIV infection and AIDS;
- counseling;
- compensation; and
- restitution.

The victim of rape should be kept informed about the progress of the criminal investigation (National Center for Victims of Crime, 1998).

Sexual Harassment

Sexual harassment is unwanted sexual behavior that ranges from making sexual comments to forcing another person into unwanted sexual acts. Sexual harassment affects females and males in a variety of circumstances and relationships. Numerous cases of sexual harassment in the workplace have appeared in magazines and newspapers, suggesting that sexual harassment is an issue in the professional and private lives of many people. Although sexual harassment often affects females, males also experience sexual harassment. In a recent case before the United States Supreme Court, the complaint of Joseph Oncale against his employer, Sundowner Offshore Services, for same-sex harassment resulted in further evaluation of factors that led to the complaint including sex-related physical assaults and threats of rape (United States Supreme Court, 1999).

There have been many ambiguities surrounding what actually constitutes sexual harassment and how it differs from a healthful flirtation. There have been misconceptions about the relationship between the perpetrator and the victim.

Simply stated, sexual harassment involves unwanted verbal or physical sexual advances and requests for sexual favors. Because sexual harassment often occurs in the workplace, the Equal Employment Opportunity Commission (EEOC) has provided a more detailed description as follows:

Unwelcome sexual advances, requests for sexual favors, and other verbal or physical conduct of a sexual nature constitute sexual harassment when (1) submission to such conduct is made either explicitly or implicitly a term or condition of an individual's employment; (2) submission to or rejection of such conduct by an individual is used as the basis for employment decisions affecting such individual; or (3) such conduct has the purpose or effect of unreasonably interfering with an individual's work performance or creating an intimidating, hostile, or offensive working environment. (EEOC)

Sexual harassment can occur in many forms. In verbal form, sexual harassment could include such behaviors as comments about a person's body, sexually explicit or demeaning jokes, leering, or sexual proposals. Unwanted touching, hugging, kissing, and more extreme behaviors such as rape or attempted rape are forms of physical sexual harassment. Most people who have been sexually harassed feel embarrassed, demeaned, intimidated, and angry about the experience.

Although both males and females might be victims of sexual harassment, it appears that the incidence rate is much higher among females. Sexual harassment is a serious issue at all levels of education from elementary and secondary schools to colleges and universities.

Title IX of the Education Amendments of 1972 forbids sex discrimination including sexual harassment. Sexual harassment might occur during any school activity within classrooms, halls, cafeterias, dormitories, and other areas. Sexual harassment sometimes causes learning difficulties, or the decision to dropout of a class or school. The experience of sexual harassment also is associated with social isolation, loss of self-esteem, and fear for personal safety. Under Title IX, schools are required to adopt and publish grievance procedures and to have at least one employee coordinate compliance (United States Department of Education, 1997).

If sexual harassment occurs in the workplace, workers might leave their jobs to avoid an intolerable situation. If sexual harassment occurs in a school setting between a teacher or coach and a student, the student might feel anxious about going to school and his or her school performance might suffer.

Sexual harassment is exploitative and unlawful sexual behavior and should never be tolerated by either males or females in any situation. Therefore, it is important to have the facts about such behavior so that ambiguities can be clarified.

There are at least three distinctions between sexual harassment and a flirtation. First, sexual harassment is unwanted. When a male or female states that he or she is not interested in pursuing a relationship, having a date, or having a sexual encounter, it is clear that any further request or advance is unwanted. Second, sexual harassment is degrading. Comments about a person's body, sexually explicit or demeaning jokes, leering, and sexual proposals that are inappropriate degrade a person and do not promote loving, caring, and healthful relationships. Third, sexual advances, favors, or comments that occur because one person is in a position of authority can be viewed as attempts to control another person. This is especially true when refusal leads to threats of harm against the person being sexually harassed. Behavior in which one person manipulates and controls another does not contribute to healthful and responsible relationships.

The perpetrator and victim relationship often is difficult to understand by those not involved in such a relationship. People who are perpetrators are usually people who desire to control, manipulate, and dominate. Because of these tendencies, perpetrators are more likely to select a person who is vulnerable. In the workplace, the person's advancement might be dependent on the perpetrator's review. The perpetrator, such as a school coach, might use sexual harassment against a student. The perpetrator might select a person who perceives the perpetrator as an authority figure. The perpetrator might practice sexual harassment in a situation in which a person is vulnerable. For example, a male leering at a female walking down the street has selected a public situation in which a female might experience embarrassment and be less likely to respond.

Because sexual harassment often occurs in vulnerable situations, victims might find it difficult to respond in spite of feelings of anger. There often is confusion about the lapse in time between the beginning of the harassment and the victim's report to a person in authority or to a family member or a friend. This lapse in time might lead to mistaken beliefs that suggest the victim desired the sexual advances. Victims often are embarrassed that they tolerated inappropriate or harmful behavior and comments for such a long time period. This might lead others to question the motives of the victim who delayed taking action. In fact, some victims accept blame for sexual harassment because of self-doubt. When victims experience more self-confidence, the report of sexual harassment might be made at a later time. The victim often does not report or share incidents of sexual harassment until information is obtained that other people have reported similar complaints about the perpetrator. When this happens, the victim might feel more confident that the report will be believed. In addition, a similar complaint by another person might relieve self-doubt or confusion about the event.

It is important for young people to have guidelines to follow when sexual harassment occurs. Table 2.4 can be used to educate young people as to appropriate guidelines.

Stalking

Stalking is harassing someone with the intent to threaten or harm that person. People who stalk others are usually obsessed with the person they stalk. More than 1 million cases of stalking occur each year. Most people who practice stalking are males. Most people being stalked are females. However, males also are stalked, resulting in an annual rate of incidence involving more than 350,000 males (USDOJ, 1999b). People who stalk are trying to form or re-establish a relationship with the person being stalked. Most stalking occurs as the result of situations involving domestic violence. An abuser might stalk a person to regain control

| Table 2.4 | **Guidelines to Follow When Sexual Harassment Occurs** |

1. Tell the person who is practicing sexual harassment in specific terms to stop the behavior.

2. Record the date of the sexual harassment, the place where it occurred, and the specific behaviors and comments of the perpetrator.

3. Identify people who might have heard or otherwise been aware of the sexual harassment. Record their observations in detail.

4. Discuss the situation with parents or a guardian and/or other trusted adult.

5. File a grievance with the appropriate person (the superintendent or principal at school, the employer or supervisor at work). If the perpetrator is one of these people, an adult can assist in identifying the appropriate authority with whom to file the grievance.

6. File a grievance with the Equal Employment Opportunity Commission if sexual harassment occurred in the workplace.

7. Consider filing civil or criminal charges against the offender in cases of sexual assault including rape.

8. Contact an attorney if you are uncertain about the steps to take.

(USDOJ, 1999b). There is no established psychological or behavioral profile for a stalker. By stalking, a person might believe that he or she can attract the other person's attention. The stalker might fantasize about a relationship with a person and decide to take action. In some cases, a stalker takes violent action, leading to injury or murder. Stalking also might begin when a relationship has just ended. The stalker might be upset and apply scare tactics to force the victim into continuing the relationship. Table 2.5 provides a list of self-protection strategies to follow when being stalked.

Table 2.5   **Self-Protection Strategies When Being Stalked**

1. **Check state laws to determine the limits of protection against stalking.** All states have passed anti-stalking legislation. However, it is important to know the rights of people who are stalked and the most effective way to implement these rights, since protection might be limited. Effective enforcement of anti-stalking legislation can substantially reduce the incidence of stalking crimes.

2. **Contact the police.** A report of stalking to the police department might result in intervention by law enforcement officials and prosecutors, leading to effective resolution of the stalking. Pressing charges against the perpetrator might frighten and stop the person.

3. **Seek safety if there is immediate danger.** Seek safety at a police station, a residence unknown to the perpetrator, a domestic violence shelter, or a public place that might discourage violent behavior.

4. **Keep records.** Each event in which stalking occurs provides evidence that might be used to enforce protection. Therefore, a person being stalked should document occurrences by listing the date, time, what was said, and what happened. All written evidence, including pertinent notes and letters and answering machine tapes with recorded messages, should be saved in a secure place. If anyone witnessed the event, his or her name and contact information should be recorded.

5. **Obtain a restraining order.** A restraining order requires that a person who practices stalking stay away from the person being stalked. A violation of a restraining order might result in incarceration and/or payment of a fine. Restraining orders usually are obtained through a magistrate's office or a local court. However, a person who is being stalked should be aware that restraining orders might not be applicable beyond certain areas of jurisdiction. Sometimes, protective orders might be obtained only against former spouses or people of intimate relationship.

6. **Inform a trusted adult.** A minor should report any incident of stalking to a parent, guardian, or other trusted adult who might assist in protection strategies. A photo or description of the person who is stalking and a description of any vehicle that is used should be provided to heighten alertness to stalking activities. When possible, arrange for screening of incoming telephone calls.

7. **Seek counseling.** A person being stalked might obtain counseling and assistance from various sources including domestic violence shelters, rape crisis programs, and victim assistance coordinators in the prosecutor's office. If these services do not exist in the person's area, the person should contact law enforcement agencies.

8. **Practice safety precautions.** A person being stalked should practice safety by establishing preventive strategies. These might include:
   • installing solid core doors with dead bolt locks;
   • installing better outside lighting;
   • trimming back bushes around the residence;
   • establishing an unlisted phone number;
   • changing travel routes frequently;
   • avoiding traveling alone; and
   • remaining in public areas.

   When a person feels threatened in a public area, he or she should yell "fire" to attract attention.

9. **Develop a plan.** A person being stalked should develop a contingency plan in the event that danger might be imminent. The plan should include a strategy for safe departure from a dangerous location (National Center for Victims of Crime, 1997c).

Strategies for Recovering and Healing from Violent Relationships

People who have experienced violent behavior and survived must develop strategies for recovering and healing from the violence. The success of such strategies is associated with the ability to cope. Coping skills enable a survivor of violence to practice acceptance of the traumatic event and to manage related health issues effectively.

Strategies involving the use of coping skills might include

- a medical examination;

- management of STDs and/or HIV infection;

- issues involving unintended pregnancy;

- Post-Traumatic Stress Disorder (PTSD) and Rape-Related Post-Traumatic Stress Disorder (RR-PTSD);

- treatment for substance abuse

- the practice of safety (self-protection strategies);

- avoidance of risk behaviors and risk situations;

- development of healthful relationships; and

- custody issues.

This section of the chapter will discuss strategies for recovery from sexual assault, strategies for recovery from domestic abuse, steps to take when leaving an abusive relationship, steps to take after leaving an abusive relationship, the effects of domestic violence on children and adolescents, strategies for recovery from child abuse and neglect, and strategies for recovery from homicide.

Strategies for Recovery from Sexual Assault

It is estimated that 700,000 to 1 million females are raped each year. About 40 percent of these females experience more than one rape. Unintended pregnancies occur in about 5 percent of the cases. Females at highest risk for sexual assault are between the ages of 16 and 19, live in urban settings, and have incomes of less than $10,000 a year (APA, 1999).

During the early 1980s, Post-Traumatic Stress Disorder (PTSD) was identified as the emotional discomfort and stress resulting from memories of a severe trauma that impaired a person's perception of safety from harm. Symptoms of the disorder previously were associated with specific trauma such as Shell Shock, Combat Fatigue, Battered Women's Syndrome, Disaster Victim's Disorder, Concentration-Camp Syndrome, and Rape Trauma Syndrome. Rape-Related Post-Traumatic Disorder (RR-PTSD) has since been established as a form of PTSD resulting from sexual assault or rape.

The four major symptoms of RR-PTSD discussed earlier in this chapter include

- continuous reliving of the trauma;

- social withdrawal;

- avoidance behaviors and actions; and

- increased alertness to the environment.

People who experience RR-PTSD might abuse alcohol and other drugs in an attempt to dull the emotional pain.

It is important that recovery from RR-PTSD includes a medical examination. Although the incidence of STDs and HIV infection as a result of sexual assault is low, medical tests are recommended. The incidence of pregnancy resulting from a rape also is low. Negative test results for STDs, HIV infection, and pregnancy will likely result in some psychological relief.

Adolescent females who have experienced rape report symptoms that include phobias and "acting out" behaviors, such as running away from home, truancy, and promiscuity. Thus parental support is necessary to help manage symptoms. Some parents might feel angry or blame the adolescent for the rape. Parents who participate in family counseling can learn ways to help their adolescents recover, as well as resolve their own feelings of anger, shame, and blame.

Although some people who have been raped do not seek professional advice, supportive counseling helps ease the trauma. There are rape crisis centers nationwide. Other recommendations also might be considered.

- It is important to remember that the information provided about a rape or attempted rape might prevent another person from becoming a victim.

- The report of a rape should include information about the perpetrator including a detailed description of physical characteristics, clothes, and vehicle used.

- Prompt medical attention should be obtained. The rape survivor should not bathe or change clothes. Semen, hair, and materials under the fingernails and on clothing might help identify the perpetrator.

Rape also might be a very traumatic experience for the spouse or intimate partner of the person who was raped. In particular, males whose partners have been raped are likely to feel angry, inadequate, and have a sense of guilt. Males might worry that the female partner is infected with an STD including HIV. The reactions of male partners can have a profound influence on the recovery of the female who was raped and the future of their relationship. Therefore, males should seek to resolve issues that might interfere with recovery of the female. It is important that males use coping skills including acceptance of the trauma and the female's reactions as well as support of the female's decisions.

The husband or intimate partner of the female who was raped also might experience long-term difficulties. Erectile dysfunction might occur or the male's sexual desire might be affected by anger or disgust. In such instances, therapy might be beneficial.

Most people who commit rape are repeat offenders, and imprisonment does not generally prevent reoccurrence. For these people, many states have initiated specialized treatment programs that generally consist of a combination of prescribed drugs and psychotherapy. The drug medroxyprogesterone is used to reduce male sexual arousal by reducing the level of testosterone in the blood.

Strategies for Recovery from Domestic Abuse

Factors that affect the level of violence in relationships between spouses or other intimate partners include previous warning signs in the relationship, substance abuse, and the state of mind of the abuser.

People remain in abusive relationships because of
• a belief in commitment;
• a desire not to hurt the other person;
• a fear of social or personal blame;
• protection of children and parents;
• financial security; and
• the marriage commitment.

Steps to Take When Leaving an Abusive Relationship

Steps to take when leaving an abusive relationship include packing an emergency suitcase with changes of clothing, money, identification, and important personal documents such as birth certificate, passport, medical prescriptions, medications, and phone numbers. A person who was abused should report the situation to the police and a responsible adult, such as a neighbor or a friend.

If a restraining order has been obtained, the person who was abused might establish a plan for safety at home by changing the locks and the phone number and alerting other people to the situation. The person who was abused might practice safety at work by changing his or her daily schedule and having calls screened.

In recent years, a growing number of people who have been abused have appeared on television talk shows. This has led to concerns about the effect of such programs on the health and safety of the victims. An abused person should not agree to participate in a television talk show before counseling and legal advice are obtained. Such participation might jeopardize the investigation of criminal behavior. An abused child, especially a younger child, is at high risk for adverse effects of media exposure that could harm personal development and peer relationships. Therefore, an abused child should not participate in a television talk show without evaluation by a child victim advocate (National Center for Victims of Crime, 1997b).

Effects of Domestic Violence on Children and Adolescents

In a national survey of 6,000 families in the United States, more than half of the male batterers abused the children in addition to the adult females. More recent studies suggest that battered females are more likely than other females to abuse a child.

Symptoms of domestic violence in children and adolescents include anxiety or Post-Traumatic Stress Disorder (PTSD), withdrawal, eating and sleeping difficulties, and physical complaints such as headaches. Young children might develop stuttering and bedwetting. Aggressive behavior is more likely to occur in young males while physical symptoms are more likely to occur in young females (AMA, 1999a).

Often, it is difficult for children and adolescents to talk about exposure to domestic violence because of warnings or threats about discussion outside the family. However, when domestic violence in a family that includes children is suspected, school personnel such as a school psychologist or a social worker should be notified. Treatment might include self-expression through talking, writing, drawing, or painting.

Strategies for Recovery from Child Abuse and Neglect

Child abuse can occur in various forms including physical abuse, sexual abuse, and emotional abuse. Child neglect results from unmet necessities ranging from inadequate physical care to lack of emotional support (AMA, 1999a).

Sexual assault of children affects 15 per 1,000 children ages 18 and under. About 80 percent of the perpetrators were the parents, 10 percent were relatives, and 2 percent were foster parents or child care providers.

Children should be taught about the "bathing suit rule": only a physician has the right to touch areas that the bathing suit covers. Children should be encouraged to ask questions about safe and unsafe touches and to talk about visits to caregivers and time spent with child-sitters. A child who reports abuse should be taken seriously. Professional help should be obtained.

Strategies for Recovery from Homicide

People who survive the murder of a family member or friend usually experience multiple reactions including shock and anger. The suddenness of an unexpected and sometimes brutal death also produces confusion. While families and friends who survive the murder of a loved one must face the necessity of making funeral arrangements, the use of coping skills also is necessary. Coping skills include

- counseling,
- developing strategies for self-protection, and
- joining a grief support group.

Since people who survive homicide might be afraid for their personal safety, strategies for self-protection should be considered. These strategies should be developed in consultation with law enforcement.

Self-Protection Strategies

Self-protection strategies are strategies that can be practiced to protect oneself and others from harm. When people do not practice self-protection strategies, they are at risk for violence. This section of the chapter will discuss self-protection strategies that include self-defense strategies, self-protection strategies for the home, self-protection strategies for social situations, and self-protection strategies for traveling.

Self-Defense Strategies

Crime statistics suggest that nearly every person in the United States will be the victim of some form of criminal behavior in a lifetime. The prevalence of crime in the United States under-scores the importance of developing self-defense strategies as a means of self-protection. Self-defense strategies include the following:

- self-defense classes;
- self-defense devices; and
- self-defense posturing.

Self-Defense Classes

Self-defense classes are classes that provide training in techniques to protect people from bodily harm. Self-defense techniques are especially useful to females who might experience assault, since the striking ability of many females who have not been trained is ineffective against most males. Training in karate techniques teaches self-defense applications that affect vital areas of the body. A person should be aware that the practice of certain self-defense applications might effectively disable a perpetrator of violence. Disabling techniques include poking or flicking the fingers to the eyes, striking the side of the neck with the elbow or fist, kicking the groin area, or kicking the knee. People should be aware that the application of severe strikes to the throat, the temple, the base of the skull, or the top of the head might result in death.

A number of law enforcement agencies offer training in self-defense techniques or can direct a person to self-defense classes.

Self-Defense Devices

People might use self-defense devices to help secure protection. **Self-defense devices** are protective devices such as chemical sprays, whistles, personal sirens, cellular telephones, and reflective material that can be worn while jogging at dawn or at night. Chemical defense sprays might be used to thwart violent behavior by spraying the perpetrator's eyes. Spraying will result in a burning sensation and block vision temporarily, allowing the person being harmed to escape.

Security devices might be installed at home that include a home alarm system and/or a video surveillance system. Both systems are deterrents to burglary. An alarm system issues a warning of intrusion through a door or a window. A video surveillance system might be as simple as the installation of a camcorder or as sophisticated as a closed-circuit television system. Security systems that are professionally installed might include cameras that can be adjusted for tilting and rotation and/or cameras with a built-in infrared illuminator.

Self-Defense Posturing

Self-defense posturing is the exhibiting of verbal and nonverbal behavior that indicates self-confidence and self-protection. A demeanor that shows confidence and self-assurance suggests purposeful direction. Wherever a person might be—on the street, in an office building or a shopping mall, waiting for a bus, or driving—it is important to remain alert to the surroundings. A person should be familiar with neighborhoods of employment and residency.

People should be wary of isolated areas such as apartment laundry rooms, public parking garages and parking lots, and office buildings after business hours. At night, a person should walk with a friend or neighbor, a coworker, or a security guard.

A person should practice preventive behavior. A purse should be carried close to the body. A wallet should be put in an inside coat or front pants pocket. Shoes and clothing should not limit movement.

If a person is being followed on foot, he or she should change direction toward a well-lighted public area. In the event of approaching danger, screaming will attract the attention of other people. A person being followed by car should drive to the nearest police station, fire station, gas station, or an open store. Persistent honking of the car horn might dissuade the perpetrator from further pursuit. If a person experiences harassment on public transportation, shouting "Leave me alone!" or activating an emergency device might end the harassment (National Crime Prevention Council, 1999c).

Self-Protection Strategies for the Home

The use of self-protection strategies at home is an important part of maintaining personal safety since one out of ten homes are burglarized each year (Table 2.6). Two deterrents to burglary are sturdy locks and the alertness of neighbors (National Crime Prevention Council, 1999b).

Table 2.6

Self-Protection Strategies for the Home

1. Lock windows and doors at all times, even when you are at home.

2. Install extra-security deadbolts on all entry doors.

3. Do not use chain locks, as they are easily ripped off a door.

4. Secure sliding glass doors by insertion of a dowel in the inside track. To prevent the door from being lifted, drill a hole through the slide doorframe and fixed frame.

5. Contact the local police department for a home security survey.

6. Consider installing a home security alarm and/or video surveillance system.

Continued on page 43

Table 2.6 continued

7. Consider getting a dog and posting "Beware of Dog" signs on a property.

8. Prune shrubbery to prevent a burglar from hiding while breaking into a home. Prune tree limbs to prevent entry through an upstairs window.

9. Do not share house keys with anyone other than trusted friends.

10. Do not hide extra keys outside the house.

11. Consider installing a one-way viewer or peephole in entry doors.

12. Leave on one or more lights at night.

13. Install outside lights and keep them on at night.

14. Discontinue mail, newspaper, and other services during extended absences.

15. Ask a trusted friend to check the house when absent.

16. Have house keys ready before going to the door.

17. Do not go inside the house if there are signs of entry. Seek a safe place and call the police.

18. Do not admit a stranger into the house unless certain of safety.

19. Give the impression you are not alone when speaking on the phone.

20. Check the identification of repair people before allowing them into your house.

21. Do not open the door to someone asking to make an emergency phone call. Make the call for the person while he or she waits outside.

22. Report any stranger without identification to the police.

23. Practice caution while giving out personal information.

24. Hang up on "crank" calls immediately.

25. Report continuous, obscene, or bothersome phone calls to the telephone company and the police.

26. Keep a list of emergency phone numbers, including the local police and fire departments, by the telephone.

Self-Protection Strategies for Social Situations

Self-protection strategies for social situations are ways that people might reduce the risk of harm in social relationships (Table 2.7).

Table 2.7
Self-Protection Strategies for Social Situations

1. Avoid places that might result in being alone with a person with whom you feel uneasy.

2. Do not accompany a stranger, even if the destination includes other people.

3. Trust your instincts about people and situations.

4. Include other people when socializing with a person who is not known well.

5. Do not use alcohol or drugs.

6. Set and communicate boundaries for expressing affection.

7. Do not be pressured to drink alcohol or to engage in sexual activity. A perpetrator of sexual assault who has been drinking is accountable. A person who has been drinking and experiences sexual assault is unable to give legal consent.

8. Avoid behavior that might be interpreted as sexually teasing or seductive.

9. Respect the boundaries of people. People should not be pressured into sexual activities.

10. Communicate feelings of confusion that include confusion over mixed sexual messages.

11. Do not assume that a person wants to express affection in the same way that you do.

12. Use physical force if unwanted sexual behavior persists.

13. Consider attending workshops, seminars, or classes regarding acquaintance rape.

14. Be aware of warning signs associated with possible harm, such as disrespect, domination, extreme jealousy, unnecessary physical roughness, and/or a history of violent and/or abusive behavior.

Self-Protection Strategies for Traveling

Because of increased incidents of carjacking, self-protection strategies for traveling are an essential means of safety for many people who drive vehicles (National Crime Prevention Council, 1999a). Carjacking occurs nationwide and often late at night. Risk factors for carjacking include intersections with stoplights or signs, garages and parking lots, car washes and self-serve gas stations, bank machines, residential streets and driveways, and highway ramps that result in reduced speed. Therefore, it is important for people who drive to practice caution and use preventive measures (Table 2.8).

Table 2.8   **Self-Protection Strategies for Traveling**

1. Park in a safe and well-lighted area with other people and cars.

2. Be aware of the exact parking location of your car.

3. Lock your car at all times and put the keys in a purse or an inside or front pocket.

4. Walk with another person to the car whenever possible.

5. Check the front and back seats of the car before entering.

6. Do not leave infants or small children unattended in a car, even for a brief time.

7. Do not leave the keys in the ignition or leave the engine running.

8. Take the keys when leaving the car.

9. Hide wallets, purses, unattached stereos, and other valuables out of sight.

10. Keep the gas tank filled. Do not let the car run out of fuel.

11. Fuel the car only during daylight hours.

12. Keep the car in good condition to prevent breakdowns.

13. Try to drive in safe, well-lighted areas, especially after dark.

14. Install a car phone for use in case of emergency.

15. Keep a "Send Help" sign in the car to use in the event of a breakdown on the road.

16. Store a flashlight and road flares in the trunk.

17. Stay in the car, keep the doors locked and the windows rolled up, keep watch for passing patrol cars, and honk the horn if the car breaks down.

18. Do not exit the car if a person other than a police officer stops to offer help. The person who stops should be asked to call the police.

19. Ask a person who offers to help to drive to a nearby phone and call 911 to send road assistance.

20. Do not pick up hitchhikers.

21. Do not drive home when being followed. Drive to a police station, a store, or well-lighted area with other people. Report the incident to the police.

22. Practice caution with a person or people who approach the car when stopped.

23. Lock car doors and roll up windows at all times to prevent carjacking. Roll windows down a crack if ventilation is needed. Keep the sunroof closed. Avoid driving in a convertible with the top down.

24. Keep the car in gear at a stoplight or stop sign. Allow enough distance between cars for the car ahead to drive away.

25. Do not give car keys to other people.

26. Install an inside latch for the trunk to provide escape in the event that a person is forced into the trunk.

27. Do not rent cars that are marked as rental cars.

28. Practice courtesy on the road. If another driver causes anger, ignore the incident.

References

American Academy of Pediatrics. 1999. "Study Reports on Voluntary Use of 'Rape Drug.'" Article Online (January). Accessed 8/1999. http://www.aap.org.

American Medical Association. 1999a. "Facts About Domestic Violence." Article Online (July). Accessed 8/1999. http://www.4journals.com.

———. 1999b. "Facts About Sexual Assault." Article Online (June). Accessed 8/1999. http://www.ama-assn.org/public/releases/assault/facts.htm.

———. 1998. "Child Pornography." Article Online. Accessed 8/1999. http://www.4journals.com.

———. 1996. "Advocacy and Communications—'Facts About Virtual Violence'—Violence in Entertainment—Television and Movie Violence." *The Journal of the American Medical Association* (July). Accessed 8/1999. http://www.4journals.com.

American Psychological Association. 1999. "Funding for Violence Against Women Act (VAWA) Programs Under the Departments of Health and Human Services and Justice." Article Online (March). Accessed 8/1999. http://www.apa.org.

———. 1996. "Sex, Drugs, Rock-and-Roll, Suicide, Teen Motherhood, Tattoos and Body Piercing." Article Online (July). Accessed 8/1999. http://www.apa.org.

Kübler-Ross, Elisabeth. 1975. *Death: The Final Stage of Growth.* Englewood Cliffs, New Jersey: Prentice-Hall.

Mediascope. 1998. "The National Television Violence Study—1994–1995—Summary of Findings and Observations." Article Online (October). Accessed 8/1999. http://www.mediascope.org.

———. 1996. "Media Ratings: Design, Use and Consequences." Article Online (June). Accessed 8/1999. http://www.mediascope.org.

National Center for Victims of Crime. 1998. "Acquaintance Rape." Article Online (April). Accessed 8/1999. http://www.ncvc.org.

———. 1997a. "Campus Crimes—Colleges and Universities." Article Online (April). Accessed 8/1999. http://www.ncvc.org.

———. 1997b. "Domestic Violence Safety Plan Guidelines." Article Online (April). Accessed 8/1999. http://www.ncvc.org.

———. 1997c. "Stalking Safety Plan Guidelines." Article Online (April). Accessed 8/1999. http://www.ncvc.org.

———. 1992. "Rape-Related Post-Traumatic Stress Disorder." Article Online (April). Accessed 8/1999. http://www.ncvc.org.

National Crime Prevention Council. 1999a. "Carjacking." Article Online (May). Accessed 8/1999. http://www.ncpc.org.

———. 1999b. "Home Security." Article Online (May). Accessed 8/1999. http://www.ncpc.org.

———. 1999c. "Personal Safety." Article Online (May). Accessed 8/1999. http://www.ncpc.org.

National Institute on Drug Abuse. 1999. "Ecstasy." Article Online (March). Accessed 8/1999. http://www.nida.nih.gov.

National Institutes of Health. 1999. "Research on Child Neglect." Article Online (March). Accessed 8/1999. http://www.nind.nih.gov.

National Institute of Mental Health. 1994. "Chapter: Family Processes and Social Networks." Article Online (July). Accessed 8/1999. http://www.nimh.nih.gov.

United States Department of Education. 1997. "Sexual Harassment: It's Not Academic." Article Online (August). Accessed 8/1999. http://www.ed.gov.

United States Department of Justice. 1999a. "Flunitrazepam (Rohypnol)." Article Online. Accessed 11/1999. http://www.usdoj.gov/dea/pubs/rohypnol/rohypnol.htm.

———. 1999b. "Office of Justice Programs—News—1.4 Million Stalking Victims Annually; Justice Department Reports Latest Findings Regarding Stalking." Article Online (November). Accessed 8/1999. http://www.usdoj.gov.

———. 1995a. "Child Maltreatment 1995." Article Online (April). Accessed 8/1999. http://www.usdoj.gov.

———. 1995b. "Federal Bureau of Investigation —Criminal Justice Information Services (CJIS) Division—Hate Crime—1995." Article Online (July). Accessed 8/1999. http://www.fbi.gov.

United States Supreme Court. 1999. "*Syllabus v. Certiorari to the United States Court of Appeals for the Fifth Circuit* No. 96–568— Argued December 3, 1997—Decided March 4, 1998." Article Online (July). Accessed 8/1999. http://www.findlaw.com.

United States Supreme Court. 1998. "*Roth v. United States* (1957)—Certiorari to the United States Court of Appeals for the Second Circuit No. 582—Argued April 22, 1957—Decided June 24, 1957." Article Online. Accessed 11/1999. http://www. caselaw.findlaw.com/cgi-bin/getcase. pl?court=US&vol=354&invol=476.

Friendship, Dating, and Abstinence
Content for Teachers *Only*

A Word from the Authors

This chapter provides content for teachers on the topics of friendship, dating, and abstinence from sex. The content on friendship provides concepts that teachers of all grade levels will find useful. The content on dating and abstinence from sex is intended for teachers at the middle and high school levels. The overwhelming majority of parents and guardians want their adolescents to practice abstinence from sex. Most state guidelines require that abstinence from sex should be the focus of the sex education curriculum. One approach to abstinence education does not permit facts about birth control methods to be taught. This approach is referred to as the "abstinence *only*" approach. The federal government has set aside Title V monies that can be used for the "abstinence *only*" approach.

Teachers should check and adhere to the guidelines in their school districts to determine the policy regarding abstinence. Remember, it is in the best interest of middle and high school students to abstain from sex. AND, the majority of parents and guardians want teachers to reinforce family guidelines regarding abstinence from sex.

The Criteria Required by Federal Law for the Funding of Abstinence Education Programs

These criteria state that a program must:

1. have as its exclusive purpose teaching the social, psychological, and health gains to be realized by abstaining from sexual activity;

2. teach abstinence from sexual activity outside of marriage as the expected standard for all school age children;

3. teach that abstinence from sexual activity is the only certain way to avoid out-of-wedlock pregnancy and sexually transmitted diseases;

4. teach that a mutually faithful monogamous relationship within the context of marriage is the expected standard of human sexual activity;

5. teach that sexual activity outside the context of marriage is likely to have harmful psychological and physical effects;

6. teach that bearing children out of wedlock is likely to have harmful consequences for the child, the child's parents, and society;

7. teach young people how to reject sexual advances and how alcohol and drug use increase vulnerability to sexual advances; and

8. teach the importance of attaining self-sufficiency before engaging in sexual activity.

Friendships

A **healthful friendship** is a balanced relationship that promotes mutual respect and healthful behavior. Children and adolescents need to have healthful friendships. Having healthful friendships improves the quality of their life. Friends take a personal interest in each other. They support one another when they are successful. They encourage one another through difficult times. They enjoy social activities together. This section of the chapter will explain how children and adolescents can initiate friendships and handle rejection and why it is important for them to maintain balanced friendships. A **balanced friendship** is a friendship in which two people give and receive acts of kindness between each other. This section also will explain why some children and adolescents are people pleasers.

Initiating Friendships

There is a saying, "Make new friends, but keep the old. One is silver, and the other gold." Some friendships are the "gold" ones—they have stood the test of time, and as a result are valued highly. Other friendships are the "silver" ones—they are newer friendships that have the potential to be long-lasting. Both kinds of friendships have something in common—someone had to initiate the friendship.

When initiating a friendship or making a gesture of interest in being a friend, children and adolescents are wise to make a "background check." The background check might be similar to what an employer does before hiring an employee. The employer "checks out" the potential employee. Children and adolescents might consider a "background check" that includes questions they ask themselves regarding a potential friend. Questions might include the following:

- What do I know about this person's behavior?
- Does this person have good character?
- Do my parents or guardians know this person?
- Will my parents or guardians approve of my spending time with this person?

Children and adolescents should pursue a friendship only if the potential new friend has good character and their parents or guardians approve. There is always an element of risk involved when pursuing a friendship. After all, they might not be certain that a potential new friend wants to pursue a friendship in return. Children and adolescents should consider the possible opening moves they might make. For example, an adolescent might wait in the hall after class and begin a conversation or call a potential new friend on the telephone. An opening move involves risk as well as the possibility of reward. They risk the possibility of being rejected, but they also might be rewarded with the opportunity to develop a new friendship. Children and adolescents should be encouraged to make opening moves towards a potential new friend.

Their success in developing new friendships often depends on their ability to carry on a conversation. A **conversation** is a verbal exchange of feelings, thoughts, ideas, and opinions. Conversation Keepers/Conversation Killers (Table 3.1) describes effective and ineffective conversation styles.

Handling Rejection

Everyone experiences rejection at times. **Rejection** is the feeling of being unwelcome or unwanted. Children and adolescents might feel ignored by their peers. They might feel left out if they are not included in plans, or they might not be called for a date. They should not bury their hurt feelings, nor should they become overtly angry and try to even the score. They can take the following actions to express their feelings of hurt, anger, or disappointment in healthful ways:

- They might use I-messages to share their feelings with the peer who rejected them. An **I-message** is a statement describing a specific behavior or event, the effect that behavior or event has on a person, and the feelings that result. For example, an adolescent might say "When I wasn't included in plans for the weekend, and you went out without me, I was disappointed."

© 2001 Everyday Learning Corporation

Table 3.1

Conversation Keepers	Conversation Killers
• Asking questions	• Talking about yourself
• Showing interest in what someone else is saying	• Appearing uninterested in what someone else is saying
• Listening carefully	• Interrupting someone
• Responding to others	• Changing the topic
• Considering other ideas	• Being a know-it-all
• Using correct grammar	• Using slang words
• Encouraging another person	• Bragging
• Being positive	• Complaining
• Sharing your ideas and feelings	• Talking about others
• Encouraging someone to talk	• Dominating the conversation
• Making eye contact	• Avoiding eye contact

- Children and adolescents should share their feelings with a trusted adult if they cannot share them with the peer who rejected them.

- Children and adolescents should remember that they are worthwhile even when a peer does not want to be their friend or when they are left out.

Maintaining Balanced Friendships

A friendship requires the commitment of two people. A **balanced friendship** is a friendship in which two people give and receive acts of kindness between each other. Giving and receiving are valuable to a friendship. There are many ways children and adolescents can give to a friendship. For example, they can listen when a friend is discouraged. They can help a friend celebrate a success. On a special occasion, they might make or buy a friend a special gift. There are ways to receive in a friendship, too. If one of their friends has experienced a disappointment, they can listen to his or her feelings. They might give a friend a gift or offer help with a task. When friends go the extra mile for one another, the recipient should express his or her gratitude.

In balanced friendships, there is generally an equal exchange of giving and receiving. The giving and receiving might not be balanced at all times. For example, sometimes one of the friends has to do more giving than usual if the other friend is sick or going through difficult times. That friend might need more than he or she can give in return. However, after a period of time, the friend is able to reciprocate. This shift back and forth is healthful.

Some children and adolescents form one-sided friendships. A **one-sided friendship** is a friendship in which one person does most of the giving and the other person does most of the receiving. There are at least two reasons why children and adolescents might choose to do most of the giving.

First, they might be people pleasers. A **people pleaser** is a person who constantly seeks the approval of others. Children and adolescents who are people pleasers are insecure. They choose to do most of the giving so that they will be liked and noticed by others. However, their giving does not result in what they want—healthful and balanced friendships. The second reason children and adolescents might do most or all of the giving in their friendships is because they do not know how to accept acts of kindness from others. They are uncomfortable accepting gifts of time or support from others. They have never learned to rely on others to meet any of their needs. As a result, they play the role of the giver in most of their friendships.

Children and adolescents who do most or all of the receiving in their friendships often are described as "users." They take from others or use others to get their own needs met. They have little interest in meeting the needs of their friends. They believe they should always come first. They want to be in control of most decisions. For example, they always expect to select the movies they see with their friends. They are self-centered and selfish. Children and adolescents who are users do not have healthful and balanced relationships. They do not know how to become close to others.

Children and adolescents should examine the balance in their friendships and ask themselves these questions:

- Do I make an effort to be flexible and consider the needs of my friends?
- Do my friends and I alternate making plans?
- Am I willing to be supportive of my friends even if it is not convenient for me?
- Do my friends ever consider my needs?
- Are my friends willing to give me time and support?

It is important for children and adolescents to examine their friendships often to be certain that they are healthful and balanced.

> ### Table 3.2 **Benefits and Risks of Dating**
>
> **Benefits of dating:**
> - Strengthening self-esteem
> - Improving social skills
> - Becoming secure with one's masculinity or femininity
> - Developing skills in intimacy
> - Understanding personal needs
>
> **Risks of dating:**
> - Rejection
> - Sex-role stereotyping
> - Superficial relationships

Dating

During adolescence, some adolescents begin to date. **Dating** is having social plans with another person. Some adolescents refer to having a date as "going out" or "hanging out" with someone. Adolescents should be made aware of the benefits and risks of dating. Parents and guardians can discuss dating standards with them. Adolescents who are permitted to date can develop dating skills. This section of the chapter includes a discussion of the benefits of adolescent dating, the risks of adolescent dating, dating standards, and dating skills.

Benefits of Dating

Table 3.2 identifies the benefits and risks of dating. Consider some of the benefits adolescents might derive from dating. These benefits help prepare adolescents for adulthood when they might choose to marry and plan a family.

Strengthening self-esteem

Being liked and accepted by members of the opposite sex is especially important during adolescence. Asking someone to share an activity and having this person accept affirms an adolescent's belief about his or her attractiveness and desirability. Being seen with a person of the opposite sex who is well-liked by peers also reinforces self-esteem. Successful dating experiences provide the foundation for continuing to take risks in the dating game. In other words, when adolescents feel that a date was successful, they gain

confidence that they are successfully managing their social life. They are developing dating skills. **Dating skills** are competencies that help a person when he or she has a date.

Improving social skills

Adolescents often have concerns about the social skills needed for dating. "What do I talk about with my date?" "What do I do if I can't think of what to say?" "What activities might I suggest if he or she asks me what I want to do?" Dating provides the opportunity to practice social skills. Some of these skills might include meeting someone's parents or guardians for the first time, mutually deciding on enjoyable activities, initiating and contributing to meaningful conversation, and using good manners.

Becoming secure with one's masculinity or femininity

Two important developmental tasks of adolescence are accepting the body changes that are occurring as a result of puberty and becoming comfortable with one's sex role. The issue of masculinity and femininity is especially important. Males need the opportunity to test their feelings about the masculine sex role. Is it masculine to be macho? To be vulnerable? To express feelings? To cry? Females need the opportunity to test their feelings about the feminine sex role. Is it feminine to be strong-willed? To be independent? To play sports? To express emotions? An adolescent's comfort level with his or her masculinity or femininity is reinforced by being able to express several aspects of his or her personality, being able to have a wide variety of interests, and gaining acceptance.

Developing skills in intimacy

Healthful relationships are about closeness. This closeness is referred to as intimacy. A lack of intimacy in important relationships such as those between close friends, marriage partners, and parents and their children can be very painful for everyone involved. Almost everyone has had the experience of being with a friend or being in a crowd yet still feeling lonely. Lack of intimacy can lead to feelings of alienation and unworthiness. The skills needed to have intimate relationships must be practiced. A sense of trust and of caring and compassion are of particular importance to the development of intimacy. While dating, adolescents have the opportunity to display trust and to interact in caring and compassionate ways. Intimacy is such a fundamental need of humans that it is discussed in depth in Chapter 8.

Understanding personal needs

In a healthful relationship, people have an understanding of each other's needs and desire to meet those needs in healthful ways. Therefore, it is essential for adolescents to be in touch with their needs and to be able to share those needs in appropriate ways with significant others. While dating, adolescents can learn ways to have needs met in healthful ways. In addition, they can learn about the needs that other people have and how these needs can be met in healthful ways. For example, some adolescents need to have more time alone than others. Some adolescents need more encouragement in the form of compliments to feel supported in a significant relationship.

Risks of Adolescent Dating

Some risks also accompany dating. As with all learning situations, some of the lessons might be painful.

Rejection

Adolescents are especially sensitive to rejection. Feeling left out by peers can be devastating. When a social activity is planned, whether it is a group activity or a one-to-one dating activity, and an adolescent is not included, he or she might question his or her self-worth. It is extremely important to encourage adolescents to share these feelings with caring adults. Feelings of rejection can result in a loss of self-esteem.

Sex-role stereotyping

Ideally, the dating experience will assist adolescents in becoming comfortable with their masculinity or femininity and their sex roles. However, it must be remembered that an adolescent has obtained previous information about masculinity and femininity almost entirely from his or her family. Adolescents tend to model the examples that have been set for them. Adolescents who have learned sex-role stereotyping might continue these attitudes and the accompanying behaviors in their dating relationships. Thus, while one person is learning to express his or her masculinity or femininity and sex role, the other person might be providing unhealthy feedback. When this occurs, adolescents should be encouraged to discuss the situation with trusted adults.

Superficial relationships

Because peer acceptance is so important, adolescents might go through the motions of dating to be a part of the group rather than to obtain the benefits outlined previously. For example, an adolescent might date someone only because he or she is in a popular clique. This kind of relationship is superficial. Neither the quality of the relationship nor the well-being of the other person involved is a priority. Some destructive behaviors might accompany superficial relationships. These behaviors might include leading someone on in order to continue dating, lying about feelings, and/or failing to pay attention to the other person's needs. If an adolescent obtains the desired benefit—acceptance from the peer group—he or she might receive enough personal satisfaction from superficial relationships that a pattern for this kind of relationship develops.

There is no doubt that dating provides the opportunity for adolescents to learn more about themselves and others. For most adolescents, the benefits of dating outweigh the risks. Moderate dating during high school is considered to be dating once or twice a week. Moderate dating that follows dating standards can contribute to emotional, social, and psychological growth.

Dating Standards

A common concern of parents, guardians, and adolescents is the appropriate time to begin dating. Parents and guardians do not want dating to interfere with their adolescent's emotional, social, and psychological development.

Adolescents who begin dating before age 15 might seem to be confident and self-assured, but they tend to be more superficial than their peers. Many adolescents prefer steady dating because it provides a reliable partner for parties and other activities and prevents the anxiety-provoking situation of getting to know someone new (Greydamus, 1999). However, early dating can interfere with an independent sense of identity. Adolescents who begin dating early might base their identity on their dating experiences rather than on developing their uniqueness.

Table 3.3

Six Important Dating Standards

1. Obtain background information on the person with whom you will have a date.

2. Tell a parent or guardian about your exact plans.

3. Arrange for safe transportation.

4. Establish a reasonable curfew.

5. Establish a code of conduct.

6. Establish the expected code of conduct for the other person.

Before accepting a date, adolescents need to establish standards for dating (Table 3.3). These standards should be shared with an adolescent's parents or guardians and the person he or she plans to date.

Obtain background information on the person with whom you will have a date

What is his or her name? How old is he or she? Where does he or she attend school? How can his or her parents or guardians be reached? This information is needed by parents and guardians to determine the appropriateness of dating a particular person.

Tell a parent or guardian about your exact plans

When will the date occur? What activity has been planned? Adolescents need to share details with their parents or guardians. The timing of the date should not interfere with family activities or with school or work responsibilities. The activity should be appropriate.

Arrange for safe transportation

If adolescents have driver's licenses, their parents or guardians will emphasize that they must obey traffic laws and speed limits and must not drink alcohol or use other illegal drugs. If neither adolescent has a driver's license, he or she might rely on their parents or guardians for transportation. If so, dating arrangements must fit the parents' or guardians' schedules. Adolescents also might rely on older friends or siblings for transportation. Parents and guardians will want to check out anyone who is driving their adolescent. Adolescents must make it clear that drinking alcohol or using other drugs will not be tolerated. They need to have a plan about what to do if the person they date violates traffic laws or exceeds the speed limit. Adolescents must never get into a car if the driver has been drinking alcohol or using other drugs. They should call home for help if a problem occurs.

Establish a reasonable curfew

A **curfew** is a fixed time when a person is to be at home. Adolescents' parents or guardians will establish how late they can stay out. Having a curfew helps promote safety and relieves parents and guardians of needless worry. Parents can consult with pediatricians to establish their adolescent's curfew and responsibilities (Spivak, et al., 1999). It is important for parents and guardians to be consistent when carrying out the punishment for a missed curfew. Except under extenuating circumstances—for example, if the car breaks down—an adolescent should not be able to talk or negotiate his or her way out of being penalized for a missed curfew or a similar violation of the rules (Greydamus, 1999).

Establish a code of conduct

The privilege to date is accompanied by the responsibility to use wise judgment. Issues regarding wise judgment need to be clear. For example, parents and guardians of adolescents will have certain expectations regarding adult supervision of activities. Are adolescents permitted to be at someone's home when no adults are present? Money is another issue to discuss. How much can adolescents spend? Who should pay for what? Adolescents should be aware of their parents' or guardians' guidelines for sexual behavior. It should be remembered that parents or guardians establish guidelines to protect their adolescents.

Establish the expected code of conduct for the other person

Adolescents' parents and guardians might discuss the importance of being respected by anyone they date. **Respect** is liking that comes from having esteem for someone's admirable characteristics and responsible and caring actions. A person whom an adolescent chooses to date should never act in a way that shows disrespect for the adolescent or his or her parents or guardians. The person an adolescent chooses to date should never encourage the adolescent to disobey his or her parents' or guardians' guidelines, say cruel words to the adolescent, hit or physically harm the adolescent, force the adolescent to show affection or be sexually active, or drink alcohol and/or use other drugs. Parents or guardians can discuss with their adolescents what to do if any of these actions occur.

Dating Skills

Each of us has a need to be liked, especially by those who are important to us. **Liking** is affection and respect for another person. **Affection** is a fond or tender feeling that a person has toward another person. It is experienced as emotional warmth, or closeness. **Respect** is liking that comes from having esteem for someone's admirable characteristics and responsible and caring actions. In a relationship, there might be respect, affection, neither, or both. Table 3.4 identifies characteristics demonstrated by adolescents who are worthy of the respect of others. This section of the chapter discusses the ten characteristics identified in Table 3.4.

Table 3.4 Characteristics of Adolescents Who Deserve Respect

An adolescent who is admirable and worthy of respect demonstrates ten characteristics. It is wise to look for these characteristics in the person one chooses to date.

1. Self-loving behavior
2. Trust and honesty
3. Healthful expression of feelings
4. Adherence to family guidelines
5. Goals and plans to reach them
6. Interdependence
7. Balance
8. Avoidance of abusive behavior
9. Drug-free lifestyle
10. Abstinence from sex

Self-loving behavior

An adolescent who has self-loving behavior places value on himself or herself. His or her behavior is not destructive. For example, this adolescent would not continually make degrading comments about himself or herself. He or she would try his or her best and would accept his or her shortcomings. This adolescent would not smoke cigarettes or use illegal drugs. Adolescents need to be in tune to the messages that others send about themselves.

Trust and honesty

A healthful relationship demands an investment of both time and energy. In return, most people expect trust and honesty. What are some behaviors that indicate that a person is trustworthy and honest? An adolescent shows that he or she is trustworthy by keeping confidences when asked to do so. When a trustworthy adolescent promises to do something, he or she follows through and does what is expected. If he or she is unable to follow through, a reasonable explanation is given. An honest adolescent tells the truth, even when it might be easier to lie. Trust and honesty are important in a relationship because they help people feel secure. They enable partners in a relationship to count on one another. Adolescents should expect trust and honesty in their dating relationships.

Healthful expression of feelings

In order to feel close to other persons, people must mutually share feelings. Only when feelings are shared can people genuinely respond to each other. There are behaviors and actions that indicate that an adolescent is able to express feelings in healthful ways. An adolescent might communicate with I-messages and engage in active listening. An **I-message** is a statement describing a specific behavior or event, the effect that behavior or event has on a person, and the feelings that result. When a person uses I-messages, it makes it easier for another person to respond honestly to what has been said. The adolescent does not blame or shame the other person. An adolescent can indicate that another person's feelings are important by using

active listening. **Active listening** is a way of responding to show that a person hears and understands. Active listening encourages sharing at a greater depth and does not block communication. When evaluating a relationship, consider the degree of sharing of feelings and how feelings are shared. If an adolescent does not share feelings or shares them in a hostile way, such as shouting or throwing objects, it would be difficult to become close to that adolescent. Adolescents need to examine ways that feelings are shared in their dating relationships and to assess whether or not they are healthful.

Adherence to family guidelines

An adolescent's willingness to follow his or her family's guidelines is important in a dating relationship. For example, an adolescent should arrive home before curfew. He or she should introduce a date to parents if they request it. An adolescent who is unwilling to demonstrate commitment to family might not have the moral fabric that is needed to sustain a healthful relationship. Adolescents need to evaluate carefully whether potential dates observe their family's guidelines. They need to share their family's guidelines with people they choose to date so that both individuals know what is expected of them.

Goals and plans to reach them

Hugh Prather said, "The way to be the best for others is to be the best for me right now" (Prather, 1970). In other words, an adolescent striving to do his or her best can have a positive influence on others. Setting goals and working toward their achievement requires energy and enthusiasm. Energy and enthusiasm tend to be contagious. When a person is around others who are energetic and enthusiastic, he or she tends to be more energetic and enthusiastic about setting his or her own goals. In addition, adolescents who set goals and work to achieve them usually are supportive of others who do the same. Adolescents should observe how much effort other people put toward achieving their goals. They can share their goals and plans to reach them. For example, does a person make time to work on achieving goals? Is the person self-disciplined? Is the person willing to delay immediate gratification in order to meet long-range goals? Adolescents need to examine the effects that specific relationships might have on their own goals and dreams.

Interdependence

In a healthful relationship, there are boundaries. Each person maintains personal identity, but at the same time works to have a cooperative relationship. There is give and take that does not require either person to meet the needs of the other by sacrificing his or her personal needs. A healthful relationship can be contrasted with a codependent relationship, which results in one or both people losing personal identity. A **codependent** is a person who wants to rescue and control another person. One person in a codependent relationship might be described as a "giver" and the other as a "taker." The "giver" strives to please the "taker" at all costs. This means that the needs of the "giver" are not met.

Healthful relationships require the give and take of both people involved. Adolescents need to examine this aspect of their dating relationships. Answering the following questions can help determine if there is healthful interdependence or whether there is destructive codependence.

• Does the other person try to meet my needs?

• Does the other person care about my feelings?

• Are my feelings a concern to this person?

• Is this person willing to do things for me?

• Do I try to meet the other person's needs?

• Am I concerned with this person's feelings?

• Am I willing to do things for this person?

Other questions can be used to examine boundaries.

• Do I have a sense of who I am, or am I defining myself by who this person is or by what this person does?

• Does the other person in the relationship define himself or herself through me rather than through his or her interests, qualities, and abilities?

For example, an adolescent male who is a talented athlete might date a female who derives her identity from being the girlfriend of an athlete. She gains her self-esteem from being seen with him and wearing his team jersey. She lets him choose their friends and activities. She doesn't form her identity based on her own qualities and talents.

An adolescent should be able to recognize characteristics of codependence in relationships so he or she can make adjustments and form healthful relationships.

Balance

Adolescents need guidance to achieve balance in dating relationships. Achieving balance allows time for the dating relationship as well as time for family relationships and for other friendships. A balanced relationship is not "suffocating;" both people are able to have quality time with others outside of their relationship. Having balance also means that there is time to meet responsibilities. In a healthful relationship, a person has balance and can meet his or her social, physical, mental, and spiritual health needs. For example, a person in a balanced relationship has time to do homework, participate in school activities, exercise, and enjoy family activities. Adolescents can be encouraged to examine balance within their lives.

Avoidance of abusive behavior

Abusive behavior—physical, emotional, and/or sexual—is not acceptable in a dating relationship. Adolescents must understand that such behavior is a warning signal to avoid becoming involved in a relationship. For example, a date should not hit, slap, or physically harm another person. A date should not belittle or ignore another person. Date or acquaintance rape is an act of violence and a crime. Date and acquaintance rape will be discussed later in this chapter. Abusive behavior must be reported to a trusted adult. Adolescents must recognize abuse and be willing to stop abusive relationships immediately.

Drug-free lifestyle

Drug abuse has had a devastating effect on the lives of many people. Drug abuse has resulted in many traffic deaths, homicides, and suicides. It is involved in many crimes. Drug abuse is a contributor to harmful relationships. Separated and divorced men and women were three times as likely as married men and women to say they had been married to an alcoholic or problem drinker (NCADD, 1998). Many situations in which children have been physically, emotionally, and/or sexually abused are directly related to drug abuse. Drugs change how people think and act and impair judgment. Drug abuse is illegal. Adolescents need to evaluate the effects of drug abuse on relationships. They need to recognize that relationships in which a person uses drugs are destructive. Adolescents must end relationships that involve drug abuse immediately. They need to discuss these relationships with a responsible adult.

Abstinence from sex

Later in this chapter, the benefits adolescents derive from practicing abstinence from sex will be discussed in detail. Practicing abstinence from sex until marriage is a responsible decision. Adolescents who practice abstinence from sex recognize the risk of giving in to instant gratification. **Instant gratification** is choosing an immediate reward regardless of potentially harmful effects. Throughout life, there will be temptations. Adolescents need to be encouraged to avoid giving in to instant gratification and to make responsible decisions.

Dating Skills

Dating skills are competencies that help a person when he or she has a date. The Dating Skills Checklist (Table 3.5) is a guide for a person to rate his or her dating skills.

Date Rape

In social situations, adolescents must be concerned about their safety and the safety of

Table 3.5 **Dating Skills Checklist**
1. I do not base my self-worth on my ability to get a date.
2. I ask questions and get the facts before I accept a date.
3. I decline a date when there will be pressure to drink or be sexually active.
4. I honor my dating commitments and do not change plans if something better comes along.
5. I recognize the advantages of dating different people rather than going steady.
6. I would make a fast exit instead of staying in a situation that is against my parents' or guardians' guidelines.
7. I would not hesitate to call my parents or guardians if I were on a date and needed help.
8. I am comfortable staying home when I do not want to date.
9. I am clear as to my expectations when I give or receive a gift in a dating situation.
10. I am honest and kind when I turn down someone for a date.

others. **Rape** is the threatened or actual use of physical force to get someone to have sex without giving consent. Rape usually is motivated by a combination of power, anger, and sexual desire. The majority of rape cases involve a form of rape known as acquaintance rape. **Acquaintance rape** is rape in which the rapist is known to the person who is raped. **Date rape** is rape that occurs in a dating situation. The National Crime Victimization Survey states that 92 percent of rapes were committed by people known to the victim. About half of all rapes and sexual assaults are committed by friends and acquaintances, and 26 percent are by intimate partners (CDC, 1998).

Date rape is more likely to be an impulsive act rather than a planned activity. Acquaintance rape and date rape both are forms of violence.

This section of the chapter discusses facts about date rape, drug use and date rape, kinds of date rape drugs, laws concerning date rape, recovery from date rape, and guidelines to follow to reduce the risk of date rape.

Facts About Date Rape

Adolescents might believe that sex without consent is OK in some situations. This belief might be based on male sex role stereotyping, negative attitudes towards women, alcohol consumption, and acceptance of rape myths by men (CDC, 1998). However, sex without consent is NEVER OK. Table 3.6 includes the facts that all adolescents should know about date rape.

Drug Use and Date Rape

Drinking alcohol and taking drugs are often associated with date rape. Three reasons why most cases of date rape involve the use of alcohol are identified and explained in the following discussion.

1. Drinking alcohol or using other drugs increases the likelihood that adolescents might be in a risk situation.

Suppose a female has been drinking alcohol or smoking marijuana. As a result, she is not thinking clearly. She is in a risk situation in which she normally would not be. For example, she might leave the party with a male she does not know. She might go to a male's home when no adults are there and listen to music in his bedroom. She is in a risk situation as it might be difficult for her to defend herself from sexual advances or rape.

2. Drinking alcohol or using other drugs interferes with judgment.

Suppose a male has a strong sexual desire for a female he is dating. The female tries to make her limits for expressing affection clear to him. She says NO. However, the male has been drinking or using other drugs. He is unable to think clearly and to respond in an appropriate way. He does not respect his female companion's "no" response. He rapes her because his judgment is impaired. In one study, 75 percent of the males who were identified as having committed date rape had taken drugs or had been drinking alcohol just prior to the rape (Curtis, 1997).

Table 3.6   **Facts About Date Rape**

Fact: Sex without consent is rape. Circumstances do not change this definition of unlawful behavior.

1. Suppose a female puts herself in a risk situation. Perhaps she goes into a male's bedroom when no adults are home. Do her actions indicate consent to have sex even if she says "no?" NO. If a male forces a female to have sex when she is in a risk situation, he has committed rape. Caution to females: Do not put yourself in risk situations. If you do, it can be very difficult to defend yourself. No one will hear your call for help should sexual advances occur. If date rape occurs, others might believe that you said "yes" even if you did not.

2. Suppose a female wears sexy clothes, such as a very short skirt, a tight sweater, or a low-cut dress. Is she "asking for it because she dresses this way?" NO. If a male assumes she wants to have sex and forces her to do so, he has committed rape. Caution to females: Dress in an appropriate way to avoid sending mixed messages. Remember, the way you dress affects your reputation.

3. Suppose a male believes the male role is to be the aggressor and the female role is to be the resister. He might believe that his sex role includes making forceful sexual advances. In addition, he might believe that when a female says "no" she really means "maybe," and when she says "maybe" she really means "yes." As a result, he ignores messages of nonconsent and forces the female to have sex, especially if he encounters little physical resistance. He is guilty of committing rape. Caution to females: Be consistent. Say "no" clearly. Do not encourage sexual advances.

4. Suppose a male misinterprets signs of affection. He might believe that cuddling or kissing indicate a desire to have sex. He might interpret a female's "no" as token resistance. He might believe that she does not want to appear too easy and that she needs to be more forceful. As a result, he ignores her resistance and forces sex. He is guilty of committing rape. Caution to females: Keep your limits clear when you express affection. If a male becomes more forceful, offer more than token resistance. Say "no" firmly and yell, scream, or run away if necessary.

---

3. Drinking alcohol and using other drugs intensifies feelings and the need for control.

Date rape is an act of violence. A male who is a rapist often has an increased need to control a female companion. He also is more likely to act upon that need after using alcohol or other drugs. Indeed, many rapes are reported after alcohol or other drug use has occurred.

Date Rape Drugs

Flunitrazepam, or **Rohypnol**, is an odorless, colorless sedative drug. On the street, the drug is known as "roofies," "rope," "the forget pill," and "roach." Flunitrazepam has effects similar to Valium, but is approximately ten times more potent (National Women's Health Information Center, 1999a). The drug is associated with impaired judgment and impaired motor skills and can make a victim unable to resist a sexual attack (National Women's Health Information Center, 1999a). Like alcohol, it makes some users fearless and aggressive. It is referred to as "the date-rape drug" because it can cause a blackout with complete or partial loss of memory. A male can slip a "roofie" into a female's drink and commit date rape after she blacks out. Flunitrazepam can cause decreased blood pressure, memory impairment, drowsiness, visual disturbances, dizziness, confusion, gastrointestinal disturbances, and urinary retention (National Women's Health Information Center, 1999a). Law enforcement officers are concerned about the increasing number of rapes associated with "roofies." There also is concern about the potential for addiction to flunitrazepam and overdosing on the drug. Other date rape drugs include GHB and MDMA (ecstasy).

Laws and Date Rape

Adolescents should know about laws concerning date rape.

- A female who is under the influence of alcohol or other drugs cannot give legal consent to have sex. In other words, having sex with a female who has been drinking or using drugs can be considered date rape in a court of law, even if the female did not say "no."

- Drunkenness or being high on drugs is not a legal defense against date rape. In other words, if a male has been drinking alcohol or using drugs before he commits a rape, this is not a legal excuse. He still has committed rape.

Consult individual state laws for more information.

Recovery from Date Rape

An adolescent who has been raped might need treatment for both physical injuries and emotional harm. A medical exam is needed to determine health status and to collect evidence. In most hospitals, a "rape kit" is used to collect evidence. A "rape kit" is a standard kit that has little boxes, microscope slides, and plastic bags in which evidence is stored (American Academy of Family Physicians, 1999). An adolescent who has been raped should not take a shower or bath until a medical examination has been performed. He or she might have become infected with HIV or other sexually transmitted diseases. STDs commonly found in persons who have been raped include gonorrhea, trichomoniasis, genital warts, chlamydia, and genital herpes. Females who have been raped might become pregnant.

Adolescents who have been raped should participate in special efforts to heal the pain they have experienced. After the rape, they might be in shock or feel frightened or guilty. They might feel responsible for the rape. Some rape survivors experience Rape-Related Post-Traumatic Stress Disorder. **Rape-Related Post-Traumatic Stress Disorder**, or **RR-PTSD**, is a condition in which a rape survivor experiences emotional responses and physical symptoms over a period of time. Adolescents who have been raped might feel ashamed, angry, afraid, guilty, and powerless. Rape-Related Post-Traumatic Stress Disorder might include symptoms of reexperiencing the violent trauma in play, dreams, and intrusive images and sounds. Psychic numbing, sleep disorders, avoidance behaviors, an exaggerated startle reaction, trauma-specific fears, and difficulty forming close personal relationships also are common symptoms (Kaufer Christoffel, et al., 1996). About half of all people who are raped report being depressed during the first year after the attack (American Academy of Family Physicians, 1999). Adolescents who have been raped might experience problems when becoming close with a person of the opposite sex.

Many resources are available to help adolescents who have been raped in their recovery. Rape crisis centers are available in many communities. They are staffed with medical personnel and volunteers. Hospitals and women's centers also offer counseling and support groups.

Guidelines to Follow to Reduce the Risk of Date Rape

There are many ways that adolescents can reduce their risk of date rape. Table 3.7 shows the guidelines adolescents might follow to reduce the risk of date rape. Adolescents should be familiar with these guidelines when they are ready to begin dating.

There are several other steps adolescents can take to avoid situations that might lead to date rape. Adolescents can:

- be prepared to find transportation home. Carry change for a phone call to a friend or family member and enough cash for a taxi;

- avoid leaving a social situation with someone they just met;

- be aware of situations in which they do not feel relaxed and in charge; and

- trust their instincts.

Abstinence from Sex

Abstinence from sex is choosing not to be sexually active. When adolescents practice abstinence from sex, they benefit in many ways. This section of the chapter will discuss ways that abstinence from sex until marriage promotes the institution of marriage and reasons why practicing abstinence from sex is a responsible decision. This section tells adolescents how to set limits for expressing physical affection. It also tells adolescents how to say NO if they are pressured to be sexually active and outlines the ten steps adolescents who have been sexually active can take to change their behavior.

| Table 3.7 | **Guidelines to Follow to Reduce the Risk of Date Rape** |

1. Set clear limits for sexual behavior.
2. Communicate your limits to people whom you date.
3. Avoid sending mixed messages in which you say NO while continuing to encourage sexual advances.
4. Firmly tell a person to stop when you experience unwanted sexual advances.
5. Respond by yelling, screaming, or running away if the person does not stop unwanted sexual advances.
6. Avoid dating or being in the company of someone who is very controlling or demanding.
7. Avoid drinking alcohol and using other drugs that interfere with your judgment and ability to respond.
8. Avoid being in places where there is no one who will hear your call for help should unwanted sexual advances occur.
9. Report date rape to the police should it occur.
10. Obtain prompt medical attention should date rape occur.

Abstinence from Sex Until Marriage Promotes the Institution of Marriage

A **traditional marriage** is an emotional, spiritual, and legal commitment a male and a female make to one another. This commitment includes the pledge to love, honor, and respect each other. It extends to include the promise to love and care for children of the marriage. Focusing on this commitment gives each person assurance and confidence about the relationship.

Waiting until marriage to have sex preserves traditional marriage.

The tradition of marriage adds stability to a society. This is important because the family structure is the strength of a society. Actions that preserve traditional marriage preserve the family. Actions that weaken traditional marriage lead to the breakdown of family life and much unhappiness.

Waiting until marriage to have sex increases sexual satisfaction.

Waiting until marriage to have sex gives a couple a chance to develop other aspects of their relationship. In healthful marriages, sex takes its natural place beside the intellectual, emotional, and practical aspects of life. The increased communication and trust the couple develops enhances sexual satisfaction.

Waiting until marriage to have sex protects physical health.

A marriage commitment implies sexual fidelity. **Sexual fidelity**, or **sexual faithfulness**, is a promise in a marriage to have sex only with one's marriage partner. If a male and a female wait until marriage to have sex and practice sexual fidelity, they protect each other from sexually transmitted diseases including HIV.

Waiting until marriage to have sex protects emotional health.

Marriage offers a major psychological advantage for both marriage partners. It helps prevent the feeling "I am just on trial" and offers a feeling of stability. Marriage also provides the self-confidence that accompanies the belief "I am accepted and loved as a total person—not just as a sexual partner." A married couple has made the commitment to be together after having sex.

Waiting until marriage to have sex protects against unwanted pregnancy.

The majority of unwanted pregnancies occur outside of marriage. When a couple is married, the couple has the kind of commitment to each other that is needed to raise a child in a loving, stable home. Children raised in homes with married parents have the opportunity to live and interact with both their mother and father. A single, unwed parent has difficulty fulfilling the role of two parents. A single, unwed parent is less able to provide for a child. Statistics show that about 80 percent of the children born to unmarried adolescents who dropped out of high school are poor (National Women's Health Information Center, 1999b).

Abstinence from Sex Is a Responsible Decision

Throughout an adolescent's life, he or she will have many important decisions to make. The quality of his or her life will be determined by his or her decisions. Chapter 1 included information on how to make responsible decisions. A **responsible decision** is a choice that leads to actions that

- promote health,
- protect safety,
- follow laws,
- show respect for self and others,
- follow the guidelines of parents and other responsible adults, and
- demonstrate good character.

Practicing abstinence from sex until marriage is a responsible decision.

Practicing abstinence from sex promotes health

Practicing abstinence from sex reduces the risk of becoming infected with HIV and developing AIDS.

Since AIDS is the sixth leading cause of death in young adults ages 15 to 24 and the development of AIDS averages 10 years, the infection in these cases occurred during adolescence (NIAID, 1999). The incidence of AIDS cases reported yearly over the past ten years has increased substantially among adolescents ages 13 to 19. In 1986, there were 53 cases of AIDS among adolescents. By 1996, the number of cases had increased nearly eight times. Through June 1997, 2,953 adolescents had AIDS (NIAID, 1999). To date, there is no cure for AIDS. When adolescents practice abstinence from sex, they help protect themselves from HIV infection and AIDS.

Practicing abstinence from sex reduces the risk of becoming infected with sexually transmitted diseases (STDs).

To date, there are treatments but no cure for genital herpes and genital warts. Adolescents infected with either of these STDs can have reoccurrences for the rest of their lives. There is an increase in the number of cases of pelvic inflammatory disease (PID) in adolescent females. PID can lead to permanent scarring of the Fallopian tubes, which can result in sterility.

When adolescents practice abstinence from sex, they protect themselves from infection with STDs.

Practicing abstinence from sex prevents adolescents from becoming teenage parents.

More than one million females under the age of 20 become pregnant annually (Felice, et al., 1998). Many become pregnant more than once as teens. Fifty percent of adolescents who have a baby become pregnant again within two years of the baby's birth (Felice, 1999b). Most adolescent females who have babies are not married. They do not have the emotional support of a loving husband. Their babies do not live with a father who can love and nurture them. Adolescents who marry have a lower continuing financial status than they would have if they had married and had children in their twenties or older. When adolescents practice abstinence from sex, they do not risk becoming pregnant or getting someone pregnant.

Practicing abstinence from sex protects safety

Practicing abstinence from sex reduces the risk of violence that is associated with adolescent parenthood.

- Suicide is the second leading cause of death among adolescents ages 15 to 19 (APA, 1998). One of the leading risk factors for adolescent suicide is unplanned pregnancy.

- Although there is no evidence that adolescent mothers are more likely to abuse their children, adolescents might be more neglectful of their children (Felice, et al., 1999a).

When adolescents practice abstinence from sex, they reduce the risk of being a teen parent who is under stress and more at risk for being violent.

Practicing abstinence from sex follows laws

Practicing abstinence from sex prevents adolescents from being in situations in which they can be prosecuted for having sex with a minor.

In most states, having sex with a person before the legal age of consent is considered corruption of a minor. The **legal age of consent** is the age when a person is legally able to give permission to have sex. A person who is mentally disabled might not understand what it means to give permission and be legally unable to give permission, even if he or she is not a minor. A person can be prosecuted for having sex with a minor or with someone who is mentally disabled.

Practicing abstinence from sex will prevent adolescents from being in situations in which they can be prosecuted for date rape.

When adolescents practice abstinence from sex, they will not be guilty of having sex with an unwilling partner. They will not be accused of date rape.

Practicing abstinence from sex shows respect for self and others

Practicing abstinence from sex helps adolescents maintain a good reputation.

Self-respect is a high regard for oneself because one behaves in responsible ways. Practicing abstinence from sex is a responsible behavior. When adolescents practice abstinence from sex, they maintain self-respect. Adolescents show respect for others when they support others' decision to be responsible by practicing abstinence from sex. They will respect those who behave in responsible ways. Other adolescents will be comfortable and confident dating those who practice abstinence from sex because there will be no pressure to be sexually active. Adolescents who practice abstinence from sex maintain a good reputation.

Practicing abstinence from sex follows the guidelines of parents and other responsible adults

Practicing abstinence from sex will prevent teens from having conflicts with their parents or guardians because they follow their parents' or guardians' guidelines.

Most parents and guardians of adolescents want them to practice abstinence from sex. Parents and guardians want their adolescents to live a quality life. They set high standards for the behavior of their adolescents because they know their adolescents will benefit. They know the serious consequences that can occur from being sexually active. Parents of adolescents want to protect them.

Practicing abstinence from sex demonstrates good character

Practicing abstinence from sex requires adolescents to use self-discipline and delay gratification to uphold family values.

A **value** is a standard or belief. **Character** is a person's use of self-control to act on responsible values. When adolescents have good character, they uphold family values and practice abstinence. They recognize the importance of delayed gratification and are willing to postpone sexual intercourse until marriage. As a result, they do not feel guilty or anxious about their behavior. They can concentrate on other aspects of life, including dating relationships.

Limits for Expressing Physical Affection

Knowing how to set limits for expressing affection helps adolescents maintain self-respect and the respect of a dating partner. Setting limits helps adolescents keep their sexual feelings under control. **Sexual feelings** are feelings that result from a strong physical and emotional attraction to another person. Sexual feelings might occur when a person sees a certain person, looks at a picture, reads certain material, and has certain thoughts.

It is important for adolescents to know how sexual feelings intensify when they express physical affection. When two people are attracted to each other, they might express physical affection by kissing or hugging. These ways of expressing physical affection are enjoyable. Kissing and hugging, in turn, might result in sexual feelings.

A couple's expressions of affection might not stop with a hug or a casual kiss. They might continue to prolonged kissing. Prolonged kissing further intensifies sexual feelings. Caressing or touching also intensifies sexual feelings. Intimate expressions of physical affection cause physical changes to occur in the body. There is increased blood flow to the reproductive organs. In the male, the penis fills with blood and becomes erect. This intensifies sexual feelings in the male. In the female, there is increased blood flow to the vagina, creating a warm feeling.

These physical changes prepare the body for sex even if the couple had previously decided to practice abstinence from sex. Each of their bodies now says, "YES, I am ready for sex," even though their brain says, "NO, I do not want to be sexually active."

Setting limits for physical affection

There is an important reason why adolescents need to set limits of expressing affection in a physical manner. If adolescents become too involved, their bodies' message "YES, I am ready to have sex," might attempt to override their brains' message "NO, I do not want to be sexually active." Adolescents must keep their brains' message in charge in order to practice abstinence from sex. Table 3.8 lists ways that adolescents can set limits for expressing physical affection.

Resisting Pressure to Be Sexually Active

Resistance skills are skills that help a person say NO to an action or to leave a situation. Table 3.9 contains a list of eight suggested ways to resist negative peer pressure to be sexually active.

Table 3.8   **Setting Limits for Expressing Physical Affection**

1. Limit your expressions of affection to hand holding, hugging, and casual kissing to keep your brain in control of your decisions and actions.
2. Tell a person your limits before expressing affection.
3. Do not date someone who does not respect your limits.
4. Avoid drinking alcohol and/or using other drugs that dull your brain and interfere with wise judgment.
5. Do not date someone who drinks alcohol or uses other drugs that dull his or her brain and interfere with his or her wise judgment.

Steps Sexually Active Teens Must Take to Change Behavior and Practice Abstinence from Sex

Wisdom is good judgment and intelligence in knowing what is responsible and appropriate. People gain wisdom as they gain more knowledge and experience. Some adolescents who have been sexually active in the past learn from their experience. They gain knowledge as they experience the negative consequences of their activity. They begin to recognize that being sexually active was not the best choice. They begin to understand the benefits of sexual abstinence. They might feel guilty or anxious about their behavior. They might take another look at the facts—the risk of HIV infection, the risk of infection with other STDs, unwanted parenthood. These teens might regret that they have not followed family guidelines. They might have given in to pressure to have sex and now they regret having done so. If adolescents practice abstinence from sex, they can be proud of their behavior. If they are sexually active, they must change their behavior.

Make a written list of the reasons to choose abstinence from sex.

Adolescents should review this list often. This list will keep adolescents aware of the risks they take when they are sexually active. It will serve as a constant reminder to them of why they should practice abstinence. For example, adolescents might list "I do not want to become infected with HIV" or "I do not want to be pregnant or get someone pregnant."

Talk to a trusted adult about the decision to practice abstinence from sex.

Parents or guardians might be angry when they learn that their adolescent has been sexually active. However, they will support their adolescent's decision to change his or her behavior. Adolescents should remember the role of parents or guardians is to guide their

children. Parents or guardians can offer suggestions to strengthen their adolescent as he or she makes the necessary changes. They can help their adolescent with the relationship in which he or she is involved. They can help set new guidelines for expressing affection.

Consider the health consequences that might have occurred from being sexually involved.

Sexually active adolescents and any partners they have had might have become infected with HIV or another STD. A sexually active adolescent might be pregnant. Sexually active adolescents should discuss with their parents or guardians what medical examinations might be needed.

Set new guidelines for expressing affection.

Obviously, the adolescent's old guidelines did not work. Adolescents must be honest with themselves and avoid temptation. They should remember that parents or guardians can help them.

Have a frank discussion with the partner with whom an adolescent was sexually involved.

Adolescents should explain that they regret having been sexually active. They should share their reasons for making a renewed commitment to practicing abstinence from sex.

Adolescents should get reassurances from their partners that they will practice abstinence from sex.

In a healthful relationship, two people acknowledge mistakes and work together to correct them. They help each other avoid temptation. They look at ways to improve the quality of their lives.

Break off a relationship with a partner who will not agree to practice abstinence from sex.

Adolescents in this situation should remember that they have examined their values and beliefs and know that this decision is the right one. Any partner who continues to pressure another at this point does not show respect.

Table 3.9

How to Use Resistance Skills If You Are Pressured to Be Sexually Active

1. **Be confident and say, "NO, I do not want to be sexually active."**
   Look directly at the person to whom you are speaking. State your limits for expressing physical affection.

2. **Give reasons why you practice abstinence from sex.**
   Use the six questions from The Responsible Decision-Making Model to develop your reasons for saying "NO, I do not want to be sexually active."

   I practice abstinence from sex to promote my health.
   • I do not want to become infected with HIV and develop AIDS.
   • I do not want to become infected with other STDs, such as genital herpes and genital warts.
   • I do not want to become a teenage parent.

   I practice abstinence from sex to protect the safety of others.
   • I do not want to risk being a stressed teen parent who might neglect or abuse a child.

   I practice abstinence from sex to follow laws.
   • I do not want my partner or myself to be prosecuted for having sex with a minor.
   • I do not want to be accused of date rape.

   I practice abstinence from sex to show respect for myself and others.
   • I want to protect my good reputation and the reputations of others.
   • I want to uphold my personal values.
   • I want to protect my health and the health of others.

   I practice abstinence from sex to follow the guidelines of my parents and other responsible adults.
   • I do not want to disappoint or disobey my parents or guardians.
   • I want to practice family values.

   I want to demonstrate good character.
   • I want to have a good reputation.
   • I do not want to feel guilty or anxious.
   • I want to postpone sexual intercourse until marriage.

3. **Use the broken record technique and repeat several times the same reason you practice abstinence from sex.**
   For example, you might say, "NO, I do not want to be sexually active. I practice abstinence to promote my health. I do not want to become infected with HIV and develop AIDS." If you continue to get pressure, repeat this response several times. You will sound like a broken record. But each time you give the same response, you will be more convincing.

4. **Use nonverbal behavior to support your message that you do not want to be sexually active.**
   Do not lead someone on or "go too far" when you express affection. These behaviors do not match the limits you have set.

5. **Avoid being in situations in which you might be pressured to be sexually active.**
   Do not spend time in situations in which you might be vulnerable, such as being in someone's bedroom. Do not go to parties at which adolescents will be drinking alcohol or using other drugs. Avoid watching movies, videos, and television shows that imply adolescent sex is OK. Avoid reading books and magazines that are filled with pictures and stories that encourage adolescent sex.

6. **Avoid being with anyone who pressures you to be sexually active.**
   Expect someone whom you are dating to respect your limits and do not date this person if he or she pressures you to have sex. Avoid being with adolescents who brag about "scoring" or having "sexual conquests." Date people your own age. Older people might exert additional sexual pressure. Pay attention to what your parents or guardians say when they advise against being with certain people.

7. **Know the laws regarding sex that protect you and follow them.**
   Tell a parent or guardian if an adult makes sexual advances toward you. Tell a parent or guardian if you suspect date rape.

8. **Influence your friends to practice abstinence from sex.**
   Be confident and share with friends your decision to practice abstinence from sex. Encourage friends to practice abstinence from sex.

© 2001 Everyday Learning Corporation

Sexually active adolescents should reevaluate the influence of the group of friends with whom they associate.

Most people are drawn to friends who support what they are doing. This is often the case with people who are doing something wrong. They are most comfortable with friends who say it is OK to do whatever they are doing. In fact, these friends also might be choosing wrong actions. When adolescents gain wisdom and want to change, these friends might continue to encourage wrong actions. After all, if one person changes, they might have to think more about what they are doing. Any time an adolescent needs to change his or her behavior, it is best to look at the role his or her friends play. If they support wrong behaviors, they are enablers. An **enabler** is a person who supports the harmful behavior of others. Adolescents should avoid being with friends who are enablers. Instead, they should select friends who challenge them to be at their best. Adolescents should choose friends who would pressure them to change wrong behavior.

Adolescents should be honest and direct about their commitment to practice abstinence from sex in new relationships.

Adolescents should set standards for expressing affection with dating partners at the beginning of the relationship. They should stick to these standards.

Adolescents should avoid behaviors, such as using alcohol or other drugs and being in tempting situations that impair their wise judgment.

Adolescents might have the best intentions and say that they will practice abstinence from sex. But certain behaviors might affect their ability to stick with what they say that they will do. Most adolescents who have been sexually active were under the influence of alcohol, placed themselves in tempting situations, or continued to "go too far" without setting limits.

References

American Academy of Pediatrics. 1993. "Adolescents and Human Immunodeficiency Virus Infection: The Role of the Pediatrician in Prevention and Intervention." *Pediatrics* 92/4 (October): 626–630. Accessed 10/1999. http://www.aap.org/policy/05071.htm.

American Academy of Family Physicians. 1999. "Rape: What to Do If You're Raped." *Information From Your Family Doctor.* Accessed 10/1999. http://www.familydoctor.org/handouts/314.html.

American Psychiatric Association. 1998. "Let's Talk Facts About Teen Suicide." Article Online. Accessed 10/1999. http://www.psych.org/public_info/teen.html.

Center for Disease Control and Prevention. 1998. "Rape Fact Sheet." Article Online (September). Accessed 10/1999. http://www.cdc.gov/ncipc/dvp/fivpt/spotlite/rape.htm.

Curtis, David G., Ph.D. 1997. "Perspectives on Acquaintance Rape." *The American Academy of Experts in Traumatic Stress.* Accessed 10/1999. http://www.medlineplus.nlm.nih.gov.

Felice, Marianne E., M.D., et al. 1999a. "Adolescent Pregnancy: Current Trends and Issues." *Pediatrics* 103/2 (February). Accessed 10/1999. http://www.aap.org/policy/re9828.html.

——. 1999b. "Fact Sheet on Adolescents Who Have Babies." *Ask NOAH.* Accessed 10/1999. http://www.cfoc.org/statsfactsheet.html.

——. 1998. "Counseling the Adolescent About Pregnancy Options." *Pediatrics* 101/5 (May): 938–940. Accessed 10/1999. http://www.aap.org/policy/re9743.html.

Greydamus, Donald E., M.D. 1999. "Caring for Your Adolescent: Ages 12–21." Article Online. Accessed 10/1999. http://www.aap.org/pubserv/teendat.htm.

Kaufer Christoffel, Katherine, M.D., M.P.H., et al. 1996. "Adolescent Assault Victim Needs: A Review of Issues and a Model Protocol (RE9643)." *Pediatrics* 98/5 (November): 991–1001. Accessed 10/1999. http://www. aap.org/policy/00991.html.

National Council on Alcoholism and Drug Dependence. 1998. "Alcoholism and Alcohol-Related Problems." Article Online (August). Accessed 10/1999. http://www. ncadd.org/problems.html.

National Institute of Allergy and Infectious Diseases. 1999. "HIV/AIDS Statistics, NIAID Fact Sheet." Article Online. Accessed 12/1999. http://www.niaid.nih. gov/factsheets/aidstat.htm.

National Women's Health Information Center. 1999a. "'Date Rape' Drug." Article Online. Accessed 10/1999. http://www.4woman. gov/faz/rohypnol.htm.

——. 1999b. "Teen Pregnancy." Article Online. Accessed 10/1999. http://www.4woman. gov/x/faq/teenpregnancy.htm.

Prather, Hugh. 1970. "Notes to Myself." Lafayette, CA: Real People Press.

Spivak, Howard, M.D., et al. 1999. "The Role of the Pediatrician in Youth Violence Prevention in Clinical Practice and at the Community Level (RE9832)." *Pediatrics* 103/1 (January): 173–181. Accessed 10/1999. http://www.aap.org/ policy/re9832.html.

Male Reproductive Health

Content for Teachers *Only*

A Word from the Authors

Male sexuality is very complex. A male, like a female, is a sexual being from head to toe. His brain functions in arousal as much as his penis. His neck and ear lobes are as sexual as his testes and scrotum. To understand him, it is important to learn about his body, his organs and their functions, his thoughts, his psychological makeup, and his feelings. Chapter 4, however, is limited to male anatomy, male physiology, and male reproductive health and sexual concerns.

Male Anatomy

The organs and structures in the male reproductive system include the scrotum, testes, seminiferous tubules, epididymis, vas deferens, seminal vesicles, ejaculatory duct, prostate gland, Cowper's glands (bulbourethral glands), urethra, and penis (Figure 4.1).

The Scrotum

The **scrotum** is a sac-like pouch in the groin that has two basic functions: to hold the testes and to regulate the temperature of the testes.

The scrotum is divided into two compartments. These compartments contain the testes. Each testis is suspended in the scrotum by the spermatic cord. The spermatic cord contains blood vessels, nerves, and muscles. It also contains the vas deferens, which will be discussed later in this chapter.

The scrotum's role in temperature regulation is very important in reproduction. Sperm cannot be produced at a temperature that is as high as the normal, internal body temperature. They are produced at a temperature that averages 3 fahrenheit degrees (16 celsius degrees) lower than normal body temperature. To maintain the cooler temperature, the scrotum holds the testes away from the body. In hot weather, the scrotum enlarges, causing the testes to be farther removed from the heat of the body. In

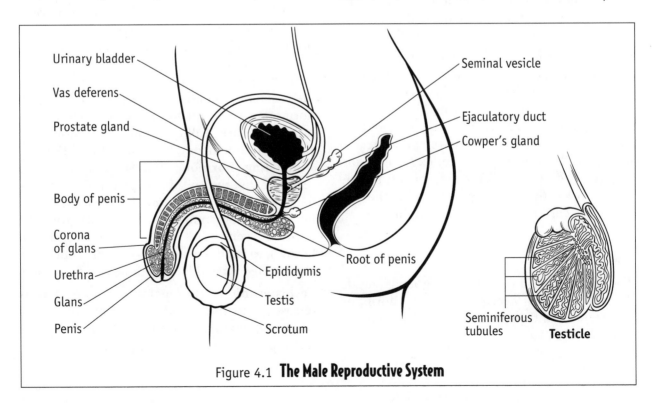

Figure 4.1 **The Male Reproductive System**

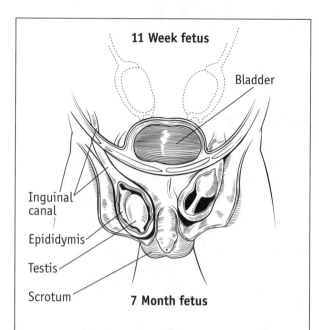

11 Week fetus

Bladder

Inguinal canal

Epididymis

Testis

Scrotum

7 Month fetus

Figure 4.2 **Descent of the Testes**

During the eighth and ninth months of fetal life, the testes descend through a tunnel-like passageway in the abdominal cavity into a sac-like pouch outside the body cavities. The tunnel is called the inguinal canal; the sac-like pouch is called the scrotum.

colder weather, or after a cold shower or swim, the scrotum draws the testes to the body for warmth. The scrotum is richly supplied with sweat glands to help regulate temperature. The evaporation of perspiration from the scrotum provides a cooling effect.

In addition, there are muscles in the scrotum that are attached to the testes. The **cremaster muscles** are muscles that contract to pull the testes closer to the body to warm them and relax to lower the testes away from the body to cool them. This muscle response to temperature and touch is called the cremaster reflex (Moglia and Knowles, 1997). In most males, the left testicle hangs lower than the right because the left spermatic cord is longer than the right one.

The Testes

The **testes** are the two male gonads inside the scrotum that secrete the male hormone testosterone and produce sperm. **Gonads** are reproductive glands.

The testes begin to evolve during the seventh or eighth week of embryonic development. Initially, they develop in the abdominal cavity at a level just below the upper border of the hip bone. During the eighth and ninth months of fetal life, the testes, stimulated by their own testosterone secretion, normally leave the pelvic cavity and move downward. They descend through a tunnel-like passageway in the abdominal cavity into a sac-like pouch outside the body cavities (Figure 4.2). The tunnel is called the inguinal canal; the sac is called the scrotum.

Sometimes the testes do not descend as they should. **Cryptorchidism** is a condition in which one or both testes do not descend through the inguinal canal into the scrotum before birth. This condition might result from premature birth, low hormonal stimulation, or blockage in the inguinal canal. The most frequent cause is premature birth with the testes usually descending shortly after birth. When the testes do not descend, they can be relocated with hormone treatments or surgery to prevent sterility. **Sterility** is the inability to produce offspring. Degeneration of the testes will occur if the condition is untreated. Male secondary sex characteristics also might not develop.

Puberty is the stage of growth and development when both the male and female body become capable of producing offspring. Puberty normally begins in males between the ages of 10 and 15. About two years before the signs of puberty appear, the pituitary gland (located in the base of the brain) increases secretion of two hormones that initiate puberty. These two hormones are follicle-stimulating hormone (FSH) and luteinizing hormone (LH). **Follicle-stimulating hormone (FSH)** is a hormone secreted by the pituitary gland that causes follicles to grow. **Luteinizing hormone (LH)** is a hormone that stimulates a special group of testicular cells, the interstitial cells (cells of Leydig), to produce testosterone. This hormone also is called interstitial cell-stimulating hormone.

Testosterone is the male hormone that is released into the bloodstream from the testes and causes male secondary sex characteristics to develop during puberty (Figure 4.3).

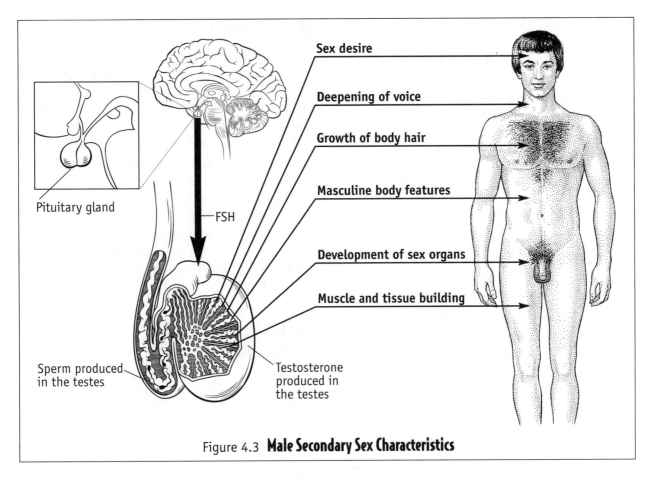

Figure 4.3 **Male Secondary Sex Characteristics**

Male secondary sex characteristics that develop include the following:

- creation of the sex drive with more frequent and possibly spontaneous erections;
- increased metabolic rate;
- deepened voice;
- growth of body hair on the face and chest;
- increased activity of the sweat glands;
- development of a V-shaped torso with more muscle mass;
- thicker and tougher skin;
- development of pubic hair;
- enlargement of the penis, scrotum, and testes about eight-fold until the age of 20;
- longer and heavier bones; and
- larger muscles.

The Seminiferous Tubules

A whitish, fibrous sheath surrounds each testis and divides the testis into several sections. **Seminiferous tubules** are a coiled network of tubes that fill the sections in each testis. With the onset of puberty, FSH stimulates the seminiferous tubules to initiate the production of sperm. Final maturation of immature sperm also requires testosterone.

Spermatogenesis is sperm production, which takes place in the seminiferous tubules in the testes. Uncoiled, the seminiferous tubules would extend 750 feet (228.6 m).

A **spermatogonium** is the earliest form in the development of mature sperm cells. A spermatogonium develops in the cells lining the outer wall of the seminiferous tubules. It is thought that these cells secrete nutritional substances for the developing sperm. As these cells grow, they move toward the center of the tubules.

As a spermatogonium grows, it moves into the first stage of sperm development, a primary spermatocyte. The primary spermatocyte then divides to form two secondary spermatocytes. As the secondary spermatocytes move toward the center of the seminiferous tubules, they divide into spermatids. The spermatid, in turn, reorganizes its nucleus to form a compact head and becomes a mature sperm.

Spermatogenesis usually begins at age 12, but mature sperm usually are not found in the growing male until he is nearly 14 years of age. The characteristics of mature sperm are as follows:

- they are very tiny, measuring only about 0.0024 inch (.005 cm);
- they have a head, a neck, a midpiece, and a tail;
- the hereditary material is located in the head of the sperm;
- the tail of the mature sperm moves and propels it from one place to another;
- the mature sperm has 23 chromosomes; and
- the mature sperm carries either an X or a Y chromosome.

Numerous environmental factors affect spermatogenesis. Stress can reduce the number of sperm produced. High altitude and radiation might inhibit or block spermatogenesis. Variations in temperature can increase or inhibit spermatogenesis.

Immersion of the testes into very hot water might produce temporary sterility. On the other hand, enclosing the scrotum in ice for one-half hour daily might increase the sperm count by 10 percent in some males. After a prolonged fever, sperm production might be reduced for as long as two months.

Some communicable diseases, such as mumps, affect sperm production. Young adult or older males who were not vaccinated for mumps prior to puberty are susceptible to the mumps virus. Mumps in post-pubescent males can result in orchitis. **Orchitis** is a condition that causes the seminiferous tubules to swell and lose their function, resulting in sterility. In most cases, one testicle becomes swollen and painful about 7 to 10 days after the parotid salivary glands have swollen. Sometimes both testicles are affected. Symptoms include high fever, chills, headache, nausea, and vomiting. As the fever subsides, testicular pain and swelling subside (Annunziato, 1999). To avoid this condition, males should have the MMR (measles, mumps, rubella) vaccine prior to puberty.

The Epididymis

Sperm produced in the seminiferous tubules move to the epididymis. The **epididymis** is a comma-shaped structure found on the back and upper surface of each testis. Sperm mature for about 2 to 6 weeks in the epididymis. Some sperm will remain in the epididymis for storage, but most move to the vas deferens after maturation.

Epididymitis is an inflammation of the epididymis. It is associated with urinary tract infections in males older than age 35. In younger males, the condition is usually caused by a sexually transmitted disease. Symptoms include testicular pain and tenderness as well as swelling of the epididymis.

The Vas Deferens

The **vas deferens** are two long, thin cords that extend from the epididymis in the scrotum, up through the inguinal canal, and into the abdomen. Each vas deferens functions as both a passageway for sperm and a place for sperm storage. Eventually, each vas deferens turns downward.

The Seminal Vesicles

The **seminal vesicles** are two small glands at the ends of each vas deferens that secrete an alkaline fluid rich in fructose, a sugar nutrient that is a source of energy for sperm. The amount of this fluid in the seminal vesicles at the time of ejaculation is thought to be related to the intensity of the sexual experience—the more seminal fluid, the greater the intensity of the male orgasm. Thus, if a male has multiple ejaculations, the first orgasm usually is the most intense. In subsequent orgasms, there is less seminal fluid.

The Ejaculatory Duct

Each vas deferens is joined by the ducts of the seminal vesicles to form the ejaculatory duct. The **ejaculatory duct** is a short, straight tube that passes into the prostate gland and opens into the urethra.

© 2001 Everyday Learning Corporation

The Prostate Gland

The **prostate gland** is a gland that produces an alkaline fluid that aids sperm longevity. It lies beneath the bladder and surrounds the urethra. The milky, alkaline prostatic fluid neutralizes the acidic secretions of the vagina as well as acidity in the male urethra.

As males age, the prostate gland commonly becomes enlarged. Monitoring of the prostate gland for possible signs of cancer is very important since it is estimated that prostate cancer will affect almost 20 percent of males in the United States during their lifetime. For 1999, 37,000 deaths from prostate cancer are predicted in the United States (Landis and Bolden, et al., 1999).

The Cowper's Glands (Bulbourethral Glands)

The **Cowper's glands**, or **bulbourethral glands**, are two small pea-sized glands located on each side of the urethra and secrete a lubrication fluid. Small ducts from these glands open into the urethra. When a male becomes sexually aroused, the Cowper's glands secrete a fluid, which is sometimes called precoital fluid. A drop of this fluid can be noticed at the tip of the penis before intercourse. The fluid is alkaline and might aid in lowering the acidity in the urethra, making it easier for sperm to live. Although this fluid precedes ejaculation, sperm have been found in it. Thus, precoital fluid might contain sperm that can impregnate a female even though ejaculation does not occur.

The Urethra

The **urethra** is a tubelike passageway that extends from the urinary bladder to the outside tip of the penis in the male or the vaginal opening in the female and serves as a passageway for semen in the male and urine in the male and the female. The urethra is about 9 inches (22.8 cm) long. The urethra passes through the prostate gland, where it is joined by the ejaculatory duct. Before ejaculation, the opening of the bladder closes. As a result, urine and semen are not in the urethra at the same time.

The Penis

The **penis** is the male organ of sexual pleasure, reproduction, and urination. The **root**, or **base**, is the part of the penis that is attached to the pelvic area. The **body**, or **shaft**, is the main part of the penis. The **corona** is the rim or crown where the glans rises slightly over the shaft. The **glans** is the tip of the clitoris or penis. The glans forms the head of the penis and is slightly enlarged. The **foreskin**, or **prepuce**, is a circular fold of loose skin that covers the glans of the penis in males who are not circumcised. The **frenulum** is the underside of the penis where the glans is attached to the foreskin.

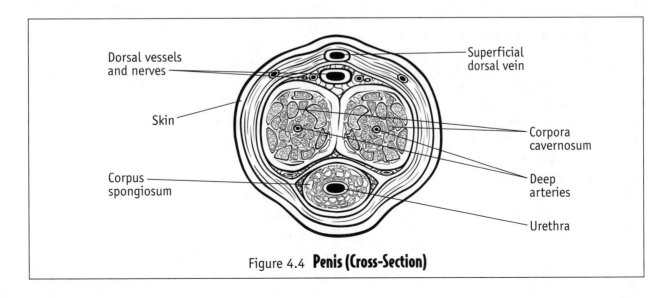

Figure 4.4 **Penis (Cross-Section)**

Male Physiology

The male organs involved in reproduction produce hormones, produce sperm, transfer sperm to the female, and provide sexual satisfaction. Male sexual physiology involves erection, orgasm, and ejaculation.

Erection

The penis is composed of three cylinders, each containing erectile tissues (Figure 4.4). The **corpus cavernosum** are the two upper cylinders containing erectile tissue on the top of the penis. The **corpus spongiosum** is the single cylinder containing erectile tissue beneath the penis. Each of these three cylinders contains many spaces and resembles a sponge. Thus, these three cylinders are called the three spongy layers. The three spongy layers are richly supplied with blood vessels and nerves. Crossbars of smooth muscle separate the spaces in them.

Erection is an involuntary process that occurs when the spongy layers inside the penis are engorged with blood and the penis elongates. Erection is produced by an involuntary reflex. There are receptors in the penis, scrotum, and thighs that, when touched, produce a neural signal that is sent to the sacral, or lowest, portion of the spinal cord. This signal causes the smooth muscles to become relaxed.

This signal also causes the parasympathetic nervous system to send a message to the arteries leading into the penis, causing them to dilate or expand. Blood then rushes into the arteries in the spongy layers under relatively high pressure, which has the same effect as soaking a sponge with water. At the same time, the flow of venous blood away from the penis is partially reduced, causing a further increase in pooling of blood.

The penis is made up of loose folds of skin. When the penis is engorged with blood, it swells, elongates, and becomes erect. The nonerect penis, which is usually 2 1/2 to 4 inches (6.4 to 10 cm) long, will increase in size to about 6 inches (15 cm) long.

Orgasm

Orgasm is an explosive discharge of neuromuscular tensions at the peak of sexual response and is marked by rhythmic contractions and a sense of physiological and psychological release. In males, orgasm is usually accompanied by ejaculation. However, ejaculation might occur without orgasm, and orgasm might occur without ejaculation. A **retrograde ejaculation** is an ejaculation in which semen is expelled into the bladder instead of out of the penis. Orgasm lasts less than a minute and normally affects only the genital area in males.

Ejaculation

Ejaculation is the sudden expulsion of seminal fluid from an erect penis. The reflex action producing ejaculation operates in the following manner: When the penis is stimulated orally, manually, or coitally, messages are transmitted to the lumbar and sacral portions of the spinal cord. These messages also might be a result of psychological stimulation. As a result of spinal reflexes, the sympathetic nervous system causes the smooth muscles in the internal organs involved in ejaculation to contract. Rhythmic contractions occur in the smooth muscles in the walls of the testes, epididymis, vas deferens, and ejaculatory ducts. At the same time, there are rhythmic contractions in the seminal vesicles and prostate gland, as well as in the skeletal muscles at the base of the erectile tissue. The pressure within the erectile tissue aids in forcing semen through the urethra.

The order of events during ejaculation that serves to facilitate the safe passage of sperm is as follows:

- Fluid from the Cowper's glands is secreted. This fluid lubricates the tip of the penis and lowers the acidity of the urethra;

- Fluid from the prostate gland is released. This fluid is alkaline and neutralizes the acidity of the seminal fluid and later will neutralize the acidity in the vagina, enhancing sperm viability;

- Sperm move through the vas deferens; and

- Fluid is ejected from the seminal vesicles. The seminal fluid is alkaline, and it contains the nutrient fructose that nourishes the sperm.

The seminal fluid leaves in spurts that correspond with the rhythmic contractions. The first contractions occur at 0.8 second intervals. The normal male ejaculate of 3 ml (less than a teaspoon) contains approximately 360 million sperm.

After ejaculation, sympathetic impulses cause constriction of the arteries leading to the erectile tissue in the penis and blood flow into the penis is reduced. The smooth muscles within the vascular spaces contract, enabling the veins to carry the excess blood from the spaces in the spongy layers. The penis returns to a flaccid or nonerect state.

Erectile Dysfunction

Erectile dysfunction is the inability to sustain an erection sufficient for sexual intercourse. This condition affects 10 to 30 million males in the United States (NIH, 1999b). Erectile dysfunction is not associated with aging. Although emotional factors can cause erectile dysfunction, 80 percent of the cases have a physical basis. These often include an emotional component since most males with physically based erectile dysfunction might experience low self-esteem and become anxious and depressed. Erectile dysfunction might be caused by side effects from drug therapy or certain conditions, such as heart disease, arteriosclerosis, hypertension, diabetes, alcoholism, liver failure, and high cholesterol level. The greatest risk factor for erectile dysfunction is considered to be smoking (Barnes, 1999).

Erectile dysfunction usually is treatable. Due to the diversity of causes, treatment should begin with a comprehensive and individualized clinical evaluation. In the past, a penile prosthesis sometimes was implanted to remedy the condition, and this device might still be used to treat males who do not tolerate other therapy. However, alternative treatments, such as penile injection therapy and sildenafil (Viagra), are used more often (Harin and Wayne, et al., 1997).

Studies show that sildenafil is the only oral drug to treat erectile dysfunction successfully. This drug is not recommended for males who have angina and are taking medication to widen

coronary arteries. Infrequently, sildenafil has been reported to cause priapism or a prolonged erection lasting more than four hours. Other drugs, such as testosterone and yohimbine hydrochloride, were previously prescribed for erectile dysfunction. These drugs have been problematic. Testosterone is useful only in cases of hormonal imbalance associated with less than 5 percent of the males with erectile dysfunction; and yohimbine hydrochloride is an aphrodisiac with no established effectiveness. Certain drugs such as fluoxetine (Prozac), sertraline (Zoloft), and trazodone (Desyrel), which are prescribed for psychological or emotional disorders, might cause erectile dysfunction and delayed ejaculation (Barnes, 1999).

Male Reproductive Health and Sexual Concerns

A male's knowledge and understanding of his reproductive organs and their reproductive as well as sexual functions help him understand and appreciate his sexuality. This knowledge and information also is necessary for maintaining optimal physical, emotional, and psychological health. This section of the chapter includes a discussion of hernia, circumcision, penis size, nocturnal emissions, morning erection, anabolic steroids, testicular cancer, prostatitis, prostate cancer, and andropause.

Hernia

In the eighth or ninth month of fetal life, the testes pass through the inguinal canal and become located in the scrotum. The inguinal canal then closes to prevent other tissues from descending into the scrotum. Thus, the inguinal canal is partly or totally obliterated in 80 percent of infants over two months of age. If the inguinal canal fails to close or for some reason opens again, an organ or part of an organ located in the abdominal cavity might pass into this tunnel-like passageway. An unclosed inguinal canal also can lead to the return of one or both testes to the abdominal cavity.

Herniation is the protrusion of the contents of one of the body's cavities through an abnormal opening in the cavity wall. A hernia might occur elsewhere in the body, but a male is especially susceptible to a hernia through the inguinal canal. An **inguinal hernia** is a hernia in which some of the intestine pushes through the inguinal canal into the scrotum (Figure 4.5). This condition affects about 2 percent of males in the United States. When the testicles descend into the scrotum, an area in the abdominal wall weakens. This is the internal ring. An indirect inguinal hernia, the most common type of inguinal hernia, occurs at the internal ring in the groin area. The less common direct inguinal hernia occurs near the internal ring and is usually associated with aging or injury after age 40 (Young, 1998a). Symptoms of an inguinal hernia include a lump in the groin near the thigh, groin pain, and partial or complete blockage of the intestine caused by strangulation of the blood supply to the intestine. Blockage to the intestine might result in blood in the stool, constipation, fever, severe pain, vomiting, and shock. Therefore, an inguinal hernia is potentially dangerous and usually requires surgical correction. Hernia repair surgery, or herniorrhaphy, sometimes involves the use of steel mesh or wire to reinforce the weak abdominal area. Studies suggest that laparoscopic repair might lead to more rapid recovery and fewer recurrences of inguinal hernia (Liem, et al., 1997).

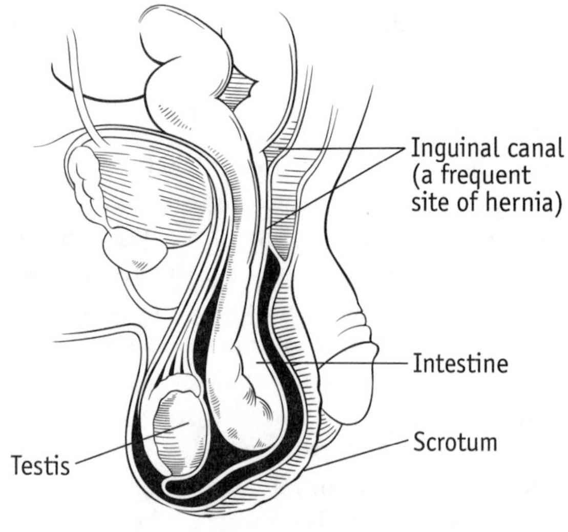

Circumcision

The **foreskin**, or **prepuce**, is a circular fold of loose skin that covers the glans of the penis in males who are not circumcised. The foreskin might cover the entire glans or a portion of the glans of the penis. It usually is easily drawn back, or retracted, from the glans.

Circumcision is the surgical removal of the foreskin from the penis (Figure 4.6). The National Center for Health Statistics estimates that 64.1 percent of male infants born in 1995 were circumcised (CDC, 1998). It is further estimated that 1.2 million male infants are circumcised in the United States every year. The rate of circumcision is higher among Caucasians than among African-Americans or Hispanics (Lannon, et al., 1999). The majority of male infants who are circumcised are circumcised on the second day after birth for a variety of ritual, religious, physical, and hygienic reasons.

Routine neonatal circumcision is a controversial subject. In 1999, the American Academy of Pediatrics issued a Circumcision Policy Statement regarding the medical benefits and risks of infant male circumcision. According to the Academy statement, there are some potential medical advantages and some minor risks in performing circumcision (AAP, 1999).

Figure 4.5 Inguinal Hernia

An **inguinal hernia** is a hernia in which some of the intestine pushes through the inguinal canal into the scrotum.

Inguinal canal (a frequent site of hernia)

Intestine

Scrotum

Testis

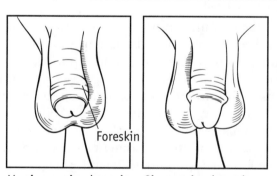

Uncircumcised penis   Circumcised penis

Foreskin

Figure 4.6 Circumcision/Non-Circumcision

Circumcision is the surgical removal of the foreskin from the penis. The **foreskin**, or **prepuce**, is a circular fold of loose skin that covers the glans of the penis in males who are not circumcised.

Complications associated with circumcision are rare. These might include abnormal urination within 6 to 8 hours of the procedure, continued bleeding, and redness around the penile tip that worsens after 3 to 5 days. Some believe that the removal of the foreskin might cause penile irritation and urination difficulties and that the penile tip might become less sensitive, decreasing sexual pleasure in later life.

Studies suggest that during the first year of life, a circumcised male is at slightly less risk than an uncircumcised male for developing a urinary tract infection. This might result from bacteria that adhere to the mucosal surface of the foreskin (NIH, 1999b).

Neonatal circumcision has many potential advantages. The medical advantages are related to reduced cancer risk and reduced risk of infection. The risk of infection might be due to secretions from the foreskin of the penis in the male who is not circumcised. The **preputial glands** are a number of small glands located in the foreskin that secrete an oily, lubricating substance. These secretions begin at puberty. During the childhood years, these glands are mostly inactive.

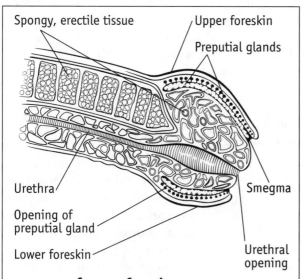

Figure 4.7 **Smegma Secretion**

Smegma is a cheesy substance that forms under the foreskin. A male who is not circumcised can prevent smegma from collecting under the foreskin by pulling the foreskin back and gently but thoroughly washing the area with soap and warm water.

The secretions of the preputial glands might combine with dead skin cells and form smegma. **Smegma** is a cheesy substance that forms under the foreskin (Figure 4.7). A male who is not circumcised can prevent smegma from collecting under the foreskin by pulling the foreskin back and gently but thoroughly washing the area with soap and warm water. However, if regular cleansing is ignored and smegma is allowed to collect, it develops a strong, unpleasant odor. Infection-causing microorganisms might collect and grow in smegma.

The research concerning links between circumcision and sexually transmitted diseases including syphilis and HIV/AIDS is complicated. There is substantial evidence that uncircumcised males are at increased risk for HIV infection. This might be due to the increased potential for viral attachment to the mucous membrane of the foreskin. However, HIV risk seems to be more related to behavioral factors (Lannon, et al., 1999).

Penile cancer, a rare kind of cancer in males in the United States, occurs as a result of malignant cells found on the skin and in the tissues of the penis. Several studies have established a risk for penile cancer in uncircumcised males. Phimosis, a condition wherein the prepuce is tight, has been established as a major risk factor for penile cancer. This condition is preventable with circumcision. However, the relationship between phimosis, hygiene, and the disease is not clear. Each year in the United States, penile cancer occurs in 9 to 10 cases among 1 million males (AAP, 1999).

The chance for recovery from penile cancer and the choice of treatment depend on the stage of the cancer, whether it is localized or has spread to other areas of the body, as well as the general health of the male. In its earliest stages, penile cancer is highly curable. Microsurgery or laser surgery might be performed to remove the cancerous cells. Radiation therapy, chemotherapy, and biological therapy also might be used to treat penile cancer.

In severe cases only, a partial or total penectomy involving partial or total amputation of the penis might be necessary (National Cancer Institute, 1998).

Penis Size

A male's attitude toward and acceptance of his body influence his sexuality and self-esteem. His feelings about his penis are particularly important in feeling masculine and sexually adequate. Some males worry unnecessarily about the size of their penis. This worry stems from the mistaken notion that a large penis is necessary for adequate sexual function.

This worry can be eliminated by the knowledge that it is primarily the external organs of the female (the labia and clitoris) that are excitable, so penis size is not an important factor. The female vagina stretches to accommodate the size of the penis. Furthermore, a penis that appears small when not erect tends to increase more in size during erection than an already large penis.

It is impossible to tell the size of a man's penis from his other physical characteristics. Penis size is not related to size of feet, length of fingers, body shape, height, or weight. There is no difference in the penis size of males of different races. It is impossible to enlarge the size of the adult penis permanently, either by surgery or hormonal treatment. Injection of a substance such as silicone might completely destroy the capacity for erection. And recent evidence suggests that using silicone in the body might cause cancer.

Nocturnal Emissions

Nocturnal emissions, or **wet dreams**, are spontaneous ejaculations that occur during sleep. Onset of nocturnal emissions occurs in puberty. Usually puberty begins between ages 10 and 15. Nocturnal emissions occur frequently during male adolescence as a result of the changes in hormonal concentrations. Adolescents who have not learned that wet dreams are normal might be frightened, uncomfortable, and embarrassed by their occurrence. Wet dreams also might occur as a result of having erotic dreams. Kinsey reported that almost all males, regardless of age, report having erotic dreams (Kinsey, et al., 1998).

Morning Erection

A **morning erection** is an erection that results from waking up during rapid eye movement (REM) or the dreaming stage of sleep or from having a full bladder. The latter might cause an erection by stimulating nerves near the base of the penis (Moglia and Knowles, 1997). Morning erections are quite common.

Anabolic Steroids

Anabolic steroids are drugs produced from male sex hormones. These drugs have some therapeutic value. The FDA has approved the use of certain anabolic steroids in the treatment of some conditions and diseases. These include specific types of anemia, some breast cancers, osteoporosis, endometriosis, and hereditary angioedema, a rare disease that causes parts of the body to become swollen (NIH, 1999a).

Male sex hormones, produced by the body, increase muscle mass and strength at puberty. This has led body builders and athletes to use anabolic steroids to further increase muscle mass and strength for sports. The use of anabolic steroids for non-medical purposes such as this is associated with major adverse effects including strokes, myocardial infarctions, and the loss of limbs (NIH, 1999a). The long-term effects on the development of coronary artery disease have not been determined (Anderson, et al., 1997). The International Olympics Committee has banned 17 anabolic steroids and related compounds because use of these drugs precludes fair competition. (NIH, 1999a).

Users of anabolic steroids should be aware that adverse effects might occur without warning. These might range from nonlife-threatening conditions, such as acne and baldness, to potentially fatal results including malignancies or thrombotic phenomena (Anderson, et al., 1997). Anabolic steroids increase the likelihood of aggressive behavior and can cause testicular atrophy. Withdrawal symptoms from the use of these drugs include severe depression and thoughts of suicide.

There is a further danger from using these drugs. Anabolic steroids usually are injected into a vein. Often the needles are shared by two or more people. Sharing a needle to inject anabolic steroids into the body is a risk behavior for HIV infection.

Because of the physiological and psychological risks, males who are using anabolic steroids should stop this practice and seek medical help and counseling.

Testicular Cancer

Although testicular cancer represents 1 percent of all cancers in males in the United States, the incidence of cases has doubled in the United States over the past 50 years (Young, 1998b). Testicular cancer is the most common malignancy in males between the ages of 20 and 40. Risk factors for testicular cancer include

1. having a family history of testicular cancer;

2. having undescended testicles by age 3;

3. having mumps resulting in orchitis after puberty;

4. having a rare condition in which the testicles do not develop normally; and

5. being Caucasian.

Some males whose mothers took diethylstilbestrol (DES) during pregnancy have testicular abnormalities. However, prenatal exposure to DES has not been established as a risk for testicular cancer. Injury to the scrotum also has been associated with testicular cancer in some males. However, such an injury is not considered to be a risk factor for testicular cancer.

An early sign of testicular cancer is a testicular mass that feels hard when palpated with the fingertips. The mass might be painless or tender when palpated. Occasionally, there are other symptoms such as a heaviness or dragging sensation in the groin or scrotum, fever, and/or tenderness in the breasts and nipples. There also might be pain in the lower abdomen or the testicle, an open sore on the scrotum, urination difficulty, a cough, or breathing difficulty.

With early detection and treatment, the most common form of testicular cancer (semicoma) is nearly 100 percent curable. Thus, regular testicular self-examination is very important. **Testicular self-examination (TSE)** is observation

and palpation of the testicles to locate any mass or tenderness. The recommended procedure is as follows (Figure 4.8):

- perform testicular self-examination after a hot shower or bath as the heat causes the scrotal skin to relax and the testes to descend;

- assume a comfortable sitting or standing position or lie on the back;

- visually examine each testicle for any changes;

- then place the thumbs of both hands on the top of a testicle and the index and middle fingers on the underside of the testicle;

- roll the testicle between the thumb and fingers applying a small amount of pressure; and

- check to see that the surface of the testicle is firm and smooth.

Each testicle should be examined in its entirety for about 30 seconds to 1 minute. The epididymis that is normally firm to the touch should not be mistaken for a cancerous lump (Young, 1998b).

Any sign of a mass or of tenderness should be reported to a physician immediately. A growth or mass on a testicle might be a sign of cancer or hernia, a cyst, or an enlarged blood vessel.

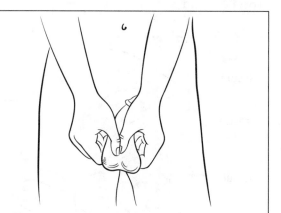

Figure 4.8 Testicular Self-Exam

Visually examine each testicle for any changes. Place the thumbs of both hands on the top of a testicle and the index and middle fingers on the underside of the testicle. Roll a testicle between the thumb and fingers applying a small amount of pressure. Check to see that the surface of the testicle is firm and smooth.

If the testicles are sensitive to touch, this might be a sign of an infection or a sexually transmitted disease. Treatment for testicular cancer usually involves surgery, although radiation therapy or chemotherapy might be used. In most cases, neither testicle is affected. Therefore, fertility is not at risk (Young, 1998b). Treatment for testicular cancer rarely results in erectile dysfunction or other problems with sexual function.

Prostatitis

Prostatitis is the inflammation of the prostate gland. Although this condition can occur in younger males, it is primarily a condition associated with aging. Prostatitis usually is caused by a viral or bacterial infection. In rare cases, it is associated with changes in the frequency of ejaculations.

The symptoms of prostatitis include backache, pain in the pelvic area, a cloudy discharge from the penis, and changes in urination. Bacterial prostatitis is treated with antibiotics. Nonbacterial prostatitis is treated with prostatic massage. The physician inserts a gloved, lubricated finger into the rectum and presses rhythmically against the prostate gland.

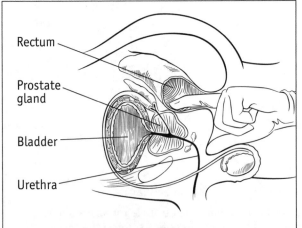

Rectum

Prostate gland

Bladder

Urethra

Figure 4.9 **Digital Rectal Examination of the Prostate**

A **digital rectal examination** is an examination in which the physician inserts a gloved, lubricated finger into the rectum and examines the prostate and rectum for hard or lumpy areas.

Prostate Cancer

Prostate cancer is second only to skin cancer as the most common type of cancer in males in the United States (Lukk, et al., 1999).

The American Cancer Society recommends that men over the age of 50 be screened for prostate cancer. Screening includes an annual digital rectal examination and a blood test (American Cancer Society, 1999). A **digital rectal examination** is an examination in which the physician inserts a gloved, lubricated finger into the rectum and examines the prostate and rectum for hard or lumpy areas (Figure 4.9).

A blood test called the prostate-specific antigen (PSA) blood test might suggest the presence of prostate cancer or a noncancerous condition. Although the blood test results alone are not conclusive, high levels of PSA might indicate a cancerous condition. Another test called the transrectal ultrasonography might be used to make a more definitive diagnosis. **Transrectal ultrasonography** is a test in which a probe inserted into the rectum sends sound waves that create a picture or sonogram on a screen.

Other diagnostic tests include an intravenous pyelogram, a series of X-rays of the urinary tract, and cystoscopy involving the insertion of a thin, lighted tube into the urethra and bladder.

If the diagnostic examination suggests the presence of prostate cancer, a biopsy will be performed.

Annual examination of the prostate gland after the age of 50 is essential to male health. The incidence and mortality associated with prostate cancer increases with a male's age. Between 1973 and 1992, the rate of prostate cancer cases increased quickly. Then the rate of incidence declined in the mid-1990s. This decline has been attributed to PSA screening (Sieve, 1998).

Those males who are at higher risk for prostate cancer include all males age 65 or older and African-American males who have a first-degree relative with prostate cancer. High dietary fat intake might increase the risk for prostate cancer, however, the connection is unclear (Sieve, 1998).

Recent studies suggest an association between DNA changes in genes and the development of prostate cancer. Researchers have identified genes in the human genome that might cause an inherited tendency toward this type of cancer (American Cancer Society, 1999).

There are usually no symptoms of prostate cancer in its early stages other than the changes that can be detected from the digital rectal examination and/or ultrasound. Signs and symptoms that indicate that medical attention should be sought include the following:

- loss in force of the urinary stream;
- dribbling;
- increased frequency of urination;
- blood in the urine or semen;
- painful ejaculation;
- passing urine at night;
- pain in the pelvic area; and
- lower back pain.

Examination might indicate that a male has benign prostatic hyperplasia (Meyeroff, 1998). **Benign prostatic hyperplasia** is a condition in which the prostate gland increases in size and puts pressure on the urethra, causing a decrease in urine flow. Symptoms might be relieved by transurethral resection of the prostate. This involves removal of the tissue that is creating pressure against the upper part of the urethra. Some short-term surgical risks include bleeding, temporary urinary discomfort, and retrograde ejaculation that moves semen back into the bladder. Alternative surgery involving an incision of the prostate without the resection might reduce side effects. However, the results of this surgery might be less permanent than with the resection (Meyeroff, 1998).

When prostate cancer is detected, a prostatectomy might be performed. A **radical prostatectomy** is the surgical removal of the entire prostate gland. The gland and some nearby lymph nodes might be removed through an abdominal incision or through an incision between the scrotum and the anus. An antiandrogen such as Lupron or Zolodex also might be used to block the effect of any male hormones produced by the adrenal glands. The surgical removal of the testicles might be necessary (Pienta, et al., 1999). Radiation therapy is another treatment option for prostate cancer.

Some side effects are associated with the various methods of treatment. Use of female sex hormones might interfere with erectile function. Males might experience hot flashes and growth of breast tissue (Sieve, 1998). Surgical treatments might cause permanent sterility and urinary incontinence, although these are rare occurrences. A new technique, nerve-sparing surgery, might prevent permanent injury to the erectile nerves as well as damage to the bladder opening. However, males whose prostate has been removed will no longer produce semen, resulting in dry orgasms. The surgical risks for radical prostatectomy are low. The hospital stay is only a few days.

With early diagnosis and treatment of localized prostate cancer, the five-year survival rate for males is 100 percent. Fifty-eight percent of the cases are discovered at this stage. The five-year survival rate drops to 31 percent after prostate cancer has spread to other parts of the body. Eleven percent of the prostate cancer cases are diagnosed at the metastasized stage (Sieve, 1998).

Some older males with localized prostate cancer might prefer "watchful waiting" as a treatment. This treatment is recommended to males who have serious medical illnesses or a reduced life expectancy less than 10 years. Males who have small, localized prostate tumors might be candidates for this non-aggressive treatment that only requires frequent monitoring (Sieve, 1998).

Andropause

Males have a decrease in testosterone between the ages of 40 and 55, although hormonal changes can occur in males as early as age 35 and as late as age 65. There is no clear biological marker to indicate the end of the male reproductive years (Diamond, 1997). **Andropause**, or the **male climacteric**, is the decrease in male sexual function that results from diminished testosterone. This might involve hot flashes, fatigue, nervousness, headache, and depression. The male climacteric, although somewhat rare, is as real for some males as it is for some females. Many of these males, when given testosterone in adequate amounts, claim to experience improvement. In most cases of androgen deficiency, testosterone therapy has been established as safe and effective (Winters, 1999).

Some research suggests possible improvement of symptoms through the use of dehydroepiandrosterone (DHEA), which is produced by the adrenal glands (Diamond, 1997). However, the National Institute on Aging warns that existing studies do not provide clear proof of the risks and benefits of DHEA use and that evidence is lacking to support claims for the use of DHEA dietary supplements. Research further suggests that when DHEA is taken even for short duration, liver damage might result.

References

American Academy of Pediatrics. 1999. "Circumcision: Information for Parents." Article Online. Accessed 7/1999. http://www.aap.org.

American Cancer Society. June 1999. "Prostate Cancer: Detection and Symptoms." Article Online. Accessed 7/1999. http://www.cancer.org.

Anderson, Steven J., M.D., Chair, et al. (Committee on Sports Medicine and Fitness, 1996 to 1997). 1997. "Adolescents and Anabolic Steroids: A Subject Review (RE9720)." *Pediatrics* 99/6 (June). Accessed 7/1999. http://www.aap.org.

Annunziato, Paula, M.D. (Medical Reviewer). 1999. "Mumps." *Journal of the American Medical Association—American Medical Association Health Insight—Infections and Immunizations* (June). Accessed 7/1999. http://www.4journals.com.

Barnes, Laura M. 1999. "Understanding Erectile Dysfunction." *Journal of the American Medical Association—American Medical Association Health Insight—Family Focus* (March). Accessed 7/1999. http://www.4journals.com.

Center for Disease Control and Prevention. 1998. "Vital and Health Statistics." 13/139 (November). Accessed 10/1999. http://www.cdc.gov/nchswww.data/sr13_139.pdf.

Diamond, Jed. 1997. *Male Menopause.* Naperville, Illinois: Sourcebooks.

Harin Padma-Nathan, Wayne J.G., et al. 1997. "Treatment of Men with Erectile Dysfunction with Transurethral Alprostadil." *New England Journal of Medicine* 336/1 (January). Accessed 7/1999. http://www.4journals.com.

Kinsey, Alfred C., et al. 1998. "Nocturnal Sex Dreams and Orgasms." *KICAT—Data From Alfred Kinsey's Studies—Alfred Kinsey's 1948 and 1953 Studies.* Excerpted from Kinsey, Alfred C. et al., *Sexual Behavior in the Human Male*, Bloomington, IN: Indiana University Press, pp. 518–19.

Landis, Murray T., S.H., Bolden S., et al. 1999. "Prevention of Prostate Cancer." *Screening and Prevention—Health Professionals* (May). Accessed 7/1999. http://www.nci.nih.gov.

Lannon, Carole M., M.D., Chairperson, et al. (Task Force on Circumcision 1998–1999). 1999. "AAP Circumcision Policy Statement." *Pediatrics* 103/3 (March): 686–693. Accessed 7/1999. http://www.aap.org.

Liem, Mike S.L., et al. 1997. "Comparison of Conventional Anterior Surgery and Laparoscopic Surgery for Inguinal-Hernia Repair." *New England Journal of Medicine* 336/2 (May): 1541–7. Accessed 7/1999. http://www.4journals.com.

Lukk, Tiiu, et al. 1999. "Prostate Cancer." CapCURE. Accessed 9/1999. http://www.205.139.28.245

Meyeroff, Wendy. 1998. "Real Patient Cases from JAMA 'Clinical Crossroads' Case History: Enlarged Prostate." *Journal of the American Medical Association—American Medical Association Health Insight—Family Focus* (April). Accessed 7/1999. http://www.4journals.com.

Moglia, Robert Filiberti and Joe Knowles (eds). 1997. *All About Sex: A Family Resource on Sex and Sexuality.* New York: Three Rivers Press.

National Cancer Institute. 1998. "Penile Cancer." Article Online. Accessed 7/1999. http://www.cancernet.nc8i.nih.gov.

National Institute of Health. 1999a. "Anabolic Steroids." NIDA Research Report Series. Accessed 7/1999. http://www.nida.nih.gov.

———. 1999b. "Care of the Uncircumcised Penis." Article Online. Accessed 7/1999. http://www.nih.gov-http://www.aap.org.

Pienta, Kenneth J., et al. 1999. "Treatment of Localized Prostate Cancer." University of Michigan. Accessed 9/1999. http://www.cancer.med.umich.edu/ prostcan/treatment.com.

Sieve, Vonne. 1998. "Understanding Prostate Cancer." *Journal of the American Medical Association—American Medical Association Health Insight—Family Focus* (August). Accessed 7/1999. http://www.nci.nih.gov.

Winters, Stephen J., M.D., 1999. "Current Status of Testosterone Replacement Therapy in Men." *Journal of the American Medical Association—Archives in Family Medicine* (May/June): 257–263. Accessed 7/1999. http://www.4journals.com.

Young, Timothy P. 1998a. "The Causes and Surgical Treatment of Abdominal Hernia." *Journal of the American Medical Association— American Medical Association Health Insight— Family Focus* (November). Accessed 7/1999. http://www.4journals.com.

———. 1998b. "Understanding and Detecting Testicular Cancer." *Journal of the American Medical Association—American Medical Association Health Insight—Family Focus* (September). Accessed 7/1999. http://www.4journals.com.

Female Reproductive Health

Content for Teachers *Only*

A Word from the Authors

Self-knowledge is necessary for a female to understand herself as a whole person. Certainly, knowledge of the female anatomy and physiology is a necessity for a female who desires self-acceptance. It also is helpful in appreciating her sexuality and in recognizing signs and symptoms of disease that need prompt medical attention. Males also need to learn about the female body. It would be difficult indeed for a male to have responsible and caring sexuality without any knowledge or appreciation of the female body and how it functions. A male's knowledge of a female's body is helpful to him in appreciating what it means to be female, planning for contraception, and preventing and discovering disease. Chapter 5 focuses on the external female reproductive organs, the internal female reproductive organs, the menstrual cycle, menstrual health, female reproductive health, the regular examination, and female sexual concerns.

The External Female Reproductive Organs

The **vulva** is the external organs of the female reproductive system. The external organs of the female reproductive system (Figure 5.1) consist of the mons pubis, the labia majora, the labia minora, the clitoris, the urethral opening, the vestibule, the vaginal opening, the hymen, the Bartholin's glands, and the perineum. Although the breasts are not considered an external female reproductive organ, they will be discussed in this section of the chapter because of their relationship to the reproductive system.

The Mons Pubis

The **mons pubis** is a pad of fatty tissue that covers the front of the pubic bone and serves as a protective cushion for the female reproductive organs. During puberty, hair covers the mons pubis in a triangular pattern. When a female is sexually aroused, the vagina secretes moist lubricants. The pubic hair covering the mons pubis might trap the scent of these secretions and further arouse both male and female.

The Labia Majora

The **labia majora** are the outer lips, or heavy folds of skin, surrounding the opening of the vagina. The labia majora are richly supplied with nerve endings and blood vessels and are sensitive to touch. During sexual arousal, the labia majora become engorged with blood.

The Labia Minora

The **labia minora** are two smaller lips, or folds of skin, located between the labia majora. The labia minora extend from the clitoral hood downward, past the openings to the urethra and the vagina. They vary in size, shape, and color. These smaller lips contain sweat and oil glands. They are richly supplied with nerve endings and blood vessels.

The Clitoris

The **clitoris** is a small, highly sensitive, cylindrical body about 3/4 inch (2.00 cm) long and about 3/16 inch (0.50 cm) in diameter projecting between the labia minora. The clitoris is composed of an external shaft and glans covered by the clitoral hood. The hood covering the shaft and glans is similar to the foreskin covering the glans of the penis. The **glans** is the tip of the clitoris or penis. The hood covers the very sensitive glans, which is richly supplied with blood vessels and nerve endings.

The shaft of the clitoris contains two small spongy bodies, the cavernosa bodies. These spongy bodies become engorged with blood during arousal and are responsible for what is sometimes called clitoral erection.

The Urethral Opening

The **urethra** is a tubelike passageway that extends from the urinary bladder to the outside tip of the penis in the male or the vaginal opening in the female and serves as a passageway for semen in the male and urine in the male and the female. The urethra opens into the floor of the vestibule, midway between the glans of the clitoris and the vaginal opening.

The Vestibule

The **vestibule** is the space between the labia minora into which open the urethra, the vagina, and the ducts of the Bartholin's glands.

The Vaginal Opening and the Hymen

The **vaginal opening** is the opening from the vagina to the outside of the body. The vaginal opening is also called the vaginal introitus. The **hymen** is a thin membrane that stretches across the vaginal introitus. There is a perforation in the center of the hymen. It is through this perforation that the menstrual flow leaves the body and through which tampons can be inserted during menstruation. **Imperforate hymen** is a condition in which there is no central perforation in the hymen. As a result, the menstrual flow is blocked, and the hymen must be opened by an incision to eliminate this condition. The hymen and virginity are discussed at the end of this chapter.

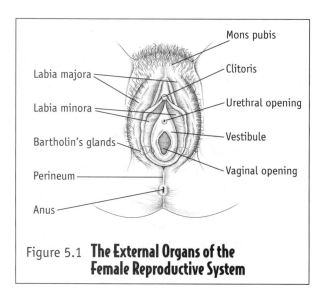

Labia majora
Labia minora
Bartholin's glands
Perineum
Anus
Mons pubis
Clitoris
Urethral opening
Vestibule
Vaginal opening

Figure 5.1 **The External Organs of the Female Reproductive System**

The Bartholin's Glands

The **Bartholin's glands** are a pair of bean-shaped glands that are located near the labia minora and that secrete a few drops of fluid during sexual excitement. The secretions from these glands provide the genital scent that contributes to sexual arousal.

The Perineum

The **perineum** is the area between the vaginal opening and the anal opening. It is a smooth area of skin that is richly supplied with nerve endings. Thus, the perineum is very sensitive.

The Breasts

The **breasts** are organs consisting of fatty tissue and mammary gland tissue. The breasts have two functions in reproduction and sexuality.

1. The mammary gland tissue produces milk for the newborn.
2. The breasts, which are richly supplied with nerve endings, provide a female with sensations during sexual arousal.

The **areola** is the darkened area in the center of each breast, and it contains oil-producing sebaceous glands. The secretions from the sebaceous glands lubricate the nipples, keeping them from cracking during breastfeeding. The **nipple** is the tip of a female's breast. Both nipples are richly supplied with nerve endings and are very sensitive to touch. The nipples might protrude, might be slightly turned inward, or might be level with the areola. The nipples might become erect when a female feels cold or when she is sexually aroused.

The Internal Female Reproductive Organs

The internal female reproductive organs (Figure 5.2) consist of the vagina, the uterus, the fallopian tubes, and the ovaries. The structure and function of these organs will be discussed in this section of the chapter. The diseases and conditions that affect them will be discussed in the section on female reproductive health.

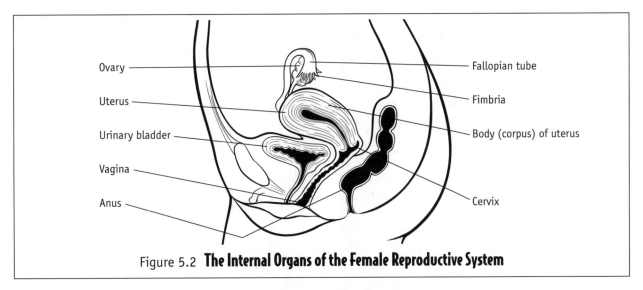

Figure 5.2 **The Internal Organs of the Female Reproductive System**

Labels: Ovary, Uterus, Urinary bladder, Vagina, Anus, Fallopian tube, Fimbria, Body (corpus) of uterus, Cervix

The Vagina

The **vagina** is a muscular passageway that lies between the bladder and the rectum, and it serves as the female organ of intercourse, the birth canal, and the passageway for the menstrual flow and the arriving sperm. This collapsed muscular tube, approximately 4 to 5 inches (10.16 to 12.70 cm) in length leads from the vulva upward to the uterus. It is composed of three layers: (1) a mucous layer richly supplied with blood vessels; (2) a muscular layer; and (3) an elastic, fibrous layer.

The vagina can best be described as a "potential space." Normally, the vaginal walls lie close together. However, when anything enters the vagina, the vaginal walls stretch apart. During sexual intercourse, the vagina stretches to accommodate the penis. During childbirth, it expands to form an opening four or five times its usual size.

The vagina is usually moist and acidic. The pH in the vagina is approximately 4.0 to 5.0. During sexual excitement, the amount of moisture increases when the walls of the vagina secrete a mucoid material by a "sweating phenomenon."

The amount of moisture in the vagina also varies with the different stages of the menstrual cycle. A continuous secretion of dead cells mixed with lubricating fluid comes from the cervix and the vagina. This continuous secretion has a self-cleansing quality that, in combination with a pH of 4.0 to 5.0, eliminates the need for douching the vagina except for prescribed medical reasons.

The Uterus

The **uterus** is the organ that prepares each month to receive a fertilized ovum, to support the fertilized ovum during pregnancy, and to contract during childbirth to help with delivery. The uterus, or womb, is a hollow, muscular, pear-shaped organ in the pelvic cavity, and is located between the bladder and the rectum. In the nonpregnant state, the uterus is about 3 inches (7.62 cm) long and 2 inches (5.08 cm) wide at the top, narrowing down to the cervix where it is normally about 1/2 inch (1.27 cm) to 1 inch (2.54 cm) in diameter.

The uterus is divided into three anatomical parts. The **corpus**, or **body**, is the upper muscular division of the uterus. The **isthmus** is the constricted area of the uterus below the corpus. During pregnancy, the isthmus lengthens and thins out. In this way, it helps the corpus enlarge the womb for the growing embryo.

The **cervix** is the lowest part of the uterus. The narrowed cervix keeps the growing embryo inside the womb during pregnancy. The cervix contains no nerve endings. However, it does contain mucus-secreting glands. There is a continuous secretion of dead cells and mucus from the cervix. During a regular health examination, cells are scraped from the wall of the cervix for a Pap smear. The Pap smear will be discussed in the section on reproductive health.

Besides the three anatomical parts of the uterus, there are three uterine layers—the perimetrium, the myometrium, and the endometrium. The

perimetrium is the outermost layer of the uterus. The **myometrium** is the muscular layer of the uterus. There are many interweaving fibers within the myometrium, with arteries and veins lying between them. At the culmination of pregnancy, arteries within the myometrium are prevented from hemorrhaging because the muscular fibers constrict.

The **endometrium** is the inner lining of the uterus. It consists of spongy tissue that is richly supplied with secretory glands and blood vessels. It is 1/2 to 3/16 inch (3 to 4 mm) in thickness. The endometrium grows each month to prepare a place for the fertilized ovum to implant and grow. When there is no fertilized ovum, the endometrium is shed as the menstrual flow.

The Fallopian Tubes

The **fallopian tubes**, or **oviducts**, are tubes that extend from near the ovaries to the uterus. The fallopian tubes lie close to the ovaries and extend to the corners of the uterus. The **fimbria** are the fingerlike projections at the end of each oviduct.

The function of the fallopian tubes is to transport ova to the uterus. When ovulation occurs, the musculature of the fallopian tubes and ligaments by which they are suspended tend to draw the flared ends of the fallopian tubes and the ovaries together. Contractions of the muscular walls of the fallopian tubes create a suction that directs an ovum into the fallopian tubes.

The process is further aided by the constant beating of cilia. **Cilia** are hairlike projections on the inner surface of the oviducts. Their beating action creates a constant current in the female reproductive system. Ordinarily, ova from the right ovary enter the right fallopian tube and those from the left ovary enter the left fallopian tube. However, numerous cases on record indicate that cross-over occurs (the left fallopian tube might move over to pick up an ovum from the right ovary).

An ovum also might float to one of the fallopian tubes. Once inside the fallopian tube, an ovum is moved by the peristaltic contractions of the fallopian tube itself. An ovum moves at a rate of 1 inch (2.54 cm) every 24 hours. An ovum is viable (healthy and alive) for approximately 24 to 48 hours; thus, fertilization usually occurs in the upper 2 inches (5.08 cm) of the fallopian tube.

The Ovaries

The **ovaries** are two almond-shaped female sex glands that produce ova and secrete hormones. The ovaries are located at the brim of the pelvis. Each ovary is about 1 inch (2.54 cm) wide, 1 1/2 inches (3.81 cm) long, and 1/4 inch (0.64 cm) thick.

At birth, the ovaries of a female baby contain many primary follicles. **Primary follicles** are podlike structures that contain immature, or unripened, ova. It is estimated that there are between 200,000 and 400,000 primary follicles in each ovary at birth. These follicles continually degenerate. About 10,000 of them remain at puberty, and by age 50 most of them have disappeared. During the reproductive years, only about 375 of the primary follicles are sufficiently developed to expel ova.

When a female is approximately eight years old, the pituitary gland, which is at the base of the brain, increases its secretion of follicle-stimulating hormone (FSH). **Follicle-stimulating hormone (FSH)** is a hormone secreted by the pituitary gland that causes follicles to grow. FSH travels to the ovaries through the bloodstream and causes the ovaries to secrete estrogen. **Estrogen** is a female sex hormone that produces female secondary sex characteristics and affects the menstrual cycle.

When a female is between the ages of 10 and 14, the influence of estrogen on the female body becomes noticeable. The female body is being prepared for reproduction. The uterus, vagina, and external female genitalia increase in size and physiological maturity. Female secondary sex characteristics that develop include the following (Figure 5.3):

- deposition of fat in the breasts, accompanied by development of an elaborate duct system;
- development of soft and smooth skin;
- broadening of the pelvis, which changes from a narrow, funnel-like outlet to a broad, oval outlet;

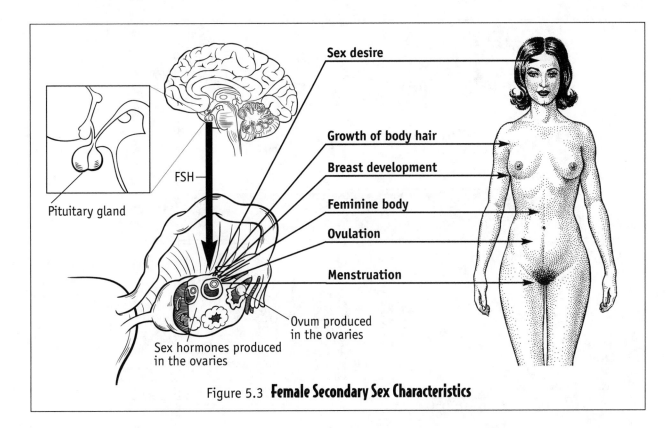

Figure 5.3 **Female Secondary Sex Characteristics**

- development of pubic hair with a flat upper border;
- deposition of fat in the thighs and buttocks; and
- early uniting of the growing end of long bones with the bone shaft (females without estrogen usually grow several inches taller than the average female).

Accompanying these anatomical changes during puberty are important physiological changes. These physiological changes include ovulation and menstruation.

The Menstrual Cycle

The **menstrual cycle** is a rhythmic cycle of approximately one month in which hormonal levels fluctuate to prepare a female's body for the possibility of pregnancy (Figure 5.4). Each monthly cycle is divided into three phases: the proliferative phase, the secretory or progestational phase, and the menstrual phase.

The Proliferative Phase

The word *proliferate* means "to grow by the rapid production of new cells." The **proliferative phase**, or **estrogen phase**, is the first phase of the menstrual cycle when FSH causes 15 to 20 primary follicles to grow in the ovaries and when ovulation occurs.

Each month shortly after menstruation begins, the pituitary gland secretes FSH. FSH travels to the ovaries through the bloodstream and stimulates some of the primary follicles in the ovaries to grow. The follicles enlarge because of an accumulation of fluids similar to the swelling of a blister.

These growing follicles secrete estrogen that causes the uterine lining, or endometrium, to grow. The endometrium attains a thickness of more than 1/16 inch to 1/8 inch (2 to 3 mm).

The **Graafian follicle** is an immature primary follicle that balloons into full maturity in the middle of a female's menstrual cycle. The **stigma** is a small dot or nipplelike protrusion that develops on the surface of the Graafian follicle. As the stigma develops, the pituitary gland secretes luteinizing hormone (LH).

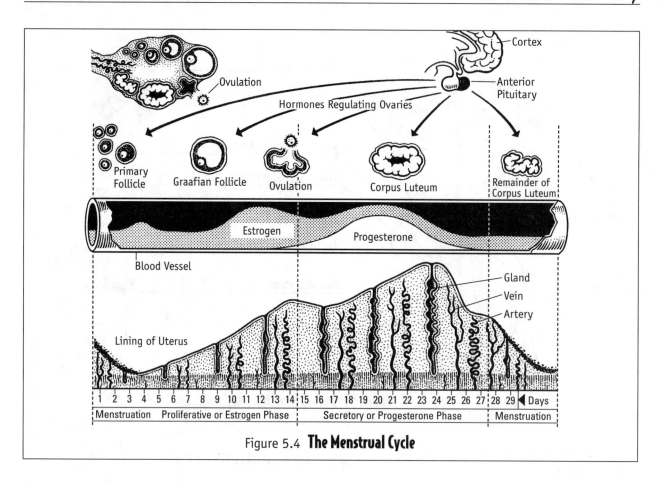

Figure 5.4 **The Menstrual Cycle**

Luteinizing hormone causes the stigma to disintegrate. This disintegration causes the Graafian follicle to rupture and release an ovum.

Ovulation is the release of a mature ovum by an ovary and occurs on or about the fourteenth day before the expected beginning of the next menstrual period. The other growing primary follicles degenerate. It is in the proliferative phase that variation in the length of a female's menstrual cycle occurs.

The Secretory Phase or Progestational Phase

The **secretory phase**, or **progestational phase**, is the second phase of the menstrual cycle, and during this phase the corpus luteum secretes progesterone and estrogen to prepare a female's body for the implantation of a fertilized ovum. The sequence of events in the secretory phase is as follows:

Shortly after ovulation, the follicular cells from the ruptured Graafian follicle are transformed into a temporary endocrine gland by the action of

luteinizing hormone (LH). The **corpus luteum** is the yellow glandular body that is formed in the ovary from the follicular remains. To prepare the female reproductive system for the reception of an ovum, the corpus luteum secretes estrogen and progesterone.

Progesterone is a hormone secreted by the corpus luteum to initiate the nourishing secretions for the ovum in the fallopian tube, to inhibit the contraction of the muscular layer of the uterus, to stimulate the breasts' ducts, and to thicken the uterine lining to receive the ovum. The secretion of progesterone is what gives this part of the menstrual cycle its name.

The corpus luteum also secretes additional amounts of estrogen. Estrogen and progesterone work together to cause the endometrium to thicken. They cause an increase in the blood supply in the lining of the uterus, and cause glands in the lining to secrete endometrial fluid. Estrogen and progesterone also inhibit the release of FSH and LH, so that no new primary follicles begin to mature.

The Menstrual Phase

The **menstrual phase** is the third phase of the menstrual cycle, and during this phase the corpus luteum degenerates, the secretion of estrogen and progesterone sharply decreases, and the menstrual flow occurs. The menstrual phase, like the proliferative and secretory phases, is under hormonal influence. It is related to the function of the corpus luteum.

The corpus luteum remains active for about 10 to 12 days. During this time, it secretes estrogen and progesterone, and these hormones work together to prepare the lining of the uterus as well as to block FSH and LH so that no new primary follicles begin to grow. However, when fertilization does not occur, the corpus luteum degenerates after 10 to 12 days.

Two days before the beginning of the menstrual flow, the secretion of estrogen and progesterone decreases sharply as the corpus luteum degenerates. The lining of the uterus, the endometrium, is no longer stimulated. The cells of the endometrium shrink to about 65 percent of their previous size. The day before the menstrual flow begins, the blood vessels to the lining of the uterus are closed off. Without a fresh supply of blood, the lining of the uterus dies.

This dead layer of cells separates from the rest of the uterus. The dead tissue and the small quantity of blood in the uterine cavity cause uterine contractions. **Menstruation** is the process by which the lining of the uterus is expelled each month that an ovum is not fertilized.

During menstruation, approximately 1 fluid ounce (35 ml) of blood, 1 ounce (35 ml) of fluid, and the lining of the uterus are expelled. The bleeding lasts from 2 to 8 days, the average being 5 days. The menstrual flow marks the end of the three-phase female cycle.

Unless some abnormal condition exists, the menstrual period will not drastically alter a female's life. She will not bleed heavily nor feel tired or run-down. She will need some form of protection to absorb the menstrual flow. Commercial products such as sanitary napkins and tampons can be used for this purpose.

Menopause

Menopause is the cessation of the monthly menstrual cycle pattern as part of the natural process accompanying aging. Menopause occurs on average at age 51. Some females, especially cigarette smokers and underweight females, might start menopause as early as age 40. Females who are overweight usually start menopause at a later age (Slupik, 1997).

During this time, the ovaries stop producing a monthly ovum. The circulating levels of both estrogen and progesterone are decreased. Previously, these hormones were needed to prepare the female body for a pregnancy. But without an ovum and without estrogen and progesterone, the lining of the uterus no longer builds up. Eventually, menstruation ceases entirely.

It is not true that females who begin their periods early will go through menopause earlier, nor is it true that females who take birth control pills build up an excess number of ova and continue to menstruate years beyond other females.

Menopause might result from an oophorectomy. An **oophorectomy** is the surgical removal of the ovaries. However, if only one ovary is removed, the other ovary will increase its secretion of estrogen, and menopause will not be initiated.

There are two rather common symptoms that might accompany menopause—hot flashes and decrease in the moisture and elasticity of the vagina. About 75 percent of females will experience hot flashes. These might last only a month or five years or more and vary in intensity and frequency (Slupik, 1997). Hot flashes are an indication that the body is trying to adjust to changing hormonal levels. When estrogen and progesterone decrease, the secretion of FSH and LH increases. FSH and LH appear to upset hormonal balance and thus trigger a vasomotor response, a response that changes the size of the blood vessels.

During a hot flash, arteries dilate and blood rushes quickly to the skin. The increased blood supply makes a female feel hot and sweaty. Usually, this sensation lasts from one to three minutes and might occur as often as five times a day. Sometimes, hot flashes are followed by a chilly feeling, and the same vasomotor response might cause dizziness, swollen ankles, and rapid heartbeat. At the start of menopause, a female might experience hot flashes only at night called "night sweats." Hot flashes also might result from stress. The most effective treatment for hot flashes is estrogen replacement therapy (ERT). This takes effect within one to two weeks and reaches maximum effectiveness within four to eight weeks (Slupik, 1997). Females who cannot take estrogen might find relief using drugs such as clonidine or a mild combination of belladonna, ergotamine, and phenobarbital. The latter combination has been effective in about 50 percent of cases (Slupik, 1997).

Avoiding spicy foods, hot beverages, alcohol, caffeinated beverages, and cigarettes might alleviate the discomfort of hot flashes. Soy products also might relieve symptoms (Koop, 1998).

Another symptom accompanying menopause and diminishing estrogen levels in females is vaginal dryness. A female might experience a loss of elasticity in the vaginal walls, a thinning out of the mucous membranes in the vagina, and a decrease in the width and length of the vaginal barrel. With increased dryness, intercourse might become more difficult for some females. With the thinner vaginal wall, some females might experience pain during intercourse. The dryness can be reduced with a lubricant, preferably a K-Y jelly. An estrogen cream as well as hormone therapy can be used to provide lubrication. Frequent sexual activity is helpful in maintaining adequate lubrication.

When a female's estrogen levels lower, the vagina is no longer as acidic and there is increased susceptibility to infection. If intercourse is painful or vaginal infections persist, medical attention should be sought.

Other symptoms that might accompany menopause include insomnia, headaches, fatigue, diminished pleasure from touch, itchy or burning skin, numbness in the hands and feet, short-term memory loss, difficulty in concentrating, anxiety, and depression. In some females, the depression is a result of feelings and environmental factors rather than a direct result of physiological changes. At present, there is insufficient evidence to establish a causal relationship between menopause and depression (Nicol-Smith, 1996).

Hormone replacement therapy (HRT) is the use of supplemental estrogen and progesterone to supplement or replace the decreasing amounts of hormones produced during menopause. There are both benefits and potential risks from HRT. The benefits of HRT include the following.

- HRT is the most effective remedy for hot flashes, sleep disturbances, depression, and mood swings (NIH, 1997).

- HRT prevents and treats osteoporosis, or loss of bone density, which results in increased protection against hip fracture (Administration on Aging (NIH, 1997).

- Estrogen with or without progestin reduces the risk of heart disease and stroke in females over age 50 (NIH, 1997).

- HRT is beneficial to continued sexual response as the hormones help with vaginal lubrication, clitoral sensitivity, sexual interest, and orgasmic response. Some risks are associated with HRT. An increased risk of ovarian cancer might be associated with extended use of HRT (Garg, et al., 1998).

The causal relationship between HRT and breast cancer is unclear. Numerous observational studies have produced inconsistent results ranging from no risk or reduced risk to increased risk of breast cancer. The Iowa Women's Health Study, a large, well-conducted population-based study of more than 37,000 postmenopausal women ages 55 to 69, suggests a risk relationship between HRT and breast cancer (Gaspatur, 1999). Another study suggests that increased risk of breast cancer might be related to weight gain, especially in women who do not use HRT (Huang, 1997).

Menstrual Health

Many conditions are associated with menstruation, and both males and females should have knowledge and understanding of these. Included among them are menarche, amenorrhea, oligomenorrhea, dysmenorrhea, menorrhagia, premenstrual syndrome (PMS), and toxic shock syndrome.

Menarche

Menarche is the term used to describe the first menstrual bleeding. The average age of menarche among females in the United States is 12 years, although it is normal for a female to start menstruating as early as age 11 or as late as age 15 (Herman-Giddens, et al., 1997). Better nutrition and leanness are associated with the earlier onset of menarche (FDA, 1997). Conversely, if menarche has not occurred by age 16 or if development of female secondary sexual characteristics has not progressed by age 13 or 14, further evaluation might be needed.

Factors that are related to the timing of a female's first menstrual cycle include heredity, general health, altitude, body weight, and percentage of body fat.

The normal menstrual cycle lasts 28 days with a range of 23 to 35 days. The amount and duration of the menstrual flow also varies.

In the first year or two after menarche, menstrual periods are usually highly irregular. In addition, many adolescent females do not ovulate each month. Nevertheless, 50 percent of adolescent females who are sexually active can and do become pregnant within the first 6 months after beginning sexual relationships.

Amenorrhea

Amenorrhea is the absence of menstruation. There are two classifications of amenorrhea. **Primary amenorrhea** is the absence of menarche more than four years after the female's body shows signs of pubertal development (usually age 15). Malformed or underdeveloped female organs, glandular disorders, general poor health, and emotional factors might cause primary amenorrhea.

Secondary amenorrhea is the prolonged cessation (for 6 months or more) of menstrual bleeding after menarche has been established. Secondary amenorrhea occurs in about 4 percent of females of reproductive age (NIH, 1998b).

In many cases, particularly in adolescents, pregnancy is the cause of secondary amenorrhea. For this reason, a female's sexual history is usually taken and a urine or serum pregnancy test is likely to be performed.

Secondary amenorrhea in females who are not pregnant might be caused by emotional stress, certain drugs including contraceptives, extreme exercise (especially without proper conditioning), body fatness less than 15 to 17 percent, obesity, and hormonal supplements. Less common causes are chronic illness, disorders of the ovaries, and malfunction of the hypothalamus.

Increased female participation in organized sports has resulted in increased potential for medical disorders. The "female athlete triad" is a syndrome that includes eating disorders, osteoporosis, and amenorrhea (NIH, 1998b).

Secondary amenorrhea is normal during pregnancy and while breastfeeding. It might occur sporadically during the first and last months of a female's childbearing years. Amenorrhea is a symptom of infertility. Medical assistance is needed when amenorrhea persists.

Oligomenorrhea

Oligomenorrhea is scanty, irregular bleeding and/or a condition in which a female who is two years past menarche has one to six cycles a year. An excess of androgens from the ovaries is often the cause. Pelvic ultrasonography and serum testosterone levels are used for diagnosis. Treatment might consist of combination pill oral contraceptives, which lower androgen levels. Females with oligomenorrhea require medical diagnosis and treatment from an experienced gynecologist or endocrinologist.

Dysmenorrhea

Dysmenorrhea is very painful menstruation. There might be cramping, bloating, and pressure in the pelvic region as well as headaches, backaches, and nausea. The highest incidence of dysmenorrhea occurs among females in their late teens and early twenties (NIH, 1998c). There are two kinds of dysmenorrhea—primary and secondary. **Primary dysmenorrhea** is caused by uterine contractions and usually starts within three years of menarche and lasts 1 to 2 days each month.

Over time or after the female has given birth, this type of menstrual pain might lessen. However, it might continue until menopause. **Secondary dysmenorrhea** is associated with pelvic inflammatory disease, endometriosis, or uterine fibroids and usually starts later in life. The presence of disease might be indicated if similar pain recurs during sexual intercourse or at other times of the menstrual cycle.

Primary dysmenorrhea is the most common menstrual difficulty and the leading cause of short-term absence from school in female adolescents. The stages of dysmenorrhea in adolescents might be described as follows.

- Abdominal pain begins from several hours to 1 or 2 days before the onset of the menstrual period.

- Mild to severe pain continues 1 or more days and might be associated with nausea and vomiting as well as changes in bowel function (NIH, 1998b)

Primary dysmenorrhea also is associated with sexually transmitted diseases among adolescents (NIH, 1998c).

Other causes of dysmenorrhea might include inflammation, constipation, psychological stress, and hormonal imbalance. Prostaglandins have been indicated as a major contributing cause of dysmenorrhea.

Prostaglandins are hormonelike substances produced by the uterus and other body tissues. They cause smooth muscles to contract and restrict the flow of blood in blood vessels. Females with severe cramping have been found to have high levels of prostaglandins. These substances cause uterine contractions, inhibit the supply of oxygen to the uterus, and heighten nerve sensitivity. Each of these actions is believed to contribute to dysmenorrhea.

Anti-inflammatory drugs, such as aspirin, nonsteroidal anti-inflammatory drugs (NSAIDS) including ibuprofen, and the prescription drug indomethacin might be helpful in treating dysmenorrhea. These drugs relieve pain and also reduce nausea, vomiting, dizziness, and weakness.

Oral contraceptives have been used in the treatment of severe cases of dysmenorrhea and other disorders, such as endometriosis. Oral contraceptives regulate hormonal levels in the body and might be prescribed to alleviate dysmenorrhea in adolescent females (NIH, 1998c).

However, if pain lasts past the end of the menses or is not relieved by NSAIDS or oral contraceptives, further investigation is warranted.

Menorrhagia

Menorrhagia is an abnormally heavy menstrual flow. This affects about 20 percent of females of reproductive age worldwide (NIH, 1999a). Menorrhagia might be a symptom of disease, endocrine disorder, or abnormalities of the reproductive organs. Excessive bleeding should be reported to a physician. Treatment for menorrhagia might include a hysterectomy or a transcervical resection of the endometrium (TCRE) (O'Connor, et al., 1997).

Premenstrual Syndrome

Premenstrual syndrome (PMS) is a combination of severe physical and psychological symptoms during the four premenstrual and first four menstrual days of the menstrual cycle. PMS affects 3 to 7 percent of females of reproductive age in the United States. The physical and psychological symptoms include food craving, hot flashes, breast pain, sadness, anxiety, bloating, irritability, and impaired function. Research suggests that there is a causal link between these symptoms and female sex hormones (Schmidt, et al., 1998).

The following are ways to manage the symptoms of PMS.

- Eat six small meals each day to stabilize blood sugar.

- Avoid or reduce the intake of sugar, salt, alcohol, caffeine, red meats, and fats.

- Drink 6 to 8 glasses of water daily.

- Do regular bipedal exercise, such as walking, swimming, or bicycling (NIH, 1998a).

A diagnosis of PMS is made from a menstrual cycle diary or calendar in which a female charts her physical and psychological symptoms. Treatment includes hormone therapy, vitamins, exercise, nutritional supplements, dietary changes, counseling, and peer support.

Toxic Shock Syndrome

Toxic shock syndrome (TSS) is a rare, serious disease caused by certain toxin-producing strains of *Staphylococcus aureus* bacterium.

The early symptoms of TSS include a high fever of more than 102°F (38.9°C), vomiting, diarrhea, dizziness, fainting, and a rash that appears like a sunburn. These symptoms might progress to a dangerous drop in blood pressure. Urine output often is decreased, and patients might be disoriented or combative. Adult respiratory distress syndrome or cardiac dysfunction might also occur (CDC, 1999).

In the past, 95 percent of the reported cases of TSS in females occurred in those who were menstruating (CDC, 1999). The *Staphylococcus aureus* bacterium was localized in the vagina. The bacteria probably made and secreted a toxin that entered the bloodstream. Nonmenstrual-related TSS might account for up to 54 percent of recent cases. Surgical TSS infections after mammoplasty with saline breast implants have been reported (Stevens, 1995). The use of certain barrier contraceptive devices, such as the diaphragm, the cervical cap, and the vaginal contraceptive sponge, have all been associated with nonmenstrual-related TSS cases.

In May 1980, the CDC examined the risk factors for TSS. A significant relationship was shown between TSS and tampon use. TSS occurred mainly in tampon users under the age of 30, with females between the ages of 15 and 19 at greatest risk. TSS was most likely to develop during or just after a menstrual period. Therefore, tampons might have played a contributing role by:

- carrying the organism from the fingers or the introitus into the vagina during insertion of the tampon;

- providing a favorable environment for growth of the organism or elaboration of toxin regardless of the manner in which the organism is introduced;

- traumatizing the vaginal mucosa and thus facilitating local infection with *Staphylococcus aureus;* and

- absorbing the toxin from the vagina.

Based on the results of the epidemiological and laboratory studies, as well as on legal and financial considerations, the manufacturers of tampons dramatically altered the products they marketed. The incidence of menstrual-related TSS has declined substantially. Only five confirmed menstrual-related TSS cases were reported in 1997 compared to 812 similar cases reported in 1980 (CDC, 1999).

Although the exact relationship between TSS and tampon use remains unclear, research indicates that the use of some high absorbency tampons increases the risk of TSS. The FDA requires manufacturers to measure and describe the specific absorbency range on tampon packaging. There also is no evidence that the rayon fibers in tampons cause TSS.

Menstruating females should be well-informed about the use of tampons. These additional precautions can be taken during menstruation to prevent TSS:

- using sanitary pads or napkins instead of tampons;

- changing tampons 4 to 5 times a day;

- using a sanitary pad or napkin at least once during each 24-hour period;

- using sanitary pads or napkins at night;

- choosing tampons with minimum absorbency; and

- using tampons only when actively menstruating.

Females who have had TSS are more likely to become infected than those who have never had an occurrence. These at-risk females should seek medical advice before using tampons. A physician might prescribe certain antibiotics to reduce the risk of getting TSS again.

Currently, scientists at the National Institute of Allergies and Infectious Diseases are studying ways to inhibit immune cells from response to toxic shock syndrome (NIAID, 1998).

Female Reproductive Health

Optimal health is attained through having adequate knowledge and understanding of one's body, taking responsibility for health, performing necessary self-examinations, and having routine medical examinations. This section of the chapter provides information on the following topics: breast self-examination, mammography, fibrocystic breast condition, breast cancer, breast implants, uterine and cervical cancer, ovarian cancer, vaginal cancer, vaginitis, cystitis, endometriosis, endometritis, polyps, dilation and curettage (D and C), and fibroids.

Breast Self-Examination

Breast self-examination (BSE) is a cancer screening procedure in which a female visually examines her breasts, palpates them to detect any lumps, and squeezes her nipples to check for any clear or bloody discharge. A female should begin self-examinations as soon as she begins to menstruate regularly. A female who uses oral contraceptives should examine her breasts on the day that she starts a new pill pack (Huang, 1997). Although breast problems are rare in the early teens, the practice of breast

self-examination establishes familiarity with the breasts, promotes self-acceptance, and establishes a lifelong habit. A female will have her breasts examined during her regularly scheduled check-ups and whenever she finds any lumps or changes.

The best time to do a breast self-examination is a few days after menstruation, when any swelling has subsided. The breast self-examination should be done at the same time each month. It should consist of a visual examination before a mirror and a palpating, or feeling, examination while in the shower or while lying down. The procedures for breast self-examination are illustrated in Figure 5.5.

Mammography

Mammography is a highly sensitive X-ray screening test used to detect breast lumps and is a highly effective tool in the early detection of cancer. During mammography, low levels of radiation create an image of the breast on film or paper. A **mammogram** is the image of the breast tissue created by mammography and is read by a qualified physician to detect breast lumps. Mammography is especially useful in

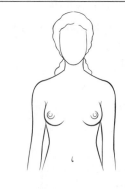

1. Stand in front of a mirror with arms at your sides. Examine breasts carefully for anything unusual—puckering, dimpling, changes in skin texture.

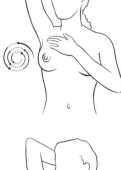

3. Raise your left arm. Use the fingers of the other hand to examine the left breast. Start at the outermost top edge of the breast. Go in circles toward the nipple. Fingers flat, press gently in small circles. Move the circles slowly around the breast. Include the area between the breast and the armpit and the armpit itself. Raise your right arm, and examine the right breast.

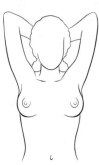

2. Clasp your hands behind your head. Press your hands forward. Look carefully for changes in size, shape, and contour of each breast.

4. Gently squeeze each nipple between your thumb and index finger. Look for discharge.

Figure 5.5 **Breast Self-Examination**

detecting breast lumps that are one centimeter or smaller because most lumps this small cannot be detected by palpation.

The American Cancer Society makes the following recommendations regarding mammography:

- a female age 40 or older should have a screening mammogram every year;

- a female between the ages of 20 and 39 should have a clinical breast examination by a health professional every three years;

- a female over age 40 should have a clinical breast examination by a health professional every year; and

- a female age 20 or older should perform a breast self-examination (BSE) every month.

Sometimes ultrasound or sonography is used to evaluate breast abnormalities and can detect the presence of a fluid-filled cyst. The FDA recently approved a new breast-imaging device called the T-Scan 2000 that can aid diagnostic evaluation when mammograms are ambiguous. This device might reduce the number of negative biopsies and help identify females who should be referred for early biopsy (FDA, 1999).

Fibrocystic Breast Condition

Mastodynia is the term used for the swelling and painful tenderness of the breasts accompanying the menstrual cycle. Each month there is a buildup of fluid and fibrous tissue in preparation for pregnancy. When conception does not occur, the body must reabsorb these unneeded substances. Many lymphatic vessels run through the breasts and empty into the lymph nodes, without which these unneeded substances drain. Sometimes drainage is difficult, and there is congestion.

A **cyst** is a sac that is formed when fluid becomes trapped in a lymph duct. A **fibroadenoma** is a lump that is formed when fluid becomes trapped in a lymph duct. The lump is not attached to any structure in the breast and usually is painless. **Fibrocystic breast condition** is a condition in which the cysts and fibroadenomas cause lumpiness and breast tenderness and discomfort. The exact causes of this condition are unknown but are believed to be hormonally related.

Drainage of cysts might resolve the condition (Gupta, 1998). Some females have reported an improvement in breast conditions when caffeine and other stimulants found in coffee, tea, chocolate, and many soft drinks are avoided. However, related studies have not confirmed a causal relationship between these stimulants and breast symptoms. Several vitamin supplements have not proven effective in reducing symptoms. When taken in large doses, some vitamin supplements have dangerous side effects. Reduced intake of dietary fat might reduce symptoms.

Breast Cancer

Breast cancer is a disease in which malignant tumors grow in the breast tissue. The National Cancer Institute (NCI) has developed the Breast Cancer Risk Assessment Tool, which is a computer program designed to assist females and health care providers in determining the risk for breast cancer based on established risk factors. Data are included concerning the drug tamoxifen, which might help reduce development of breast cancer in females at high risk. Risk factors for breast cancer include the following (NCI, 1998c):

- two breast tissue abnormalities;

- being older than 50;

- having menarche prior to age 12;

- having no pregnancies;

- having a first child born after the age of 30;

- having breast cancer among "first-degree relatives";

- having breast biopsies, especially if a biopsy showed a change in breast tissue known as atypical hyperplasia; and

- being Caucasian, although African American females who are diagnosed with breast cancer are more likely to die of the disease.

Other possible risk factors have not been established as conclusive. These include age at menopause, dense breast tissue, use of birth control pills or hormone replacement therapy, obesity, use of alcohol, and exposure to radiation and environmental pollutants.

Warning signs for breast cancer include changes in the nipple or in the symmetry of the breast. There might be a dark or bloody discharge from the nipple, or the nipple might be drawn inward or pointing in a new direction. There might be dimpling in the breast.

Most breast lumps are noncancerous (Huang, 1997). When a breast lump is detected during breast self-examination, routine physical examination, or mammography, further diagnosis is needed. A **needle aspiration** is a procedure in which a needle is inserted into the lump to determine if it contains fluid. When fluid is detected, the lump is usually a cyst and it can be drained. When no fluid is detected, a biopsy is usually done. A **biopsy** is the removal of tissue from a lump to determine if cancerous cells are present. A new, less invasive procedure is a large core needle biopsy that does not require surgical excision (Gaspatur, et al., 1999).

There are several means by which breast cancer might be treated. Treatment might include radiation, chemotherapy, hormone therapy, immunotherapy, and/or mastectomy or lumpectomy. A **preventive mastectomy**, or **prophylactic mastectomy**, is the surgical removal of one or both breasts. A **radical mastectomy** is the surgical removal of the entire breast, the underlying pectoral muscle, and the lymph nodes. This procedure helps ensure that all of the affected tissue is removed; however, there might be difficulty in arm movement following the removal of the pectoral muscles. This once standard operation is now used only when the chest muscles are cancerous. A **modified radical mastectomy** is the surgical removal of the breast, some lymph nodes under the arm, the lining over the chest muscles, and sometimes part of the chest wall muscles.

A **total mastectomy**, or **simple mastectomy**, is the surgical removal of the entire breast and possibly a few lymph nodes.

A **lumpectomy** is the surgical removal of the lump itself and a small bit of surrounding tissue. Usually some lymph nodes under the arm are removed for additional diagnosis. A **partial mastectomy**, or **segmental mastectomy**, is the surgical removal of the lump, some breast tissue, the lining over the chest muscles beneath the tumor, and some lymph nodes. Radiation therapy is used to destroy cancer cells that might not have been removed by surgery.

Research indicates that long-term survival rates are the same for lumpectomy with radiation therapy as they are for mastectomy (NIH, 1999b). With early detection and treatment, the survival rate of females with breast cancer is almost 100 percent after a five-year period.

Breast Implants

Breast implants are materials that are surgically implanted into breast tissue to improve the size and shape of a breast. Breast implant surgery has been the choice of females for cosmetic purposes and for reconstructive purposes following a mastectomy.

In April 1990, the Food and Drug Administration (FDA) reported that the polyurethane foam used to cover some implants could break down and form 2-toluene diamine (TDA), a chemical known to cause cancer in rats. The FDA advised physicians not to use the polyurethane-covered implants until further data could be collected and analyzed. In 1991, these implants were taken off the market. About 10 percent of breast implants were made with this type of foam (FDA, 1997).

The question arose as to whether or not females who have foam implants should have them removed. Although a small quantity of TDA was discovered in the urine of females with foam-coated implants, the risk of cancer was determined to be negligible over a female's lifetime. The FDA estimates that there is a one in ten thousand to one in a million chance of developing cancer from the use of foam implants. Therefore, the FDA does not recommend their removal on the basis of a female's exposure to TDA (FDA, 1997).

In the 1990s, concerns were raised about the safety of silicone-gel-filled breast implants. Some females with silicone-gel-filled breast implants have reported symptoms of degenerative auto-immune disorders, such as Lupus. Symptoms include swelling of the skin, the glands or lymph nodes, the hands and the feet, muscle weakness or burning, headaches, extreme fatigue, abnormal hair loss, and memory difficulties. However, these symptoms have been found in persons without autoimmune and connective tissue disorders or breast implants. Some women with silicone implants have produced antibodies to their own collagen. Whether the presence of these antibodies heightens the risk for a disorder of the immune system is unknown.

In 1996, a large study of 400,000 women with breast implants was conducted at the Harvard Medical School. The results of the study established that less than 1 percent of women with silicone implants will develop autoimmune or connective tissue disease as a result of these implants.

There is some concern but scant data about the risk of cancer from saline implants (FDA, 1997).

Uterine and Cervical Cancer

Cancer of the uterus is the most common cancer of the female genital tract. Although the cause of uterine cancer is unknown, a number of risk factors for it have been established. These risk factors include the following:

- being older than 50;
- having endometrial hyperplasia;
- using estrogen replacement therapy, although combined estrogen and progesterone therapy reduces the risk linked with estrogen alone;
- being overweight since fat converts certain hormones into estrogen and excess estrogen is known to increase the risk;
- having diabetes and high blood pressure;
- having a history of other cancers;
- using tamoxifen for the treatment of breast cancer; and
- being Caucasian.

Other risk factors related to increased estrogen levels include few or no pregnancies or late menopause (NCI, 1998b).

About 15,000 females in the United States develop cervical cancer each year. Some sexually transmitted viruses might cause changes in cervical cells resulting in cancer

(NCI, 1998a). The following evidence supports the viral theory as the cause of cervical cancer.

- The earlier that an adolescent female has intercourse, the more susceptible she is to developing cervical cancer; this suggests that the virus or viruses might be spread through sexual intercourse.
- The greater the number of sexual partners a female has, the greater her risk; again, suggesting the greater possibility of exposure to the virus.
- Females who are celibate, such as nuns, rarely develop cervical cancer.
- Females who have had genital warts, which are caused by the human papillomavirus (HPV), have an increased risk of developing cervical cancer.

A **Pap smear** is a screening test for cervical cancer in which cells are scraped from the cervix and examined for abnormalities. To obtain a Pap smear, a speculum is inserted into the vagina to hold the vaginal walls apart. A small wooden spatula is used to scrape cells from the cervix. These cells are smeared on a slide and sent for screening to a special laboratory.

Although the Pap smear has been an important tool in the early detection and treatment of cervical cancer, the test does have some limitations. Blood, mucus, or cervical inflammation might compromise the Pap smear, forcing the patient to return for a second test. A new Pap test, called ThinPrep, has been approved as a test for cervical cancer. This test improves the quality of the sample taken during a cervical exam, reducing the likelihood of a compromised test.

Because there are no nerve endings on the cervix, the Pap smear procedure should not be uncomfortable or painful. This screening test should be performed every one or two years. It should be performed more often in females who are at risk. At risk females are those who have had multiple sex partners, a history of genital warts, and/or early first sexual intercourse.

The laboratory results for the Pap smear are reported in five different classes.

1. A class I Pap smear indicates normal tissue and thus is negative.

2. A class II Pap smear usually indicates inflammation of the cervix due to vaginitis; however, it also might indicate precancerous cells.

3. A class III Pap smear indicates the presence of abnormal cells on the surface of the cervix; frequent Pap smears are recommended to follow up on this condition and to be certain it clears up rather than progresses.

4. A class IV Pap smear indicates the possible presence of cancerous cells on the surface of the cervix.

5. A class V Pap smear indicates the presence of cancerous cells.

When a female has a class III, IV, or V Pap smear, further screening tests might be performed. These screening tests might include a colposcopy and a cervical biopsy. A **colposcopy** is a screening exam in which a microscope is used to detect abnormal and cancerous cells. A **cervical biopsy** is the surgical removal of cervical tissue for the purpose of laboratory examination.

Several treatments can be used when cancer is detected. **Cryosurgery** is a procedure in which the tissue is frozen in order to remove small numbers of cancerous cells from the surface of the cervix. A cervical biopsy might also be used. This is more extensive than a biopsy that might have been performed for screening purposes. Cauterization or diathermy or laser surgery might be performed (NCI, 1998c).

A hysterectomy is done when abnormal cells are found inside the opening of the cervix. A **hysterectomy** is the surgical removal of the entire uterus and cervix, but not the ovaries. This procedure might be done when a female is known to have a malignancy. There are different techniques for surgically removing the uterus. When the uterus is not enlarged nor awkwardly positioned, the surgeon might remove the uterus through the vagina. This technique has fewer possible surgical complications. When this technique is not possible, the uterus is removed through an incision made in the abdominal wall. This latter technique involves the same risks for complications as any other major surgery involving an incision in the abdominal wall.

Sometimes a surgeon will recommend removing the ovaries. An **oophorectomy** is the surgical removal of the ovaries. If the ovaries are removed, there will be a decrease in lubrication of the vagina and in sex drive. Hormone replacement therapy (HRT) might be recommended.

A hysterectomy without an oophorectomy will not result in vaginal dryness and reduced sex drive. However, there might be some changes in sexual response. The vasocongestion and elevation of the uterus during sexual arousal heightens the sexual response in some females. These females experience contraction of the uterus during orgasm that provides sexual pleasure. However, most females do not report feeling less aroused or less satisfied with sexual intercourse following a hysterectomy. And most females have intercourse about as frequently as they did before the surgery.

Ovarian Cancer

Ovarian cancer is a disease in which there are cancerous cells and/or malignant tumors in one or both of the ovaries. More than 22,000 females in the United States develop ovarian cancer each year. Treatment for ovarian cancer includes an oophorectomy, chemotherapy or radiation therapy or a combination of treatments. Studies are being done to evaluate the effectiveness of biological therapy in females with recurrent or advanced ovarian cancer. Biological therapy uses substances that improve the immune system's response to cancer (NCI, 1998d).

The risk factors for ovarian cancer include the following:

• being 40–50 years of age;

• having a history of ectopic pregnancies;

• having a history of infertility problems; and

• having endometriosis.

Vaginal Cancer

Vaginal cancer is a disease in which cancerous cells and/or malignant tumors are present in the vagina. Vaginal cancer was rare in this country until the early 1970s. In 1970, it was discovered that vaginal cancer was more likely to occur in females whose mothers had taken diethylstilbestrol (DES) during pregnancy.

Diethylstilbestrol (DES) is a drug that was used to prevent miscarriage. A relationship between DES and vaginal cancer has been confirmed. Some 3 million females were exposed to DES in utero. Animal studies suggest that DES might suppress a gene associated with reproductive tract development. This supports findings in the females exposed to DES who have exhibited tissue or structural changes in the uterus, the cervix, or the vagina (Stewart, et al., 1997). However, a recent study of these females whose average age is 38 has not established any increased risk for other cancers except for vaginal clear cell adenocarcinoma (CCA). Further monitoring is necessary to determine the cancer risk for these females during their menopausal years (Stewart, et al., 1997).

Although a Pap smear is recommended for high-risk females every six months and annually for all other females, it does not always confirm a malignancy in the vagina. A better test is painting the vaginal and cervical area with an iodine stain to highlight abnormal cells.

Treatment for vaginal cancer involves chemotherapy, radiation, and/or surgery. Some physicians also recommend preventive procedures for DES-exposed females, such as using contraceptive jellies on the cervical and upper vaginal area. Physicians also recommend that DES-exposed females avoid any exposure to estrogen, such as the use of birth control pills.

Vaginitis

Vaginitis is an irritation or inflammation of the vagina usually accompanied by a discharge. Despite the high incidence of vaginitis, many females are not well informed about vulvovaginal health (Stewart, et al., 1997). Vaginitis can be caused by organisms, such as bacteria, yeast, or viruses, as well as hormonal changes, allergies, and irritations.

There are three main types of vaginitis. The most common type is called a "yeast" infection, and is caused by the fungus *Candida albicans*. Trichomoniasis is caused by a protozoan. Gardnerella is caused by a bacterium.

In vaginitis, the natural acidic pH of 4.0 to 5.0 of the vagina is altered. This natural pH promotes a healthy mucosa. When there is a change, the normal secretions and the natural balance of bacteria are altered. The vagina and vulva are irritated and begin to itch. The secretions might take on a disagreeable odor. Douching further irritates the lining and increases the vaginitis.

Vaginitis should be treated and cured. A female can avoid vaginitis that is not the result of sexually transmitted diseases. She can

- wear cotton panties or nylon panties with a cotton crotch to allow ventilation;
- eat a well-balanced diet low in sugar;
- bathe regularly, washing the vulva carefully;
- avoid the use of feminine hygiene sprays, perfumed douches, bubble bath, and similar products; a couple of tablespoons of white vinegar mixed with a quart of warm water is more effective as a douche because it helps restore normal pH;
- use a white vinegar douche when taking antibiotics for an extended period of time;
- focus on good toilet habits; wipe carefully from front to back; use white toilet tissue that is not perfumed; and
- consult with a physician if chronic vaginitis exists and she is using the birth control pill.

Cystitis

The urethral opening is close to the vaginal and anal openings. Therefore, bacteria from defecation and infectious agents from sexual contact easily are transmitted from the anus and vagina to the urethra. They might travel through the urethra and infect the bladder. **Cystitis** is the inflammation of the urinary bladder.

In most cases, cystitis is caused by the bacterium *Escherichia coli*. The symptoms of cystitis include pain during intercourse, frequent urination, blood and/or pus in the urine, a burning sensation during urination, backache, and pelvic pain.

The diagnosis of cystitis is based on the symptoms and/or a urine sample that is analyzed to confirm the presence of *Escherichia coli.* Treatment is with an antibiotic, although recent data suggests resistance to certain often-prescribed antibiotics (Gupta, 1998).

Endometriosis

Endometriosis is a condition in which the endometrial tissue grows somewhere other than in the lining of the uterus. The endometrial tissue might grow abnormally in the ovaries, fallopian tubes, rectum, bladder, vagina, cervix, or lymph glands. The exact location of the endometrial tissue determines the symptoms a female will experience. However, most females with endometriosis have unusually painful periods with excessive bleeding.

Mild endometriosis is common among infertile females, but the cause-and-effect relationship is unclear. Research has confirmed that resection or ablation of lesions enhances fertility in infertile females.

Severe endometriosis is considered a leading cause of infertility. Yet, while pregnancy rates among females with endometriosis are lower than among other females in good reproductive health, most females with endometriosis do not experience fertility problems (NIH, 1999b).

Treatment of endometriosis usually involves laser surgery in which the endometrial tissue is removed. Physicians usually recommend that females with endometriosis have their children as early as possible, because this extra lining is stimulated to grow by hormonal secretions each month.

Endometritis

Endometritis is the inflammation of the uterine lining. The symptoms include pelvic pain, a foul-smelling discharge, and a tenderness during examination. Sometimes there are no symptoms.

Endometritis requires treatment. Ampicillin and tetracycline are taken orally. Treatment also includes bed rest and no sexual intercourse for at least two weeks.

Polyps

Polyps are long tubelike protrusions that grow from mucous membranes inside the uterus or along the cervix. They are rarely malignant. The symptoms that indicate possible polyps are irregular menstrual periods, a heavy menstrual flow, and bleeding between periods. The treatment for polyps is dilation and curettage (D and C).

Dilation and Curettage (D and C)

Dilation and curettage (D and C) is a surgical procedure in which the cervical opening is dilated by means of probes of increasingly larger sizes until a metal loop curette can be inserted to scrape the uterine lining.

The procedure can be performed under local anesthesia on an outpatient basis. Recovery will take 8 to 24 hours when a local anesthesia is used. If a general anesthesia is needed, the procedure is performed in a hospital, and the recovery time is longer.

There is bleeding for several days following a D and C. To prevent infection, sanitary napkins are used to collect the blood rather than tampons. Danger signals following a D and C are excessive bleeding and/or cramping and a high fever.

The D and C is performed:

- as a cleansing procedure before any gynecological surgery;
- for diagnosis of cancer of the uterus or oviducts;
- for a diagnosis when there is abnormal bleeding or blood clotting;
- for a diagnosis when infertility is suspected.

© 2001 Everyday Learning Corporation

Fibroids

Fibroids are benign, slow-growing growths in the uterus. About 20 to 30 percent of females of childbearing age have fibroids. In a small study, close clinical examination indicated more widespread presence of fibroids suggesting that there might be a higher incidence of these growths than previously thought (NIH, 1999c). Most fibroids do not cause symptoms and do not require treatment. Fibroids rarely become malignant or cancerous. They are most likely to occur when tissue builds up in the endometrial lining each month and is not completely sloughed off.

Studies are inconclusive regarding risk factors for fibroids. However, athletic females seem to be at lower risk than females who do not participate in athletic activity.

Fibroids might cause problems during a pregnancy, and they might make delivery difficult. Fibroids also might push against the bladder or rectum, and they might facilitate urinary tract infections. Sometimes they are the cause of menstrual irregularities and a heavy menstrual flow. They might make a female feel bloated in her abdominal area. When menopause occurs, fibroids shrink because of the diminished secretion of estrogen.

The Regular Examination

A regular gynecological examination should be viewed as an opportunity to gather information, record important findings, restore confidence, and continue optimal care; not as a check to see what is wrong with a female. A healthy reproductive system depends on the general health of the female. The following examinations provide the information needed for a health profile.

- health history
- thyroid palpation
- breast examination
- blood tests and blood pressure check
- lung tests
- urinalysis
- pelvic examination including Pap smear

Health History

A **health history** is a detailed description of a person's health status that includes information about diseases, disorders, and conditions as well as about healthful behaviors and risk behaviors in which a person engages. In order to assist the physician in gathering a complete health history, a female should keep a menstrual cycle journal or calendar.

She should record the days when she is menstruating. She should write down any additional information about her periods. Did she have cramps? Was her menstrual flow heavy? How did she feel emotionally and physically?

If she is sexually active, she should make a check on the days she has had intercourse and make a note about what type of contraception, if any, was used. She should record any noticeable changes, such as a vaginal discharge, a lump in the breast or groin. If she is taking birth control pills, she should indicate when she began her pill pack and mark down any day that she forgot to take a pill.

Thyroid Palpation

The **thyroid gland** is an endocrine gland located just below the larynx (voice box) and in front and to the side of the trachea (windpipe). This gland secretes hormones that influence growth and stimulate activity in the nervous system.

During the young adult years, the thyroid gland might enlarge, or lumps or tumors might develop on it. These conditions affect thyroid function which, in turn, affects growth and the functions of the reproductive system. During the annual examination, the physician palpates, or feels, the thyroid to determine whether or not there are any lumps or tumors, and also to determine whether or not the thyroid gland is enlarged.

Breast Examination

It is important for a female to perform breast self-examination each month after her menstrual period. The physician can check her technique to be certain she is performing breast self-examination correctly. The physician also performs a breast examination.

Blood Tests and a Blood Pressure Check

Blood tests and a blood pressure check provide information about general health status. These checkups are particularly important for females who are sexually active.

Blood Tests

A female should have a complete blood count. A blood sample should be sent to a laboratory to determine the hemoglobin level. **Hemoglobin** is a substance that combines with oxygen in the blood. It gives blood its red color. During the reproductive years, many females fail to get enough iron. These females risk anemia. **Anemia** is a condition in which the oxygen-carrying pigment in the blood is below normal. Some females need iron or other supplements.

Every female of childbearing age should know her Rh factor. The **Rh factor** is an inherited protein substance in red blood cells. **Rh positive (Rh+)** is the presence of Rh in a person's blood. **Rh negative (Rh–)** is a lack of Rh in a person's blood. The Rh factor is genetic. Rh positive is dominant over Rh negative. The importance of the Rh factor will be discussed in Chapter 9 Pregnancy and Childbirth.

In addition to having the complete blood count checked, the level of triglycerides and cholesterol in the bloodstream might be checked. **Triglycerides** are substances stored in fat tissue and are associated with a risk of cardiovascular diseases. **Cholesterol** is a saturated fat that is normally found in the brain, nerves, and skin and is associated with a risk of cardiovascular disease.

In addition to these blood tests, some females have their blood tested for syphilis and for human immunodeficiency virus (HIV). Syphilis and HIV will be discussed in Chapters 6 and 7.

Blood Pressure Check

Blood pressure is the force exerted by the flowing blood against the walls of arteries. Changes in blood pressure can indicate either an improved state of health or stresses on the body that can lead to a variety of problems.

Levels of hormones circulating in the bloodstream can affect the circulatory system. For this reason, physicians do not like to prescribe birth control pills or hormone replacement therapy for females who have high blood pressure. Blood pressure will vary within a normal range. It is important for a female to know her blood pressure in order to detect changes.

Lung Tests

A physician will listen carefully to the heart and lungs. If a female is a smoker, the physician will recommend a smoking-cessation program. Smoking during the child-bearing years is accompanied by increased health hazards. Smoking during pregnancy affects the developing fetus (see Chapter 9), and smoking while taking birth control pills increases the risk of blood clots.

Urinalysis

A **urinalysis** is a chemical or microscopic examination of the urine collected under special conditions. Usually, a female collects a urine sample in a cup at the laboratory or at the physician's office.

Urine is analyzed for several reasons. It can be checked for evidence of infection. For example, whenever cystitis is suspected, urinalysis is used for confirmation. Urine is also checked for excess sugar as a test for diabetes. **Diabetes** is a disease in which the body is unable to process sugar in food in normal ways.

The Pelvic Examination

The **pelvic examination** includes the following:
- an inspection of the external genitalia;
- a speculum examination;
- a bimanual vaginal examination; and
- a rectovaginal examination.

Inspection of the external genitalia

The first part of a thorough pelvic examination is a careful inspection of the external genitalia. A check is made for any irritation, lumps, swelling, or discoloration. Of particular concern is a vaginal discharge or adhesions of the clitoris. Then the physician or practitioner inserts a finger into the vagina to see whether or not:

- urine will flow involuntarily;
- there is pus in Bartholin's glands; and
- the muscles in the pelvic floor are strong.

The speculum examination

A metal or plastic speculum is inserted inside the vagina to hold apart the vaginal walls. The metal speculum might feel cold. During speculum insertion, it is important for the female to relax.

With the speculum in place, it is easy for the physician or nurse practitioner to do a visual internal examination to look for the following:

- evidence of lesions;
- an unusual discharge;
- any inflammation of the vaginal walls;
- infection;
- growths; and
- abnormal mucous membranes.

Two routine tests are then performed. The first test is a Pap smear, which was previously discussed. The second test involves collecting a sample of vaginal discharge with a long cotton swab. The specimen is collected for a microscopic examination and for cultures to test for gonorrhea and chlamydia.

Bimanual pelvic examination

After the speculum examination, a bimanual pelvic examination is performed. A **bimanual pelvic examination** is a procedure in which a physician or nurse practitioner inserts the index and middle finger of one hand into the vagina and puts the other hand on the abdomen to check reproductive organs.

The hands are pressed together so that the size, shape, consistency, and position of the uterus, ovaries, and oviducts can be felt. Any unusual growths or inflammation can be detected. Any source of pelvic pain and its location can be determined.

Rectovaginal examination

A **rectovaginal examination** is a procedure in which a physician or nurse practitioner places one finger in the vagina and another finger in the rectum and presses together to check for rectal lesions. The tone of the rectal sphincter muscle (important in bowel movements) also can be checked, as well as the alignment of the organs in the pelvis.

Female Sexual Concerns

Having adequate knowledge and understanding about the female reproductive system and about sexual functioning is helpful in alleviating unnecessary concerns. In this section, female concerns about breast size and about the hymen and virginity will be discussed.

Breast Size

The breasts are comprised of mammary gland tissue and fat tissue. The mammary gland tissue is milk-producing tissue. All females have nearly the same amount of mammary gland tissue and are able to produce nearly the same amount of milk during lactation, so that the overall size of a female's breasts has little bearing on her ability to nurse her baby.

Surrounding the mammary or glandular tissue is fat tissue. The fat tissue protects and cushions the mammary glands. The amount of fat tissue varies in females and is responsible for variations in breast size. There might be more fatty tissue in one breast than in the other. Females with very small breasts and females with large breasts might both be self-conscious.

The Hymen and Virginity

Contrary to popular belief, a hymen that is not intact is not a sign that a female is no longer a virgin, nor is an intact hymen an absolute sign of virginity. Females have come to the delivery of their first child with an intact hymen. On the other hand, females who are virgins have been known to have a poorly developed or a broken hymen.

If the hymen is intact, it will usually rupture and tear at several points during the first coitus. The amount of bleeding accompanying the coital tearing varies. Generally, there is a slight bleeding if the hymen is intact at the first coitus; however, this is not an absolute sign of virginity.

In rare cases, the hymen is resistant to coital tearing and must be surgically divided before intercourse can take place. A physician can rupture the hymen to prevent a female's difficulty during her first sexual intercourse.

References

Centers for Disease Control and Prevention. 1999. "Toxic Shock Syndrome—United States." Article Online (March). Accessed 7/99. http://www.cdc.gov.

Food and Drug Administration. 1999. "FDA Approves New Imaging Device." *FDA Talk Paper* (April). Accessed 7/99. http://www.fda.gov.

———. 1997. "Illness and Conditions Elsewhere in the Body and Breast Implants." Article Online (March). Accessed 7/99. http://www.fda.gov.

Garg, Pushkal P., et al. 1998. "Hormone Replacement Therapy and the Risk of Epithelial Ovarian Carcinoma: A Meta-Analysis." *Obstetrics and Gynecology* 92 (September): 472–479. Accessed 7/99. http://www.4journals.com.

Gaspatur, Susan M., Ph.D. 1999. "Women's Health Information Center—Hormone Replacement Therapy and Risk of Breast Cancer with a Favorable Histology." *Journal of the American Medical Association* (June). Accessed 7/99. http://www.4journals.com.

Gupta, Kaplana, M.D. 1998. "AMA Health Insight—Atlas of the Body—The Breast-Disorders." *Journal of the American Medical Association* 1998–1999. Accessed 7/99. http://www.4journals.com.

Herman-Giddens, M., et al. 1997. "Secondary Sexual Characteristics and Menses in Young Girls Seen in Office Practice: A Study from the Pediatric Research Office Settings Network." *Pediatrics* 99: 505–512.

Huang, Zhiping M.D., Ph.D. 1997. "Dual Effects of Weight and Weight Gain on Breast Cancer Risk." *Journal of the American Medical Association* (November). Accessed 7/99. http://www.4journals.com.

Koop, Everett, M.D. 1998. "Menopause/Hot Flashes." Article Online (May). Accessed 7/99. http://www.nlm.nih.gov/medlineplus or http://www.drkoop.com.

National Cancer Institute. 1998a. "Estimating Breast Cancer Risk." Article Online (October). Accessed 7/99. http://www.nci.nih.gov.

———. 1998b. "Cancer of the Uterus." Article Online (September). Accessed 7/99. http://www.nci.nhi.gov.

———. 1998c. "Cancer of the Cervix." Article Online (September). Accessed 7/99. http://www.nci.nhi.gov.

———. 1998d. "Ovarian Cancer." Article Online (September). Accessed 7/99. http://www.nci.nhi.gov.

National Institute of Allergies and Infectious Diseases. 1998. "Toxic Shock Syndrome." Article Online (March). Accessed 7/99. http://www.niaid.nih.gov.

National Institute of Health. 1999a. "Modern Treatments of Menorrhagia Attributable to Dysfunctional Uterine Bleeding." *Obstetrics Gynecology Survey 1999* (January). Accessed 7/99. http://www.nlm.nih.gov.

———. 1999b. "Facts about Endometriosis." Article Online (June). Accessed 7/99. http://www.nih.gov/nichd/publications.

———. 1999c. "Uterine Fibroids." Article Online (June). Accessed 7/99. http://www.nih.gov/nichd/publication.

———. 1998a. "The Female Athlete: The Triad of Disordered Eating, Amenorrhea, and Osteoporosis." *Sports Medicine* (August). Accessed 7/99. http://www.nlm.nih.gov.

———. 1998b. "Menstruation, painful." *Medical Encyclopedia* 1998–1999. Accessed 7/99. http://www.nlm.nih.gov.

———. 1998c. "FAQs—PMS." Article Online (August). Accessed 7/99. http://www.womenshealth.com.

——. 1997. "Cancer Facts —Menopausal Hormone Replacement Therapy." Article Online (September). Accessed 7/99. http://www.cancernet.nci.nih.gov.

Nicol-Smith, Louise. 1996. "Causality, Menopause, and Depression: A Critical Review of the Literature." *British Medical Journal* 313: 1229–1232. Accessed 7/99. http://www.4journals.com.

O'Connor, Hugh, et al. 1997. "Medical Research Council Randomized Trial of Endometrial Resection versus Hysterectomy in Management of Menorrhagia." *Journal of the American Medical Association* 349 (April): 897–901. Accessed 7/99. http://www.4journals.com.

Schmidt, Peter J., et al. 1998. "Differential Behavioral Effects of Gonadal Steroids in Women with and Those Without Premenstrual Syndrome." *New England Journal of Medicine* 338/4 (January). Accessed 7/99. http://www.4journals.com.

Slupik, Ramona I., M.D. 1997. "AMA Health Insight—Women's Health—Menopause." *Journal of the American Medical Association* (May). Accessed 7/99. http://www.4journals.com.

Stevens, Dennis L., Ph.D., M.D. 1995. "Streptococcal Toxic Shock Syndrome: Spectrum of Disease, Pathogenesis, and New Concepts in Treatment." Article Online (July). Accessed 7/99. http://www.nih.gov.

Stewart, Elizabeth G., et al. 1997. "Women's Health Information Center— Over-the-Counter Alternative Medicines in the Treatment of Chronic Vaginal Symptoms." *Journal of the American Medical Association* (July). Accessed 7/99. http://www.4journals.com.

6 Sexually Transmitted Diseases

Content for Teachers *Only*

A Word from the Authors

An estimated 15 million Americans become newly infected with a sexually transmitted disease (STD) each year. Thirty percent of these cases occur in adolescents and nearly two thirds occur in people younger than 25 years of age (NIAID, 1999). STDs can be serious and life-threatening. This chapter includes information about the transmission and prevention of STDs, the common STDs, and other, less common STDs. It also includes *The Prevention Model for Educating Adolescents About STDs.* The prevention message emphasizes that abstinence from sex and monogamous marriage reduce the risk of infection with STDs.

Transmission of STDs

Sexually transmitted diseases (STDs) are diseases caused by pathogens that are transmitted from an infected person to an uninfected person during intimate sexual contact. **Pathogens** are germs that cause disease. At present, there are about 20 pathogens that are known to be transmitted sexually (NIAID, 1999). Some of these pathogens are regarded as the "second generation" of STD pathogens. The **second generation of STD pathogens** are those pathogens that cause STDs that have mutated and are more difficult to treat and control. Table 6.1 identifies the risk behaviors and risk situations through which the pathogens causing STDs can be transmitted. A **risk behavior** is an action a person chooses that threatens health and can cause disease, injury, and premature death. A **risk situation** is a circumstance that threatens health and can cause disease, injury, and premature death. This section of the chapter discusses the risk behaviors and risk situations for transmission of STDs.

Table 6.1 Risk Behaviors and Risk Situations for Transmission of STDs

The following are risk behaviors and risk situations for transmission of STDs. These risk behaviors and risk situations do not carry the same degree of risk.

1. Having intimate sexual contact
2. Engaging in open-mouth kissing with a person whose mouth contains lesions, ulcers, blisters, or chancres that contain pathogens that cause STDs
3. Sharing needles, syringes, or other injection equipment for injecting drugs
4. Sharing a needle to make tattoos or to pierce ears or other body parts
5. Sharing a needle and mixing blood in a ceremony to become a blood sister or blood brother
6. Having contact with the blood or other body fluids, mucous membranes, or broken skin of a person infected with an STD
7. Having a blood transfusion with blood or blood products infected with HIV, hepatitis B, or syphilis
8. Having a tissue transplant from a person infected with HIV, hepatitis B, or hepatitis C
9. Touching the genital area and/or touching other mucous membranes after having contact with lesions or blisters containing pathogens for STDs
10. Being infected with an STD through perinatal transmission
11. Having contact with infected objects, clothing, and/or bed linen

1. Having intimate sexual contact

Intimate sexual contact is a risk behavior for the transmission of STDs. During intimate sexual contact, there is the possibility that body fluids can be exchanged between partners. Pathogens can pass from an infected partner to an uninfected partner through openings in the skin. The passage of these pathogens can cause infections.

2. Engaging in open-mouth kissing with a person whose mouth contains lesions, ulcers, blisters, or chancres that contain pathogens that cause STDs

Most people have tiny cuts or tears in the mucous membranes of the mouth. During open-mouth kissing, pathogens causing STDs might enter through these small cuts or tears. Then, symptoms might appear at the site of entry. For example, a person with syphilis might have chancres in the mouth, and a person who has herpes might have blisters in the mouth. During open-mouth kissing, a person who is not infected might be exposed to the pathogens from the chancres or from the blisters. In addition, small traces of blood from one person's mouth might get into small cuts or tears in the mouth of the other person. This is one way that HIV, viral hepatitis, and syphilis can be transmitted. According to the Centers for Disease Control and Prevention, to date there has been one documented case of HIV infection through open-mouth kissing.

3. Sharing needles, syringes, or other injection equipment for injecting drugs

An **injecting drug user** is a person who injects illegal drugs into the body with syringes, needles, and other injection equipment. Persons who share syringes, needles, and other injection equipment are at risk for becoming infected with pathogens that cause HIV, viral hepatitis, and syphilis. When an infected person injects drugs, droplets of blood containing pathogens that cause HIV, viral hepatitis, and syphilis might remain in the syringe or on the needle or injection equipment. A second person who shares a needle, syringe, or other injection equipment to inject drugs might get the infected blood into his or her body. Then this person will be infected. Any person who has intercourse (penile-vaginal, penile-anal, or oral genital) with the infected injecting drug user might become infected.

4. Sharing a needle to make tattoos or to pierce ears or other body parts

Droplets of blood infected with HIV, viral hepatitis, and/or syphilis might remain on the needle when a person who is infected uses a needle to make a tattoo or to pierce ears or other body parts. The droplets of infected blood might be invisible to the eye. A second person who shares the needle might get the infected blood into his or her body and become infected.

5. Sharing a needle and mixing blood in a ceremony to become a blood sister or blood brother

The ceremony to become a blood sister or blood brother involves two or more persons pricking the finger to draw a droplet of blood. Then the fingers of the persons involved are placed together to mix blood. The sharing of the needle and the mixing of blood are risk behaviors. In both cases, blood from a person infected with HIV, viral hepatitis, or syphilis might enter a person who is not infected.

6. Having contact with the blood or other body fluids, mucous membranes, or broken skin of a person infected with an STD

The pathogens that cause syphilis, hepatitis, and HIV/AIDS grow and multiply in the bloodstream. People who handle the body fluids of a person who is infected with pathogens from these STDs risk having these pathogens enter their bodies though small cuts or tears on the skin or through a splash in the eyes. Touching the mucous membranes or broken skin of a person infected with these STDs might result in contact with exposed blood vessels. Infected blood can enter the body through small cuts or tears on the skin. People who share something such as a razor or toothbrush that contains droplets of infected blood are at risk for being infected with pathogens from STDs. The pathogens from STDs might enter their bodies through small cuts or tears in the mucous membranes or skin.

7. Having a blood transfusion with blood or blood products infected with HIV, hepatitis B, or syphilis

In the United States, the FDA controls blood donations, blood donor centers, and blood labs. All donors are screened. After donation, blood is tested for HIV, hepatitis B, and syphilis. The risk of infection has been decreased to nearly zero due to screening. However, people traveling to countries other than the United States should inquire about the safety of the blood supply. A person cannot become infected with HIV, hepatitis B, or syphilis by donating blood.

8. Having a tissue transplant from a person infected with HIV, hepatitis B, or hepatitis C

In the United States, screening and testing procedures have reduced the risk of being infected by human tissue transplants. Potential donors for all human tissues must be tested for HIV, hepatitis B, and hepatitis C. They also must be screened to determine if they have engaged in risk behaviors and to check for symptoms of HIV infection and hepatitis. Imported tissues must be accompanied by records showing that the tissues were screened and tested. If no records are available, tissues are shipped under quarantine to the United States. People having tissue transplants outside the United States should check screening and testing procedures.

9. Touching the genital area and/or touching other mucous membranes after having contact with lesions or blisters containing pathogens for STDs

HSV-1 usually causes cold sores or fever blisters in the mouth or lips, while HSV-2 generally is associated with sores or lesions in the genital area. However, HSV-1 can be transmitted to the genital area if a person touches the cold sores or fever blisters and then touches the genital area, and HSV-2 can be transmitted to the mouth if a person touches the sores or lesions in the genital area and then puts fingers in the mouth.

In addition, a person might touch the cold sores or fever blisters in the mouth or lips and/or the sores or lesions in the genital area and then rub the eyes with contaminated fingers.

10. Being infected with an STD through perinatal transmission

Perinatal transmission is the transfer of an infection to a baby during pregnancy, delivery, or breastfeeding. A pregnant female infected with HIV, viral hepatitis, or syphilis can transmit these pathogens through the umbilical cord to her developing embryo or fetus. A baby can be infected while passing through the vagina at birth. Infected blood in the vagina can enter the baby's blood through a cut on the baby's body. Pathogens from infected mucous membranes, chancres, or blisters can enter the mucous membranes in the baby's eyes. A nursing baby can become infected with some STDs through the breast milk of an infected mother.

11. Having contact with infected objects, clothing, and/or bed linen

Lice can live outside the body for as long as a day, and it is possible for both lice and scabies to be transmitted by sleeping on infected sheets or by wearing clothing worn by someone who is infected. It also is possible for someone who is being treated for lice or scabies to become reinfected by sleeping on previously infected sheets and/or by wearing infected clothing. For this reason, the bed linen and clothing of someone who has been infected must be disinfected by washing in hot water and soap.

Common Sexually Transmitted Diseases

The number of cases of STDs has been increasing steadily—in some cases to epidemic proportions. About 45 million Americans are estimated to have genital herpes infections and as many as 24 million Americans might be infected with the virus that causes genital warts (NIAID, 1998).

This section of the chapter will focus on those STDs that occur in such numbers that they are considered to be common: bacterial vaginosis, candidiasis, trichomoniasis, chlamydia, gonorrhea, nongonococcal urethritis, syphilis, genital herpes, genital warts, pediculosis pubis, and viral hepatitis. The discussion of each of these STDs will include the name of the pathogen causing the disease, method of transmission, symptoms, diagnosis, and treatment.

Bacterial Vaginosis

Bacterial vaginosis is an STD caused by the *Gardnerella vaginalis* bacterium. Although these bacteria are found normally in the vagina at low levels, an increase in their growth produces typical symptoms of the disease. An increase in the number of *Gardnerella vaginalis* bacteria might occur when changes in the natural conditions of the vagina cause an overgrowth of these organisms.

Transmission Bacterial vaginosis is spread from an infected partner to an uninfected partner through penile-vaginal intercourse.

Symptoms Symptoms in a female include a foul-smelling discharge, possible irritation of vaginal tissue, and burning during urination. As with other STDs, females might be infected and show no symptoms. Males also might be infected without having the typical symptoms of foreskin inflammation, inflammation of the urethra, and cystitis (bladder infection).

Diagnosis Diagnosis is made through microscopic examination of vaginal or urethral discharges.

Treatment The antibiotics metronidazole and clindamycin are reported to be most effective in the treatment of bacterial vaginosis. During and following metronidazole therapy for at least three days, a person should not drink alcohol for 24 hours from the last metronidazole treatment (Majeroni, 1999). Currently, the Centers for Disease Control and Prevention (CDC) do not recommend that treatment of sexual partners is necessary. However, in cases of repeated infections, females would very likely benefit if their partners also were treated.

Candidiasis

Candidiasis is an STD caused by the fungus, *Candida albicans*. It is commonly referred to as a yeast infection. Another name for this infection is moniliasis. The *Candida albicans* organism is present normally in the vagina of many females and will begin to multiply when the vaginal environment has been altered.

The vaginal environment can be altered by several factors that change the sugar concentration in vaginal tissue, such as pregnancy, the use of birth control pills, or diabetes. Many potent antibiotics available today destroy resident vaginal bacteria that normally keep fungal growths under control. Females who take antibiotics over a period of time commonly experience bouts of candidiasis. Frequent douching also increases the likelihood of candidiasis.

Transmission The fungus causing candidiasis can be spread from an infected female to an uninfected male through penile-vaginal intercourse. Also, the fungus causing candidiasis can be found under the foreskin of the penis of an infected male and can be transmitted from male to female during penile-vaginal, penile-anal, and oral-genital intercourse.

Symptoms Symptoms of candidiasis in females include a white, foul-smelling discharge and itching. Males with candidiasis might experience itching and burning during urination.

Diagnosis A physician diagnoses candidiasis from the symptoms.

Treatment Miconazole, clotrimazole, or teraconazole cream, tablets, or vaginal suppositories are used for treatment. It is important to keep the affected area clean and dry. A female might wear a sanitary pad to protect her clothing.

Trichomoniasis

Trichomoniasis is an STD caused by the parasitic protozoan *Trichomonas*, which might infect the vagina, urethra, or prostate gland. This disease affects about 10 to 15 percent of people who are sexually active (CDC, 1997).

Transmission Trichomoniasis is transmitted from an infected female to an uninfected male through penile-vaginal intercourse. It is transmitted from an infected male to an uninfected female through penile-vaginal, oral-genital, and penile-anal intercourse.

Trichomoniasis also can be transmitted nonsexually. A female who uses vaginal sprays and douches might change the natural flora of her vagina enough to create a favorable atmosphere for this parasite to flourish. The protozoa might survive for 24 hours on damp towels, making the sharing of infected towels a means of transmission.

Symptoms Approximately half of the females who are infected with trichomoniasis are asymptomatic for the first six months. When symptoms appear, there is a frothy, greenish-yellow vaginal discharge that has an odor. Vaginal tissue might become inflamed. There might be itching, burning, and pain during urination.

Most infected males have no symptoms. Males who have symptoms usually suffer from urethritis and pain and burning during urination. A male partner who is asymptomatic still can spread trichomoniasis to an uninfected partner.

Diagnosis Diagnosis is made through microscopic examination of vaginal or urethral discharges, through urinalysis, or by a Pap smear.

Treatment Metronidazole is a prescription drug used in the treatment of trichomoniasis, under the trade name Flagyl. When being treated with Flagyl, a person should not drink alcohol for at least 24 hours following the last treatment.

Chlamydial Infections

Chlamydial infections are STDs caused by the bacterium *Chlamydia trachomatis,* that might result in inflammation of the urethra and epididymis in males and inflammation of the vagina and cervix in females. Chlamydial infections are quite prevalent in the United States and have serious consequences. Chlamydial infection is the most common

bacterial sexually transmitted disease in the United States today, with over 4 million new cases diagnosed yearly (NIAID, 1998).

Transmission Chlamydial infections primarily are transmitted through penile-vaginal intercourse; however, it is possible to transmit chlamydial infections during penile-anal and oral-genital intercourse. Chlamydial infections can be transmitted from an infected mother to her baby during vaginal delivery, resulting in conjunctivitis and pneumonia. Most babies born with these conditions respond favorably to antibiotic treatments.

Symptoms Chlamydial infections often are referred to as "silent" STDs because frequently there are either no symptoms or very mild symptoms. In females, chlamydial infections involve the vagina and cervix. Most females with lower reproductive tract infections experience no symptoms. If symptoms occur, they include irritation and itching in the genital area, burning during urination, and a vaginal discharge.

If the infection is not checked, the upper reproductive tract also might be involved. This latter condition is known as pelvic inflammatory disease (PID). Chlamydia and gonorrhea are the leading causes of PID (ASHA, 1996). Symptoms of PID include fever, abdominal pain, nausea, vomiting, tachycardia, and disrupted menstrual periods. Some ectopic pregnancies and cases of sterility have been linked to PID.

In males, chlamydial infections involve the urethra and epididymis, and cause a discharge and burning during urination. A male might not have the symptoms of PID for years, but meanwhile, internal organs are being infected and damaged. The vas deferens might become blocked, preventing the movement of sperm from the testes and causing sterility.

Diagnosis Chlamydial infections are diagnosed through microscopic examination of vaginal and urethral discharges.

Treatment The bacterium *Chlamydia trachomatis* can successfully be treated with antibiotics.

Drugs such as tetracycline, erythromycin, and doxycycline have been proven to be effective. Both the infected person and his or her sex partner should be treated (NIAID, 1998).

Gonorrhea

Gonorrhea is an STD caused by the bacterium *Neisseria gonorrhoeae,* which infects the epithelial surfaces of the genitourinary tract of males and females (Figure 6.2).

Transmission The bacterium causing gonorrhea can be transmitted from an infected partner to an uninfected partner during penile-vaginal, penile-anal, and oral-genital intercourse, and it can be transmitted from an infected mother to her baby during vaginal delivery. The infected baby will be born with gonorrheal ophthalmia neonatorum, a severe eye infection. Symptoms include a purulent discharge from the eyes two to three days after birth and edema of the eyelids. Unless the baby is treated immediately, this infection can result in blindness. To prevent this from happening, laws require that every newborn baby be given antibiotic eye drops or other preventative treatments to prevent infection with *Neisseria gonorrhoeae.*

Symptoms The signs and symptoms of gonorrhea vary with the site and duration of the infection as well as the particular characteristics of the infecting strain of the bacteria. Females

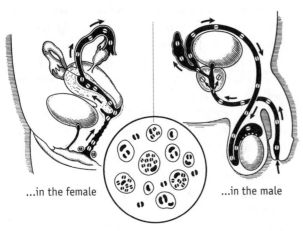

...in the female   ...in the male

Figure 6.2 Gonorrhea infects the epithelial cells of the genitourinary tract of males and females.

infected with these bacteria often have no visible symptoms. Symptoms, when they occur, are increased vaginal discharge, genital irritation, and pain during urination. There might be increased urination and abnormal menstrual bleeding as well as abdominal tenderness. Infection might be present in the urethra, vagina, cervix, pharynx, or rectum. If left untreated, gonorrhea will spread to the uterus, ovaries, and Fallopian tubes. Gonorrhea is a common cause of sterility in females.

More males than females are apt to show signs and symptoms of infection with *Neisseria gonorrhoeae.* However, as many as 40 percent of infected males might have no symptoms. Symptoms, which might appear in two days to a week after exposure, include a purulent urethral discharge from the penis, pain, and increased frequency of urination. In males who become infected during penile-anal and oral-genital intercourse, there might be a discharge from the pharynx or rectum with accompanying pain. Early symptoms often disappear, but the bacteria are still present, and the male can infect others.

A male can be cured at any time with appropriate treatment. However, if left untreated, the infection will spread to the prostate gland, the seminal vesicles, and the epididymis. Infection in these tissues can be serious enough to cause permanent sterility.

Diagnosis A sure diagnosis of gonorrhea is made by a culture test of mucous membranes from the cervix (Figure 6.3), pharynx, and/or rectum in females and the urethra (Figure 6.4), pharynx, and/or anus (Figure 6.5) in males.

Treatment Penicillin has been an effective treatment for gonorrhea. Recently there has been evidence of strains of *Neisseria gonorrhoeae* that are resistant to penicillin. Current recommended treatment is a combination of ceftriaxone (an antibiotic) and doxycycline or azithromycin (NIAID, 1998). This combination also is effective in the treatment of chlamydial infections, which are often present with a gonorrheal infection. People being treated for gonorrhea are advised to have a culture one to two weeks after treatment and then again in about six months to be certain they are no longer infected.

Untreated gonorrhea poses serious health risks, some of which are life-threatening. Systemic gonorrheal infections might result in complications such as meningitis, endocarditis, and joint destruction. Females might develop PID with accompanying fever, abdominal pain, nausea, vomiting, tachycardia, and disrupted menstrual periods.

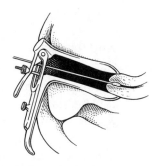

Figure 6.3 An endocervical culture is a culture test to detect pathogens in the mucous membranes of the cervix.

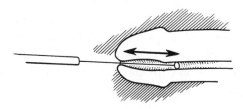

Figure 6.4 A urethral culture is a culture test to detect pathogens in the urethra.

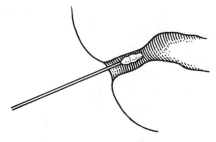

Figure 6.5 An anal culture is a culture test to detect pathogens in the anus.

Nongonococcal Urethritis

Nongonococcal urethritis (NGU) is an STD caused by pathogens other than *Neisseria gonorrhoeae*, which cause an infection and inflammation of the urethra. The infection is probably caused by the pathogens *Chlamydia trachomatis* and *Ureaplasma urealyticum.*

Transmission NGU can be transmitted from an infected partner to an uninfected partner during penile-vaginal, penile-anal, and oral-genital intercourse. This STD also can be transmitted from an infected mother to her baby during vaginal delivery.

Symptoms Unfortunately, many females are asymptomatic. When symptoms occur, they usually are mild and include itching and burning during urination. However, these symptoms might be so mild that the female is unaware that she is infected. If left untreated, a female might develop PID and cervical inflammation.

As many as two million males might become infected each year with NGU. Symptoms of NGU in males are similar to those of gonorrhea and include painful and frequent urination as well as purulent urethral discharge. The symptoms might disappear temporarily without treatment. However, the pathogens are still in the body and a male can infect others even when he has no symptoms.

Diagnosis Diagnosis of NGU is done through a culture of the discharge. A laboratory diagnosis is essential so that the correct treatment is prescribed.

Treatment Penicillin is not effective against NGU. Tetracycline or doxycycline is the usual treatment, but erythromycin is used for people who are allergic to tetracycline. People being treated for NGU are advised to have a culture one to two weeks after treatment and then again in about six months to be certain that they are no longer infected.

Syphilis

Syphilis is an STD caused by the bacterium *Treponema pallidum,* which penetrates mucous membranes and abrasions in the skin and causes lesions that might involve any organ or tissue.

Transmission Transmission is through direct contact with infected lesions during penile-vaginal, penile-anal, and oral-genital intercourse. *Treponema pallidum* also can be transmitted by having direct contact with bodily fluids or by having a transfusion with infected blood (a rare occurrence). In addition to these modes of transmission, the bacterium can be transmitted from a pregnant female to the fetus through the placenta.

Symptoms The *Treponema pallidum* bacteria easily penetrate the skin and mucous membranes. From this point of entry, they quickly spread into the lymphatic system and the bloodstream resulting in a systemic infection. Usually the bacteria have been carried throughout the body before the first signs and symptoms of syphilis appear.

Untreated syphilis progresses through four stages of development—primary, secondary, latent, and tertiary stages (Figure 6.6). There are characteristic signs and symptoms for each of these stages. However, some people who are infected are asymptomatic.

The primary stage of syphilis is characterized by chancres. **Chancres** are hard, round, painless sores with raised edges resulting from syphilis. Chancres appear mostly in the genital area of the body three weeks or longer after exposure. A chancre develops where the pathogen entered the body, so it is not unusual to find a chancre in the mouth if a person has engaged in oral-genital intercourse. Chancres also might appear on the lips, tongue, fingers, or nipples. A chancre might be the size of a dime or as small as a pimple. Since a chancre is full of *Treponema pallidum* bacteria, any contact with the chancre might result in transmission of the bacteria to an uninfected partner.

In females, chancres usually appear on the labia or within the vagina or cervix. Because chancres are painless, they often go unnoticed if they develop in internal areas of the body. In males, chancres appear on the penis, the scrotum, or in the pubic area. They often appear on the anus or within the rectum of males who are receptive partners in penile-anal intercourse. Chancres heal and disappear without treatment within a few weeks, giving the infected person a false sense of security in thinking that the condition has cured itself. An infected person might have no further symptoms for a period of time after a chancre has disappeared. However, this infected person who has no symptoms can infect others during this time.

The secondary stage of syphilis is characterized by a skin rash with macular, papular, and/or pustular lesions. The skin rash and lesions appear on the palms of the hands and the soles of the feet. The rash might cover the entire body, and it does not itch. In moist areas of the body, the lesions might open and become contagious. The infected person experiences fever, weight loss, swollen lymph nodes, and even hair loss. Again, these secondary stage symptoms will subside without treatment after a few weeks, and the person will experience relief because the symptoms have disappeared. An infected person is very contagious in the secondary stage.

Congenital syphilis is the transmission of syphilis to a fetus from an infected pregnant female. About one quarter of these pregnancies result in stillbirth or neonatal death. Between 40 and 70 percent of such pregnancies will result in a syphilis-infected infant (NIAID, 1998). Congenital syphilis can cause mental disturbance or retardation and other birth defects.

A pregnant woman might transmit *Treponema pallidum* to her developing fetus as early as the fourth month of pregnancy. This infection results in stillbirth or neonatal death in 20 percent of infected infants. However, syphilis can be treated with penicillin, and this treatment usually will result in a cure for the fetus as well. The child should be carefully monitored after birth and given further treatment if necessary.

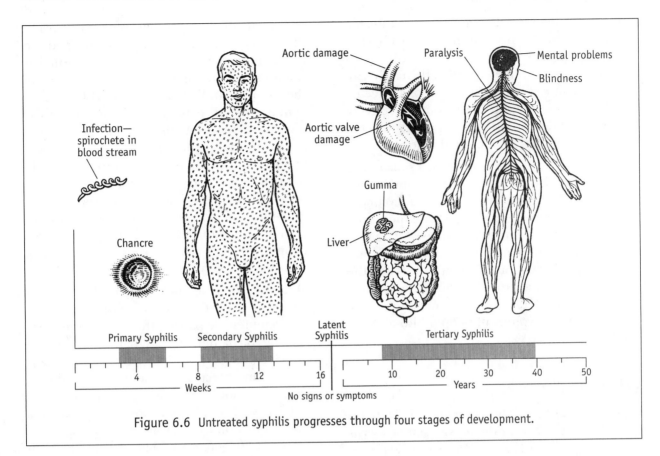

Figure 6.6 Untreated syphilis progresses through four stages of development.

Without treatment during the primary and secondary stages, syphilis progresses to the third, or latent, stage. During latent syphilis, there usually are no symptoms in infected people even though the *Treponema pallidum* are affecting tissues and organs in the body. Many people who have syphilis stay in the latent stage for the remainder of their lives.

People who do not obtain treatment through the primary, secondary, and latent stages experience the final stage of syphilis, the tertiary stage. During the tertiary stage of syphilis, symptoms including blindness, paralysis, liver damage, and mental problems occur. These conditions might arise many years after the initial infection with syphilis. The tertiary stage of syphilis might result in death.

Diagnosis In the primary stage, syphilis is diagnosed by culture and examination of the chancre. After the primary stage, diagnosis of syphilis might be made through a fluorescent treponemal antibody-absorption (FTA-ABS) test. A Venereal Disease Research Laboratory (VDRL) and a cerebrospinal fluid (CSF) examination also might be used for diagnosis.

Treatment The preferred treatment for syphilis during all stages is with penicillin G and doxycycline. Tetracycline or erythromycin is used in people who are allergic to penicillin. The infected person should keep all lesions dry throughout treatment. VDRL testing should be used during the treatment to be certain that all *Treponema pallidum* bacteria have been eradicated.

Treatment is usually effective for the primary and secondary stages of syphilis. Unfortunately, any organ damage acquired during the tertiary stage might be irreversible.

Untreated syphilis might result in heart disease, central nervous system disease, and musculoskeletal diseases and disorders.

In the United States, cases of primary and secondary syphilis reached an all-time low in 1956. Then a "roller coaster" course began and lasted until 1977. Syphilis rates have been declining over the last two decades and have reached their lowest rate ever, falling to about 70,000 new cases annually (American Medical News, 1998). However, a new concern is the increased likelihood that a person infected with syphilis will become infected with HIV. During intimate sexual contact, bodily fluids from a person infected with HIV easily can enter a chancre on a partner who is infected with syphilis. During the secondary stage of syphilis, bodily fluids from a person infected with HIV can enter an eroded lesion.

Public health care providers also are concerned about treating syphilis in people infected with HIV. Penicillin or tetracycline is usually prescribed, with larger doses necessary in the latent and tertiary stages. There is evidence that infection with HIV alters not only the progression of syphilis but also the person's response to penicillin. Research is ongoing to determine the most effective treatment for syphilis in people who also are infected with HIV.

Genital Herpes

Genital herpes is a highly contagious STD that is caused by two forms of the herpes simplex virus (HSV), HSV-1 and HSV-2. HSV-1 usually causes cold sores or fever blisters in the mouth or on the lips. HSV-2 usually causes sores or lesions in the genital area (Figure 6.7). However, HSV-1 has been known to cause genital lesions and HSV-2 has been known to cause oral lesions.

Transmission A person with genital herpes is highly contagious if any lesions are present. The blisters eventually erupt and the fluid containing the virus particles is released. This is a highly contagious period when the virus can be transmitted by touch alone. The virus can be transmitted if a lesion on an infected person erupts and the virus particles enter a partner's body during penile-vaginal, penile-anal, and oral-genital intercourse. Transmission can occur even during kissing or touching if contact is made with a lesion. The risk is less when the lesions have healed.

The use of condoms reduces the risk of infection by virus particles from lesions that erupt during sexual intercourse. However, there still is some risk if the areas infected with lesions are not completely covered or if the condom breaks.

A person infected with herpes can transmit the infection from one area of the body to another through touch. If the person has lesions in the mouth and places the fingers in the mouth and then touches his or her genitals, the virus might be spread from the mouth to the genitals. If the person has lesions in the genital area and touches these lesions and then puts fingers into the mouth, the virus might spread to the mouth. It also is possible to spread the virus to the eyes by touching infected lesions in the mouth or genital area and then rubbing the eyes. People infected with herpes need to keep their hands clean for this reason.

Other modes of transmission for genital herpes include the possibility of an infected pregnant female passing the virus to the fetus, causing birth defects. A baby also can be infected during a vaginal delivery, especially during an infected mother's first outbreak with the lesions. Because the virus moves in nerve tissue, an infected baby might develop a brain infection that causes brain damage. As many as 50 percent of babies infected with herpes die or suffer neurologic damage. To eliminate the risk of infecting the baby, cultures might be done on a pregnant female during the last six weeks of the pregnancy. A positive herpes culture might determine that a cesarean section will be performed. In the event of infection of the baby, early detection and treatment with acyclovir will greatly improve the outcome (NIAID, 1998).

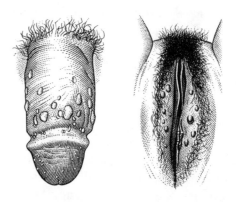

Figure 6.7 HSV-2 usually causes sores or lesions in the genital area.

© 2001 Everyday Learning Corporation

Symptoms Genital herpes has two stages, and unlike other STDs, it tends to recur spontaneously. Stage 1 of genital herpes is referred to as the active stage and usually occurs between 2 and 12 days after exposure. During the active stage of herpes, males and females develop characteristic skin lesions on their genitals. These skin lesions appear as shallow, ulcerated vesicles or blisters.

In a female, these blisters appear on the labia, the inner vaginal area, and the cervix. In a male, blisters appear on the penis, in the urethra, and in the area of the anus. These blisters might rupture during urination, sexual intercourse, or irritation from clothing and cause acute pain and itching. Other generalized symptoms of genital herpes include fever, headaches, tiredness, and swollen lymph nodes. Females also might experience leukorrhea, a discharge containing white blood cells.

The length of the acute stage of genital herpes varies. Eventually the blisters heal and disappear and the other symptoms vanish. Then genital herpes enters the latent stage. During the latent stage, there are no signs and symptoms of genital herpes although the virus is still present in the body. At present, there is no known procedure to rid the body of the virus.

Many people infected with HSV-1 and HSV-2 have recurrent attacks of genital herpes; others have no further episodes. The number and pattern of outbreaks can vary over an individual's lifetime, making prediction of outbreaks difficult (NIAID, 1998). Some studies indicate that the likelihood of recurrences tends to be linked to physical and psychological health. Circumstances such as prolonged stress, trauma, or disease also might be triggers for recurring symptoms of genital herpes.

Diagnosis Diagnosis of genital herpes is made through clinical inspection and culture and examination of fluid drawn from the blisters. A blood test can be used to distinguish between HSV-1 and HSV-2.

Treatment There is no known cure for genital herpes. One drug, acyclovir, sold under the trade name of Zovirax, is helpful on a short-term basis for relieving some symptoms. Acyclovir relieves symptoms but might also keep the virus from reproducing. Personal hygiene is essential when lesions are present. Research to develop a vaccine for genital herpes continues.

The consequences of being infected with genital herpes are serious. An infected person always must be cautious because this STD is highly contagious during the acute stage and might be transmitted to a partner. Females who are infected with genital herpes are at increased risk for developing cervical cancer and should have regular Pap smears and pelvic examinations. Males and females who are infected with genital herpes and have an outbreak of the blisters are at increased risk of becoming infected with HIV from an HIV-infected partner during sexual contact (NIAID, 1998). HIV can enter the body through the broken blisters.

Genital Warts

Genital warts are dry, wart-like growths that are caused by the human papillomavirus (HPV). Genital warts usually are painless and have a cauliflower shape (Figure 6.8).

Transmission HPV is transmitted during penile-vaginal, oral-genital, and penile-anal intercourse. Genital warts also might be spread through direct contact with infected bed linen, towels, and clothing.

Symptoms Genital warts appear three to eight months after infection with HPV. They might last for a few weeks or longer. In females, the genital warts usually appear on the labia and in the vagina. In males, genital warts appear on the penis and occasionally in the urethra. In both females and males, genital warts can spread to the perineal area. The size of genital warts varies from pin-like dots to much larger, irregular masses.

Figure 6.8 Genital warts usually are painless and have a cauliflower shape.

Diagnosis Diagnosis usually is made by clinical inspection. The warts are a yellow-gray color and look like tiny cauliflowers when they appear on dry skin areas. They are soft and pink in color when they appear in moist skin areas such as in the vagina. The same virus can cause "flat warts" that usually appear on the cervix or on the penis. "Flat warts" are diagnosed by microscopic examination of the tissue that has been treated with vinegar, which causes the warts to become white in color. The presence of flat warts has a strong connection to cervical cancer and can be diagnosed by a Pap smear.

Treatment The Centers for Disease Control and Prevention report that there is no treatment available to eradicate HPV completely (CDC, 1998a). The usual treatment involves topical medications such as podophyllin and trichloroacetic acid to erode the warts. The treatment should not be self-administered; a qualified health care professional should be consulted for treatments. Podophyllin is not used if a female is pregnant. Laser surgery also is a means of removing warts by burning them away, or warts might be frozen and removed by using liquid nitrogen. None of these treatments will erase the possibility of the warts recurring, because the virus remains in the body tissues.

There is much concern about genital warts. Genital warts are the most common symptomatic viral STD in the United States, with more than three million cases diagnosed each year. There seems to be an increased risk of becoming infected with genital warts if a person had sexual intercourse at a young age.

Pediculosis Pubis

Pediculosis pubis is infestation with *Phthirus pubis*, pubic or crab lice. Lice are parasitic insects that are yellowish-gray in color and about the size of a pinhead (Figure 6.9). The lice attach themselves to pubic hairs and burrow into the skin where they feed on blood. Female lice produce eggs, or nits, that attach to body hair. The eggs hatch in six to eight days and mature in 21 days. Since each female lays as many as 50 eggs, an infestation can increase in a very short time.

Transmission Lice can be transmitted from one person to another through close sexual contact. Since lice can live outside the body for as long as a day, it is possible for a person to become infected by sleeping on infected sheets, wearing infected clothing, sharing infected towels, and sitting on a toilet seat that has been used by an infected person.

Symptoms Little black spots, which are lice, might be visible on body parts that have dense hair growth. In addition, a person will feel intense itching where the lice are attached.

Diagnosis Self-diagnosis is possible if a louse is located, or a physician can diagnose pediculosis pubis after clinical inspection.

Treatment A prescription drug, Lindane, sold under the trade name of Kwell, kills lice, but this method is not recommended for pregnant women (CDC, 1998a). Over-the-counter preparations such as A-200 pyrinite and Nix also are effective treatments. Petroleum jelly is used to control lice by suffocating them. There are no known major complications associated with pubic lice.

When a person is infected with pediculosis pubis, he or she should avoid sexual intimacy and close contact until after treatment. All clothing, towels, and bed linen should be disinfected by thorough washing in hot water or by dry cleaning. Toilet seats that have been used by an infected person should be disinfected. A post-treatment checkup should occur to be certain that the lice have been eradicated.

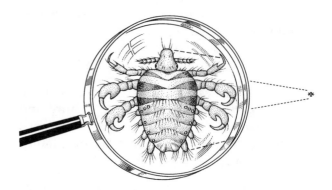

Figure 6.9 Pubic lice are yellowish-gray in color and about the size of a pinhead.

Viral Hepatitis

Viral hepatitis is an inflammatory infection of the liver caused by viruses. There are four types of viral hepatitis, all caused by a different virus. The four types are designated as hepatitis A (infectious hepatitis), hepatitis B (serum hepatitis), hepatitis C (sometimes called non-A/non-B hepatitis), and hepatitis D (delta hepatitis). The diseases caused by these viruses are very similar.

Transmission Hepatitis A can be transmitted by infected people who handle food and who do not practice ordinary sanitary habits of washing their hands after bathroom use. Shellfish from contaminated waters that are eaten raw or that are not cooked properly are a source of hepatitis A infection.

Hepatitis B is a common type of viral hepatitis. The hepatitis B virus is found in blood, blood products, saliva, semen, and vaginal secretions. The hepatitis B virus can be transmitted during intravenous drug use when an infected person shares a needle with infected blood on it with another person who then uses it to inject a drug.

Hepatitis C has been a mystery. It was previously referred to as non-A/non-B until the C virus was identified. It can be transmitted from an infected person to an uninfected person during intravenous drug use. Transmission also can result when infected blood is used for a blood transfusion.

Hepatitis D is more common in the Mediterranean and Middle East than in the United States. Hepatitis D is present only with the hepatitis B virus. Hepatitis D is transmitted in the same ways as hepatitis B.

Symptoms Symptoms of hepatitis A include fatigue, abdominal pain, fever, and occasional jaundice (a yellowing of the skin). Symptoms of hepatitis B include profound fatigue, jaundice, nausea, and abdominal pain. Fatigue might cause severely limited physical activity and can last for months. Most patients recover from the infection and eventually eliminate the virus. The infection is fatal to about 4 percent of patients; 5 to 10 percent become chronic hepatitis B carriers (CDC, 1998b). There is a danger in that these carriers can transmit the virus to others.

Symptoms for hepatitis C might vary from mild to severe. An infected person might have diarrhea, poor appetite, and fatigue and experience high fever and jaundice. Symptoms for hepatitis D are similar to those of hepatitis B. Hepatitis D infection is severe, often causing permanent liver damage and death.

Diagnosis Diagnosis of hepatitis is made through blood tests for hepatitis antibodies.

Treatment General treatment for all types of hepatitis is bed rest and fluid intake, which is important to prevent dehydration. No effective medication is available at present. Antibiotics might be prescribed to prevent secondary infection. The disease eventually runs its course, although recovery might take several months.

Prevention of viral hepatitis is a major focus of public health efforts. Shots of immune serum globulin give partial immunity to people exposed to hepatitis A. However, in many cases, a person can be exposed to hepatitis A for a long time without knowing it. As many as 400,000 new cases are reported in the United States each year. Physicians and other health care givers are urged to wear protective clothing including gloves and eye protectors to reduce the risk of infection when treating a person who has tested positive for viral hepatitis.

A vaccine is available to prevent hepatitis B. People who are at risk include those who have had multiple sex partners, have used intravenous drugs, are routinely exposed to blood or blood products as a health care provider, or have a family member who is infected with hepatitis B. Everyone who might be exposed to hepatitis B is encouraged to get the vaccine.

Other Sexually Transmitted Diseases

In the preceding Section, those STDs that are prevalent in large numbers were discussed. Many other STDs occur less frequently and so receive less attention. In this section of the chapter, the following less common STDs will be discussed: molluscum contagiosum, scabies, shigellosis, chancroid, lymphogranuloma venereum, and granuloma inguinale. The discussion of each of these STDs will include the name of the pathogen causing the disease, method of transmission, symptoms, diagnosis, and treatment.

Molluscum Contagiosum

Molluscum contagiosum is an STD caused by a large virus of the pox group.

Transmission The molluscum contagiosum virus is transmitted from an infected to an uninfected partner.

Symptoms Molluscum contagiosum is characterized by small, raised lesions that appear on the external genitals, the buttocks, thighs, and the abdomen. Lesions appear three to six weeks after exposure to an infected person, and secondary infection with *Staphylococcus* bacteria might occur.

Diagnosis Diagnosis is made by clinical examination and by a culture and examination of fluid from the lesions.

Treatment Treatment involves squeezing out the center core of each lesion or freezing the lesions with liquid nitrogen. A caustic chemical such as podophyllin, trichloroacetic acid, or silver nitrate also might be used on the lesions. If left untreated, the lesions usually disappear within six months. However, if every lesion is not treated in some way, the disease might recur.

Scabies

Scabies is a skin infestation by *Sarcoptes scabiei*, microscopic mites that are parasites. The female mite burrows under the skin and deposits eggs.

Transmission Scabies is transmitted through close physical contact in which the females mites infesting one person begin to infest a second person. Transmission also can occur from direct contact with infested clothing, bed linen, towels, or toilet seats. Thus, scabies is not a true STD.

Symptoms The symptoms of scabies include itching and the presence of welts or small blisters. There may be reddish-brown nodules one or more months after infection has occurred.

Diagnosis Diagnosis for scabies is made by observing the symptoms and by taking a medical history to learn if a person has had exposure to a partner infected with scabies within the previous two months. A definite diagnosis can be made by observing scrapings from a blister for mites and/or eggs under a microscope.

Treatment Treatment for scabies can be with special creams: Permethrin or Lindane and Elinite. Permethrin is more expensive than Lindane, but Lindane resistance has been reported in some parts of the United States (CDC, 1998a). These drugs are applied to the entire body for a specific period of time and then scrubbed off. The clothing, bed linen, and towels used by an infected person should be washed carefully to prevent re-infection. Toilet seats used by an infected person should be disinfected.

Shigellosis

Shigellosis is an STD caused by the *Shigella* bacterium.

Transmission Shigellosis is transmitted by direct contact with infected feces.

Symptoms Symptoms of shigellosis include fever, diarrhea, and inflammation of the large intestine.

Diagnosis Diagnosis is made by a culture and examination of fecal material.

Treatment Shigellosis can be treated with tetracycline or ampicillin.

Chancroid

Chancroid is an STD caused by the *Hemophilus ducreyi* bacterium. It is a common cause of genital ulcers. These ulcers are similar to syphilis chancres but are soft in comparison to the harder chancres associated with syphilis.

Transmission Chancroid is transmitted from an infected person to an uninfected person during intimate sexual contact. It may be transmitted by direct contact with an infected ulcer or by intravenous drug use in which an infected person shares a needle with an uninfected person. Chancroid is more prevalent in developing countries; however, it is increasing in incidence among prostitutes and their clients. It is believed that intravenous drug use among prostitutes is the reason for this increase.

Symptoms Females are usually asymptomatic, but they may have one or more ulcer-like lesions in the genital area. In males, a single ulcer-like lesion usually appears on the penis or anus. Eventually, the lesions erupt with a foul-smelling discharge. The presence of the lesions might be accompanied by swollen lymph nodes.

Diagnosis Diagnosis is made by culture and examination of fluid from the ulcer-like lesion.

Treatment Chancroid is treated with erythromycin and sulfa drugs.

Lymphogranuloma Venereum

Lymphogranuloma venereum, or **LGV**, is an STD caused by the *Chlamydia trachomatis* bacterium.

Transmission LGV is transmitted from an infected person to an uninfected person through penile-vaginal, penile-anal, and oral-genital intercourse and also can be transmitted by touching an infectious ulcer.

Symptoms Symptoms appear from three days to three weeks after contact with an infected person. The first symptom is small ulcers on the genitals. This may be followed with a sensation of stiffness and aching in the groin. Other symptoms include swollen lymph nodes and fever.

Diagnosis LGV is often confused with chancroid. Diagnosis requires isolating *Chlamydia trachomatis* to confirm that it is LGV.

Treatment Doxycycline, tetracycline, and erythromycin are three medications used to treat this STD.

Granuloma Inguinale

Granuloma inguinale is an STD caused by the bacterium *Calymmatobacterium granulomatis*.

Transmission Granuloma inguinale can be transmitted by touching an infectious lesion.

Symptoms Small bumps that look like pimples appear on the thighs and in the genital area. When these lesions burst, a sour liquid that has a strong odor can spread to nearby tissues.

Diagnosis Diagnosis is made by microscopic examination of scrapings of the lesions. It is important to treat these lesions as quickly as possible so that tissues in the genital area will not be damaged. Granuloma inguinale can damage the genital organs, and might spread to other parts of the body (New York State Department of Health, 1999).

Treatment Erythromycin and tetracycline are two of the medications that are used to treat this disease.

The Prevention Model for Educating About STDs

Health care providers, researchers, educators, and parents all agree that the key to eliminating the widespread epidemic of STDs is through educational efforts aimed at prevention. This section of the chapter focuses on *The Prevention Model for Educating About STDs* (Table 6.10).

Table 6.10
The Prevention Model for Educating About STDs

Step 1: Teach the Facts

Step 2: Send a Clear Message: Choose Abstinence from Sex and Monogamous Marriage

Step 3: Promote Self-Respecting Behavior

Step 4: Emphasize Prevention: Use Resistance Skills

Step 5: Encourage Honest Talk Within Relationships

Step 1: Teach the Facts

Step 1 in *The Prevention Model for Educating About STDs* involves teaching the facts about STDs. This involves teaching these facts about each STD:

- Name of the STD
- Pathogen that causes the STD
- Transmission—the risk behaviors and risk situations
- Symptoms
- Diagnosis
- Treatment

Step 2: Send a Clear Message: Choose Abstinence from Sex and Monogamous Marriage

Step 2 in *The Prevention Model for Educating About STDs* involves sending a clear message about family values. Adolescents should be encouraged to practice abstinence from sex now and, when and if they choose to marry, to commit themselves to a monogamous marriage. A **monogamous marriage** is a marriage in which both people remain sexually faithful to one another. Chapter 3 examines the advantages of practicing abstinence from sex during adolescence. Chapter 8 includes a discussion of the advantages of monogamous marriage.

Step 3: Promote Self-Respecting Behavior

Step 3 in *The Prevention Model for Educating About STDs* involves helping adolescents develop self-respecting behavior. **Self-respect** is a high regard for oneself because one behaves in responsible ways. Health education traditionally has focused on "how to be healthy." Yet, some adolescents who know "how to be healthy" participate in risk behaviors and risk situations. Therefore, teaching "how to be healthy" is not enough. Adolescents must believe they have "something to be healthy for."

Adolescents who have self-respect believe they are worthwhile and have "something to be healthy for." As a result, they choose self-respecting behavior. **Self-respecting behavior** is treating oneself in healthful and responsible ways. Adolescents who have self-respect and choose self-respecting behavior delay gratification and resist peer pressure. They have reasons to avoid STDs (Table 6.11).

Step 4: Emphasize Prevention: Use Resistance Skills

Step 4 of *The Prevention Model for Educating About STDs* includes a discussion of ways to prevent STDs. Adolescents should be encouraged to resist pressure to participate in risk behaviors

---

Table 6.11
Reasons to Avoid Infection with STDs

Because I like myself and believe myself to be of value:

1. I want to live a long, productive, and healthful life.
2. I want to keep my body healthy.
3. I want my reproductive organs to function as they should.
4. I want to keep my body free of recurring symptoms of STDs such as those that recur from genital herpes and genital warts.
5. I want to avoid embarrassing myself and my family.
6. I want to avoid unnecessary medical expenses and to help keep health care costs reasonable.
7. I want to be able to tell a future marriage partner that I have practiced abstinence from sex and have never been infected with an STD.
8. I want to have a healthful, satisfying sexual relationship within marriage and do not want to risk having symptoms from an STD.
9. I want to remain fertile so that I have the option of becoming a parent someday.
10. I do not want to infect my offspring with an STD if I choose to marry and become a parent.

---

and risk situations for transmission of STDs. **Resistance skills** are skills that help a person say NO to an action or to leave a situation. Some classroom time should be devoted to practicing resistance skills.

- Have students role play situations in which they are pressured to engage in risk behaviors and risk situations for transmission of STDs. Have students practice saying NO with self-confidence. Then have students give their reasons for saying NO to risk behaviors and risk situations for transmission of STDs. They might use one of the reasons from Table 6.10. Continue the role play by escalating the pressure. Have students repeat their reasons for saying NO to risk behaviors and risk situations for transmission of STDs. During the role play situations, students should use nonverbal behavior to match their verbal NO.

- Have students identify situations they should avoid because they will be pressured to participate in risk behaviors and risk situations for transmission of STDs.

- Encourage students to avoid peers who might pressure them to participate in risk behaviors and risk situations for transmission of STDs.

- Have students tell ways they might influence others to avoid risk behaviors and risk situations for transmission of STDs.

Step 5: Encourage Honest Talk Within Relationships

Step 5 in *The Prevention Model for Educating About STDs* involves teaching adolescents the importance of honest talk. **Honest talk** is the straightforward sharing of feelings. This prepares adolescents for adulthood when they might choose to marry and plan a family. It is important to know if a potential marriage partner has engaged in risk behaviors or risk situations that might have resulted in infection with one or more STDs. It is important to know if a potential marriage partner has a recurring STD such as genital herpes or genital warts.

Asking questions and providing accurate information when asked questions helps protect personal health and the health of others. In addition, honest talk also prevents lawsuits. The courts decided in the late 1980s that a person who has contracted genital herpes from a sex partner who has failed to disclose that he or she is infected can seek compensation through the legal system.

Preparing adolescents for the future includes helping them examine the risk behaviors and risk situations other people choose. For some adolescents, high school will be the last educational experience in which they discuss sexuality, reproductive health, risk behaviors and risk situations for STD infection, and the impact that STD infection might have on their future.

References

American Medical News. 1998. "STD Numbers Higher Than Estimated." Article Online (December). Accessed 3/1999. http://www. web4.searchbank.com/itw/session/268/963/ 8678219w5/144!prv_6.

Centers for Disease Control and Prevention. 1998a. "1998 Guidelines for Treatment of Sexually Transmitted Disease." Article Online (July). Accessed 3/1999. http://www.cdc.gov/ nchstp/dst.htm.

——. 1998b. "Hepatitis B Factsheet." Article Online (July). Accessed 3/1999. http://www.cdc. gov/ncidod/diseases/hepatitis/b/fact.htm.

Centers for Disease Control and Prevention: Office of Women's Health. 1997. "Sexually Transmitted Diseases." Article Online (November). Accessed 3/1999. http://www. cdc.gov/od/owh/whstd.htm.

Majeroni, Barbara, A., M.D. 1999. "Bacterial Vaginosis: An Update." *American Academy of Family Physicians* (May). Accessed 7/1999. http://www. aafp.org/afp/980315ap/majeroni.html.

National Institute of Allergy and Infectious Diseases. 1999. "Fact Sheet: An Introduction of Sexually Transmitted Diseases." Article Online (July). Accessed 7/1999. http://www.niaid.nih.gov/ factsheets.htm.

——. 1998. "Fact Sheet." Article Online (July). Accessed 3/1999. http://www.niaid.nih.gov/ factsheets.htm.

New York State Department of Health. 1999. "Communicable Diseases Fact Sheet." Article Online (February). Accessed 7/1999. http:// www.health.state.ny.us/nysdoh/consumer.htm.

7 HIV/AIDS

Content for Teachers *Only*

A Word from the Authors

Being well-educated about healthful sexuality and loving and caring relationships must include a discussion of the emotional and physical threats to relationships. Perhaps the greatest concern to the emotional and physical health of a relationship today is the prospect of transmitting HIV, which results in the life-threatening condition known as AIDS. Professionals must provide youth with knowledge about HIV and AIDS, but more than this, they must instill the skills youth need to form healthful relationships in which the risk of HIV transmission is avoided. In other words, education about HIV and AIDS must focus on the message, "You can reduce your risk of becoming infected with HIV and developing AIDS if you avoid risk behaviors and risk situations and have open, honest relationships." This chapter includes information about transmission of HIV, tests for HIV infection, the progression of HIV infection and AIDS, treatment for HIV infection and AIDS, and *The Prevention Model for Educating Adolescents About HIV Infection and AIDS.*

HIV Infection

The **human immunodeficiency virus (HIV)** is a pathogen that destroys infection-fighting helper T cells in the body. HIV causes AIDS. **Acquired Immune Deficiency Syndrome (AIDS)** is a condition that results when infection with HIV causes a breakdown of the body's ability to fight other infections. Being infected with HIV and having AIDS are two different conditions. This section of the chapter includes a discussion of how the body defends itself from pathogens and how the body responds to HIV.

How the Body Defends Itself from Pathogens

To understand how HIV infection affects the body, it is important to review how the body defends itself from pathogens. Body defenses are the body's means of defending itself from foreign substances including pathogens. Unbroken skin keeps pathogens from entering the body. Oils and perspiration on the skin trap and help kill some pathogens. Tears contain chemicals that help kill some pathogens. Tears help keep some pathogens from entering the body through the eyes. If pathogens enter through the nose, mucous in the nasal passages traps them. Cilia, hair-like projections, beat back and forth and force the pathogens back out. Cilia also line the windpipe or trachea and help keep some pathogens from entering the lungs. If pathogens enter the mouth, saliva helps destroy some of them.

Suppose pathogens are not kept out of the body. The **immune system** is the body system that removes harmful substances from the blood and combats pathogens. The **lymphatic system** is the part of the immune system that includes lymph vessels, lymphocytes, lymph nodes, the thymus gland, tonsils, and the spleen. The lymphatic system carries fluid away from the body tissues to the circulatory system thereby helping maintain fluid balance in the body. The lymphatic system also filters blood and lymph so that pathogens are removed from the body.

Lymphocytes are white blood cells that circulate throughout the lymphatic system to help the body fight pathogens. **Neutrophils** are white blood cells produced in the tissue that lies in the hollow part of the bone known as bone marrow. Neutrophils account for 54 percent to 62 percent of the white blood cells in the body. Neutrophils also fight pathogens.

Helper T cells and B cells are two types of lymphocytes that help the body fight pathogens. **Helper T cells**, or **CD4+T cells**, are white blood cells that signal B cells to make antibodies. A healthy person has 800 to 1,200 helper T cells per cubic milliliter of blood. **B cells** are the blood cells that produce antibodies. **Antibodies** are proteins produced by B cells that help destroy pathogens inside the body. Antibodies then travel through lymph vessels to destroy pathogens. Antibodies can make pathogens ineffective and susceptible to macrophages. **Macrophages** are white blood cells that surround and destroy pathogens. Antibodies help macrophages by attaching to pathogens and making them easier to engulf and digest. Digested pathogens enter lymph and are destroyed in the lymph nodes and removed by the spleen.

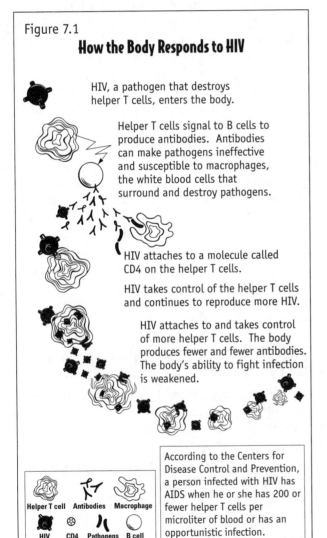

Figure 7.1

How the Body Responds to HIV

HIV, a pathogen that destroys helper T cells, enters the body.

Helper T cells signal to B cells to produce antibodies. Antibodies can make pathogens ineffective and susceptible to macrophages, the white blood cells that surround and destroy pathogens.

HIV attaches to a molecule called CD4 on the helper T cells.

HIV takes control of the helper T cells and continues to reproduce more HIV.

HIV attaches to and takes control of more helper T cells. The body produces fewer and fewer antibodies. The body's ability to fight infection is weakened.

| Helper T cell | Antibodies | Macrophage |
| HIV | CD4 | Pathogens | B cell |

According to the Centers for Disease Control and Prevention, a person infected with HIV has AIDS when he or she has 200 or fewer helper T cells per microliter of blood or has an opportunistic infection.

How the Body Responds to HIV

Suppose HIV, a pathogen that destroys helper T cells, enters the body. Helper T cells signal to B cells to produce antibodies. Antibodies can make pathogens ineffective and susceptible to macrophages, the white blood cells that surround and destroy pathogens. HIV attaches to a molecule called CD4 on the helper T cells. HIV takes control of the helper T cells and continues to reproduce more HIV. HIV attaches to and takes control of more helper T cells. The body produces fewer and fewer antibodies and its ability to fight infection is weakened. Some signs of HIV infection include flu-like symptoms, such as fever, sore throat, skin rash, diarrhea, swollen glands, loss of appetite, and night sweats. These signs come and go as the helper T cell count fluctuates. According to the Centers for Disease Control and Prevention, a person infected with HIV has AIDS when he or she has 200 or fewer helper T cells per microliter of blood or has an opportunistic infection. An **opportunistic infection** is an infection that develops in a person with a weakened immune system. Figure 7.1 illustrates the progression of HIV infection to AIDS.

Transmission of HIV

People who are infected with HIV have HIV in most of their body fluids. HIV is spread from an infected person to others by contact with certain body fluids. These body fluids are blood, semen, vaginal secretions, and, in a few cases, breast milk. Minute traces of HIV have been found in saliva, sweat, and tears. To date, there have been no documented cases of HIV transmission through saliva and tears. Table 7.2 includes a list of ways HIV is not transmitted. This section of the chapter discusses the risk behaviors and risk situations for transmission of HIV (Table 7.3).

> ### Table 7.2 **Ways HIV Is Not Transmitted**
>
> To date, there have been no documented cases of HIV transmission through saliva, sweat, or tears. According to the Centers for Disease Control and Prevention, HIV is not spread through casual contact, such as
>
> - Closed-mouth kissing
> - Hugging
> - Touching, holding, or shaking hands
> - Coughing or sneezing
> - Sharing food or eating utensils
> - Sharing towels or combs
> - Having casual contact with friends
> - Sharing bathroom facilities or water fountains
> - Sharing a pen or pencil
> - Being bitten by insects
> - Donating blood
> - Eating food prepared or served by someone else
> - Attending school
> - Using a telephone or computer used by someone else
> - Swimming in a pool
> - Using sports and gym equipment

> ### Table 7.3 **Risk Behaviors and Risk Situations for Transmission of HIV**
>
> 1. Having intimate sexual contact
> 2. Engaging in open-mouth kissing with a person infected with HIV
> 3. Sharing needles, syringes, or other injection equipment for injecting drugs
> 4. Sharing a needle to make tattoos or to pierce ears or other body parts
> 5. Sharing a needle and mixing blood in a ceremony to become a blood sister or blood brother
> 6. Having contact with the blood or other body fluids, mucous membranes, or broken skin of a person infected with HIV
> 7. Having a blood transfusion with blood or blood products infected with HIV
> 8. Having a tissue transplant from a person infected with HIV
> 9. Being born to a mother infected with HIV

1. Having intimate sexual contact

Intimate sexual contact is a risk behavior for the transmission of STDs. During intimate sexual contact, there is the possibility that body fluids can be exchanged between partners. Pathogens can pass from an infected partner to an uninfected partner through openings in the skin. The passage of these pathogens can cause infections.

2. Engaging in open-mouth kissing with a person infected with HIV

During open-mouth kissing, small traces of blood from one person's mouth might get into small cuts, tears, or sores in another person's mouth. According to the Centers for Disease Control and Prevention, to date there has been one documented case of HIV infection through open-mouth kissing.

3. Sharing needles, syringes, or other injection equipment for injecting drugs

An **injecting drug user** is a person who injects illegal drugs into the body with syringes, needles, and other injection equipment. Persons who share syringes, needles, and other injection equipment are at risk for becoming infected with HIV. When a person infected with HIV injects drugs, droplets of blood containing HIV might remain in the syringe or on the needle or injection equipment. A second person who shares a needle, syringe, or other injection equipment to inject drugs might get HIV-infected blood into his or her body. Then this person will be infected with HIV. Any person who has intercourse (penile-vaginal, penile-anal, or oral-genital) with an HIV-infected injecting drug user might become infected.

4. Sharing a needle to make tattoos or to pierce ears or other body parts

Droplets of HIV-infected blood might remain on the needle when a person infected with HIV uses a needle to make a tattoo or to pierce ears or other body parts. The droplets of HIV-infected blood might be invisible to the eye. A second person who shares the needle might get the HIV-infected blood into his or her bloodstream and become infected with HIV.

5. Sharing a needle and mixing blood in a ceremony to become a blood sister or blood brother

The ceremony to become a blood sister or blood brother involves two or more persons pricking their fingers to draw a droplet of blood. Then the fingers of the persons involved are placed together to mix blood. The sharing of the needle and the mixing of blood are risk behaviors. HIV-infected blood from one person might enter the bloodstream of the other person.

6. Having contact with the blood or other body fluids, mucous membranes, or broken skin of a person infected with HIV

HIV multiplies in the bloodstream. People who handle the body fluids of a person infected with HIV risk having HIV enter their bodies through small cuts or tears on the skin or through splash in the eyes. Touching the mucous membranes or broken skin of a person infected with HIV might result in contact with exposed blood vessels. HIV-infected blood can enter the bloodstream through small cuts or tears on the skin. People who share something such as a razor or toothbrush that contains droplets of HIV-infected blood may be at risk for being infected with HIV. HIV might enter their bodies through small cuts or tears in the mucous membranes or skin.

7. Having a blood transfusion with blood or blood products infected with HIV

In the United States, the FDA controls blood donations, blood donor centers, and blood labs. All donors are screened. After donation, blood is tested for HIV. In the United States, the risk of HIV infection from having a blood transfusion has been decreased to nearly zero due to screening.

However, people traveling to countries other than the United States should inquire about the safety of the blood supply.

8. Having a tissue transplant from a person infected with HIV

In the United States, screening and testing procedures have reduced the risk of being infected by human tissue transplants. Potential donors for all human tissues must be tested for HIV. They also must be screened to determine if they have engaged in risk behaviors and to check for symptoms of HIV infection. Imported tissues must be accompanied by records showing that the tissues were screened and tested. If no records are available, tissues are shipped under quarantine to the United States. People having tissue transplants outside the United States should check screening and testing procedures.

9. Being born to a mother infected with HIV

Perinatal transmission is the transfer of an infection to a baby during pregnancy, delivery, or breastfeeding.

During Pregnancy

A pregnant female who is infected with HIV can transmit HIV to her developing baby through the umbilical cord. Tiny capillaries in the umbilical cord allow oxygen and nutrients to pass from the mother to her developing baby. Waste products including carbon dioxide pass from the developing baby into its mother's bloodstream for elimination from her body. Babies born to mothers infected with HIV might or might not be infected with HIV.

During Childbirth

A pregnant female who is infected with HIV can transmit HIV to her baby during childbirth. During labor and delivery, small cuts or tears might occur on the baby. HIV might enter microscopic openings on the baby's body and enter the baby's bloodstream. A pregnant female infected with HIV can greatly reduce this risk by taking AZT during pregnancy. **AZT**, or **zidovudine**, is a drug that slows down the rate at which HIV multiplies.

During Breastfeeding

Breast milk has been established as a source of HIV infection in some babies. A mother who is infected with HIV transmits HIV to her baby through the colostrum or breast milk (NIAID, 1999c).

Tests for HIV Infection

Persons who have engaged in risk behaviors and/or risk situations for transmission of HIV and persons who have symptoms of HIV infection should be tested for HIV. There are at least two important reasons why. First, persons who test positive for HIV infection benefit from getting early medical care. Second, persons who test positive for HIV should protect others from possible HIV infection. This section of the chapter includes a discussion of diagnostic tests for HIV and HIV status.

Diagnostic Tests for HIV

ELISA, or **enzyme-linked immunosorbent assay**, is a blood test used to check for antibodies for HIV. If an ELISA test is positive, it is repeated to confirm the results. If two or more ELISA tests are positive, a Western blot test is given. **Western blot** is a blood test used to check for antibodies for HIV and to confirm an ELISA test. It is more specific and takes longer to perform. Tests are available that can use blood, oral fluids from the mouth, or urine to detect HIV antibodies. The **Orasure Western blot** is a test for HIV in which a tissue sample is collected using a cotton swab between the gum and cheek. Because many people do not like to get their finger pricked or have a blood sample drawn, more people may agree to be tested with this newer test. Used together, ELISA and Western blot are correct more than 99.9 percent of the time. **Amplicor HIV-1 monitor test** is a test that measures the level of HIV in the blood. Higher levels of HIV in the blood can be correlated with an increased risk that HIV infection will progress to AIDS and can help patients and physicians make treatment decisions.

The FDA has approved use of a few home collection kits for HIV antibody testing. A **home collection kit for HIV antibody testing** is a kit that allows a person to take a blood test sample at home, place drops of blood on a test card, mail the card to a lab, and call a toll-free number for the results of the test. The blood sample contains a personal identification number that the caller gives when using the toll-free number for the test results. If the person tests positive, a counselor discusses the results with the person over the telephone. Many health care professionals are concerned about people being told over the telephone that they have tested positive for HIV infection. Adolescents who need to be tested for HIV infection should talk to their parents or guardian and decide together where to have testing and get results.

HIV Status

HIV status is a term used to describe whether or not a person has antibodies for HIV present in the blood. **HIV positive** is a term used to describe a person whose test results indicate the presence of HIV antibodies in the blood. **HIV negative** is a term used to describe a person whose test results do not indicate the presence of HIV antibodies in the blood. It is possible for a person to have a false negative test for HIV. A false negative test is a term used to describe a person who is infected with HIV but whose test results do not indicate the presence of HIV antibodies in the blood.

The development of HIV antibodies usually occurs within three months after HIV infection. Thus, a person who has an ELISA test during the first months after HIV infection might have a false negative test. In rare cases, it can take up to six months for a person infected with HIV to test HIV positive.

People who engage in high risk behaviors such as being an injection drug user, engaging in male-to-male intercourse, or having multiple sex partners need to be tested and regularly retested for HIV status. This testing is necessary because of the false sense of security they might have if they test HIV negative. They might test

HIV negative with the ELISA test because antibodies have not yet developed at the time they were tested. Only by retesting will they know their HIV status for certain. While waiting to be retested, people who engage in high risk behaviors should refrain from engaging in risk behaviors that might infect other people with HIV.

In some states, people who are HIV positive and know their HIV status, but do not tell others with whom they are sexually intimate, can be held accountable. They can be fined or incarcerated for not telling a sexual partner that they are HIV positive.

People who test HIV positive should receive counseling. Counseling can help people who are HIV positive examine their options. They might examine possible options for obtaining medical, social, and emotional support. And they might examine resources available to pay for treatment.

Progression of HIV and AIDS

In Western countries, the median time period between being infected with HIV and developing AIDS is about 10 years. However, this time period differs among people who are infected with HIV. Some people might develop AIDS and die within a few months after HIV infection occurs. About 5 percent of people infected with HIV remain asymptomatic for 12 or more years (NIAID, 1999a). This section of the chapter discusses the initial signs and symptoms of HIV infection and progression to the opportunistic infections associated with AIDS.

Initial Signs and Symptoms

Many people infected with HIV do not experience initial signs and symptoms. Other people might exhibit a mononucleosis-like illness that might last only a few days. The most prominent symptom is lymphadenopathy. **Lymphadenopathy** is the presence of swollen lymph glands. Other symptoms might include a fever, sore throat, skin rash, diarrhea, loss of appetite, and night sweats. These signs and symptoms might disappear and be followed by an asymptomatic period. **Asymptomatic** is being without signs and symptoms. During the asymptomatic period, people infected with HIV might feel healthy, but HIV continues to destroy their helper T cells. Also, people infected with HIV can infect others even when they are asymptomatic.

After the initial asymptomatic period, people infected with HIV might experience a number of symptoms. Lymphadenopathy might recur and last for a period of three months. The lymph glands in the head and neck, groin, and armpits might be swollen and painful. Other symptoms include fatigue, frequent and persistent yeast infections (oral and vaginal), persistent skin rashes, flaky skin, pelvic inflammatory disease that does not respond to treatment, and short-term memory loss (NIAID, 1999b).

Diarrhea and wasting syndrome also are common. **Wasting syndrome** is an unexplained loss in body weight of more than ten percent of the total body weight. Night sweats and a high fever of up to 106 degrees Fahrenheit are not uncommon. HIV is attacking the nervous system.

Opportunistic Infections

According to the Centers for Disease Control and Prevention, a person infected with HIV has AIDS when he or she has 200 or fewer helper T cells per microliter of blood or has an opportunistic infection. An **opportunistic infection** is an infection that develops in a person with a weakened immune system. The risk factors for opportunistic infections include a reduced number of helper T cells and an increased viral load. Viral load refers to the amount of HIV in the bloodstream. Antiretroviral therapy helps reduce the incidence of opportunistic infections. However, not all persons infected with HIV respond to antiretroviral therapy (AMA, 1997). Therefore, many opportunistic infections continue to affect people infected with HIV and people who have AIDS (Table 7.4). It is important to note that it is the opportunistic infections and diseases that cause death, not AIDS itself. However, AIDS usually is listed as the cause of death on death certificates. This section of the chapter includes a discussion of several opportunistic infections.

Table 7.4   **Opportunistic Infections**

Protozoan Infections		
	Important Points	**Signs and Symptoms**
Pneumocystis carinii pneumonia	Caused by protozoan, although there is some thought it may be better classified as a fungus. Pulmonary disease caused by PCP occurs in 65%–85% of individuals with AIDS	Fever and cough Pneumonia
Toxoplasmosis	Intracellular protozoan infection Invades the host cell and multiplies Cats are a primary host Can be transmitted to a fetus by placental transfer	Fever, headache, mental status changes, and seizures Lesions on the brain—detectable by MRI scans
Cryptosporidiosis	Caused by protozoan that enters the digestive system	Frequent heavy, watery diarrhea accompanied by cramps and weight loss
Isosporiasis	A protozoan infection	Profuse watery diarrhea and weight loss

Viral Infections		
	Important Points	**Signs and Symptoms**
Cytomegalovirus Infection	A virus in the herpes group Can be latent and then become active Transmitted by contact with infected body fluids	Retinitis that can threaten sight Decreased visual acuity Hormonal imbalance Nausea
Herpes Simplex Virus Infection	Primary or recurrent mucocutaneous disease Common among HIV-positive persons	Enlarging and painful throat and genital ulcerations Fever and nausea
Varicella-Zoster Infection	Can infect organs inside the body Can affect the eyes and throat	Skin lesions
Epstein-Barr Virus Infection	Diagnosis is based upon presence of lesions May involve central nervous system	Oral hairy leukoplakia Lesions do not scrape off of tongue

Mycobacterial Infections		
	Important Points	**Signs and Symptoms**
Mycobacterium Avium Disease	Can be found in soil, water, and wild animals Can be acquired through inhalation or ingestion	Fever, weight loss, sweats, and cough Signs and symptoms are more serious than TB among persons who do not have AIDS
Mycobacterium Tuberculosis	Has increased in incidence along with AIDS Common among persons who have AIDS and live in urban areas	Similar to those of tuberculosis

Fungal Infections		
	Important Points	**Signs and Symptoms**
Candidiasis	Organisms are thin-walled yeast cells Can be found on skin and female genital tracts	Oral thrush and vaginitis White patches on oral mucosa and tongue
Cryptococcosis	An encapsulated yeast May be found in pigeon feces	Attacks central nervous system Impaired mental status and seizures

Cancers		
	Important Points	**Signs and Symptoms**
Kaposi's Sarcoma	Most common type of cancer in persons with AIDS Affects 15%–20% of homosexual males who have AIDS	Purple, raised skin lesions Appears on lower and upper extremities and face Lesions are painless
Non-Hodgkin's Lymphoma	Occurs in advanced HIV infection Affects 2%–3% of persons who have AIDS	Affects central nervous system Headache, fever, and seizures

Source: Kessler, Harold A., Bick, Joseph A., Pottage, John C., and Benson, Constance A. *Disease-a-Month, AIDS: Part II.* Volume XXXVIII, No. 10, October, 1992.

Candidiasis

Candidiasis is an STD caused by the fungus, *Candida albicans.* It is commonly called a yeast infection. Symptoms of candidiasis depend upon the tissue that is infected. **Thrush** is an overgrowth of the yeast *Candida* in the mouth, esophagus, and vagina. White, painful patches form in the mouth. There is a mesh of white lines or curdlike material on the sides of the tongue. It can be wiped away and leaves a surface that might bleed. The white, painful patches might spread down the esophagus making it difficult to swallow. Females might develop a severe yeast infection in the vagina. It is very difficult to treat.

Shingles

Shingles is an infection that produces a severely painful skin eruption of fluid-filled blisters. It is caused by herpes zoster, the virus that causes chickenpox. The initial infection might be in the form of chickenpox. Then the virus enters the spinal or cranial nerves and remains latent there. Shingles occurs when the virus is reactivated. Reactivation occurs when the body's immunity is compromised. This is why shingles might occur in people who have AIDS.

Hairy leukoplakia

Hairy leukoplakia is an opportunistic infection characterized by the presence of white patches on the surface of the tongue. Hairy leukoplakia might sometimes be thought to be cancer because its signs are similar. Unlike some other infections, hairy leukoplakia is found only on the tongues of people who have AIDS.

Pneumocystis carinii pneumonia

Pneumocystis carinii **pneumonia**, or **PCP**, is a form of pneumonia that results from a weakened immune system. The symptoms include fever, shortness of breath, and a dry cough. These symptoms usually present themselves over a period of several weeks. Sulfa drugs have been used to treat persons who have PCP. However, with recurring bouts of PCP, the sulfa drugs lose their potency.

Tuberculosis

Tuberculosis is a contagious, potentially fatal, bacterial infection of the lungs. The transmission of HIV worldwide has accelerated the resurgence of tuberculosis. Up to one-third of persons infected with HIV and living in developing countries die from tuberculosis (WHO, 1997). The World Health Organization estimates that by the end of this century there will be 1.4 million new cases of TB associated with HIV infection (WHO, 1996). Unlike other opportunistic infections, TB presents major concerns because it can be transmitted through the air. This means health care workers are at risk if they care for a person with AIDS who sneezes, coughs, or expectorates.

In the early stages of TB, a person infected with HIV has the same signs and symptoms as other persons who have tuberculosis and are not infected with HIV. These signs and symptoms include weight loss, night sweats, fever, and coughing. When a person is in the late stages of AIDS, the signs and symptoms of tuberculosis might differ. The signs and symptoms might mimic other opportunistic infections such as those for PCP. Tuberculosis might cause inflammation of the heart tissue, bones, and joints. Several drugs are being tested as treatment for people infected with HIV who have tuberculosis.

Cytomegalovirus

Cytomegalovirus, or **CMV**, is a virus in the herpes group. CMV is a common virus that recurs in many people. CMV is very serious in people who have AIDS. Signs and symptoms include infection of the retina of the eyes, resulting in increased "floaters" in the eye and possible blindness. The adrenal glands might be affected resulting in hormonal imbalance. There are no drugs to cure CMV. CMV can cause death in people who have PCP (AMA, 1997).

Kaposi's sarcoma

Kaposi's sarcoma, or **KS**, is a type of cancer that is a common opportunistic infection in people who have AIDS. Signs and symptoms include the presence of pink, purple, or brown tumors and lesions. The lesions might appear on the arms and legs. Eventually, they spread to the linings inside the body. KS is difficult to control once it has spread to the linings inside the body. Chemotherapy might be initiated, but any chance for successful treatment is limited.

AIDS dementia complex

AIDS dementia complex is a loss of brain function caused by HIV infection. Gradually, people who are infected with HIV experience diminished ability to think and move. Signs of AIDS dementia complex include forgetfulness, personality changes, and loss of coordination. As the condition worsens, persons become more and more confused. They suffer severe memory loss and lose the ability to perform simple, routine tasks.

Treatment for HIV Infection and AIDS

To date, there is no cure for HIV infection and AIDS. Treatment focuses on slowing the progression of the virus by keeping the immune system healthy and taking drugs. Early treatment is critical in slowing the rate at which HIV multiplies. This, in turn, delays the progression of HIV to AIDS. This section of the chapter will include a discussion of keeping the immune system healthy, drugs used as treatment for HIV infection and AIDS, and universal precautions for health care workers.

Keeping the Immune System Healthy

Persons infected with HIV and/or living with AIDS should practice healthful behaviors. By doing so, they keep their immune system healthy. This helps slow the progression of HIV infection and AIDS.

Avoid alcohol, tobacco, and other harmful drugs.

Alcohol, tobacco, and other harmful drugs impair the immune system. This makes it easier for HIV to destroy helper T cells and for opportunistic infections to develop.

Practice stress management skills.

Too much stress reduces the number of helper T cells. Too much stress can interfere with rest and sleep.

Get enough rest and sleep.

The body needs rest and sleep to replenish its energy level. The immune system requires energy to fight opportunistic infections. HIV will replicate faster and destroy the immune system more quickly if a person is fatigued.

Reduce exposure to ultraviolet radiation.

Some evidence shows that exposure to ultraviolet radiation increases the ability of HIV to replicate. HIV will replicate faster and destroy the immune system more quickly.

Obtain medical advice before receiving a vaccine.

Some vaccines contain live viruses. Persons who have a weakened immune system might not be able to ward off the harmful effects the virus might produce.

Protect against infection spread by animals.

People who have AIDS might get infections transmitted by animals. They should avoid contact with stray animals. They should wash their hands with soap and water after touching animals. They should not kiss their pets. They should avoid contact with an animal's feces. Cat feces are a source of toxoplasmosis. Toxoplasmosis is an infection that resembles mononucleosis but might cause extensive damage to the brain, eyes, skeletal and cardiac muscles, liver, and lungs. Cats can be tested for toxoplasmosis. Persons infected with HIV should avoid cleaning a litter box or should wear disposable gloves and a mask to reduce the risk of infection. Cats also are a source of other infections. Rough play with cats might result in scratches or bites that result in severe infections. All wounds caused by cats should be washed immediately (AMA, 1997).

Make wise food choices.

Persons infected with HIV and living with AIDS should avoid foods that might be contaminated. They should avoid eating raw and undercooked eggs including raw eggs used to prepare hollandaise sauce, mayonnaise, and creamy salad dressings. They should avoid or reheat ready-to-eat foods such as hot dogs and cold cuts to reduce the risk of listeriosis. Listeriosis is an infection that produces meningitis and endocarditis. Persons infected with HIV and living with AIDS should wash fruits and vegetables carefully. They should avoid eating raw fish such as sushi. They should eat meat and poultry that is prepared well done to avoid bacterial infections.

Limit travel to areas of the world with a safe water supply.

Travel outside the United States might put persons infected with HIV and living with AIDS at risk. In some countries, people get sick from drinking the water.

Drugs Used As Treatment for HIV Infection and AIDS

The Food and Drug Administration has approved many drugs for treatment of HIV infection.

- **AZT**, or **zidovudine**, is a drug that slows down the rate at which HIV multiplies.

- **ddI** is a drug that slows the rate at which HIV multiplies.

- **Aerosolized pentamidine isethionate** is a drug to prevent *Pneumocystis carinii* pneumonia (PCP).

- **Interferon alfa-2a** and **Interferon alfa-2b** are drugs to treat Kaposi's sarcoma (KS).

- **Protease inhibitors** are antiviral drugs that decrease the amount of HIV in the blood and increase the helper T cell count.

- **Highly active antiretroviral therapy**, or **HAART**, is a combination of protease inhibitors and two reverse transcriptase inhibitors, such as AZT and ddI.

- **Fusion inhibitors** are a class of drugs that reduce the presence of HIV in persons with viral strains that are resistant to combination therapy.

The first group of antiretroviral drugs to be approved included AZT and ddI. Laboratory studies showed that AZT prevented replication of HIV in an early stage, suggesting that AZT could slow the spread of HIV and delay the onset of opportunistic infections. However, AZT only partially blocked the replication of HIV. This led clinicians to stop treating HIV infection with AZT only and to combine drug therapies (Blakeslee, 1997).

A newer treatment is HAART. Known as the triple drug "cocktail," it has helped transform the progression of AIDS into a chronic manageable disease. Some of the people who have AIDS who switched to the cocktail have experienced a normal helper T cell count and restored functioning of the immune system (FDA, 1999). Despite the effectiveness of HAART, there are some concerns about its use. These include its high cost, the possible consequences of poor treatment management, potential side effects, and reduced prevention strategies. Correct treatment management is essential because the use of protease inhibitors might result in new HIV strains that are resistant to treatment.

Possible side effects from HAART include diabetes and abnormalities in fat distribution. The improved sense of well-being for persons taking HAART might result in reduced prevention strategies. The viral load is reduced substantially, but it is not eliminated. Therefore, persons infected with HIV who take HAART might not have symptoms, but they are capable of infecting others with HIV (FDA, 1999).

Research has established that HAART therapy might be used for all babies, children, and adolescents being treated with drugs for the management of HIV infection. During the first six weeks of life, babies exposed to HIV can be treated only with AZT. However, babies who are diagnosed with HIV while being treated with AZT should be given combination therapy (FDA, 1999). A class of drugs called fusion inhibitors might reduce the presence of HIV in persons who have viral strains that are resistant to combination therapy (FDA, 1999).

Universal Precautions for Health Care Workers

Universal precautions are steps taken to prevent the spread of disease by treating all human blood and certain body fluids as if they contained HIV, hepatitis B virus (HBV), and other pathogens. Table 7.5 identifies universal precautions for health care workers. Universal precautions are standard in the health care industry. However, surveillance of AIDS cases through the end of 1998 reported that 5.1 percent of more than 400,000 AIDS cases occurred among health care workers. Since then, the Centers for Disease Control and Prevention also has reported the deaths of 75 percent of the health care workers who had AIDS including physicians, surgeons, nurses, dental workers, and paramedics (CDC, 1999).

Table 7.5
Universal Precautions for Health Care Workers

1. Wear disposable vinyl or latex gloves when handling blood and certain body fluids;
2. Do not wear disposable gloves more than once;
3. Wash hands well with soap and water after the gloves have been removed;
4. Wear a face mask or protective goggles to prevent exposure to contaminated splash;
5. Wear a face mask or shield when giving first aid for breathing;
6. Do not wear a face mask or shield more than once without disinfecting it;
7. Cover any body cuts, scrapes, and rashes with plastic wrap or a sterile dressing;
8. Do not eat or drink when giving first aid;
9. Do not touch your mouth, eyes, or nose while providing care;
10. Wear a gown or apron to protect clothing from contaminated splash;
11. Wash immediately if contaminated with blood or body fluids;
12. Dispose of used syringes and needles immediately and properly.

The Prevention Model for Educating About HIV Infection and AIDS

Since the first multidisciplinary session at the VIII International Conference on AIDS in Amsterdam in July 1992, the number of AIDS cases has declined while the number of people living with HIV infection has grown. The effectiveness of triple drug therapy has increased the need to educate people about the presence of HIV in the population and the continued risk for becoming infected. Since the long-range effectiveness of triple drug therapy is not yet known, more aggressive prevention efforts aimed at reduction of risk behaviors are necessary (CDC, 1998). This section of the chapter focuses on *The Prevention Model for Educating About HIV Infection and AIDS* (Table 7.6).

Table 7.6 The Prevention Model for Educating About HIV Infection and AIDS

Step 1: Teach the Facts

Step 2: Send a Clear Message: Choose Abstinence from Sex and Monogamous Marriage

Step 3: Promote Self-Respecting Behavior

Step 4: Emphasize Prevention: Use Resistance Skills

Step 5: Encourage Honest Talk Within Relationships

Step 1: Teach the Facts

Step 1 in *The Prevention Model for Educating About HIV Infection and AIDS* involves teaching these facts about HIV infection and AIDS:

- How the body defends itself from pathogens
- How the body responds to HIV
- Risk behaviors and risk situations for HIV infection
- Tests for HIV infection
- Progression of HIV Infection and AIDS
- Treatment for HIV Infection and AIDS
- Universal precautions

Step 2: Send a Clear Message: Choose Abstinence from Sex and Monogamous Marriage

Step 2 in *The Prevention Model for Educating About HIV Infection and AIDS* involves sending a clear message about family values. Adolescents should be encouraged to practice abstinence from sex now and, when and if they choose to marry, to commit themselves to monogamous marriage. A **monogamous marriage** is a marriage in which both people remain sexually faithful to one another. Chapter 3 examines the advantages of practicing abstinence from sex during adolescence. Chapter 8 includes a discussion of the advantages of monogamous marriage.

Step 3: Promote Self-Respecting Behavior

Step 3 in *The Prevention Model for Educating About HIV Infection and AIDS* involves helping adolescents develop self-respecting behavior. **Self-respect** is a high regard for oneself because one behaves in responsible ways. Health education traditionally has focused on "how to be healthy." Yet some adolescents who know "how to be healthy" participate in risk behaviors and risk situations. Therefore, teaching the facts or "how to be healthy" is not enough. Adolescents must believe they have "something to be healthy for."

Adolescents who have self-respect believe they are worthwhile and have "something to be healthy for." As a result, they choose self-respecting behavior. **Self-respecting behavior** is treating oneself in healthful and responsible ways.

Adolescents who have self-respect and choose self-respecting behavior delay gratification and resist peer pressure. They practice the following ten life skills:

1. They practice abstinence from sex.

HIV is transmitted during intimate sexual contact in which body fluids are exchanged. High risk behaviors for HIV infection include having multiple sex partners and having sex with a prostitute.

2. They do not engage in open-mouth kissing with a person infected with HIV.

Although the risk is low, the CDC warns against open-mouth kissing because of the possible contact with infected blood.

3. They change their behavior if they have been sexually active.

Adolescents who have been sexually active need tests for HIV and other STDs. They should begin to abstain from sex right away. Then they should make an appointment with a physician or go to a clinic and be tested for HIV and other STDs. Their parents or guardian can give them help and support.

4. They plan to have a monogamous marriage if they should marry in the future.

Sexual fidelity protects both partners from sexual transmission of HIV provided neither partner was infected with HIV at the time of marriage.

5. They do not inject illegal drugs.

Sharing a needle, syringe, or injection equipment for injecting drug use is a risk behavior for HIV infection.

6. They agree to change their behavior if they have injected illegal drugs.

Adolescents who have injected illegal drugs need tests for HIV and other STDs. They should stop injecting illegal drugs right away. Then they should make an appointment with a physician or go to a clinic and be tested for HIV and other STDs. Their parents or guardian can give them help and support.

7. They do not share a needle to make a tattoo or to pierce ears and other body parts.

Adolescents should be encouraged to obtain permission from their parents or guardian before getting a tattoo or piercing ears and other body parts. Sharing a needle to make a tattoo or to pierce ears or other body parts is a risk behavior. These procedures should be performed by qualified people who use sterile equipment.

8. They follow universal precautions.

Universal precautions are steps taken to prevent the spread of disease by treating all human blood and certain body fluids as if they contained HIV, HBV, and other pathogens. Adolescents should be taught the following:

Always follow universal precautions when you have contact with the blood, other body fluids, mucous membranes, or broken skin of a person. Wear disposable vinyl or latex gloves and wash your hands with soap and water or waterless antiseptic hand cleanser after removing them. Use a face mask or shield with a one-way valve if you perform first aid for breathing emergencies. Avoid touching objects that have had contact with a person's blood. Do not eat or drink anything while performing first aid. Do not touch your mouth, eyes, or nose while performing first aid.

9. They ask their dentist if he or she autoclaves dental pieces and accessories.

To **autoclave** is to sterilize with steam under pressure. The FDA, CDC, and American Dental Association recommend autoclaving.

10. They inquire about the safety of having a transfusion or tissue transplant if they should need one.

The FDA regulates blood donations in the United States. All donors are screened and checked against a list. After donation, blood is tested for HIV, hepatitis B, and syphilis. As a result, there is little risk of HIV infection when having a blood transfusion in the United States. If a person travels to countries other than the United States, he or she should inquire about the safety of the blood supply. Imported tissues must be accompanied by records showing the tissues were screened and tested.

Step 4: Emphasize Prevention: Use Resistance Skills

Step 4 of *The Prevention Model for Educating About HIV Infection and AIDS* includes a discussion of

ways to prevent HIV infection. Adolescents should be encouraged to resist pressure to participate in risk behaviors and risk situations for HIV infection. **Resistance skills** are skills that help a person say NO to an action or to leave a situation. Some classroom time should be devoted to practicing resistance skills.

- Have students role play situations in which they are pressured to engage in risk behaviors and risk situations for transmission of HIV. Have students practice saying NO with self-confidence. Then have students give their reasons for saying NO to risk behaviors and risk situations for transmission of HIV. Continue the role play by escalating the pressure. Have students repeat their reasons for saying NO to risk behaviors and risk situations for transmission of HIV. During the role play situations, students should use nonverbal behavior to match their verbal NO.

- Have students identify situations they should avoid because they will be pressured to participate in risk behaviors and risk situations for transmission of HIV.

- Encourage students to avoid peers who might pressure them to participate in risk behaviors and risk situations for transmission of HIV.

- Have students tell ways they might influence others to avoid risk behaviors and risk situations for transmission of HIV.

Step 5: Encourage Honest Talk Within Relationships

Step 5 in *The Prevention Model for Educating About HIV Infection and AIDS* involves teaching adolescents the importance of honest talk. **Honest talk** is the straightforward sharing of feelings. This prepares adolescents for adulthood when they might choose to marry and plan a family. It is important to know if a potential marriage partner has engaged in risk behaviors or risk situations that might have resulted in HIV infection.

Asking questions and providing accurate information when asked questions help protect personal health and the health of others. In addition, honest talk also prevents lawsuits. The courts have prosecuted people who knew they were infected with HIV but did not disclose their HIV status to a sex partner.

Preparing adolescents for the future includes helping them examine the risk behaviors and risk situations other people choose.   For someadolescents, high school will be the last educational experience in which they discuss sexuality, reproductive health, risk behaviors and risk situations for HIV infection, and the consequences of HIV infection.

References

American Medical Association. 1997. "HIV/AIDS Information Center—SPHS/IDSA Guidelines for the Prevention of Opportunistic Infections in Persons Infected with Human Immunodeficiency Virus: A Summary." *MMWR Recommendations and Reports*. 44/RR-8 (June). Accessed 7/1999. http://www.4journals.com.

Blakeslee, Dennis, Ph.D. 1997. "JAMA HIV/AIDS Information Center—The Failure of AZT—An Enzyme Bottleneck." *Newsline* (August). Accessed 7/1999. http://www.4journals.com.

Centers for Disease Control and Prevention. 1999. "Surveillance of Health Care Workers with HIV/AIDS." *CDC Update* (March). Accessed 7/1999. http://www.cdc.gov.

——. 1998. "Combating Complacency in HIV Prevention." *CDC Update* (July). Accessed 7/1999. http://www.cdc.gov.

Food and Drug Administration. 1999. "Attacking AIDS with a 'Cocktail' Therapy." *FDA Consumer Magazine* (July–August). Accessed 7/1999. http://www.fda.gov.

Kessler, H. A., Bick, J. A., Pottage, J. C., and Benson, C. A. 1992. "AIDS—Part II." *Disease-a-Month* 38 (10): 720.

National Institute of Allergy and Infectious Diseases. 1999a. "HIV/AIDS Statistics." *Fact Sheet* (May). Accessed 7/1999. http://www.niaid.nih.gov.

——. 1999b. "Basic Information About AIDS and HIV." *AIDS Vaccine Site* (March). Accessed 7/1999. http://www.niaid.nih.gov.

——. 1999c. "HIV Infection and AIDS." *Fact Sheet* (June). Accessed 7/1999. http://www.niaid.nih.gov.

World Health Organization. 1997. "World TB Day 1997—Let's Get Serious About the Dual Epidemics." *Global Tuberculosis Programme*. Accessed 7/1999. http://www.who.int.

——. 1996. "Global Tuberculosis Programme—World TB Day 1996—Fact Sheet N104 (Revisited)." Article Online (March). Accessed 7/1999. http://www.who.int.

8 Marriage, Parenthood, and Family Living

Content for Teachers *Only*

A Word from the Authors

A **commitment** is a pledge or promise that is made. In a relationship, a commitment involves a pledge or promise that is made to another person regarding the relationship. The marriage commitment is a promise to love and nurture a spouse for a lifetime. The wedding ceremony is a public promise to honor the marriage commitment. The parenthood commitment is a promise to love and nurture a child for a lifetime. Ideally, couples should discuss their intentions about parenthood before they marry. A commitment to marriage and to parenthood cannot be taken lightly. After all, the family is the institution that serves as the foundation of society. As teachers ponder the true meaning of success and commit themselves to teaching skills that promote success, it is important to place education about marriage and parenthood at the top of the list! This chapter provides background information on marriage, parenthood, and family living. It emphasizes the risks associated with adolescent marriage and parenthood.

Marriage

More than 90 percent of Americans marry at least once. Those who marry have high expectations. Marriage can provide intimacy and companionship as well as feelings of well-being. Marriage can provide a framework for sustaining the family unit and for having and raising children. This section of the chapter will examine factors to predict success in marriage, intimacy in marriage, the marriage commitment, and risks associated with adolescent marriage.

Factors to Predict Success in Marriage

There are ten factors that help predict whether or not a marriage will be a success.

1. *Age.* Couples who marry during adolescence have a high divorce rate. Couples who marry when they are in their twenties or older usually enjoy more success. Marriage partners who are similar in age are at similar stages in development and have greater success in marriage than marriage partners with large age differences.

2. *Reasons for marriage.* Couples who marry to love and nurture one another are more likely to succeed at marriage than those who marry to escape a difficult and unhappy family situation, to get even with parents, or to escape loneliness.

3. *Length of the relationship and engagement.* Longer relationships and engagements provide the opportunity for couples to examine their relationship. Longer relationships usually are associated with success in marriage.

4. *Similar attitudes about children and childraising.* Discussing attitudes toward having and raising children contributes to a successful marriage. Couples should discuss these issues before they are married—if and when they want children, how many children they want, and how they intend to raise children. Couples should work through any disagreement on these issues before they are married.

5. *Similar interests.* Although marriages can sustain differences in interests, the old saying "opposites attract" might not apply when predicting success at marriage. Differences provide stressors that must be worked out. Studies report that couples who are similar with regard to race, ethnic background, religious beliefs, socioeconomic

status, education, and intelligence are more likely to succeed at marriage.

6. *Commitment to sexual fidelity.* Physical intimacy in marriage provides a closeness and a feeling of security. Sexual fidelity is important in establishing trust. Couples who honor a commitment to sexual fidelity and who trust each other are more likely to succeed at marriage.

7. *Good character.* People who have good character make responsible decisions. They are self-disciplined. They are aware that their actions will affect the quality of their marriage.

8. *Parents' success at marriage.* People whose parents are divorced are more likely to become divorced themselves. This might be because they have not lived in a family in which parents resolved conflicts and maintained their marriage.

9. *Parental attitudes toward the potential marriage partner.* A marriage is more likely to succeed when a person's parents approve of the future spouse.

10. *Careful selection of a marriage partner.* A marriage is more likely to succeed when people are cautious when selecting mates. They should consider these factors that contribute to successful marriage when considering a partner.

Intimacy in Marriage

Intimacy is a deep and meaningful kind of sharing between two people. When people talk about intimacy in marriage, they might confuse sex with intimacy. While sex is an important part of intimacy in marriage, there are many other factors that create intimacy. There are many kinds of intimacy, but for a marriage to be sustained over the years, four kinds of intimacy are of particular importance. The four kinds of intimacy are philosophical, psychological, creative, and physical.

Philosophical intimacy is the sharing of beliefs and values. Marriage partners share how their beliefs influence their decisions as well as the values that determine day-to-day priorities. For example, one partner might value his or her

relationship with parents. As a result, spending holidays with parents is a priority to this partner. The other partner recognizes and respects this priority even though this particular value might not be as important to him or her.

Psychological intimacy is the sharing of needs, emotions, weaknesses, and strengths. Marriage partners share their needs, such as the need for a hug or the need to have someone who will listen. Marriage partners share and rejoice in their individual successes. They ask one another for support when a disappointment occurs. In a healthful relationship, there is a trading back and forth of strength and vulnerability, which is a sign of trust in a relationship (Herring, 1996). When married partners share weaknesses, they feel accepted rather than rejected. Psychological intimacy deepens through the years.

Creative intimacy is the sharing of efforts to accomplish tasks and projects. This kind of sharing goes beyond discussion and emotional responses. Marriage partners engage in many cooperative efforts. For example, they might work together to make their apartment or house a home. They might choose furniture together, plant a garden, and select wallpaper. Marriage partners might plan a vacation together. They might take lessons to learn a sport they enjoy together. Raising children also involves creative intimacy. Marriage partners plan activities in which they can participate with their children. They share child-raising responsibilities, such as discipline. For marriage partners to have creative intimacy, each partner must do his or her share of the work with a willing attitude. Marriage partners must agree on expectations and on who does what.

Physical intimacy is the sharing of physical affection. Physical intimacy includes a wide range of behaviors that express warmth and closeness. Marriage partners show physical affection when they touch, caress, hold hands, and kiss. Marriage partners express physical affection when they have sexual intercourse. To be physically intimate, marriage partners should be sexually attracted to each other. Each marriage partner should have a healthful attitude about sex. Each marriage partner benefits from the commitment of marriage. The commitment that the marriage partners make to each other provides a real sense of security to each partner. This enhances physical intimacy.

Potential marriage partners can assess the warmth and closeness that each partner feels for the other without having sexual intercourse. Sex before marriage does not predict sexual satisfaction during marriage. Sex before marriage does not involve a commitment, so there is no feeling of security.

The Marriage Commitment

Today, because of rising divorce rates, it seems wise to examine two important ways marriage partners can help ensure that their marriage will last.

1. Marriage partners must be committed to actions that honor their wedding vows.

2. Marriage partners must work together to master the developmental stages of marriage.

Wedding Vows

Marriage partners must be committed to actions that honor their wedding vows. When two people marry, they make promises called vows. This is what commitment is. There are two ways partners can view marriage. One view of marriage is commitment-motivated: "I will behave in my marriage in the ways I have promised." Another view of marriage is feelings-motivated: "I will behave in my marriage according to how I feel about my marriage at the moment."

Examine the differences between these two views of marriage and the potential consequences. A partner who is commitment-motivated behaves as he or she has vowed rather than as he or she happens to "feel" at the time. Suppose this partner does not "feel" like being supportive of the other person's needs but uses discipline in order to do so to honor the marriage commitment. Suppose this partner does not "feel" like being sexually faithful but uses discipline to say "no" to tempting situations. When a partner acts in these ways without feeling resentment, he or she indicates that the marriage commitment is a priority. These kinds of actions reinforce the marriage commitment.

Now examine the opposite type of marriage. Suppose a partner believes in a feelings-motivated marriage. This partner believes how he or she feels at any given moment determines whether or not he or she should keep the vows that were made. When this partner "feels" like loving the other partner at times during the marriage, the marriage thrives. But suppose, at times, the partner does not "feel" like being loving or being loved. The partner might not "feel" like being supportive or listening or being faithful. The partner decides to honor these sexual "feelings" rather than the promises made in the wedding vows. Habits that interfere with the marriage commitment begin to creep into the marriage. This partner acts on his or her feelings and is not supportive, doesn't listen, and is not sexually faithful. The consequences are loss of trust, loss of security, and loss of commitment.

Responsible actions cause good "feelings"; however, "feelings" might or might not cause responsible actions. No one can promise how he or she will feel for a lifetime. However, he or she can promise how he or she will act.

The Developmental Stages of Marriage

Marriage partners must work together to master the developmental stages of marriage. The **developmental stages of marriage** are five stages of marriage during which couples must master certain tasks in order to develop and maintain intimacy. The five stages and the tasks to be mastered in each stage are identified in The Major Tasks of the Five Stages of Marriage (Table 8.1). The appropriateness of the tasks within each stage depends on the ages of the married partners and the length of the marriage. The tasks are designed for people who marry in their twenties and stay married to the same person. People who marry much older or much younger might experience other stressors that affect the tasks. They might need to master tasks from different stages at the same time. These people might be working on tasks that are different from those of their peers who married in their twenties and stayed married.

Table 8.1   **The Major Tasks of the Five Stages of Marriage**

The First Stage: The First Two Years	The Second Stage: The Third Through the Tenth Years	The Third Stage: The Eleventh Through the Twenty-fifth Years	The Fourth Stage: The Twenty-sixth Through the Thirty-fifth Years	The Fifth Stage: The Thirty-sixth Year and On
The newly married couple overcome their idealistic notions of marriage and begin to form a family. The partners strive to:	The couple gain a realistic view of their marriage and of each other and must settle into dealing with their individual weaknesses and make an effort to avoid dysfunctional behaviors. Their goals are to:	The couple establish and maintain individual identity and deal with issues of forgiveness, aging, adolescent children, and intimacy. They recognize the need to:	The couple must master tasks from the first three stages that were not previously mastered, confront changes in sexuality, and grieve over their losses. They strive to:	The couple find new reasons for existing after the major life tasks of achieving financial security and nurturing their family have been completed; partners confront their feelings about death. They agree to:
• maintain individual identity at the same time as they form a family; • develop cooperation and reduce the need to control the other; • develop a sexual bond with the other that leads to a deeper intimacy; • develop an effective decision-making style; • recognize the difficulties in their parents' marriages and anticipate how those difficulties might affect their marriage.	• recognize and confront the weaknesses of both partners; • examine their relationship and avoid dysfunctional behaviors; • reaffirm their commitment to sexual intimacy, including sexual fidelity; • examine the influence of children on their marriage and agree upon child-raising methods.	• reexamine and maintain individual identity and develop mutual dependence; • recognize that each other will not be perfect; • forgive one another for shortcomings and mistakes; • confront the crisis of middle age, including aging, sexuality, job and financial security, and the struggle for individuality; • reevaluate and make a plan for maintaining and developing intimacy.	• reevaluate the tasks from the previous stages and determine if they have been successfully mastered; • recognize the physical changes that accompany aging and affect sexuality and rekindle romance; • grieve over losses such as the death of parents and children leaving home.	• prepare for retirement; • renew intimacy and develop ways to continue sexual intimacy; • prepare for death and for the death of the marriage partner; • accept death as a stage of life.

(Adapted from Minirth, et al. *Passages of Marriage*, 1991)

Risks Associated with Adolescent Marriage

One way to reduce the number of separations and divorces is to reduce the number of adolescent marriages. More than 75 percent of adolescent marriages end in divorce. There are many reasons why adolescent marriages do not succeed. Adolescents need to master the developmental tasks of adolescence before tackling the tasks that are appropriate for the five stages of marriage. Robert Havinghurst, a sociologist, identified eight developmental tasks of adolescence. A **developmental task** is an achievement that needs to be mastered to reach the next level of maturity. The following discussion explains why adolescent marriage interferes with reaching the next level of maturity necessary for a successful marriage.

Task 1: Adolescent marriage does not give adolescents enough time to develop healthful friendships with members of both sexes. During adolescence, adolescents need to have friendships with members of both sexes. They need to learn how to communicate and how to develop friendships. To do this, they must identify characteristics of people they admire. Examining issues such as trust, honesty, and loyalty is important. Having friendships with members of both sexes helps adolescents learn more about themselves, which is an important aspect of forming personal identity. Adolescents need to gain a sense of who they are. Marriage cuts short the time they need to develop friendships with members of both sexes. Adolescents who marry are less likely to have a support network of mature friends who will be helpful during the stressful first years of marriage.

Task 2: Adolescent marriage does not give adolescents enough time to become comfortable with their maleness or femaleness. Dating helps adolescents learn to respond to people of the opposite sex. Having the opportunity to date different people is very beneficial. Adolescents can test ways of interacting they have learned from their role models. They might become aware of harmful patterns in their behavior and the need for change. Adolescents who marry are robbed of the time they need to become comfortable with their maleness or femaleness. They pass up much of the fun that their peers have participating in social activities.

Task 3: Adolescent marriage does not give adolescents enough time to become comfortable with their bodies. Adolescent bodies are still growing and developing. Hormonal changes that accompany puberty cause new feelings as well as body changes. **Puberty** is the stage of growth and development when both the male and female body become capable of producing offspring. Adolescents might notice that their moods change. They need time to adjust to these changes in their emotions. They need time to become comfortable with changes in their bodies. Adolescents who marry might do so because they have a strong sexual attraction to one another. They might lack the skills needed to tell the difference between love and sexual attraction. As a result, they might make mistakes in selecting a marriage partner.

Task 4: Adolescent marriage does not give adolescents enough time to become emotionally independent from adults. One of the reasons adolescents are described as rebellious is that they challenge their parents or guardians. They might challenge their parents or guardians as a way to show their independence. At times, they still might want to be dependent on their parents or guardians, while at other times they want to break away from adult influence. This is normal. After all, adolescents are learning to be adults and preparing to run their own lives. During adolescence, they need the safety and security that parents and guardians provide. Parents or guardians help adolescents test their ways of becoming independent. Adolescents who marry are faced with adulthood without the safety and security of being parented themselves when they really need it. If adolescents marry and live with parents or guardians who continue in the parent role, they are unable to master one of the primary tasks of the first stage of marriage—to mold into one family with their partner.

Task 5: Adolescent marriage does not give adolescents enough time to learn skills for successful marriage and parenthood. As adolescents mature and complete different developmental tasks, they acquire skills they can use later when they marry and become parents. They need to develop effective communication skills to help them achieve intimacy in adulthood. They also need to develop conflict resolution skills to learn how to settle disagreements when they are married and become parents. Adolescents who marry do not have time to fully develop these and other skills necessary for marriage and parenthood.

Task 6: Adolescent marriage does not give adolescents enough time to prepare for a career. Adolescents are gaining skills and knowledge about themselves to help them prepare for a career. Getting an education should be a top priority. An adolescent's goal is to have the skills needed to get a job, be self-supporting, and be financially independent. Adolescents who marry usually have difficulty completing their education. When they try to get a job, they have difficulty competing with their skilled peers who remained in school. As a result, they earn less money. If they rely on parents or guardians for financial support, they are not able to achieve their own financial independence. Living with very limited income places stress on marriage.

Task 7: Adolescent marriage does not give adolescents enough time to have a clear set of values to guide their behavior. A **value** is a standard or belief. An adolescent's parents or guardians teach many values that help guide choices and behaviors. Adolescents begin to achieve emotional independence from their parents or guardians. As a result, they have time to take a second look at the values they have learned from their parents or guardians. They gain confidence when they move from "these are my parents' or guardians' values" to "these are my values." Adolescents who marry might do so before they are certain of their own values. They might marry someone who has different values.

Task 8: Adolescent marriage does not give adolescents enough time to understand and achieve socially responsible behavior. Adolescence has been described as the "me" stage. During early and middle adolescence, adolescents often focus on their own needs. They might spend much of their time thinking about their appearance, their social life, and their friends. In the next few years, this focus will change. They will look at the world around them and identify ways to be helpful. Adolescents who marry do not have the time to get involved in their community and help others. The demands of adolescent marriage take up all of their time.

Parenthood

The most important profession—being a parent—is the profession for which the least amount of education is provided. It is never too early to begin educating about parenthood and parenting skills. This section of the chapter discusses factors to consider before becoming a parent, the parent-child relationship, understanding growth and development, and the risks associated with being an adolescent parent.

Factors to Consider Before Becoming a Parent

A person's marital status and the quality of his or her marriage is an important consideration before choosing parenthood. A father and mother who are married and who love and respect one another provide the greatest benefit to children. Many children do not live with both of their parents. Perhaps a parent died or their parents are divorced. The parent with whom they live might be very loving and have good parenting skills. Some children live with both parents, but only one is loving and the other one is abusive. These kinds of situations change the structure of a family. The ideal situation is for children to live with two loving, married parents. There are three "Rs" to consider before becoming a parent.

R: The REASONS a person wants to have a child.

R: The RESOURCES a person will need to raise a child.

R: The RESPONSIBILITIES a person will have as a parent.

Table 8.2   **Reasons People Want to Become Parents**

1. To build up one's ego
   - To have a child who looks like me
   - To have a child who will carry on the family name
   - To have a child who will inherit the family business, money, or property

2. To compensate for something that is missing in one's life
   - To try to save one's marriage
   - To make up for one's unhappy childhood
   - To help one feel more secure as a male or female

3. To conform to what peers are doing or what others expect
   - To please one's parents or guardian
   - To do what one's peers are doing
   - To keep from being criticized for being childless

4. To love and to guide someone
   - To have the satisfaction of loving a child
   - To help a child grow and develop
   - To teach a child how to be responsible

(Adapted from Peck and Granzig. *The Parent Test,* 1978.)

Reasons to Become a Parent

The reasons for having children can be grouped into four categories. These four categories and examples from each appear in Table 8.2, Reasons People Want to Become Parents. Suppose a person chooses one or more of the first three reasons in Table 8.2. This person will focus more on his or her own needs than on the child's needs. Being ready for parenthood means being ready to focus on needs in addition to one's personal needs. The fourth reason, the desire to love and guide a child, is the best reason to become a parent.

Resources Needed for Parenthood

Suppose a married couple wants to purchase a car. The cost of the car and of various options for the car would be considered. If the purchase could not be financed, the decision to buy the car would have to be delayed. Financial resources also must be evaluated when a couple considers having a child. Some of the costs a couple might expect are the following:

- health and hospitalization insurance;
- prenatal care for the mother-to-be;
- maternity clothes for the mother-to-be;
- delivery and postpartum care for the mother and baby in a hospital or birth center or at home;
- hospitalization for the baby;
- pediatrician's hospital visits, regular well-baby checkups, required immunizations, sick visits, medications;
- nursery furnishings—bassinet, crib, bedding, linens, bathtub, stroller, highchair, chest, car seat, infant carrier, toys;
- clothing for the baby;
- diapers and/or a diaper service;
- formula, food, and vitamins for the baby;
- baby supplies—bottles, swabs, baby wipes, diaper rash ointment, tissues, powder, baby soap and shampoo, oil;
- the possible need for child care or day care.

For many families, there is the additional cost of lost income during the mother's maternity leave. One of the parents might cut back to part-time work or stop working altogether after the birth of a baby. The first year of childrearing is very expensive. These financial considerations are a must when deciding if and when to become parents.

Responsibilities of Parenthood

When people become parents, they take responsibility for raising a child. Whether the child is a newborn or adopted, there are certain promises parents should make. These ten promises are listed in Table 8.3 in The Parent Pledge to a Child.

Table 8.3 **The Parent Pledge to a Child**

1. I will set aside a quantity of time as well as quality time to spend with you.

2. I will learn about your age-appropriate development so that I can have realistic expectations for you.

3. I will teach you rules to ensure your health and safety.

4. I will give you love and affection.

5. I will teach you with a positive attitude, avoiding criticism.

6. I will teach you my moral and ethical values.

7. I will teach you self-discipline and self-control with effective discipline, not child abuse.

8. I will provide economic security for you.

9. I will recognize that you have rights, and I will respect those rights.

10. I will raise you in a stable, secure family that is free from substance abuse (free from the abuse of alcohol, marijuana, and other drugs).

The Parent-Child Relationship

Parenting involves having more than loving feelings for a child. To **parent** is to guide a child to responsible adulthood. Being a responsible and caring parent is not an easy task. It involves developing intimacy with a child, understanding growth and development, helping a child develop self-discipline and self-control, and selecting responsible people as childsitters.

Developing Intimacy with a Child

Developing intimacy with a child is one of the responsibilities of parenting. The early lessons a child learns from parents with regard to intimacy influence the child's ability to become intimate with others.

Philosophical intimacy. Responsible parents teach their children beliefs and values. They discipline their children when they act in wrong ways. This helps children know how to behave. It helps them develop good character.

Psychological intimacy. Responsible parents are trustworthy and accepting. Their children can talk to them about sensitive topics. Responsible parents encourage and support their children when their children have disappointments.

Creative intimacy. Responsible parents give their children their first feelings of teamwork. They ask their children to help with tasks in the home. They share fun projects.

Physical intimacy. Responsible parents express physical affection for children in appropriate ways. Babies who receive soft touches and are spoken to, held, and looked at frequently by their mothers and fathers in the first few days of life cry less and smile and laugh more than babies who are not treated in these ways. Children who are loved learn to feel secure in ways of expressing affection. They are able to receive affection from others.

Understanding Growth and Development

Responsible parents help their children develop emotional, social, verbal, intellectual, and motor skills. They understand that age-appropriate skills help keep their children safe from harm. They understand emotional development and reassure their children if they are fearful or anxious. They obtain medical help for their children when needed. Table 8.4 highlights the growth and development of a child from birth through six years.

Table 8.4	**Growth and Development of a Child: Ages Birth to Six Years**

Birth to Six Months

Emotional and Social Skills A newborn cries to get attention and stops crying when held or when hearing a comforting voice. At about two months, a baby begins to recognize parents using the body senses of sight, smell, and sound. The baby becomes interested in others, particularly in their facial expressions and eyes. Thumbsucking is common and is used to reduce tension. Beginning at about four months, the baby enjoys laughing and smiling and makes mouth sounds to attract attention.

Verbal Skills Shortly after birth, the baby makes different crying sounds to indicate needs such as diaper change or feeding. First sounds are usually coos and chuckles followed by distinct vowel sounds such as "oo" and "aah." At about four to five months, the baby verbalizes with one-syllable sounds such as "da."

Intellectual Skills At three or four months, the baby explores the environment by looking at objects and people. Body parts such as fingers and toes and feet are intriguing and the focus of play. The baby begins to recognize his or her bottle and familiar toys such as a rattle and begins kicking and reaching toward them.

Motor Skills The newborn baby keeps his or her head turned to the side when lying on his or her back. When held by someone, the baby is able to lift his or her head. Beginning at two months, the baby can turn over from stomach to back. The baby enjoys kicking his or her legs and holding a rattle placed in the hand. As the baby gets older, he or she will be able to raise his or her head and chest using the arms and the hands. The baby can sit up with support and can roll completely over.

Continued on pages 159, 160, 161, and 162.

Table 8.4 continued

Six Months to Twelve Months

Emotional and Social Skills A six-month-old baby becomes attached to the primary caregiver and will express anxiety when separated. The baby differentiates between those who are familiar and those who are strangers. A baby recognizes his or her name by nine months and will turn toward someone saying his or her name. A favorite pastime becomes playing games such as peekaboo. The baby will hold his or her arms out toward the primary caregiver when wanting to be held.

Verbal Skills Beginning at six months, a baby will babble "da-da" and "ma-ma" without knowing these refer to parents. The baby has an understanding of some words. He or she will look toward a familiar object when the parents say the word, such as bottle. The baby understands the word "no" and may shake his or her head to indicate no. The baby begins to imitate and respond to parents. When parents say "bye-bye," the baby may wave or repeat "bye-bye." A ten-month-old baby will seek parent's attention by saying "ma-ma" or "da-da."

Intellectual Skills The baby learns by touching, shaking, and throwing objects. Toys that can be shaken and those that make noise are of particular interest. When these are dropped, the baby will look for them. When someone makes a noise, the baby looks to see who it was. A nine-month-old baby associates a name with a person or pet. When asked, "Where's Daddy?" the baby will look for daddy. The baby enjoys picture books. He or she likes to play with stacked toys that can be taken apart and restacked. The baby likes to imitate the primary caregiver and may offer his or her bottle to someone.

Motor Skills A six-month-old baby enjoys standing with the help of someone to support his or her arms or hands for balance. The baby might jump or bounce in this position. He or she can now keep a sitting position without being supported. At seven months, the baby creeps by slowly moving his or her belly. This is followed by crawling on the hands and knees. The baby begins self-feeding and feels successful when holding his or her bottle and using fingers to put food into the mouth. Soon the baby begins pulling himself or herself to the standing position by holding someone's hand or a piece of furniture. The baby begins to move around by holding on to something and then something else. The baby takes a few steps by himself or herself.

Twelve Months to Eighteen Months

Emotional and Social Skills The baby begins to communicate needs and feelings by making sounds and pointing. When parents do not understand, the baby seems frustrated. The baby initiates interaction with others. He or she may kiss or hug parents spontaneously and give toys to others. The baby wants to be the center of attention and might resist parents at times. Familiar routines such as bathing or storytelling at bedtime are comforting. A soiled diaper is uncomfortable and the baby will indicate that he or she needs to be changed by some movement or words. The baby enjoys communicating with parents and will laugh and smile.

Verbal Skills The baby begins to communicate using words. At twelve months, the baby usually knows only four or five simple words such as "ma-ma" and "da-da," but by fifteen months the baby knows ten to twelve words. The baby may say one-word sentences such as "milk" to convey meaning. Voice fluctuation is used to convey meaning such as a firm "no-no." The baby also might make up words to use for familiar objects. At about eighteen months, the baby is able to respond to some communication. The baby might respond to the command, "Please give me the toy." When parents read a picture book to the baby, the baby shows understanding by pointing to the correct object or person upon hearing a familiar word.

Intellectual Skills At twelve months, the baby is fascinated with the ways in which things fit together. Toys that open and close keep his or her attention. The baby also is fascinated by shaped boxes in which he or she fits simple pieces into similarly shaped holes. The baby places toys right side up. He or she continues to explore objects with the hands and mouth. Playing in sand and mud is fascinating. At about sixteen months, the baby begins to imitate life-like situations such as pretending to talk on the phone.

Table 8.4 continued

Motor Skills At twelve months, the baby takes several steps. By fourteen months, the baby has mastered walking and will sit down when beginning to lose balance. The baby is challenged by getting up and down the stairs using all fours and then walking up and down with the help of parents. The baby enjoys push toys such as a toy vacuum for housework or toy lawnmower for yardwork. These provide the opportunity to imitate parents. The baby takes off socks and pulls at clothes to imitate dressing. Hand-eye coordination is developing. The baby throws a ball, but with little control. He or she also begins to scribble with large crayons. Gradually the scribbling becomes an attempt to make the same mark over and over again.

Eighteen Months to Two Years

Emotional and Social Skills The toddler becomes very independent, yet at the same time wants to be assured of parents' or a caregiver's whereabouts. He or she enjoys playing with a parent and is possessive of parents and of his or her toys. When siblings want a parent's attention or to play with toys, the toddler may show frustration and disapproval with tantrums.

Verbal Skills The baby begins to speak in sentences of two words to convey meaning. For example, he or she might say "bye-bye da-da." The number of vocabulary words used increases to more than fifty. This is a time of rapid learning of new words. Reading picture books and playing rhyming games help the toddler learn words. Singing familiar songs is also valuable. The toddler is aware of his or her name and uses it to refer to himself or herself.

Intellectual Skills This is a time of rapid intellectual growth. The toddler learns to name his or her body parts and points to them to show what he or she knows. Books that help the toddler learn to name things are helpful. For example, the toddler will learn the names of farm animals when the parent reads a picture book. The toddler increases his or her memory. When a familiar person is not present, a toddler has a mental image of this person. The toddler has a sense of self and recognizes himself or herself in a picture with others.

Motor Skills The toddler usually is ready for toilet training. He or she has gained the coordination necessary to zip and unzip zippers, put on shoes, and wash hands. He or she can walk backwards as well as forward, can jump up and down, and imitate a simple dance. The toddler enjoys climbing on furniture and playground equipment. He or she is able to hold a crayon correctly and has more agility when making marks with it.

Two Years to Two and One-Half Years

Emotional and Social Skills The toddler is in what is referred to as the "terrible twos." He or she resists parents, is very demanding, and yet does not know what he or she wants. Temper tantrums are at their peak. The toddler wants to be close and secure with parents and at the same time wants to be independent. He or she is very demanding and aggressive with siblings and yet is very meek when strangers appear. The toddler may express fears about objects and/or people.

Verbal Skills The toddler is rapidly increasing his or her vocabulary and by two and a half years may know more than 250 words and use sentences containing four or more words. The toddler begins to differentiate between the present and the past using words such as "has" and "had" appropriately. He or she follows conversations more closely and listens intently to television.

Intellectual Skills The toddler asks many questions at this age. He or she wants to grasp cause and effect. He or she tends to think about behavior before acting. The toddler conceptualizes both time and amount. He or she is very good at matching shapes to fit in puzzles and identifying colors. When listening to familiar stories, songs, or nursery rhymes, the toddler will join in indicating words recalled.

Motor Skills The toddler begins to dress himself or herself with help from parents. With help, he or she practices grooming skills such as brushing teeth and using the toilet. The toddler resists being carried and instead wants to walk and/or run by himself or herself. He or she can stand on tiptoes

Table 8.4 continued

and can stand on one foot for several moments without falling. The toddler can begin other ways of playing. He or she can catch a ball and pedal a tricycle. The toddler can use the fine agility of the hands and fingers. He or she begins to cut with scissors and to draw curved lines. The toddler enjoys holding a book and turning the pages while a parent reads.

Two and One-Half Years to Three Years

Emotional and Social Skills The child becomes more independent and does not experience discomfort when parents or a caregiver leaves. The child likes to be helpful and wants to help with simple chores. He or she understands simple rules, such as "Please put toys away after playing." The child imitates parents and gives orders to other children and siblings. Rather than having a temper tantrum, the child expresses anger directly toward siblings and other children. At this age, the child can participate in simple group games.

Verbal Skills The child expands his or her vocabulary. He or she can provide his or her complete name, recite nursery rhymes and familiar stories, and use a vocabulary of more than 900 words. Most of the time, the child makes sense when he or she speaks. He or she asks many questions and wants detailed answers that include the "what," "where," and "when" of the situation. The child wants to participate in "reading" and will share stories from familiar books.

Intellectual Skills The child shows further comprehension and can be given directions that include two to three commands. His or her attention span increases. The child may engage in play with dolls and stuffed toys and have conversations with these objects.

Motor Skills The child's motor skills improve. He or she can draw a circle with a large crayon and can cut paper in half with scissors. The child can hold a pencil correctly. He or she can jump without falling and climb the stairs putting one foot on each step. The child can throw with more force and kick a ball with more force by bringing his or her leg back to gain momentum. The child can dress himself or herself with help. He or she can use silverware and can pour liquids from a container to a glass. He or she might use the toilet without help.

Three Years to Four Years

Emotional and Social Skills The child is very self-centered, yet he or she begins to pay attention to other people's needs and feelings and begins to share. He or she begins to form friendships with other children. The child may also have an imaginary friend. This friend may take the blame for anything the child feels he or she has done wrong. During this period, the child shows much affection toward the parent of the opposite sex. He or she may indicate that one day he or she will marry this parent.

Verbal Skills The child experiments more with language and as a result might make mistakes on verb tenses and double negatives. He or she improves listening skills. At this age, the child begins to practice new words that are introduced by the parent.

Intellectual Skills The child will imitate phrases used by parents and other adults. He or she enjoys using the hands and fingers and likes fingerpainting, building sand castles, and putting together puzzles. The child is able to make some decisions by himself or herself. He or she likes to engage in play in which he or she plays a role such as mother, father, or doctor. When asked, the child will use his or her fingers to indicate how old he or she is.

Motor Skills The child becomes more capable of activities that require coordination such as turning a somersault, doing a sit-up, and/or doing jumping jacks. He or she is more adept at games that require hopping on one foot or jumping a very low rope. The child can more easily run fast and climb on play equipment.

Table 8.4 continued

Four Years to Five Years

Emotional and Social Skills The child demonstrates a rapid growth in emotional and social skills. He or she becomes more self-assured, tries new things, and may brag about new accomplishments. The child shows more interest in others, demonstrates good manners, and selects other children to be good friends. He or she enjoys playing outdoors and can do so without much supervision as long as there are clear guidelines. At this age, the child is especially curious about sexuality. He or she wants to know where babies come from and why boys' and girls' genitals are different. Children typically play doctor at this age. They also emulate parents and show attitudes toward sex roles.

Verbal Skills The child talks quite a bit. He or she can use between 1,500 and 2,000 words and can understand many more. Often a child tells detailed stories using new words. The child is particularly interested in death and in violent actions. He or she asks many questions that begin with "how" and "why." It is particularly important to give clear answers because the child listens carefully. At this age, it is normal for a child to repeat what he or she has heard and to use words that he or she believes will shock parents.

Intellectual Skills The child rapidly gains skills such as counting to 30, matching words with related pictures, and reading a clock from the position of the clock's hands. He or she begins to understand time and seasons and can anticipate what seasons are accompanied by important holidays.

Motor Skills The child has the motor skills to care for himself or herself. These include the ability to lace shoes, comb hair, brush teeth, and wash hands and face. He or she demonstrates proficiency in motor skills by being able to make U-turns and dodge obstacles when riding a tricycle. Hand-eye coordination improves and the child can throw and catch a ball in both hands. The child also begins to draw objects more realistically. Human figures at first take the form of stick figures and then the child gradually begins to add hair, fingers, eyes, etc. The child can fold paper as directed and can use scissors to cut. At this age, the child can be taught to print words and is especially interested in learning to print his or her name.

Five Years to Six Years

Emotional and Social Skills The child is able to differentiate among emotions and to share what he or she is feeling with others. When feeling anxious, the child may revert to thumbsucking or might choose behaviors such as kicking the foot or biting nails. The child is eager to please parents and/or teacher and knows which behavior is pleasing and which is disturbing. He or she becomes more socially conscious and will care for younger sisters and brothers as well as family pets. The child is aware of the need for sharing in interactive play.

Verbal Skills The child enjoys using an expanded vocabulary. He or she enjoys reading familiar books, memorizing the stories, and telling them to parents/teacher. He or she is eager to learn the meaning of new words and to use the words. The child is also interested in spelling simple words such as "dad," "mom," and "cat." He or she is fascinated with the telephone and may want to talk to grandma or grandpa for an extended length of time.

Intellectual Skills The child can be taught safety skills such as being able to print his or her name and state his or her correct street address. He or she begins to demonstrate skills necessary for reading, such as being familiar with the alphabet and recognizing certain words in books. Games involving recall and matching reinforce skills. The child knows which hand is dominant. He or she can select the appropriate colors when completing a picture. During play, the child is very creative in making up stories and situations.

Motor Skills The child continues to improve at grooming skills. He or she can tie shoelaces and dress himself or herself without help. He or she has the finer skills needed to cut food into bite-size pieces when eating and to carry a glass full of milk without spilling it. Eye-hand coordination continues to improve. The child can put yarn through the eye of a needle and can complete a sewing card. He or she can hop on one foot, playing games such as hopscotch. He or she can catch a bounced ball, dodge out of the way of a ball, and throw a ball to a specific place. The child can do simple calisthenics such as toe touches and jumping jacks.

Helping a Child Develop Self-Discipline and Self-Control

Responsible parents teach their children self-discipline and self-control (Table 8.5). **Discipline** is training that develops self-control. There are different disciplinary techniques.

Preventive discipline is a disciplinary technique in which a parent explains correct behavior and the consequences of wrong behavior. Suppose a child gets a new bicycle for his or her birthday. The parent explains his or her expectations for the child's behavior. For example, the parent says he or she expects the child to put the bicycle away after riding it. The parent further explains that if the bicycle is not put away, the child will not be permitted to ride the bicycle for three days.

Behavior modification is a disciplinary technique in which positive rewards are used to encourage desirable behavior and negative consequences are used to stop undesirable behavior. For example, a parent might praise a child for remembering to put away his or her bicycle. The parent might plan a special reward. On the other hand, the parent wants to change undesirable behavior. The child who leaves the bicycle in an unsafe place might not be permitted to ride the bicycle for three days.

Logical consequences discipline is a disciplinary technique in which the child is allowed the opportunity to experience the results of undesirable behavior so that he or she will want to change the undesirable behavior. An example might be a child who looks for inappropriate web sites on his or her home computer. The parent disciplines the child by taking away computer privileges for a period of time and must be supervised on the computer after that.

Physical punishment is a disciplinary technique in which an act is used to teach a child not to repeat undesirable behavior. Slapping and spanking are examples of physical punishment. Slapping and spanking appear to be helpful in only two instances. First, when a child is young, a parent might slap the child's hand to prevent a behavior that might harm the child. For example, the parent might slap the child's hand if he or she tries to put a fork in an electrical outlet. Second, a parent might use a very light slap on the young child's buttocks or hand to get the child's attention. The slap should not be severe enough to hurt or injure the child.

Spanking is usually ineffective in teaching long-range self-discipline and self-control. For example, consider the two examples mentioned above—the child who did not put away his or her bicycle and the child who looked for inappropriate web sites. If a child is spanked for either of these behaviors, the physical punishment creates fear rather than changing the undesirable behavior. The other disciplinary techniques that were discussed are more effective than physical punishment in teaching the desired behavior. Spanking usually creates hostility and anxiety in children.

Selecting Responsible Persons as Childsitters

A **childsitter** is a person who provides care for infants and children with the permission of a parent or guardian. A responsible childsitter is

- observant and alert;
- calm during emergencies;
- able to follow instructions;
- trained in first aid;
- able to recognize safety hazards;
- able to communicate with adults;
- able to communicate with young children;
- able to supervise young children;
- patient; and
- friendly.

Before parents place a child in the care of a childsitter, an interview should take place and references should be requested and scrutinized. This is the time for direct questions and answers

---

Table 8.5 **Responsible Parents Teach Children Self-Discipline and Self-Control**

Responsible parents

1. set limits for their children,
2. are consistent in their actions,
3. are neither too strict nor too permissive,
4. discuss acceptable behavior with their children,
5. listen to their children and pay attention to their feelings.

---

and also an opportunity for the parents' instincts to come into play.

Parents might prepare a sheet of vital information for their childsitter and leave it in a convenient place, such as directly over the telephone. The list should include the following:

1. The parents' names, home address, and telephone number. This may seem unnecessary, but in an emergency, childsitters have been known to "blank out" while trying to give this critical information over the telephone.

2. The telephone numbers of the family doctor, the police department, and the fire department.

3. The name, address, and telephone number where the parents can be reached.

4. The names and telephone numbers of nearby neighbors to be contacted in an emergency. (Consent should be obtained from neighbors.)

5. The telephone number and name of a relative or close friend to be used as a backup.

6. The time parents expect to return. If there is any change in plans, and parents are going to be late, they should be sure to let the childsitter know. There might be people the childsitter will need to notify so they won't worry about him or her (Child Development Institute, 1999a).

Each family and situation are different, but there are general rules and procedures that should be covered in any childsitting situation.

1. Is the sitter allowed to use the telephone for personal calls? It is often wise to specify the length of telephone calls in case parents will need to reach home.

2. Is the sitter allowed to invite a friend for company or to work on a homework assignment? What if the friend is of a different sex? More than one friend? A group of friends on a childsitting assignment usually should not be permitted.

3. What are the rules about answering the door? A childsitter shouldn't let anyone he

or she doesn't know into the apartment or house, no matter who he or she claims to be. The childsitter should contact the parents if someone comes to the door.

4. What are instructions on how to answer the telephone? If the parents are expecting an important call, they might describe how they would like it handled. Should the sitter take a message? Ask the caller to call back?

5. What time should the child go to bed? Should a night light be turned on? Is the door to his or her room left ajar? Does the child have special stuffed animals he or she likes to take to bed?

6. Does the child have homework? If so, is the childsitter willing and able to help?

7. Is the childsitter expected to do any household chores, such as washing dishes? If so, is extra pay involved?

8. Are there any special words the child uses for certain items or activities? If so, these should be jotted down for the childsitter. (Child Development Institute, 1999a)

Many adolescents offer their services as childsitters. Adolescents who offer their services as childsitters should be prepared. They can use The Childsitter's Check Sheet (Table 8.6). They can develop the skills identified in The Childsitter's List of Skills for the Care of Infants and Toddlers (Table 8.7). They can develop the skills identified in The Childsitter's List of Skills for the Care of Young Children (Table 8.8).

Risks Associated with Being an Adolescent Parent

An **unnecessary risk** is a chance that is not worth taking after the possible outcomes are considered. There are risks associated with being a baby born to adolescent parents. There are risks associated with being a pregnant adolescent and an adolescent mother. There are risks associated with being an adolescent father. A discussion of these risks follows Table 8.6, Table 8.7, and Table 8.8.

Table 8.6   **The Childsitter's Check Sheet**

A responsible childsitter is prepared. It is a childsitter's responsibility to obtain the information needed before childsitting. Adolescents who might wish to childsit should use The Childsitter's Check Sheet to make sure they are prepared.

1. I have taken a first-aid course, and I am familiar with universal precautions.
2. I have taken the childsitting course offered by the American Red Cross or by another organization.
3. I have a parent's or guardian's approval to childsit.
4. I have checked to make sure I am available to childsit.
5. I have discussed with the parents or guardians the hours I will childsit and the payment.
6. I have arranged for transportation to and from the job.
7. I have met the child or children and learned their name(s) and age(s).
8. I have familiarized myself with the house and where everything is.
9. I have discussed pets and rules for them.
10. I have discussed what privileges I will have in regard to such things as the telephone, food, and visitors.
11. I know the address and telephone number of the home where I will be childsitting.
12. I know what time to arrive.
13. I know what time the parents or guardians will be home.
14. I know the address and telephone number of the parents or guardians.
15. I know whom to contact if the parents or guardians cannot be reached.
16. I know emergency telephone numbers, including police, fire department, and poison control.
17. I know if 9-1-1 service is available.
18. I know the name and telephone number of the child's physician.
19. I know the child's mealtime(s).
20. I know the child's naptime(s) and bedtime(s).
21. I know what health problems the child has.
22. I know what medications the child needs.
23. I know what allergies the child has.
24. I know what the child is and is not allowed to do.
25. I know what the child's favorite activities and toys are.

Table 8.7 ### The Childsitter's List of Skills for the Care of Infants and Toddlers

Responsible childsitters need certain skills to provide responsible care for an infant or toddler. Childsitters should consult The Childsitter's List of Skills for the Care of Infants and Toddlers to make sure they have the skills needed.

Know what to do when a baby cries.

Responsible childsitters determine why the baby is crying. Ask yourself if the baby is too warm, too cold, hungry, teething, or ill. Is the diaper wet or soiled? Does the baby want company or attention? Then, take the appropriate action.

Know what to do if you think an infant or toddler is sick.

Call the parents or guardians. Tell them the signs and symptoms you have observed. Follow the parents' or guardians' instructions.

Know how to diaper a baby.

Follow universal precautions and wear rubber gloves. Have everything ready that you will need—diaper, baby wipes or a washcloth, ointment, water, cotton balls, safety pins (for cloth diapers). Take off the soiled or wet diaper and clean the baby's bottom with a baby wipe or damp washcloth. Place the baby on the new diaper and bring the bottom of the diaper up between the baby's legs. First, bring one side across the front. Then, bring the other side across the front and fasten the diaper. Dispose of the soiled diaper appropriately.

Know how to bathe a baby.

Give the baby only a sponge bath if the baby still has an umbilical cord. Otherwise, bathe the baby in a plastic baby tub or in a sink. Warm the room, have ready water, a soft washcloth, and baby soap. Fill the baby tub or sink with several inches of warm water. Then, place the baby on a flat surface and undress him or her. Place the baby in the water, supporting the baby's head and keeping the baby's face out of the water. Wash the entire body and rinse the baby with clean, warm water from a cup. When you are finished, wrap the baby up in a towel to dry. Make sure the baby's head is covered.

Know how to give a baby a bottle.

Ask the parents or guardians for instructions. Follow the instructions for preparing the bottle. Pick up the baby and hold him or her in your arms to feed. Make sure the bottle nipple is always full of milk.

Know how to burp a baby.

Put a towel or diaper on your shoulder and pick up the baby. Hold the baby upright with his or her head resting on your shoulder. Support the baby's head and back. Pat the baby's back gently with your other hand. Or, lay the baby stomach down on your lap. Place one hand on the baby's bottom and use the other hand to gently pat his or her back. Or, sit the baby on your lap. Support the baby's chest with one hand. Gently pat the baby's back with your other hand.

Know how to pick up and hold a baby.

Slide your arm under the baby's body. Cradle the baby against your body. Or, support the baby against your shoulder. Support the baby's head with one hand. Also support the shoulders. Be very careful when touching the two soft spots on the top of the baby's head.

Table 8.8   **The Childsitter's List of Skills for the Care of Young Children**

Responsible childsitters need certain skills to provide responsible care for young children. Childsitters should consult The Childsitter's List of Skills for the Care of Young Children to make sure they have the skills needed.

Know what to do when the child is afraid. Talk quietly with the child and show the child that you are not afraid. Find out exactly why the child is afraid. If an object frightens the child, move it out of the child's sight. Give the child a favorite toy or stuffed animal to hold.

Know what to do if a child has a tantrum. Ask the parents or guardians ahead of time how to respond to a tantrum. Find out why the child is angry. Quietly and calmly tell the child that a tantrum is not appropriate or acceptable. Tell the child that you will not pay attention to his or her wants until the tantrum stops. If it does not stop in a short amount of time, tell the child that he or she will have a time out. A time out is a calming-down period of time. Tell the child that he or she can play again after becoming calm.

Know how to help a young child learn. Smile at the child. Talk to and play games with the child. Use safe toys and games that interest the child.

Know what to do when a child refuses to go to bed. Find out if the child does not want to be alone or is afraid of the dark. Read the child a story to help him or her relax. Or sit and quietly talk to the child for a short period of time. Assure the child that you will be close by and will check him or her very soon.

Know what to do if you think a young child is sick. Call the parents or guardians. Describe the signs and symptoms you have observed. Follow the parents' or guardians' instructions about what steps to take.

Risks Associated with Being a Baby Born to Adolescent Parents

A discussion of adolescent pregnancy and parenthood often begins with the risks to the adolescent mother and father. But let's begin with the correct focus. A loving, caring, and responsible person considers the effect of his or her behavior on others. Adolescents are at risk for producing babies whose health status has been compromised.

An adolescent female's body is still developing and maturing. Her body needs adequate and balanced nutrition for proper growth. Many adolescent females do not have healthful habits. Since a developing baby relies on the mother-to-be for its nutrition, whatever the mother-to-be eats, smokes, or drinks gets into the baby's bloodstream. Even if an adolescent female changes her habits as soon as she knows she is pregnant, the developing baby has already relied on her until her pregnancy was confirmed. This means the baby might have been inadequately nourished for six to eight weeks or more. Most pregnant adolescents delay getting prenatal care and many do not receive any prenatal care. As a result, adolescent mothers are at risk for having a baby with a low birth weight. A **low birth weight (LBW)** is a weight at birth that is less than 5.5 pounds (2.5 kilograms). Low birth weight babies are more likely to have physical and mental problems than do babies of normal birth weights. The costs of providing neonatal and postnatal health care for LBW infants are three times higher on average than the costs for normal birth weight babies (Crouse and Larson, 1992). The incidence of low birth weight among babies born to adolescent mothers is more than double the rate for adult mothers, and the neonatal death rate (within 28 days of birth) is almost three times higher among babies born to adolescent mothers (AAP, 1999d).

The health habits of an adolescent father-to-be also affect a developing baby. The habits of the father-to-be affect the quality of the hereditary material contained in his sperm. Some substances that can damage a male's sperm are related to poor lifestyle choices such as smoking, drinking alcohol, and taking other drugs. Lead, pesticides, benzene, and anesthetic gases also can damage sperm. Males who plan to be fathers should avoid these substances for at least three months prior to conception. Since most adolescent pregnancies are not planned, an adolescent female should understand that the habits of a father-to-be might seriously affect the quality of his sperm.

Babies born to adolescent parents are at risk for having parents with inadequate parenting skills. Parenting takes knowledge and skill. Every parent has a 24-hour job. However, an adolescent has responsibilities that also include school, his or her social development, and other learning experiences. Having a baby in addition to these responsibilities can be overwhelming to an adolescent. In addition, as an infant becomes a toddler, a firm value system is required in order to discipline the toddler. This is hard work and many adolescent parents become frustrated with the process. This explains why the incidence of child abuse is very high among adolescent parents. Child abuse is a problem among adolescent parents because they tend to lack adequate parenting skills and are under the additional stress caused by poverty and lack of a job or a low-paying job (AAP, 1999d). A child deserves to be raised by parents equipped to handle frustration and who will not be abusive.

Risks Associated with Being a Pregnant Adolescent and Adolescent Mother

Pregnancy places many demands on a female's body. The demands on a female who is an adolescent are even greater because her body is still growing. A pregnant adolescent is at risk for developing anemia and toxemia of pregnancy. **Anemia** is a condition in which the oxygen-carrying pigment in the blood is below normal. If a pregnant adolescent is anemic, the developing baby will be seriously affected because the baby depends on the mother's blood for oxygen and nutrients. **Toxemia of pregnancy** is a disorder of pregnancy characterized by high blood pressure, tissue swelling, and protein in the urine. If severe, toxemia of pregnancy can progress to seizures and coma.

Pregnant adolescents and adolescent mothers are at risk in other ways. Pregnancy and parenthood disrupt education and career plans. Most adolescent females who become pregnant unexpectedly postpone finishing their education and therefore initially do not have sufficient skills and training to adequately support themselves and their children (Ikemoto, 1995). Dating opportunities are limited for an unmarried adolescent raising a child. An unmarried adolescent mother does not have as much time or money as her peers. Males might not want to get involved with a female who has a baby.

Risks Associated with Being an Adolescent Father

Adolescent fathers have the responsibility of providing for the care of their babies. Some states have passed laws that require adolescent fathers to pay child support until their child is 18. Adolescent fathers are similar to adolescent mothers; they are more likely than their peers to have poor academic performance, higher high school drop-out rates, limited financial resources, and reduced income potential (AAP, 1999d). Many adolescent fathers drop out of school to earn money to provide child support. They are less likely to graduate from high school or college than their peers who did not become fathers when they were adolescents. Adolescent fathers usually do not marry the mothers of their children. And, pregnancy is a key factor in terminating relationships, as "more than 85 percent of all males who impregnate adolescent females will eventually abandon them." (Ikemoto, 1995). If adolescent males do marry the mother of their child, they often divorce within five years. As a result, adolescents who become fathers spend little time with their children. Only one in three fathers who live apart from their children visit their children at least once a week. Many adolescent fathers do not know how to be involved in their children's lives, and many current programs in adolescent pregnancy and parenting are exploring ways to reach and engage adolescent fathers in the lives of their children (AAP, 1999d). Children do not thrive when there is a lack of contact with their father. Fathers also can feel the emptiness of not being close to their children.

© 2001 Everyday Learning Corporation

Family Relationships

A **family** is a group of people who are related by blood, adoption, or marriage. **Family relationships** are the connections a person has with family members, including extended family members. **Extended family members** are the members of a family in addition to parents, brothers, and sisters. A person's family relationships influence his or her behavior. The parents or adults who raise a person have the greatest influence on that person. Parents or other adults who "parent" a person serve as role models for relationships. This section of the chapter will examine ideal family relationships and dysfunctional family relationships.

Ideal Family Relationships

An **ideal family** is a family that has all the skills needed for loving, responsible relationships. The ideal family is the family that is visualized as being perfect. Although few families are perfect, it is important to recognize what is ideal. Then, children have a model toward which they can work.

In an ideal family, parents teach children the following twelve skills: self-respecting behavior, healthful attitudes toward sexuality, effective communication skills, a clear sense of values, responsible decision making, ways to resolve conflict, effective coping skills, ways to delay gratification, ways to express affection and integrate love and sexuality, how to give and receive acts of kindness, a work ethic, and respect for authority.

Self-Respecting Behavior

Self-respecting behavior is treating oneself in healthful and responsible ways. Self-respecting behavior is an outgrowth of the ways children were treated by the adults who raised them from birth. If they received love and felt accepted, then they began to feel good about themselves. If they were well cared for, they learned how to take care of themselves. As a result, they learned how to treat themselves in healthful and kind ways. They learned behaviors that would not cause harm to themselves. Children raised in an ideal family also learn the difference between

self-respecting and self-centered behavior. **Self-centered behavior** is actions that fulfill personal needs with little regard for the needs of others. Self-centered behavior does not contribute to healthful family relationships.

Healthful Attitudes Toward Sexuality

Sexuality is the feelings and attitudes a person has about his or her body, sex role, and relationships. A person's sexuality is influenced from birth, when children are born either male or female. Parents or guardians talk to children about their bodies and shape their attitudes about being either male or female. Parents influence their children's sex role. **Sex role** is the way a person acts and the feelings and attitudes he or she has about being male or female. Sex roles also include the expectations people have for males or females. Parents and guardians help their children learn about sex roles. For example, a child might learn that it is acceptable for males as well as females to cry and share feelings. A child might learn that males and females differ but deserve equal respect. In an ideal family, parents or guardians discuss puberty with their adolescents. They explain the changes in feelings and emotions that accompany puberty. Their openness and sensitivity help adolescents learn how to accept their sexuality.

Effective Communication Skills

Communication is the sharing of emotions, thoughts, and information with another person. Children first learn to communicate in their families. Suppose a child's parents or guardians use I-messages to express feelings and listen carefully when the child speaks. Then, as the child begins to copy the parents' way of communicating, he or she develops skills in communicating with others. Suppose a child's parents or guardians know how to express anger, sadness, and disappointment in healthful ways. The child will learn healthful ways to express the same emotions. In an ideal family, children feel secure practicing communication skills and can use these communication skills in other relationships. Table 8.9 suggests Ways Parents Can Teach Their Children Effective Communication Skills.

Table 8.9 **Ways Parents Can Teach Their Children Effective Communication Skills**

- Listen carefully and with interest.
- Make and keep eye contact.
- Listen for the hidden messages in what your children are saying. What emotions are behind what they are saying?
- Show respect for your children's ideas and feelings. Stay away from hurtful teasing, blaming, belittling, and fault-finding.
- Use "I" messages when you talk. Avoid "you" messages and put-downs.
- Be honest.
- Pick good times and places for talking. If your children come home from school tired, let them rest and have a snack before you try to talk about what's on your mind. If you come home tired, take a rest. Choose a quiet, private area for talking.
- Praise or reward your children when they show good listening habits. They want to listen more carefully and follow through on what they are saying if they think you appreciate their efforts.
- Be fair as possible with your children. Use the same communication approach and style with every child. Sometimes the different make-up of each child might require altering what you say. But do not seem to play favorites or be more accepting of one child than another (AAP, 1999a).

A Clear Sense of Values

A **value** is a standard or belief. In an ideal family, parents or guardians teach their children values. For example, parents or guardians might value hard work, honesty, and close family relationships. They behave in ways that are consistent with these values. They work hard, are honest in their dealings with others, and spend time with members of their family. They discuss these values with their children. The children listen to what their parents say, and their behavior confirms what they say. Children observe their parents' everyday behavior. Children internalize their parents' values and behave in similar ways. When the children relate to others, they remember these family values. These values become the standard for what the children think and believe. They have a clear sense of values for the rest of their lives. **Manners** are rules of conduct and behavior.

Good manners reflect the values of the parents or guardians who raise children. Table 8.10 identifies Manners That Support Family Values.

Table 8.10
Manners That Support Family Values

Manners to protect privacy
- Do not open a closed door until you have knocked and waited for permission to enter.
- Do not go into anyone else's bureau, desk, box, or papers at home or anywhere else without his or her permission.
- Do not read anyone's mail or anything he or she has written (for example, a diary) unless permission was given.
- Do not discuss the private affairs of the family with outsiders (unless you need to talk to a trusted adult).

Manners for dining in a home
- Never reach for any food that is not right in front of you. Ask someone to pass it. And if you are passing something, do not help yourself along the way.
- Wait for food to cool if your food is too hot. Do not blow on it.
- Do not spit food out if you put something in your mouth that is too hot. Reach for your water and take a quick swallow.
- Do not talk with your mouth full.
- Bring your food up to your mouth rather than bending over to reach it.

Manners for dining in a restaurant
- Do not be upset if you spill something. It happens all the time. The waiter will clean it up.
- Do not use silverware if you drop it on the floor. Ask the waiter to replace it for you.
- Do not put packages or handbags on the table.
- Do not comb your hair at the table.
- Do not use a toothpick in public.

Manners for being a guest
- Do not go visiting unless you are expected.
- Do not overstay your invitation.
- Do not expect to be waited on. Offer to help.
- Do not plan to stay overnight without consulting the host/hostess and your parents.
- Do not upset the family's routine. Try to fit in and do your part.
- Do not make extra work. Make your bed, straighten up after yourself.
- Be sure to say thank you for a meal or an overnight visit at a friend's house.

Continued on next page.

Manners for being in public
- Do not walk in bunches so that you block others.
- Do not stop to chat in the middle of the sidewalk. Step to the side so that people won't have to move around you.
- Do not stare at or make fun of anyone, no matter how strange he or she might look.
- Do not be a litterbug.
- Do not mark on buildings or other public property.
- Say you're sorry if you bump into someone or step on his or her toe (adapted from Child Development Institute, 1999b).

Responsible Decision Making

In an ideal family, parents and guardians serve as role models for decision making. Children observe their parents and guardians using the decision-making process. Parents or guardians carefully evaluate options before deciding what to do. They weigh the consequences of possible actions. They make responsible decisions and teach their children to do the same. In an ideal family, parents and guardians expect responsible behavior from their children. They set guidelines and make expectations clear. There are consequences for breaking family guidelines. Children learn that there are always consequences for wrong behavior. This helps them when they are pressured by peers. Children think about possible consequences and say "no" to wrong behaviors. When children have difficulty saying "no," they turn to their parents and/or guardians for support. If they make a mistake, their parents or guardians help them learn from it.

Ways to Resolve Conflict

A **conflict** is a disagreement between people or between choices. In every relationship, there are conflicts. In an ideal family, parents and guardians teach their children to resolve conflicts in healthful ways. They listen to both sides of a disagreement and work to find an acceptable solution. In an ideal family, conflicts are resolved without violence. Children learn healthful ways to resolve conflicts in other relationships.

Effective Coping Skills

There are five emotional responses that people use to cope with a life crisis. People might

1. deny or refuse to believe what is happening;
2. become angry about what is happening;
3. bargain or make promises hoping it will change what is happening;
4. become depressed when it is obvious that the outcome is unlikely to change;
5. accept what is happening, adjust, and bounce back.

In an ideal family, parents and guardians want their children to develop emotional strength. They understand and recognize ways people deal with a life crisis. Suppose a child's parents or guardians encourage him or her to share his or her feelings during a life crisis. He or she will learn how to cope during difficult times he or she might experience later in life.

Ways to Delay Gratification

In an ideal family, parents or guardians teach their children the importance of delayed gratification. **Delayed gratification** is voluntarily postponing an immediate reward in order to complete a task before enjoying a reward. If children learn how to delay gratification, they are patient. They are not tempted to choose something that they want right now rather than wait for a more appropriate time. Being able to delay gratification is especially important in relationships. During adolescence, adolescents experience sexual feelings. This is healthy and normal. Parents and guardians should talk to their adolescents about sexual feelings and sexual behavior. They should make it clear that it is not appropriate for adolescents to be sexually active. Waiting until marriage to express intimate sexual feelings protects health and follows family guidelines. There are emotional risks if an adolescent has sex. The adolescent might regret the decision when he or she is older or feel guilty, frightened, or ashamed (AAP, 1999c).

Ways to Express Affection and Integrate Love and Sexuality

Affection is a fond or tender feeling that a person has toward another person. In an ideal family, parents or guardians teach their children how to express affection. For example, parents or guardians might hug their children, kiss them good-night or good-bye, or hold them when they are sad. Their expressions of warm feelings help their children feel loved. They also teach children appropriate ways to express affection. Children learn who has the right to touch them, when, and how. For example, a child might allow a doctor to touch certain parts of his or her body during a physical examination. However, a child learns when it is not appropriate for someone to touch his or her body. In an ideal family, parents and guardians teach their children that sex and love belong together in a committed marriage. Adolescents learn that sex belongs in marriage, and they practice abstinence from sex.

How to Give and Receive Acts of Kindness

In an ideal family, parents or guardians demonstrate acts of kindness and express thankfulness. They do kind things for family members and for other people in the community. They accept and are grateful for acts of kindness from others. As children observe their parents or guardians giving and receiving, they learn to act in similar ways. They are willing to give to others and express thankfulness. They are able to receive kind acts from others. Giving and receiving are both needed to sustain healthful relationships.

A Work Ethic

A **work ethic** is an attitude of discipline, motivation, and commitment toward tasks. In an ideal family, parents or guardians work hard and serve as role models for their children. As children observe their parents or guardians, they learn to do their best and not give up when the work is challenging. They learn the rewards that result from hard work. They learn to demonstrate a work ethic by completing schoolwork, doing household chores, participating in athletics, holding a part-time job, and doing volunteer work.

Respect for Authority

In a healthful family, children learn to respect authority. **Authority** is the power and right to apply laws and rules. Authority is first learned within the family. In an ideal family, children respect the authority of their parents or guardians. Parents or guardians set and enforce guidelines for behavior. For example, parents and guardians might set a curfew. A **curfew** is a fixed time when a person is to be at home. Children respect their parents and guardians and do not break the curfew. Children recognize that if they break the curfew, there will be consequences. Their parents or guardians will then use appropriate discipline, such as taking away certain privileges. In an ideal family, parents and guardians also serve as role models for their children. They, too, respect authority by obeying laws and rules. As children observe their parents' behavior, they learn to obey laws and rules set by authority figures such as teachers, principals, and police officers.

Dysfunctional Family Relationships

The term dysfunctional family was first used to describe families in which there was alcoholism. A **dysfunctional family** is a family that lacks the skills to be successful and to function in healthful ways. The term dysfunctional family is now applied to all families in which family members relate to one another in destructive and irresponsible ways.

Causes of Dysfunctional Family Relationships

There are at least seven causes of dysfunctional family relationships.

1. *Chemical dependence in the family.* **Chemical dependence** is the compelling need to take a drug even though it harms the body, mind, or relationships. Chemical dependence also is called drug addiction and drug dependence. The lives of family members who are drug-dependent become dominated by the need to obtain and use drugs. The drugs, in turn, cause changes in thinking and behavior. There is more violence in families in which there is drug dependence. There

© 2001 Everyday Learning Corporation

also is more sexual abuse. Children who are raised in a family in which there is chemical dependence are at risk for being harmed by violence. Emotional expression is frequently forbidden and discussion about the alcohol use or related family problems is usually nonexistent. All of these factors leave children feeling insecure, frustrated, and angry (Kansas State University, 1997). They might use drugs to cope with difficult situations.

There is evidence that chemical dependence might be inherited. Children of people with alcoholism are at much higher risk for developing alcoholism than are children of people who are not chemically dependent (Kansas State University, 1997). Adolescents who have a family history of chemical dependence who experiment with alcohol and other drugs have an increased risk of developing chemical dependence. Adolescents and other family members might develop codependence. **Codependence** is a mental disorder in which a person denies feelings and begins to cope in harmful ways.

2. *Other addictions in the family.* An **addiction** is the compelling need to take a drug or engage in a specific behavior. Besides chemical dependence, the following addictions contribute to dysfunctional family life: eating disorders, exercise addiction, perfectionism, gambling addiction, nicotine addiction, relationship addiction, shopping addiction, television addiction, thrill-seeking addiction, and workaholism.

A family member who has an addiction is compelled to engage in a specific behavior and neglects family relationships. Children raised in this type of family might develop codependence. They might develop the same addiction as a way of coping.

3. *Perfectionism in the family.* **Perfectionism** is the compelling need to be accurate. Perfectionism is an addiction that is becoming more common. A family member who is a perfectionist might affect the behavior of other family members. Parents and guardians who are perfectionists are overly critical of themselves and their children. Children who

live with a parent or guardian who is overly perfectionistic might feel inadequate and insecure. They might model this behavior and become perfectionists. They might criticize others and never be satisfied with anything. They might be overly critical of themselves. Their behavior is self-destructive and harms their relationships with others.

4. *Violence in the family.* **Violence** is the use of physical force to injure, damage, or destroy oneself, others, or property. **Domestic violence** is violence that occurs within a family. Domestic violence includes physical abuse and sexual abuse. The family member who is violent usually is very controlling. Often, this family member abuses drugs. Other family members try to keep peace by avoiding disagreements with the family member who is violent. They might blame themselves when this family member has violent outbursts. Between acts of violence, the family member who is violent might be kind, gentle, and apologetic. But the cycle of drug use and violent outbursts continues.

Children who live in homes with domestic violence are at risk. They might be injured by the family member who is violent. They might copy this family member's behavior and become controlling and violent. Children are at risk for becoming juvenile offenders. A juvenile offender is a legal minor who commits a criminal act. Children who are sexually abused are at risk for becoming pregnant and/or infected with HIV and other STDs.

5. *Abuse in the family.* **Abuse** is the harmful treatment of another person. **Child abuse** is the harmful treatment of a minor. **Spouse abuse** is the harmful treatment of a husband or wife. **Parent abuse** is the harmful treatment of a parent. **Elder abuse** is the harmful treatment of an aged family member.

There are four kinds of abuse. **Physical abuse** is harmful treatment that results in physical injury to the victim. The Federal Child Abuse Prevention and Treatment Act defines physical abuse as "the infliction of physical injuries such as bruises, burns, welts, cuts, and bone or skull fractures; these are caused by kicking, punching, biting, beating, knifing, strapping, paddling, etc." (Kansas State University, 1997). **Emotional abuse** is "putting down" another person and making the person feel worthless. **Neglect** is failure to provide proper care and guidance. **Sexual abuse** is sexual contact that is forced on a person. Sexual abuse happens to both males and females. It is perpetrated by both males and females. It cuts across lines of race, socioeconomic level, education level, and religious affiliation. In most cases, sexual abuse is part of an overall family pattern of dysfunction, disorganization, and inappropriate role boundaries (Kansas State University, 1997).

A family member who is abusive is controlling and moody. Often, family members who are abusive are drug-dependent. Their need for control and their moodiness increase when they are under the influence of drugs. Children who live with a family member who is abusive might be afraid and confused. They cannot understand why the family member can be loving at one moment and abusive the next. They want to believe that they are loved by the family member who is abusive. For this reason, they deny their feelings and cover up the behavior of the family member who is abusive. They might blame themselves and believe they deserve to be abused. They tend to be self-punishing and have considerable difficulties with relationships and with sexuality.

6. *Abandonment in the family.* **Abandonment** is removing oneself from those whose care is one's responsibility. Parents who abandon their children are not available for them. Their absence from their children's lives might cause their children pain, suffering, and confusion. For example, a married couple might separate and divorce. Later, one parent might not want any contact with children. The children feel a great loss. They might begin to feel unlovable, worthless, or guilty. They might think, "Why doesn't my parent want to be a part of my life? What did I do wrong? I must not be lovable." They might experience the same feelings in other relationships. Children who have been abandoned have difficulty getting close to others. They might feel that if they get too close to someone, that person might abandon them. Children who have been abandoned might push away others. Or, they might be very needy. They might demand the attention of others to fulfill needs that were not met.

7. *Mental disorders in the family.* A **mental disorder** is a mental or emotional condition that makes it difficult for a person to live in a normal way. Families in which one or more family members have a mental disorder have special stressors. Suppose a family member suffers from clinical depression. In an ideal family, other family members might respond in a healthful way. They might recognize that this family member has a mental disorder that requires treatment. They are sensitive to this but do not let this person's depression dominate their lives. In a dysfunctional family, family members do not respond in a healthful way. They might feel responsible for the family member's depression and feel guilty. They might try to "fix" the family member's depression and attempt to alleviate or lessen his or her depression. When the family member remains depressed, they feel personally responsible. The family member's depression dominates family life.

Codependent Family Relationships

Family members living in a dysfunctional family might develop codependence. People who have codependence are called codependent.

The Tree of Codependence (Figure 8.11) illustrates how dysfunctional family life can lead to codependence. The roots are labeled with behaviors that occur in dysfunctional families. The branches are labeled with feelings and behaviors that describe people who are codependent.

People who are codependent struggle in their relationships. They cannot develop intimacy. Intimacy is a deep and meaningful kind of sharing between two people. People who are codependent avoid intimacy by choosing one extreme or another. They might focus on trying

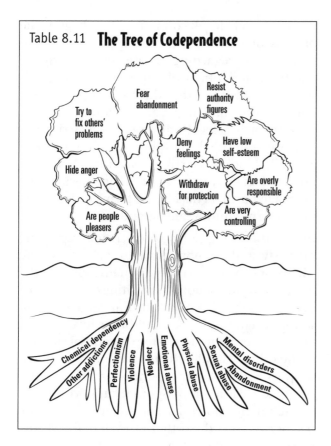

Table 8.11   **The Tree of Codependence**

to please others and deny their own needs, or they might avoid being close to others to keep from being hurt.

How to Improve Dysfunctional Family Relationships

Individual and group therapy can help ensure recovery from codependence. In individual therapy, a skilled therapist works one-on-one with the codependent. He or she assists the codependent in discovering how much of what he or she feels and believes was shaped by the dysfunctional family. Then the therapist helps the codependent learn healthful ways to express feelings and relate to others.

In group therapy, a skilled therapist works with a group of people to help them learn healthful ways to express feelings and relate to others. The group members practice new ways of relating within the safety of the group. These new ways of relating are transferred into real-life situations.

Recovery programs help people bounce back from codependence. A **recovery program** is a

group that supports members as they change their behavior to be responsible. One of the first recovery programs was Alcoholics Anonymous. **Alcoholics Anonymous (AA)** is a recovery program for people who have alcoholism.

Recovery programs for family members of people who have alcoholism also exist. **Al-Anon** is a recovery program for people who have friends or family members with alcoholism. **Alateen** is a recovery program for adolescents who have friends or family members with alcoholism.

Today, there are many different recovery programs. There are recovery programs for codependence, gambling, workaholism, and many other addictions.

Family Changes

A **life change** is an event or situation that requires a person to make a readjustment. Life changes are stressors. When people undergo life changes, their mental, physical, and emotional health is at risk. For this reason, it is necessary to make healthful adjustments to life changes as soon as they occur. Family changes are the most stressful of life changes, particularly for young children and adolescents. The most common stressors in marriage are changes in financial status, changes in living arrangements, changes in work situations, illness of a family member, abuse, infidelity, poor communication, alcohol and other drug misuse and abuse, and other drug dependency.

This section of the chapter will include a discussion of family changes that might occur if marriage partners have conflict, if parents divorce, if children live in a single-custody family, if a parent remarries, if a parent loses a job, and if a parent goes to jail.

If Marriage Partners Have Conflict

In order for marriages to succeed and be satisfying, marriage partners need to pay attention to the status of their relationship. When a marriage is taken for granted, the quality of the marriage declines and intimacy declines.

Marital conflict resolution is a process in which married partners identify their problems, agree upon solutions, and reestablish intimacy. The attitude of each partner is important in marital conflict resolution. In a healthful and caring marriage, each partner is willing to work on problems. Marital conflict resolution is impossible if both partners are not committed to restoring the quality of the marriage.

Sometimes marriage partners need help with marital conflict resolution. They might need assistance identifying their problems or finding solutions. In some cases, one partner is aware there is a problem and has resolved to do something about the situation, but the other partner does not recognize there is a problem. This is often the case in a marriage in which one partner abuses drugs. The partner who abuses drugs denies a problem exists. Outside intervention might be needed to help resolve the problem.

A married couple might recognize a problem but not be able to solve it. A marriage counselor, such as a member of the clergy, psychologist, psychiatrist, or social worker, might help present possible solutions. If the solution involves new ways of behaving, the counselor might help assist one or both partners to change behavior. Again, attitude and commitment are key. A counselor cannot help marriage partners change their ways of behaving if they do not want to do so.

If Parents Divorce

Married couples are not always able to solve problems and reestablish intimacy. **Marital separation** is the living apart of marriage partners. **Divorce** is a legal way to end a marriage in which a judge or court decides the terms with respect to property, custody, and support. Most married couples who divorce experience a six-stage process. Marital separation might occur at any time during the six stages, but it often occurs in an earlier stage.

In the first stage of divorce, the marriage deteriorates and partners show less affection and begin to detach from one another. One or both partners do not meet the needs of the other. This first stage might last up to several years. In the second stage of divorce, one or both

partners seek legal counsel. This begins the process of discussing grounds for the divorce and issues regarding property, custody of children, and financial support. During this stage of divorce, the different options for ending the marriage are examined. An **annulment** is a legal way to end a marriage in which it is decided that what was thought to be a legally binding marriage was not. A **dissolution** is a legal way to end a marriage in which the marriage partners decide the terms with respect to property, custody, and support.

In the third stage of divorce, issues regarding property and support payments are finalized. The property in a marriage usually refers to the home and household furnishings the couple owns, jewelry, cars, life insurance, money in savings accounts, stocks, and other investments. One partner might agree to pay spousal support to the other. Usually, the partner paying spousal support is the partner who has the greater ability to earn money. Spousal support often is based on the potential earning power of one partner versus the other, the length of the marriage, and the other assets in the marriage.

In the fourth stage of divorce, issues of custody, visitation rights, and child support are negotiated. **Single custody** is an arrangement in which one parent keeps legal custody of a child or children. The **custodial parent** is the parent with whom a child or children live and the parent who has the legal right to make decisions about the health and well-being of the child or children. Sometimes the parents or the court decide on joint custody of a child or children. **Joint custody** is an arrangement in which both parents keep legal custody of a child or children. A child or children might live with one parent or might alternate living arrangements, spending time with one parent and then the other. In joint custody, both parents maintain the legal right to make decisions about the health and well-being of the child or children. This arrangement requires that meaningful communication between the parents be maintained after the marriage has ended.

Visitation rights are guidelines set for the visitation of children by the parent who does not have custody. In some cases, visitation rights are very specific and include the exact number of days and a specific amount of time during which the parent can spend time with a child or children. Some guidelines might be set with regard to a parent moving to a new location and the effects of the move on visitation. Recently, the court has begun to look at other aspects of visitation such as grandparents' rights. **Grandparents' rights** are the visitation rights with grandchildren courts have awarded grandparents when their son's or daughter's marriage ends.

In the fifth stage of divorce, each of the partners establishes a new identity with family, friends, and co-workers. This stage often is difficult. In fact, some people going through divorce delay telling others about the divorce because they fear it will affect their relationships with them. These relationships might have been based on being part of a couple. Some family members and friends might take sides and feel angry or disappointed with one or both partners.

In the sixth stage of divorce, each of the partners makes emotional adjustments to the new lifestyle that results from being divorced. This stage of divorce affects both marriage partners and their children. Tables 8.12, 8.13, and 8.14 give suggestions for families in which a divorce occurs.

Table 8.12   **Suggestions for Parents on How to Talk to Children About Divorce**

1. Be completely honest and open about circumstances. Talk about the divorce in simple terms. For example, "Your dad and I are having some trouble getting along" or "Your mother and I are thinking we might need to separate."

2. Make sure your children know they are not responsible. Children often will think it is their fault that one parent has left. They might blame themselves or feel alone, unwanted, or unloved. Let your children know the changes are not their fault, that you love them and will not leave them.

3. Try not to blame your ex-spouse. Explain that parents sometimes make adult decisions to live separately.

4. Be patient with questions. You do not have to have all the answers. Sometimes just carefully listening to your children's concerns is more helpful than talking (AAP, 1999d).

Table 8.13   **Suggestions for Adolescents Whose Parents Divorce**

1. Practice stress management skills. Remember, you have experienced a life change.

2. Avoid using alcohol and other drugs as a way of coping. Work through feelings of anger, disappointment, and sadness.

3. Practice abstinence from sex. Becoming sexually active will not fill the emptiness created by a family breakup. In most cases, being sexually active will make you feel very empty and lonely.

4. Choose healthful ways to express your angry feelings about the family breakup. Participating in delinquent behavior will only get you in trouble.

5. Ask for help to resolve any feelings of betrayal or rejection. These feelings can affect your other relationships if you don't.

Table 8.14   **Suggestions for Parents Who Divorce**

1. Never force your children to take sides. Most children will have loyalty to both parents.

2. Do not involve your children in arguments between the two of you.

3. Do not criticize each other in front of your children or when your children might be listening to a conversation you are having with someone else. If you find out the other parent is saying negative things about you, explain to your children that when people get angry they sometimes say things that are hurtful.

4. Discuss your concerns and feelings with your children's other parent when and where your children cannot hear.

5. Avoid fighting in front of your children (AAP, 1999e).

What Kinds of Adjustments to Expect

Divorce is intended to fulfill at least two purposes for the married partners involved. First, divorce is intended to end a marriage that at least one spouse believed was intolerable. Second, separation and divorce are intended to be the beginning of building a new life. This second task is of particular importance to both the former marriage partners and their child or children.

Adjustments made by former marriage partners. Often, one marriage partner has a more difficult time adjusting to the divorce than the other. Usually, one partner feels that he or she is much better off for getting divorced, while the other partner feels that he or she is not better off. Usually, the partner who initiated the divorce feels as though he or she is better off.

The immediate response of partners varies. Some partners become very involved in work, others begin to date excessively to be reassured of their attractiveness, others withdraw, and some might be very depressed. Females who divorce usually require three years to regain balance in their lives. Males who divorce usually require two to two-and-one-half years. Females usually must make more economic adjustments than males. Many females experience a drop in their standard of living and must adjust to living on much less money. Both females and males who divorce are more at risk for health problems because of added stress.

Adjustments made by children after parents separate and divorce. Separation and divorce are very different experiences for children and adults. At least one of the married partners wanted the divorce and felt it was for the best. Children do not have this kind of control over the situation. They usually feel that they had no control over a decision that influences something fundamental in their development—an intact family structure.

The initial reactions of all children to separation and divorce usually are similar. They feel very vulnerable and fearful. Young children exhibit these fears by having difficulty sleeping or having nightmares. Adolescents exhibit these fears through a loss of concentration and a need to cling to others or withdraw from others.

Children commonly will react to parents separating or divorcing by developing signs of distress, or symptoms, and it is normal for them to do so (Frankel, 1996). Parents should be aware if there are signs of persistent stress in their children. These might include loss of motivation for school, for making friends, or even for having fun. Other warning signs include sleeping too much or too little, or being unusually rebellious and argumentative within the family (American Academy of Child and Adolescent Psychiatry, 1996). If children show increasing or prolonged signs of distress (more than a month or so), it is usually wise to seek a consultation with a mental health professional who specializes in working with children and adolescents. Psychotherapy, or brief counseling, can help alleviate some of the stress associated with divorce (Frankel, 1996).

Divorced parents might spend less time with their children. Most divorced fathers do not have custody of their children. They have infrequent or no contact with their children. Any lack of parenting takes its toll on the children. Many children have a decline in their grades. Many are at risk for becoming depressed, becoming sexually active, abusing alcohol and other drugs, and having delinquent behavior.

Some children might have to adjust to parental dating. This can cause stress. If parental dating begins before or soon after the divorce, children might feel angry. They might believe that the new person caused the breakup. Children often fantasize about their parents getting back together. They might continue to hope for a reconciliation for many years.

When parents date, children might resent the time and attention given to someone new. They might be jealous of the people the parent dates. They might set out to disrupt the relationship and regain the parent's attention.

Children of divorce have two traits in common —fear of rejection and fear of betrayal. These traits affect all of their relationships. For example, adolescent females whose parents divorce often fear abandonment. As a result, they might try to have many boyfriends at the same time so that there always will be a backup. They might seek an older boyfriend to be the father figure they do not have. They are more likely to get into harmful relationships and not end them.

Adolescent males whose parents divorce often feel awkward with females. They might hold back their feelings in dating and have difficulty trusting others. In some cases, they throw themselves into sports and/or work, rather than into developing and maintaining relationships.

If Children Live in a Single-Custody Family

A **single-custody family** is a family in which a child or children live with one parent who has custody. This term, rather than "single-parent" family, is used because a child or children might have two living parents. However, only one of the parents has custody or responsibility for them. When both parents have custody and responsibility, a child or children live in a joint-custody family.

Although mothers still are more likely to maintain custody of their children, more and more fathers are now taking on this role. While there is no evidence that one form of custody is better than another, all children need a stable place where they feel secure (AAP, 1999c).

There often are differences between living in a single-custody family and living in a joint-custody family. In most cases, children raised in a single-custody family live with their mothers. They are more likely to be economically disadvantaged. This means that they will lack many of the resources that other families have available. These resources range from good medical care to clothing. Their family might lack resources such as food and shelter. This makes living in a single-custody family more stressful than living in a two-parent family.

In a two-parent, or joint-custody family, there is a male and female role model for the children. After divorce, many children who live in single-custody families with their mothers have little or no contact with their fathers. Unless there is another male figure, such as a grandfather in their lives, they do not experience the benefits of having a male role model.

The single-custody parent has the sole responsibility of supervising children. If he or she works outside the home, there is less time for supervising the children and for being involved in their academic performance. This accounts for the fact that children whose parents divorce spend less time with parents and are at risk for getting poorer grades. Table 8.15 gives suggestions for adolescents who live in a single-custody family to help them handle the stresses and difficulties that they might encounter. Table 8.16 gives suggestions that single parents might choose to follow to reduce stress in their home lives.

Table 8.15 Suggestions for Adolescents Who Live in a Single-Custody Family

1. Recognize the financial pressures your parent has. Discuss ways to control expenses.

2. Schedule quality time with your parent. Do not let friends or social activities interfere with the time you have set aside.

3. Talk to your parent about having a mentor. A mentor can give you additional adult support. Organizations such as Big Brothers and Big Sisters can provide names of mentors.

4. Do not let your grades decline. Ask your parent about getting a tutor if you are having difficulty in school.

5. Discuss parental dating. Share concerns with your parent so he or she can reassure you.

Table 8.16 Tips for a Parent to Reduce Stress in a Single-Custody Family

1. Get control of finances.
2. Talk often, especially at the beginning.
3. Find support and use it.
4. Take time for family.
5. Take time for yourself.
6. Keep a daily routine.
7. Maintain consistent discipline.
8. Treat kids like kids.
9. Stay positive.
10. Take care of yourself (AAP, 1999b).

If a Parent Remarries

A **remarriage** is a marriage in which a previously married person marries again. A **blended family**, or **stepfamily**, is a family consisting of the marriage partners, children one or both of them had previously, and the children whom they have by their marriage to one another. More than half the Americans alive today have been, are now, or eventually will be in one or more stepfamily situations during their lives. One-third of all children alive today are expected to become stepchildren before they reach the age of 18. One out of every three Americans is currently a stepparent, stepchild, stepsibling, or some other member of a stepfamily. By the year 2000, more Americans are predicted to be living in stepfamilies than in nuclear families (Arnold, 1998).

Blended families often include a stepfather whose new wife has custody of her children. Eighty-six percent of stepfamilies are composed of a biological mother and a stepfather (Arnold, 1998). At the same time, the stepfather might have visitation rights for children of his former marriage. In some blended families, the father has custody of his children, but this arrangement is less common. Some blended families include joint-custody arrangements.

The two greatest sources of conflict in a blended family are determining which set of rules the children will follow and adjusting to a new budget. Often, children have been raised with specific rules that might not be the same as those they are expected to follow in the blended family. Suppose one set of children in a blended family was raised with very clear guidelines in which consequences were identified for inappropriate behavior. However, the other children in the family had little discipline and were allowed to behave as they pleased. Blending these two sets of children into one framework for discipline will likely cause conflict.

Another issue is the rules for children who live with the other parent and come to visit the blended family. All parents and stepparents involved need to communicate about the ways to blend these children into the family during visitation, rules that the children must follow, and how to discipline the children.

Decisions about the budget in a blended family can be challenging. Parents and stepparents have many decisions to make about how to spend money. When money is spent on one child for a birthday or other special circumstances, it might not be available for the needs of other children. The two sets of children might have been accustomed to having different guidelines for spending money.

Other issues that are important in blended families arise from the new relationships that are formed. The success of the blended family often depends on how stepsiblings interact. Clear guidelines for interaction must be set by parents. For example, adolescents from different families who are living together might find each other attractive. Parents must establish that acting on the attraction is not acceptable. Guidelines for resolving conflict also must be set for the family.

Many children who live in blended families resent their stepparent. They might think that their stepparent does not like them, or that their stepparent does not treat them well. However, with effective communication and mutual respect they can establish a healthful relationship with their stepparent. Children who are close to their stepparents are more likely to be satisfied with their family and perform better in school. But children from a family that consists of both biological parents are still more likely to be more satisfied and perform better in school (Americans for Divorce Reform, 1999). Table 8.17 gives suggestions to children whose parents remarry in order to help them make a smooth transition into the new family structure.

Table 8.17

Suggestions for Children Whose Parents Remarry

1. Respect the guidelines set for your behavior.
2. Respect the family budget and keep your spending within it.
3. Interact with stepbrothers, stepsisters, and a stepparent in healthful ways.
4. Show respect for your stepparent.

If a Parent Loses a Job

There are a number of reasons why a parent might lose a job. One reason is that the company or factory at which the parent worked might have downsized. To **downsize the workforce** is to reduce the number of employees in a company. Downsizing often affects people who have performed well at their jobs. Downsizing might not be tied to job performance but rather to economics.

Another reason a parent might lose a job has to do with job performance. A parent might not have had the appropriate skills for the job. Or the parent might have had problems, such as alcoholism, that resulted in a poor work record. These are only a few of the reasons why a parent might lose a job. There are many others.

The loss of a job can be devastating to a parent and very stressful for the family. The parent who loses the job might become depressed and disappointed. He or she might lose confidence and feel embarrassed. The parent might worry that family members and friends will lose respect for him or her. The parent might be anxious or worried about how the family will survive. There might be an adjustment period before he or she feels energized and ready to find another job. He or she might need training or other help before getting another job.

Children who have a parent who has lost a job also might be anxious or worried. They might wonder: "What should I say to my parent? What should I say to other people? What changes will this bring about in where and how we live? How will the loss of income affect me?" Table 8.18 gives suggestions for children who have a parent who loses a job. These suggestions might help children handle stress in this difficult time.

Table 8.18 **Suggestions for Children Who Have a Parent Who Loses a Job**

1. Encourage your parent by being supportive.

2. Discuss what family changes might occur, such as the family budget.

3. Discuss what to say to people outside the family. Determine what facts are to be kept private and what facts can be shared.

If a Parent Goes to Jail

When a parent is sentenced to jail, his or her family experiences a great deal of stress. One of the most immediate stressors might be a shortage of money, if the parent was the main source of income for the family. Legal fees can be very expensive, and arrangements must be made to pay these fees. The family might be eligible for money from the government for rent and food stamps. However, the family might be left with no source of support.

The loss of income might result in other changes. The family might have to move to another place or move in with relatives. The parent who goes to jail might be a single parent. Children who live with this parent might end up living with other relatives or being placed in foster care. **Foster care** is an arrangement in which another unrelated adult or adults assume temporary responsibility for a child or children.

Children who have a parent who is sentenced to jail might have to deal with the response from society. If the crime was widely publicized, people might make cruel remarks. They might become angry at the child because of the behavior of the child's parents. This might require a child to be resilient. It can be very embarrassing to listen to comments about the wrong behavior of a parent. Other people might assume that the child is like the parent who committed a crime and that the child also will participate in criminal behavior.

Children who have a parent who is sentenced to jail must recognize that they are not responsible for what happened. Their guilty parents chose wrong actions for which there are consequences. The children did not choose this behavior. They do not have to behave in similar ways. These children can choose to follow the law. Table 8.19 gives suggestions for children who have a parent in jail. These suggestions might help adolescents handle stress and cope more effectively with their situation.

Table 8.19

Suggestions for Children Who Have a Parent in Jail

1. Discuss your feelings with a trusted adult. You might feel ashamed, angry, confused, betrayed, and anxious. Your other parent, counselor, or teacher can help you.

2. Ask questions about what changes might occur. Questions you might want answers to include

   • Will there be any changes in my living arrangement?

   • Will my family's financial situation change?

   • Will my family responsibilities change (such as looking after younger siblings)?

   • Will I be able to have contact with my parent who is in jail?

   • When will my parent be eligible for parole or release from jail?

3. Do not accept blame for a parent's wrong actions. A parent who breaks the law is responsible for his or her actions. Suppose you notified the police about a parent's illegal actions and the parent was jailed. You protected others.

4. Pledge that you will not engage in illegal behavior. Children who have a parent in jail are more at risk for committing illegal acts themselves.

References

American Academy of Child and Adolescent Psychiatry. 1996. "Children and divorce." ParenthoodWeb: United Advertising Publications, Inc., 1996–99. Accessed 9/1999. http://www.parenthoodweb.com/articles/phw62.htm.

American Academy of Pediatrics. 1999a. "Communication Do's and Don'ts." Adapted from "Caring for Your School-Age Child: Ages 5–12." Accessed 9/1999. http://www.aap.org/advocacy/childhealthmonth/talk2.htm.

——. 1999b. "Divorce and Children." Article Online. Accessed 9/1999. http://www.aap.org/family/divorce.htm.

——. 1999c. "Single Parenting: What You Need to Know." Article Online. Accessed 9/1999. http://www.aap.org/family/single.htm.

——. 1999d. "Talking to Your Young Adolescent About Sex and Sexuality." Article Online. Accessed 9/1999. http://www.aap.org/family/adolescentsex.htm.

——. 1999e. "Tips for Parents of Adolescents." Article Online. Accessed 9/1999. http://www.aap.org.family/tipsadol.htm.

Americans for Divorce Reform. 1999. "Children of Divorce: Stepfamilies." Divorce Reform Page. Accessed 9/1999. http://www.divorcereform.org/step.html.

Arnold, Chandler. 1998. "Children and Stepfamilies: A Snapshot." Center for Law and Social Policy, Inc. Accessed 9/1999. http://www.clasp.org/pubs/familyformation/stepfamiliesfinal.BK!.htm.

Child Development Institute. 1999a. "Choosing a Baby Sitter." Article Online. Accessed 9/1999. http://www.cdipage.com/choosing_baby_sitter.htm.

——. 1999b. "Helping Children with Manners." Article Online. Accessed 9/1999. http://www.cdipage.com/manners.htm.

Crouse, Gilbert, and Larson, David. 1992. "Cost of Teenage Childbearing: Current Trends." Office of Family, Community, and Long-Term Care Policy. Accessed 9/1999. http://www.aspe.os.dhhs.gov/rn/Rn03.htm.

Frankel, Alan L. 1996. "The Effects of Divorce on a Child." ParenthoodWeb: United Advertising Publications, Inc. Accessed 9/1999. http://www.parenthoodweb.com/articles/pw977.htm.

Herring, Jeff. 1996. "Key Ingredients of a Good Marriage." Tallahassee Democrat. Accessed 9/1999. http://www.tdo.com/features/health/herring/0708/herring.htm.

Ikemoto, A. Soares Taku. 1995. "Risks of Premature Sexual Activity Among Adolescents." Article Online. Accessed 9/1999. http://www.hi-ho.ne.jp/taku77/papers/adolescent560.htm.

Kansas State University. 1997. "Dysfunctional Families: Recognizing and Overcoming Their Effects." University Counseling Services. Accessed 9/1999. http://www.ksu.edu.ucs.dysfunc.html.

Minirth, Frank, et al. 1991. *Passages of Marriage*. Nashville: Thomas Nelson Publishers.

Peck, E., and Granzig, W. 1978. *The Parent Test*. New York: G.P. Putnam's Sons.

9 Pregnancy and Childbirth

Content for Teachers *Only*

A Word from the Authors

Statistics concerning pregnancy are just that—statistics—until a pregnancy is experienced. Then it becomes a very significant event to both the male and the female who are involved. Today, the well-informed female can avail herself of the latest scientific information in regard to prenatal care. The focus for both parents becomes one of doing whatever is necessary to have a pregnancy that will result in the birth of a healthy baby. The focus for both parents must then extend to the experience of bonding with the baby and being involved in the baby's development. This chapter includes a short and simplified discussion of the cellular basis of human reproduction followed by these related topics: lifestyle habits to adopt before planning to have a baby, the process of conception, pregnancy, childbirth, and the postpartum period.

Cellular Basis of Human Reproduction

The human body is made up of trillions of cells that are the basis of the structure and function of the body. All cells in a human body originate from a single cell, the fertilized ovum, which undergoes differentiation as embryonic development proceeds. **Differentiation** is the process by which cells become more complex and assume adult forms. Differentiation results in a variety of cell types, such as bone, blood, nerve, and skin. This section of the chapter will include a discussion of the parts of a cell, DNA, cell division, the sex chromosomes and sex determination, dominant and recessive characteristics, and sex-linked characteristics.

Parts of a Cell

Cells are highly organized units that are microscopic and make up all living things. Cells are composed of living matter called protoplasm. A cell membrane gives the cell its shape and contains the cytoplasm, which is the material within the cell that surrounds the cell nucleus. The nucleus is the part of the cell that controls the activities of the cell. Other structures within the cell are called organelles. Organelles perform specific cellular functions.

The nucleus is essential in the process of reproduction. Chromosomes within the nucleus contain genes that team up to determine the characteristics, the hereditary blueprint of each individual. A **chromosome** is a threadlike structure that carries genes. A **gene** is a unit of hereditary matter. Despite the great variety of cells in the human body, the number of chromosomes remains constant. Each body cell, with the exception of the gametes (the reproductive cells), contains 23 pairs of chromosomes with an estimated 60,000 to 100,000 genes. One chromosome of each pair is inherited from the mother; one is inherited from the father.

DNA

Deoxyribonucleic acid (DNA) is a large molecule that contains all the genetic information needed to form and sustain life. All living creatures from bacteria to humans have DNA. It directs every cell in the body and coordinates all organic functions.

DNA is nearly identical between two individuals. However, variations in DNA can cause a genetic illness or predispose an individual to a disease. This information is "spelled out" in DNA. Knowing in advance the risk for transmission to offspring of genetic diseases can help reduce their risk through medical monitoring and lifestyle changes.

The Human Genome Project, a global research effort established in 1990, will complete the first international effort to identify, map, and sequence every human gene by 2003. The information will enable scientists to identify and to understand the function of human genes (National Human Genome Research Institute, 1998).

Cell Division

Mitosis is the process of cell division in which a cell divides to form two "daughter" cells that have the same number of chromosomes as the "parent" cell. In this process, the chromosomes duplicate themselves and the nucleus divides to form two new nuclei, and thus two new cells. In the human body, mitosis occurs throughout life. For example, new skin cells and new blood cells are continually being produced.

Not all cells reproduce by mitosis. If an ovum and a sperm each contained 46 chromosomes, the result of their union would be a cell containing 92 chromosomes. This does not happen, because sperm and ova are formed by a special type of cell division called meiosis. **Meiosis** is a form of cell division that results in cells that have half the number of chromosomes that other body cells have. A sperm and an ovum each have 23 chromosomes. Thus, when a sperm and ovum unite, the resulting cell has 46 chromosomes.

The Sex Chromosomes and Sex Determination

In a female, the 23 pairs of chromosomes are homologous. **Homologous cells** are cells that are identical. In a male, one pair of chromosomes is not made up of identical chromosomes. In both males and females, one pair is called the sex chromosomes. In females, the sex chromosomes are identical and are called XX. Every ovum produced by a female contains an X sex chromosome. In males, the sex chromosomes are not identical and are called XY. Sperm produced by a male contain either an X chromosome or a Y chromosome. The Y chromosome is essential for the development of male characteristics.

The sex of a baby is determined by the sex chromosome it receives from the father (Figure 9.1). When a sperm fertilizes an ovum, a full complement of 46 chromosomes (23 from the father and 23 from the mother) is present in the resulting cell. If a sperm with a Y chromosome fertilizes an ovum, the resulting cell will have an XY pair of sex chromosomes and will develop into a male offspring. If a sperm with an X chromosome fertilizes an ovum, the resulting cell will have an XX pair of sex chromosomes and will develop into a female offspring.

Dominant and Recessive Characteristics

Hereditary characteristics are determined by genes carried on chromosomes. Genes determine the traits that are inherited from parents. Genes are arranged on chromosomes something like beads on a necklace. Just as chromosomes are paired, so are genes. There

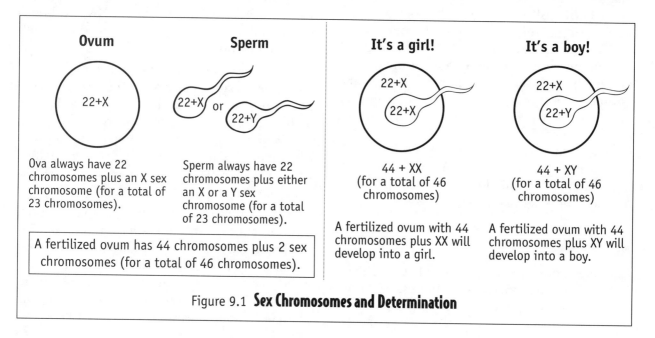

Figure 9.1 **Sex Chromosomes and Determination**

are two genes for every trait, one located on each chromosome that makes up a pair. One chromosome of each pair is inherited from the mother and one from the father.

If the maternal and paternal genes for a trait are different, one will override the other. A **dominant gene** is a gene that overrides the expression of the other gene. A **recessive gene** is a gene whose expression is overridden by the other gene. For example, a paternal gene for brown eyes might line up with a maternal gene for blue eyes. In this case, the gene for brown eyes will keep the gene for blue eyes from being expressed. The gene for brown eyes is dominant because if it is present, it will be expressed. The gene for blue eyes is recessive because it is not expressed when the dominant gene for eye color is present. Other examples of dominance in humans are curly hair over straight hair and dark hair over blond hair. If the offspring inherits recessive genes for eye color from both parents, the offspring will have blue eyes.

Codominance is a condition that occurs when two different variations of a gene, called alleles, are inherited from the mother and the father. In this case, if one allele is for blue eyes and one allele is for brown eyes, the gene will be expressed as one blue eye and one brown eye. Incomplete dominance occurs when two alleles result in a blend. Thus, if one allele is for brown eyes and the other allele is for blue eyes, the gene will be expressed as hazel eyes.

When a defective gene overrides its normal counterpart, dominant and recessive genetic disorders occur. In a dominant disorder, the mother or the father has a disease-causing allele, and each child has a 50 percent risk of inheriting the disease allele and the disorder. In a recessive disorder, both healthy parents each have one normal allele and one disease-causing allele, and each child has a 50 percent risk of inheriting one normal allele and one disease allele and being a carrier like the parents. Each child also has a 25 percent risk of inheriting both disease alleles and the disease (NIH, 1999c).

There are numerous genetic disorders. **Sickle cell disease** is a genetic disorder caused by an abnormal type of hemoglobin. It is one of the most prevalent genetic disorders among the African-American population. It affects many parts of the body in both males and females (March of Dimes Birth Defects Foundation, 1999). **Turner's syndrome** is a genetic disorder caused by the lack of or defectiveness of the X chromosome in one or more cells and affects females only. Depending on the number of affected cells, the syndrome can limit sexual development and produce infertility as well as mental defects (AMA, 1998). **Fragile X syndrome** is a genetic disorder caused by breakage or weakness at the end of the X chromosome and is associated with mental retardation (NIH, 1999b).

Sex-Linked Characteristics

The pair of sex chromosomes carries genes like other chromosomes. The hereditary characteristics transmitted on the sex chromosomes are said to be sex-linked. **Sex-linked characteristics** are genetic conditions that affect either the X or the Y chromosome, and therefore will only be expressed in one gender. The X chromosome carries genes for traits such as color vision and blood clotting. The Y chromosome does not carry matching genes for those or other traits. Therefore, when the X and Y chromosomes are together, the genes on the X chromosome control the traits. If a recessive gene, such as red-green color blindness is present on an X chromosome inherited by a male offspring, the offspring will be color-blind.

In contrast, recessive defects carried on the maternal X chromosome are far less likely to manifest themselves in female offspring. The reason is that genes carried on the X chromosome inherited from the father will dominate any recessive genes on the X chromosome inherited from the mother. However, if both maternal and paternal X chromosomes carry recessive genes for a trait, the recessive trait will appear in female offspring. Genetic traits carried by sex-linked genes are far more likely to appear in male than in female offspring.

Lifestyle Habits to Adopt Before Planning to Have a Baby

Planning a year ahead for pregnancy is especially important for a female. She should be in a loving, committed relationship with a healthy male. The lifestyle the couple chooses should include proper nutrition and exercise, childbirth and health education, and the avoidance of drug use and other risk behaviors.

During this time of preparation, a female should consult her primary health care provider to resolve any health issues that could develop. Prenatal and genetic counseling can help reduce possible complications in a pregnancy by establishing a program suited to the female's specific needs and requirements. If transmission of a genetic disorder to the fetus is likely to occur, close medical monitoring will be necessary.

Two primary aspects of prenatal care for which the female must take primary responsibility are nutrition and the avoidance of risk behaviors, such as eating disorders and the use of drugs that will adversely affect the embryo and the fetus.

Healthful Diet

A healthy female is more likely to have a healthy baby. If a female is overweight, she should begin to lose weight slowly and steadily at a rate of one-half to one pound a week. Reaching her optimum weight level before pregnancy is important since she should not diet during pregnancy and risk depriving the fetus of nutrients necessary for development (Cnattingius, 1998).

A female should choose a well-balanced diet based on the dietary guidelines established by the Food and Drug Administration. She needs to make food choices from the Food Guide Pyramid (Figure 9.2). These should include 6 to 11 servings from the bread, cereal, rice, and pasta group; 3 to 5 servings from the vegetable group; 2 to 4 servings from the fruit group; 4 to 6 servings from the milk, yogurt, and cheese group; and 3 to 4 servings from the meat, poultry, fish, dry beans, eggs, and nuts group. In particular, a female should eat iron-rich foods, such as lean meats and whole-grain or enriched white bread. She also should eat less fatty foods and sweets.

Drinking plenty of fluids, including 6 to 8 glasses of water each day, is highly recommended. Fruit juice and milk, an essential source of calcium, also are important.

Nutrition Facts Labels will help a female make healthful decisions about her food choices. However, she should be aware that nutrition facts labels are not required for certain foods including coffee and tea, which contain caffeine and no significant amounts of nutrients.

A female should have 400 micrograms of folic acid daily just before conception and in the early weeks of pregnancy. Natural sources of folic acid include orange juice, green leafy vegetables, beans, peanuts, broccoli, asparagus, peas, lentils, and enriched grain products. During pregnancy, prenatal supplements can provide a female with higher levels of some vitamins.

Responsible Use of Medicine

Drugs that are present in a pregnant female's blood can enter the fetal bloodstream through the umbilical cord. It is difficult to pinpoint all the drugs that adversely affect a developing fetus and to ascertain the period during pregnancy at which each drug might pose a potential risk. Therefore, it is vital that a female be aware of

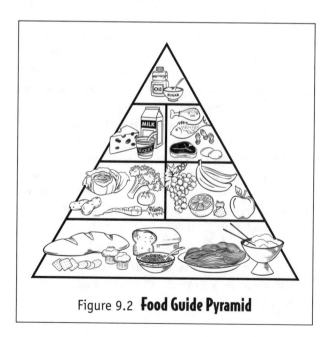

Figure 9.2 **Food Guide Pyramid**

warnings associated with the prescription drugs she uses that might be harmful to a fetus.

Drugs used to control certain disorders in a female can cause birth defects in a baby if the drugs are taken during pregnancy. If a female has diabetes, epilepsy, or high blood pressure, these should be treated and under control before pregnancy occurs. Tranquilizers might cause fetal malformations and profound birth defects. Accutane, a drug frequently prescribed for acne, can cause miscarriage or birth defects. Hormones, such as those in birth control pills, also might cause birth defects. Long-term exposure by a fetus to drugs used for connective tissue disorders can result in systemic problems, head and face abnormalities, and restricted growth (Rayburn, 1998).

Over-the-counter drugs, such as aspirin, might interfere with blood clotting in both a pregnant female and a fetus. All drugs, whether prescription or over-the-counter, should be taken only under medical supervision.

Maintenance therapy to control asthma in a pregnant female is important because she is "breathing for two." Uncontrolled asthma can cause preeclampsia in a pregnant female and seizures in a fetus (Moran, 1998).

Drug-Free Lifestyle

According to the Centers for Disease Control and Prevention (CDC), alcohol consumption among pregnant females has increased over the last several years. Problems related to substance abuse during pregnancy are well documented. Since no safe level of alcohol intake during pregnancy has been established, females who are trying to conceive should not drink alcoholic beverages. **Fetal alcohol syndrome (FAS)** is a birth defect characterized by growth retardation, facial abnormalities, and central nervous system dysfunction (CDC, 1998b).

Females who want to conceive should consider the effect of smoking cigarettes on a fetus. Research indicates that pregnant females who smoke might have preterm babies or low birth weight babies with breathing and other health problems. In later childhood, these babies also might have learning and behavioral problems. Smoking during pregnancy is associated with higher rates of complications in pregnancy, miscarriage, and sudden infant death syndrome (SIDS) (March of Dimes, 1994). SIDS causes a baby who seems healthy to die without warning (National Center for Health Statistics, 1999a). Babies of mothers who smoke might be predisposed to heart attacks in adulthood (FDA, 1996).

Other addictive drugs, such as cocaine, heroin, and amphetamines, are hazardous to the health of a pregnant female and a fetus. If such substances are present in a female's blood at conception, they can enter the fetal bloodstream through the placenta. Babies born to mothers who are addicted to such substances might be born prematurely or have low birth weight. These babies might be born addicted to a substance and forced to suffer the pain of withdrawal. According to the National Pregnancy and Health Survey, nearly half of all females in the childbearing age group of 15 to 44 in the United States are drug abusers. The drug abuse of pregnant females affected more than 200,000 babies in 1999 (National Institute on Drug Abuse, 1999).

Physical Activity and Fitness

Moderate physical activity during most days of the week is essential to the health of a female. If she has been sedentary and is considering pregnancy, she should develop a daily regimen that includes walking, swimming, or bicycling for at least thirty minutes. When possible, she should use stairs rather than elevators. She should park her car farther than usual from her destination in order to increase her walking distance.

Although there is some evidence that a healthy, well-conditioned female might take part in exercise during pregnancy without harm to the fetus (Kardel, 1998), strenuous training can cause complications (James, 1998).

Habits Specific to Males

At one time, pregnancy and childbirth were thought to be a female's sole domain and responsibility. Today, she shares the experiences of pregnancy with her partner, the father-to-be of her baby. It is not too soon for the once-forgotten male to take an active role before conception.

The father-to-be's participation is crucial since the success of conception will partly depend on his lifestyle, which can affect the number and quality of his sperm. Alcohol and drugs including marijuana, nicotine, and certain med-ications, can temporarily reduce sperm quality (Nodenberg, 1997).

There also are many decisions to be made and shared concerning the baby's birth. Issues concerning the pregnancy, parenting, work, and finances should be discussed and mutual strategies developed for a healthful pregnancy. The father-to-be should encourage the mother-to-be to eat well and to avoid drinking and smoking. The male should not smoke around the female if she is trying to stop smoking. The male also should be aware that secondhand smoke might be harmful to the fetus.

The Process of Conception

Human reproduction is based on the union of gametes, a male sperm and a female ovum. **Fertilization** is the union of a sperm and ovum. A basic knowledge of the factors that can affect fertilization is essential in understanding the reproductive process. This section of the chapter will include a discussion of fertilization, infertility, increasing fertility and the probability of conception, and assisted reproductive technologies.

Fertilization

One ovum matures and is released from an ovary each month. **Ovulation** is the release of a mature ovum by an ovary and occurs on or about the fourteenth day before the expected beginning of the next menstrual period. Once

an ovum is released, it enters the fallopian tube. The **fallopian tubes**, or **oviducts**, are tubes that extend from near the ovaries to the uterus. As an ovum moves through the fallopian tube, it can be fertilized if sperm are present. Fertilization usually occurs in the upper third of the fallopian tube.

In an ejaculation, millions of sperm can be released into a female's vagina. Sperm move through the vagina into the uterus and fallopian tubes. An ovum in the fallopian tube is surrounded by many sperm, but only one penetrates it. An ovum has a fertilizable life of approximately 24 hours, but it remains fertilizable longer than it can produce a normal embryo (Pollard, 1994).

Conception is the union of a sperm and ovum. A **zygote** is the cell that forms from the fertilized ovum. Remaining unsuccessful sperm die and disintegrate. An ovum that is not fertilized also disintegrates.

Infertility

To be **fertile** is to be capable of producing offspring. A female who produces mature ova is said to be fertile. To be **infertile** is to be incapable of producing offspring. To be sterile is to be infertile. A person who is infertile still has the same desire and ability to perform sexually. A male who is infertile is not necessarily impotent.

Infertility is the inability to conceive a child after a year of unprotected sexual intercourse. The male or the female, and sometimes both, might be infertile. In most cases, the causes of infertility can be explained. Only 20 percent of infertility cases cannot be explained (American Society of Reproductive Medicine, 1998a).

Male Infertility

About one-third of the infertility cases are the result of a male factor (American Society of Reproductive Medicine, 1998a). The most pre-dominant cause of this infertility is a low sperm count. The production of abnormal sperm also has been shown to be a frequent cause of male infertility. Sperm might be considered abnormal if they lack motility. **Motility** is the ability of sperm to propel themselves to reach an ovum. Normal motile sperm have the ability to move about 3 to 5 inches (7.62 to 12.70 cm) per hour. Another common cause of male infertility is an inadequate volume of seminal fluid.

Another cause of male sterility is the result of diseases such as mumps or sexually transmitted diseases that affect the reproductive organs. Other possible causes of male sterility are undescended testicles that are not corrected before puberty, exposure to radiation, testicular injury, continual elevation of the testes from wearing tight-fitting underwear or athletic supporters, fever, high altitude, stress, inadequate hormone production, and testicular cancer. In addition, it has been noted that the use of drugs, including alcohol, tobacco, and some illegal drugs, as well as a variety of prescription medications, can alter fertility.

The treatment of male infertility might require something as simple as changing from tight-fitting underwear to boxer trunks, changing medications, or reducing alcohol consumption. While drug therapies have all been used effectively, there also might be a need for psychological intervention to help minimize performance anxiety. Some conditions might necessitate more aggressive medical intervention, such as surgery. Unfortunately, however, the success rate of curing more complex causes of male infertility is poor.

Female Infertility

The most common reason for female infertility is the failure to ovulate at the same time each month. Irregular ovulation can be related to several situations, such as a change in diet, poor nutrition, eating disorders, low body fat caused by excessive exercise and/or dieting, ovarian disorders, cigarette smoking, drug addiction and abuse, physical and emotional stress, illness, hormonal imbalance, and fallopian tube damage. A leading cause of fallopian tube damage is the STD chlamydia (Cates, Jr., 1999).

If inability to conceive continues and a female's partner has been diagnosed as being fertile, the next step is to determine the cause of the female's infertility. The first action will likely be to make sure that the female ovulates on a regular basis. After that, a physician might choose to determine if sperm are being denied passage to the ovum. Side effects of infections such as STDs can cause fallopian tubes to be blocked. This blockage can prevent an ovum from passing through the fallopian tube. Infections in the vagina and uterus also might prevent sperm from reaching an ovum. Infections, such as pelvic inflammatory disease (PID), can cause scar tissue to form in and around the fallopian tubes and the ovaries.

Endometriosis is a condition in which the endometrial tissue grows somewhere other than in the lining of the uterus. This condition can result in blocked fallopian tubes. Although considered to be one of three major causes of female infertility, the cause-effect relationship of endometriosis is unclear. The disease affects between 10 and 20 percent of females of child-bearing age in the U.S. Many of these problems can be remedied through medication and/or surgery.

Although antibody production is essential to human health, it can sometimes cause problems. An estimated 10 to 30 percent of female infertility might be associated with the development of antibodies that attack sperm. In some cases, when sperm come in contact with cervical mucus, the female's body produces antibodies that incapacitate sperm and thus prevent pregnancy. There is some evidence that this condition can be corrected. If a couple uses condoms for six months, the level of sperm antibodies will be reduced and the chances of pregnancy are increased.

Psychological factors also might influence infertility. There are stories of females who became pregnant after being told by their doctors that they should not conceive. This type of situation has led to the belief that the ability to become pregnant is, to a large degree, dependent upon a female's frame of mind. This is a highly controversial idea. Science has not shown that a significant relationship exists. In fact, psychological stress is more likely to be the result than the cause of infertility (Nodenberg, 1997). However, the possibility that an emotional state might be a factor in a female's ability to conceive cannot be discounted.

Increasing Fertility and the Probability of Conception

There are several methods and techniques that can be used to increase the chances of conception.

Timing of Sexual Intercourse

The time of the month is an important factor to consider in conception. The rhythm method of birth control can be used to enhance the chances of conception. By using the basal body temperature (BBT) method, a female can determine when she ovulates. Once an ovulation pattern is established, a female might wish to begin having intercourse about one to two days before she ovulates, since sperm can survive for up to 72 hours after being released into the vagina.

Another way to increase the chances of conception is to measure hormone levels. Over-the-counter home urine tests are available that measure the level of luteinizing hormone (LH) in a female. These tests can detect the increase in LH that normally occurs prior to ovulation. Although these tests are expensive, they are much more accurate than the BBT method.

Frequency of Sexual Intercourse

The frequency with which a couple has intercourse might need to be modified to enhance the odds of achieving conception. For example, if the usual frequency of intercourse is once a month, the couple should consider increasing the frequency. However, if a couple engages in intercourse once a day, the couple should consider reducing the frequency. A high sperm count at ejaculation is important to ensure conception. With frequent subsequent ejaculations, the number of sperm cells is reduced. A period of at least 24 hours is necessary to replenish all 300 million+ sperm. Therefore, if a female is about to ovulate, it would be wise for a male not to ejaculate for about two days before having intercourse in order to coincide with ovulation.

Position During Sexual Intercourse

The position in which a couple chooses to engage in intercourse is an important factor in conception. The man-on-top, face-to-face position is considered the position most beneficial for increasing the chances of conception. Before ejaculation has occurred in this position, the female should draw her knees up to her chest. She should remain in this position for approximately 20 minutes after the male has ejaculated. It also might be helpful to place a pillow under her buttocks to prevent semen from escaping from the vagina. During ejaculation, the male should penetrate as deeply as possible, and not thrust. His penis should remain in the vagina for several minutes and then be removed as gently as possible to prevent disturbing the pool of semen.

Fertility Drugs

Between 80 and 90 percent of infertility cases are treated with drugs or surgery. Clomid or a more potent hormone stimulator usually is recommended to females with ovulation disorders. Couples seeking treatment should be aware that multiple births occur in 10 to 20 percent of births resulting from fertility drug therapy.

Surgical Procedures

There are many surgical procedures for the enhancement of fertility. The surgical treatment of abnormalities including fallopian tube obstruction, endometriosis, uterine fibroids, and pelvic scarring in the female and vas obstruction in the male has a high rate of success. Once the normal reproductive function is restored, pregnancy can occur naturally.

Psychosocial Issues

A female who fears pregnancy for health or emotional reasons should resolve these issues with the help of her health care provider. The support and encouragement of a female's partner also are necessary. The decision to share equal responsibility for a healthful pregnancy is an important step toward resolution of a female's fears.

Assisted Reproductive Technologies

Traditional penile/vaginal intercourse is not the only technique that can result in conception. Many other techniques are available that can make conception possible.

Intrauterine Insemination (IUI)

Intrauterine insemination (IUI) is the process of introducing semen into the vagina or uterus by sperm preparation techniques so that conception can occur (Figure 9.3). IUI was practiced on animals as long ago as the 14th century. It now is used successfully on humans and often is combined with fertility drug therapy to treat unexplained infertility, endometriosis, certain sperm problems, and other conditions (American Society of Reproductive Medicine, 1998a).

IUI is used if the father-to-be has a low sperm count. The father-to-be's sperm, donor sperm, or a mix of father-to-be and donor sperm is placed in the female's vagina. If the father-to-be's sperm is used, several ejaculates can be collected and held under proper conditions. However, in most cases of intrauterine insemination donor sperm is used.

The number of sperm banks, also known as human semen cryobanks, has increased over the years. Sperm that has been frozen for therapeutic

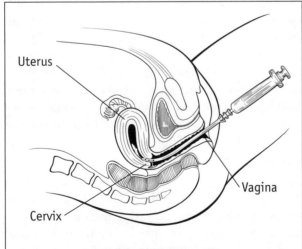

Uterus

Vagina

Cervix

Figure 9.3 **Intrauterine Insemination**

Intrauterine insemination is the process of introducing semen into the vagina or uterus by sperm preparation techniques so that conception can occur.

donor insemination might be purchased from semen banks nationwide. Criteria for sperm donor selection can include not only the intelligence and general health of the donor, but also preferred physical traits.

Despite the widespread use of donor semen specimens in fertility treatment, there are no federal laws regulating consumer safety in human semen cryobanks. However, the American Association of Tissue Banks provides stringent criteria for the collection, testing, storage, and tracking of semen (Fertilitext, 1998).

Male Factor Infertility Treatments

Various new treatments are available for male sexual dysfunction. Viagra, the first effective oral medication for erectile dysfunction, has been shown to be successful in treating erectile dysfunction in males with hypertension, coronary artery disease, diabetes, depression, and spinal cord injury. Other treatments that have proven effective include assisted fertilization or micromanipulation, microinsemination, and intracytoplasmic sperm injection. **Micromanipulation** is the use of tiny instruments attached to a microscope to examine or work with minute objects. **Microinsemination** is the use of a micromanipulator to fertilize an ovum. **Intracytoplasmic sperm injection** is a technique for fertilizing an ovum through surgical means, in which an ovum is injected with one sperm to produce an embryo that can implant and grow in the uterus (American Society of Reproductive Medicine, 1998b).

In Vitro Fertilization (IVF)

In vitro fertilization (IVF) is a procedure in which mature ova are removed from a female's hormone-stimulated ovary and placed in a lab dish to be fertilized by sperm. After 48 to 72 hours, any developing embryos are placed directly into the female's uterus for implantation to take place. This procedure has been used in cases of infertility caused by blocked or absent fallopian tubes. In 1995, the live birth rate for IVF was 22.5 percent. This rate is almost equivalent to the 20 percent chance in any given month that a reproductively healthy couple has of achieving pregnancy and carrying it to term (American Society of Reproductive Medicine, 1998a).

In vitro fertilization is considered to be one of the very best treatments for many fertility problems. Since in vitro fertilization was introduced into the United States, many couples have chosen this procedure. It has been the most popular method of assisted reproductive technology.

Gamete Intrafallopian Transfer (GIFT)

Gamete intrafallopian transfer (GIFT) is a procedure in which sperm and ova are placed directly in a fallopian tube where fertilization takes place naturally. This procedure requires the presence of at least one functioning fallopian tube and is beneficial when infertility is caused by such conditions as endometriosis and the destruction of sperm by cervical antibodies or chemicals present in cervical mucus.

Both IVF and GIFT might result in multiple births because the chances are increased that more than one fertilized ovum will implant in the uterus and develop.

Zygote Intrafallopian Transfer (ZIFT)

Zygote intrafallopian transfer (ZIFT) is a combination of IVF and GIFT. Ova and sperm are collected, fertilized in vitro, and then placed in a fallopian tube. With ZIFT, as with IVF, fertilization is assured before placement of the zygote in a female's body.

Donor Egg IVF

Ova also might be given to females who do not ovulate, who do not have ovaries, or who wish to prevent passing along an inheritable disease. Some ova donors, such as a close relative or a friend, are chosen. Others might be anonymous. Females using IVF themselves sometimes contribute extra ova, and in some cases, ova donors are paid.

This treatment is becoming a standard form of care for females with failed or impaired ovarian function, for carriers of genetic disease, and for

females whose fertility is declining with age or who are past menopause. The success rate for females over 40 years of age using donor egg IVF is 31 percent (American Society of Reproductive Medicine, 1998a).

Embryo Freezing

Frequently, more ova than necessary are removed for IVF. Since only a few fertilized ova are used in the procedure, the remainder might be frozen for possible later use. Conservation of these embryos provides the opportunity for reimplantation should the first procedure fail. This also avoids having to repeat the surgical procedure to retrieve ova. This not only is energy and cost efficient, but also reduces the possibility of multiple births. While healthy live births have been accomplished using frozen embryos, there are many unanswered questions concerning the effects of freezing and thawing on the embryo. These include moral and ethical questions as well as those involving the medical aspects of this procedure.

Surrogate Mothers

Another alternate method of procreation is the use of a surrogate mother. In this arrangement, an infertile couple contracts for a fee with a fertile female. There are two kinds of surrogacy. A surrogate mother might provide an ovum to be artificially inseminated by the father-to-be's sperm, or the infertile female might provide an ovum. In the latter case, the ovum is transferred to the surrogate mother by GIFT along with the father-to-be's sperm and an embryo transfer to the surrogate mother's uterus is performed. Surrogacy might be used when a female does not ovulate, or if a female should not or cannot carry a fetus to full term for reasons of age or personal health.

After the pregnancy has reached full term and the baby is born, the baby is given to the couple for adoption. Obviously, this means of procreation is subject to much legal and moral criticism. Several cases already have occurred in which the welfare of the baby has been placed in jeopardy because the contractual agreement was broken by one of the parties involved.

Therefore, it is of the utmost importance that the couple and the surrogate mother consider the future of the child. In order to reduce the possibility of a dispute, the receiving couple should be present at the baby's birth and care for the baby in the hospital.

Pregnancy

A **trimester** is one of three three-month periods during a human pregnancy. The **first trimester** is the first three months after conception. The **second trimester** is the fourth, fifth, and sixth months after conception. The **third trimester** is the seventh, eighth, and ninth months after conception. This section of the chapter includes a discussion of detecting pregnancy, establishing the delivery date, development of the embryo and fetus, the importance of prenatal care, the effects of pregnancy on the mother-to-be, the effects of pregnancy on the father-to-be, sexual activity during pregnancy, atypical conditions during pregnancy, and ways to detect birth defects. The risks associated with adolescent pregnancies also are discussed.

Detecting Pregnancy

The first sign that indicates a pregnancy is the absence of a menstrual period when it is expected. However, a missed period does not necessarily indicate that conception has occurred. In fact, most females at one time or another skip a menstrual period for a month or are late because of diet, physical activity, stress, or other circumstances. If conception has occurred, however, the female might experience additional symptoms, such as tenderness in the breasts, nausea, vomiting, fatigue, and a change in appetite. Some females might experience spotting or light, irregular menstrual flow. After eight weeks, the uterus will be enlarged with a soft cervix.

When a female has missed a period and has other accompanying symptoms of pregnancy six weeks after the first day of her last menstrual cycle, she should be tested for pregnancy. A trained professional, such as a nurse practitioner or a physician, can perform a pelvic examination and generally detect pregnancy at this six-week period. Blood and urine tests also can confirm a diagnosis of pregnancy.

In pregnancy, the placenta, even in its most elementary state, produces large quantities of a hormonal substance called human chorionic gonadotrophin (HCG). This substance can be detected in a female's blood as early as six to eight days after fertilization of an ovum.

HCG also is found in urine. One of the most common methods used to determine pregnancy is a urine test. Thus, if HCG is detectable, fertilization has occurred. When a urine or blood test is performed by a medical professional, accuracy of results is assured.

Over-the-counter home pregnancy kits are now available in most pharmacies. These tests can be performed in a few minutes and reportedly can detect pregnancy as early as 12 days after a missed menstrual period. While many of them claim to be accurate, there is always the problem that users might not follow the instructions carefully, thereby causing false readings. The diagnostic efficiency of home pregnancy kits depends largely on the characteristics of the users. While do-it-yourself tests can be highly reliable when performed and interpreted accurately, no test for pregnancy is 100 percent certain. Any negative test result, therefore, should be followed up with a retest in about a week. Diagnosis of early pregnancy should not rely on home pregnancy tests or clinical examination but on a laboratory test (Bastian, 1997).

Establishing the Delivery Date

The average length of a human pregnancy is 266 days, or approximately nine months. Many physicians have been taught to think in terms of 10 lunar cycles (months) of 28 days or 40 weeks from the beginning of the last menstrual period for a total of 280 days. This method of calculation adds two weeks to the length of pregnancy over other methods of calculation. However, it is only a mathematical average, and few babies arrive exactly according to schedule. Statistics show, in fact, that only 4 percent of births occur on the so-called due date, while 60 percent occur within five days of the predicted date. Generally, a baby might be born one to four weeks before or after the due date.

Another method of calculating the due date is by counting back three months from the first day of the last menstrual period and adding seven days and one year. For example, if the last menstrual period began on September 3, 1999, the delivery date would be computed as follows:

September 3, 1999 minus 3 months = June 3, 1999

June 3, 1999 plus 7 days and 1 year = June 10, 2000 the delivery date

Development of the Embryo and Fetus

The zygote formed by the fertilization of an ovum by a sperm divides to form two cells about 18 to 39 hours after fertilization. These two cells divide to form four cells, which divide to form eight cells, and so on to form a multi-celled mass. At this stage of development, the mass of cells is called a morula. Three or four days later, the morula might contain as many as 32 cells. When the mass develops a hollow inner portion, or cavity, it is called a blastocyst. The cavity that forms in the blastocyst is called a blastocele.

Surrounding the blastocyst is a single layer of cells called the trophoblast. The trophoblast secretes enzymes that digest the endometrium, the inner lining of the uterus. As the mass of cells plants itself in the uterine wall, cells of the trophoblast along with the uterine tissues become the placenta, the structure that nourishes the embryo. Implantation usually occurs eight to ten days after ovulation (Wilcox, 1999).

The placenta enlarges after implantation, reaching approximately three inches (7.6 cm) in length by the fourth month and eight inches (20 cm) by the eighth month. At birth, the placenta weighs about one pound.

In the first eight weeks of pregnancy, the developing mass is called an embryo. A membrane called the amnion forms around the fluid-filled sac called the amniotic sac that surrounds the developing embryo. The embryo floats in this fluid, cushioned and kept at a constant temperature. This fluid protects the developing embryo from injury.

The placenta is connected to the embryo by the umbilical cord, which contains two arteries and one vein. Oxygen and essential nutrients from the mother's blood reach the fetus through the umbilical cord. At the same time, waste materials produced by the metabolism of the developing embryo move through the cord to the mother's bloodstream and are excreted from her body. The exchange of materials takes place in the placenta. The circulatory systems of the mother and the embryo are separate. There is no mixing of the mother's blood with the embryo's blood. This separation of the two circulatory systems remains throughout a female's pregnancy.

Although the blood of the mother and the blood of the embryo do not mix, all substances in the mother's blood enter the blood of the embryo. If a pregnant female is not well-informed, she might inadvertently use substances that will harm the embryo. Substances such as nicotine, alcohol, narcotics, and pathogens, will adversely affect the embryo.

The First Trimester

The first three months after conception is the first trimester. By the end of the second month, the embryo is recognizable as a human and is called a fetus.

At the end of the first month, the embryo has a heartbeat, a two-lobed brain, and a spinal cord. After two months, the embryo has started to form arms and legs, fingers and toes, ears, and the beginnings of eyes and facial features. At the end of the third month, the major internal organs have been differentiated and have begun to function. The limbs have continued to develop and the fetus can be visibly identified as male or female. By the end of the first trimester, the fetus is about four inches (10.16 cm) long and weighs about one ounce (28 g).

The Second Trimester

By the end of the fourth month, fingernails and toenails, and eyebrows and eyelashes have developed. Teeth begin to form, lips appear, and head hair might start to grow. Movement of the fetus can be felt by the mother.

During the fifth month, a fetal heartbeat can be detected using a stethoscope. During the fifth and sixth months, growth is rapid. By the end of the second trimester, the fetus begins to open its eyes. It is about 12 inches (30.48 cm) long and weighs approximately 1.5 pounds (0.68 kg).

The Third Trimester

If a baby is born prematurely at the beginning of the seventh month, it has a 20 percent chance of surviving. Optimal development occurs at about 40 weeks' gestation.

A **preterm baby**, or **premature baby**, is a baby that is born before 37 weeks of pregnancy. A baby born between 38 and 40 weeks of pregnancy is considered to be full-term. Full-term babies are usually 19 to 21 inches (48.26 cm to 53.34 cm) long and might weigh between six and nine pounds (2.7 kg and 4.05 kg) by the end of the third trimester.

Importance of Prenatal Care

The prenatal care a mother-to-be and her baby receive and the lifestyle she chooses during her pregnancy should support the nutritional regimen the female started before conception. Her prenatal care also should include routine medical examinations, reasonable exercise, extra rest and relaxation, and childbirth and child care education. A pregnant female also should be fully recovered from any risk behaviors such as the use of illegal drugs or alcohol. Medical monitoring will help ensure the success of the prenatal care program that was established for the female with the help of her primary care provider before conception. This cooperative effort should be maintained during pregnancy and after the birth of the baby.

Diet During Pregnancy

Adequate prenatal nutrition during pregnancy provides the fetus with nutrients essential for development. Inadequate prenatal nutrition deprives the fetus of these vital nutrients. Fetal growth will be affected. Inadequate nutrition can be the cause of premature birth and low birth weight, which is known to be associated with mental retardation and a high incidence of infant death.

Gestational Diabetes

Gestational diabetes, like any form of diabetes, is a disorder that interferes with the body's ability to use food properly. However, gestational diabetes begins during pregnancy and disappears after the baby's birth. Screening for gestational diabetes is recommended since approximately 3 to 5 percent of all females in the United States are diagnosed with the disease. Factors that increase a female's risk for gestational diabetes include obesity, family history of diabetes, prior birth to a very large baby, a stillbirth, a baby with a birth defect, or too much amniotic fluid. Females older than 25 are at greater risk than younger females (Intelihealth, 1999).

Screening Tests for STDs During Pregnancy

Because STDs can harm a fetus, all pregnant females should be tested at the first prenatal visit. A test for HIV infection should be offered at the same time. The test for chlamydia should be done in the third trimester for females at higher risk. These include females younger than 25 years old and females who have new or multiple sex partners (Atkins, 1998).

Drug Use During Pregnancy

The primary health care provider should monitor drug use during pregnancy. If a pregnant female develops even the mildest illness, she should advise her health care provider. She should not take over-the-counter drugs or use alternative therapies such as herbal supplements without supervision. There are no federal guidelines governing supplements, such as St. John's wort, which is used for mood-enhancement. Certain prescription drugs are known to cause complications in pregnancy. Neither lithium nor benzodiazepines, for example, are recommended during the first trimester. Antidepressants might cause premature labor, and babies might be less healthy at birth. Asthma medications, on the other hand, are generally considered safe for pregnant females. Every effort should be made to avoid acute exacerbation of asthma since it can deprive the fetus of oxygen (Moran, 1998). However, the bronchodilator theophylline is secreted into breast milk that might result in irritability and insomnia in the newborn. Since many drugs are excreted through human milk, a pregnant female should be aware of the implications for breastfeeding (Chambers et al., 1996).

Preventing Preterm Labor

Many females who are not at risk for preterm delivery have their babies before they reach full-term. However, some females are at higher risk than others for preterm labor. The following females are at the highest risk:

1. Females who are younger than 17 years old or older than 35.

2. Females who are carrying twins or any multiple pregnancy.

3. Females who have had more than three miscarriages.

4. Females who have previously had a preterm baby.

5. Females who engage in strenuous activity at work.

All pregnant females should be aware of the symptoms for preterm labor. These include menstrual-like cramps; low, dull backache; pelvic pressure; abdominal cramping; and frequent uterine contractions.

The symptoms for preterm labor should not be ignored. A female who experiences any of these symptoms should be cautious. She should stop doing any activity, such as exercise, that might have caused her to have symptoms. She should contact her health care provider. Her health care provider will give her instructions. She might be advised to lie down on her left side and rest for an hour. She might be advised to drink two or three glasses of water. Her health care provider will advise her when it is all right for her to resume normal activities.

However, a female who has experienced preterm labor symptoms might need to adjust her daily activities. All pregnant females, especially those at risk for preterm labor, need rest. Standing can bring on symptoms in some females. It is important for a female at risk to plan her day with periodic breaks from standing. If physical activity at work brings on symptoms, a female should consider reducing her work hours for a few months or changing her schedule to avoid commuting during peak traffic times. Sports activities, climbing stairs, heavy lifting, and heavy housework can all bring symptoms of preterm labor. Females with symptoms of preterm labor should avoid taking long trips until after the baby is born. If a female must travel, she should stop at least once an hour and walk around. Most pregnant females do not need to restrict sexual activity. However, sexual activity should be restricted if symptoms of preterm labor are experienced. All females should take precautions during pregnancy against urinary tract infections. While current evidence does not support universal testing for bacterial vaginosis (BV), a test might be done early in the second trimester if a female has a history of preterm delivery. Regular prenatal care and drinking plenty of water daily can help a pregnant female avoid vaginal infections (Atkins, 1998).

Ultrasound Examination

An **ultrasound** is a diagnostic technique that uses sound waves to create pictures of internal body structures (Figure 9.4). Gel or oil is smoothed on the woman's abdomen to give an air tight seal. A scanner is slowly moved across the female's abdomen. High frequency sound waves are transformed into a picture of the developing baby and shown on a monitor. The procedure is noninvasive and safe for both the mother-to-be and the developing baby.

An ultrasound has made it possible to visualize the embryo as early as six to eight weeks after a female has missed her last menstrual period. A physician can monitor the rate of growth and determine if it is normal for the gestational age. The physician also can check for missing arms and legs and detect if the baby has kidney disease, obstruction of the intestines, or some brain abnormalities. An ultrasound might be used when there is question about whether the fetus has died in the uterus. It might be used to visualize the fetus if surgery must be performed in-utero. If an ultrasound is performed at 18 to 20 weeks into the pregnancy, it might reveal the sex of the baby.

An ultrasound can be used to obtain information that might help during the birth process. The position of the placenta and the baby's position in the womb can be determined. An ultrasound can be used to confirm that the mother-to-be will give birth to more than one baby.

Effects of Pregnancy on the Mother-to-Be

As a fetus grows within a female's uterus, the female's body undergoes many physical and physiological changes necessary to support the new life. These, as well as some psychological factors, affect the mother-to-be throughout the trimesters of the pregnancy.

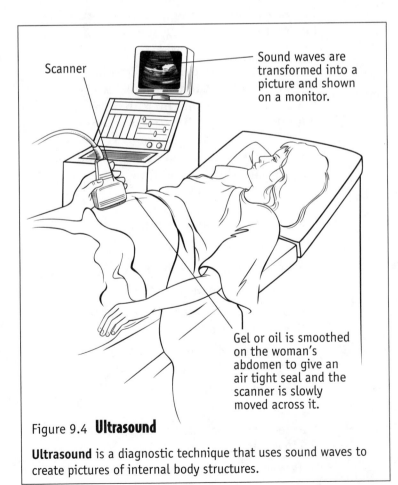

Scanner

Sound waves are transformed into a picture and shown on a monitor.

Gel or oil is smoothed on the woman's abdomen to give an air tight seal and the scanner is slowly moved across it.

Figure 9.4 **Ultrasound**

Ultrasound is a diagnostic technique that uses sound waves to create pictures of internal body structures.

The First Trimester

Most of the physical changes that occur in a pregnant female are due to increased production of the hormones estrogen and progesterone. The mammary glands develop further as the result of the increased production of hormones. The breasts become fuller and might be tender to the touch. The nipples, as well as the areolae, might become darker and slightly puffy. In addition, there might be a tingling sensation around the nipples.

The increase in hormone production causes more water to be retained in the female's body. In addition, as the uterus expands, it exerts pressure on the bladder. Since this pressure is the normal stimulus to urinate, an expectant mother might feel a need to urinate more frequently. This is a normal occurrence. Bowel movements also might become irregular because of pressure exerted on the rectum by the expanding uterus. Constipation might become a problem if the mother reduces her activity, which in turn will cause her to feel tired most of the time.

During the first trimester, a female might experience nausea or frequent vomiting. This condition is referred to as morning sickness, although it might occur at any time during the day. The physiological cause of morning sickness is unknown, but there are two theories.

1. The placental secretions of human chorionic gonadotrophin (HCG) in the early stages of pregnancy might be responsible. According to this theory, the body develops a tolerance to HCG during the later stages of pregnancy.

2. Morning sickness might be caused by chemicals released from cells that are destroyed in the uterine lining as the zygote implants itself. In support of this theory, it has been observed that degeneration of other tissues produces nausea.

Early in pregnancy, an expectant mother might feel very tired and desire more sleep than usual. This might be due to the effects of morning sickness, depression, or the production of high levels of progesterone.

The psychological state of the expectant mother during the first trimester is dependent on a variety of factors surrounding her personal situation.   For example, she might wonder about her career plans and/or her financial situation. She might have concerns as to how a baby will fit into her lifestyle.

A wide range of emotions might surface during this period. If she is pregnant because she wants to be, an expectant mother might be effervescent and "up." This often is true if the mother has tried to conceive over a long period of time. Conversely, an expectant mother who does not want to be pregnant might feel depressed. This might be due to uncertainty in a relationship. Expectant mothers also might feel depressed during this first trimester because they feel physically fatigued.   The expectant mother's mental and physical state often go hand in hand. Some expectant mothers experience no changes at all.

Because of hormonal changes, moodiness is not unusual during pregnancy. Hormonal changes can affect the emotions and create psychological ups and downs. Although each expectant mother has her own unique responses to pregnancy, most find it a fulfilling time.

The Second Trimester

During the second trimester, a fetal heartbeat can be heard, and many observable physical changes take place for the mother-to-be. Her waistline begins to expand, and she will experience quickening. **Quickening** is the awareness of feeling the fetus move for the first time.   As the fetus continues to grow, the female's abdomen distends, causing the skin to stretch. Stretch marks might appear. They are normal and are more pronounced in some females than in others. In general, there is nothing that can be done about stretch marks.

The physical symptoms of morning sickness and fatigue that are associated with the first trimester become minimal or disappear. However, as a result of retaining water in her body, the female's hands, face, and feet might

swell. This condition is known as edema. As the fetus grows, increased pressure is placed on internal organs and the female might experience indigestion and constipation as well as varicose veins and hemorrhoids. During this trimester, the breasts might secrete colostrum. **Colostrum** is a yellowish fluid that is secreted by the mammary glands in preparation of milk production.

The second trimester is often the most peaceful trimester. The mother-to-be might feel better emotionally because many of the earlier physical problems have passed. Barring any complications, she should be able to continue most of her normal everyday tasks.

The Third Trimester

During the last three months of pregnancy, the fetus is very active—kicking, turning, and pushing against the mother-to-be's abdomen. She might have an increased desire for food. Hormonal changes might account for an increase in her appetite, but psychological factors that might cause her to eat more than she needs must be considered.

The weight of the expectant mother will affect the weight of the fetus. Females who overeat during pregnancy might gain as much as 50 pounds (22.5 kg). The recommended weight gain is 25 to 35 pounds (11.25 kg to 15.75 kg) for females of average weight and height. Weight gain during this time is distributed in the following manner:

Baby's weight: 6 to 8 pounds (2.7 kg to 3.6 kg)

Placenta: 1 to 2 pounds (0.45 kg to 0.9 kg)

Amniotic fluid: 2 to 3 pounds (0.9 kg to 1.35 kg)

Increased uterine weight: 2 pounds (0.9 kg)

Enlargement of breasts: 1 to 2 pounds (0.45 kg to 0.9 kg)

Increased blood volume: 3 to 4 pounds (1.35 kg to 1.80 kg)

Increased fluid volume: 2 to 3 pounds (0.9 kg to 1.35 kg)

Increased store of fats and proteins: 6 to 8 pounds (2.7 kg to 3.6 kg)

(Fats and proteins are important for lactation.)

Excessive weight gain is a potential hazard to both the female and the fetus. Medical complications, such as higher than usual blood pressure, might occur. Pregnant females who are overweight prior to conception might gain as little as 15 pounds (6.75 kg) under medical supervision. However, the addition of too little weight during pregnancy also can predispose the female and fetus to medical problems. Pregnant females who are underweight prior to conception might gain up to 40 pounds (18 kg) during pregnancy. In either case, weight should be carefully monitored (March of Dimes, 1999d).

The third trimester is probably the most uncomfortable. The expectant mother might experience shortness of breath because of pressure on her lungs. Heartburn and indigestion are common because of pressure exerted on the abdominal organs. Pressure on the bladder will cause frequent urination. Fatigue will increase. During pregnancy, a female's metabolic rate increases to support the physiological changes that are taking place in her body. She might experience sensations of unusual warmth because the extra weight carried during pregnancy contributes to extra heat production.

Because weight gain is at its peak during this trimester, a pregnant female's center of gravity might be affected. She might try to compensate for the distention of her abdomen by trying to keep her shoulders and back straight. Overcompensation causes the "waddle" type of walking that is often evident during the last days of pregnancy. Back pains are common.

During the last three months, a female might experience Braxton Hicks contractions. **Braxton Hicks contractions** are irregular, painless contractions of the uterine muscles. Many females often mistake these contractions for the onset of labor.

At the beginning of the ninth month, the uterus might begin to descend. This occurs in most pregnancies and indicates that the fetus has begun to sink into the pelvic area. In lay terms, it is called lightening or dropping. Medically, it is known as engagement of the fetus. This event occurs earlier in first pregnancies because there is a greater pressure surrounding the fetus since

the abdominal wall and the uterus have not been stretched by a previous pregnancy and childbirth.

For many females, this trimester is difficult emotionally. It seems to last forever, especially the ninth month. As a result, the mother-to-be might feel anxious and impatient and more irritable than usual. She might begin to worry about the health of the fetus, particularly if the due date has passed. It is important for her to receive support from the father-to-be during this time.

Danger Signs During Pregnancy

Any abnormal or unexplained symptoms during pregnancy might indicate a medical problem that could compromise the health of the female or the fetus. The expectant mother should report any of the following classic danger signs to her physician:

- Bleeding from the vagina, rectum, nipple, or lungs (coughing blood);
- Swelling or puffiness of the face or hands;
- A sudden large weight gain;
- Persistent severe swelling of the legs;
- Severe or repeated headaches;
- Dimness, blurred vision, flashes of light, or spots before the eyes;
- Sharp or prolonged pain in the abdomen;
- Chills and/or fever; and
- Sudden escape of fluid from the vagina (NIH, 1998).

Effects of Pregnancy on the Father-to-Be

The father-to-be can gain insight into a pregnancy by various means. There are numerous books available as well as thousands of articles from medical journals and government sources on the Internet that can help the father-to-be. By accompanying the expectant mother to appointments with her obstetrician, the father-to-be can ask questions about the progress of the pregnancy. He can listen to the fetus's heartbeat. At home, he can feel the movements of the fetus against the mother's abdomen. The expectant mother and father also can attend pregnancy education and childbirth preparation classes together.

Although preparation for the male's future role might have started before conception, the father-to-be usually feels some anxiety during a pregnancy. The couple should discuss its worries and fears and help each other through the emotional ups and downs of pregnancy. While the father-to-be is reassuring and comforting to his partner during the pregnancy, it is important for him to share his feelings. He might experience the same uncertainties and fluctuating emotions as his partner. And he might have additional concerns. Something that might seem unimportant to one partner might be disturbing to the other. Each partner needs to be understanding and patient and to know that each one has special needs.

The father-to-be might worry about the changes in his life and about the changes in his relationship with the mother-to-be. He can reduce his anxiety by talking about these changes with her and with the health care provider. Maintenance of healthful lifestyle habits will help alleviate the father-to-be's concerns and encourage a healthy pregnancy. Taking daily walks together is recommended. By sharing the housework, especially the heavy work, the father can help protect the fetus. He also can protect the fetus from the potentially harmful fumes of aerosol sprays or cleaning fluids. If the couple has a cat, the father should empty or clean the litter box and wear disposable or washable, waterproof gloves. This will protect the mother from exposure to an infection called toxoplasmosis found in cat feces that can endanger the health of the fetus.

Although planning for the baby's arrival might have started before conception, further decisions must be made and shared concerning the baby's birth. Imminent decisions include purchasing a nursery, the roles the expectant parents intend to play, employment, maternity and paternity leave from jobs, and health needs. The father-to-be might decide to take time off from work to assist and give further emotional support.

Some males become so involved in their partner's pregnancy that they experience a sym-

pathetic pregnancy. **Couvade** is a condition in which a male experiences the same physical and psychological symptoms of pregnancy that the expectant mother experiences, including depression, nausea, vomiting, and labor pains.

Since postnatal care will affect both the mother and father, they should be informed about current hospital practices. Widespread publicity about the decline in hospital stays for childbirth has raised concerns for the health of mothers and their babies. Federal legislation enacted in 1996 prohibited insurers from restricting these hospital stays to less than two days for vaginal deliveries and four days for cesarean deliveries. Although the legislation did not take effect until 1998, state laws and changes in insurance coverage occurred in anticipation of the federal law. The welcome increase in hospital stays for mothers and their newborns helps reduce the amount of care from the father (National Center for Health Statistics, 1999b).

Sexual Activity During Pregnancy

Sexual relations during the first trimester can continue as they were before conception occurred. However, for many couples, morning sickness and fatigue act as deterrents. Except for females who are pregnant for the first time, decreased sexual interest during the first trimester generally is not common.

Some psychological changes that are a result of pregnancy might affect sexual relations. For example, if a female is anxious about her pregnancy, she might not be able to be aroused. This disinterest might make sexual intercourse painful because of the lack of vaginal lubrication. Increased breast sensitivity might reduce her desire to become intimate during the first trimester.

Some females are concerned that intercourse might cause miscarriage. However, there is no evidence to support this notion. The fetus is well protected within the confines of the uterus.

During the second trimester, females often experience increased sexual response. In fact, some females might experience orgasm for the first time; others might develop a multiorgasmic response. This experience might be due to the increased pelvic vascularity, which is brought on by pregnancy. Sexual activity also might decrease over the course of a pregnancy.

During the second trimester, a couple might use the full range of coital positions, provided they do not find them awkward or uncomfortable. For many couples, there is abstention from intercourse during the third trimester for physical as well as psychological reasons. Some couples believe that intercourse during this time might cause premature labor. That is not true in pregnancies where there are no risk factors. While orgasm in a pregnant female might trigger contractions, these contractions usually are not related to the onset of labor.

Many physicians feel that sexual relations are in no way harmful at any time during a pregnancy. However, some physicians advise their patients to refrain from sexual activity during the last four to six weeks of pregnancy if there are pre-existing causes for concern. Any concerns should be discussed with the primary care provider.

Sexual intercourse during the third trimester might require creativity and an adventurous spirit. As the due date approaches, the man-on-top position becomes uncomfortable for the pregnant female. The side-to-side position might be more suitable. Experimenting with other positions is recommended if each partner is comfortable.

If, at any time during pregnancy, a female experiences preterm labor symptoms, she should restrict sexual activity and consult her health care provider.

Atypical Conditions During Pregnancy

Most females have relatively uneventful pregnancies and deliver full-term, healthy babies. However, there are times when the unexpected or the unusual occurs.

Pseudocyesis

False pregnancy, or **pseudocyesis**, is a condition wherein a female believes that she is pregnant and shows some of the signs and symptoms of

pregnancy, even though she is not pregnant. The female might experience absence of menses, breast changes, nausea, and vomiting. Her abdomen might even swell, due to gaseous distention of the bowel. Despite medical assurance to the contrary, the patient might insist that she is pregnant. In fact, she might go into a false labor at the end of nine months. More frequently, she has a heavy menstrual period and claims to have had a miscarriage.

Many females who experience pseudocyesis are childless and perhaps have an abnormal longing for a baby. These females can be treated by counseling or psychotherapy.

Ectopic Pregnancy

An **ectopic pregnancy** is a condition wherein a fertilized ovum implants itself in any place other than in the lining of the uterus (Figure 9.5). More than 95 percent of ectopic implantations occur in the fallopian tubes, thus the term tubal pregnancy (Mayo Clinic, 1995). Rarely do ectopic pregnancies occur in the abdominal cavity, cervix, or ovaries. Ectopic pregnancies generally are caused by blockages such as tumors, scar tissue, or structural defects in the reproductive system that prevent an ovum from reaching the uterus.

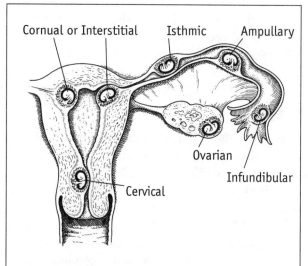

Figure 9.5 **Ectopic Pregnancies**

An **ectopic pregnancy** is a condition wherein a fertilized ovum implants itself in any place other than in the lining of the uterus.

An ectopic pregnancy ordinarily is diagnosed by the occurrence of lower abdominal pain several days or weeks after a period is missed. Vaginal bleeding might occur, which might be mistaken for a menstrual period. Since these symptoms can be typical of many conditions, an ectopic pregnancy is difficult to diagnose. If it is suspected, however, an ultrasound might be used to confirm the diagnosis and determine the location of the implantation.

Ectopic pregnancies cannot be carried full term. Some embryos might spontaneously abort and be released into the abdominal cavity. In this case, if the embryo is young enough and the oviduct has not been damaged, the embryo might disintegrate. However, if the embryo has begun to grow and stretches the tube, the tube might rupture. This could present a life-threatening situation to the female. Surgery should be performed as soon as possible after diagnosis to preserve the tube intact and to prevent rupture and subsequent hemorrhage.

Most ectopic pregnancies occur in females between the ages of 35 and 44. Pelvic inflammatory disease (PID) poses the greatest risk for ectopic pregnancy. Other risk factors include advancing age, previous ectopic pregnancy, tubal surgery, several induced abortions, and infertility problems or medication to stimulate ovulation.

Ectopic pregnancies occur in 7 of every 1,000 reported pregnancies in the United States. Death from ectopic pregnancy is rare because of new techniques that can detect the disorder at an early stage.

Rh Factor

When a female first becomes pregnant, as part of her checkup her doctor will determine if her blood has the Rh factor. The **Rh factor** is an inherited protein substance in red blood cells. **Rh positive (Rh+)** is the presence of Rh in a person's blood. **Rh negative (Rh–)** is a lack of Rh in a person's blood. The Rh factor is present in 85 percent of the Caucasian population and 93 percent of the African American population. The Rh factor can present problems in a pregnancy.

Every female should be tested early in pregnancy or before pregnancy to determine if she is Rh negative. To prevent Rh disease, an injection of a blood product called Rh immunoglobulin (RhIg) should be given to an Rh-negative female within 72 hours of delivery of an Rh-positive baby. Less often, the injection is given at about 28 weeks of pregnancy and after delivery (March of Dimes, 1997). During the latter part of a pregnancy or during birth, fetal blood might mix with the mother's blood. If the mother is Rh– and the fetus is Rh+, the mother will produce antibodies against the Rh factor. If these antibodies cross the placenta and enter the fetal blood, they can destroy the fetal red blood cells. If this condition is not treated, it can result in fetal anemia, mental retardation, or the birth of a stillborn baby. The treatment consists of slowly removing the baby's blood at birth and replacing it with Rh-negative blood. In this way, if any antibodies remain in the baby's circulation, they will not destroy the red blood cells.

There is very little risk of incompatibility between an Rh– mother and an Rh+ fetus in a first pregnancy because the level of antibodies is too low to cause a problem. However, there is a chance that succeeding pregnancies might present a problem.

Rubella

A pregnant female should avoid exposure to rubella (German measles) so as not to expose the fetus to possible blindness, deafness, heart defects, mental and growth retardation, or liver, spleen, and bone marrow problems. When a female contracts rubella during the first trimester of pregnancy, there is a 25 percent chance that her baby will be born with an abnormality. If the disease is contracted after the twentieth week of pregnancy, however, the chances of congenital rubella syndrome are slim (Koop, 1999).

Due to immunization of younger children and adolescents, fewer cases of congenital rubella occur. Estimates are that 10 percent of young females of childbearing age are susceptible to rubella (Novitt-Moreno, 1999).

Multiple Births

Multiple births might occur unexpectedly. Though heredity seems to play a role, multiple births are not definitely known to be an inherited trait. Over the past two decades, there has been a substantial increase in the number of multiple births. This is due to the rise in births to females in their thirties who use fertility drugs and techniques. The increase in triplet births is associated with ovulation-enhancing drugs and assisted reproductive techniques, such as in vitro fertilization. Multiple heartbeats during pregnancy often can be detected, and a sonogram usually can show if more than one fetus is in the uterus. Multiple births might produce twins, triplets, quadruplets, quintuplets, and even greater numbers. Many multiple-birth babies die as a result of low birth weight. The average weight of a triplet at birth is half that of a single birth child. The period of gestation is about seven weeks shorter for multiple births than for a single birth child (National Center for Health Statistics, 1997).

Twins might be of two types—identical and fraternal. **Identical twins** are twins that develop from a single ovum fertilized by a single sperm that divides after fertilization to form two zygotes. Since they inherit the same chromosomes, identical twins are always the same sex. They share the same placenta but have separate amniotic sacs as well as separate umbilical cords (Figure 9.6).

Fraternal twins might result when ovulation occurs more than once during a menstrual cycle. **Fraternal twins** are twins that develop from two separate ova that are fertilized by two different sperm. Fraternal twins develop in separate amniotic sacs and have separate umbilical cords and placentas. Fraternal twins can be the same or different sex. They look no more alike than any other two children by the same parents because they do not share identical chromosomes.

Conjoined twins, or **Siamese twins**, are twins who are physically joined at birth. This joining occurs when a cell mass does not separate completely. As a result, the twins might be joined at any part of the body. Depending on which organs the twins share, surgery to separate conjoined twins can be successful.

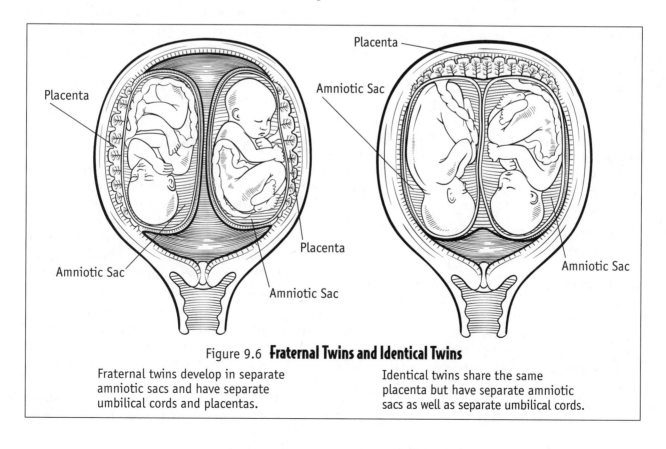

Figure 9.6 **Fraternal Twins and Identical Twins**

Fraternal twins develop in separate amniotic sacs and have separate umbilical cords and placentas.

Identical twins share the same placenta but have separate amniotic sacs as well as separate umbilical cords.

In most cases, triplets result from the fertilization of two ova, one of which divides into two zygotes, producing identical twins and a third baby. Triplets also can result from the fertilization of three different ova. Quadruplets most often are the result of two fertilized ova that separate and form two sets of identical twins.

Between 1980 and 1995, triplet births per 100,000 births increased 272 percent. In 1997, twin births increased 3 percent and triplet births rose 16 percent while quadruplet and quintuplet deliveries decreased slightly (National Center for Health Statistics, 1999c).

Miscarriage

A **miscarriage**, or **spontaneous abortion**, is a natural expulsion of the embryo or fetus before it has reached a point of development at which it can survive outside the mother's body. Many pregnancies end before they are detected, or even before any symptoms of pregnancy are experienced, such as a missed period. About one in every six pregnancies ends in a miscarriage (CDC, 1999). In the past, it was estimated that pregnancy loss due to miscarriage was 10 to 15 percent.

Spotting, or vaginal bleeding, is frequently the first sign of a miscarriage, particularly in the early stages of pregnancy. Later on in a pregnancy, an impending miscarriage might be indicated by bleeding and cramping as well as the disappearance of the symptoms of pregnancy. Many miscarried fetuses have deformities or biological malfunctions. Miscarriage might be nature's way of trying to insure that full-term babies are healthy and have the greatest chance of survival.

There are varied reasons for miscarriages. If an ovum or a sperm is damaged, the fertilized ovum cannot survive. A female's hormone system might be impaired. Fetal development might be abnormal. The uterus or the cervix might have physical problems (CDC, 1999). Age also poses a risk factor. Females older than 35 years of age have a high incidence of miscarriage, many of which are due to chromosomal abnormalities. Some other causes of miscarriage are illness, malnutrition, STDs, trauma, and drug use. However, most miscarriages have no known cause and therefore are not preventable. Females with recurrent miscarriages associated with certain conditions are treated with aspirin and heparin. This has resulted in a significantly higher rate of live births (Rai et al., 1997).

Preterm or Premature Birth

Preterm birth, or **premature birth**, is birth before the 37th week of gestation. Toxemia is one cause of premature birth. **Toxemia**, or **preeclampsia**, is a condition characterized by high blood pressure, edema, the presence of protein in the urine, and rapid weight gain during pregnancy. All of these signs frequently are associated with poor nutrition. Obesity in females before pregnancy increases the risk of late fetal death (Cnattingius, 1998).

Whether or not the administration of low doses of aspirin prevents preeclampsia in females at high risk for the disease has not been established. In a recent study, the use of low-dose aspirin did not reduce the occurrence of preeclampsia (Caritis, 1998). Previous studies suggested that calcium supplementation during pregnancy might reduce the risk of preeclampsia. However, additional calcium intake did not prevent preeclampsia in more recent trials. Other causes of premature birth include abnormalities of the uterus or cervix, heavy cigarette smoking, alcoholism, drug use, poor nutrition, and generally poor health.

Ways to Detect Birth Defects

According to recent statistics, birth defects occur among 150,000 American families every year. These defects can be physical or mental or both. Various new studies are being developed to consider possible genetic and environmental causes including exposure to pesticides, heat, and drinking water contaminants (CDC, 1998a).

Prenatal screening for birth defects can reveal the presence of chromosomal abnormalities in a fetus. **Amniocentesis** is a simple diagnostic procedure in which a needle is inserted through the uterus to extract fluid from the amniotic sac. It is often done during the 14th to 16th week of pregnancy (Figure 9.7). Amniocentesis usually is not offered to all pregnant females because there is some small risk of miscarriage. Before

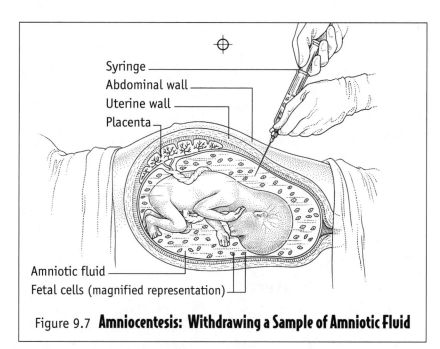

Syringe
Abdominal wall
Uterine wall
Placenta

Amniotic fluid
Fetal cells (magnified representation)

Figure 9.7 **Amniocentesis: Withdrawing a Sample of Amniotic Fluid**

the procedure is performed, ultrasound is used to locate the fetus and the placenta. Afterward, the abdomen is cleansed. Then the amniocentesis needle is inserted through the abdominal wall into the uterine cavity and a sample of amniotic fluid containing fetal cells is withdrawn. Ultrasound is used again to check that the fetal heartbeat is normal. Fetal cells are analyzed for genetic defects, such as sickle-cell disease, muscular dystrophy, and Down Syndrome. Not all genetic abnormalities in a fetus can be diagnosed with this procedure (March of Dimes, 1999a).

Another test for detecting genetic defects prior to birth is chorionic villi sampling (CVS). This test can diagnose most of the same birth defects as amniocentesis. The chorion is an outer sac surrounding the fetus, and in early pregnancy it is covered with root-like projections called villi. These projections are fetal tissue, a part of which will later differentiate into the placenta. One of these projections easily can be biopsied in early pregnancy with no real discomfort to the pregnant female. However, CVS might pose a small risk of birth defects of the fingers and the toes (March of Dimes, 1999a).

Screening tests for a variety of genetic defects can be performed on the cells obtained by CVS. Although CVS has certain advantages over amniocentesis, research suggests that CVS seems to have a slightly higher risk of miscarriage

and other complications than amniocentesis.

A recent study indicates that maternal serum screening with or without the use of ultrasound can detect Down Syndrome during the first trimester (Haddow et al., 1998). Other research suggests that serum screening also can detect many other chromosomal abnormalities (Scott, 1995).

There are pregnancy situations in which it is reasonable to suspect that a fetus might have inherited genetic defects. The following are considered candidates for screening tests:

• Females older than 35 years of age

• Females who have or whose partner has a parent with a chromosomal defect

• Females with a previous child born with a defect

• Females in whose families there is a predisposition toward birth defects

Although there is a risk of causing miscarriage with these tests, the information provided by them needs to be weighed against any disadvantages. When screening tests reveal that the fetus has a chromosomal abnormality, the parents can explore their options.

Risks Associated with Adolescent Pregnancy

Each year, nearly one million adolescents become pregnant (March of Dimes, 1999c). This statistic is alarming by itself. However, it is even more alarming when considering the statistics regarding sexually transmitted diseases in adolescents. STDs affect three million adolescents each year. This represents 25 percent of all cases reported annually. The threat of HIV infection is the greatest in the adolescent population (March of Dimes, 1999c). Thus, adolescent females who are sexually active risk becoming pregnant and being infected with sexually transmitted diseases including HIV.

Many adolescents cling to the notion that a female cannot conceive the first time she has sexual intercourse. Many still believe that "it can't happen to me."

The risks to the fetus are great in the cases of adolescent pregnancies. An adolescent female's body is still growing. If she does not have good prenatal care and if her diet is not balanced, her baby is more likely to have low birth weight. A low birth weight baby weighs less than 5.8 pounds (2.61 kg) at birth. Low birth weight babies represent 7 percent of all births but account for about two-thirds of all infant deaths. Very low birth weight babies weighing less than 3.5 pounds (1.58 kg) represent 1 percent of all births each year but account for one-half of all infant deaths. Low birth weight babies, if they survive, are more apt to have developmental problems, both physical and mental, than babies of normal weight (March of Dimes, 1999b).

Adolescent parents find that the 24-hour-a-day demands of a baby make it difficult for them to fulfill the developmental tasks of adolescence. Many of them drop out of school. Without an education, their future is dim. After giving birth, almost half of all unmarried adolescents receive welfare during the next two years (March of Dimes, 1999c).

Childbirth

The delivery of a baby from the mother's uterus is an extremely complex process that might take several hours. This section of the chapter will include a discussion of birthplace alternatives, childbirth preparation, pain management in childbirth, stages of labor, and positions in childbirth.

Birthplace Alternatives

Not all females are content to give birth in the traditional, sometimes impersonal hospital setting. A number of other options are available, such as birthing rooms within hospitals, birth centers, and home births.

Birthing Rooms

Many hospitals have birthing rooms. These rooms are specially designed to simulate a home environment and, yet, are furnished with traditional equipment and supplies found in labor and delivery rooms. Because the birthing room is located within the hospital, emergency equipment is available if needed. Unlike the traditional hospital, however, labor and delivery take place in the same room. In addition, family members, including children, might be welcome in a birthing room and might participate in the birth experience.

Birth Centers

During the past decade, birth centers have appeared throughout many parts of the country. They might be associated with a hospital or be an independent health care facility. A birth center, like the birthing room within a hospital, is designed to look like a home. The accommodations might consist of a double hospital bed and chairs, a living room, a dinette, and a nurse's station. In this environment, a couple, along with the couple's obstetrician or nurse-midwife and pediatrician, draws up a plan that directs the staff of the birthing center. This plan considers the needs and preferences of the mother-to-be, including her wishes regarding the use of intravenous infusions and anesthetics.

The homelike atmosphere of the birthing center is conducive to relaxation with friends and family. During labor, the mother might walk around and have the support of those close to her. Usually, no unexpected medical professionals or other visitors are allowed to enter unless an emergency arises.

Females who choose to use a birthing center are prescreened to determine if they are at risk for developing complications. Generally, only those who are considered not to be at risk are accepted. Despite the prescreening, unpredictable problems might arise. Guidelines for conditions that might require transfer out of a birth center's care to a nearby hospital vary. Therefore, it is important for females to be aware of the services and options offered by the center.

Home Births

Giving birth at home is becoming more and more popular. Home births can be a safe experience if the following preparations have been made:

- proper prenatal care;
- screening for complications;
- the availability of a skilled assistant; and
- the availability of emergency medical transportation in the event it is needed.

The increasing number of trained nurse midwives and their greater acceptance by some obstetricians have facilitated the accessibility of the choice of home births. In 1995, certified nurse midwives delivered 6 percent of all births in the United States compared with 3 percent in 1989. The first study to examine infant mortality risks for all babies delivered by certified nurse midwives in the United States reports excellent birth outcomes. The risk of infant death was 19 percent lower for births attended by certified nurse midwives than for births attended by physicians. The risk of infant death during the first 28 days of life was 33 percent lower. The risk of delivering a low birth weight infant was 31 percent lower (National Center for Health Statistics, 1998).

Although the role of the nurse midwife is primarily clinical, he or she also might provide emotional and physical support to the laboring mother. A doula also might join the expectant couple in the home during the early stages of labor. A **doula** is an assistant to the new mother during birth and in the first few days after giving birth. This person enters the home to assist with household duties and attend to the new mother's needs. Doulas have a great deal of experience with very young children and help the new mother learn what to expect in the months ahead. Doulas do not interfere with a clinical caregiver but serve as support to the new family (Wickersham, 1999).

The practice of home birth is controversial among medical professionals. Many hospitals would revoke the privileges of physicians who deliver babies at home. Further, the fear of malpractice suits resulting from birth complications might dissuade some physicians and midwives from taking part in home deliveries.

There are advantages to a home birth.

- It provides a familiar surrounding.
- It allows bonding to begin immediately without interruption.
- It allows immediate breastfeeding without time limits.
- It places the decision-making responsibility on the couple.
- It costs much less than a hospital delivery.
- It might allow the expectant mother to be less anxious than she would be in a hospital.
- It avoids procedures the expectant mother might consider objectionable and unnecessary (McDonald, 1999).

There are disadvantages to a home birth.

- Emergency medical treatment is not as readily available as in a hospital.
- There is risk of infection.
- There is the risk of an unexpected emergency.

Childbirth Preparation

Childbirth preparation combines education about the birth process before delivery with techniques that facilitate the birth process. The following discussion includes the Dick-Read method, the Lamaze method, the Leboyer method, the Bradley method, and the Waterbirth method.

The Dick-Read Method

The term "natural childbirth" was coined by Grantly Dick-Read. He believed that the pain of childbirth was caused by fear and tension. To alleviate fear and tension, Dick-Read proposed a program that combined education about the birth process before delivery with exercise and relaxation techniques. Dick-Read made it clear that natural childbirth was not necessarily painless childbirth. Although medication is not usually recommended, an anesthesia is used if it is needed or wanted. Natural childbirth usually involves relaxation and comfort techniques. The parents are involved in decisions about the birth of their baby.

Several other methods of prepared childbirth based on the Dick-Read natural childbirth technique are available today. These include the Bradley method, the Gomper method, and the Kitzinger, Simkin, and Noble approaches. All include relaxation and comfort techniques and encourage parents to make informed decisions regarding such options as birthplace, the use of a physician or nurse-midwife, and the use of anesthetics. Prepared childbirth techniques are popular among couples who want to actively participate in and share the birth process.

The Lamaze Method

The most widely used technique of prepared childbirth in the United States today is the Lamaze method. In 1970, Dr. Fernand Lamaze developed what he called a psycho-prophylactic or "mind prevention" method in which two techniques, relaxation and controlled breathing, could help an expectant mother become distracted from the pain of labor and delivery. Lamaze is based on a conditioned response technique in which the mother learns to respond to pain by relaxing and controlling her breathing instead of becoming tense. This technique is designed to break the fear-tension-pain cycle, and is taught to the female and her coach (usually her partner) who work together during the pregnancy as well as through labor and delivery. Massage and abdominal stroking (effleurage) are two other practices used in the Lamaze method to decrease the sensation of pain.

The Leboyer Method

In 1975, Frederick Leboyer introduced his philosophy and method of childbirth to the United States. Unlike those of Dick-Read and Lamaze, Leboyer's approach focuses on the birth experience of the infant. Leboyer believed that the process of birth is traumatic based on the following observations:

- The baby goes from the curled, fetal position in which it has been for nine months, to a straight-backed position in which it lies on its back when it is born.
- The baby goes from nine months of darkness to glaring lights.

- The baby goes from quietness and the sounds of its mother's heartbeat to noise.
- The baby goes from an environment of warmth to an environment that might be more than 20°F (−6.67°C) cooler.

Leboyer thought that the baby's transition from the inner world to the outer world should be less traumatic. To best mediate this transition, Leboyer advocated that the following conditions should be met in the delivery room at the time of birth:

- The baby should be placed in a tub of water at body temperature when the baby is born.
- The lights used in the delivery room should be dimmed.
- Soft music should be played and low voices used.
- The umbilical cord should be cut after it ceases to pulsate.
- The baby should have skin-to-skin contact with its mother's abdomen.

Leboyer's philosophy sounds very rational. However, most hospitals in the United States have not set up such an environment and few have adopted his method. The effect of such a delivery on a baby is speculative.

The Bradley Method

Dr. Robert A. Bradley developed his method of childbirth in the late 1940s. Designed to involve fathers in the birth process, the Bradley Method teaches effective coaching techniques during pregnancy. Positive communication and deep relaxation are practiced to reduce pain without medication during labor and delivery. The importance of bonding and the father's role in breastfeeding are stressed to help couples adjust to the transition to parenthood.

The Waterbirth Method

One of the newest methods of prepared childbirth is the waterbirth method. The use of a pool or tub of lukewarm water for delivery suggests that a waterbirth might be especially effective during long labors. Hypnotherapy, such as the Leclaire Method and Body-Centered Hypnosis, is associated with reduced discomfort during pregnancy and birth.

Pain Management in Childbirth

Medications for managing pain are sometimes used during labor and delivery. Labor pains can be managed with tranquilizing, narcotic, barbiturate, and amnesic drugs. Because these medications can have adverse effects on the mother as well as on the fetus and reduce the strength of contractions, some physicians recommend that they be avoided whenever possible. There are medical situations, however, when their use is required. The benefits should be weighed against the possible adverse effects, and, under all circumstances, caution should be used.

Obstetrical anesthesia is used commonly in childbirth. This section of the chapter will include a discussion of anesthetics used to prevent pain and will be divided into three major types—local anesthetics, regional anesthetics, and general anesthetics.

Local Anesthetics

Local anesthetics are drugs used to eliminate pain in small specific areas for short periods of time. The paracervical block and the pudendal block are two types of local anesthetics used in obstetrics. The benefit of local anesthetics is that they do not impede movement or interfere with the pushing movements necessary for the baby to move through the birth canal.

A **paracervical block** is an injection of an anesthetic around the cervix in order to numb the cervix and uterus before delivery. The disadvantage of the paracervical block is that it might cause slowing of the fetal heart rate.

A **pudendal block** is an injection of an anesthetic around the nerves on each side of the vagina in order to numb the perineum and vulva. It is administered shortly before the delivery.

Regional Anesthetics

Regional anesthetics are drugs used to affect a larger area of the body, and although they are temporary, they might be longer lasting than local anesthetics. Regional anesthetics used in obstetrics include the spinal and the epidural.

A **spinal anesthetic** is an injection of an anesthetic administered into the spinal fluid surrounding the lower spinal cord. It is given as close to delivery as possible. Spinal anesthetics numb the body from the waist down, thereby eliminating pain completely. There are some drawbacks, however. Spinal anesthetics can slow down or stop labor, and the resulting loss of muscle control below the waist might prevent the ability of the mother to push. If the mother cannot help the baby pass through the birth canal, forceps are required for delivery. The use of forceps, however, might harm the baby. For this reason, spinal anesthetics are not usually the anesthetic of choice for normal vaginal deliveries. However, they are highly recommended and frequently used in cesarean sections performed on a routine rather than an emergency basis.

A **saddle block** is an injection of an anesthetic into the spinal fluid that numbs only those parts of the body that would touch a horse's saddle.

An **epidural** is an injection of an anesthetic into the back that eliminates pain below the waist. Unlike spinal anesthetics, it does not enter the spinal fluid. An epidural might be administered after the first stage of labor has been established. It not only eliminates pain below the waist but also allows the mother to be more effective during delivery because all muscle control is not lost. An epidural might be administered early in the birth process so that the pain associated with the later stages of labor is eliminated.

Epidurals are used often because of their superiority to other kinds of anesthetics during labor. A new technique that combines the spinal and the epidural is being widely used. The advantages of combining the spinal and epidural include rapid effectiveness and decreased motor block, allowing the mother to walk during labor.

General Anesthetics

A **general anesthetic** is an anesthetic used to eliminate pain in the whole body, creating temporary but complete unconsciousness. General anesthetics are absorbed quickly into the bloodstream. The major argument against the use of general anesthetic is that it enters the fetus' circulation through the placenta and might depress the central nervous system and lungs. The baby then is born sleepy, not alert, and might have sluggish respiration. In rare cases, newborn babies have died from the effects of general anesthetics, and some mothers have become ill.

There is no doubt that anesthetics are a tremendous asset to the process of childbirth. Once the obstacle of pain has been removed, a mother might feel more at ease during delivery and be able to more fully appreciate the birth of her baby. On the other hand, some mothers-to-be believe that the administration of anesthetics detracts from the excitement of the birth experience. There also is the contention that anesthetics are sometimes used unnecessarily and therefore increase the chances of harm to the mother and the baby.

Stages of Labor

Parturition is the technical name for the process of childbirth. Labor is the common name. The positioning of the baby during the birth process is illustrated in Figure 9.8. Parturition is initiated by a combination of hormonal and mechanical factors.

Some evidence suggests that irritation or stretching of the cervix stimulates the release of oxytocin, a hormone produced by the pituitary gland. The increase in the level of oxytocin at the time of labor in turn causes uterine contractions. The vaginal application of prostaglandin E2 gel also can stimulate uterine contractions (Hannah, 1996).

Stretching of the uterus is thought to stimulate uterine contractility. For example, as pregnancy progresses and the growth and movement of the fetus increase, the smooth muscles that line the uterus become stretched. This stretching, in turn, might cause the uterus to contract.

Although the amniotic sac usually ruptures after labor begins, it might occur before the first contractions. A discharge or gushing of water from the vagina indicates that this has happened. A more dependable sign that labor is about to begin, however, is the discharge of the mucous plug that sealed the cervix during pregnancy. This is called "show" or "bloody show." Another indication of ensuing labor is the beginning of irregular contractions. There are three distinct stages of labor. In each stage, specific events take place.

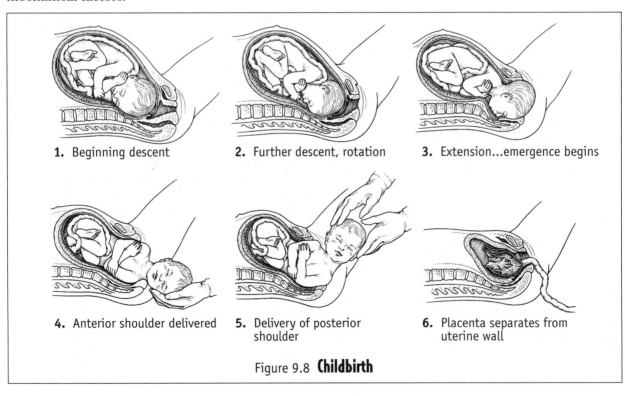

1. Beginning descent

2. Further descent, rotation

3. Extension...emergence begins

4. Anterior shoulder delivered

5. Delivery of posterior shoulder

6. Placenta separates from uterine wall

Figure 9.8 **Childbirth**

Stage 1: Dilation of the Cervix

The first stage of labor is the longest stage. It can last from two hours to an entire day. The contractions in the beginning of Stage 1 are short, weak, and spaced far apart. During this stage, effacement takes place. **Effacement** is the thinning out of the cervix. **Dilation** is the widening of the cervix. Effacement and dilation occur at the same time.

As the mother moves through Stage 1, the contractions become more intense, last longer, and occur more frequently. The cervix continues to dilate during this time.

Transition is the end of Stage 1. The contractions are very strong, lasting a minute or more, and occur every one to three minutes. During this stage, the cervical opening enlarges to 8 to 10 cm (3 1/8 to 3 15/16 inch) wide, a width sufficient for delivery. Dilation of the cervix is complete and the baby moves into the birth canal.

Stage 2: Delivery of the Baby

This stage of labor begins with the cervix fully dilated and ends with the delivery of the baby. At the beginning of Stage 2, the baby has dropped farther down into the birth canal, usually head first. Subsequent contractions of the uterus accomplish delivery. This stage of labor can last from several minutes to an hour or more.

During Stage 2, the mother experiences an urge to push the baby out. **Crowning** is the beginning of the head emerging during birth. During crowning, an episiotomy might be performed. An **episiotomy** is a cut made in the perineum to facilitate easier passage of the baby's head through the vagina and to prevent the vaginal tissues from tearing. An episiotomy might or might not be performed with local anesthetics. Because of the great pressure of the baby's head on the perineum, the incision might not be felt by the mother. Once the baby has been eased out of the birth canal and begins to breath on its own, the umbilical cord is cut.

An episiotomy is no longer performed as a routine procedure. There is evidence that contradicts the expected results from having this procedure. Having an episiotomy does not necessarily preserve muscle tone. And, having an episiotomy might cause tears in the perineum.

Stage 3: Delivery of the Placenta

In the final stage of labor, the placenta is expelled. The **afterbirth** is the placenta that is expelled in the final stage of labor. If the afterbirth is not expelled naturally, the physician removes it by hand. It is important that the placenta be intact and that no placental fragments remain in the uterus. Shortly after delivery, the uterus contracts tightly to close off the blood vessels that supplied the placenta through the uterine wall.

Positions in Childbirth

Approximately 99 percent of all babies during childbirth adopt a longitudinal position in the uterus. The majority of these have a cephalic, or head-first, presentation. In this position, the baby is delivered head first with the face rotated to the side as the rest of the body emerges from the birth canal.

Two to four percent of all longitudinal births are in the breech position. A **breech birth position** is a position in which the baby's buttocks is presented first (Figure 9.9a). If the physician is aware that the fetus is in a breech position, he or she might try to manipulate the baby so that the head will present first (Walkinshaw, 1997).

In 1 in 200 births, the fetus might lie across the birth canal. A **transverse birth position** is a position in which the baby's shoulder, arm, or hand is presented first (Figure 9.9b).

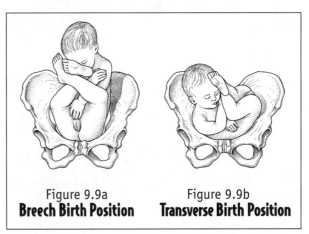

Figure 9.9a	Figure 9.9b
Breech Birth Position	**Transverse Birth Position**

When a baby cannot be delivered vaginally, a cesarean section must be performed. A **cesarean section**, or **c-section**, is the surgical removal of the fetus through an incision made in the mother's abdomen and uterus (Figure 9.10). The most common reasons for cesarean sections include the following:

- A pelvis too small for the baby to pass into the vagina.
- Breech or transverse presentation of the baby.
- Failure of the cervix to dilate.
- Premature separation of the placenta from the uterus.
- Infection in the vaginal tract.
- Exhaustion of the mother.
- Fetal distress.
- Incapacitation of the mother because of injury or trauma.

The number of cesarean sections in the United States rose through the 1970s and the 1980s to a high of 25 percent of all births. Throughout the 1990s, cesarean rates steadily declined until 1997, when the rate seemed to have leveled off at 21 percent of all births. (National Centers for Health Statistics, 1999a).

Some physicians, as well as expectant mothers, believe that once a c-section has been performed, all future babies born to that mother must be delivered surgically. However, this is true only in certain circumstances, such as in the case of a female who has a small pelvis. In general, a vaginal delivery can be safe subsequent to a c-section. It is important to note that a female can have more than one cesarean delivery.

Induced Labor

Induced labor is a procedure that involves dilating the cervix and administering a hormone intravenously to initiate rhythmic uterine contractions and thus initiate labor. Prelabor rupture of fetal membranes at term poses a risk of infection to the fetus and to the mother. The risk increases as the interval increases between the rupture and delivery. Therefore, induced labor using intravenous oxytocin or the vaginal prostaglandin E2 gel might be necessary. Research indicates that induced labor with intravenous oxytocin results in lowered risk of maternal infection (Hannah et al., 1996).

Induced labor also might be used in severe cases of preeclampsia. If preeclampsia progresses to eclampsia, then hypertension, convulsions, and death might result. The only cure for eclampsia is immediate delivery of the baby (National Institute of Child Health and Human Development, 1998).

The Postpartum Period

The **postpartum period** is the first several weeks after delivery. During this time, the mother undergoes many physical and psychological changes. The postpartum period is a period of adjustment for the entire family. This section of the chapter will include a discussion of the adjustments of the mother, bonding, breastfeeding, and sexual intercourse after childbirth.

Figure 9.10 **Procedure for Cesarean Section Delivery**

A **cesarean section**, or **c-section**, is the surgical removal of the fetus through an incision made in the mother's abdomen and uterus.

Adjustments of the Mother

Physically, the mother begins to return to "normal" immediately after giving birth. The uterus decreases in weight by one-half within a week, and by four to six weeks, it returns to its normal state. The cervical opening decreases to less than one centimeter (3/8 inch) in size and the overstretched vagina shrinks, although not quite to pre-delivery size. After childbirth, hormone levels decline sharply. During the first two to three weeks after delivery, there is a uterine discharge called lochia. **Lochia** is a thick, dark red fluid consisting of blood, mucous, and tissue. As the uterus rebuilds itself, the discharge changes to pink and then eventually becomes clear.

Psychologically, the postpartum period is a time for mixed feelings and emotions. Happiness can turn to sadness, confidence to anxiety, and energy to extreme fatigue. At times the new mother might have spur-of-the-moment episodes of crying and depression known as postpartum depression, or "baby blues." Usually postpartum depression is transient and has no adverse consequences (National Institute of Mental Health, 1999b).

Such highs and lows might be due to the rapid hormonal changes in the mother's body. Hormones affect brain chemistry that controls the emotions and moods, but no specific biological mechanism explaining hormonal involvement is known (National Institute of Mental Health, 1999a). Coupled with the stresses of new parenthood and immense changes in lifestyle, strong emotional responses are not unusual for the mother. Relationships among family members take on new dimensions and might become strained as demands on time and attention increase. All this is normal and should not last long. The postpartum period is a time of adjustment.

Bonding

Bonding is a process in which people develop a feeling of closeness. Bonding between a baby and its parents begins with soft touches, words, and physical closeness. The importance of the baby bonding with both the mother and the father, as well as siblings, is without question. The baby's early development should be shared and enjoyed. There is some debate, however, regarding the existence of a critical period for the initiation of bonding and the impact this has on the future happiness of the baby. Bonding as an integral part of the birth experience has long been perceived as a way to humanize the clinical process of childbirth. Past research suggested that increased postnatal contact between the mother and her baby resulted in positive attachment behavior patterns. New data suggests a direct relationship between the mother's sense of competence toward her baby and close contact during the two-day period following delivery (Tessier et al., 1998).

Breastfeeding

During pregnancy, high levels of estrogen and progesterone cause the duct system of the breasts to expand and form an extensive network. Additional fat tissue also is deposited, resulting in enlarged breasts. Although these hormones do not produce milk in the breasts, their high levels inhibit milk production by another hormone, prolactin.

After parturition, the levels of estrogen and progesterone decrease. Prolactin then stimulates the production of milk in the mammary glands. During the first one to three days after childbirth, colostrum is produced. **Colostrum** is a yellowish fluid that is secreted by the mammary glands in preparation of milk production. Colostrum and milk are not only the source of the baby's nutrition but also the source of antibodies that help protect the baby from infections.

Lactation is the production of milk in the mother's breasts following childbirth. Milk produced in the breasts is stored until the baby nurses. The release of milk is the result of a reflex response. As the baby suckles, a nerve impulse is transmitted to the mother's brain. The brain signals the pituitary gland to release the hormone oxytocin. Oxytocin is released into the bloodstream and stimulates the ends of the milk ducts to contract and release milk in a process called milk letdown.

The amount of prolactin in the mother's blood returns to its nonpregnant level a few weeks after childbirth. However, each time the mother nurses her baby, a nerve impulse causes an increase in the production of prolactin. Thus, continual nursing causes continued production of milk, a process that could last for several years. Milk production stops within a few days in the absence of the nerve impulse stimulated by the baby's nursing.

After childbirth, the uterus returns to its normal size more rapidly in lactating mothers than in mothers who do not breastfeed their babies. This occurs because of a diminution in the amount of estrogen secreted during lactation.

Physiological factors associated with lactation might prevent normal menstrual cycles for the first few months after childbirth. Breastfeeding might act to inhibit ovulation in some females, especially if they breastfeed their babies around the clock. However, lactating females also might have normal cycles, in which case they are capable of becoming pregnant again.

Breastfeeding facilitates bonding between mother and baby. The warmth of body-to-body contact and the sound of the mother's heartbeat have a calming effect on many babies. Babies that are breastfed tend to be less fretful and less likely to suffer from stomach upsets because breast milk is easier to digest.

For females who must work, breastfeeding might not be practical because the milk must often be stored for later use, and storage conditions might not be optimal. Human milk can be stored safely either at (59° F) 15° C for 24 hours or at (77° F) 25° C for 4 hours (Hamosh et al., 1996). The use of a breast pump, however, might be feasible under such circumstances to provide breast milk for the infant. It also would have the added benefit of allowing the father to feed his child.

Research indicates that the addition of oral Vitamin K supplements to the mother's diet will increase the concentration of Vitamin K in her breast milk, resulting in serum concentrations in breastfed babies that are similar to those in formula-fed babies. Past studies indicate that formula-fed babies were at less risk for hemorrhagic disease (Greer et al., 1997).

The advantages of breastfeeding are numerous, but there are some disadvantages. The genitals of a nursing mother tend to be sensitive, and sexual intercourse might be uncomfortable. This is because of the lack of lubrication caused by low levels of estrogen in the blood. The breasts also might be tender and secrete milk when a female is sexually aroused. For some females this might be uncomfortable and embarrassing.

Sexual Intercourse After Childbirth

Historically, the great majority of physicians advised couples to refrain from engaging in sexual intercourse until after the six-week, post-delivery office visit. However, in recent years, the exact amount of time that a couple is advised to wait has become an individual matter dependent on physical and psychological factors. Three to four weeks after delivery, the lochia discharge in most females is clear. Also, if an episiotomy incision was made or vaginal lacerations occurred, these have healed. The two most important factors for couples to consider before engaging in sexual intercourse are the comfort of the mother and whether or not she has a desire for sexual intercourse.

Increased time with the newborn might reduce time that the mother and the father spend together. The decreased time spent alone as a couple for first-time parents often is a factor in declining marital satisfaction and changes in their sexual relationship. Maintaining shared responsibility for the newborn and continuing the communication style that was established before conception can lead to greater intimacy.

When physical and psychological problems are overcome and sexual intercourse is resumed, the couple should remember to use a birth control method if another pregnancy is not desired.

References

American Medical Association. 1998. "Turner's Syndrome." *AMA Medical Glossary* (September). Accessed 6/1999. http://www.ama-assn.org.

American Society of Reproductive Medicine. 1998a. "Frequently Asked Questions about Infertility." Article Online (June). Accessed 6/1999. http://www.asrm.org.

——. 1998b. "From Psychological Interventions to Viagra: Treatments for Male Sexual Dysfunction." Article Online. Accessed 6/1999. http://www.asrm.org.

Atkins, David M.D., M.P.H., et al. 1998. "1998 Guidelines for Treatment of Sexually Transmitted Disease." *Morbidity and Mortality Weekly Report* (January). Accessed 6/1999. http://www.cdc.gov.

Bastian, Lori A., M.D., M.P.H., and Joanne T. Piscitelli, M.D. 1997. "Is This Patient Pregnant?" *Journal of the American Medical Association* 280. Accessed 6/1999. http://www.4journals.com.

Cartitis, Steve, et al. 1998. "Low-Dose Aspirin to Prevent Preeclampsia in Women At High Risk." *New England Journal of Medicine* (March). Accessed 6/1999. http://www.4journals.com.

Cates, Willard, Jr., M.D., M.P.H. 1999. "Chlamydia Infections and the Risk of Ectopic Pregnancy." *Journal of the American Medical Association* 281. Accessed 6/1999. http://www.4journals.com.

Centers for Disease Control and Prevention. 1999. "The Effects of Workplace Hazards on Female Reproductive Health." Article Online (March). Accessed 6/1999. http://www.cdc.gov/niosh.

——. 1998a. "Centers for Birth Defect Research and Prevention." Article Online (October). Accessed 6/1999. http://www.cdc.gov/genetics.

——. 1998b. "Prevention of Fetal Alcohol Syndrome." Article Online (October). Accessed 6/1999. http://www.cdc.gov.

Chambers, Christina D., et al. 1996. "Birth Outcomes in Pregnant Women Taking Fluoxetine." *New England Journal of Medicine* (October). Accessed 6/1999. http://www.4journals.com

Cnattingius, Sven, M.D., Ph.D., et al. 1998. "Prepregnancy Weight and the Risk of Adverse Pregnancy Outcomes." *New England Journal of Medicine* (January). Accessed 6/1999. http://www.4journals.com.

Fertilitext. 1998. "Fertilitext Information on Sperm and Tissue Banks." Article Online. Accessed 6/1999. http://www.fertilitext.org.

Food and Drug Administration. 1996. "Evidence for Link Between Prenatal and Adult Health Growth." *Science and Medicine* 9026. Accessed 6/1999. http://www.fda.gov.

Greer, Frank R., et al. 1997. "Improving the Vitamin K Status of Breastfeeding Infants With Maternal Vitamin K Supplements." *Pediatrics* (March). Accessed 6/1999. http://www.pediatrics.org.

Haddow, James E., et al. 1998. "Screening of Maternal Serum for Fetal Down Syndrome in the First Trimester." *New England Journal of Medicine* (April). Accessed 6/1999. http://www.4journals.com.

Hamosh, M., et al. 1996. "Breastfeeding and the Working Mother: Effect of Time and Temperature of Short-Term Storage on Proteolysis, Lipolysis, and Bacterial Growth in Milk." *Pediatrics* (April). Accessed 6/1999. http://www.pediatrics.org.

Hannah, Mary E., et al. 1996. "Induction of Labor Compared with Expectant Management for Prelabor Rupture of the Membranes at Term." *New England Journal of Medicine* (April). Accessed 6/1999. http://www.4journals.com.

Intelihealth. 1999. "Understanding Gestational Diabetes." Johns Hopkins University and Health System. Article Online. Accessed 6/1999. http://www.diabetes.net.com.

James, William H., Ph.D. 1998. "The Health and Hormone Status of Female Cadets and Active-Duty Women in the US Armed Forces." *Archives of Pediatrics & Adolescent Medicine* (January). Accessed 6/1999. http://www.4journals.com.

Kardel, Kristine R., M.S., et al. 1998. "Training in Pregnant Women: Effects on Fetal Development and Birth." *American Journal of Obstetrics and Gynecology* (February). Accessed 6/1999. http://www.4journals.com.

Koop, Everett, M.D. 1999. "Rubella." *Medical Encyclopedia.* Accessed 6/1999. http://www.drkoop.com.

March of Dimes. 1999a. "Amniocentesis." Article Online (October). Accessed 6/1999. http://www.modimes.org.

——. 1999b. "Low Birth Weight." Article Online. Accessed 6/1999. http://www.modimes.org.

——. 1999c. "Teen Pregnancy Fact Sheet." Article Online. Accessed 6/1999. http://www.modimes.org.

——. 1999d. "Weight Gain." *Birth Defects Information.* Accessed 6/1999. http://www.mod.org.

——. 1997. "Rh Disease." Article Online (September). Accessed 6/1999. http://www.nih.gov.

——. 1994. "Give Your Baby a Healthy Start: Stop Smoking." *Ask NOAH About Pregnancy.* Accessed 6/1999. http://www.noah.cuny.edu.

March of Dimes Birth Defects Foundation. 1999. "Sickle Cell Disease." Article Online. Accessed 6/1999. http://www.modimes.org.

Mayo Clinic Foundation for Medical Education and Research. 1995. "Mayo Clinic Foundation for Medical Education and Research, 1995–1997." Article Online (October). Accessed 6/1999. http://www.4journals.com.

McDonald, Sandra, CPM. 1999. "What Are Some Advantages of Having My Baby At Home?" *Pregnancy Today.* Accessed 6/1999. http://www.pregnancy.com.

Moran, Mark. 1998. "Allergists: Continue Asthma Medication During Pregnancy." *American Medical News* (December). Accessed 6/1999. http://www.4journals.com.

National Center for Health Statistics. 1999a. "Healthy People 2000: Maternal and Infant Health Progress Reviews." Article Online (September). Accessed 6/1999. http://www.cdc.gov.

——. 1999b. "Longer Hospital Stays for Childbirth." Article Online (September). Accessed 6/1999. http://www.cdc.gov.

——. 1999c. "Teen Birth Rate Down in All States." Article Online (April). Accessed 6/1999. http://www.hhs.gov.

——. 1998. "New Study Shows Lower Mortality Rates for Infants Delivered by Nurse Midwives." Article Online (May). Accessed 6/1999. http://www.cdc.gov.

——. 1997. "Multiple Births Multiply During Past Two Decades." Article Online (November). Accessed 6/1999. http://www.cdc.gov.

National Human Genome Research Institute. 1998. "Genome Project Leaders Announce Intent to Finish Sequencing the Human Genome Two Years Early." Article Online (September). Accessed 6/1999. http://www.nhgri.nih.gov.

National Institute of Child Health and Human Development. 1998. "Researchers Identify Risk Factors for Preeclampsia in Hypertensive Women." Article Online (September). Accessed 6/1999. http://www.nih.gov.

National Institute on Drug Abuse. 1999. "Pregnancy and Drug Use Trends." *National Pregnancy and Health Survey.* Accessed 6/1999. http://www.nida.nih.gov.

National Institute of Health. 1999a. "Facts About Endometriosis." Article Online (October). Accessed 6/1999. http://www.nih.gov/nich.d/publication.

——. 1999b. "Facts About Fragile X Syndrome." Article Online. Accessed 6/1999. http://www.nih.gov/nichd.

——. 1999c. "Understanding Gene Testing: Altered Dominant Genes." Article Online. Accessed 6/1999. http://www.nih.gov.

——. 1998. "Problems of Pregnancy." *Family Web.* Accessed 6/1999. http://www.noah.cuny.edu.

——. 1995. "Pregnancy and Perinatology Branch—Report to the NACHHD Council January 1995—Predictive Factors for Spontaneous Preterm Birth." Article Online (January). Accessed 6/1999. http://www.nih.gov.

National Institute of Mental Health. 1999. "Causes of Depression." Article Online. Accessed 6/1999. http://www.nimh.nih.gov.

——. 1999b. "The Many Dimensions of Depression in Women: Women At Risk." Article Online. Accessed 6/1999. http://www.nimh.nih.gov.

Nodenberg, Tamar. 1997. "Overcoming Infertility." Article Online (February). Accessed 6/1999. http://www.fda.gov.

Novitt-Moreno, Anne, M.D. 1999. "Rubella (German Measles)." *Journal of the American Medical Association.* Accessed 6/1999. http://www.4journals.com.

Pollard, Irina. 1994. *A Guide to Reproduction: Social Issues and Human Concerns.* Cambridge, U.K. and New York: Cambridge University Press.

Rai, R., et al. 1997. "Randomized Controlled Trial of Aspirin and Aspirin Plus Heparin in Pregnant Women with Recurrent Miscarriage Associated with Phospholipid Antibodies." *Journal of the American Medical Association* (January). Accessed 6/1999. http://www.4journals.com.

Rayburn, William F., M.D. 1998. "Connective Tissue Disorders and Pregnancy: Recommendations for Prescribing." *Journal of Reproductive Medicine* 43. Accessed 6/1999. http://www.4journals.com.

Scott, F., A. Boogert, S. Smart, J. Anderson. 1995. "Maternal Serum Screening and Routine 18-Week Ultrasound in the Detection of All Chromosomal Abnormalities." *Australia/New Zealand Journal of Obstetrics and Gynecology* 35/2. Accessed 6/1999. http://www.ncbi.nih.gov.

Tessier, Rejean, et al. 1998. "Kangaroo Mother Care and the Bonding Hypothesis." *Pediatrics* (June). Accessed 6/1999. http://www.pediatrics.org.

Walkinshaw, S.A. 1997. "Pelvimetry and Breech Delivery at Term." *The Lancet* 350/9094. Accessed 6/1999. http://www.thelancet.com.

Wickersham, Rachel. 1999. "What Is a Doula?" *Pregnancy Today.* Accessed 6/1999. http://www.pregnancy.com.

Wilcox, Alan J., et al. 1999. "Time of Implantation of the Conceptus and Loss of Pregnancy." *New England Journal of Medicine* (June). Accessed 6/1999. http://www.4journals.com.

The Meeks Heit K–12 Sexuality and Character Education Curriculum Guide Abstinence Edition

Table of Contents

Goals and Philosophy

The Meeks Heit K–12 Sexuality and Character Education Curriculum Abstinence Edition is an organized, sequential curriculum that teaches knowledge, behaviors, attitudes, and skills that promote committed family relationships, good character, healthful sexuality, and reproductive health.

The Meeks Heit Umbrella of Sexuality and Character Education K–12 Abstinence Edition illustrates concepts that describe the purpose of the curriculum. At the top of *The Meeks Heit Umbrella of Sexuality and Character Education K–12 Absinence Edition* are two stripes, each of which illustrates an important component of a comprehensive sexuality and character education curriculum: Health Literacy and The National Health Education Standards. These might be defined as follows:

> **Health Literacy** is competence in critical thinking and problem-solving, responsible and productive citizenship, self-directed learning, and effective communication. When young people are health literate, they possess skills that protect them from risk behaviors and risk situations.

> **The National Health Education Standards** are standards that specify what students should know and be able to do regarding health. There are seven National Health Education Standards. Young people are protected from risk behaviors and risk situations that harm relationships, character, and reproductive health when they

> 1. comprehend concepts related to health promotion and disease prevention;
>
> 2. demonstrate the ability to access valid health information and health-promoting products and services;
>
> 3. demonstrate the ability to practice health-enhancing behaviors and reduce health risks;
>
> 4. analyze the influence of culture, media, technology, and other factors on health;
>
> 5. demonstrate the ability to use interpersonal communication skills to enhance health;
>
> 6. demonstrate the ability to use goal-setting and decision-making skills that enhance health;
>
> 7. demonstrate the ability to advocate for personal, family, and community health.

The Meeks Heit Umbrella of Sexuality and Character Education K–12 Abstinence Edition is divided into ten sections. These ten sections represent content areas in which young people need to gain health knowledge, practice life skills, and learn objectives.

> **Health knowledge** consists of information that is needed to become health literate, to maintain and improve health, to prevent disease, and to reduce health-related risk behaviors.

> **Life Skills** are healthful actions students learn and practice for the rest of their lives.

> **Objectives** are statements that describe what students need to know and do in order to practice the life skills.

Goals and Philosophy (continued)

The Content Areas for Sexuality and Character Education are

Character in Relationships

Harmful and Violent Relationships

Friendship, Dating, and Abstinence

Male Reproductive Health

Female Reproductive Health

Sexually Transmitted Diseases

HIV/AIDS

Marriage, Parenthood, and Family Living

Pregnancy and Childbirth

Students who participate in **The Meeks Heit K–12 Sexuality and Character Education Curriculum Abstinence Edition** and who master The National Health Education Standards are enthusiastic, radiant, and energetic. They are confident and empowered because they

- have health knowledge,

- demonstrate good character,

- choose healthful behaviors,

- choose to be in healthful situations,

- choose to have healthful relationships,

- make responsible decisions,

- use resistance skills when appropriate,

- possess protective factors,

- are resilient, and

- are health literate.

The Meeks Heit Umbrella of Sexuality and Character Education K-12 Abstinence Edition

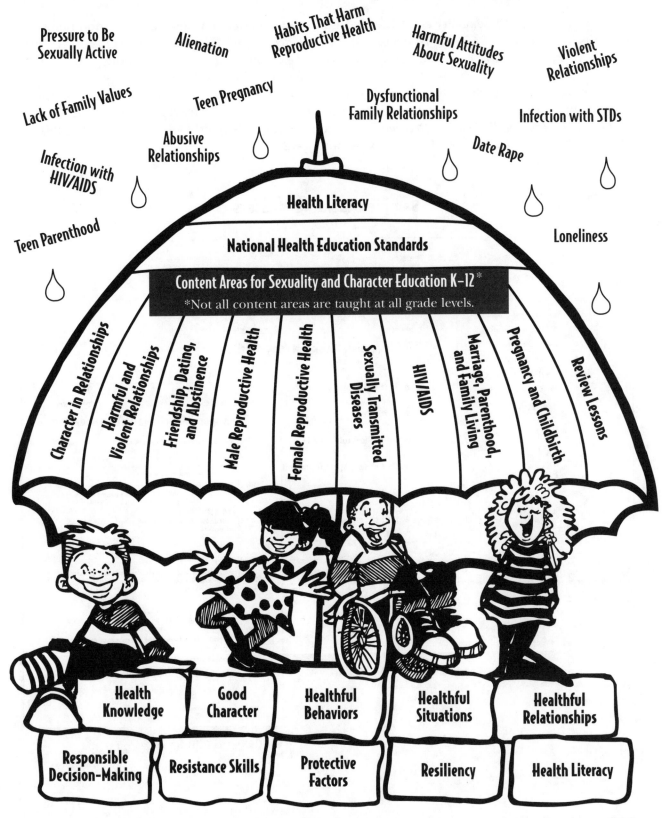

Pressure to Be Sexually Active

Alienation

Habits That Harm Reproductive Health

Harmful Attitudes About Sexuality

Violent Relationships

Lack of Family Values

Teen Pregnancy

Dysfunctional Family Relationships

Infection with STDs

Abusive Relationships

Date Rape

Infection with HIV/AIDS

Teen Parenthood

Loneliness

Health Literacy

National Health Education Standards

Content Areas for Sexuality and Character Education K-12*

*Not all content areas are taught at all grade levels.

Character in Relationships

Harmful and Violent Relationships

Friendship, Dating, and Abstinence

Male Reproductive Health

Female Reproductive Health

Sexually Transmitted Diseases

HIV/AIDS

Marriage, Parenthood, and Family Living

Pregnancy and Childbirth

Review Lessons

Health Knowledge

Good Character

Healthful Behaviors

Healthful Situations

Healthful Relationships

Responsible Decision-Making

Resistance Skills

Protective Factors

Resiliency

Health Literacy

The Meeks Heit
Guidelines for Making Responsible Decisions™

The Meeks Heit K–12 Sexuality and Character Education Curriculum Abstinence Edition helps students learn to make responsible decisions. The *Guidelines for Making Responsible Decisions™* are a series of steps to follow to assure that the decisions a person makes result in actions that protect health, protect safety, follow laws, show respect for oneself and others, follow family guidelines, and demonstrate good character. Three versions of the *Guidelines for Making Responsible Decisions™* correspond to three different reading levels. *Make Wise Decisions™* is used for Grades K–2, *Guidelines for Making Responsible Decisions™* is used for Grades 3–4 and 5–6, and *The Responsible Decision-Making Model™* is used for Grades 7–8 and 9–12.

Sample Blackline Masters

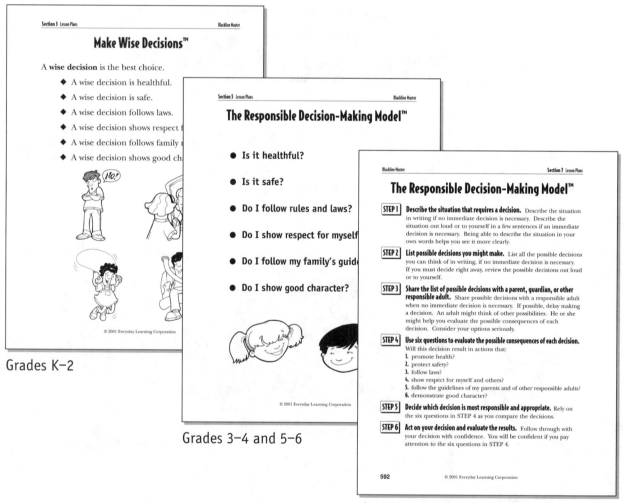

Grades K–2

Grades 3–4 and 5–6

Grades 7–8 and 9–12

The Meeks Heit Models for Using Resistance Skills

The Meeks Heit K–12 Sexuality and Character Education Curriculum Abstinence Edition helps students learn to use resistance skills. **Resistance skills** (Grades 3–12), or **say NO skills** (Grades K–2), are skills that are used when a person wants to say NO to an action or to leave a situation. **The Model for Using Resistance Skills** is a list of ways to resist negative peer pressure.

Sample Blackline Masters

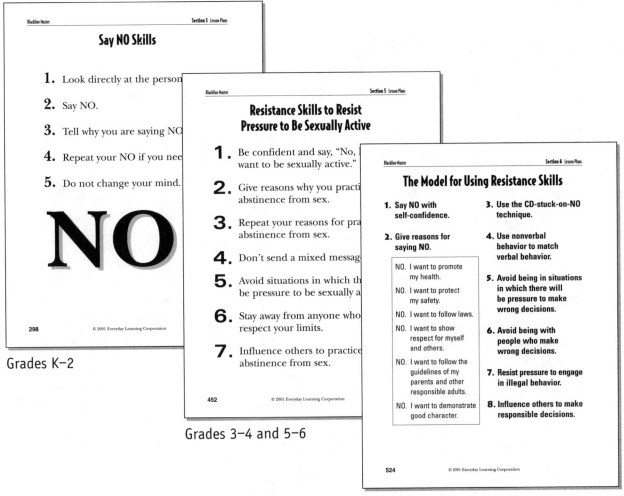

Grades K–2

Grades 3–4 and 5–6

Grades 7–8 and 9–12

The Meeks Heit Lesson Plans with Totally Awesome® Teaching Strategies

The Meeks Heit K–12 Sexuality and Character Education Curriculum Abstinence Edition includes Lesson Plans with *Totally Awesome® Teaching Strategies* for every grade level. *Totally Awesome® Teaching Strategies* are creative Lesson Plans designed to help students become health literate and master The National Health Education Standards.

Sample Lesson Plan

Grades 9–12

The Meeks Heit Lesson Plans with Totally Awesome® Teaching Strategies (continued)

Totally Awesome® Teaching Strategies contain the following features:

Clever Title A clever title is set in boldfaced type in the center of the page.

Designated Content Area The content area for which the Lesson Plan is designed appears in the upper left-hand corner. The content areas include the following: Character in Relationships; Harmful and Violent Relationships; Friendship, Dating, and Abstinence; Male Reproductive Health; Female Reproductive Health; Sexually Transmitted Diseases; HIV/AIDS; Marriage, Parenthood, and Family Living; Pregnancy and Childbirth; and Birth Control Methods (OPTIONAL).

Designated Grade Level The grade level for which the Lesson Plan is appropriate appears in the upper left-hand corner.

Health Literacy Health literacy is competence in critical thinking and problem-solving, responsible and productive citizenship, self-directed learning, and effective communication. The Lesson Plans are designed to promote competency in health literacy. A symbol designating one of the four components of health literacy appears in the upper right-hand corner.

Curriculum Infusion Curriculum infusion is the integration of a subject area into another area of the curriculum. The Lesson Plans are designed to be infused into several curriculum areas other than health education. These areas include art studies, foreign languages, home economics, language arts, physical education, math studies, music studies, science studies, social studies, and visual and performing arts. The curriculum area into which the Lesson Plan is designed to be infused is designated by a symbol that appears in the upper right-hand corner.

Life Skills Life skills are healthful actions students learn and practice for the rest of their lives.

Lesson Objectives Objectives are statements that describe what students need to know and do in order to practice life skills.

National Health Education Standards The National Health Education Standards are standards that specify what students should know and be able to do regarding health. They involve the knowledge and skills essential to the development of health literacy.

Materials The materials are items that are needed to do the Lesson Plan. The materials used in the Lesson Plans are readily available and inexpensive.

Blackline Masters Blackline Masters are masters that can be made into transparencies or copied for student worksheets.

Teaching the Lesson Plan Step-by-step directions to follow are provided for teachers to use when they teach the Lesson Plan. The Lesson Plan includes a *Totally Awesome® Teaching Strategy* that can be used to teach the health content and skills students need to master The National Health Education Standards and life skills.

Assessment An assessment that tests student mastery of the life skills and objectives is included at the end of each Lesson Plan. The assessment is designed to make students think critically about the information in the Lesson Plan and to apply the life skills and objectives.

Lesson Plans That Promote Good Character

The Meeks Heit K–12 Sexuality and Character Education Curriculum Abstinence Edition contains Lesson Plans and *Totally Awesome® Teaching Strategies* that promote good character. **Good character** is the effort a person uses to act on responsible values. In Grades K–2 and 3–4, children are taught three responsible values: tell the truth, be fair, and show respect. In Grades 5–6, 7–8, and 9–12, the following responsible values are emphasized: honesty, fairness, respect, self-discipline, healthful behavior, determination, courage, citizenship, responsibility, and integrity.

Grades 7–8

Sample Lesson Plan

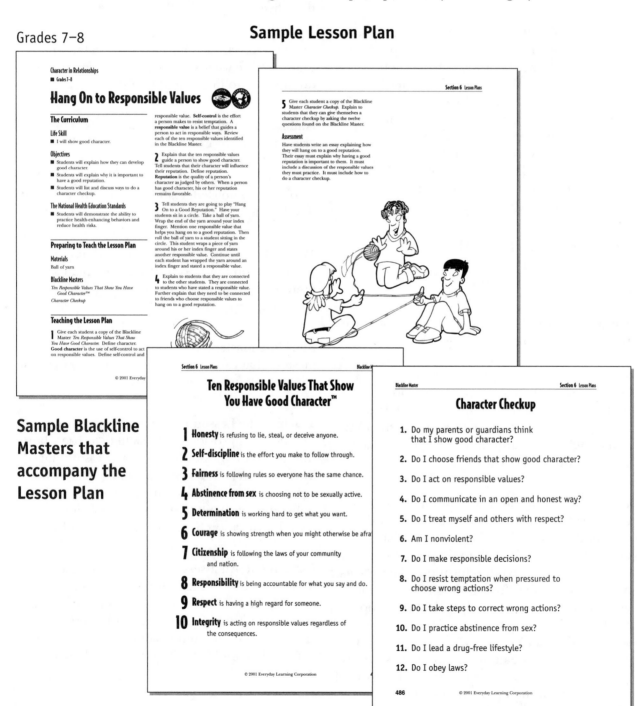

Sample Blackline Masters that accompany the Lesson Plan

Lesson Plans That Promote Abstinence from Sex

The Meeks Heit K–12 Sexuality and Character Education Curriculum Abstinence Edition contains Lesson Plans and *Totally Awesome® Teaching Strategies* that beginning at Grades 5–6 promote abstinence from sex. **Abstinence from sex** is choosing not to be sexually active. The Lesson Plans and *Totally Awesome® Teaching Strategies* meet the criteria required by federal law for the funding of abstinence education programs.

The Criteria Required by Federal Law for the Funding of Abstinence Education Programs

These criteria state that a program must

1. have as its exclusive purpose teaching the social, psychological, and health gains to be realized by abstaining from sexual activity;

2. teach abstinence from sexual activity outside of marriage as the expected standard for all school age children;

3. teach that abstinence from sexual activity is the only certain way to avoid out-of-wedlock pregnancy and sexually transmitted diseases;

4. teach that a mutually faithful monogamous relationship within the context of marriage is the expected standard of human sexual activity;

5. teach that sexual activity outside the context of marriage is likely to have harmful psychological and physical effects;

6. teach that bearing children out of wedlock is likely to have harmful consequences for the child, the child's parents, and society;

7. teach young people how to reject sexual advances and how alcohol and drug use increase vulnerability to sexual advances; and

8. teach the importance of attaining self-sufficiency before engaging in sexual activity.

Curriculum Infusion

The Meeks Heit K–12 Sexuality and Character Education Curriculum Abstinence Edition emphasizes skills needed to master Health Literacy, life skills, objectives, and The National Health Education Standards. The Lesson Plans and *Totally Awesome® Teaching Strategies* are designed so that they can be infused into curriculum areas other than health education, including the following:

Health Literacy

The Meeks Heit K–12 Sexuality and Character Education Curriculum Abstinence Edition is designed to promote Health Literacy. A **health literate person** is a person who is skilled in critical thinking, responsible citizenship, self-directed learning, and effective communication. The Lesson Plans and *Totally Awesome® Teaching Strategies* include the following symbols for Health Literacy:

Effective Communication

is skill in expressing knowledge, beliefs, and ideas. It includes expressing oneself in different ways—oral, written, artistic, graphic, and technological. It also includes showing empathy and respect for others.

Self-Directed Learning

is skill in gathering and using health knowledge. It involves having current information about health throughout life.

Critical Thinking

is skill in evaluating information from reliable sources before making decisions. It includes knowing how to make responsible decisions.

Responsible Citizenship

is skill in practicing responsible behavior. It involves choosing healthful, safe, legal behavior that shows respect for oneself and others, follows family guidelines, and demonstrates good character. It includes behaviors that promote a healthful community, nation, and world.

218

Assessment and Evaluation

Assessment An assessment that tests student mastery of the life skills and objectives is included at the end of each Lesson Plan. The assessment is designed to make students think critically about the information in the Lesson Plan and to apply the life skills and objectives.

Worksheet Masters are provided with certain Lesson Plans. The Worksheet Masters are another tool for teachers to test a student's understanding of the concepts presented in the Lesson Plan. While performing the tasks on the Worksheet Masters, students will think critically about the information in the Lesson Plan and apply the life skills and objectives.

Grades 5–6 Sample Assessment at
            the end of a Lesson Plan

Grades 5–6 Sample Worksheet Master
            from a Lesson Plan

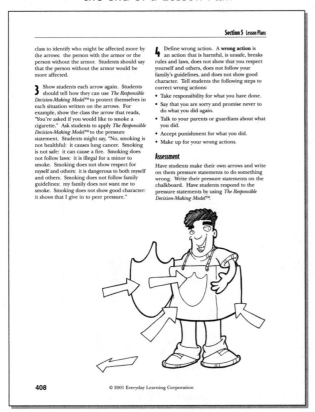

Section 5 Lesson Plans

class to identify who might be affected more by the arrows: the person with the armor or the person without the armor. Students should say that the person without the armor would be more affected.

3 Show students each arrow again. Students should tell how they can use *The Responsible Decision-Making Model*™ to protect themselves in each situation written on the arrows. For example, show the class the arrow that reads, "You're asked if you would like to smoke a cigarette." Ask students to apply *The Responsible Decision-Making Model*™ to the pressure statement. Students might say, "No, smoking is not healthful: it causes lung cancer. Smoking is not safe: it can cause a fire. Smoking does not follow laws: it is illegal for a minor to smoke. Smoking does not show respect for myself and others: it is dangerous to both myself and others. Smoking does not follow family guidelines: my family does not want me to smoke. Smoking does not show good character: it shows that I give in to peer pressure."

4 Define wrong action. A **wrong action** is an action that is harmful, is unsafe, breaks rules and laws, does not show that you respect yourself and others, does not follow your family's guidelines, and does not show good character. Tell students the following steps to correct wrong actions:

• Take responsibility for what you have done.
• Say that you are sorry and promise never to do what you did again.
• Talk to your parents or guardians about what you did.
• Accept punishment for what you did.
• Make up for your wrong actions.

Assessment

Have students make their own arrows and write on them pressure statements to do something wrong. Write their pressure statements on the chalkboard. Have students respond to the pressure statements by using *The Responsible Decision-Making Model*™.

408 © 2001 Everyday Learning Corporation

Section 5 Lesson Plans   **Worksheet Master**

All About Boys Word Search

A	X	A	I	T	I	L	P	Q	P	M	V	U	E	T	T
H	O	R	M	O	N	E	S	T	E	P	C	W	R	E	W
U	Y	Q	P	E	N	E	O	A	N	X	P	S	E	U	A
R	U	Z	Z	L	I	Q	S	D	I	K	E	N	C	I	X
E	S	C	R	O	T	U	M	T	S	W	N	I	T	V	J
T	E	S	T	O	S	T	E	R	O	N	E	E	I	P	E
H	Y	S	T	E	O	P	Q	U	D	I	I	S	O	O	M
R	P	U	B	E	R	T	Y	W	D	V	U	K	N	B	Z
A	W	D	R	H	O	N	B	J	S	Q	P	L	C	R	C
P	R	O	T	E	C	T	I	V	E	C	U	P	G	H	U

1. _____ are chemicals that control certain body processes.
2. _____ is a hormone that produces secondary sex characteristics.
3. The _____ is the male sex organ used to pass urine and to reproduce.
4. The _____ is the sac-like pouch that holds the testes.
5. _____ is the period of growth when your body matures and becomes like that of an adult.
6. The _____ is a narrow tube through which urine and semen pass out of the body.
7. An _____ is when the penis fills with blood and becomes hard.
8. A _____ is an undergarment that supports the testes and penis.

© 2001 Everyday Learning Corporation   439

K–12 Scope and Sequence Chart

The Scope and Sequence Chart serves as a blueprint for **The Meeks Heit K–12 Sexuality and Character Education Curriculum Abstinence Edition.** The Scope and Sequence Chart correlates the K–12 Lesson Plans to The National Health Education Standards. The chart identifies the life skills and objectives used in each Lesson Plan.

The heading at the top of each page identifies one of the content areas in **The Meeks Heit K–12 Sexuality and Character Education Curriculum Abstinence Edition.** For example, in the scope and sequence chart below, the heading identifies the content area as "1 Character in Relationships."

The first column, **Life Skills**, identifies the life skills covered in the Lesson Plans. For example, in the scope and sequence chart below, the first life skill is "I will develop good character."

The second column, **The National Health Education Standards**, identifies the standards covered by the Lesson Plans. For example, in the scope and sequence chart below, the first National Health Education Standard is "Students will demonstrate the ability to practice health-enhancing behaviors and reduce health risks."

The third column, **Objectives**, identifies the objectives for the Lesson Plans. For example, in the scope and sequence chart below, the first objective is "Tell what good character is."

The Scope and Sequence Chart is divided by grade levels.

Content Area		**1 Character in Relationships**			
Life Skills	**The National Health Education Standards**	**Grades K–2 Objectives**	**Grades K–2 Lesson Plans**	**Grades 3–4 Objectives**	**Grades 3–4 Lesson Plans**
I will show good character.	Students will demonstrate the ability to practice health-enhancing behaviors and reduce health risks.	• Tell what good character is. • Tell ways to show good character. • Tell what to do if you do something wrong.	**The Gift of Good Character**	• Tell three actions that make up good character. • Explain why you need good character. • Explain why your heroes should have good character. • Explain what to do if you do something wrong.	**Good Character Is Priceless**
I will make responsible decisions.	Students will demonstrate the ability to use goal-setting and decision-making skills that enhance health.	• Tell six questions to ask before you make a decision. • Tell how to make wise decisions.	**If You Make Wise Decisions and You Know It**	• List six questions to ask before you make a decision. • Explain the difference between a responsible decision and a wrong decision.	**Good Character Is Priceless**
I will use resistance skills when necessary.	Students will demonstrate the ability to use goal-setting and decision-making skills that enhance health.	• Tell what a wrong decision is. • Name Say NO skills. • Show ways to say NO to wrong decisions.	**If You Make Wise Decisions and You Know It**	• Explain how to use resistance skills. • Explain when to use resistance skills. • Show how to use resistance skills. • Explain why a peer might pressure you to make a wrong decision.	**Good Character Is Priceless**
I will share feelings in healthful ways.	Students will demonstrate the ability to use interpersonal communication skills to enhance health.	• Tell different feelings you have. • Tell healthful ways to share feelings. • Explain what to do if you are angry or afraid.	**Angry Inside**	• Tell questions to ask to help understand your feelings. • Explain why you need to express feelings in healthful ways. • Describe healthful ways to express feelings.	**Coated with Kindness**
I will settle conflict in healthful ways.	Students will demonstrate the ability to use interpersonal communication skills to enhance health.	• Tell ways to work out conflict.	**Angry Inside**	• Discuss ways to settle conflict. • Explain how you can control angry feelings. • Discuss what to do if someone wants you to fight.	**Coated with Kindness**

© 2001 Everyday Learning Corporation

261

1 Character in Relationships

Content Area

Life Skills	The National Health Education Standards	Grades K–2 Objectives	Grades K–2 Lesson Plans	Grades 3–4 Objectives	Grades 3–4 Lesson Plans
I will show good character.	Students will demonstrate the ability to practice health-enhancing behaviors and reduce health risks.	• Tell what good character is. • Tell ways to show good character. • Tell what to do if you do something wrong.	**The Gift of Good Character**	• Tell three actions that make up good character. • Explain why you need good character. • Explain why your heroes should have good character. • Explain what to do if you do something wrong.	**Good Character Is Priceless**
I will make responsible decisions.	Students will demonstrate the ability to use goal-setting and decision-making skills that enhance health.	• Tell six questions to ask before you make a decision. • Tell how to make wise decisions.	**If You Make Wise Decisions and You Know It**	• List six questions to ask before you make a decision. • Explain the difference between a responsible decision and a wrong decision.	**Good Character Is Priceless**
I will use resistance skills when necessary.	Students will demonstrate the ability to use goal-setting and decision-making skills that enhance health.	• Tell what a wrong decision is. • Name Say NO skills. • Show ways to say NO to wrong decisions.	**If You Make Wise Decisions and You Know It**	• Explain how to use resistance skills. • Explain when to use resistance skills. • Show how to use resistance skills. • Explain why a peer might pressure you to make a wrong decision.	**Good Character Is Priceless**
I will share feelings in healthful ways.	Students will demonstrate the ability to use interpersonal communication skills to enhance health.	• Tell different feelings you have. • Tell healthful ways to share feelings. • Explain what to do if you are angry or afraid.	**Angry Inside**	• Tell questions to ask to help understand your feelings. • Explain why you need to express feelings in healthful ways. • Describe healthful ways to express feelings.	**Coated with Kindness**
I will settle conflict in healthful ways.	Students will demonstrate the ability to use interpersonal communication skills to enhance health.	• Tell ways to work out conflict.	**Angry Inside**	• Discuss ways to settle conflict. • Explain how you can control angry feelings. • Discuss what to do if someone wants you to fight.	**Coated with Kindness**

2 Harmful and Violent Relationships

Content Area					
Life Skills	**The National Health Education Standards**	**Grades K–2 Objectives**	**Grades K–2 Lesson Plans**	**Grades 3–4 Objectives**	**Grades 3–4 Lesson Plans**
I will protect myself from people who might harm me. I will follow safety rules to protect myself from violence.	Students will demonstrate the ability to practice health-enhancing behaviors and reduce health risks.	• Tell ways you can stay safe from strangers. • Tell what to do if you get an unsafe touch.	**Code Word: Safety** **The Danger Stranger** **Private Body Parts**	• Tell safety rules to follow when you are home with someone besides your parents or guardians. • Tell ways to stay safe from strangers when you are away from home. • Tell safety rules to stay safe from strangers in cars. • Tell what to do if someone gives you an unsafe touch.	**Telephone Safety** **Car Caution**
I will choose healthful entertainment. I will develop media literacy.	Students will analyze the influence of culture, media, technology, and other factors on health.	• Tell what healthful entertainment is. • Tell guidelines to use to choose healthful entertainment. • Choose computer games that are healthful entertainment. • Choose TV shows that are healthful entertainment.	**Entertainment Detective**	• List guidelines for choosing healthful entertainment. • List questions to check out whether or not TV shows are healthful entertainment. • List questions to check out whether or not books are healthful entertainment. • List questions to check out whether or not movies are healthful entertainment. • List questions to check out whether or not computer games are healthful entertainment.	**Turn Off the TV**

Content Area

3 Friendship, Dating, and Abstinence

Life Skills	The National Health Education Standards	Grades K–2 Objectives	Grades K–2 Lesson Plans	Grades 3–4 Objectives	Grades 3–4 Lesson Plans
I will work to have healthful friendships. I will make wise decisions with friends. I will show respect for others.	Students will demonstrate the ability to use interpersonal communication skills to enhance health.	• Tell what a good friend is. • Tell six questions to ask when you make decisions with friends. • Tell what respect is. • Tell ways to show respect for yourself and others.	Friendship Tree Friendship Recipe	• Tell ways to make a true friend. • Explain how friends can make responsible decisions. • Tell why you need to show respect for yourself. • Explain ways you can show respect for other people. • List ways you can tell if someone does not show respect for you. • Discuss what to do if someone does not show respect for you. • Explain what to do if you feel left out.	Take a Second Look Left Out

Content Area   **4** **Male Reproductive Health**   and   **5** **Female Reproductive Health**

Life Skills	The National Health Education Standards	Grades K–2 Objectives	Grades K–2 Lesson Plans	Grades 3–4 Objectives	Grades 3–4 Lesson Plans
I will take care of my body. I will learn ways my body changes. I will have checkups.	Students will comprehend concepts related to health promotion and disease prevention.	• Name body parts. • Tell ways to take care of body parts. • Tell ways you will grow. • Tell why you need checkups.	**The Growth Line** **You've Left Your Mark**	• Name private body parts. • Tell signs you are growing. • Tell ways your body will change. • Tell why you need medical checkups.	**Body Part Name Game**
I will be well-groomed. I will choose safe and healthful products.	Students will demonstrate the ability to practice health-enhancing behaviors and reduce health risks. Students will demonstrate the ability to access valid health information and health-promoting products and services.	• Tell how you can groom yourself. • Tell ways you can look sharp. • Name grooming products you have seen in ads.	**Grooming Collage**	• Discuss rules for the safe use of grooming products. • Name kinds of media used to sell health products and services. • Tell how you can check out commercials for health products.	**I Need Privacy**

6 Sexually Transmitted Diseases

Content Area

Life Skills	The National Health Education Standards	Grades K–2 Objectives	Grades K–2 Lesson Plans	Grades 3–4 Objectives	Grades 3–4 Lesson Plans
I will choose habits that prevent the spread of germs. I will recognize symptoms and get treatment for communicable diseases.	Students will comprehend concepts related to health promotion and disease prevention.	• Tell how germs are spread. • Tell how to protect yourself and others from germs. • Tell what a symptom is.	**A Spray of Germs** **Super Soap: A Germ Fighter**	• List kinds of pathogens that cause disease. • Explain ways pathogens from people enter your body. • List body defenses that fight pathogens.	**Germ Stop** **Name Those Defenses**

7 HIV/AIDS–OPTIONAL

Content Area

Life Skills	The National Health Education Standards	Grades K–2 Objectives	Grades K–2 Lesson Plans	Grades 3–4 Objectives	Grades 3–4 Lesson Plans
I will choose habits that prevent the spread of germs.	Students will comprehend concepts related to health promotion and disease prevention.	• Explain what HIV does to helper T cells.	**I Love Gloves**	• Tell when a person has AIDS.	**What to Know About HIV and AIDS**
I will recognize symptoms and get treatment for communicable diseases.		• Tell what HIV is.	**Blood Brothers/ Sisters—NOT!**	• Tell ways HIV is spread.	**The Truth About HIV and AIDS**
		• Tell ways HIV is spread.		• Tell ways HIV is not spread.	
		• Tell ways HIV is not spread.		• Tell ways to keep from getting HIV.	
		• List ways to prevent HIV infection.		• Explain what HIV does to body defenses.	
		• Tell what AIDS is.		• Tell symptoms that appear in people who have HIV.	
		• Tell ways HIV is spread from sharing a needle with blood on it, from touching blood.			
		• Tell why health care workers wear gloves.			

Content Area

8 Marriage, Parenthood, and Family Living

Life Skills	The National Health Education Standards	Grades K–2 Objectives	Grades K–2 Lesson Plans	Grades 3–4 Objectives	Grades 3–4 Lesson Plans
I will get along with my family. I will follow my family's guidelines.	Students will demonstrate the ability to use interpersonal communication skills to enhance health.	• Tell what a family rule is. • Tell why you should follow family rules. • Tell ways to get along with your family.	**Family Building Blocks** **Memory Matters**	• Tell the special names for each person who belongs to a family. • Explain how to be a loving family member. • Explain reasons why you should follow family guidelines. • Discuss reasons why it is important to be close to your family. • Tell ways you can cooperate with family members.	**Family Cultures** **TLC for Older Family Members**
I will adjust to family changes in healthful ways.	Students will demonstrate the ability to practice health-enhancing behaviors and reduce health risks.	• Name ways families change. • Tell what to do if you have family changes. • Tell things to talk about if you have family changes. • Tell ways to help with a newborn baby.	**Memory Matters**	• Explain how a family changes when there is a new baby or child. • Explain how a family changes if parents divorce or remarry. • Tell ways a family might adjust if —a family member is ill or injured. —a family member dies. —a parent or guardian loses a job. —it has to move. —parents divorce.	**The Blended Family**

9 Pregnancy and Childbirth—OPTIONAL

Life Skills	The National Health Education Standards	Grades K–2 Objectives	Grades K–2 Lesson Plans	Grades 3–4 Objectives	Grades 3–4 Lesson Plans
I will learn facts about pregnancy and childbirth.	Students will comprehend concepts related to health promotion and disease prevention.	• Tell what a cell is. • Tell what an egg cell and a sperm cell are. • Tell that a baby is made when an egg cell and a sperm cell join. • Tell that an unborn baby grows inside its mother during pregnancy.	Do You Copy?	• Tell what fertilization is. • Tell actions a mother-to-be can take to care for a baby while it is growing inside her. • Tell how a baby is born.	**Seed Needs** **How a Baby Is Made** **How a Baby Is Born**

Content Area

1 Character in Relationships

Life Skills	The National Health Education Standards	Grades 5–6 Objectives	Grades 5–6 Lesson Plans	Grades 7–8 Objectives	Grades 7–8 Lesson Plans
I will show good character.	Students will demonstrate the ability to practice health-enhancing behaviors and reduce health risks.	• Tell reasons to show good character. • Give examples of family values. • Tell actions that show you have self-respect. • Tell what to do if others don't respect you. • Tell ways to show respect for others. • Tell reasons to participate in The Family Round Table.	The Character Connection	• Explain how you can develop good character. • Explain why it is important to have a good reputation. • List and discuss three ways to do a character checkup.	Hang On to Responsible Values
I will make responsible decisions.	Students will demonstrate the ability to use goal-setting and decision-making skills that enhance health.	• Use the *Guidelines for Making Responsible Decisions™*. • Tell the difference between a responsible action and a wrong action. • Tell steps to correct wrong actions.	Armor of Responsibility	• Use *The Responsible Decision-Making Model™* to make decisions. • Identify six questions to ask to evaluate the possible outcomes of a risk or dare before you take it. • Tell the difference between an unnecessary risk and a calculated risk.	The CD Stuck on NO
I will use resistance skills when appropriate.	Students will demonstrate the ability to use goal-setting and decision-making skills that enhance health.	• Identify resistance skills you can use to resist pressure to make a wrong decision. • Show how to use resistance skills. • Explain what to do if a friend plans to do something wrong.	Armor of Responsibility	• Identify resistance skills you can use to say NO to negative peer pressure. • Demonstrate resistance skills if you are pressured to do something wrong. • Explain what to do if you give in to negative peer pressure.	The CD Stuck on NO

1 Character in Relationships

Content Area

Life Skills	The National Health Education Standards	Grades 5–6 Objectives	Grades 5–6 Lesson Plans	Grades 7–8 Objectives	Grades 7–8 Lesson Plans
I will express feelings in healthful ways.	Students will demonstrate the ability to use interpersonal communication skills to enhance health.	• Tell the three parts of an I-message. • Use I-messages to express feelings. • Explain how to listen and respond when someone else shares feelings.	**I-Message Match-Up**	• Use honest talk. • Use I-messages and active listening. • Avoid sending mixed messages. • Describe anger cues and signs of hidden anger. • Explain how to use anger management skills. • Discuss how nonverbal behavior and mixed messages affect communication.	**Talk the Talk**
I will use conflict resolution skills.	Students will demonstrate the ability to use interpersonal communication skills to enhance health.	• Explain how settling internal conflict protects your health. • Explain how settling conflict with others protects your health. • Explain how to use conflict resolution skills. • Explain how a trusted adult can help you with mediation.	**I-Message Match-Up**	• Explain how to use conflict resolution skills. • Identify the six questions from *The Responsible Decision-Making Model™* that you can use to evaluate possible solutions to conflict. • Explain how to deal with people who settle conflict in harmful ways. • Explain how an adult mediator can help teens resolve conflicts.	**Talk the Talk**

2 Harmful and Violent Relationships

Content Area

Life Skills	The National Health Education Standards	Grades 5–6 Objectives	Grades 5–6 Lesson Plans	Grades 7–8 Objectives	Grades 7–8 Lesson Plans
I will practice protective factors to reduce the risk of violence. I will practice self-protection strategies. I will participate in victim recovery if I am harmed by violence.	Students will demonstrate the ability to practice health-enhancing behaviors and reduce health risks.	• Discuss why people might harm themselves and others. • Tell ways to recognize violence. • Identify protective factors to reduce the risk of violence. • Discuss ways you can protect yourself from people who might harm you. • Explain how you can get help if you are a victim of violence.	**Hang Up** **Hurting Inside**	• Explain how to recognize violence. • Discuss protective factors that reduce your risk of being involved in violence. • Identify self-protection strategies you can practice. • Discuss guidelines you can follow to reduce the risk of rape. • Explain the steps in victim recovery.	**Stop in the Name of Love**
I will choose healthful entertainment. I will develop media literacy.	Students will analyze the influence of culture, media, technology, and other factors on health.	• Identify guidelines for choosing healthful entertainment. • Discuss ways you can judge ads.	**Click Off That Computer Screen**	• Discuss reasons why you need to choose healthful entertainment. • Identify *Guidelines for Choosing Entertainment That Promotes Responsible Behavior.* • Give examples of TV programs, movies, and computer games that show healthful relationships. • Recognize and evaluate media messages. • Describe appeals used in advertisements.	**Smash or Trash?** **Web Wise**

3 Friendship, Dating, and Abstinence

Content Area

Life Skills	The National Health Education Standards	Grades 5–6 Objectives	Grades 5–6 Lesson Plans	Grades 7–8 Objectives	Grades 7–8 Lesson Plans
I will develop healthful relationships. I will recognize harmful relationships.	Students will demonstrate the ability to use interpersonal communication skills to enhance health.	• Explain the effects a healthful relationship and a harmful relationship can have on you. • List and discuss guidelines for friendships. • Explain why you should choose friends your parents or guardian like. • Explain why you should choose friends other people respect. • Discuss reasons to avoid being in a clique. • Discuss steps you can take to do something about a harmful relationship. • Discuss when and how you would end a friendship.	Want Ad for a Friend	• Explain why it is more important to be respected than it is to be popular. • Describe the balance of giving and taking in a healthful relationship. • List the six criteria to use to evaluate decisions made with friends. • Give examples of "sick" relationships and tell what to do about them. • Explain when and how to end a friendship.	Maintaining a Healthful Balance
I will develop dating skills.	Students will demonstrate the ability to use interpersonal communication skills to enhance health.	• Make a list of social activities you can do in a group with people your age of the same and opposite sex. • Ask your parent or guardian for guidelines to follow when spending time with a person of the opposite sex. • Tell how to be a good friend to a person of the opposite sex.	Top Ten List of Activities	• Explain how to stick to limits for expressing affection. • List your parents' or guardians' guidelines for dating. • List and explain do's and don'ts for dating. • List the questions in *The Respect Checklist™* that tell you whether someone of the opposite sex shows respect for you. • Discuss ways to reduce the risk of date rape.	Do You Want to be Prepared for Dating?

232   © 2001 Everyday Learning Corporation

3 Friendship, Dating, and Abstinence

Content Area

Life Skills	The National Health Education Standards	Grades 5–6 Objectives	Grades 5–6 Lesson Plans	Grades 7–8 Objectives	Grades 7–8 Lesson Plans
I will practice abstinence from sex. I will use resistance skills when appropriate.	Students will demonstrate the ability to practice health-enhancing behaviors and reduce health risks. Students will demonstrate the ability to use goal-setting and decision-making skills that enhance health.	• Name *The Top Ten List of Reasons to Practice Abstinence™*. • Tell reasons to keep sex within marriage. • Tell how practicing abstinence from sex protects psychological health. • Give reasons why you want to avoid teen marriage, teen pregnancy, and teen parenthood. • Give reasons why you want to keep from being infected with an STD. • Give reasons why you want to keep from being infected with HIV. • Tell how to set limits for expressing affection. • Demonstrate resistance skills to use if you are pressured to be sexually active. • Tell how being drug-free supports your decision to practice abstinence from sex. • Use guidelines for choosing entertainment that supports family values.	**Top Ten List of Activities**	• Discuss the benefits of a monogamous traditional marriage. • Use *The Responsible Decision-Making Model™* to explain why abstinence is the expected standard for teens. • Identify the harmful consequences that can result from having babies outside of marriage. • Explain how abstinence reduces your risk of becoming infected with HIV and STDs. • Identify *The Top Ten List of Reasons to Practice Abstinence™*. • Outline resistance skills you can use if you are pressured to be sexually active. • Explain how a drug-free lifestyle supports your decision to practice abstinence.	**Resisting Temptation** **Looking Ahead** **You Booze, You Lose** **Unfriendly Persuasion**

Content Area

4 Male Reproductive Health and 5 Female Reproductive Health

Life Skills	The National Health Education Standards	Grades 5–6 Objectives	Grades 5–6 Lesson Plans	Grades 7–8 Objectives	Grades 7–8 Lesson Plans
I will recognize habits that protect male reproductive health.	Students will comprehend concepts related to health promotion and disease prevention.	• Tell ways that a girl's body changes during puberty.	**Puberty—All About Boys**	• Accept body changes that occur during puberty.	**Masculine/Feminine**
I will recognize habits that protect female reproductive health.	Students will demonstrate the ability to access valid health information and health-promoting products and services.	• Name the organs in the female reproductive system.	**Puberty—All About Girls**	• Practice habits that protect male reproductive health (if you are male).	**Reproductive Health: Media Literacy**
I will have regular examinations.	Students will demonstrate the ability to advocate for personal, family, and community health.	• Explain what happens during the menstrual cycle.	**Picture Perfect**	• Practice habits that protect female reproductive health (if you are female).	
I will keep a personal health record.	Students will demonstrate the ability to practice health-enhancing behaviors and reduce health risks.	• Identify products used for menstruation.		• Explain what happens during the menstrual cycle.	
I will be well-groomed.		• Identify symptoms of toxic shock syndrome (TSS).		• Explain why smoking is NOT sexy.	
I will learn ways my body changes.		• Tell healthful habits that girls your age can practice.		• Tell why you need regular medical checkups.	
		• Tell ways that a boy's body changes during puberty.		• Tell why you need to keep a personal health record.	
		• Name the organs in the male reproductive system.			
		• Tell why boys should wear an athletic supporter and protective cup for sports.			
		• Tell healthful habits that boys your age can practice.			

6 Sexually Transmitted Diseases

Content Area					
Life Skills	The National Health Education Standards	Grades 5–6 Objectives	Grades 5–6 Lesson Plans	Grades 7–8 Objectives	Grades 7–8 Lesson Plans
I will choose behaviors to reduce my risk of infection with sexually transmitted diseases. I will not misuse or abuse drugs. I will use resistance skills when appropriate.	Students will demonstrate the ability to use goal-setting and decision-making skills that enhance health. Students will demonstrate the ability to practice health-enhancing behaviors and reduce health risks.	• Give reasons why you want to keep from being infected with an STD. • Outline signs and symptoms of, diagnosis and treatment for, and health problems that result from the following STDs: chlamydial infection, gonorrhea, syphilis, genital herpes, genital warts, candidiasis, trichomoniasis, and pubic lice. • Tell how abstinence from sex reduces the risk of STDs. • Tell how a drug-free lifestyle reduces the risk of STDs. • Discuss ways to stick with abstinence and reduce the risk of STDs. • Use resistance skills if you are pressured to be sexually active or to use drugs.	**What a Glittering Handshake** **STD FACT-O**	• Identify the cause, transmission, symptoms, diagnosis and treatment, and complications for the following STDs: chlamydia, genital herpes, genital warts, gonorrhea, pubic lice, syphilis, trichomoniasis, and viral hepatitis. • Discuss ways to reduce your risk of becoming infected with STDs. • Explain why you should abstain from sex until you are married. • Tell why you must change your behavior and be tested for STDs and HIV if you have been sexually active. • Explain why you should have a monogamous traditional marriage if you choose to marry in the future. • Tell why it is important to choose a drug-free lifestyle. • Explain why you should avoid the use of injection drugs. • Tell why you should change your behavior if you use drugs. • Explain why you should avoid sharing a needle to make tattoos or to pierce ears and other body parts. • Explain why you should follow universal precautions.	**STDs: Questions and Answers** **The Pressure Builds**

© 2001 Everyday Learning Corporation

235

7 HIV/AIDS

Life Skills	The National Health Education Standards	Grades 5–6 Objectives	Grades 5–6 Lesson Plans	Grades 7–8 Objectives	Grades 7–8 Lesson Plans
I will choose behaviors to reduce my risk of HIV infection. I will use resistance skills when appropriate.	Students will demonstrate the ability to use goal-setting and decision-making skills that enhance health.	• Describe how HIV destroys the immune system. • Discuss risk behaviors and risk situations for HIV infection. • Explain why a person can spread HIV before testing positive for HIV. • Discuss treatment for HIV infection and AIDS. • State ways to reduce your risk of HIV infection. • Give reasons why you want to keep from being infected with HIV.	**Did You Know?** **Compassion** **HIV and AIDS: The Facts**	• List ways HIV is and is not spread. • Explain why practicing abstinence protects you from HIV infection. • Explain why saying NO to injecting drugs, using alcohol and other drugs, and sharing a needle to make tattoos or to pierce ears or other body parts protects you from HIV infection. • Explain why you need to follow universal precautions to protect yourself from HIV infection. • Discuss tests used to determine HIV status. • Explain how HIV infection progresses to AIDS. • Discuss the latest treatments for HIV and AIDS. • Identify ways in which HIV and AIDS threaten society. • Outline resistance skills you can use if you are pressured to choose risk behaviors for HIV infection.	**HIV: You Have Entered** **Infected Needles** **Pass That Cookie**

Content Area

8 Marriage, Parenthood, and Family Living

Life Skills	The National Health Education Standards	Grades 5–6 Objectives	Grades 5–6 Lesson Plans	Grades 7–8 Objectives	Grades 7–8 Lesson Plans
I will develop healthful family relationships. I will work to improve difficult family relationships.	Students will demonstrate the ability to use interpersonal communication skills to enhance health.	• Explain how you can be a loving family member. • Explain why you need to follow family guidelines. • Tell reasons to participate in the Family Round Table. • Discuss ways to cope with difficult family relationships.	**Family Sculpture** **The Parenting Magazine**	• Identify different kinds of family patterns. • Discuss actions that can help you develop healthful family relationships. • Discuss reasons why you should follow family guidelines. • Identify three kinds of problems that can occur in dysfunctional families. • Explain steps that can be taken to improve dysfunctional family relationships.	**Difficult Family Relationships**
I will develop skills to prepare for marriage. I will develop skills to prepare for parenthood.	Students will demonstrate the ability to use goal-setting and decision-making skills that enhance health.	• Tell reasons why monogamous marriage protects society. • Tell reasons why children need responsible parents. • Tell ways to help care for younger children. • Give reasons why you want to avoid teen marriage, teen pregnancy, and teen parenthood.	**The Parenting Magazine**	• Discuss the benefits of monogamous marriage. • Outline responsibilities of married adults and parents. • Identify reasons why you should be an adult before you marry or become a parent. • Explain why teens who feel unloved are more at risk for teen marriage and teen parenthood.	**The Costs of Rearing a Child**
I will make healthful adjustments to family changes.	Students will demonstrate the ability to practice health-enhancing behaviors and reduce health risks.	• Discuss ways families might change. • Discuss ways to make healthful adjustments to family changes.	**Family Sculpture**	• Discuss changes that might occur in family relationships. • Describe ways you can adjust to changes in family relationships. • Discuss ways parents' divorce can affect a teen's future relationships.	**Difficult Family Relationships**

Content Area

9 Pregnancy and Childbirth

Life Skills	The National Health Education Standards	Grades 5–6 Objectives	Grades 5–6 Lesson Plans	Grades 7–8 Objectives	Grades 7–8 Lesson Plans
I will learn facts about pregnancy and childbirth.	Students will comprehend concepts related to health promotion and disease prevention.	• Explain where and how fertilization takes place. • Explain how the sex of a baby is determined. • Explain the difference between a dominant gene and a recessive gene. • Explain how an unborn baby gets healthful substances from its mother. • Tell what is included in prenatal care. • Tell how a father-to-be who smokes can affect his unborn baby. • Name harmful substances that can pass from the mother-to-be's blood into her unborn baby's blood. • Tell how harmful substances can affect the unborn baby. • Explain how identical twins and fraternal twins are produced. • Tell what happens during labor and childbirth.	**It's a Boy! It's a Girl!** **What's KNOT Good for an Unborn Baby**	• Explain the process of conception. • Explain what happens in the first week after conception. • List the signs of pregnancy. • Discuss the importance of prenatal care. • Explain ways a mother-to-be's behaviors can affect the health of her baby. • Describe the development of a baby from conception through birth. • Explain ways a father-to-be's behavior can affect the health of his baby. • Identify problems that can occur during pregnancy. • Explain what happens during labor and childbirth.	**I Am a Responsible Parent** **Teen Pregnancy Misfortune**

1 Character in Relationships

Content Area

Life Skills	The National Health Education Standards	Grades 9–12 Objectives	Grades 9–12 Lesson Plans
I will develop good character.	Students will comprehend concepts related to health promotion and disease prevention. Students will demonstrate the ability to use interpersonal communication skills to enhance health.	• Explain why it is important to know how to practice moderation and be able to delay gratification. • Identify the responsible values that make up good character. • Explain why you must demonstrate each of the responsible values that make up good character to have healthful relationships. • Identify reasons why you need good character.	**Brown Bag**
I will make responsible decisions.	Students will demonstrate the ability to use goal-setting and decision-making skills that enhance health. Students will demonstrate the ability to advocate for personal, family, and community health.	• Identify three decision-making styles and explain how each one might affect the quality of your relationships. • Use *The Responsible Decision-Making Model*™ to make decisions.	**Deep Thoughts, By Me**
I will use resistance skills when appropriate.	Students will demonstrate the ability to use interpersonal communication skills to enhance health. Students will demonstrate the ability to advocate for personal, family, and community health.	• Differentiate between positive peer pressure and negative peer pressure. • Demonstrate resistance skills that can be used to resist pressure to do something wrong. • Explain why it is important to show remorse for wrongful behavior. • Identify steps to take to correct wrong actions. • Give examples of restitution including ways to pay back and pay forward.	**A Me Advertisement**
I will express emotions in healthful ways.	Students will demonstrate the ability to use interpersonal communication skills to enhance health. Students will demonstrate the ability to advocate for personal, family, and community health.	• Construct sample I-messages to express different emotions. • Demonstrate ways to implement active listening. • Give examples of ways people relate using nonverbal communication. • Explain how sending mixed messages might affect the quality of your relationships.	**A Pat on the Back**
I will use conflict resolution skills.	Students will demonstrate the ability to practice health-enhancing behaviors and reduce health risks. Students will demonstrate the ability to use interpersonal communication skills to enhance health.	• Identify three conflict response styles and explain how each one might affect the quality of your relationships. • Demonstrate how to use conflict resolution skills.	**A Pat on the Back**

Content Area

2 Harmful and Violent Relationships

Life Skills	The National Health Education Standards	Grades 9–12 Objectives	Grades 9–12 Lesson Plans
I will practice protective factors to reduce the risk of violence.	Students will demonstrate the ability to practice health-enhancing behaviors and reduce health risks. Students will demonstrate the ability to use interpersonal communication skills to enhance health.	• Identify and discuss risk factors for harmful and violent relationships. • Describe profiles of people who relate with others in harmful ways. • Explain why some people match-up to form harmful relationships. • Discuss steps to prevent and/or resolve harmful relationships. • Discuss four types of abusive relationships: physical, emotional, neglect, and sexual.	**A Dis-Heartening Experience** **I'm Harassed**
I will practice self-protection strategies.	Students will demonstrate the ability to use goal-setting and decision-making skills that enhance health.	• Discuss *Guidelines to Follow to Reduce the Risk of Rape.* • Discuss *Guidelines to Follow When Sexual Harassment Occurs.* • Discuss *Steps to Take When Being Stalked.* • Identify and describe kinds of self-defense strategies. • Identify *Self-Protection Strategies for the Home.* • Identify *Self-Protection Strategies for the School.* • Identify *Self-Protection Strategies for Traveling.*	
I will participate in victim recovery if I am harmed by violence.		• Discuss recovery strategies for victims and survivors of violence.	
I will choose healthful entertainment.	Students will analyze the influence of culture, media, technology, and other factors on health.	• Discuss reasons to avoid viewing television shows, movies, and videotapes; reading materials; saying raps and listening to and singing song lyrics that have a violent message.	
I will develop media literacy.	Students will demonstrate the ability to use goal-setting and decision-making skills that enhance health.	• Explain how being media literate can help protect you from becoming desensitized to violence. • List guidelines that help you choose healthful entertainment. • Identify *Guidelines to Follow to Stay Safe When Using the Internet.*	

Content Area

3 Friendship, Dating, and Abstinence

Life Skills	The National Health Education Standards	Grades 9–12 Objectives	Grades 9–12 Lesson Plans
I will develop healthful friendships.	Students will demonstrate the ability to practice health-enhancing behaviors and reduce health risks. Students will demonstrate the ability to use interpersonal communication skills to enhance health. Students will comprehend concepts related to health promotion and disease prevention.	• Explain how to initiate friendships. • Discuss ways to handle rejection. • Explain how to maintain balanced friendships. • Identify behaviors that indicate respect in a relationship.	**The Perfect Match**
I will develop dating skills.	Students will demonstrate the ability to use interpersonal communication skills to enhance health. Students will demonstrate the ability to use goal-setting and decision-making skills that enhance health.	• List and discuss standards for dating. • Discuss each of the items on the *Dating Skills Checklist*. • Discuss *Guidelines to Follow to Reduce the Risk of Rape* (refer to Harmful and Violent Relationships).	**Values Tug of War**
I will practice abstinence from sex. I will practice resistance skills when appropriate.	Students will demonstrate the ability to practice health-enhancing behaviors and reduce health risks. Students will demonstrate the ability to use goal-setting and decision-making skills that enhance health. Students will demonstrate the ability to use interpersonal communication skills to enhance health. Students will demonstrate the ability to advocate for personal, family, and community health.	• List and explain reasons to wait until marriage to have sex. • Identify the *Top Ten List of Reasons to Practice Abstinence™*. • Use *The Responsible Decision-Making Model™* to outline reasons why abstinence from sex is a responsible decision. • Explain how to set limits for expressing physical affection. • Identify choices that reinforce your decision to practice abstinence from sex. • Outline resistance skills that can be used to say NO if you are pressured to be sexually active. • List and discuss steps teens who have been sexually active can take to change their behavior.	**Values Tug of War** **Unexpected Reaction**

4 Male Reproductive Health

Content Area

Life Skills	The National Health Education Standards	Grades 9–12 Objectives	Grades 9–12 Lesson Plans
I will recognize habits that protect male reproductive health.	Students will comprehend concepts related to health promotion and disease prevention.	• Discuss the physical and emotional changes males experience during puberty.	**Reproduce My System**
	Students will demonstrate the ability to practice health-enhancing behaviors and reduce health risks.	• Name and give the function of the organs in the male reproductive system.	**Balloon Blow Up**
I will have regular examinations.	Students will demonstrate the ability to access valid health information and health-promoting products and services.	• Discuss male reproductive physiology: erection, orgasm, and ejaculation.	
I will keep a personal health record.	Students will analyze the influence of culture, media, technology, and other factors on health.	• Discuss information pertaining to male reproductive health: hernia, circumcision, penis size, nocturnal emissions, morning erection, anabolic steroids, testicular cancer, testicular self-examination, prostatitis, prostate cancer, and andropause.	
I will be well-groomed.	Students will demonstrate the ability to use goal-setting and decision-making skills that enhance health.	• Identify habits males must practice to protect reproductive health.	
		• Explain why males should keep a personal health record.	
		• Discuss ways for males to be well-groomed.	

Content Area

5 Female Reproductive Health

Life Skills	The National Health Education Standards	Grades 9–12 Objectives	Grades 9–12 Lesson Plans
I will recognize habits that protect female reproductive health.	Students will comprehend concepts related to health promotion and disease prevention.	• Discuss the physical and emotional changes females experience during puberty. • Name and give the function of the organs in the female reproductive system. • Outline the physiological changes that occur in a menstrual cycle.	**My Body, My System** **All Blown Up**
I will have regular examinations.	Students will demonstrate the ability to practice health-enhancing behaviors and reduce health risks.	• Discuss information pertaining to menstrual health: menarche, amenorrhea, oligomenorrhea, dysmenorrhea, menorrhagia, premenstrual syndrome, and toxic shock syndrome.	
I will keep a personal health record.	Students will demonstrate the ability to access valid health information and health-promoting products and services.	• Discuss information pertaining to female reproductive health: breast self-examination, mammography, fibrocystic breast condition, breast cancer, breast implants, uterine and cervical cancer, ovarian cancer, vaginal cancer, vaginitis, cystitis, endometritis, endometriosis, polyps, dilation and curettage, and fibroids.	
I will be well-groomed.	Students will analyze the influence of culture, media, technology, and other factors on health.	• Discuss what is included in a pelvic examination. • Identify habits females must practice to protect female reproductive health.	
	Students will demonstrate the ability to use goal-setting and decision-making skills that enhance health.	• Explain why females should keep a personal health record. • Discuss ways for females to be well-groomed.	

Content Area

6 Sexually Transmitted Diseases—OPTIONAL

Life Skills	The National Health Education Standards	Grades 9–12 Objectives	Grades 9–12 Lesson Plans
I will choose behaviors to reduce my risk of infection with sexually transmitted diseases.	Students will demonstrate the ability to access valid health information and health-promoting products and services.	• Identify and discuss risk behaviors and risk situations for transmission of STDs.	**All My Diseases**
	Students will demonstrate the ability to use goal-setting and decision-making skills that enhance health.	• Discuss the cause, transmission, symptoms, diagnosis, and treatment for common STDs: chlamydia, genital herpes, genital warts, gonorrhea, pubic lice, syphilis, trichomoniasis, viral hepatitis.	
I will not misuse or abuse drugs.	Students will demonstrate the ability to practice health-enhancing behaviors and reduce health risks.	• Discuss ways to reduce the risk of infection with STDs.	
I will practice abstinence from sex.		• Outline resistance skills that can be used to resist pressure to engage in risk behaviors and risk situations for transmission of STDs.	
I will use resistance skills when appropriate.			

© 2001 Everyday Learning Corporation

Content Area

7 HIV/AIDS

Life Skills	The National Health Education Standards	Grades 9–12 Objectives	Grades 9–12 Lesson Plans
I will choose behaviors to reduce my risk of HIV infection.	Students will comprehend concepts related to health promotion and disease prevention.	• Explain how the immune system responds to most pathogens.	**Defend That Line**
		• Explain how the immune system responds when HIV enters the body.	**It Just Keeps on Spreading**
I will not misuse or abuse drugs.	Students will demonstrate the ability to practice health-enhancing behaviors and reduce health risks.	• Identify and discuss risk behaviors and risk situations for transmission of HIV.	**HIV Conference**
		• Identify and discuss ways HIV is not transmitted.	**The Odds Aren't Great**
I will practice abstinence from sex.	Students will demonstrate the ability to use goal-setting and decision-making skills that enhance health.	• Discuss tests used to determine HIV status.	**The AIDS News of the Day**
		• Explain the progression of HIV infection and AIDS including the opportunistic infections that might develop.	
		• Discuss treatment for HIV infection and AIDS.	
I will use resistance skills when appropriate.		• Discuss ways to reduce the risk of HIV infection.	
		• Outline resistance skills that can be used to resist pressure to engage in risk behaviors and risk situations for transmission of HIV.	

8 Marriage, Parenthood, and Family Living

Content Area

Life Skills	The National Health Education Standards	Grades 9–12 Objectives	Grades 9–12 Lesson Plans
I will develop skills to prepare for marriage. I will discuss skills to prepare for parenthood.	Students will demonstrate the ability to practice health-enhancing behaviors and reduce health risks. Students will demonstrate the ability to use interpersonal communication skills to enhance health. Students will demonstrate the ability to advocate for personal, family, and community health.	• Identify factors used to predict success in marriage. • Explain four kinds of intimacy in marriage. • Explain two important ways marriage partners can ensure that their marriage will last. • Discuss the risks associated with teen marriage. • Discuss ways teen marriage interferes with mastery of the eight developmental tasks of adolescence. • Explain the three "Rs" (reasons, resources, responsibilities) to consider before becoming a parent. • Explain four kinds of intimacy in the parent-child relationship. • Outline the growth and development of a child: from birth to six months, six months to twelve months, twelve months to eighteen months, eighteen months to two years, two years to two and one-half years, two and one-half years to three years, three years to four years, four years to five years, and five years to six years. • Explain ways parents and guardians help their children develop self-discipline and self-control. • Identify skills that must be developed by teens who plan to childsit.	**Stressors of Teen Marriage** **Handle That Crying**
I will develop healthful family relationships. I will work to improve difficult family relationships.	Students will demonstrate the ability to use interpersonal communication skills to enhance health. Students will demonstrate the ability to use goal-setting and decision-making skills that enhance health.	• Contrast ideal family relationships with dysfunctional family relationships using *The Family Continuum.* • List and explain skills children who have ideal family relationships learn from their parents or guardians. • Discuss the causes of dysfunctional family relationships. • Discuss feelings and behaviors that describe family members who are codependent. • Outline ways to improve dysfunctional family relationships.	**Family Circles**
I will make healthful adjustments to family changes.	Students will demonstrate the ability to practice health-enhancing behaviors and reduce health risks. Students will demonstrate the ability to use interpersonal communication skills to enhance health.	• Discuss adjustments children might make if their parents divorce. • Discuss adjustments children might make if they live in a single-custody family. • Discuss adjustments children might make if a parent or parents remarry. • Discuss adjustments children might make if a parent(s) loses a job. • Discuss adjustments children might make if a parent goes to jail.	**Family Circles**

Content Area

9 Pregnancy and Childbirth

Life Skills	The National Health Education Standards	Grades 9–12 Objectives	Grades 9–12 Lesson Plans
I will learn about pregnancy and childbirth.	Students will comprehend concepts related to health promotion and disease prevention. Students will demonstrate the ability to access valid health information and health-promoting products and services.	• Explain how a baby's sex and inherited traits are determined. • Discuss lifestyle habits that a couple should adopt before the couple plans to have a baby. • Explain fertilization. • Discuss male and female infertility. • Discuss ways to increase fertility and the probability of conception. • Identify assisted reproductive technologies. • Explain how pregnancy and the estimated delivery date are determined. • Describe the development of the embryo and fetus during the three trimesters of pregnancy. • Discuss the importance of prenatal care. • Describe the effects of pregnancy on the mother-to-be and father-to-be. • Identify atypical conditions that might occur during pregnancy. • Discuss ways birth defects are detected. • Discuss the risks associated with teen pregnancy. • Discuss birthplace alternatives and childbirth preparation. • Discuss pain management alternatives for childbirth. • Discuss what happens during each of the three stages of labor. • Discuss the postpartum period including breastfeeding and parental bonding.	**Pregnancy Test** **Childbirth Class**

Grades K–2
Lesson Plans and Blackline Masters

Table of Contents

The Gift of Good Character

The Curriculum

Life Skill
■ I will show good character.

Objectives
■ Students will tell what good character is.
■ Students will tell ways to show good character.
■ Students will tell what to do if they do something wrong.

The National Health Education Standards
■ Students will demonstrate the ability to practice health-enhancing behaviors and reduce health risks.

Preparing to Teach the Lesson Plan

Materials
One shoe box
Decorative wrapping paper
Glue or tape
Small mirror
Chalkboard
Chalk

Teaching the Lesson Plan

Make a gift box using a shoe box. Use decorative wrapping paper to cover the shoe box. Glue or tape a small mirror to the inside of the shoe box lid.

1 Stand in front of the class holding the gift box. Allow students to observe the gift box. Students will be curious about what is inside the gift box.

2 Ask students whether they have ever received gifts. Students will probably answer that they have. Allow students time to share information about gifts they have received. Ask students whether they have ever tried to guess what is inside a gift box. They will probably answer that they have. Explain to students that you are holding a gift box that contains something very special. Tell students that they will be allowed to see what is inside the gift box. Emphasize to students that they will see a special gift when they open the gift box.

3 Explain that you are going to pass the gift box around the class. Tell students that they are not to tell anyone what they see inside the gift box. As you come to each person, open the lid so that the student can look inside the gift box. (When students open the lid, they will see their faces reflected in the mirror.) Ask students to think about what was so special about the gift each one saw. Students might say that they saw themselves and they are special.

4 Ask students to share the special characteristics they saw. Students might say that they saw a good friend, a hard worker, or an honest person. Explain that these characteristics help make up good character. Define good character. **Good character** is telling the truth, showing respect, and being fair. Explain to students that the gift of good character is a gift that they can share with others. Just as students might share material gifts with others, they can share the values that make up good character, such as honesty and fairness.

5 Discuss some of the special gifts that students have. Write the following sentences on the board: "I have good character. I have the gift of _____." Tell students to share the special values they have that make up good character. Students might give the following examples:

- I have the gift of being honest.
- I have the gift of being a good friend.
- I have the gift of playing games in a fair way.
- I have the gift of respecting others.
- I have the gift of showing others I care about them.
- I have the gift of being responsible.

After students have shared their statements, you can share statements about gifts you have. You might give the following examples:

- I have the gift of being a role model of good character.
- I have the gift of having respect for students.
- I have the gift of teaching you how to show good character.

Assessment

Write the following poem on the board: "I look in the mirror, and what do I see? I see someone special. It is me."

Underline the last two sentences. Have students repeat the poem. Then ask each student to substitute his or her own last two lines. Students might give the following examples:

"I look in the mirror, and what do I see? I see someone responsible. It is me."

"I look in the mirror, and what do I see? I see someone truthful. It is me."

If You Make Wise Decisions and You Know It

The Curriculum

Life Skills

■ I will make responsible decisions.

■ I will use resistance skills when necessary.

Objectives

■ Students will tell six questions to ask before they make a decision.

■ Students will tell how to make wise decisions.

■ Students will tell what a wrong decision is.

■ Students will name NO skills.

■ Students will show ways to say NO to wrong decisions.

The National Health Education Standards

■ Students will demonstrate the ability to use goal-setting and decision-making skills that enhance health.

Preparing to Teach the Lesson Plan

Materials

None

Blackline Masters

Make Wise Decisions™

Say NO Skills

Teaching the Lesson Plan

1 Ask students to sit on the floor in a circle. Tell students that they are going to sing a song called "If You're Happy and You Know It." The words to the song are as follows:

> "If you're happy and you know it, clap your hands.
>
> If you're happy and you know it, clap your hands.
>
> If you're happy and you know it, and you really want to show it,
>
> if you're happy and you know it, clap your hands."

Have students sing the song three times.

2 Give each student a copy of the Blackline Master *Make Wise Decisions*™. Define wise decision. A **wise decision** is the best choice. Explain that a wise decision is healthful. A wise decision is safe. A wise decision follows laws. A wise decision shows respect for others. A wise decision follows family rules. A wise decision shows good character. Give examples of wise decisions, such as staying away from tobacco, getting plenty of physical activity, and wearing a safety belt in a car. Tell students that you are going to ask them to name wise decisions they have made.

3 Define wrong decision. A **wrong decision** is a choice you will not be proud of. Explain to students that sometimes someone might try to get them to make a wrong decision. Ask students what they would do. Students might answer that they would say "no." Give each student a copy of the Blackline Master *Say NO Skills*. Review the *Say NO Skills* with the class.

4 Explain to students that they are going to sing the same song, but this time with different words. Tell the class that after a student shares a wise decision that he or she has made, the class will substitute the words of the original song with the person's name and the wise decision that the person has made. Ask for a student volunteer. Ask the student volunteer to name a wise decision he or she has made. The student volunteer might say that he or she wears a safety belt while riding in a car. Suppose the student volunteer is named Danni. You would have students substitute the words of the song with the following words:

"Danni wears a safety belt every day (clap clap).

Danni wears a safety belt every day (clap clap).

Danni makes a wise decision and she really wants to show it,

Danni wears a safety belt every day (clap clap)."

5 Repeat the activity for each student in the class. You can change the activity by asking students to name wise decisions other students have made. Then the class will sing the song using the name of the student who has made the wise decision.

Assessment

Ask students to repeat the wise decision they and other students have made. Write several of these wise decisions on the board. Point to a wise decision.

Ask students the following questions:

- Is the decision healthful?
- Is the decision safe?
- Does the decision follow laws?
- Does the decision show respect for others?
- Does the decision follow family rules?
- Does the decision show good character?

© 2001 Everyday Learning Corporation

Make Wise Decisions™

A **wise decision** is the best choice.

◆ A wise decision is healthful.

◆ A wise decision is safe.

◆ A wise decision follows laws.

◆ A wise decision shows respect for others.

◆ A wise decision follows family rules.

◆ A wise decision shows good character.

Say NO Skills

1. Look directly at the person.

2. Say NO.

3. Tell why you are saying NO.

4. Repeat your NO if you need to.

5. Do not change your mind.

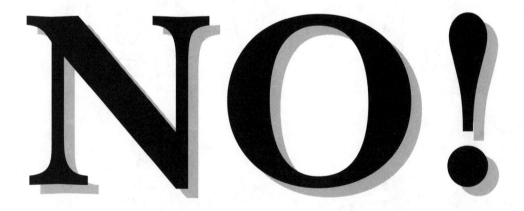

© 2001 Everyday Learning Corporation

Angry Inside

The Curriculum

Life Skills

■ I will share feelings in healthful ways.

■ I will settle conflict in healthful ways.

Objectives

■ Students will tell different feelings they have.

■ Students will tell healthful ways to share feelings.

■ Students will explain what to do if they are angry or afraid.

■ Students will tell ways to work out conflict.

The National Health Education Standards

■ Students will demonstrate the ability to use interpersonal communication skills to enhance health.

Preparing to Teach the Lesson Plan

Materials

Knife

Apple

Blackline Master

You Can Work Out Conflict

Teaching the Lesson Plan

Use a bright, shiny apple for this lesson plan. With the knife, slice a vertical wedge from the apple about one-half inch thick. Let the apple sit for at least an hour in a place where students cannot see it.

1 Hold the apple so that only the bright, shiny section is visible to students. Ask students to describe the apple. Students might say that the apple looks delicious and that it is bright and shiny.

2 Explain to students that there is an outside and an inside of the apple. Tell students that they have just described what they see when they look at the outside of the apple. Ask students to describe what they believe the inside of the apple looks like. Students might say that the apple is crisp and delicious on the inside. Ask students if they would like to take a bite out of the apple. Students might say that they would like to take a bite out of the apple.

3 Show students the part of the apple from which the slice was removed. Because the inside of the apple has been exposed to air, it will look bruised and will have brown spots. Ask students what they see. Students might say that the inside of the apple is bruised. Explain that there was no way to know that the apple was bruised until they saw the inside.

4 Tell the class that you are now going to talk about sharing feelings. Use the analogy that each person has an outside and an inside. Every person has feelings. Define feelings. **Feelings** are the ways you feel inside. Explain that a person can show feelings on the outside by laughing, crying, smiling, and speaking. Explain that a person also has feelings on the inside. A person can have happy feelings on the inside. But a person also can have sad, hurt, or angry feelings. Define angry. **Angry** is feeling very upset with someone or something. A person might choose not to share the feelings he or she has on the inside. This person might appear cheerful and happy on the outside just like the apple that appeared bright and shiny. But this person might be hurt or angry on the inside just like the apple that was bruised on the inside.

5 Ask students what they believe will happen to the bruise on the apple if it sits overnight. Students might answer that the bruise will become worse or will darken. Explain that when a person has angry feelings, these feelings do not go away either. Angry feelings are much like the bruise on the apple. Angry feelings can eat away at a person. Angry feelings can cause body changes. A person with angry feelings might get a stomachache or a headache. A person might have difficulty sleeping. Holding angry feelings inside can cause the heart to beat faster. Holding angry feelings inside can cause a person to breathe more often. Holding angry feelings inside can make digesting food more difficult.

6 Explain to students that if they have angry feelings, they should not do anything wrong. They should not start fights or say bad words. They should not break anything. They should stay calm and share feelings.

7 Tell students that it is healthful to share feelings. When students are angry, they should ask themselves four questions:

1. What am I feeling?

2. Why do I feel this way?

3. What are some ways I might express my feelings?

4. Which ways of expressing feelings are healthful?

Explain that if a person asks these four questions each time he or she has angry feelings, it will help the person know what he or she is feeling. It will make it easier for the person to share these feelings with others. A person can talk about his or her feelings and these four questions with a trusted adult.

8 Define conflict. A **conflict** is a disagreement. Give each student a copy of the Blackline Master *You Can Work Out Conflict.* Explain to students that sometimes they will have conflicts with others. Tell students that they can work out conflicts. They should not fight or say bad words. They should talk in a calm way. Tell students that they should listen to the other person. They should share their feelings. They should think of ways to work things out. They should agree on a way to work things out.

Assessment

Tell students to repeat the four questions to ask if they are angry. Tell students to repeat the ways to work out conflict. Ask students to tell how the body changes because of angry feelings. Give students scenarios such as the following: "A friend has plans to spend the day with you. The friend never appears at your house as planned. You learn that your friend spent the day with someone else." Ask students to name healthful ways to deal with this situation. Ask them how they could use the four questions to deal with their anger.

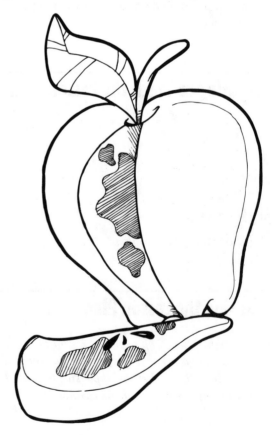

You Can Work Out Conflict

1. Do not fight.

2. Do not say bad words.

3. Talk in a calm way.

4. Listen to the other person.

5. Share your feelings.

6. Think of ways to work things out.

7. Agree on a way to work things out.

8. Walk away if the other person or people want to fight.

9. Ask a trusted adult for help.

Code Word: Safety

The Curriculum

Life Skills

■ I will protect myself from people who might harm me.

■ I will follow safety rules to protect myself from violence.

Objective

■ Students will tell ways they can stay safe from strangers.

The National Health Education Standards

■ Students will demonstrate the ability to practice health-enhancing behaviors and reduce health risks.

Preparing to Teach the Lesson Plan

Materials

None

Blackline Master

Stay Safe from Strangers

Teaching the Lesson Plan

1 Ask students whether they have ever been picked up from school at the end of the school day. Students might say that they have. Ask students who has picked them up from school. Students might say that a family member or guardian has picked them up. Ask students whether they have ever been picked up from school by a family friend. Students might say that they have been picked up by a family friend. Ask students how they knew they were supposed to go with this person. Students might say that a parent told them that the family friend would pick them up. Ask students whether they were concerned about leaving school with someone who was not a member of their family. Students might say that they were not concerned.

2 Tell students that it is usually safe to take a ride home from school with a friend of the family. However, tell students that parents and guardians want them to follow safety rules to protect them from harm. Define stranger. A **stranger** is a person you do not know well. Explain to students that most strangers are kind. But explain to students that some strangers might harm a person. Give each student a copy of the Blackline Master *Stay Safe from Strangers*. Tell students to follow these safety rules to stay safe from strangers:

• Tell your parents or guardians where you will play.

• Run away if a stranger talks to you.

• Do not play alone.

• Do not talk to a stranger.

3 Tell students that another way to stay safe from strangers is to have a secret code word. Tell students that having a secret code word can help them know when it is safe to leave with a person other than a family member. Explain to students that they can have a secret code word with their parents or guardians. Tell students that only the student and the parents or guardians should know the secret code word. The parents or guardians can tell the secret code word to a family friend or childsitter who might pick up their child from school. Suppose a family friend or childsitter picks you up from school. That person should know the secret code word.

A student should ask the person, "What is the secret code word?" If the person does not know the secret code word, the child should not go with this person. If that person does not know the secret code word, the student should tell a teacher or other responsible adult. The teacher might call the student's parents or guardians to find out whether or not the student should leave school with the person.

4 Tell students that if they use a secret code word once, they should choose a new secret code word in case someone overheard the secret code word.

Assessment

Tell students to role play safety rules by using a secret code word. Ask for two student volunteers. Tell one of the volunteers to pretend that he or she is a child leaving school. Tell the other volunteer that he or she is an adult who is picking up the child from school. This student should say, "Can I give you a ride home?" The child leaving school should ask, "What is the secret code word?" Tell students that if the adult does not know the secret code word or if the child feels threatened for any reason, he or she should tell a teacher or other responsible adult what happened. Now tell the student volunteer playing the adult a secret code word. Tell the students to role play the situation again. Ask the class how the situations were different. Students might say that this time the stranger knew the secret code word. Ask whether or not the student should go with the stranger this time. Students might say that the student should go with the stranger if he or she knows the secret code word.

What is the
secret code word?

Stay Safe from Strangers

Do

✓ Do tell your parents or guardians where you will play.

✓ Do run away if a stranger talks to you.

Do NOT

✗ Do not play alone.

✗ Do not talk to a stranger.

The Danger Stranger

The Curriculum

Life Skills

■ I will protect myself from people who might harm me.

■ I will follow safety rules to protect myself from violence.

Objective

■ Students will tell ways they can stay safe from strangers.

The National Health Education Standards

■ Students will demonstrate the ability to practice health-enhancing behaviors and reduce health risks.

Preparing to Teach the Lesson Plan

Materials

Index cards

Raincoat

Hat

Sunglasses

Chalkboard

Chalk

Teaching the Lesson Plan

Write one of the following on each of three index cards: Stranger #1: NO; Stranger #2: NO; Stranger #3: YES.

1 Explain to students that they are going to play a guessing game called the Danger Stranger. Tell students that you are going to play the role of three different strangers. Explain that two of the strangers are nice people and would not harm anyone. Explain that one of the strangers you will play is a person who would harm someone.

2 Pretend you are Stranger #1. In this role, you might wear a raincoat, a hat, and sunglasses. Walk around the room acting tough. You might ask students questions, such as what their names are, in a threatening voice. Then say to the class, "Remember Stranger #1."

3 Pretend you are Stranger #2. In this role, you might appear messy. Your hair might appear uncombed, your shirt or blouse might not be tucked in at your waist, and your shoes might be untied. You might glare at the class without saying a word. Then say to the class, "Remember Stranger #2."

4 Pretend you are Stranger #3. In this role, you should appear neat and well-groomed. Walk around the room acting friendly. You might say to the students, "I like your shirt," or "You look great today." You might shake someone's hand. Then say to the class, "Remember Stranger #3."

5 Hold the blank side of your index cards toward the students. Tell students that the answer to who is the danger stranger is on one of the cards. Tell students that they will vote on who is the danger stranger. Place the tallies on the board. After all votes have been cast, ask students to give reasons why they voted for their choice. Students might say that they picked Stranger #1 or Stranger #2 because of the way that person looked and acted.

6 Tell students that you will hold up the three index cards one by one. First hold up the card with the words "Stranger #1: NO." Students will understand that the danger stranger was not Stranger #1. Then hold up the card with the words "Stranger #2: NO." Students will understand that the danger stranger was not Stranger #2. Then hold up the card with the words "Stranger #3: YES." Students will understand that the danger stranger was Stranger #3. Explain to students that they cannot tell by looking at someone whether or not that person would harm them. Stranger #3 was clean-cut and neat. Nor can they tell by the way a person acts whether or not that person is dangerous. Stranger #3 was friendly and personable.

7 Tell students that they can take action if a stranger bothers them. Tell students to tell their parents or guardians, a teacher, a police officer, or another responsible adult if a stranger bothers them. Tell students that if a stranger bothers them, they should try to remember what the stranger looks like. If they remember what the stranger looks like, it might help the police. The police might ask these questions:

- What color hair did the stranger have?
- How old was the stranger?
- What was the stranger wearing?
- Was the stranger in a car?
- What color was the car?
- What was the license plate number of the car?

8 You might choose to modify this activity by changing what is written on the index cards. You might change the cards to read that each of the strangers was a danger stranger. You would indicate to students that any stranger potentially can be dangerous.

Assessment

Show students pictures of people involved in different activities, such as an athlete, a physician, a teacher, and a construction worker. Ask students to tell why any of these people could be a danger stranger. Students might say that they cannot tell by looking at someone whether or not that person would harm them. Remember to tell students that most strangers are nice and would not harm anyone.

Private Body Parts

The Curriculum

Life Skills

■ I will protect myself from people who might harm me.

■ I will follow safety rules to protect myself from violence.

Objectives

■ Students will tell ways they can stay safe from strangers.

■ Students will tell what to do if they get an unsafe touch.

The National Health Education Standards

■ Students will demonstrate the ability to practice health-enhancing behaviors and reduce health risks.

Preparing to Teach the Lesson Plan

Materials

Crayons or markers

Blackline Masters

Private Body Parts

Follow Rules If You Get an Unsafe Touch

Teaching the Lesson Plan

1 Tell students that the following activity will teach them how to be safe if they get an unsafe touch. Define unsafe touch. An **unsafe touch** is a touch that is not right. Tell students to suppose someone gives a person an unsafe touch. Someone might tickle the person where he or she does not want to be tickled. Someone might touch the person on a private body part. Define private body part. A **private body part** is any part of your body that your bathing suit covers. Give each student a copy of the Blackline Master *Private Body Parts*. Give each student crayons or markers. Tell students to color the girl's bathing suit using crayons or markers. Tell students to color the boy's bathing suit using crayons or markers.

2 Give each student a copy of the Blackline Master *Follow Rules If You Get an Unsafe Touch*. Tell students that no one should give them an unsafe touch. If someone does give them an unsafe touch, they should follow safety rules:

• Tell the person to stop.

• Yell as loud as you can.

• Run away.

• Tell your parents, guardians, or another trusted adult right away.

3 Tell students that you are going to read them some situations. Tell students to yell "stop" as loud as they can if the touch you describe is an unsafe touch. Tell students to remain quiet if the touch is a safe touch. Read these situations:

• Your mother hugs you before you go to school (students should remain quiet).

• Your father holds your hand to cross the street (students should remain quiet).

• A person tickles you in a way you do not want to be tickled (students should yell "stop").

• A doctor listens to your heartbeat (students should remain quiet).

• The school nurse gives you first aid for a scrape (students should remain quiet).

• A person touches you on a body part that your bathing suit covers (students should yell "stop").

Assessment

On a sheet of paper, have students write the names of three grown-ups that they trust. Tell students that the grown-ups should be people who they can tell about an unsafe touch. Tell students that if they tell a grown-up about an unsafe touch and the grown-up does nothing, students should tell another grown-up right away.

Private Body Parts

Follow Rules If You Get an Unsafe Touch

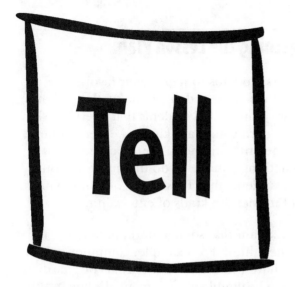

1. Tell the person to stop.

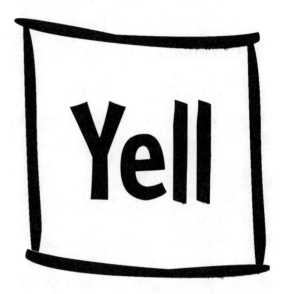

2. Yell as loud as you can.

3. Run away.

4. Tell your parents, guardians, or another trusted adult right away.

Entertainment Detective

The Curriculum

Life Skills

■ I will choose healthful entertainment.

■ I will develop media literacy.

Objectives

■ Students will tell what healthful entertainment is.

■ Students will tell guidelines to use to choose healthful entertainment.

■ Students will choose computer games that are healthful entertainment.

■ Students will choose TV shows that are healthful entertainment.

The National Health Education Standards

■ Students will analyze the influence of culture, media, technology, and other factors on health.

■ Students will demonstrate the ability to use goal-setting and decision-making skills to enhance health.

Preparing to Teach the Lesson Plan

Materials

Crayons or markers

Blackline Master

Healthful Entertainment

Worksheet Master

Entertainment Detective

Teaching the Lesson Plan

1 Ask students to name their favorite TV shows. Ask students to name their favorite board games. Tell students that television shows and board games are kinds of entertainment. Define entertainment. **Entertainment** is something you see or do that interests you. Tell students that TV shows, computer games, and movies are kinds of entertainment.

2 Explain that some entertainment is healthful. For example, computer games that have the OK of your parents or guardians can be healthful entertainment. Define healthful entertainment. **Healthful entertainment** is entertainment that keeps your mind and body healthy. Give each student a copy of the Blackline Master *Healthful Entertainment*. Tell students that entertainment is healthful if it meets the following guidelines:

• follows family rules;

• shows people who have good character;

• does not show violence; and

• does not show people saying bad words.

3 Ask students to name kinds of healthful entertainment. Students might say that TV shows for the whole family are healthful entertainment. Explain that healthful entertainment also keeps your mind alert. It helps you learn facts. Healthful entertainment helps you to act in responsible ways.

4 Give each student a copy of the Worksheet Master *Entertainment Detective*. Tell students that the Worksheet Master shows two televisions and two computer games. One television shows healthful entertainment. The other television shows harmful entertainment. One computer game shows healthful entertainment. The other computer game shows harmful entertainment. Tell students that they are going to be entertainment detectives. They are going to find which TV show is healthful entertainment. Tell students to color the TV that shows healthful entertainment. Tell students to put an X on the TV that shows harmful entertainment. Tell students to color the computer game that is healthful. Students should put an X on the computer game that is harmful entertainment.

Assessment

Tell students to look at their Worksheet Masters. Ask students why the TV show they did not color was harmful entertainment. Ask students why the computer game they did not color was harmful entertainment. Have students write one of the guidelines for healthful entertain-ment under the TV. Have students write another one of the guidelines for healthful entertainment under the computer screen.

Healthful Entertainment

1. **Follows family rules**

2. **Shows people who have good character**

3. **Does not show violence**

4. **Does not show people saying bad words**

Entertainment Detective

Put an X on pictures that show harmful entertainment.

Color the pictures of healthful TV and computer games.

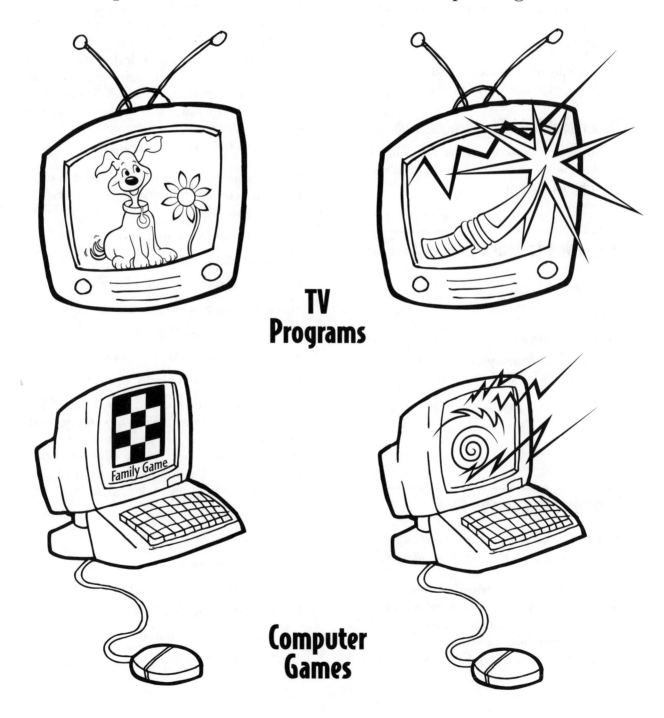

TV Programs

Computer Games

Friendship Tree

The Curriculum

Life Skill

■ I will make wise decisions with friends.

Objective

■ Students will tell six questions to ask when they make decisions with friends.

The National Health Education Standards

■ Students will demonstrate the ability to use interpersonal communication skills to enhance health.

Preparing to Teach the Lesson Plan

Materials

Scissors

Plain white paper

Green construction paper, one sheet for each student

Chalkboard

Chalk

Glue or tape

Teaching the Lesson Plan

Cut circles from plain white paper (five per student). Circles should be large enough for students to write on.

1 Define friend. A **friend** is someone you know and like. A friend will not cause you harm. A friend is someone you can trust. A friend is someone you can talk to. A friend is someone you can share feelings with. Teach students the song "Make New Friends, But Keep the Old." The lyrics are as follows:

"Make new friends, but keep the old.
One is silver and the other gold."

Practice the song with the class several times to be certain that students know the words. Tell the class that they will sing the song in a round. Divide the class in half. Tell the students on one half of the room to begin singing, "Make new friends, but keep the old." Then tell the students on the other half of the class to begin singing, "Make new friends, but keep the old." Have both halves continue singing.

2 Ask students to name things friends can do together. Students might give the following answers:

• Friends can play together.

• Friends can do chores together.

• Friends can go to school together.

• Friends can talk to each other.

• Friends can share feelings.

• Friends can exercise together.

• Friends can eat healthful foods together.

Write the responses on the board that show healthful activities. Explain to students that they also can make wise decisions with friends. Define wise decision. A **wise decision** is the best choice. Tell students that they can ask six questions before they make a decision:

1. Is it healthful?

2. Is it safe?

3. Do I follow laws?

4. Do I show respect for others?

5. Do I follow family rules?

6. Do I show good character?

"Yes" answers show wise decisions.

3 Give each student a piece of green construction paper and a pair of scissors. Tell students to cut out the shape of a tree with a trunk. Tell students that this will be their friendship tree.

4 Give each student five of the circles. Tell students to choose a partner. Their partner should be someone that they do not know well. Tell the students that they are going to learn about new friends by asking questions. Write the following questions on the board:

• What is your favorite game?

• What is your favorite food?

• What is your favorite movie?

• How many brothers and sisters do you have?

• What do you like to do after school?

Tell students to ask their partner the questions you have written on the board. After students have asked each other the questions, they can each color a circle. Then tell students to switch circles with the other person. Ask students to glue or tape the other student's circle to their tree.

5 Tell students to repeat the activity four times with four more partners. At the end of the activity, students should have five circles glued to their trees.

Assessment

Ask students what it means to be a friend to someone. Have them share questions that they can ask to learn about a new friend. Ask them why friends should make wise decisions together. Students should answer that making wise decisions with friends keeps them healthy and safe, follows laws, shows respect for others, follows family rules, and shows good character. You can make a bulletin board called *The Friendly Forest* using the students' trees.

Friendship Recipe

The Curriculum

Life Skills

■ I will work to have healthful friendships.

■ I will make wise decisions with friends.

■ I will show respect for others.

Objectives

■ Students will tell what a good friend is.

■ Students will tell six questions to ask when they make decisions with friends.

■ Students will tell what respect is.

■ Students will tell ways to show respect for themselves and others.

The National Health Education Standards

■ Students will demonstrate the ability to use interpersonal communication skills to enhance health.

Preparing to Teach the Lesson Plan

Materials

Crayons or markers

Worksheet Masters

Recipe for a True Friend

Show You Care Cookie

Teaching the Lesson Plan

1 Ask students whether or not they have ever helped their parents or guardians cook food. Tell students that they might have followed a recipe to cook food. A recipe is a list of all the ingredients that are in a food. Tell students to suppose a person makes cookies. The ingredients are flour, sugar, butter, eggs, and baking soda. Tell students to suppose the person forgets one of the ingredients, such as sugar. Then the cookies will not taste good. Suppose the person forgets baking soda, then the cookies will be flat. Suppose the person forgets the eggs and butter, then the cookies will be dry. Tell students that every ingredient of the cookie is important.

2 Explain to students that the ingredients that go into friendships also are important. No ingredient should be left out. Ask students what they think are the important ingredients in a friendship. Students might say that respect and honesty are important ingredients in a friendship. Define true friend. A **true friend** is a friend who is responsible and cares about you. Explain to students how they can be a true friend:

• Make responsible decisions with a friend.

• Show a friend that you care.

• Take turns with a friend.

3 Tell students that they are going to make a recipe for a true friend. The recipe will have all the ingredients that make up a true friend. Tell students their recipe for a true friend should have the following ingredients:

• A true friend should be liked by your parents or guardians.

• A true friend should have an even relationship with you.

• A true friend should respect you.

Define even friendship. An **even friendship** is a friendship in which friends take turns sharing and choosing. In an even friendship, friends do some of the talking and some of the listening. Give each student a copy of the Worksheet Master *Recipe for a True Friend*. Tell students to write a recipe for a true friend on the Worksheet Master. Students should use the "ingredients" for a true friend discussed in class.

Assessment

Ask students how they can show a friend that they care. Students might say that they can show they care by helping a friend study for a test. Or they can show they care about a friend's health by doing physical activity with the friend. Tell students to draw a picture that shows they care about a friend. Tell students to draw their picture on the cookie shown on the Worksheet Master *Show You Care Cookie*. Students might draw pictures of themselves and a friend eating healthful foods or riding bikes with safety equipment.

Recipe for a True Friend

A true friend should be liked by your parents or guardians.

A true friend and you should have an even relationship.

A true friend should respect you.

Recipe for a True Friend

Recipe for a True Friend

2 parts
3 parts

Show You Care Cookie

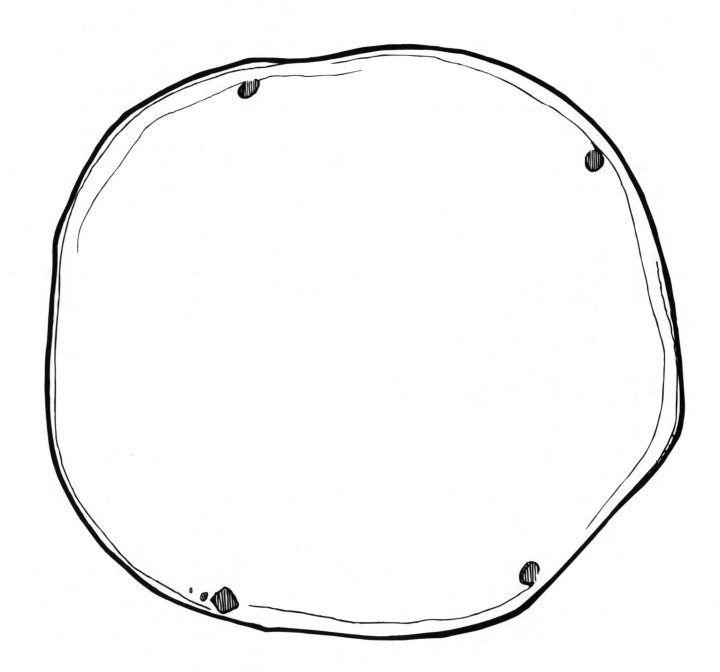

The Growth Line

The Curriculum

Life Skills

- I will take care of my body.
- I will learn ways my body changes.
- I will have checkups.

Objectives

- Students will name body parts.
- Students will tell ways to take care of body parts.
- Students will tell ways they will grow.
- Students will tell why they need checkups.

The National Health Education Standards

- Students will comprehend concepts related to health promotion and disease prevention.

Preparing to Teach the Lesson Plan

Materials

Thick cord or clothesline

Tape

Clothing of different sizes, such as socks, shirts, and pants

Clothespins

Chalkboard

Chalk

Blackline Master

Take Care of Your Bones and Muscles

Teaching the Lesson Plan

1 Use a thick cord or clothesline. Tape each end to a secure place in the classroom. Fasten the cord from one side of the front of the room to the other side. Explain to students that the cord represents a line of growth from infancy to adulthood.

2 Tell students to gather clothing of different sizes, such as socks, shirts, and pants. Be sure to have a collection of clothes that represents people of different ages.

3 Tell students to attach the clothes to the clothesline using the clothespins. Tell them to arrange the clothes by age. Students should attach the smallest clothes to the left side of the clothesline. Students should place the next larger size to the right of these clothes, and so on, until all of the clothes have been hung on the clothesline. If possible, clothes should be lined up by complete outfits. For example, the socks, shirt, and pants for a five-year-old should hang together on the clothesline.

4 Define grow. To **grow** is to become bigger. Ask students how the clothing changes as a person grows. Students might say that the socks become longer, the shirt sleeves become longer, and the pant legs become longer and wider. Students also might notice that clothing does not change as much after a person reaches a certain age.

5 Explain to students that as they grow older, they will grow larger. Their bodies will change. The changes in the size of socks show that a person's feet will grow larger. The changes in the size of shirt sleeves show that a person's arms will grow longer. The changes in the size of pant legs show that a person's legs will grow longer and wider. Explain to students that these changes show that a person's bones and muscles are growing. Define bones. **Bones** are strong, hard body parts that support the soft body parts. Define muscles. **Muscles** are body parts that help you move. Explain to students that as they grow they need to get checkups. Define checkup. A **checkup** is a check by your doctor to learn how healthy you are. Tell students that checkups are very important. Tell students the doctor checks their bodies to see how they are growing.

6 Give each student a copy of the Blackline Master *Take Care of Your Bones and Muscles.* Explain to students that they can help their bones grow and become stronger by following these healthful habits:

• Wear safety equipment to protect bones when you play.

• Drink milk.

• Eat foods made with milk.

• Get plenty of exercise.

Explain to students that they can help their muscles grow and become stronger by following these healthful habits:

• Stretch your muscles at least two to three times a week.

• Get plenty of exercise.

• Drink milk.

• Eat green, leafy vegetables and foods from the milk group.

7 Explain that there are body parts that cannot be seen, such as the heart, lungs, brain, and stomach. Tell students that even though a person cannot see them grow, these body parts also are growing.

8 Tell students that between the ages of 11 and 13, a girl might be larger than a boy of the same age. Tell students that a boy might have a growth spurt between the ages of 13 and 15. Define growth spurt. A **growth spurt** is a fast increase in height and weight. At this age, the average boy is larger than the average girl.

9 Explain that at a certain age, a person stops growing. A person will change in ways other than physical growth as he or she grows.

He or she might have different ways of thinking. He or she might change the way he or she relates to others. A person might have more responsibilities as he or she grows.

10 Write the following terms on the board:
• body changes
• changes in thoughts and feelings
• changes in relationships

Ask students to name ways they think they will change as they grow. Students might say that they will grow taller or become smarter. Ask students how they think their bodies will change. Students might say that their hands or feet will become bigger. Ask students how they think their thoughts will change. Students might say that they will learn more and become more accepting of other people's differences. Ask students how they think their relationships will change. Students might say that they will start dating and have more responsibilities. Write the changes the students name on the board.

Assessment

Have students make a book entitled, "Me Today, Me Tomorrow." Explain that this book is going to be a picture book that shows what a student looks like today and what a student will look like when he or she is older. Ask students to draw three pictures of themselves doing things they like to do right now. Then ask students to draw three to five pictures of themselves as they think they will look when they grow older. Make sure that students draw pictures of themselves as teens and as adults. Have them draw pictures of what they will be doing when they are teens and when they are adults. Ask students to share with the class how they think they will grow and change as they grow older.

Take Care of Your Bones and Muscles

Take Care of Your Bones

 Wear safety equipment to protect bones when you play.

 Drink milk.

 Eat foods made with milk.

 Get plenty of exercise.

Take Care of Your Muscles

 Stretch your muscles at least two to three times a week.

 Get plenty of exercise.

 Drink milk.

 Eat green, leafy vegetables and foods from the milk group.

You've Left Your Mark

The Curriculum

Life Skills

■ I will take care of my body.

■ I will learn ways my body changes.

Objectives

■ Students will name body parts.

■ Students will tell ways to take care of body parts.

■ Students will tell ways they will grow.

■ Students will tell why they need checkups.

The National Health Education Standards

■ Students will comprehend concepts related to health promotion and disease prevention.

Preparing to Teach the Lesson Plan

Materials

Index cards, one for each student

Crayons or markers, one for each student

Ink pad

Teaching the Lesson Plan

1 Tell students that they each have physical traits that make them special. Define special. To be **special** is to be very important. Tell students to look around the room at their classmates. Ask them to name physical traits of their classmates that they see. A student might say that he or she sees brown hair, light hair, brown eyes, blue eyes, curly hair, or straight hair.

Ask students whether they see some students with some of the same physical traits as other students. Students might say that they do.

2 Tell students to look around the room again. Tell students that this time you are going to name a physical trait that you see. Tell students to stand up if they have the physical trait that you name. Name one physical trait, such as brown hair. Many students will stand up. Next, add a physical trait to the physical trait you just named, such as *short* brown hair. Tell the students who are standing that if they do not have *short* brown hair, then they must sit down. Some students will sit down. Continue to add physical traits until only one student is standing. Tell students that it might seem that many students have the same physical traits. However, when physical traits are combined, few students have similar physical traits.

3 Explain to students that you are going to show them how each of them is special. Pass out an index card and a crayon to each student. Ask students to draw pictures on their index cards of themselves from the shoulders down. Tell students to *not* draw their heads.

4 Open the ink pad. Tell each student to place his or her thumb on the ink pad. Tell students to place their thumbprint over their drawing of themselves from the shoulders down. The thumbprint will represent the head. Tell students to compare their thumbprints. Ask them how their thumbprints look alike. Students might say that the lines are similar. Ask them how their thumbprints look different. Students might say that although the thumbprints are similar, the lines do not match exactly from one thumbprint to the next.

5 Tell students to try to match their thumbprints. Tell students to find another person's card that has a thumbprint head that matches their own. Give students time to compare their thumbprints with those of their classmates. Students will not be able to find anyone whose thumbprint matches.

6 Explain to students that no two people have the same thumbprints. No two people have the same fingerprints. Tell students that people have special physical traits. Explain that each student in your class is special. No two students look exactly the same. No two students act exactly the same. Ask students to name ways they are special. A student might say that he or she is short and has red hair. Or a student might say that he or she likes to talk a lot or that he or she is shy. Have each student share ways he or she is special.

Assessment

Tell students to draw a picture that shows ways they are special. Students can draw their special physical traits and draw themselves doing special activities. Have students pair up. Ask each student to share his or her special traits with a partner. Have the partner tell the class why the person is special. Let each pair take a turn. Switch so that each person in the pair tells why the other person is special.

Grooming Collage

The Curriculum

Life Skills

■ I will be well-groomed.

■ I will choose safe and healthful products.

Objectives

■ Students will tell how they can groom themselves.

■ Students will tell ways that they can look sharp.

■ Students will name grooming products they have seen in ads.

The National Health Education Standards

■ Students will demonstrate the ability to practice health-enhancing behaviors and reduce health risks.

■ Students will demonstrate the ability to access valid health information and health-promoting products and services.

Preparing to Teach the Lesson Plan

Materials

Poster board

Magazines

Art supplies

Blackline Master

How to Look Sharp

Teaching the Lesson Plan

1 Tell students that in this lesson they will learn about ways to stay well-groomed. They will learn about grooming products that will help them stay well-groomed. Define grooming. **Grooming** is taking care of your body and your appearance. Tell students that grooming helps them look sharp. Give each student a copy of the Blackline Master *How to Look Sharp*. Tell students there are ways they can keep their body clean:

• Keep your body clean and neat. Take a bath or shower every day. Shampoo and brush your hair often.

• Keep your fingernails clean and neat. Do not bite your fingernails. Use a nail brush to get dirt from under your nails.

• Keep clothes clean and neat. Hang up or fold clothes when you take them off. Wash them when they are dirty. Tell your parents or guardian if your clothes get torn.

2 Divide the class into groups of four students each. Give each group a piece of poster board. Give each group magazines and art supplies. Tell students to find ads for grooming products in the magazines. Define ad. An **ad** is pictures or words that try to get you to buy something. Tell students that there are three questions they can ask when they see an ad. The questions will help them decide if the ad is truthful. These three questions will help students decide if they need the product in the ad:

1. What health facts are in the ad? Tell students to suppose they find an ad for toothpaste. The ad says the toothpaste has fluoride in it. This is a health fact.

2. What health facts are left out of the ad? The toothpaste is more expensive than any other brand. The ad does not mention this.

3. Do I really need the product in the ad? The toothpaste is a grooming product. Students do not have to buy the most expensive kind of toothpaste. Other less expensive brands have fluoride.

3 Tell students to cut out ads of grooming products. Tell them to paste their ads to the poster board to make a grooming collage. Tell students to write the name of the grooming product under the ad. Collect the grooming collages. Point to an ad on one of the collages. Ask students to name health facts in the ad. Ask students to name health facts that are left out of the ad. Ask students whether or not they really need the product in the ad.

Assessment

Ask students to pick the grooming products that are wise consumer choices. Ask students to name reasons the products they picked are wise consumer choices.

How to Look Sharp

1. Keep your body clean and neat. Take a bath or shower every day. Shampoo and brush your hair often.

2. Keep your fingernails clean and neat. Do not bite your fingernails. Use a nail brush to get dirt from under your nails.

3. Keep clothes clean and neat. Hang up or fold clothes when you take them off. Wash them when they are dirty. Tell your parents or guardian if your clothes get torn.

A Spray of Germs

The Curriculum

Life Skills

■ I will choose habits that prevent the spread of germs.

■ I will recognize symptoms and get treatment for communicable diseases.

Objectives

■ Students will tell how germs are spread.

■ Students will tell how to protect themselves and others from germs.

■ Students will tell what a symptom is.

The National Health Education Standards

■ Students will comprehend concepts related to health promotion and disease prevention.

Preparing to Teach the Lesson Plan

Materials

A spray can of room deodorizer
Tissue

Teaching the Lesson Plan

1 Explain to students that germs are everywhere. Define germs. **Germs** are tiny living things that can make you sick. Germs can cause diseases, like colds and strep throat. Explain to students that germs are on objects that a person touches. Germs are in the water that a person drinks. Germs are on the food that a person eats. Germs are in the air that a person breathes.

2 Spray the deodorizer can. Cover the nozzle with a tissue. Tell students that this is like covering one's nose and mouth with a tissue when sneezing. Ask students whether or not they can smell the deodorizer. Students probably will say they cannot. Tell them that the reason they cannot smell the deodorizer is because the tissue prevented the spray from entering the air. Explain that when a person covers his or her mouth and nose with a tissue when sneezing, germs do not enter the air. Other people are not at risk for breathing the germs.

3 Tell students that germs are everywhere, even in the room in which they now are sitting. To demonstrate this, spray the deodorizer with the nozzle uncovered. Tell students that you just sprayed make-believe germs in the air. Ask students whether they see the "germs." Students will probably say they can. Explain that in a moment they will no longer be able to see the "germs." Ask students whether they smell the "germs." Students will probably say that they can. Tell students that this is because, although the "germs" can no longer be seen, they are still in the air. They can still be detected by their scent. Tell students that spraying the deodorizer without covering the nozzle with a tissue is similar to a person not covering his or her mouth and nose when he or she sneezes.

4 Tell students that they should cover their mouth and nose with a tissue when they sneeze. Tell students not to cover their mouth and nose with their hand when they sneeze. This is because after a person uses his or her hand to cover his or her nose, the person might touch an object. Germs can get on the object. If the object is touched by another person, germs can get on this person. Germs might enter the person's body. Ask students to name other ways to prevent the spread of germs. Students might say staying away from a person who is sneezing or coughing prevents the spread of germs. Tell students that there are other ways to prevent the spread of germs:

- Wash hands often.
- Cover your mouth and nose when you sneeze or cough.
- Keep your fingers out of your eyes, nose, and mouth.
- Keep objects such as pencils out of your mouth.

5 Tell students that if they have symptoms of a disease they should tell their parents or guardians. Define symptom. A **symptom** is a change from normal in a person's health. Sneezing and coughing might be symptoms of a disease caused by germs.

Assessment

Spray the deodorizer again, once with a tissue covering the nozzle and once without a tissue covering the nozzle. Ask students which of the sprays prevented the spread of "germs." Students might say that the spray that was covered by a tissue prevented the spread of "germs." Ask students to tell how covering the nozzle with a tissue is similar to what a person should do when sneezing. Students might say that a person should cover his or her mouth and nose with a tissue when he or she sneezes.

Super Soap: A Germ Fighter

The Curriculum

Life Skill

■ I will choose habits that prevent the spread of germs.

Objectives

■ Students will tell how germs are spread.

■ Students will tell how to protect themselves and others from germs.

The National Health Education Standards

■ Students will comprehend concepts related to health promotion and disease prevention.

Preparing to Teach the Lesson Plan

Materials

Petroleum jelly

Sand

Bowl of water

Soap

Blackline Master

Protect Yourself and Others from Germs

Teaching the Lesson Plan

1 Ask students to describe how they wash their hands. Students might say that they wet their hands, place the soap in their hands, and rub their hands together. Tell students that soap is a very important substance to use to wash hands. Tell students that they are going to do an experiment.

2 Ask for a student volunteer to come to the front of the room. Place petroleum jelly on the student's hand. Tell the student volunteer to rub his or her hands together to distribute the jelly to both hands. Now place sand on the student volunteer's hand. Tell the student to rub his or her hands together to distribute the sand to both hands. Explain that the petroleum jelly represents the natural oils on the skin. The sand represents germs. Tell the student volunteer to wash his or her hands in a bowl of water *without using soap*. Ask the student volunteer if the "germs" have been washed off. The student volunteer will say that they have not. Have the student volunteer again wash his or her hands, but this time, allow him or her to use soap. Ask the class and the student volunteer whether or not the "germs" are gone. Students will say that the "germs" are gone. Ask students why the "germs" are gone. Students might say because soap was used to wash the hands.

3 Tell students that using soap is more effective in cleaning hands and other body parts than not using soap. Explain that the oils in the skin are broken down by the use of soap. If soap is not used, the oils in the skin do not break down. Explain that students should always use soap to wash hands.

4 Tell students that using soap to wash hands keeps germs from spreading. Define germs. **Germs** are tiny living things that can make you sick. Explain that students can protect themselves and others from germs by washing their hands often. Explain that students should always wash their hands with soap after using the bathroom. They should wash their hands with soap before making or eating food. Tell students that there are other ways to prevent the spread of germs. Give each student a copy of the Blackline Master *Protect Yourself and Others from Germs*.

Assessment

Tell each student to make a chart on a sheet of paper. The chart should have two columns. Tell students to write the words "Used Restroom" at the top of the first column. Tell students to write the words "Used Soap" at the top of the second column. Tell students that they should make a check in the first column each time they use the restroom, whether it be at home or at school. Tell students that they should make a check in the second column each time they use soap to wash their hands after using the restroom. Tell students to hand in their charts after one week. Ask students why the number of checks in each column on their chart should be the same. Students might say that the number of checks in each column should be the same because a person should wash his or her hands with soap every time he or she uses the restroom.

Protect Yourself and Others from Germs

1. **Wash** your hands often.

2. **Wash** your hands after you use the bathroom.

3. **Wash** your hands before making or eating food.

4. **Cover** your mouth and nose with a tissue when you sneeze or cough.

5. **Wash** your hands after coughing or sneezing.

6. **Keep** your fingers out of your eyes, nose, and mouth.

7. **Keep** objects such as pencils out of your mouth.

I Love Gloves

The Curriculum

Life Skill

■ I will choose habits that prevent the spread of germs.

Objectives

■ Students will explain what HIV does to helper T cells.

■ Students will tell what HIV is.

■ Students will tell ways HIV is spread.

■ Students will list ways to prevent HIV infection.

■ Students will tell what AIDS is.

■ Students will tell why health care workers wear gloves.

The National Health Education Standards

■ Students will comprehend concepts related to health promotion and disease prevention.

Preparing to Teach the Lesson Plan

Materials

Latex gloves

Broad tip marker

Construction paper

Markers

Scissors

Teaching the Lesson Plan

1 Ask the class whether or not they have seen gloves worn by a health care worker, such as a school nurse or a dentist. Students will probably say that they have.

2 Explain that health care workers wear special gloves when helping patients. Tell the class that you are going to show why health care workers wear latex gloves. Place the latex gloves on your hands. Draw lines on the gloves using the broad tip marker. Show students the gloves. Tell students that you are pretending to be a dentist. The lines you have drawn are "germs" from a patient's mouth. Define germs. **Germs** are tiny living things that can make you sick. Explain that germs can be in a person's saliva. They also can be in a person's blood.

3 Remove the gloves. Ask students to look at your hands. Ask students whether or not they see any lines on your hands. Students might say that they do not. Tell students that your hands are free of "germs." Ask students why a dentist wear gloves. Students might say that a dentist might touch saliva or blood. Saliva and blood can contain germs. Tell students that if the dentist has a cut on his or her hand, the germs can enter his or her body. The dentist could get sick.

4 Health care workers who wear gloves are protected from a germ called HIV. Define HIV. **HIV** is a germ that causes AIDS. HIV kills helper T cells. Define helper T cell. A **helper T cell** is a cell that helps you fight diseases. Tell students they have many helper T cells in their bodies. Explain that when HIV kills many helper T cells in a person's body, that person gets AIDS. Define AIDS. **AIDS** is an illness in which the body cannot fight disease. Many times, health care workers do not know whether their patients have the germ that causes AIDS. Many people who have HIV do not have symptoms. Define symptom. A **symptom** is a change from normal in a person's health. A person who has HIV will have the germ in his or her blood. If the blood of a person who has HIV gets into the blood of a health care worker, the health care worker can get HIV. The health care worker can develop AIDS. This is why health care workers wear latex gloves.

Assessment

Give each student a piece of construction paper and a marker. Tell students to trace their hands on the paper. Then have students cut out the hand. Tell students that the hand represents a latex glove.

Write the following list on the board: teacher, truck driver, computer programmer, nurse, artist, dentist, typist, family doctor, basketball player, emergency medical technician, dental hygienist, police officer. Tell students that you are going to read the names of each professional. When you read a name, students will hold up their "gloves" if the professional must wear latex gloves on his or her job. If the professional does not wear latex gloves, the students should not hold up their "gloves." Explain to students that there are some professionals, such as police officers, who sometimes wear latex gloves. Tell students to explain why some professionals wear latex gloves while others do not.

Blood Brothers/Sisters–NOT!

The Curriculum

Life Skills

■ I will choose habits that prevent the spread of germs.

■ I will recognize symptoms and get treatment for communicable diseases.

Objectives

■ Students will tell what HIV is.

■ Students will tell ways HIV is spread.

■ Students will tell ways HIV is not spread.

■ Students will list ways to prevent HIV infection.

■ Students will tell what AIDS is.

■ Students will tell ways HIV is spread: from sharing a needle with blood on it, from touching blood.

The National Health Education Standards

■ Students will comprehend concepts related to health promotion and disease prevention.

Preparing to Teach the Lesson Plan

Materials

Crayons or markers

Blackline Master

Facts About HIV

Worksheet Master

Safe Seal of Friendship

Teaching the Lesson Plan

1 Tell students that HIV is a germ that can be found in blood. Define HIV. **HIV** is a germ that causes AIDS. Define AIDS. **AIDS** is an illness in which the body cannot fight disease. HIV can make a person sick. It gets into the blood of a person. HIV can be spread in certain ways. Give each student a copy of the Blackline Master *Facts About HIV.*

Tell students that HIV **cannot** be spread in the following ways :

• sitting next to a person;

• hugging a person;

• shaking hands with a person;

• using the same bathroom as a person;

• sharing a book or pencil with a person; and

• breathing droplets from a person's cough or sneeze.

Tell students the following ways that they can keep from getting HIV:

• Do not touch someone else's blood. A person who helps someone who is bleeding should wear gloves. The person should wash his or her hands afterwards.

• Do not become a blood brother or sister. HIV can be transmitted from the cut finger of one person to the cut finger of another person.

• Do not share a needle to pierce ears or other body parts. Do not get a tattoo. Do not use harmful, illegal drugs.

2 Tell students that sometimes friends prick their fingers with a needle. Then they press the blood of their fingers together to become blood brothers or blood sisters. Tell students that they should never do this. HIV can spread this way. Tell students that they are going to learn a safe way to seal a friendship. Give each student a copy of the Worksheet Master *Safe Seal of Friendship*. Tell students to color the Friendship Seal. Tell students to write their name on the line that reads, "_____ is my friend." Then have students exchange their seals. Make sure that each student has a seal. Tell students that these Safe Seals of Friendship represent that they have a friend. Allow students to wear their seals as buttons. Or you can display the seals on a bulletin board entitled Safe Seals of Friendships.

Assessment

Have students write on the back of the Safe Seals of Friendship one way HIV is not spread. Ask each student to stand and tell the name of the friend on his or her button and one way HIV is not spread.

Facts About HIV

HIV cannot be spread in any of these ways:

✔ Sitting next to a person

✔ Hugging a person

✔ Shaking hands with a person

✔ Using the same bathroom as a person

✔ Sharing a book or pencil with a person

✔ Breathing droplets from a person's cough or sneeze

How to keep from getting HIV

✘ Do not touch someone else's blood.

✘ Do not become a blood brother or blood sister.

✘ Do not share a needle to pierce ears or other body parts.

Safe Seal of Friendship

is my friend.

Family Building Blocks

The Curriculum

Life Skill

■ I will follow my family's guidelines.

Objectives

■ Students will tell what a family rule is.

■ Students will tell why they should follow family rules.

The National Health Education Standards

■ Students will demonstrate the ability to use interpersonal communication skills to enhance health.

Preparing to Teach the Lesson Plan

Materials

Tape

Sheets of paper

Ten large building blocks

Marker

Teaching the Lesson Plan

1 Tell students that their relationships with their families are very important. Define family. A **family** is the group of people to whom you are related. Family members can give each other support and love. Families provide shelter, food, and other things. Families also provide safe places for family members to learn, grow, develop, and share. Each family member has a responsibility to the other family members. Define family guidelines. **Family guidelines** are rules your parents or guardians expect you to follow. Ask students what family guidelines their parents or guardians expect them to follow. Students might say that they must do schoolwork before playing or that they must always ask permission to visit a friend. Explain that family guidelines help keep students healthy and safe. Tell students that when all family members follow family guidelines, the whole family benefits. But when one family member does not follow family guidelines, the whole family can suffer.

2 Tape a sheet of paper to one face of each building block. The sheet of paper should be the same size as the face of the building block. On each sheet of paper, write one of the following words:

- responsible
- respectful
- honest
- loving
- hard-working
- fair
- strong
- helpful
- kind
- caring

3 Ask for a student volunteer. Tell the student volunteer to choose four of the blocks. Tell the student volunteer to set the blocks in a row to form a foundation. Ask another student volunteer to choose three more blocks. Tell the second student volunteer to set the three blocks in a row to form the second row from the bottom. Continue until a pyramid is formed. One block should be at the top of the pyramid.

4 Tell students that the pyramid represents a family. Explain that each of the blocks is a family value. Define family value. **A family value** is something that is important to your family. Explain that family values work together to make a family strong. All of the family values are connected to one another. If one family value is missing, then the whole family is affected. To demonstrate this, tell students to suppose that one family member lies to another family member. This family member is not honest. Remove the block with the word "honest." This family member does not respect the other family member. Remove the block with the word "respectful." This family member does not act responsibly. Remove the block with the word "responsible." The pyramid probably will have fallen down. Explain to students that when one family value is missing, it affects the whole family. When one family member does not act responsibly, the whole family can be affected.

Assessment

Tell students that the class will hold a contest. The contest is to select the Outstanding Family Member of the Year. Tell students that they must nominate, or pick, someone who is an outstanding family member. On a sheet of paper, have students nominate themselves for Outstanding Family Member of the Year. Tell students to write why they are outstanding family members. Tell students to include at least three family values in their nominations. You might hold an awards ceremony in which *every* student receives an award for Outstanding Family Member of the Year.

© 2001 Everyday Learning Corporation

Memory Matters

The Curriculum

Life Skills

■ I will get along with my family.

■ I will adjust to family changes in healthful ways.

Objectives

■ Students will tell ways to get along with their families.

■ Students will name ways families change.

■ Students will tell what to do if they have family changes.

■ Students will tell things to talk about if they have family changes.

■ Students will tell ways to help with a newborn baby.

The National Health Education Standards

■ Students will demonstrate the ability to use interpersonal communication skills to enhance health.

■ Students will demonstrate the ability to practice health-enhancing behaviors and reduce health risks.

Preparing to Teach the Lesson Plan

Materials

A memento, such as a picture or a seashell

Teaching the Lesson Plan

Ask students to bring to class an object from home that represents a good memory. You might want to send a letter home with each student that explains the activity to their parents or guardians. Tell their parents or guardians that you are going to do a show-and-tell activity in which students will share good memories with the class. Each student should bring to class an object that represents a good memory. The object should be important to the student and should demonstrate his or her role in the family. For example, the student might bring a picture that shows him or her doing something meaningful with his or her family. Parents might want to discuss with their child the meaning of the object.

1 Tell students that the class is going to have a show and tell. This show and tell will be about a good memory. Define memory. A **memory** is being able to remember things. For example, a person might have a memory of an event such as going to the zoo with his or her family. Tell students that sometimes an object can help bring up a memory for a person. For example, a baseball that a person caught while watching a baseball game with another family member might bring up a memory of the big game. Or a person might have an object, such as a favorite book, that brings up a memory of a grandparent or of another family member.

2 Explain to students that not all memories are good ones. Everyone has some bad memories, too. Students might have bad memories about family changes, such as a divorce of parents. Define divorce. A **divorce** is the end of a marriage. Or they might have a bad memory about a family pet who died. Explain to students that not all family changes are bad changes. Having a newborn baby sister or brother is a happy family change. Remind students that a newborn baby needs a lot of care. Tell students that if they have a newborn baby in their family they should ask their parents for ways they can help. Tell students that they are going to talk about only good memories.

3 Ask students to bring their objects to class. Tell students to show their objects to the rest of the class. Tell each student to tell why this object brings up a good memory. Tell the other classmates to ask each student questions about his or her object.

4 Explain to students that memories are made in families. Having good memories about family members can make the family bond stronger. Good memories help a person think about the good times he or she had with his or her family. Memories help a person value his or her family.

Assessment

Tell students to draw a picture of a family memory. Ask students why the memory is valuable. Students might say that the memory is valuable because it makes their family bond stronger. Ask students how the memory makes their family bond stronger. Students might say that the memory helps them think about the good time they had with their families.

© 2001 Everyday Learning Corporation

Do You Copy?

The Curriculum

Life Skill

■ I will learn facts about pregnancy and childbirth.

Objectives

■ Students will tell what a cell is.

■ Students will tell what an egg cell and a sperm cell are.

■ Students will tell that a baby is made when an egg cell and a sperm cell join.

■ Students will tell that an unborn baby grows inside its mother during pregnancy.

The National Health Education Standards

■ Students will comprehend concepts related to health promotion and disease prevention.

Preparing to Teach the Lesson Plan

Materials

Cardboard or construction paper

Scissors

String

Paper

Tape or glue

Blackline Master

Animal Flashcards

Teaching the Lesson Plan

Make an egg cell by cutting a circle out of cardboard or construction paper. Make a sperm cell by cutting an oval out of cardboard or construction paper. Attach a string to the oval. The string represents the sperm's tail.

Make copies of the Blackline Master Animal Flashcards. Cut them out. Cut pieces of cardboard or construction paper the same size as the animal flashcards. Glue or tape the animal flashcards onto the pieces of cardboard or construction paper.

1 Tell students that they will learn about how babies are made. Explain that all living things are made from cells. Define cell. A **cell** is the smallest living part of a person's body. Show students the egg cell. Tell students that the egg cell is a special cell that comes from the mother. An egg cell is about the size of the period at the end of this sentence. Show students the sperm cell. Tell students that the sperm cell is a special cell that comes from the father. Tell students that the tail helps the sperm cell move. A sperm cell cannot be seen because it is too small. Explain that sperm cells and egg cells are special cells that help make a baby. When a sperm cell meets an egg cell inside the mother's body, the sperm cell enters the egg. The egg cell is fertilized. Define fertilization. **Fertilization** is the joining of the egg cell and the sperm cell to make a single cell. The fertilized egg cell becomes a baby.

2 Show the class one of the pictures of the animals that you copied. Tell them that you copied the picture on a copy machine. The copy machine made a copy of the picture. In the same way, a baby animal is a copy of its parents. Explain that a puppy is a baby dog that is made from a mother dog and a father dog. A baby bird is made from a mother bird and a father bird. A baby fish is made from a mother fish and a father fish. The special cells from a mother and a father help make a copy that is just like them.

3 Explain that an egg cell and a sperm cell can meet inside or outside of the mother animal. The egg can develop inside or outside of the mother. For example, a frog egg cell and a frog sperm cell meet outside the body of the mother frog. The egg develops outside of the mother, too. A chicken egg cell and a chicken sperm cell will meet inside of the mother chicken, but the egg will develop outside of the mother's body. Tell students that a human egg cell and a human sperm cell will meet inside the mother's body. The egg will develop inside the mother's body.

4 Play Animal Flashcards to show how living things come from like living things. Tell students to sit in a circle on the floor. Place all the animal mother flashcards on one side of the circle. Mix the mother animal flashcards up. Place all the animal baby flashcards on the

other side of the circle. Mix the baby animal flashcards up. Call on a student to choose a mother flashcard. Tell the student to match the mother flashcard to the baby flashcard. If the student matches the cards, ask the student where the baby will develop. Continue playing until each student has had a turn.

Assessment

Use the flashcards to quiz students. Copy the pictures onto a sheet of paper. Arrange the pictures so that the pictures of the mothers are on one side of the page and the pictures of the babies are on the other side of the page. Ask students to draw lines that connect the mother pictures to the correct baby pictures.

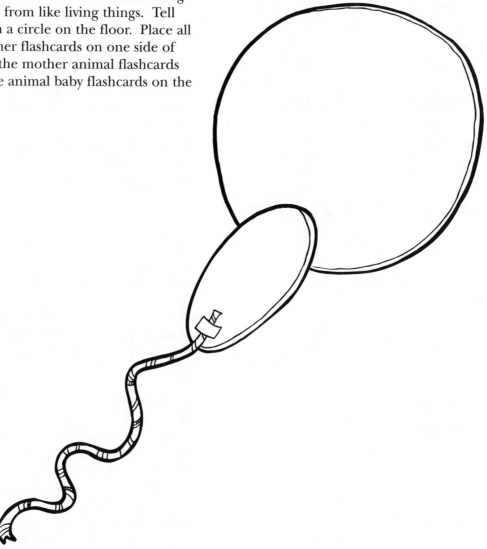

Animal Flashcards

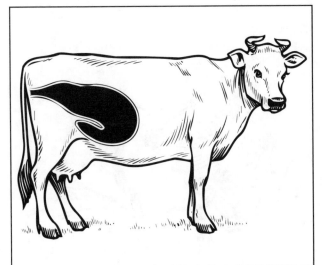

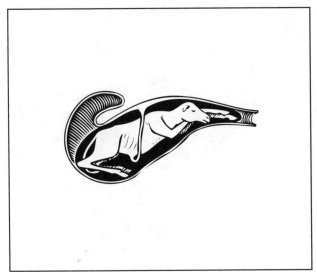
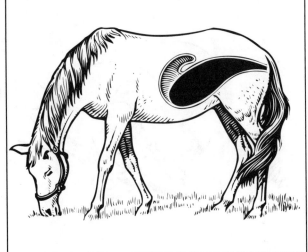

Animal Flashcards (Continued)

Animal Flashcards (Continued)

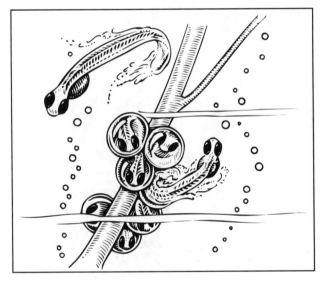

Animal Flashcards (Continued)

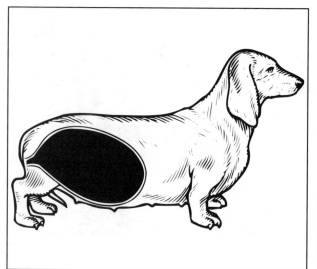

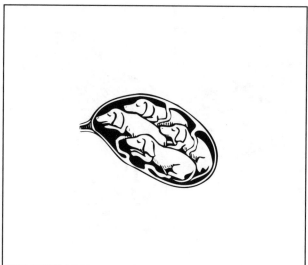

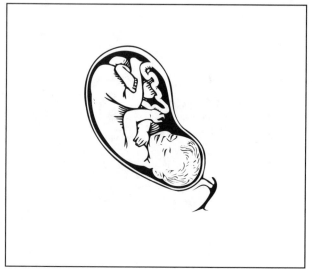

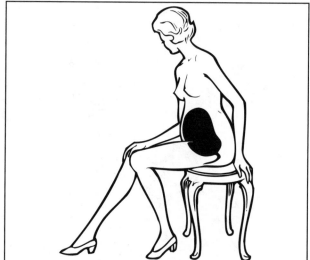

Grades 3–4
Lesson Plans and Blackline Masters

Table of Contents

Good Character Is Priceless

The Curriculum

Life Skills

■ I will show good character.

■ I will make responsible decisions.

■ I will use resistance skills when necessary.

Objectives

■ Students will tell three actions that make up good character.

■ Students will explain why they need good character.

■ Students will explain why their heroes should have good character.

■ Students will explain what to do if they do something wrong.

■ Students will list six questions to ask before they make a decision.

■ Students will explain the difference between a responsible decision and a wrong decision.

■ Students will explain how to use resistance skills.

■ Students will explain when to use resistance skills.

■ Students will show how to use resistance skills.

■ Students will explain why a peer might pressure them to make a wrong decision.

The National Health Education Standards

■ Students will demonstrate the ability to practice health-enhancing behaviors and reduce health risks.

■ Students will demonstrate the ability to use goal-setting and decision-making skills that enhance health.

Preparing to Teach the Lesson Plan

Materials

Play money bill of a high dollar amount

Scissors

Blank sheet of paper

Pencils, crayons, or markers

Tape

Chalkboard

Chalk

Teaching the Lesson Plan

As on real money, there might be a portrait in the middle of the play money bill. Cut out a shape to cover the portrait from a blank sheet of paper. Then copy and enlarge the play money bill. Make a copy of the enlarged play money bill for each student.

1 Give a copy of the play money bill to each student. Tell each student to draw his or her portrait in the center of the play money bill. As an option, you can tell students the day before the activity to bring head shots of themselves to class. Students can then glue their head shots onto the play money bills. Students should get permission from their parents or guardians to apply glue to their photos.

2 Make a bulletin board with the play money bills. Title the bulletin board, "Good Character Is Priceless." Explain to the class that what is shown on the bulletin board is worth more than any amount of money. The bulletin board shows that the good character of each person in the class is priceless. Define good character. **Good character** is telling the truth, showing respect, and being fair.

3 Write the following sentence on the board: "Money can't buy _____."

Tell students to complete the sentence with something they value. Students might give the following examples:

- Money can't buy health.
- Money can't buy good friends.
- Money can't buy respect.

Tell students that there is something else money can't buy—good character. Explain to students that telling the truth, showing respect, and being fair are values that make up good character. When a person has good character, he or she acts on these values.

4 Point to each self-portrait on the bulletin board. As you point to each self-portrait, ask a student (other than the student in the portrait) to name a value that the person has that makes up his or her good character. A student might say that the person never cheats at games or that the person always works hard.

5 Tell students that making responsible decisions is part of showing their good character. Define responsible decision. A **responsible decision** is a decision that is safe and healthful and follows laws and family guidelines. Tell students that *Guidelines for Making Responsible Decisions*™ can help them make decisions that are responsible. Students should ask the following questions to know whether or not a choice is responsible:

- Is it healthful?
- Is it safe?
- Do I follow rules and laws?
- Do I show respect for myself and others?
- Do I follow my family's guidelines?
- Do I show good character?

6 Tell students to suppose they are pressured to make a choice that is not responsible. Suppose they are pressured to do something wrong, such as smoke a cigarette. Explain that students can use resistance skills to resist pressure to do something wrong. Define resistance skills. **Resistance skills** are ways to say NO to behaviors that are wrong. Tell students they can use the following resistance skills:

- Say NO in a firm voice.
- Give reasons for saying NO.

- Match your actions with your words.
- Keep away from situations in which peers might try to talk you into wrong decisions.
- Keep away from peers who make wrong decisions.
- Tell an adult if someone tries to talk you into a wrong decision.
- Help your friends make responsible decisions.

Assessment

Tell students to write the word CHARACTER as an acrostic on a sheet of paper. Tell students to write a sentence for each letter that tells something about their good character. Each letter of the word "character" will be used for the first word in each sentence. Examples are shown below:

Choosing not to smoke is a responsible decision, so I choose not to smoke.

Having to wait to buy a new videogame until I have saved up my allowance shows self-discipline.

Always wearing my safety belt in the car shows good citizenship.

Really trying hard on something new shows determination.

Allowing myself to admit my mistakes shows integrity.

Cheating on a test does not show honesty, so I never cheat on a test.

The act of trying new things shows courage.

Eating all of the meal that my parents or guardians cooked for me shows responsibility.

Reading when I'm told to shows respect for my parents or guardians and my teacher.

In Character We Trust

Coated with Kindness

The Curriculum

Life Skills

■ I will share feelings in healthful ways.

■ I will settle conflict in healthful ways.

Objectives

■ Students will tell questions to ask to help understand their feelings.

■ Students will explain why they need to express feelings in healthful ways.

■ Students will describe healthful ways to express feelings.

■ Students will discuss ways to settle conflict.

■ Students will explain how they can control angry feelings.

■ Students will discuss what to do if someone wants to fight with them.

The National Health Education Standards

■ Students will demonstrate the ability to use interpersonal communication skills to enhance health.

Preparing to Teach the Lesson Plan

Materials

A piece of cake that crumbles easily

A chocolate-coated cookie

Tissues

Blackline Master

Steps to Keep Away from Conflicts

Teaching the Lesson Plan

Bring a small piece of cake and a chocolate-coated cookie to class. The piece of cake should be the portion size that a student in the class would eat. The piece of cake should be such that it can crumble easily when passed from one person to another.

1 Tell students that the cake represents a person. Pass the piece of cake around the class. As students pass the piece of cake, tell them to say statements they have heard that could be used to hurt a person's feelings. Students might give some of the following examples:

• "You're ugly."

• "You're mean."

• "Your hair is messy."

• "The color of your shirt is gross."

Tell students to notice that the cake begins to crumble. Tell them that the cake falls apart as it is being passed around and exposed to negative statements. This is similar to what happens when people are mean to each other and make statements that hurt each other. When someone says something harmful to another person, that person will feel hurt. The person might cry or become upset and angry.

2 Explain to students that everyone experiences anger. Define anger. **Anger** is the feeling of being mad or upset. Anger is an emotion. Define emotions. **Emotions** are the feelings that are inside you. Tell students that it is okay to feel anger. But it is not okay to harm another person in anger. It is not okay to destroy property. It is not okay to harm oneself. There are ways to control angry feelings. A person who is angry can take a timeout. A person who is angry can take a deep breath. He or she can accept a situation that he or she cannot change. Not everything in life can be controlled or predicted. A person must learn to change habits or situations that he or she *can* control. A person must learn to deal with situations that he or she *cannot* control. A person can ask three questions to help understand his or her feelings:

1. What am I feeling?

2. Why do I feel this way?

3. How might I show this feeling in a healthful way?

A person who is angry can talk to a trusted adult. A trusted adult might be a parent, guardian, other family member, teacher, or school counselor. A trusted adult can help a person work through angry feelings.

3 Explain to students that sometimes angry feelings result from a conflict. Define conflict. A **conflict** is a disagreement. A person can stay away from conflicts. Give each student a copy of the Blackline Master *Steps to Keep Away from Conflicts*. Tell the class that they can take the following steps to keep away from conflicts:

• Use self-control.

• Say you will not fight.

• Agree to talk things out.

• Agree to a responsible solution and try it.

• Walk away if the other person or people still want to fight.

• Ask a trusted adult for help.

A person also can remove himself or herself from a situation when another person is being mean. Ask students what they might do or say if someone says something mean to them. Students might answer that they would walk away from the person or that they would say, "I don't think you are being nice. Please don't talk to me like that."

4 Pass the chocolate-coated cookie around the room. Tell students that this cookie represents a different person. Ask students to say something that is thoughtful and nice as they pass the cookie. Students might give some of the following examples:

• "You're a nice person."

• "You look great today."

• "I love the way your hair looks."

Tell students to notice that as the cookie is passed, the chocolate begins to rub off on students' fingers. Explain that when people express emotions in healthful ways, the good feelings rub off. People feel good about themselves. Their self-esteem is heightened.

5 Explain the importance of expressing emotions in healthful ways. Expressing emotions in healthful ways and avoiding conflict help improve self-esteem. People who do not express emotions in healthful ways should speak to a trusted adult about their feelings. People who choose friends who express emotions in healthful ways will have those good feelings rub off on them.

6 After the chocolate-coated cookie has been passed around, give each student a tissue to wipe his or her fingers. Tell students that they must not lick the chocolate from their fingers because it contains germs from the fingers of others.

© 2001 Everyday Learning Corporation

Assessment

Divide students into groups of five. Each student in the group should say one nice statement to each of the other group members. Tell students to share how they feel after hearing others make positive statements about them. Tell two members of each group to act out a conflict. You might choose one of the following examples for students to act out, or you might ask students to think of their own conflicts to act out. Examples of conflict are

- You want to watch a sporting event on television, but your older sister wants to watch a comedy.

- Someone cuts in front of you in line in the school cafeteria. He says that if you do not let him, he will hurt you.

- You notice that your sister is wearing a ring of yours. She did not ask you if she could borrow it.

Ask students to apply the *Steps to Keep Away from Conflicts* to the situations they act out.

Steps to Keep Away from Conflicts

1. Use self-control.

2. Say you will not fight.

3. Agree to talk things out.

4. Agree to a responsible solution and try it.

5. Walk away if the other person or people still want to fight.

6. Ask a trusted adult for help.

Telephone Safety

The Curriculum

Life Skills

■ I will protect myself from people who might harm me.

■ I will follow safety rules to protect myself from violence.

Objective

■ Students will tell safety rules to follow when they are home with someone besides their parents or guardians.

The National Health Education Standards

■ Students will demonstrate the ability to practice health-enhancing behaviors and reduce health risks.

Preparing to Teach the Lesson Plan

Materials

Two toy telephones

Chalkboard

Chalk

Blackline Master

Safety Rules to Follow When Answering the Telephone

Teaching the Lesson Plan

1 Ask students whether or not they answer the telephone in their homes. Most students will say that they answer the telephone at home. Ask students if they have ever been home with just a childsitter or an older brother or sister. Students will probably say that they have. Ask students what they might do if they answered the telephone when they were at home with just a childsitter or brother or sister but did not know who was calling. Ask students what they might say if the caller asked them whether or not their parents or guardians were home. Students might say that they would not answer the question. Tell students that if a stranger on the telephone asks whether or not their parents or guardians are at home, they should say that their parents or guardians cannot come to the phone right now. Students should ask if they can take a message.

2 Place a toy telephone on your desk. Ask for a student volunteer. Give the student volunteer the other toy telephone. Tell the student volunteer to pretend he or she is home with only a childsitter or older brother or sister. Tell the student volunteer that you are going to pretend to call his or her home. Explain that the student does not know who you are. Make a ringing sound. Tell the student to answer the telephone as he or she would if he or she were at home.

The following is a sample conversation. Students might or might not respond in the ways described.

Student: Hello.

Stranger: Hi! Who is this?

Student: This is Kassandra (student's name).

Stranger: Hi, Kassandra. This is Mr. Smith. Is your mother home?

Student: No.

Stranger: Do you know when she will be home?

Student: No.

Stranger: Is anyone else home?

Student: Just my brother.

Stranger: Kassandra, I have a package your mother wanted me to deliver to your home, but I've lost your address. Could you give me your address? I'll stop by to deliver her package.

Student: Sure. I live at 1234 Fifth Street.

Stranger: Thanks. When I stop by, just open the door and I'll give you the package. Good-bye.

3 If a student gives similar answers to those in the above conversation, tell the class that this way of answering the phone does not follow safety rules. Tell the class that the student gave you too much personal information. Ask students what other safety rules the student volunteer did not follow. Students might say that the student volunteer told the caller that his or her parents were not at home. Give each student a copy of the Blackline Master *Safety Rules to Follow When Answering the Telephone*. Tell students that they can follow safety rules when they answer the phone:

• Never say your name or your family name.

• Never give your address or telephone number.

• Never tell anyone that your parents or guardians are not home.

• Never answer other questions a caller might ask.

• Hang up if the caller bothers you or says something mean or dirty.

4 Ask the student volunteer to answer the phone again, but this time following safety rules. The conversation might be similar to the following:

Student: Hello.

Stranger: Hello. Who is this?

Student: To whom do you want to speak?

Stranger: Is your mother home?

Student: My mother is busy and cannot come to the phone right now.

Stranger: I need to deliver a package to your home and I lost your address. Could I have it?

Student: Please give me your name and phone number and my mother will call you back.

Stranger: Good-bye.

Tell students that in this conversation, the student volunteer followed safety rules. Ask students which safety rules the student volunteer followed. Students will say that the student volunteer did not give out personal information and that he or she did not tell the caller that his or her parents or guardians were not home.

Assessment

Write the above conversation on the chalkboard. Leave blank the student responses. Ask students to come to the chalkboard and write appropriate responses in the blanks. You can change some of the questions the caller uses to get information from the student.

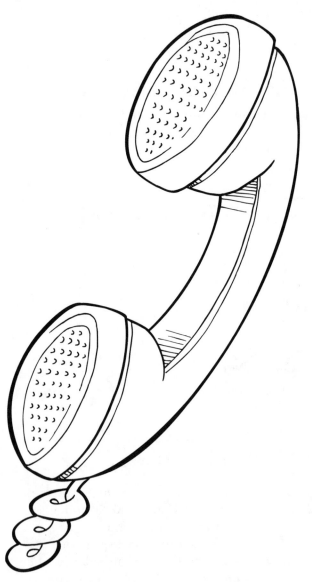

© 2001 Everyday Learning Corporation

Safety Rules to Follow When Answering the Telephone

■ Never say your name or your family name.

■ Never give your address or telephone number.

■ Never tell anyone that your parents or guardians are not home.

■ Never answer other questions a caller might ask.

■ Hang up if the caller bothers you or says something mean or dirty.

Car Caution

The Curriculum

Life Skills

■ I will protect myself from people who might harm me.

■ I will follow safety rules to protect myself from violence.

Objectives

■ Students will tell ways to stay safe from strangers when they are away from home.

■ Students will tell safety rules to stay safe from strangers in cars.

■ Students will tell what to do if someone gives them an unsafe touch.

The National Health Education Standards

■ Students will demonstrate the ability to practice health-enhancing behaviors and reduce health risks.

Preparing to Teach the Lesson Plan

Materials

Cardboard box, such as that from a
   grocery store

Scissors

Pencil

Colored markers

Chair

Magazine picture of a puppy

Blackline Master

Safety Rules to Follow Around Strangers in a Car

Teaching the Lesson Plan

Cut one of the large sides from a cardboard box. Then draw an outline of a car in the shape of a convertible or other car. Color the car a bright color. Cut around the outline of the car. Leave enough of the box sides to prop up the cutout convertible.

1 Tell students that the following activity will teach them how to be safe from strangers in cars. Place a chair behind the cardboard box. Sit on the chair so that it appears you are driving the car. Ask for a student volunteer. Tell the student volunteer to stand approximately ten feet away from the car. Tell the student to pretend he or she is walking down the street. Tell the student that he or she should do what you say to do. Show the student the magazine picture of the puppy. Say to the student, "Excuse me. I lost my puppy and I have a picture of her. Could you come here so that I can show you a picture of her? Maybe you can help me find her." As the student comes close to the car, grab his or her arm. Then tell the class that if you were a stranger who wanted to harm the student, you could have dragged him or her into the car.

2 Tell students that they should never approach a car with a stranger inside. Students should never get into a car with a stranger inside. Give each student a copy of the Blackline Master *Safety Rules to Follow Around Strangers in a Car.* Tell students these safety rules to follow around strangers in cars:

• Make a noise if a stranger in a car follows you. Other people will hear you and come to see what is wrong.

• Run to a safe place. Run home or to a nearby store.

• Do not go close to a car in which there is a stranger.

- Do not accept candy, toys, or money from a stranger. A stranger might try to get you close to the car by offering you such things.

- Do not walk over to a car to answer a question or to give directions.

- Do not let a stranger in a car follow you. Turn and run in the opposite direction.

3 Tell students that they have the right to be safe. They also have the right not to be touched in ways they do not like. Define unsafe touch. An **unsafe touch** is a touch that is wrong. It is not okay for someone to touch their private body parts. If someone gives them an unsafe touch, they should do the following:

- Tell the person to stop touching you.

- Yell as loud as you can.

- Run away from the person.

- Tell an adult.

- Tell another adult if the first adult does not believe you.

4 Explain to students that when a stranger in a car follows them, they should run in the opposite direction in which the car is moving. This way, the stranger would have to turn the car around to follow them. Tell students that it is also important to remember as much as possible about a stranger who follows them in a car. Students should remember the following about a stranger who follows them in a car:

- The color of the car.

- The kind of car.

- What the stranger looked like.

- What the stranger was wearing.

- The license plate number of the car.

Tell students to draw license plates with various numbers and letters. Attach a license plate to the cardboard car. Practice the scenario with the stranger again. Tell the class to follow safety rules around strangers in cars this time. Pretend that you stop your car. Ask a random student to come closer to see the picture of the lost puppy. The student should run in the opposite direction. The student should be able to tell the license plate number on the car. Practice the scenario several more times with different license plates.

Assessment

Review the safety rules to follow around strangers in a car. Then tell students to close their eyes. Ask students to give the safety rules to follow around strangers in cars. After students give the safety rules with their eyes closed, ask them to describe what the "stranger" in the car was wearing. Ask them to tell you the license plate number that is now on the car. Ask them to tell you the kind of car the "stranger" was in. Ask them to tell you what color the car was. Students should be able to describe your clothing and details about the car.

Safety Rules to Follow Around Strangers in a Car

Do

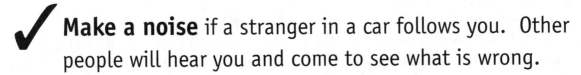

✔ **Make a noise** if a stranger in a car follows you. Other people will hear you and come to see what is wrong.

✔ **Run** to a safe place. Run home or to a nearby store.

Do Not

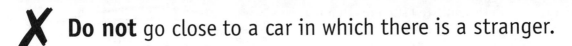

✗ **Do not** go close to a car in which there is a stranger.

✗ **Do not** accept candy, toys, or money from a stranger. A stranger might try to get you close to the car by offering you such things.

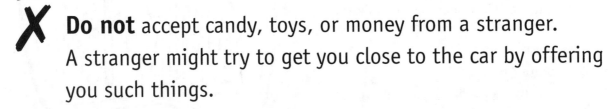

✗ **Do not** walk over to a car to answer a question or to give directions.

✗ **Do not** let a stranger in a car follow you. Turn and run in the opposite direction.

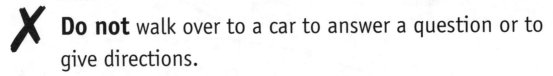

Turn Off the TV

The Curriculum

Life Skills

■ I will choose healthful entertainment.

■ I will develop media literacy.

Objectives

■ Students will list guidelines for choosing healthful entertainment.

■ Students will list questions to check out whether or not TV shows are healthful entertainment.

■ Students will list questions to check out whether or not books are healthful entertainment.

■ Students will list questions to check out whether or not movies are healthful entertainment.

■ Students will list questions to check out whether or not computer games are healthful entertainment.

The National Health Education Standards

■ Students will analyze the influence of culture, media, technology, and other factors on health.

Preparing to Teach the Lesson Plan

Materials

Cardboard

Scissors

Markers

Tape

Blackline Master

Questions to Ask to Check Out a TV Show

Teaching the Lesson Plan

Before teaching the Lesson Plan, cut the cardboard into a square 2 feet by 2 feet. Cut out a square center piece so that the cardboard resembles a TV. Draw knobs on the cardboard TV. Cut pieces from any remaining cardboard to make a television antenna. Tape the antenna to the cardboard TV with tape.

1 Define entertainment. **Entertainment** is something that interests or amuses you. Ask students what they do for entertainment. Students might say that they play soccer or that they watch movies. Tell students that there is healthful entertainment and there is harmful entertainment. Define healthful entertainment. **Healthful entertainment** is entertainment that promotes health. Ask students to name kinds of healthful entertainment. Students might name reading a book or doing physical activity. Tell students these kinds of healthful entertainment:

• **Physical activity** Physical activity is fun and keeps the body healthy. Physical activity is good for social health. It can be done with a friend or a family member.

• **Hobbies** Many hobbies are healthful kinds of entertainment. A person might like to play chess. Or a person might like to collect and play with trains. Practicing hobbies can help a person learn something well. Practicing hobbies can discipline a person. Discipline is working hard at something.

• **Reading** Learning new words helps a person's memory. Reading for fun helps a student do well in school. Reading is good for mental health.

• **Clubs** Being in clubs can be healthful entertainment. Clubs such as the Girl Scouts, Boy Scouts, and 4-H help teach young people skills. Young people learn how to camp, take care of animals, and do crafts.

• **TV shows and movies** Some TV shows and movies are healthful entertainment. TV shows and movies that show families resolving conflicts in healthful ways are healthful entertainment. TV shows and movies that teach students facts and important information are healthful entertainment.

2 Tell students that some entertainment is harmful. Harmful entertainment might show violence. Harmful entertainment might show people using illegal drugs. It might show information that is not true. Give each student a copy of the Blackline Master *Questions to Ask to Check Out a TV Show*. Tell students that they can check out whether or not a TV show is healthful entertainment. Tell students the following questions to ask to check out whether or not a TV show is healthful entertainment:

• Does the TV show tell me to follow family guidelines?

• Do the people in the TV show act in responsible ways?

• Does the TV show leave out violence?

• Does the TV show leave out bad words?

• Do I have permission from my parents or guardians to watch this TV show?

Tell students that if the answer to one of the questions is "no," they should not watch the TV show.

3 Tell students that they will name kinds of healthful entertainment that they choose. Give the cardboard TV to a student. Tell the student to hold the cardboard TV so that his or her face appears behind the "screen." Tell students that first you will name a way entertainment is harmful, such as "Violence is not

good to see." Then the student holding the cardboard TV will respond by saying, "I will turn off my TV." Then the student will name a healthful activity or entertainment choice. For example, a student might say, "I will turn off my TV. I will read a book." Tell the student to pass the television to another student. Repeat the activity until every student has named a healthful activity or entertainment choice. Name these ways entertainment can be harmful during the activity:

• "Illegal drugs aren't good to see."

• "Harmful lies aren't good to see."

• "Meanness is not good to see."

• "Disrespect is not good to see."

• "Cheaters aren't good to see."

• "Fighting is not good to see."

• "Kicking is not good to see."

Assessment

Have students keep a TV calendar for a week. Tell students to write on their calendars the length of time they watched TV each day. Tell students to write on their calendars the names of the TV shows they watched each day. At the end of the week, tell students to total the number of hours they watched television. Students should not have watched television for more than seven hours in seven days. Tell students to choose a TV show they watched. Tell students to write the name of the TV show at the top of a separate sheet of paper. Then tell students to answer the *Questions to Ask to Check Out a TV Show* on the sheet of paper. Ask students whether or not the TV show they watched was healthful entertainment.

Questions to Ask to Check Out a TV Show

◆ Does the TV show tell me to follow family guidelines?

◆ Do the people in the TV show act in responsible ways?

◆ Does the TV show leave out violence?

◆ Does the TV show leave out bad words?

◆ Do I have permission from my parents or guardians to watch this TV show?

If the answer to one of the questions is **"no,"** you should not watch the TV show.

323

Take a Second Look

The Curriculum

Life Skill

■ I will show respect for others.

Objectives

■ Students will tell why they need to show respect for themselves.

■ Students will explain ways they can show respect for other people.

■ Students will list ways they can tell if someone does not show respect for them.

■ Students will discuss what to do if someone does not show respect for them.

The National Health Education Standards

■ Students will demonstrate the ability to use interpersonal communication skills to enhance health.

Preparing to Teach the Lesson Plan

Materials

Two books

Brown wrapping paper

Markers

Magazine pictures

Tape

Glue

Chalkboard

Chalk

Blackline Master

Ways to Show Respect for Other People

Teaching the Lesson Plan

Make covers for the books using the brown wrapping paper. Decorate one of the covers using colorful markers, appealing magazine photos, and illustrations. Make this cover look really attractive. Decorate the other book cover to be only somewhat attractive. On a sheet of paper, write the following healthful behaviors: gets plenty of physical activity; avoids alcohol, tobacco, and other drugs; is well-groomed. On the same sheet of paper, write the following risk behaviors: does not show respect for others; cannot control angry feelings; does not follow family guidelines. Place the sheet of paper inside the attractive book. On another sheet of paper, write only the following healthful behaviors: follows family rules; makes responsible decisions; has good character. Place this sheet of paper inside the moderately attractive book.

1 Show the two books to the class. Tell the class that you are going to take a poll. Tell students that they are going to vote on the most attractive book. Hold up the attractive book. Ask students if they consider this book to be the most attractive. Most students probably will vote for this book. Count the raised hands. Write the tally on the board. Hold up the moderately attractive book. Ask students if they consider this book to be the most attractive. Most students probably will not vote for this book. Count the raised hands. Write the tally on the board.

2 Explain to students that they have just voted for the most attractive "friend." Tell students that they selected their friend based on outward appearance only. Tell students that they will learn more about the behaviors of the friend they selected. Open the attractive book and read the list of actions and behaviors on the sheet of paper: gets plenty of physical activity; avoids alcohol, tobacco, and other drugs; is well-groomed; does not show respect for others; cannot control angry feelings; does not follow family guidelines. Tell students that even though the friend they selected appeared attractive, that friend practices risk behaviors. Define risk behavior. A **risk behavior** is an action that can be harmful to health. Ask students to name which behaviors were risk behaviors. Students should say that the following are risk behaviors: does not show respect for others; cannot control angry feelings; does not follow family guidelines.

3 Tell students that they will learn about the actions and behaviors of the friend they did not select. Open the moderately attractive book and read the sheet of paper with these healthful behaviors: follows family guidelines; makes responsible decisions; has good character. Tell students that although this "friend" looks only moderately attractive, the actions of this friend are important. For example, a person who follows family rules has respect for others. Define respect. **Respect** is thinking highly of someone. A person who respects his parents or guardians is more likely to respect you. A person earns respect by having responsible actions. Define self-respect. **Self-respect** is thinking highly of yourself because you act in responsible ways. Give each student a copy of the Blackline Master *Ways to Show Respect for Other People.* Tell students that there are ways to show respect for other people:

- Treat other people in kind ways.
- Do not talk when other people are talking to you.
- Take your turn when you and other people are waiting.
- Be fair when you play with other people.
- Answer when other people speak to you.

Assessment

On a sheet of paper, have students make a list of the actions that they can tell about a person from the first impression of him or her. Below this list, have students make a list of actions and behaviors that they might miss from the first impression of a person. Tell students to write why it is important to take a second look at a person.

Ways to Show Respect for Other People

■ Treat other people in kind ways.

■ Do not talk when other people are talking to you.

■ Take your turn when you and other people are waiting.

■ Be fair when you play with other people.

■ Answer when other people speak to you.

Left Out

The Curriculum

Life Skills

■ I will work to have healthful friendships.

■ I will make wise decisions with friends.

■ I will show respect for others.

Objectives

■ Students will tell ways to make a true friend.

■ Students will explain how friends can make responsible decisions.

■ Students will explain ways they can show respect for other people.

■ Students will explain what to do if they feel left out.

The National Health Education Standards

■ Students will demonstrate the ability to use interpersonal communication skills to enhance health.

Preparing to Teach the Lesson Plan

Materials

Tape recorder

Music

Two index cards

Ten strips of paper

Teaching the Lesson Plan

Write the following situations on separate strips of paper:

I am at a party with a friend. Someone at the party has a cigarette. This person wants me to take a puff. I tell them "no way." I leave the party.

A friend's brother picks us up from practice. I smell alcohol on his breath. I get in the car anyway.

I am physically active, but I pig out every night on chips and dip.

I play music so loud I feel the floor shaking.

I am at a friend's house. She wants to ride bicycles. She says she has an extra bike. But she does not have an extra helmet. I say, "Let's do something else."

I am at the mall with a group of friends. One of them says, "Let's steal a jacket. Put it on, and we'll walk out of the store." I tell the person to forget it. I leave and call home to get a ride.

Both of my parents work. After school, I'm supposed to stay at a neighbor's house until my parents come home. Instead, I go to a friend's house after school. I don't tell anyone where I am.

My parents want me to watch my younger sister while they cook dinner. I teach my sister how to play a game.

A friend tells me that he needs to spend time with his family instead of with me. I am angry and make a plan to get back at my friend.

A friend tells me that she needs to spend time with her family instead of with me. I tell my friend that the two of us can do something another time. I respect my friend's need for space.

1 This lesson plan will show students what a true friend is. Ask students to name activities that they do alone each day. Students might say that they do their homework alone or that they read books alone. Tell students that everyone needs time to be alone. Define true friend. A **true friend** is a person whose actions toward you are responsible and caring.

A true friend

- stands by you;
- spends time with you;
- respects your family's guidelines;
- wants you to spend time with your family;
- lets you have other friends;
- does not tell other people things you do not want shared;
- does not put you down;
- wants you to make responsible decisions;
- wants you to take care of your health;
- wants you to have good character.

2 Explain to students that just like they need time to be alone, a true friend sometimes needs time to be alone. A true friend needs to spend time with his or her family. He or she needs to spend time with other friends. Explain to students that they also need to spend time with their families and other friends. True friends give each other space. They give each other time apart. True friends respect each other. Define respect. **Respect** is thinking highly of someone. True friends respect each other's space. Explain to students that they might feel left out at times when a friend does something without them. Students can take the following actions if they feel left out:

- Say nothing because a true friend needs space.
- Share your feelings of being hurt and left out.
- Call another person and do something else.
- Talk to your parents or guardians.

3 Tell students that they will play musical chairs. Arrange the classroom chairs to play musical chairs. Make sure there are enough chairs for every student except for one. Play tape recorded music. Tell students to walk in a circle around the chairs while the music plays. When the music stops, students should find a chair to sit in. The person who does not find a chair to sit in must name an action to follow when a person feels left out. For example, the student might say, "Talk to a parent or guardian."

4 Explain that true friends also make responsible decisions together. But how do friends know they are making responsible decisions together? Tell students that they can judge decisions that they make with friends. Tell students they can know if a decision is responsible by following the *Guidelines for Making Responsible Decisions™*. Students should ask the following questions:

- Is it healthful?
- Is it safe?
- Does it follow rules and laws?
- Does it show you respect yourself and others?
- Does it follow your family's guidelines?
- Does it show good character?

Assessment

Tell students that they will be in a mock trial. A mock trial is a trial that is make-believe. Ask for six student volunteers. Ask the six student volunteers to sit behind a table at the front of the classroom. Give each student volunteer an index card and a marker. Ask students to write "yes" on one side of the index card and "no" on the other side of the index card. Tell the class that the six student volunteers will be judges. They will judge decisions their classmates make. The first student volunteer will judge whether or not a decision is healthful, the second student volunteer will judge whether or not a decision is safe, and so on.

Pass out the ten strips of paper to ten students. Ask students to read aloud the situations on the strips. After a student reads a situation, tell the student to ask each judge one of the questions in the *Guidelines for Making Responsible Decisions™*. The judges should use the index cards to respond to the questions.

Ask students to write their own situations on sheets of paper. Collect the papers. Pick appropriate situations. Give the papers to random students. Repeat the above procedure.

Body Part Name Game

The Curriculum

Life Skills

■ I will take care of my body.

■ I will learn ways my body changes.

■ I will have checkups.

Objectives

■ Students will name private body parts.

■ Students will tell signs they are growing.

■ Students will tell ways their bodies will change.

■ Students will tell why they need medical checkups.

The National Health Education Standards

■ Students will comprehend concepts related to health promotion and disease prevention.

Preparing to Teach the Lesson Plan

Materials

Ball of string

Marker

Construction paper

Scissors

24 index cards

Teaching the Lesson Plan

1 Tell students that the body is made up of body parts. Some body parts work together to do a certain job. For example, some body parts work together to help you use food. Some body parts work together to help you breathe. Some body parts work together to help you move. Define body system. A **body system** is a group of organs that work together to do a certain job.

2 Tell students that they are going to learn about their body systems. Explain to students that they will help make a large outline of a body. This can be done in two different ways: Have a student hold a spool of string while another student unwinds it. Tell the person unwinding the string to position the string on the floor so that it forms the shape of a young person. The shape of the young person should be the size of the average student in class. Another way to shape the string is to tell a student to lie on the floor. Then tell a student to shape the string around the student lying on the floor. An outline of a student's body will be formed.

3 Draw two eyes, a nose, two ears, and a mouth on construction paper. Cut out these body parts. Tell students to place these body parts in the correct place on the string body. Explain to students that these body parts appear on the outside of the body. They can be seen. Explain that both boys and girls have these body parts.

4 Define respiratory system. The **respiratory system** is made up of organs that help you use the air you breathe. Draw outlines of the throat (pharynx), the windpipe (trachea), and the lungs on construction paper. Cut out these body parts. Tell students that these body parts are part of the respiratory system. The **throat** is the passage between the mouth and the windpipe. The **windpipe** is a tube that goes from the throat to the lungs. The **lungs** are organs that put oxygen into the blood and take carbon dioxide out of the blood. Define oxygen. **Oxygen** is a gas needed for you to live. Define carbon dioxide. **Carbon dioxide** is a gas that is a waste product of your cells. Ask students if they can name other body parts in the respiratory system. Students might say that the nose is a body part in the respiratory system.

Define circulatory system. The **circulatory system** is made up of organs that move blood throughout your body. Draw an outline of a heart. Cut out this body part. Tell students that the heart is a body part in the circulatory system. The **heart** is a muscular organ that pumps blood. Ask students if they can name other body parts in the circulatory system. Students might say that veins and arteries are body parts in the circulatory system.

Define digestive system. The **digestive system** is made up of organs that help your body use food. Draw an outline of a stomach, a small intestine, and a large intestine. Tell students that these body parts are part of the digestive system. The **stomach** is an organ that releases special juices to break down food. The **small intestine** is an organ that breaks down most of the food you eat into substances your body cells can use. The **large intestine** is the body organ through which solid waste passes.

Define urinary system. The **urinary system** is made up of organs that help the body remove wastes. Draw outlines of two kidneys. Cut out the kidneys. Tell students that the kidney is part of the urinary system. The **kidney** is an organ that removes waste in the form of urine. Help students place all the pieces where they belong on the body. Explain that both boys and girls have these same body parts.

5 Cut out a circle and place it below and between the kidneys. The circle represents the urinary bladder. Cut three pieces of string approximately six inches in length. Connect the kidneys to the urinary bladder using two pieces of string. Attach one end of a piece of string to one kidney. Attach one end of another piece of string to the other kidney. Explain to students that the circle is the urinary bladder. Define urinary bladder. The **urinary bladder** is an organ that holds urine, which contains body wastes. Explain that urine comes from the kidneys. Then urine passes into the tubes. Attach the other ends of the

© 2001 Everyday Learning Corporation

pieces of string to the circle. Explain that from these tubes urine passes into the urinary bladder. Tell students that both boys and girls have these body parts.

6 Explain that both boys and girls have a urethra. The **urethra** is a tube that carries urine from the urinary bladder to the outside of the body.

7 **OPTIONAL** Tell students that a boy has a body part called a penis. The **penis** is a male organ through which urine and sperm pass out of the body. A boy's urethra is inside his penis. When he urinates, urine from the urinary bladder passes down the urethra and out of the body. When a boy gets older, his body makes sperm. A **sperm** is a male reproductive cell. To make a baby, a sperm from a male must join an egg from a female. Sperm from inside a male's body pass out of his body through the urethra. It is important to know that urine and sperm are never in the urethra at the same time.

8 **OPTIONAL** Explain that a girl also has a urethra. When she urinates, urine from the urinary bladder passes down the urethra and out of her body. She has an opening between her legs where the urine comes out. A girl has another opening between her legs. It is the opening to the vagina. The **vagina** is tube through which sperm pass to meet an egg and through which a baby is born.

9 **OPTIONAL** Tell students that their bodies will change as they grow. As girls grow, their breasts get bigger and their hips get wider. As boys grow, hair grows on their face and chest. Their voice gets deeper.

10 Tell students that they need to have medical checkups from a doctor. A doctor will check their height and weight. A doctor will check their eyes, ears, nose, and throat. They can ask their doctor questions about their body. They can ask their doctor questions their growth.

Assessment

Use 20 index cards. Print the name of each of the following body organs on one side of a separate index card: throat, windpipe, lungs, heart, stomach, small intestine, large intestine, kidney, urinary bladder, urethra. Print the definition of each of the body organs on one side of a separate index card. Shuffle the 20 index cards. Place them on the floor with the blank sides facing upwards. Have students take turns trying to get a match. One student begins by turning over an index card. It will have either the name of a body organ or a definition of a body organ printed on it. If the index card has the name of a body organ printed on it, the student tries to turn over the index card with the corresponding definition printed on it. If the student is successful, the student has a match. If the student turns over an index card with the definition of a body organ printed on it, the student tries to turn over the index card with the corresponding name of the body organ. If the student is successful, the student has a match.

OPTIONAL Use four more index cards. Print penis on one card and its definition on another card. Print vagina on one card and its definition on another card. Add these four index cards to the set of 20 index cards.

I Need Privacy

The Curriculum

Life Skills
■ I will be well-groomed.
■ I will choose safe and healthful products.

Objectives
■ Students will discuss rules for the safe use of grooming products.
■ Students will name kinds of media used to sell health products and services.
■ Students will tell how they can check out commercials for health products.

The National Health Education Standards
■ Students will demonstrate the ability to practice health-enhancing behaviors and reduce health risks.
■ Students will demonstrate the ability to access valid health information and health-promoting products and services.

Preparing to Teach the Lesson Plan

Materials
None

Teaching the Lesson Plan

1 Tell students that they will learn about good grooming. Ask students to name ways they take care of their appearance. Students might say that they shower or bathe every day. They might say that they comb or brush their hair.

Tell students the following ways to take care of their skin, hair, and nails:
- keep skin and nails clean;
- get treatment for skin infections;
- protect your skin from the sun;
- stay out of the sun between 10 a.m. and 4 p.m. Use sunscreen with a sun protection factor (SPF) of at least 15;
- keep your hair clean and brush your hair often; and
- protect your hair and scalp from the sun. Wear a hat.

2 Ask students to name grooming products. Students might say shampoo or soap. Tell students that they can choose grooming products wisely:
- They can read the labels for grooming products. They can check out a product's ingredients.
- They can choose products to stay well-groomed. Students can stick to the basics like soap, shampoo, and conditioner.
- They should not let ads get them to buy grooming products they do not need. They should not buy products just because they like the ad. They should buy products that they need to stay well-groomed and healthy.

3 Explain to students that privacy is an important part of respecting oneself and others. Define privacy. **Privacy** is having a place and the time to be alone. Explain to students that they might want privacy when they groom themselves. Tell students to suppose they are taking a bath. They do not want their sister or brother barging into the bathroom. They want their sister or brother to respect their privacy. Students also should respect the privacy of others.

Assessment

Tell the class that they will play a game called "Go for Grooming." You might want to play this game on a playing field or in a gym. Have students stand in a large circle. One student (student #1) should stay outside the circle. Ask the students in the circle to join hands. Student #1 will walk around the outside of the circle and tag one of the students. The student who is tagged (student #2) must chase student #1 until student #1 is tagged or until student #1 names a grooming product and is allowed inside the circle. When student #1 names a grooming product, the students in the circle should lift their arms to let student #1 into the circle. If student #1 is tagged before he or she names a grooming product, then student #1 is "it" and student #2 goes into the center of the circle. Tell students that if they are tagged they must name a grooming product that has not been named by one of the students who already was tagged and named a grooming product.

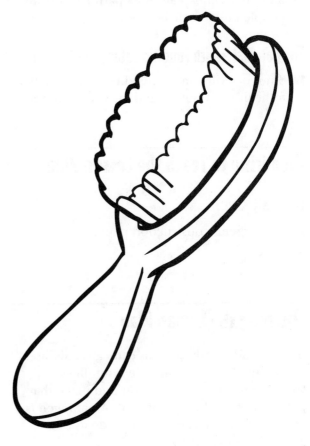

Germ Stop

The Curriculum

Life Skill

■ I will choose habits that prevent the spread of germs.

Objective

■ Students will explain ways pathogens from people enter their bodies.

The National Health Education Standards

■ Students will comprehend concepts related to health promotion and disease prevention.

Preparing to Teach the Lesson Plan

Materials

Red and green construction paper
Scissors

Teaching the Lesson Plan

1 Tell students that germs can cause disease. Define disease. A **disease** is an illness. Germs can spread to a person and make that person sick. Define pathogen. A **pathogen** is a germ that causes disease. Tell students that germs are everywhere.

2 Explain to students that pathogens can be spread from people or from the environment. Pathogens from people enter a person's body through the mouth, nose, or eyes. Pathogens from people also can enter a person's body when he or she breathes, or through the bloodstream, skin, or nails.

Suppose a person has a cold. That person sneezes and does not cover his or her mouth or nose. A person close by might breathe in droplets. These droplets contain pathogens for the cold.

Explain that pathogens from the environment can enter a person's body through the eyes, nose, and mouth. They also can enter a person's body through cuts, scrapes, and puncture wounds. Suppose a person falls down and scrapes his or her knee while playing in the yard. Usually germs in the soil will not harm a person. But they can harm a person if they enter the person's body through a cut, scrape, or other wound.

3 Pass out red and green construction paper and scissors to students. Tell students to cut out one green circle and one red circle. Both circles should be between 8 and 10 inches in diameter. Tell students that the red circle represents "stop" and the green circle represents "go."

4 Tell students that you are going to read some situations to them. The situations describe either a way to spread pathogens or a way to prevent the spread of pathogens. Ask students to hold up the red circle (stop) if you read a situation that describes a way to spread pathogens. Ask students to hold up the green circle (go) if you read a situation that describes a way to prevent the spread of pathogens.

Give students the following example: Two people are sharing a drink from the same cup. Tell students to hold up either their red circle or their green circle. Students should hold up their red circle. Choose a student who held up a red circle and ask the student why he or she chose a red circle. The student should say that the germs from the first person's mouth can get on the cup. When the second person drinks from the cup, germs can be spread to that person.

Use the following situations in this activity:

- Two friends decide to become blood brothers. They prick their fingers and rub them together to exchange blood (red circle).

- A friend sneezes near you without covering his or her mouth (red circle).

- Two friends are sharing ice cream using the same spoon (red circle).

- You take your own toothbrush when sleeping overnight at a friend's house (green circle).

- A classmate has the flu but gets on the bus for school (red circle).

- A person washes his or her hands before going to the cafeteria for lunch (green circle).

- You play in the dirt with an exposed cut on your hand (red circle).

- A person wears special gloves to give first aid to someone with a nosebleed (green circle).

- A friend washes his hands after using the restroom (green circle).

- Your hamburger looks raw. You're hungry and eat it anyway (red circle).

Assessment

Ask students to think of their own scenarios that show how germs are spread and how germs are prevented from being spread. Have students write one scenario for how germs are spread and one scenario for how germs are prevented from being spread on a sheet of paper. Collect the sheets of paper. Read the sheets of paper for appropriateness. Place the sheets of paper in a hat or container. Ask for a student volunteer to come to the front of the class and read the scenarios. As the student volunteer reads each scenario, have the class show their red or green circles.

Name Those Defenses

The Curriculum

Life Skills

■ I will choose habits that prevent the spread of germs.

■ I will recognize symptoms and get treatment for communicable diseases.

Objectives

■ Students will list kinds of pathogens that cause disease.

■ Students will list body defenses that fight pathogens.

The National Health Education Standards

■ Students will comprehend concepts related to health promotion and disease prevention.

Preparing to Teach the Lesson Plan

Materials

Construction paper

Markers

Scissors

Blackline Master

Body Defenses

Teaching the Lesson Plan

1 Tell students that they will learn about their body defenses. Define body defenses. **Body defenses** are ways the body works to fight pathogens. Body defenses protect a person from germs. They help keep germs out of the body. They help a person to keep from getting sick.

2 Give each student a copy of the Blackline Master *Body Defenses*. Explain that the body protects itself from pathogens in the following ways:

Tears in Your Eyes
Tears in your eyes help keep pathogens out of your body. Each time you blink, a fluid coats your eyes. This fluid washes away dust and other particles. It washes away pathogens, too. Tears can kill some pathogens.

Tiny Hairs in Your Nose
Tiny hairs trap pathogens when you breathe. Then you cough or sneeze to get them out of your nose. This keeps pathogens from getting into your lungs.

Saliva in Your Mouth
Saliva helps break down food that you eat. A chemical in saliva also kills some pathogens.

Acid in Your Stomach
Acid in your stomach kills some pathogens if you swallow something that has pathogens in it.

Mucus That Lines Your Nose and Throat
Mucus is a moist coating that lines your nose and throat. Mucus traps pathogens before they enter your lungs. Then you cough or blow your nose to get rid of the pathogens.

Unbroken Skin That Covers Your Body
Your skin covers your body and keeps pathogens out.

3 Explain to students that sometimes pathogens get through a person's nose, eyes, mouth, skin, and stomach. When this happens, other body defenses help protect the person from pathogens. Define white blood cell. A **white blood cell** is a cell that surrounds and destroys pathogens. White blood cells surround and attack pathogens that enter a person's body. Define antibody. An **antibody** is a substance in the blood that helps kill pathogens. Tell students to suppose a person gets chickenpox. Chickenpox is a virus that begins as an itchy rash of small red spots. A person's body makes antibodies to the chickenpox virus when he or she gets chickenpox. The antibodies stay in the person's blood after he or she is well. If chickenpox enters the person's body again, the antibodies help protect him or her from getting the disease. Define vaccine. A **vaccine** is a substance that makes a person immune to a certain communicable disease. A person can get vaccines for some diseases. Vaccines protect a person from pathogens that cause certain diseases. For example, a person can get a vaccine for chickenpox. Then the person will not get chickenpox.

4 Tell students that they will play a game called "Name Those Defenses." Ask students to form groups of two or three people each. Pass out construction paper, markers, and scissors to each group. Tell each group to draw one picture that represents one of the nine body defenses you discussed. For example, you might tell group A to draw a picture that represents tears in the eyes. Group A might draw a large eye with a tear drop. Ask groups to cut out their drawings. Write the following terms on the board: "good health" and "your body." Tape the drawings above or below the term "your body." Tell students that they will try to protect their body's good health. They will place the body defenses around the term "good health." Tell students that you will describe body defenses without naming them. For example, you might say that if a person gets these, he or she will become immune to certain communicable diseases. Instruct a student to pick the correct answer from the body defenses and to name the body defense. If the student picks the correct answer—vaccine—he or she may tape the body defense above or below the term "good health" on the board. If the student does not pick the correct answer, the student cannot move the body defense to protect "good health." You might ask students to give clues to other students. Play until all the body defenses have been moved to protect good health.

Tell students that body defenses help protect them from disease, but sometimes they get sick anyway. There are three reasons students might get sick:

1. **The number of pathogens** Sometimes a person might have too many pathogens for the body to fight.

2. **The type of pathogen** Some pathogens are more difficult to kill than other pathogens.

3. **Their health** Body defenses work best when a person takes good care of his or her health all of the time. A person should eat healthful foods, get plenty of physical activity, and get enough rest and sleep.

Assessment

Ask students to write the name of a communicable disease on a sheet of paper. Students might write chickenpox, measles, cold, or flu. Ask students to write three body defenses that might help protect them from the disease. Have students write how that body defense would protect them. For example, a student might write that a vaccine for measles would make him or her immune to the measles virus. Have students write three healthful behaviors they practice that help their bodies fight disease.

Body Defenses

Tears in Your Eyes

Tears in your eyes help keep pathogens out of your body. Each time you blink, a fluid coats your eyes. This fluid washes away dust and other particles. It washes away pathogens, too. Tears can kill some pathogens.

Tiny Hairs in Your Nose

Tiny hairs trap pathogens when you breathe. Then you cough or sneeze to get them out of your nose. This keeps pathogens from getting into your lungs.

Saliva in Your Mouth

Saliva helps break down food that you eat. A chemical in saliva also kills some pathogens.

Acid in Your Stomach

Acid in your stomach kills some pathogens if you swallow something that has pathogens in it.

Mucus That Lines Your Nose and Throat

Mucus is a moist coating that lines your nose and throat. Mucus traps pathogens before they enter your lungs. Then you cough or blow your nose to get rid of the pathogens.

Unbroken Skin That Covers Your Body

Your skin covers your body and keeps pathogens out.

Body Defenses (continued)

Other Body Defenses

A **white blood cell** is a cell that surrounds and destroys pathogens.

An **antibody** is a substance in the blood that helps kill pathogens.

A **vaccine** is a substance that makes a person immune to a certain communicable disease.

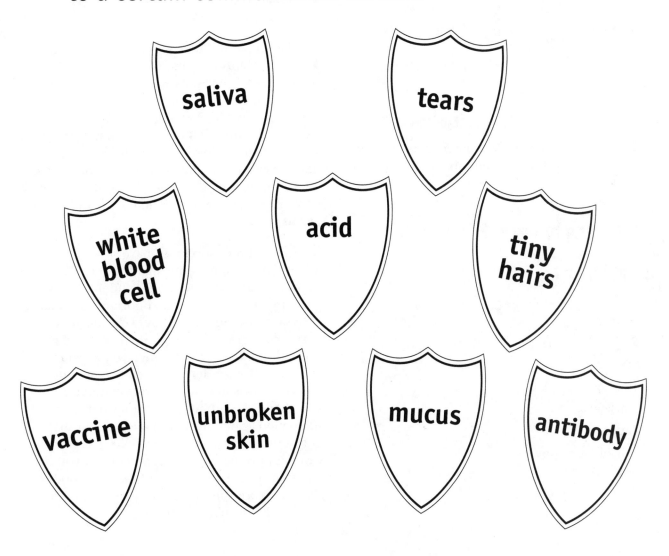

What to Know About HIV and AIDS

The Curriculum

Life Skills

■ I will choose habits that prevent the spread of germs.

■ I will recognize symptoms and get treatment for communicable diseases.

Objectives

■ Students will tell when a person has AIDS.

■ Students will tell ways HIV is spread.

■ Students will tell ways HIV is not spread.

■ Students will tell ways to keep from getting HIV.

■ Students will explain what HIV does to body defenses.

The National Health Education Standards

■ Students will comprehend concepts related to health promotion and disease prevention.

Preparing to Teach the Lesson Plan

Materials

Glass

Water

Red food coloring

Scissors

Two sheets of paper

Marker

Tape

Pair of latex gloves

Bowl

Blackline Master

Ways HIV Is and Is Not Spread

Teaching the Lesson Plan

Before class, prepare a glass of water tinted with red food coloring. Make two to three copies (depending on class size) of the Blackline Master Ways HIV Is and Is Not Spread. *Cut out one slip of paper for each student from the Blackline Master. Make two signs, one that reads "Ways HIV Is Spread" and one that reads "Ways HIV Is Not Spread." Attach them to the walls on opposite sides of the room.*

1 Place a pair of latex gloves on your hands. Ask students to name people they have seen wearing gloves. Students might answer doctors, nurses, and dentists. Explain that health care workers wear gloves when taking care of patients. Tell the class you are going to show why these workers wear gloves. Hold one hand over a bowl. Pour the glass of red-tinted water over that hand. Explain that the red-tinted water represents blood. The blood could have germs in it.

2 Take off the gloves and have students observe whether your hand is wet. Your hand should not be wet. Ask students to tell you why wearing gloves is important for health care workers. Students should answer that germs cannot pass through the glove and get on their hands. Hold an ungloved hand over the bowl. Tell students to pretend the water is blood. Pour some of the red-tinted water on your hand. Ask them to tell you what happened. Students might answer that the germs got on your hand. Explain that germs can get into the body through cuts. If you had a cut on your hand and you touched blood that had germs in it, the germs could get into your body through the cut.

3 Explain that one kind of germ that can be found in blood is HIV. Define HIV. **HIV** is the germ that causes AIDS. Define AIDS. **AIDS** is an illness in which the body cannot fight diseases. Tell students that health care workers do not always know if their patients have HIV. Many times people who have HIV have no symptoms. Define symptom. A **symptom** is a change from normal in a person's health. If blood from a person who has HIV gets into the blood of a health care worker, the health care worker can get HIV. This is why health care workers wear gloves.

4 Tell students they are going to learn how HIV makes a person ill. Define helper T cell. A **helper T cell** is a special kind of white blood cell. Helper T cells help fight germs. A person stays well when the helper T cells work as they should. Suppose HIV gets into a person's blood. HIV attacks and destroys helper T cells. There are fewer helper T cells to help fight germs. When the number of helper T cells gets very low, the person's body cannot fight off diseases. The person gets sick with certain diseases. Then the person has AIDS.

5 Explain that HIV can be spread only in certain ways. HIV can be spread by touching blood that has HIV in it. HIV can be spread by using a needle that has blood with HIV in it.

6 Tell students that they cannot get HIV from a person who has HIV if they

- sit next to the person;
- hug the person;
- shake hands with the person;
- use the same bathroom as the person;
- share a book or pencil with the person; or
- breathe droplets from the person's coughs or sneezes.

7 Discuss the following ways students can keep from getting HIV:

- Do not touch someone else's blood. Wear throw-away gloves if you help someone who is bleeding. Wash your hands with soap and water afterwards.

- Do not press your cut finger against the finger of another person. This is sometimes done to become a blood brother or sister.

- Do not share a needle. Never pierce ears or body parts without permission. Do not use harmful drugs.

Assessment

Give each student one of the slips of paper you cut out earlier. Point out the signs you have put on the walls. Tell students to read their slips to themselves and decide whether or not what is written on the slip is a way HIV is spread. If it is a way HIV is spread, they should move to the side of the room labeled "Ways HIV Is Spread." If it is not a way HIV is spread, they should move to the side of the room labeled "Ways HIV Is Not Spread." Read a slip out loud and demonstrate.

When all students have moved to a side of the room, have each student read his or her slip. Have the class decide whether the student is correct. If the student is not correct, he or she should walk over to the other side of the room.

Ways HIV Is and Is Not Spread

A person presses a tissue on someone's knee to stop bleeding. The person does not wear gloves.	A person shares a needle to pierce a body part.
A person shares a needle to pierce his or her ear.	A person sits next to a person who has HIV.
A person helps someone with a nosebleed. The person does not wear gloves.	A person hugs a person who has HIV.
	A person shakes hands with a person who has HIV.
A person presses his or her cut finger against the cut on another person's finger.	A person uses the same bathroom as a person who has HIV.
	A person shares a book with a person who has HIV.
A person shares a needle to use harmful drugs.	A person breathes droplets from the sneeze of a person who has HIV.

The Truth About HIV and AIDS

The Curriculum

Life Skills

■ I will choose habits that prevent the spread of germs.

■ I will recognize symptoms and get treatment for communicable diseases.

Objectives

■ Students will tell ways to keep from getting HIV.

■ Students will explain what HIV does to body defenses.

■ Students will tell symptoms that appear in people who have HIV.

■ Students will tell when a person has AIDS.

■ Students will tell ways HIV enters a person's body.

The National Health Education Standards

■ Students will comprehend concepts related to health promotion and disease prevention.

Preparing to Teach the Lesson Plan

Materials

None

Blackline Master

Ways HIV Is Spread

Teaching the Lesson Plan

1 Tell students they have probably heard of HIV and AIDS. Ask students if they can give definitions for HIV and AIDS. Define HIV. **HIV** is the germ that causes AIDS. Define AIDS. **AIDS** is an illness in which the body cannot fight diseases. HIV must enter the bloodstream to cause AIDS. HIV gets into helper T cells and destroys them. Define helper T cell. A **helper T cell** is a special kind of white blood cell. When helper T cells are destroyed, body defenses are weakened.

2 Explain that some people who get HIV do not have symptoms right away. They might have a fever or rash a few weeks after HIV enters the body. Several years later a person who has HIV might have weight loss, fever, tiredness, and mouth infections.

3 Tell students that a person who gets infected with HIV does not have AIDS right away. A person has AIDS when the person has a very low number of helper T cells. The person gets sick with certain diseases.

4 Explain that HIV is spread only in certain ways. HIV must get into the bloodstream. A person can get HIV in these ways:

• using a needle used by someone who has HIV;

• cutting his or her finger and rubbing it against a cut of someone who has HIV. This is done sometimes to become a blood brother or blood sister; and

• touching the blood from a nosebleed or cut of another person.

5 Tell students they can keep from getting HIV by taking the following actions:

• do not share a needle to use drugs;

• do not share a needle to pierce your ears or other body parts;

• do not share a needle to get a tattoo;

• do not cut your finger and rub it against a cut on someone else; and

• wear throw-away gloves if you help someone with a nosebleed or cut. Wash your hands with soap and water after you take off the gloves.

6 Explain that a person cannot get HIV in these ways:

• hugging;

• shaking hands;

• sharing pencils;

• using the same bathroom;

• eating food prepared by a person who has HIV; or

• breathing droplets from a cough or sneeze of a person who has HIV.

7 Give each student a copy of the Blackline Master *Ways HIV Is Spread*. Read each situation and have students check "Yes" or "No" depending on whether HIV is spread in that way. Review the answers.

Assessment

You might want to conduct this activity in the gym or on a playing field. Choose five students to represent HIV. Have the rest of the class stand in a circle and join hands. Tell these students they represent the bloodstream. They will listen as you call out situations. If you call out a situation in which HIV can get into the bloodstream, the students are to let go of each other's hands and let students who represent HIV into the circle. If you call out a situation in which HIV cannot get into the bloodstream, the students keep holding hands. The students who represent HIV stand outside the circle. They cannot get in the circle. Use the list from the Blackline Master *Ways HIV Is Spread*.

© 2001 Everyday Learning Corporation

Ways HIV Is Spread

Listen as your teacher reads the following list. Put a check in the "Yes" box if HIV is spread in that way. Put a check in the "No" box if HIV is not spread in that way.

		Yes	No
1.	You go to a party. Several people are piercing their ears. They use the same needle.		
2.	You want to join a club. The club members tell you that you must cut your finger. You must rub it against all their cut fingers.		
3.	You use a pencil that was used by a person who has HIV.		
4.	You put your bare hand over the cut of another person to try to stop the bleeding.		
5.	A person who has HIV coughs in your direction.		
6.	You hug a person who has HIV.		
7.	A person shares a needle to use drugs.		
8.	You use the same bathroom as a person who has HIV.		
9.	You shake hands with a person who has HIV.		
10.	You help a person who has a nosebleed and you wear throw-away gloves.		

The Blended Family

The Curriculum

Life Skill

■ I will adjust to family changes in healthful ways.

Objectives

■ Students will explain how a family changes when there is a new baby or child.

■ Students will explain how a family changes if parents divorce or remarry.

■ Students will tell ways a family might adjust if

—a family member is ill or injured.

—a family member dies.

—a parent or guardian loses a job.

—the family has to move.

—parents divorce.

The National Health Education Standards

■ Students will demonstrate the ability to practice health-enhancing behavior and reduce health risks.

Preparing to Teach the Lesson Plan

Materials

Three types of fruits, such as oranges, strawberries, and apples

Blender

One cup of water

Three glasses

Blackline Master

Adjusting to Family Changes

Teaching the Lesson Plan

1 Define family. Your **family** is the group of people to whom you are related. Explain that many families are blended families. A blended family might have a mother or father who has been married before. That parent might bring children from a prior marriage to the current marriage.

2 Tell students that blended families are alike and different. Show students the different fruits you brought to class. Pour the cup of water into the blender. Put the strawberries into the blender. Blend the strawberries and water together. Pour the mixture into a glass. Do the same for the other fruits, keeping fruits separated by type. After the other fruits are blended and poured into glasses, explain that each glass represents an original family. Tell students to observe the different qualities of each mixture. Students might say that the strawberry mixture has seeds. Students might say that the orange mixture has pulp. Explain that each mixture or "family" has its own special qualities.

3 Now place all the mixtures into the blender and blend them together. Pour the new mixture into one of the glasses. Explain that the new mixture looks different from the original mixture. The different "families" were blended. Define blended family. The **blended family** is a family of people from different families that give the new family a different character. Just as the new mixture might appear different from the original mixtures, the blended family will behave in ways that differ from the ways the families behaved before they were blended.

4 Explain to students that relationships will change when a family becomes a blended family. A person in a blended family might

© 2001 Everyday Learning Corporation

have to form relationships with new brothers and sisters or with a new parent. A person in a blended family might have to share belongings or property with a new brother or sister. For example, a person might have to share a bathroom. A person might need to help care for a new, younger child or baby. Parents in a blended family might have changes in responsibilities to children in the family. For example, a parent might spend time with new children in the family. Ask students what other changes might occur when a family becomes a blended family.

5 Tell students that when family changes occur, a person can adjust. Define adjust. To **adjust** is to change and make right or better. There are ways to adjust when a family becomes a blended family. Talking to parents about changes can help parents and their children understand each other's feelings. This can help them adjust to changes.

6 Explain to students that *all* families change. Even families that are not blended families undergo change. Give each student a copy of the Blackline Master *Adjusting to Family Changes*. Tell students the following ways a family might change:

• a family member is ill or injured;

• a family member dies;

• a parent or guardian loses a job; or

• a family has to move.

Assessment

Ask students to imagine that they are reporters for a magazine called *The Blended Family*. Have them select a topic for an article based on some of the changes that blended family members undergo. For example, a student might select the topic of relationships with new sisters and brothers. Based on their topics, have students write headlines for their articles. A student might write the following headline: "Sharing Shows Caring to New Brothers and Sisters." Then have students write a brief article that explains the family changes and tells how to adjust to the family changes.

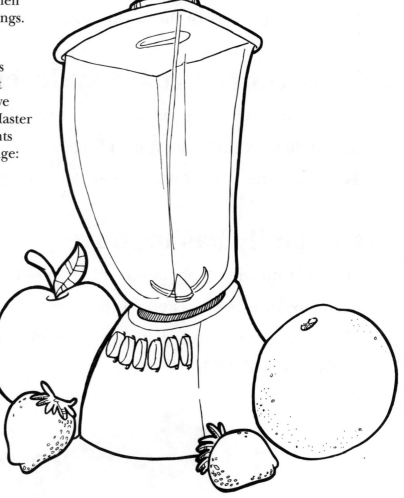

347

Adjusting to Family Changes

If a family member is ill or injured

■ Pitch in and help with chores.

■ Show the family member who is ill or injured that you care.

■ Ask your parents or guardians questions about what will happen next.

If a family member dies

■ Express grief rather than keeping it in.

■ Discuss fears with a parent or guardian.

■ Share memories of the person with other family members.

If a parent or guardian loses a job

■ Give support to the family member who lost a job.

■ Ask how to cut back on spending.

■ Ask a parent or guardian about other changes the job loss might cause.

If a family has to move

■ Talk with friends about ways to keep in touch.

■ Share your feelings about the move with family members.

■ Ask a parent or guardian any questions you have about the move.

Family Cultures

The Curriculum

Life Skills

■ I will get along with my family.

■ I will follow my family's guidelines.

Objectives

■ Students will tell the special names for each person who belongs to a family.

■ Students will explain how to be a loving family member.

■ Students will explain reasons why they should follow family guidelines.

■ Students will discuss reasons why it is important to be close to their families.

■ Students will tell ways they can cooperate with family members.

The National Health Education Standards

■ Students will demonstrate the ability to use interpersonal communication skills to enhance health.

Preparing to Teach the Lesson Plan

Materials

Family photograph

Blackline Master

Special Family Names

Teaching the Lesson Plan

Ask students to bring to class a photograph of their family during a holiday or other event. You can send a letter home to students' parents or guardians

telling them that you would like their child to bring to class a family picture. Tell the parents or guardians that the photograph should show something unique about how that family celebrates a holiday or other event. For example, a student might bring in a photograph of his or her family celebrating Hanukkah, Christmas, or Kwanza. A student might bring to class a photograph of his or her family having a family meal or attending the graduation of an older family member.

1 Explain that there are many different kinds of families. Define family. A **family** is the group of people to whom you are related. There are large families and small families. There are blended families and single-parent families. There are families whose members all live in the same city. There are families whose members do not live in the same city. Families come from many different cultures. They have many different beliefs and customs. Families are unique in some ways and similar in other ways.

2 Tell students that each family member has a special name. Give each student a copy of the Blackline Master *Special Family Names*. Tell students that every member of the family has at least one special name. Often, a family member has more than one special name. For example, a person might be a mother to one family member *and* a sister to another family member. Ask students to say all of the special names that apply to them. A student might answer that he is a son and a brother.

3 Tell students that families are different in many ways. Tell students that they are going to learn about different kinds of families. Learning about other families can help a person have respect for other families. A person can learn to respect other ways families do things.

4 Explain to the class that it is important to spend time with one's family. Sharing special times such as holidays and other celebrations with one's family brings family members closer together. It creates a bond. It creates time for family members to learn to cooperate and to respect one another. Tell students that they can show respect for other family members by following family guidelines. Define family guideline. A **family guideline** is a rule set by your parents or guardians that tells you how to act. Tell students that parents and guardians make family guidelines to protect them.

5 Ask students to show their pictures to the class one at a time. As a student shows a picture to the class, ask the other students the following questions:

- How many family members are present?
- Which family members are present?
- What are the family members wearing?
- What is the occasion or event that is shown in the picture?
- What activities are the family members doing?
- What foods are the family members eating?

Ask the student showing the picture to title the picture. A student showing a picture of a family meal might title his or her picture, "The Jones Family Is Cookin'."

Assessment

Have students pair up with other students whose photographs are similar. For example, students whose pictures show their families celebrating a holiday could pair up. Or students whose pictures show their families eating a meal together could pair up. Ask students to draw a line down the center of a sheet of paper. Have students write the word "Different" at the top of the first column. Then have students write the word "Alike" at the top of the other column. Ask students to study their partner's photograph. Then have students write under each heading the ways in which their families are alike and the ways in which their families are different. Ask students to present what is alike and what is different to the class.

Special Family Names

mother: female parent of a child.

father: male parent of a child.

daughter: female child. A girl or woman is the daughter of her mother and father.

son: male child. A boy or man is the son of his mother and father.

brother: boy or man having the same parents as another person.

sister: girl or woman having the same parents as another person.

grandmother: mother of a person's mother or father.

grandfather: father of a person's mother or father.

granddaughter: daughter of a person's son or daughter.

grandson: son of a person's son or daughter.

aunt: sister of a person's mother or father. The wife of a person's uncle.

uncle: brother of a person's mother or father. The husband of a person's aunt.

cousin: son or daughter of an aunt or uncle.

brother-in-law: brother of a person's husband or wife. The husband of a sister.

sister-in-law: sister of a person's husband or wife. The wife of a brother.

TLC for Older Family Members

The Curriculum

Life Skill

■ I will get along with my family.

Objectives

■ Students will explain how to be a loving family member.

■ Students will discuss reasons why it is important to be close to their families.

■ Students will tell ways they can cooperate with family members.

The National Health Education Standards

■ Students will demonstrate the ability to use interpersonal communication skills to enhance health.

Preparing to Teach the Lesson Plan

Materials

Tissues, one for each student

A book

Chalkboard

Chalk

Blackline Master

Help Older People with Special Needs

Teaching the Lesson Plan

1 Ask students whether they have an older family member such as a grandparent or great-grandparent. Students will probably say that they do. Explain that although most older

people are healthy, some are not. Some older people have physical handicaps. Define handicap. A **handicap** is a special need that a person has. Explain that some older people have special needs. Some older people might need help seeing. They might need help hearing. They might need help moving. An older person who needs help seeing might wear special glasses. An older person who needs help hearing might need people to speak loudly so he or she can hear. An older person who needs help moving might need a wheelchair or a walker. Define walker. A **walker** is a support to help a person walk. Define handicapped ramp. A **handicapped ramp** is a path that makes it easier for people who have special needs to go up and down.

2 Tell students that they are going to experience what it might feel like to lose some of the body functions a person loses as he or she ages. Define age. To **age** is to grow older. Have each student in the class hold a tissue in front of his or her eyes. The tissue should be thin enough for a student to see through, but not clearly. Hold up various numbers of fingers. Ask students how many fingers you are holding up. Students probably will not see the correct number of fingers. Explain to students that they just experienced what it might be like to have cataracts on their eyes. Define cataract. A **cataract** is a clouding of the lens of the eye that makes it difficult to see. Many older people have cataracts. Surgery can help correct this condition.

3 Tell students that older people also might need help moving. They might need help sitting or standing. Some older people have arthritis. Define arthritis. **Arthritis** is a condition in which joints become swollen and sore. Ask one-half of the class to stand in front of their seats. Have the other half of the class observe. Tell students that they must sit without bending their knees. Then tell students to stand without bending their knees. Ask the students who are observing to describe what they have seen. Students will say that the students stood and sat with difficulty. Tell students that arthritis affects joints such as the knee joint. It is important to be patient around older people who might have difficulty moving.

4 Explain that some older people need help hearing. Tell students to listen as you read from a book. Begin to read at a normal volume. As you read, soften your voice. Students will have difficulty hearing you. Soften your voice until you cannot be heard at all. Explain to students that some older people need help hearing. Tell students that they should speak louder if they are around a

person who needs help hearing. Give each student a copy of the Blackline Master *Help Older People with Special Needs*.

Assessment

Write the following phrases on a chalkboard:
- a person who needs help hearing;
- a person who needs help seeing;
- a person who needs help moving.

Ask students to come to the board and write under the correct phrase a way they might help a person with that special need. Students might write that they might help a person who needs help seeing by reading him or her directions or by locating his or her glasses.

Help Older People with Special Needs

- Be a friend to people who have special needs.

- Offer to help older people who have special needs.

- Do not play on a handicapped ramp or put your bike in a handicapped space.

Seed Needs

The Curriculum

Life Skill

■ I will learn facts about pregnancy and childbirth.

Objectives

■ Students will tell what fertilization is.

■ Students will tell actions a mother-to-be can take to care for a baby while it is growing inside her.

The National Health Education Standards

■ Students will comprehend concepts related to health promotion and disease prevention.

Preparing to Teach the Lesson Plan

Materials

Flower seeds in an envelope

Flowerpot

Soil

Water

Construction paper

Scissors

Teaching the Lesson Plan

Obtain an envelope that contains flower seeds. The envelope should show a picture of the flowering plant that will develop. Obtain a flowerpot and soil. Put the soil in the flowerpot.

1 Show the class the flower seeds. Select one seed. Show the class the picture on the envelope. Tell the class that this one seed can grow into the flower shown on the envelope. Tell them that the seed will need special care to grow into a flower.

2 Tell students that the seed came from a parent flower. Plant the seed in the soil according to the directions on the package. Explain to the class that the seed must be in soil for it to grow. The seed also must have water and sunlight for it to grow. The seed must be kept warm. Explain that taking care of the seed will help the seed grow.

3 Tell students that they grew from a single cell that was made by their parents. Tell them you are going to explain how the single cell from which they began was made. Explain that a male makes sperm and a female makes ova. Define sperm and ovum. A **sperm** is a male reproductive cell. An **ovum** is a female reproductive cell. Define fertilization. **Fertilization** is the joining of an ovum and a sperm to make a single cell. A **fertilized egg** is the single cell that is formed from an ovum and a sperm.

4 Remind students that the seed from the plant was placed in rich soil so that it would grow. Then it was given water and sunshine. Tell students the fertilized egg must have a special place to grow. It grows in a special place inside its mother. Asked students if they have ever seen a female who is pregnant. Tell them that a female is pregnant when she has a fertilized egg growing inside her. The fertilized egg is growing into a baby. There is a special place inside the female's body. It is a place where the fertilized egg is kept warm. It is a place where the fertilized egg is kept safe from injury. The fertilized egg gets food to grow from the female. This is why she must eat healthful foods. She also must not smoke cigarettes or cigars or breathe the smoke from other people's cigarettes or cigars. There are harmful substances in cigarette and cigar smoke that can harm the fertilized egg as it grows into a baby. A female who is pregnant also cannot drink alcohol. Define alcohol. **Alcohol** is a depressant drug found in some beverages.

5 Define pregnancy. **Pregnancy** is the time between fertilization and birth. Tell students that pregnancy lasts about nine months. The baby gets bigger and bigger inside the female who is pregnant. Then the baby is big enough to live outside her body. Then the baby will be born. A baby is usually born at a hospital.

6 Have students keep track of the growing seed. As the seed grows into a flower, students will notice that the flower begins to look like the flower on the seed's envelope. A baby will look like its parents also.

7 Ask students what they think would happen to the seed if they did not take care of it. Ask students what they think would happen if they did not water the seed or if it was not placed in sunlight. Tell students a female who is pregnant must choose actions to care for the baby growing inside her. She must not drink alcohol. She must not smoke. She must not breathe smoke from others. She must eat healthful foods.

Assessment

Give each student a piece of construction paper. Have students draw a flower with four petals on it. Have students cut out the flower. Have students write on the flower petals the four actions a female who is pregnant must choose.

How a Baby Is Made

The Curriculum

Life Skill

■ I will learn facts about pregnancy and childbirth.

Objective

■ Students will tell what fertilization is.

The National Health Education Standards

■ Students will comprehend concepts related to health promotion and disease prevention.

Preparing to Teach the Lesson Plan

Materials

Clay

Blackline Master

Fertilization

Teaching the Lesson Plan

1 Define family. A **family** is the group of people to whom you are related. Explain that one of the reasons a man and woman marry is to have a family. A married couple might choose to make a baby or to adopt a baby or an child.

2 Tell students that you are going to explain how a baby is made. Explain that it takes both a male and female to make a baby. A baby is made when a sperm from a male and an ovum or egg from a female join together. Define ovum. An **ovum** is a female reproductive cell. Take a piece of clay and roll it into a ball. Tell students that the an ovum is very tiny. A **sperm** is a male reproductive cell. Take a piece of clay and roll it into a very small ball. Tell students that a sperm is very tiny. It is even smaller than an ovum or egg.

3 Define fertilization. **Fertilization** is the joining of an ovum and a sperm to make a single cell. Take the clay ovum and the clay sperm and roll them together. Tell students that a fertilized ovum or fertilized egg is an ovum that has been joined by a sperm. Give each student a copy of the Blackline Master *Fertilization*. Explain to students that fertilization usually takes place inside the mother-to-be's body. It takes place in a special tube. Point to and say "Fallopian tube." Then explain that the fertilized egg moves down the tube to a special place. Point to the uterus. Tell students the baby grows inside this special place until the baby is ready to be born. Explain that it takes about nine months before the baby will be born.

4 Tell students that there is another way for a married couple to have a baby. They can adopt a baby. To **adopt** is to take a child of other parents into a family. Some married couples choose to adopt a newborn baby. Other married couples choose to adopt older children.

5 Tell students that a married couple is very happy when it has a baby or adopts a baby. Teach students the first two lines of lyrics for the song "You've Made Me So Very Happy" by Blood, Sweat, and Tears. The lyrics are

You've made me so very happy.

I'm so glad you came into my life.

Assessment

Ask students to define ovum, sperm, fertilization, and adopt. Give each student a copy of the Blackline Master *Fertilization*. Ask students to point to the sperm, to the ovum, and to the fertilized ovum. Ask them how long it takes for a baby to be born.

Fertilization

Fertilization usually occurs in the fallopian tube.
Fertilization is the joining of an ovum and a sperm to make a single cell.

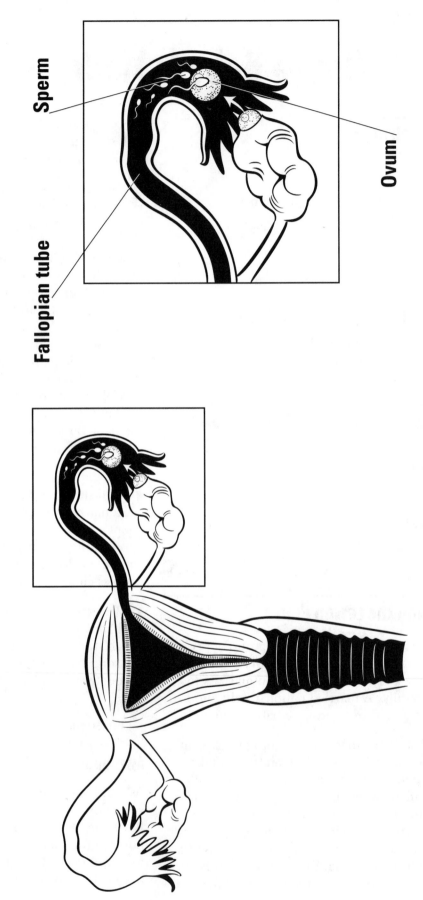

Sperm

Fallopian tube

Ovum

© 2001 Everyday Learning Corporation

358

How a Baby Is Born

The Curriculum

Life Skill

■ I will learn facts about pregnancy and childbirth.

Objectives

■ Students will tell what fertilization is.

■ Students will tell actions a mother-to-be can take to care for a baby while it is growing inside her.

■ Students will tell how a baby is born.

The National Health Education Standards

■ Students will comprehend concepts related to health promotion and disease prevention.

Preparing to Teach the Lesson Plan

Materials

A sock

A stuffed animal

Old magazines

Scissors

Two paper bags

Blackline Masters

Healthful and Harmful Substances for a Developing Baby

Childbirth

Teaching the Lesson Plan

1 Tell students that they are going to learn how a baby is born. Define fertilization. **Fertilization** is the joining of an ovum and a sperm to make a single cell. An ovum is a female reproductive cell. A sperm is a male reproductive cell. Define fertilized egg. A **fertilized egg** is the single cell that is formed from an ovum and a sperm. Fertilization usually takes place in a fallopian tube. Define fallopian tube. A **fallopian tube** is a tube that connects the ovary and the uterus. Explain that a fertilized egg moves from a fallopian tube to the uterus. The uterus is a body organ in the female that holds a developing baby. Tell students that the uterus is located near the stomach.

2 Tell students that a mother-to-be's health habits can affect a baby that is growing inside of her uterus. Give each student a copy of the Blackline Master *Healthful and Harmful Substances for a Developing Baby*.

When a mother-to-be has healthful substances in her blood, she promotes the health of her unborn baby. These healthful substances can pass from the mother-to-be's blood into the blood of the unborn baby:

• vitamins and minerals from healthful foods and supplements;

• calcium from milk and other dairy products.

The unborn baby is at risk if the mother-to-be has harmful substances in her blood. These harmful substances can pass from the mother-to-be's blood into the blood of the unborn baby:

• nicotine from cigarette smoke;

• crack or cocaine;

• alcohol;

• chemicals in glues or pesticides;

• ingredients in secondhand smoke;

• caffeine;

• HIV.

3 Tell students that this activity will show how a baby is born. Give each student a copy of the Blackline Master *Childbirth*. Define labor. **Labor** is a series of changes that results in the birth of a baby. Define childbirth. **Childbirth** is the process in which the baby moves from the uterus to the outside of the mother's body. Hold up a sock containing a small stuffed animal. Explain that the sock represents the uterus. The stuffed animal represents a baby. Tell students that the baby inside the uterus is ready to come out of the female's body. It has been growing and developing for nine months. Define contractions. **Contractions** are a tightening of the muscles in the uterus when a baby is to be born. When a baby is to be born, there are many contractions, one after another. Explain that the contractions push the baby through the opening of the uterus. Push the baby (stuffed animal) slightly through the uterus (sock). Tell students that the opening of the sock represents the opening of the uterus, or cervix. As the baby's head pushes through the uterus, the opening of the uterus widens, or dilates. The baby then moves through the uterus and into the birth canal, or vagina.

4 You can modify this activity by using the neck of the sock as the birth canal. As you push the stuffed animal through the sock, explain that the walls of the birth canal stretch to allow the baby to pass through. You also can modify this activity to explain what happens during a cesarean section. Explain that sometimes a baby cannot pass through the birth canal. A doctor will perform a cesarean section. Define cesarean section. A **cesarean section** is a procedure in which the doctor performs surgery to remove the baby. The doctor makes a cut through the stomach area into the uterus of the mother. The baby is removed from the uterus.

Assessment

Give students the old magazines. Ask students to cut out pictures of healthful substances that are good for a developing baby. Students might cut out pictures of healthful foods such as fruits. Have students also cut out pictures of harmful substances that are not good for a developing baby. Students might cut out pictures of cigarettes or alcoholic beverages. Write the word "baby" or draw a baby on each of the paper bags. When students are finished cutting out pictures, put all the pictures face down on a desk. Place the two paper bags at the opposite end of the room. Be sure to clear a path from the magazine pictures to the paper bags. Divide the class into two teams. Have the teams stand on opposite sides of the desk with the magazine pictures on it. Tell students that the object of the game is to give ten healthful substances to "the baby." One team member from one of the teams picks a picture. The team member must say what the picture is and tell whether the substance is healthful or harmful. If the substance is harmful, the picture is returned to the pile face down, and a team member from the other team takes a turn. If the substance is healthful, then the team member walks to his or her team's paper bag and places the picture in the bag. A team member from the opposite team picks a picture as soon as the team member from the first team begins walking toward the bag. The first team to give the baby ten healthful substances wins.

Healthful and Harmful Substances for a Developing Baby

When a mother-to-be has healthful substances in her blood, she promotes the health of the unborn baby. These healthful substances can pass from the mother-to-be's blood into the blood of the unborn baby:

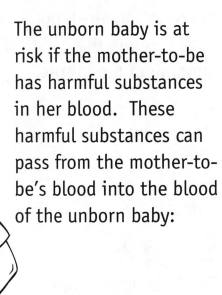

The unborn baby is at risk if the mother-to-be has harmful substances in her blood. These harmful substances can pass from the mother-to-be's blood into the blood of the unborn baby:

- **Vitamins and minerals from healthful foods and supplements**

- **Calcium from milk and other dairy products**

- **Nicotine from cigarette smoke**

- **Crack or cocaine**

- **Alcohol**

- **Chemicals in glues or pesticides**

- **Ingredients in secondhand smoke**

- **Caffeine**

- **HIV**

Childbirth

Stage 1

Contractions push the baby through the opening of the uterus.

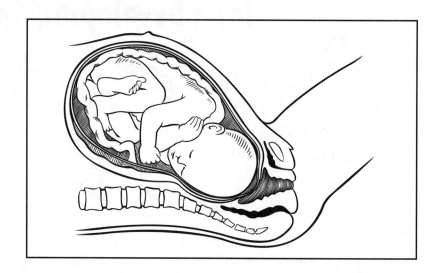

Stage 2

The baby moves into the birth canal.

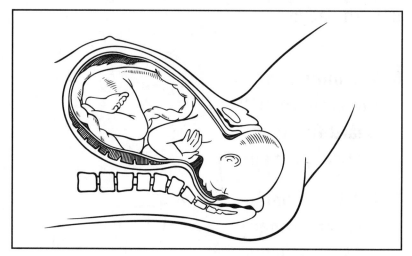

Stage 3

The walls of the birth canal stretch to let the baby pass through.

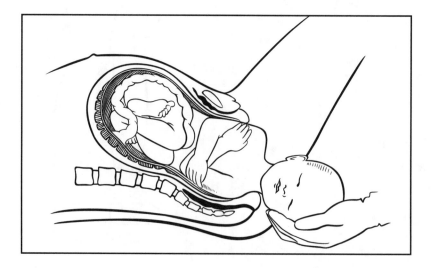

© 2001 Everyday Learning Corporation

Grades 5–6
Lesson Plans and Blackline Masters

Table of Contents

Armor of Responsibility

The Curriculum

Life Skills

■ I will make responsible decisions.

■ I will use resistance skills when appropriate.

Objectives

■ Students will use *The Responsible Decision-Making Model*™.

■ Students will tell the difference between a responsible action and a wrong action.

■ Students will tell steps to correct wrong actions.

■ Students will identify resistance skills they can use to resist pressure to make a wrong decision.

■ Students will show how to use resistance skills.

■ Students will explain what to do if a friend plans to do something wrong.

The National Health Education Standards

■ Students will demonstrate the ability to use goal-setting and decision-making skills that enhance health.

Preparing to Teach the Lesson Plan

Materials

Construction paper

Markers

Scissors

Blackline Master

The Responsible Decision-Making Model™

Teaching the Lesson Plan

Make a shield and armor from construction paper. The shield and armor should be large enough so that it covers a specific area, such as a student's chest. To make a shield, outline it using a marker. The armor can be any shape, as long as it can be recognized by students as armor.

Cut out arrows from construction paper. The arrows should be about two inches wide and from 1 to 2 feet in length. The arrows should have statements written on them that are used to pressure a student into doing something wrong. Write one of each of the following pressure statements on each of the arrows.

"Come on, smoke a cigarette."

"Come to my party. My parents won't be home."

"Can I copy your homework?"

"I dare you to put a CD in your backpack and walk out of the store."

"Let's play a practical joke on the teacher."

1 Call two students to the front of the classroom. Give one student the armor. Tell the class to pretend that the armor has *The Responsible Decision-Making Model*™ on it. Define *The Responsible Decision-Making Model*™. The ***The Responsible Decision-Making Model*** ™ is six questions to ask to make sure your decision is healthful, is safe, follows rules and laws, shows respect for yourself and others, follows your family's guidelines, and shows good character. Give each student a copy of the Blackline Master *The Responsible Decision-Making Model*™. Review the Blackline Master with students. Take each arrow and place it so that the pointed end hits the armor. Tell students that the arrows represent pressure statements to do something wrong. When the arrow strikes the armor, read what is written on the arrow.

2 Repeat the demonstration, this time with the student not wearing the armor. Ask the class to identify who might be affected more by the arrows: the person with the armor or the person without the armor. Students should say that the person without the armor would be more affected.

3 Show students each arrow again. Students should tell how they can use *The Responsible Decision-Making Model*™ to protect themselves in each situation written on the arrows. For example, show the class the arrow that reads, "You're asked if you would like to smoke a cigarette." Ask students to apply *The Responsible Decision-Making Model*™ to the pressure statement. Students might say, "No, smoking is not healthful: it causes lung cancer. Smoking is not safe: it can cause a fire. Smoking does not follow laws: it is illegal for a minor to smoke. Smoking does not show respect for myself and others: it is dangerous to both myself and others. Smoking does not follow family guidelines: my family does not want me to smoke. Smoking does not show good character: it shows that I give in to peer pressure."

4 Define wrong action. A **wrong action** is an action that is harmful, is unsafe, breaks rules and laws, does not show that you respect yourself and others, does not follow your family's guidelines, and does not show good character. Tell students the following steps to correct wrong actions:

- Take responsibility for what you have done.
- Say that you are sorry and promise never to do what you did again.
- Talk to your parents or guardians about what you did.
- Accept punishment for what you did.
- Make up for your wrong actions.

Assessment

Have students make their own arrows and write on them pressure statements to do something wrong. Write their pressure statements on the chalkboard. Have students respond to the pressure statements by using *The Responsible Decision-Making Model*™.

© 2001 Everyday Learning Corporation

The Responsible Decision-Making Model™

- **Is it healthful?**

- **Is it safe?**

- **Do I follow rules and laws?**

- **Do I show respect for myself and others?**

- **Do I follow my family's guidelines?**

- **Do I show good character?**

The Character Connection

The Curriculum

Life Skill

■ I will show good character.

Objectives

■ Students will tell reasons to show good character.

■ Students will give examples of family values.

■ Students will tell actions that show they have self-respect.

■ Students will tell what to do if others don't respect them.

■ Students will tell ways to show respect for others.

■ Students will tell reasons to participate in The Family Round Table.

The National Health Education Standards

■ Students will demonstrate the ability to practice health-enhancing behaviors and reduce health risks.

Preparing to Teach the Lesson Plan

Materials

Construction paper
Scissors
Markers
Tape

Blackline Master

Family Values

Teaching the Lesson Plan

1 Define character. **Character** is the effort you make to do what is right. Ask students how they know what is right. Tell them that their family values will help them know what is right. Define family values. **Family values** are beliefs that keep the family and society strong.

2 Give each student a copy of the Blackline Master *Family Values*. Review the following family values and definitions:

honesty Honesty is telling the truth and not misleading anyone.

self-discipline Self-discipline is the effort you make to follow through.

fairness Fairness is following the rules so that everyone has the same chance.

avoidance of risk behaviors Avoidance of risk behaviors is choosing to not participate in actions that can be harmful to you and others.

determination Determination is working hard to get what you want.

courage Courage is showing strength when you might otherwise be afraid.

citizenship Citizenship is following the laws of your community and nation.

responsibility Responsibility is being accountable for what you say and do.

respect Respect is thinking highly of someone.

integrity Integrity is acting on responsible values regardless of the consequences.

3 Give students construction paper, markers, scissors, and tape. Have students each cut a strip from the construction paper. The strip should be a foot long and two inches wide. Tell students that they will use this strip to make one link of a chain. But, first they are going to write one family value on the strip. Have students number off from one to ten. Their assigned number will correspond with one on the list of family values on the Blackline Master *Family Values.*

4 Explain to students that they are going to make a chain using the strips of paper they have prepared. Each of their strips will become one of the links in the chain. Have one student begin by reading what is written on his or her strip. Then this student will take the strip and tape its ends together to make a link. Then have a second student read what is written on his or her strip. Then this student will put his or her strip through the link of the first student and form it into a link by taping its ends together. Proceed until every student has added a link to the chain.

5 Tell students that the chain represents the family values that they must practice to have good character. Explain that the chain links are connected. Further explain that the character connection is important. To keep good character, students must choose friends who have good character. If not, they might be tempted to participate in wrong actions.

To keep good character, they need to spend time with their family. They might participate in The Family Round Table. **The Family Round Table** is a special time when family members meet as a group to talk.

6 Define wrong action. A **wrong action** is an action that is harmful, is unsafe, breaks rules and laws, does not show that you respect yourself and others, does not follow your family's guidelines, and does not show good character. Tell students to correct wrong actions.

- Take responsibility for what you have done;
- Say that you are sorry and promise never to do what you did again;
- Talk to your parents or guardians about what you did;
- Accept punishment for what you did;
- Make up for your wrong actions.

7 Define self-respect. **Self-respect** is thinking highly of yourself. Have students tell ways they show self-respect. Discuss respect for others. Define privacy. **Privacy** is having a place and the time to be alone. Explain that giving family members their privacy is a way to show respect for them.

Assessment

Have students work in groups of six to design a Character Magazine. Each group must write a table of contents for the magazine including articles to cover six objectives for this lesson. Each group can brainstorm the articles to be included. Then each of the six students in the group will write one of the articles.

Family Values

1. honesty
Honesty is telling the truth and not misleading anyone.

2. self-discipline
Self-discipline is the effort you make to follow through.

3. fairness
Fairness is following the rules so that everyone has the same chance.

4. abstinence from sex
Abstinence from sex is choosing not be sexually active.

5. determination
Determination is working hard to get what you want.

6. courage
Courage is showing strength when you might otherwise be afraid.

7. citizenship
Citizenship is following the laws of your community and nation.

8. responsibility
Responsibility is being accountable for what you say and do.

9. respect
Respect is thinking highly of someone.

10. integrity
Integrity is acting on responsible values regardless of the consequences.

I-Message Match-Up

The Curriculum

Life Skills

■ I will express feelings in healthful ways.

■ I will use conflict resolution skills.

Objectives

■ Students will tell the three parts of an I-message.

■ Students will use I-messages to express feelings.

■ Students will explain how to listen and respond when someone else shares feelings.

■ Students will explain how settling internal conflicts protects students' health.

■ Students will explain how settling conflict with others protects students' health.

■ Students will explain how to use conflict resolution skills.

■ Students will explain how a trusted adult can help you with mediation.

The National Health Education Standards

■ Students will demonstrate the ability to use interpersonal communication skills to enhance health.

Preparing to Teach the Lesson Plan

Materials

Paper

Pen or pencil

Scissors

Blackline Master

How to Settle Conflicts

Teaching the Lesson Plan

1 Tell students that they can express feelings in healthful ways by using I-messages. Define I-message. An **I-message** is a statement that includes a behavior, the effect of the behavior, and the feeling that results. Write the following example on the board:

> Suppose a classmate promises to study with you before a big exam. You promise to meet at the library. Your classmate does not show up and you are angry.

Tell students they can use the following I-message to express their feelings to the friend:

1. When you did not show up to the library to study (behavior).

2. I was not able to study as well and was less prepared for the test (the effect of the behavior).

3. I was angry and hurt (the feeling that that resulted).

2 Explain that an I-message does not put another person on the defensive. Instead it shares feelings in an honest way. This allows the other person to respond. The other person does not feel blamed or shamed. Tell students to think of a situation in which they were really angry. Have them write an I-message for this situation on a sheet of paper. Then tell students they are to take another sheet of paper and cut it into three strips. They are to write each of the three parts to their I-message on one of the three strips of paper. Divide the class into four groups. Have each group shuffle its strips of paper. Then have each group exchange their pile of paper strips with another group. Tell groups to put together the I-messages. The first group to put all its paper strips into I-messages wins. Discuss the importance of listening and responding when someone shares feelings.

3 Tell students that using I-messages can help them avoid conflicts. But sometimes conflicts are unavoidable. Define conflict. A **conflict** is a disagreement. Explain that sometimes a person might have internal conflicts with himself or herself. A person might have conflicts with others. Conflicts need to be settled. Settling conflicts protects a person's health. A person is less likely to experience the body changes from being stressed out. He or she is less likely to have health conditions, such as a headache or an upset stomach. A person will sleep better. Settling conflicts also reduces a person's risk of harm from violence. Define violence. **Violence** is an act that harms oneself, others, or property. A person protects himself from injury when he or she knows how to settle conflicts.

4 Give each student a copy of the Blackline Master *How to Settle Conflicts*. Define conflict resolution skills. **Conflict resolution skills** are steps you can take to settle disagreements in a responsible way. Tell students that they can use conflict resolution skills when they have a conflict with another person. Explain that if they cannot agree on a solution, they might need to ask a trusted adult for help. A trusted adult can help mediate a conflict. Define mediation. **Mediation** is a process in which a trusted adult helps to settle a conflict.

Assessment

Have students design a poster that reminds students their age to settle conflicts in healthful ways. The poster must include conflict resolution skills.

How to Settle Conflicts

1. **Remain calm.**

2. **Set the tone.**
   - Do not blame.
   - Do not interrupt.
   - Do not use put-downs.

3. **Talk about what happened.**

4. **Be honest about what you have said or done to cause the disagreement.**

5. **Use I-messages to express your feelings about what happened.**

6. **Listen to the feelings of the other person.**

7. **List and talk about possible solutions.**
   - Will the solution lead to actions that are healthful?
   - Will the solution lead to actions that are safe?
   - Will the solution lead to actions that follow rules and laws?
   - Will the solution lead to actions that show respect for you and others?
   - Will the solution lead to actions that follow your family's guidelines?
   - Will the solution lead to actions that show you have good character?

8. **Agree on a solution.**

9. **Keep your word and follow the solution upon which you agreed.**

10. **Ask a trusted adult for help if you cannot agree on a solution.**

Hang Up

The Curriculum

Life Skills

■ I will practice protective factors to reduce the risk of violence.

■ I will practice self-protection strategies.

■ I will participate in victim recovery if I am harmed by violence.

Objectives

■ Students will tell ways to recognize violence.

■ Students will explain how to get help if they are a victim of violence.

■ Students will discuss ways they can protect themselves from people who might harm them.

■ Students will identify protective factors to reduce the risk of violence.

■ Students will discuss why people might harm themselves and others.

The National Health Education Standards

■ Students will demonstrate the ability to practice health-enhancing behaviors and reduce health risks.

Preparing to Teach the Lesson Plan

Materials

Two toy telephones

Blackline Master

Violence Glossary

Teaching the Lesson Plan

1 Give each student a copy of the Blackline Master *Violence Glossary*. Tell students that there are many types of violence. Define violence. **Violence** is an act that harms oneself, others, or property. The following are some types of violence: bullying, discrimination, and fighting. **Bullying** is hurting or scaring someone younger or smaller. **Discrimination** is treating certain people or groups of people differently than others. **Fighting** is taking part in a physical struggle.

2 Tell students that receiving obscene or threatening phone calls also is a form of violence. Ask students whether or not they have ever received an obscene or threatening phone call. Many students will probably say that they have. Ask for a student volunteer. Tell the student volunteer to sit at your desk in front of one of the toy telephones. Tell the student to answer the phone call you will pretend to make on the other toy telephone. When the student picks up the receiver, say to the student, "I want to talk dirty to you." Allow the student to respond.

3 If the student did not hang up the phone, tell the class that he or she did not follow safety rules to protect himself or herself from violence. Tell students that if they receive an obscene or threatening phone call, they should hang up immediately. This action might discourage the caller from calling again. If a student receives an obscene or threatening phone call, he or she should tell a parent or guardian immediately. Threats such as the threat in the demonstration should be taken seriously. Threats of this kind should be immediately reported to the police and to the telephone company. The police might suggest that the threatening telephone calls be traced. In some states, people use caller-ID machines that show the phone number of the person who is threatening them. This information can help the police trace the call. Some people get unlisted phone numbers as a way to reduce the number of threatening phone calls.

4 Define victim of violence. A **victim of violence** is a person who is harmed by violence. Tell students to suppose that they are victims of violence. Suppose a caller has made threatening calls to a person. The person is afraid to leave his or her house. The person is afraid to go to school. Explain that there is help for a person who is a victim of violence. A person can talk about his or her feelings. A person can learn what to do. A victim who does not get help might risk getting hurt again.

5 Tell students that they must not act in violent ways themselves. They must not make prank phone calls. Making prank phone calls is against the law. A person can be fined and placed in jail if caught. Prank phone calls are a threat to many people.

Assessment

Write the following situations on slips of paper:

- What would you do if a caller threatened you?
- What would you do if someone called you but said nothing and stayed on the line?
- What would you do if a friend told you he or she was receiving threatening phone calls?
- What would you do if you received a prank phone call made by teens?
- What would you do if a caller asked for your address?
- What would you do if a caller asked your name?

Have students pair up. Pass out the slips of paper to pairs of students. Ask students to role play the situations using the toy telephones.

Violence Glossary

Definitions You Should Know

Abuse is the harmful treatment of another person.

Bullying is hurting or scaring someone younger or smaller.

Discrimination is treating certain people or groups of people differently than others.

Domestic violence is violence that occurs within the family.

Fighting is taking part in a physical struggle.

Homicide is killing someone on purpose or by accident.

Murder is killing someone on purpose.

Neglect is failure to provide proper care and guidance.

Parent abuse is harming a parent.

Physical abuse is excessive use of force.

Rape is forcing someone to have sex or having sex with a minor.

Sexual abuse is sexual contact that is forced on a person.

Sexual harassment is unwanted sexual comments and touches.

Spouse abuse is harming a marriage partner.

Suicide is the taking of one's life on purpose.

Hurting Inside

The Curriculum

Life Skills

■ I will practice protective factors to reduce the risk of violence.

■ I will participate in victim recovery if I am harmed by violence.

Objectives

■ Students will tell ways to recognize violence.

■ Students will explain ways to get help if they are a victim of violence.

The National Health Education Standards

■ Students will demonstrate the ability to practice health-enhancing behaviors and reduce health risks.

Preparing to Teach the Lesson Plan

Materials

Apple

Teaching the Lesson Plan

Prepare the apple. Bang it against something so that it is bruised.

1 Define violence. **Violence** is an act that harms oneself, others, or property. **Domestic violence** is violence that occurs within the family. The family member who uses force wants to control others. This person often uses drugs. Other family members might do anything to keep the violent family member calm. They might pretend the violence does not exist. But this does not work. The violent family member will continue to hurt others unless he or she gets help. The whole family might need counseling.

2 Show students the apple and ask them to describe it. They might say that the apple has been bruised. Ask them how they know that the apple has been bruised. They will probably say that they can see the bruise. Ask students what the inside of the apple is like. They probably will say that they cannot be certain but that it might be discolored. Ask students what the apple will be like if you cut into the middle of it in about a week. Most of the students will probably tell you that it will continue to discolor and might even get soggy.

3 Tell students that you used the apple to illustrate what can happen to a victim of violence who does not get help. A **victim of violence** is a person who is harmed by violence. Just like the apple a victim of violence might have injuries to the outside. The victim of violence might have been beaten. Just like the apple the victim might have injuries inside too. A victim of violence might have physical injuries that cannot be seen. The victim might have emotional injuries that cannot be seen. Just like the apple if nothing changes, the bruises in a victim of violence can get deeper and deeper. This is why a victim of violence needs to get help. A victim of violence might need the following:

• A physical exam to check for injuries and diseases

• Treatment for injuries

• Counseling for anger, fear, and trust

• Support from family and friends

4 Tell students that there is another reason why a victim of violence might need help. Some victims of violence repeat what was done to them to others. Define abuse. **Abuse** is the harmful treatment of another person. Suppose a person is abused. This person is a victim of violence. Suppose a person is abused for a long period of time and does not get any help. Then this person is at risk for behaving in the same ways. For example, suppose a person is physically abused. This person might abuse others by kicking, biting, shoving, and hitting. Suppose a person is emotionally abused. This person might abuse others by name calling or ignoring them.

5 Explain that when a victim of violence gets help, he or she produces a protective factor. A **protective factor** is something that increases the chance of a positive outcome. The victim of violence increases the chance that he or she will recover from violence. The victim of violence increases the chance that he or she will not act in violent ways. The victim of violence increases the chance that he or she will not be harmed again.

6 Tell students that they must recognize violent behaviors. Scramble each of the following words and write them on the chalkboard: *bully, fight, kick, bite, shove, push, trip, steal, punch, hit, prank, swear, tease.* Have students take turns selecting words and unscrambling them.

Assessment

Give students the following quiz:

1. What is violence?
2. What is domestic violence?
3. What kind of help might a victim of violence need?
4. Why is getting help after being a victim of violence a protective factor?
5. What are kinds of violent behaviors?

Click Off That Computer Screen

The Curriculum

Life Skills

■ I will choose healthful entertainment.

■ I will develop media literacy.

Objectives

■ Students will identify guidelines for choosing healthful entertainment.

■ Students will discuss ways they can judge ads.

The National Health Education Standards

■ Students will analyze the influence of culture, media, technology, and other factors on health.

Preparing to Teach the Lesson Plan

Materials

Cardboard

Scissors

Markers

Blackline Master

How to Choose Healthful Entertainment

Teaching the Lesson Plan

Cut the cardboard into a 2-foot-by-2-foot square. Cut out a square center piece so that the cardboard resembles a computer screen. Draw knobs on the cardboard computer.

1 Ask students what they do for entertainment. Students might say that they play tennis or that they watch TV. Tell students that there is healthful entertainment and there is harmful entertainment. Define healthful entertainment. **Healthful entertainment** is entertainment that promotes physical, mental, or social health. Ask students to name kinds of healthful entertainment. Students might name reading a book or doing physical activity. Give each student a copy of the Blackline Master *How to Choose Healthful Entertainment*. Tell students that some entertainment is harmful. Harmful entertainment might show violence. Harmful entertainment might show people using illegal drugs. Harmful entertainment might show information that is not true.

2 Tell students that some computer games are harmful entertainment. Computer games might show violence. Computer games might show information that is not true. Give the cardboard computer screen to a student. Tell the student to hold the cardboard computer screen so that his or her face appears behind it. Tell students that first you will name a way some computer games are harmful entertainment. You might say, "Violence should not be seen." Then the student holding the cardboard computer screen will respond by saying, "I will click off that computer screen." Tell the student to name a healthful activity or entertainment choice. For example, a student might say, "I will click off that computer screen. I will go read a book." Repeat the activity until every student has had a chance to name a healthy activity or entertainment choice. The following are some ways entertainment is harmful:

"Illegal drugs should not be seen."

"Guns should not be seen."

"Blood should not be seen."

"Fighting should not be seen."

"Kicking should not be seen."

3 Tell students that some people have entertainment addiction. Define entertainment addiction. **Entertainment addiction** is the uncontrollable urge to be entertained. A person with entertainment addiction might spend most of his or her time watching television or playing computer games. A person with entertainment addiction does not make time for exercise, homework, or his or her family. His or her physical, mental, and social health suffer.

Assessment

Tell students to keep a computer calendar for a week. Tell students to write on the calendar the length of time they played a computer game or used the Internet each day. Define Internet. The **Internet** is a technology that connects people around the world. Tell students to write on the calendar the names of the computer games they played or Web sites they accessed each day. Tell students to bring their calendars to class. Ask students to total the number of hours they played computer games or used the Internet. Tell students that they should limit the amount of time they spend playing computer games or using the Internet each day. Tell students to talk to their parents about limiting the time they spend playing computer games. Ask students to choose a computer game they played or a Web site they accessed. Tell students to write the name of the computer game at the top of a separate sheet of paper. Tell students to follow the Blackline Master *How to Choose Healthful Entertainment*. Ask students if the computer game they played or the Web site they accessed was healthful entertainment.

© 2001 Everyday Learning Corporation

How to Choose Healthful Entertainment

Entertainment should:

✓ follow family guidelines.

✓ be approved for your age group.

Entertainment should not:

✗ show or talk about teens having sex.

✗ show or talk about drug use.

✗ have violent or sexual language.

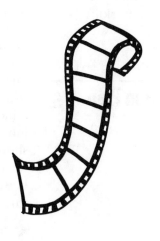

Want Ad for a Friend

The Curriculum

Life Skills

■ I will develop healthful friendships.

■ I will recognize harmful friendships.

Objectives

■ Students will explain the effects a healthful relationship and a harmful relationship can have on a person.

■ Students will list and discuss guidelines for friendships.

■ Students will explain why a person should choose friends their parents or guardians like.

■ Students will explain why a person should choose friends other people respect.

■ Students will discuss reasons to avoid being in a clique.

■ Students will discuss steps they can take to do something about a harmful relationship.

■ Students will discuss when and how they would end a friendship.

The National Health Education Standards

■ Students will demonstrate the ability to use interpersonal communication skills to enhance health.

Preparing to Teach the Lesson Plan

Materials

A want ad from the newspaper

Markers

Blackline Masters

A True Friend

Good Character Checklist
 (For Optional Grades 9–12)

Teaching the Lesson Plan

1 Ask students what they think are important traits a true friend should have. Students might say that a friend should be honest, kind, and respectful. Define friend. A **friend** is someone that is known well and liked. Explain to students that a friend is someone who does not harm them. A friend does not lead people into harmful situations. A friend is someone they can trust. A friend is a good listener. Define true friend. A **true friend** is a person whose actions toward you are responsible and caring. Give each student a copy of the Blackline Master *A True Friend*. Tell students that they should choose friends their parents or guardians like and that other people respect. Other people think you are like your friends.

2 Show students the want ad from the newspaper. Explain that a want ad is a description of something that a person is trying to find. For example, a person might place an ad in a newspaper to find a lost puppy. A person might place an ad in a newspaper to find someone to work for him or her. This ad might describe the traits a person must have in order to do the job. It might tell what kind of education a person needs in order to do the job. It might tell what special skills a person should have in order to do the job. The more detailed the description of the want ad, the better chance a person will have in trying to find what they are looking for.

3 Tell students that they each will create two want ads using paper and markers. Ask students to make one want ad for a true friend. Tell students to include traits that are important for a true friend to have, such as good character. Define good character. **Good character** is telling the truth, showing respect, and being fair. Explain that students should always choose friends who have good character. Encourage students to be very specific in their descriptions. Tell students to make a second want ad to find a person who would not be a true friend. Students should include traits that would not be desirable for a true friend. Students' want ads should look similar to those in a newspaper.

4 Explain that true friends make responsible decisions together. Define responsible decision. A **responsible decision** is a decision that is safe, healthful, and follows laws and family guidelines. Friends can know that they are making responsible decisions together by asking the following questions:

- Is the decision healthful?
- Is the decision safe?
- Does the decision show respect for you and others?
- Does the decision follow family guidelines?
- Does the decision show good character?

5 Create a bulletin board for the want ads. Make the bulletin board resemble a newspaper. The bulletin board might be entitled *True Friendship Press.* Then assign each want ad a number. Have students write a number on their want ads so that their want ads can be identified. Each want ad should have a different number. Students must remember the numbers on their want ads. Have students place their want ads on the bulletin board.

6 Tell students to read some of the want ads on the bulletin board. Ask them to select one or two want ads to which they might want to respond. Have students write letters responding to the want ads. Students should say why they would make a true friend. Collect students' letters. Choose a letter to read to the class. First, read the want ad to which the letter responds. Then read the letter. Ask

students if they think that the person who wrote the letter would be a true friend to the person who wrote the want ad. Tell students to choose many different kinds of friends. Explain that it is important to not join a clique.

7 Some want ads were not selected. The want ads that were not selected should be the want ads to find a person who would not be a true friend. Read some of the want ads on the bulletin board that were not chosen. Tell students that they should end a friendship if a friend is not responsible, if a friend does not respect their limits, or if their parents ask them to end a friendship.

OPTIONAL: For Grades 9–12
Have students make want ads for a date. Give each student a copy of the Blackline Master *Good Character Checklist.* Review the traits that make up good character. Tell students to use the *Good Character Checklist* to help them choose dates.

Assessment

Review the traits a true friend should have. Ask students to sit in a circle. Have one student begin by saying, "I'm going to choose a true friend and my true friend will _____." The student should complete the sentence by naming a trait a true friend will have. The next student should repeat the sentence, repeat the trait the first student named, and name another trait a true friend should have. Continue until everyone has named a trait.

A True Friend

A true friend:

stands by you.

spends time with you.

respects your family's guidelines.

wants you to spend time with your family.

lets you have other friends.

does not tell other people things you do not want shared.

does not put you down.

wants you to make responsible decisions.

wants you to take care of your health.

wants you to have good character.

Good Character Checklist

Yes   No

☐ ☐ **1.** Do my parents or guardians think this person shows good character?

☐ ☐ **2.** Does this person choose friends who show good character?

☐ ☐ **3.** Does this person act on responsible values?

☐ ☐ **4.** Does this person communicate in an open and honest way?

☐ ☐ **5.** Does this person treat me and others with respect?

☐ ☐ **6.** Is this person nonviolent?

☐ ☐ **7.** Does this person make responsible decisions?

☐ ☐ **8.** Does this person resist temptation when pressured to choose wrong actions?

☐ ☐ **9.** Does this person take steps to correct wrong actions?

☐ ☐ **10.** Does this person practice abstinence from sex?

☐ ☐ **11.** Does this person have a drug-free lifestyle?

☐ ☐ **12.** Does this person obey laws?

Top Ten List of Activities

The Curriculum

Life Skills

■ I will develop dating skills.

■ I will practice abstinence from sex.

■ I will use resistance skills when appropriate.

Objectives

■ Students will make a list of social activities they can do in a group with people their age of the same and opposite sex.

■ Students will ask their parents or guardians for guidelines to follow when spending time with a person of the opposite sex.

■ Students will tell how to be a good friend to a person of the opposite sex.

■ Students will name The Top Ten List of Reasons to Practice Abstinence™.

■ Students will tell reasons to keep sex within marriage.

■ Students will tell how practicing abstinence from sex protects their psychological health.

■ Students will tell how to set limits for expressing affection.

■ Students will demonstrate resistance skills to use if they are pressured to be sexually active.

The National Health Education Standards

■ Students will demonstrate the ability to use interpersonal communication skills to enhance health.

■ Students will demonstrate the ability to practice health-enhancing behaviors and reduce health risks.

■ Students will demonstrate the ability to use goal-setting and decision-making skills that enhance health.

Preparing to Teach the Lesson Plan

Materials

None

Teaching the Lesson Plan

1 Tell students that they will learn how to be a good friend with a person of the opposite sex. Tell students that having friends who are members of the opposite sex can help prepare them for when they will date. Tell students that their parents or guardians will set guidelines for them to date when their parents think think they are ready to date. Students should not begin to date until they have the approval of their parents or guardians.

Students can follow these three guidelines to choose friends of the opposite sex:

1. Choose friends of the opposite sex who make responsible decisions.

2. Choose friends of the opposite sex your parents or guardians like.

3. Choose friends of the opposite sex other people respect.

2 Ask students whether or not their parents or guardians have guidelines for them to follow when they spend time with persons of the opposite sex. Students might say that they are not allowed to be alone with members of the opposite sex and that they need to be chaperoned. Students can ask their parents or guardians for guidelines to follow when spending time with a person of the opposite sex. Students might only be allowed to spend time with a person of the opposite sex when in a group.

3 To make a new friend of the opposite sex, students might invite the person to share a group activity. Tell students that they are going to make a list called "The Top Ten List of Activities to Do in a Group with Members of the Same and Opposite Sex." Tell students that the activities they choose must follow family guidelines for entertainment. Students might write the following group activities: going to a movie theater, playing a team sport, or volunteering for a civic group.

4 You might choose to do this part of the teaching strategy tomorrow. Make a master Top Ten List. Collect students' lists. Make notes regarding the activities that students listed most frequently. Make a Top Ten List that includes the most frequently listed student responses. Activities should be listed in order of the frequency of their appearance. For example, if ten students wrote "going to the movies," and five students wrote "playing a team sport," then "going to the movies" should appear before "playing a team sport." After compiling a master Top Ten List, tell students that they will play a game called "Countdown to the Top Ten List." Divide the class into four teams. Tell students that you hold "The Top Ten List of Activities to Do in a Group with

Members of the Same and Opposite Sex." Tell students that they will have a chance to guess the top ten activities that the class listed. Keep score of how many activities on the Top Ten List each team guesses correctly. Flip a coin to choose which team goes first. If the team guesses correctly, that team can guess again. If the team guesses incorrectly, the next team guesses. Play ends when the last activity is named. You might want to ask teams to put the list in order. The first team to play guesses in what order an activity was listed on the Top Ten List. If the team guesses correctly, the team can guess again. If the team guesses incorrectly, the next team guesses.

Assessment

Tell students to talk to their parents or guardians about guidelines to follow when spending time with a person of the opposite sex. Ask students to write down these guidelines. Have students bring the guidelines to class. Using these guidelines, have students create brochures that list these guidelines and that tell the importance of following guidelines for spending time with a person of the opposite sex set by parents and guardians.

Picture Perfect

The Curriculum

Life Skill

■ I will learn ways my body changes.

Objective

■ Students will develop an understanding of the physical, mental, and social changes that they will experience as they grow.

The National Health Education Standards

■ Students will demonstrate the ability to practice health-enhancing behaviors and reduce health risks.

Preparing to Teach the Lesson Plan

Materials

Baby pictures

Thumb tacks

Squares of paper (2 per student)

Sack or hat

Blackline Master

How People Age

Teaching the Lesson Plan

1 Ask students to bring to class a picture of themselves as a baby and a recent school picture of themselves. The picture of themselves as a baby should show them at no older than one year. Tell them that you will write their names on the backs of their pictures. Tack the baby pictures to a bulletin board. Write a number for each student in the class on the squares of paper. For example, if you have 25 students, you will have 25 squares of paper, numbered 1 through 25. Tack a square of paper with a number under each picture. Then write a number for each student on the remaining squares of paper. Put the squares of paper in a sack or in a hat.

2 Tell the class that they are going to play a game called "Name That Baby." Each student will take a turn choosing a number from the sack or hat. Tell students not to share their numbers with other students. Select a student to go to the bulletin board. Have that student look for the number under the picture that matches the number he or she is holding. After the student matches the number, ask him or her to study the picture above the number. Ask the student to match the picture to a classmate.

3 Then have the student show his or her number to the class. Ask the student to go stand by the classmate that matches the picture he or she studied. Then the classmate who was picked must go stand beside the picture. Ask the student who picked this classmate to tell why they believe the classmate is the person shown in the picture. The student might identify physical traits, such as the hair color or eye color of the classmate.

The classmate who has been picked as the one in the picture then can say to the class, " I am the person in the picture," or, "I am not the person in the picture." The classmate does not have to tell the truth. Then have the class vote on whether or not the person standing in front of the picture is the person shown in the picture. After the votes have been counted, ask the classmate to tell the truth. Continue the activity with other students in the class. Depending on time, you might wish to let a few students take part in this activity each day.

4 Give each student a copy of the Blackline Master *How People Age.* Explain to students that they are growing and changing. They are moving through the stages of the life cycle. Define life cycle. The **life cycle** is the stages of life from birth to death. The first stage of the life cycle is infancy. Infancy is the stage of growth from birth to one year. Tell students that an infant changes in many ways. An infant gains weight quickly. An infant grows about an inch per month until he or she is six months old. An infant might begin to develop teeth.

5 Tell students that right now they are in their childhood. Childhood is the stage of growth from 1 to 12 years. Place the recent school pictures of students next to their baby pictures. Ask students to name ways they have changed from infancy to childhood. Students might say that they have gotten taller or that their hair has grown. They might say that they have more teeth. Explain to students that besides having physical changes, they also are experiencing mental changes. For example, students are making responsible decisions by themselves. A student might decide between eating healthful foods or unhealthful foods for lunch. Students also are experiencing social changes. They are making new friends. They are learning to share. They are showing their parents that they can be responsible. They are becoming more independent. These are some of the mental and social changes that a person experiences during childhood.

6 Explain that after childhood, students will enter the stage of growth called adolescence. Adolescence is the stage of growth from 12 to 18 years. Puberty occurs during this stage of the life cycle. Define puberty. **Puberty** is the period of growth when your body matures and becomes like that of an adult. Most girls reach puberty between the ages of 11 and 13. Most boys reach puberty between the ages of 13 and 15.

Assessment

Have students write an article to appear in a journal on aging. Their article should include a discussion of the nine stages in the life cycle. Then the article should focus on stage 4—late childhood. They should discuss ways a boy's and girl's body changes in this stage of the life cycle.

How People Age

The **life cycle** is the stages of life from birth to death. There are nine stages in the life cycle.

Stage 1: Infancy (birth to 1 year)

Stage 2: Early childhood (1 to 3 years)

Stage 3: Middle childhood (3 to 6 years)

Stage 4: Late childhood (6 to 12 years)

Stage 5: Adolescence (12 to 18 years)

Stage 6: Transition to adulthood (18 to 30 years)

Stage 7: First adulthood (30 to 45 years)

Stage 8: Second adulthood (45 to 70 years)

Stage 9: Late adulthood (70+ years)

Puberty—All About Boys

The Curriculum

Life Skills

■ I will recognize habits that protect male reproductive health.

■ I will have regular examinations.

■ I will keep a personal health record.

■ I will be well-groomed.

Objectives

■ Students will tell ways that a boy's body changes during puberty.

■ Students will name the organs in the male reproductive system.

■ Students will tell what happens during an erection.

■ Students will tell why boys should wear an athletic supporter and protective cup for sports.

■ Students will tell healthful habits that boys can practice at this age.

The National Health Education Standards

■ Students will comprehend concepts related to health promotion and disease prevention.

■ Students will demonstrate the ability to access valid health information and health-promoting products and services.

■ Students will demonstrate the ability to advocate for personal, family, and community health.

■ Students will demonstrate the ability to practice health-enhancing behaviors and reduce health risks.

Preparing to Teach the Lesson Plan

Materials

None

Blackline Masters

All About Boys Vocabulary

The Male Reproductive System

Athletic Supporters

Steps for Shaving the Face

Worksheet Master

All About Boys Word Search

Teaching the Lesson Plan

1 Give each student a copy of the Blackline Master *All About Boys Vocabulary*. Tell students the following body changes that occur in boys during puberty:

• Increase in height

• Broadening of the shoulders

• Deepening of the voice

• Increase in muscle mass

• Increase in perspiration

• Growth of hair under the arms and on the legs and chest

• Growth of hair around the pubic area (The **pubic area** is the area outside the body that includes the reproductive organs.)

• Appearance of facial hair

• Increase in size of the reproductive organs

• Production of sperm

2 Give each student a copy of the Blackline Master *The Male Reproductive System*. Tell students that the male reproductive system is made up of organs in the male body that are used to produce a baby. Tell students what happens during an erection. Define erection. An **erection** is when the penis fills with blood and becomes hard. The arteries that carry blood to the penis widen. Then blood fills the spongy tissue in the penis. The veins that take blood away from the penis narrow. This keeps blood from leaving the penis. It is normal for boys to begin to have erections during puberty.

3 Give each student a copy of the Blackline Master *Athletic Supporters.* Tell students that an athletic supporter holds the testes and penis close to the body. Then the testes and penis do not move when a boy moves during sports. An athletic supporter must fit correctly to support the testes and penis. The package in which an athletic supporter is sold will indicate a waist size. The athletic supporter will fit a boy correctly if it is the correct waist size. The protective cup also will fit correctly.

4 Tell students these healthful habits that boys their age can practice:

- Have regular checkups.
- Wear an athletic supporter to support the testes and penis when you play sports.
- Wear a protective cup for sports that require you to wear one.
- Bathe or shower each day.
- Avoid picking or squeezing acne.
- Do not share a razor, even if you have permission to shave.
- Wear clean underwear and a clean athletic supporter to prevent jock itch.
- Talk to your doctor about growing pains.
- Do not use steroids.
- Practice abstinence from sex until marriage.

Tell students these five ways to stamp out smelly feet:

- Keep your feet clean and dry.
- Wear socks that absorb moisture, such as cotton ones.
- Use powders or sprays designed for feet and shoes.
- Do not wear the same shoes two days in a row—give shoes a chance to air out.
- Wash sneakers and other shoes that can be washed.

Tell students the do's and don'ts of acne:

- Do control your stress.
- Do keep your skin clean.

- Don't pinch or pop pimples.
- Don't scrub infected areas.

5 Give each student a copy of the Blackline Master *Steps for Shaving the Face.* Tell students these steps for shaving the face:

- Wet your whiskers with warm water.
- Put shaving cream, gel, or foam on your face.
- Use a razor with a sharp blade.
- Shave downward in the same direction that whiskers grow.
- Shave the whiskers on the chin and upper lip last.
- Rinse your razor and let it air-dry.

Assessment

Give each student a copy of the Worksheet Master *All About Boys Word Search.* Words or phrases that relate to boys' reproductive health are hidden in this word search. Fill in the blanks in the sentences below the word search. Then find and circle in the word search the eight words you wrote in the blanks. The words might be written across or down.

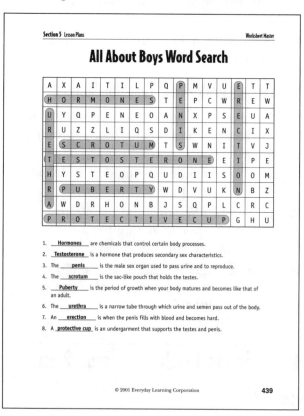

All About Boys Vocabulary

acne: a skin disorder in which pores are clogged with oil and germs.

athletic supporter: an undergarment that supports the testes and penis.

ejaculation: the passage of semen from the penis.

erection: when the penis fills with blood and becomes hard.

hormones: chemicals that control certain body processes.

jock itch: a fungal infection of the skin in the pubic area.

penis: the male sex organ used to pass urine and to reproduce.

perspiration: a salty liquid secreted by the sweat glands.

prostate gland: a gland that makes fluid that helps sperm stay alive.

protective cup: a plastic cup that is worn to protect the testes and penis.

puberty: the period of growth when your body matures and becomes like that of an adult.

secondary sex characteristics: the body changes that occur during puberty.

semen: a mixture of sperm and fluids.

seminal vesicles: two small glands that make a fluid with sugar in it to help sperm move.

testosterone: a hormone that produces secondary sex characteristics.

urethra: a narrow tube through which urine and semen pass out of the body.

vas deferens: one of two long tubes through which sperm pass from the testes to the urethra.

The Male Reproductive System

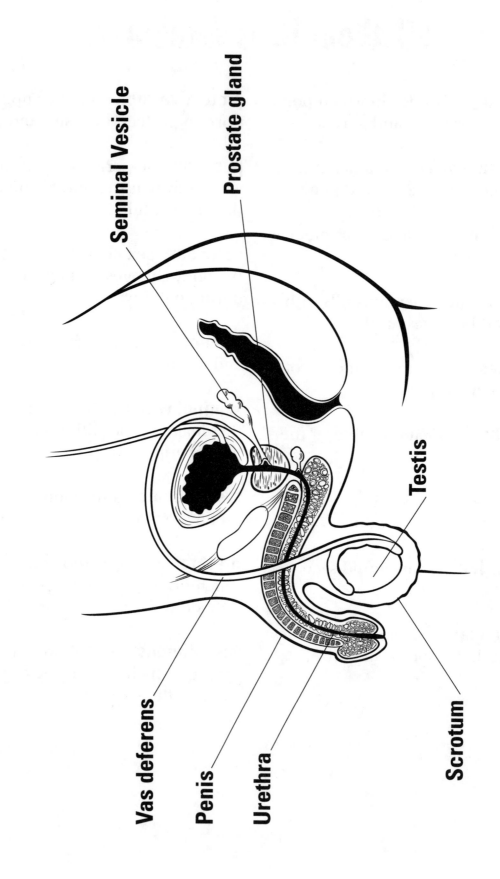

Seminal Vesicle

Prostate gland

Vas deferens

Penis

Urethra

Testis

Scrotum

Athletic Supporters

A protective cup is placed inside an
athletic supporter for protection in sports
such as baseball, football, and hockey.

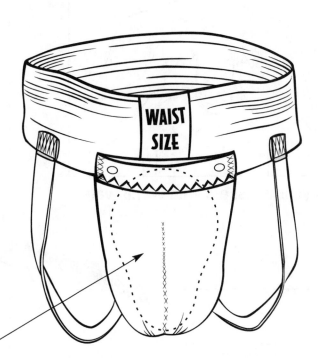

An athletic supporter is an
undergarment that supports
the testes and penis.

Athletic Supporter

A protective cup is a plastic
cup that is worn to protect
the testes and penis.

Protective cup

Steps for Shaving the Face

Wet your whiskers with warm water.

Put shaving cream, gel, or foam on your face.

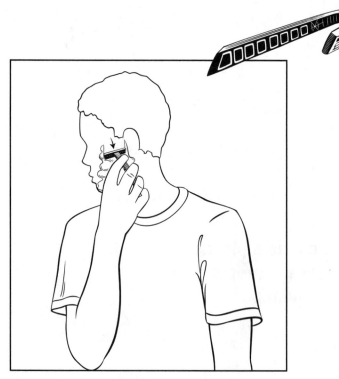

Shave downward in the same direction that whiskers grow.

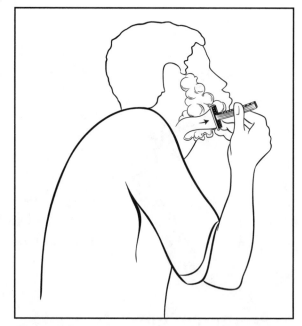

Shave the whiskers on the chin and upper lip last.

All About Boys Word Search

A	X	A	I	T	I	L	P	Q	P	M	V	U	E	T	T
H	O	R	M	O	N	E	S	T	E	P	C	W	R	E	W
U	Y	Q	P	E	N	E	O	A	N	X	P	S	E	U	A
R	U	Z	Z	L	I	Q	S	D	I	K	E	N	C	I	X
E	S	C	R	O	T	U	M	T	S	W	N	I	T	V	J
T	E	S	T	O	S	T	E	R	O	N	E	E	I	P	E
H	Y	S	T	E	O	P	Q	U	D	I	I	S	O	O	M
R	P	U	B	E	R	T	Y	W	D	V	U	K	N	B	Z
A	W	D	R	H	O	N	B	J	S	Q	P	L	C	R	C
P	R	O	T	E	C	T	I	V	E	C	U	P	G	H	U

1. _____ are chemicals that control certain body processes.

2. _____ is a hormone that produces secondary sex characteristics.

3. The _____ is the male sex organ used to pass urine and to reproduce.

4. The _____ is the sac-like pouch that holds the testes.

5. _____ is the period of growth when your body matures and becomes like that of an adult.

6. The _____ is a narrow tube through which urine and semen pass out of the body.

7. An _____ is when the penis fills with blood and becomes hard.

8. A _____ is an undergarment that supports the testes and penis.

397

Puberty—All About Girls

The Curriculum

Life Skills

■ I will recognize habits that protect female reproductive health.

■ I will have regular examinations.

■ I will keep a personal health record.

■ I will be well-groomed.

Objectives

■ Students will tell ways a girl's body changes during puberty.

■ Students will name the organs in the female reproductive system.

■ Students will explain what happens during the menstrual cycle.

■ Students will identify products used for menstruation.

■ Students will identify symptoms of toxic shock syndrome (TSS).

■ Students will tell healthful habits that girls their age can practice.

The National Health Education Standards

■ Students will comprehend concepts related to health promotion and disease prevention.

■ Students will demonstrate the ability to access valid health information and health-promoting products and services.

■ Students will demonstrate the ability to advocate for personal, family, and community health.

■ Students will demonstrate the ability to practice health-enhancing behaviors and reduce health risks.

Preparing to Teach the Lesson Plan

Materials

None

Blackline Masters

All About Girls Vocabulary

The Female Reproductive System

The Menstrual Cycle

Menstrual Products

How to Insert a Tampon

Tampon Safety

Bra Measurement

Worksheet Master

All About Girls Word Search

Teaching the Lesson Plan

1 Give each student a copy of the Blackline Master *All About Girls Vocabulary.* Tell students the following body changes that occur in girls during puberty:

• Increase in height

• Increase in breast size

• Growth of hair under the arms

• Increase in perspiration

• Growth of thicker and darker hair on the legs

• Growth of hair around the pubic area (The **pubic area** is the area outside the body that includes the reproductive organs.)

• Widening of the hips

• Increase in size of the reproductive organs

• Onset of menstrual periods

2 Give each student a copy of the Blackline Master *The Female Reproductive System.* Tell students that the female reproductive system is made up of organs in the female body that are used to produce a baby.

Give each student a copy of the Blackline Master *The Menstrual Cycle.* Explain the menstrual cycle to students. Define menstrual cycle. The **menstrual cycle** is a series of changes in the female body that includes the build-up of blood in the lining of the uterus, the release of an ovum, and the period. Each month a female's body prepares for the release of an ovum, or egg. Define ova. **Ova** are female reproductive cells. Estrogen causes blood to build up in the lining of the uterus. Define estrogen. **Estrogen** is a hormone that produces secondary sex characteristics and influences the menstrual cycle. This makes the the lining of the uterus very thick. Then ovulation occurs. Define ovulation. **Ovulation** is the release of a mature ovum from the ovary. The ovum is released into one of the Fallopian tubes. The ovum travels down the Fallopian tube toward the uterus. Define uterus. The **uterus** is an organ that supports a fertilized ovum during pregnancy. The bloody lining in the uterus is not needed if an ovum is not fertilized. The bloody lining breaks away from the uterus. Blood then trickles down the vagina. Define vagina. The **vagina** is a tube that connects the uterus to the outside of the body. The blood is red, pink, or brown. Blood trickles out for about five days. Then the menstrual cycle starts again. Each menstrual cycle lasts about 28 days.

3 Give each student a copy of the Blackline Master *Menstrual Products*. Define pad. A **pad** is a soft piece of material worn outside the body to absorb the menstrual blood. Define panty liner. A **panty liner** is a thin piece of material that is worn inside underpants to keep them fresh or to provide a backup for a tampon. Define tampon. A **tampon** is a small roll of material that is put inside the vagina to absorb the menstrual blood. Give each student a copy of the Blackline Master *Tampon Safety*. Tell students that a girl should change her tampon at least every four hours. Give each student a copy of the Blackline Master *How to Insert a Tampon*. Tell students that a bra is worn for support and comfort. A bra also is worn for privacy. A bra covers a girl's breasts so her breasts cannot be seen if she wears a sleeveless shirt. A bra keeps a girl's nipples from showing if she wears a thin shirt. Give each student a copy of the Blackline Master *Bra Measurement*.

4 Tell girls that they should practice the following healthful habits:

- Have regular medical checkups.
- Do not share a razor, even if you have permission to shave.
- Bathe or shower each day.

- Avoid picking or squeezing acne.
- Change pads, panty liners, and tampons often.
- Tell your parents or guardians and your doctor right away if you have symptoms of toxic shock syndrome.
- Limit caffeine, take a warm bath, and get mild exercise to lessen menstrual cramps.
- Choose responsible actions if you have mood swings.
- Keep a calendar of your menstrual periods.
- Practice abstinence from sex until marriage.

Tell students the do's and don'ts of acne:

- Do control your stress.
- Do keep your skin clean.
- Don't pinch or pop pimples.
- Don't scrub infected areas.

Assessment

Give each student a copy of the Worksheet Master *All About Girls Word Search*. Words or phrases that relate to girls' reproductive health are hidden in this word search. Fill in the blanks in the sentences below the word search. Then find and circle in the word search the eight words you wrote in the blanks. The words might be written across or down.

All About Girls Word Search

I	T	M	W	Q	P	C	V	P	L	T	C	J	H	E	B
P	O	H	R	B	S	T	A	H	R	E	E	B	C	X	L
U	R	C	W	J	B	T	G	U	P	E	R	B	X	Q	A
B	U	G	P	A	D	P	I	C	E	R	V	V	G	T	D
E	S	T	R	O	G	E	N	Y	K	D	I	L	S	A	E
R	E	D	J	R	J	C	A	P	J	R	X	E	O	B	O
T	U	T	N	D	F	K	P	X	Q	H	M	Y	K	X	V
Y	T	P	M	E	N	S	T	R	U	A	T	I	O	N	A
U	V	A	G	I	W	X	O	V	A	Z	I	U	C	H	R
Y	O	V	U	L	A	T	I	O	N	H	O	E	M	V	Y

1. A _____pad_____ is a soft piece of material worn outside the body to absorb the menstrual blood.
2. ___Puberty___ is the period of growth when your body matures and becomes like that of an adult.
3. ___Estrogen___ is a hormone that produces secondary sex characteristics and influences the menstrual cycle.
4. An ___ovary___ is a gland that produces estrogen and ova.
5. The ___cervix___ is the lower part of the uterus that connects to the vagina.
6. The ___vagina___ is a tube that connects the uterus to the outside of the body.
7. ___Ovulation___ is the release of a mature ovum from the ovary.
8. ___Menstruation___ is the time when blood from the lining of the uterus trickles down and out of the vagina.

    449

    399

All About Girls Vocabulary

abstinence from sex: choosing not to be sexually active.

acne: a skin disorder in which pores are clogged with oil and germs.

bra: an undergarment that holds the breasts close to the chest.

breast bud: a hard lump that forms behind a nipple.

cervix: the lower part of the uterus that connects to the vagina.

estrogen: a hormone that produces secondary sex characteristics and influences the menstrual cycle.

Fallopian tube: a four-inch-long tube through which ova move from an ovary to the uterus.

fertilization: the joining of an ovum and a sperm to make a single cell.

harassment: unwanted and disrespectful comments and actions.

hormones: chemicals that control certain body processes.

menstrual cramps: dull aches or pains in the lower abdomen or back.

menstrual cycle: a series of changes in the female body that includes the build-up of blood in the lining of the uterus, the release of an ovum, and the period.

menstruation: the time when blood from the lining of the uterus trickles down and out of the vagina.

ovary: a gland that produces estrogen and ova.

ovulation: the release of a mature ovum from the ovary.

pad: a soft piece of material worn outside the body to absorb the menstrual blood.

panty liner: a thin piece of material that is worn inside underpants to keep them fresh or to provide a backup for a tampon.

perspiration: a salty liquid secreted by the sweat glands.

puberty: the period of growth when your body matures and becomes like that of an adult.

secondary sex characteristics: the body changes that occur during puberty.

tampon: a small roll of material that is put inside the vagina to absorb the menstrual blood.

toxic shock syndrome (TSS): a severe illness caused by toxins from *Staphylococcus* bacteria.

uterus: an organ that supports a fertilized ovum during pregnancy.

vagina: a tube that connects the uterus to the outside of the body.

The Female Reproductive System

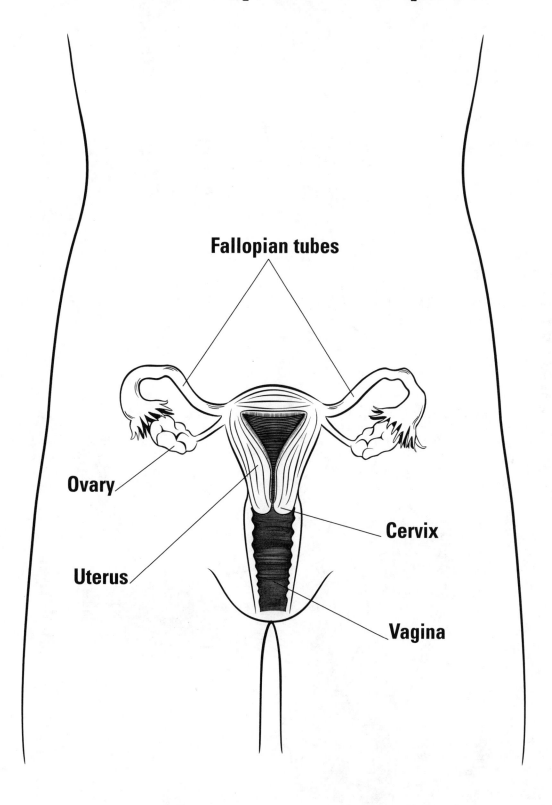

Fallopian tubes

Ovary

Cervix

Uterus

Vagina

The Menstrual Cycle

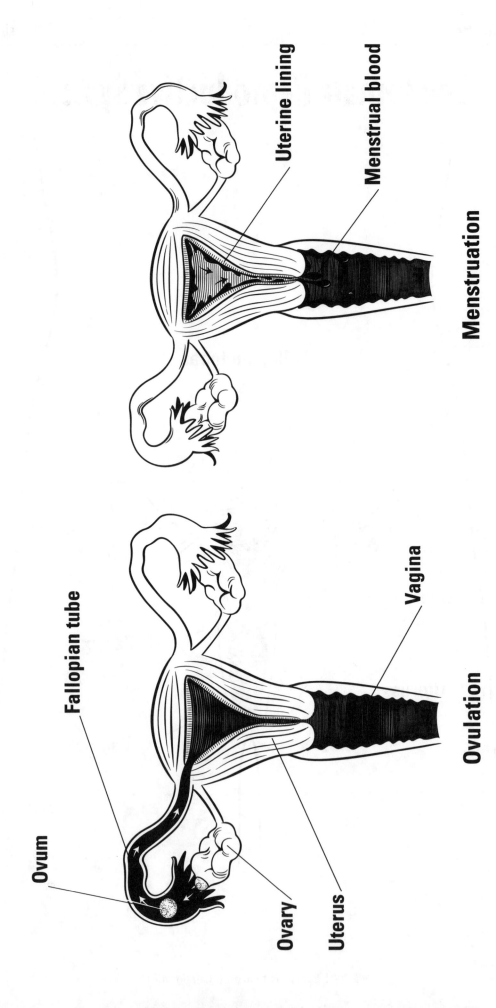

Fallopian tube

Ovum

Ovary

Uterus

Vagina

Ovulation

Uterine lining

Menstrual blood

Menstruation

© 2001 Everyday Learning Corporation

402

Menstrual Products

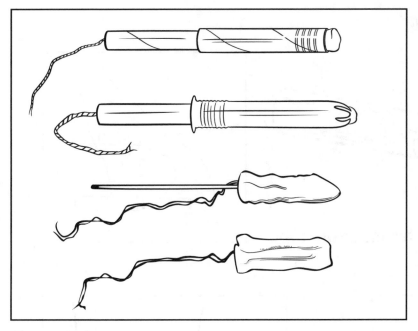

A tampon is a small roll of material that is put inside the vagina to absorb the menstrual blood.

Tampons

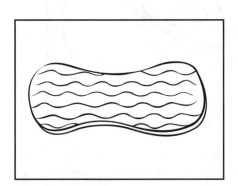

Panty liners

A panty liner is a thin piece of material that is worn inside the underpants to keep them fresh or to provide a backup for a tampon.

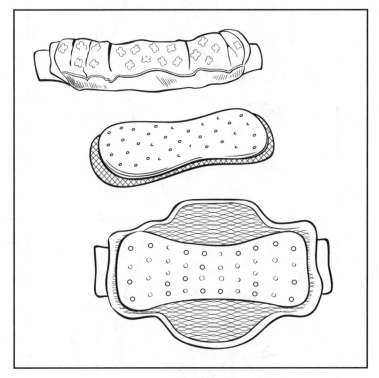

Pads

A pad is a soft piece of material worn outside the body to absorb the menstrual blood.

How to Insert a Tampon

Tampon

Withdraw cord

Inner plunger tube

Outer insertion tube

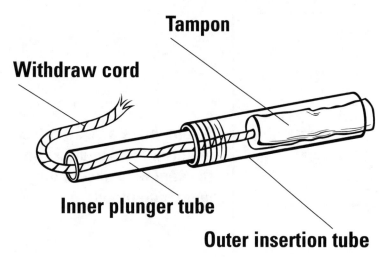

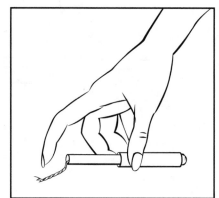

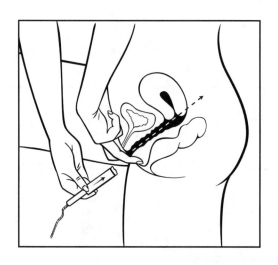

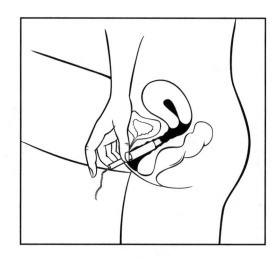

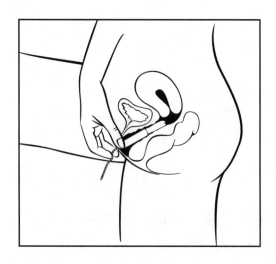

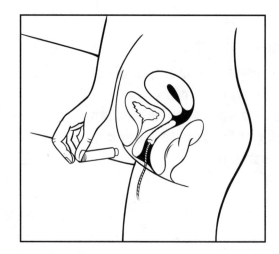

Tampon Safety

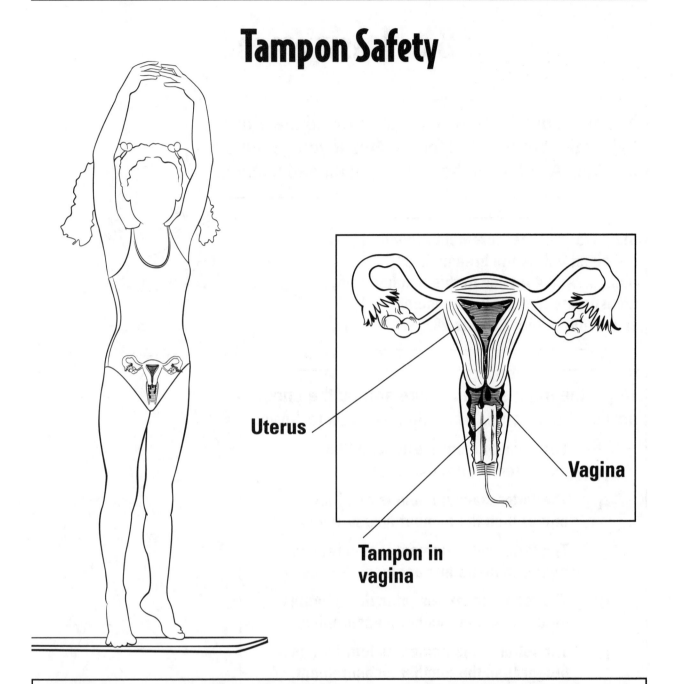

Uterus

Vagina

Tampon in
vagina

Toxic Shock Syndrome (TSS)

Toxic Shock Syndrome (TSS) is a severe illness caused by toxins from Staphylococcus (STA·fuh·loh·KAH·kuhs) bacteria. Girls who use super-absorbent tampons during their periods are at the highest risk for getting TSS.

Symptoms of TSS are fever, vomiting, diarrhea (DY·uh·REE·uh), fainting, and a skin rash. Tell your parents or guardians right away if you have symptoms of TSS. They can call a doctor.

Reduce the risk of getting TSS. Change tampons every four hours. Use low-absorbency tampons. Use pads instead of tampons at night.

Bra Measurement

To get the number size, measure around the chest below the breast. Add four inches if you get an even number. Add five inches if you get an odd number.

Suppose your measurement around the chest below the breasts is 24 inches. Add 4 inches to this number measurement to get your number size. Your number size is 28.

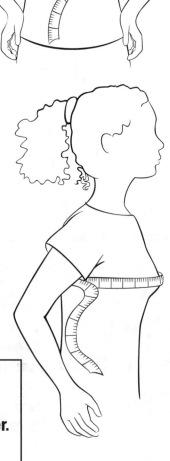

To get the letter size, measure around the chest across the nipples. The cup size is as follows:

AA or **AAA**   The number measurement and letter measurement are the same.

A   The letter measurement is one inch bigger than the number measurement.

B   The letter measurement is two inches bigger than the number measurement.

C   The letter measurement is three inches bigger than the number measurement.

D   The letter measurement is four inches bigger than the number measurement.

DD   The letter measurement is five inches bigger than the number measurement.

Suppose your measurement around the chest across the nipples is 25 inches. If your measurement is 24 inches, your letter measurement around the chest is one inch bigger. Therefore, your letter size is A. Your bra size is 28A.

All About Girls Word Search

I	T	M	W	Q	P	C	V	P	L	T	C	J	H	E	B
P	O	H	R	B	S	T	A	H	R	E	E	B	C	X	L
U	R	C	W	J	B	T	G	U	P	E	R	B	X	Q	A
B	U	G	P	A	D	P	I	C	E	R	V	V	G	T	D
E	S	T	R	O	G	E	N	Y	K	D	I	L	S	A	E
R	E	D	J	R	J	C	A	P	J	R	X	E	O	B	O
T	U	T	N	D	F	K	P	X	Q	H	M	Y	K	X	V
Y	T	P	M	E	N	S	T	R	U	A	T	I	O	N	A
U	V	A	G	I	W	X	O	V	A	Z	I	U	C	H	R
Y	O	V	U	L	A	T	I	O	N	H	O	E	M	V	Y

1. A _____ is a soft piece of material worn outside the body to absorb the menstrual blood.

2. _____ is the period of growth when your body matures and becomes like that of an adult.

3. _____ is a hormone that produces secondary sex characteristics and influences the menstrual cycle.

4. An _____ is a gland that produces estrogen and ova.

5. The _____ is the lower part of the uterus that connects to the vagina.

6. The _____ is a tube that connects the uterus to the outside of the body.

7 _____ is the release of a mature ovum from the ovary.

8. _____ is the time when blood from the lining of the uterus trickles down and out of the vagina.

What a Glittering Handshake

The Curriculum

Life Skills

■ I will choose behaviors to reduce my risk of infection with sexually transmitted diseases.

■ I will use resistance skills when appropriate.

Objectives

■ Students will discuss ways to stick with abstinence and reduce the risk of STDs.

■ Students will use resistance skills if they are pressured to be sexually active or to use drugs.

The National Health Education Standards

■ Students will demonstrate the ability to practice health-enhancing behaviors and reduce health risks.

Preparing to Teach the Lesson Plan

Materials

Glitter in a small container

Blackline Master

Resistance Skills to Resist Pressure to Be Sexually Active

Teaching the Lesson Plan

1 Place a small amount of glitter on your hand. Spread the glitter around your hand so that it covers most of your palm and fingers. Then with that hand, shake the hand of one of your students.

2 After shaking hands, have the student look at his or her hand. Ask the student what he or she sees. The student will say that he or she sees pieces of glitter. Tell students to imagine that the glitter represents pathogens. Tell students that the pathogens were spread from you to the student.

3 Tell the student whose hand you shook to shake the hand of a classmate. Then tell the classmate to shake the hand of another student. Ask the three students who shook hands to look at their hands. Ask them what they see. The students should say that they have glitter on their hands. Explain to students that even though you did not directly touch the other students, the pathogens were still spread to them.

4 Tell students that the glitter represents pathogens that cause a sexually transmitted disease (STD). Define sexually transmitted disease. A **sexually transmitted disease (STD)** is a disease caused by germs that are spread from an infected person to an uninfected person during intimate sexual contact. Tell students that the first student received glitter from you directly. In other words, the first student had contact with you and this is how the first student got pathogens from you. Further explain that the second student received glitter from the first student. However, the glitter originally came from your hand. The second student got the glitter on his or her hand indirectly from you. But, you were the source. Further explain to students that STDs spread the same way. Suppose a person who has an STD has sexual contact with a second person. The second person might become infected. If the second person has sexual contact with a third person who becomes infected, the source for the pathogens was really the first person.

5 Tell students that they are expected to practice abstinence from sex and to avoid misuse and abuse of drugs. Then they will reduce their risk of being infected with sexually transmitted diseases. Explain that they can use resistance skills if they are pressured to be sexually active or use drugs. **Resistance skills** are ways to say NO to wrong actions. Give each student a copy of the Blackline Master *Resistance Skills to Resist Pressure to Be Sexually Active.*

Assessment

Have students make palm cards that include the list of seven resistance skills. Then ask students to memorize the list of seven resistance skills. Pass a piece of chalk around the class for ten seconds and then say stop. The student who has the piece of chalk in his or her hand must state the list of resistance skills by memory. Repeat several times. Ask students to identify behaviors that reduce their risk of infection with STDs.

Resistance Skills to Resist Pressure to Be Sexually Active

1. Be confident and say, "No, I do not want to be sexually active."

2. Give reasons why you practice abstinence from sex.

3. Repeat your reasons for practicing abstinence from sex.

4. Don't send a mixed message.

5. Avoid situations in which there might be pressure to be sexually active.

6. Stay away from anyone who does not respect your limits.

7. Influence others to practice abstinence from sex.

STD FACT-O

The Curriculum

Life Skills

■ I will choose behaviors to reduce my risk of infection with sexually transmitted diseases.

■ I will not misuse or abuse drugs.

Objectives

■ Students will outline signs and symptoms of, diagnosis and treatment for, and health problems that result from the following STDs: chlamydial infection, gonorrhea, syphilis, genital herpes, genital warts, candidiasis, trichomoniasis, and pubic lice.

■ Students will give reasons why they want to keep from being infected with an STD.

■ Students will tell how abstinence from sex reduces the risk of STDs.

■ Students will tell how a drug-free lifestyle reduces the risk of STDs.

The National Health Education Standards

■ Students will demonstrate the ability to use goal-setting and decision-making skills that enhance health.

■ Students will demonstrate the ability to practice health-enhancing behaviors and reduce health risks.

Preparing to Teach the Lesson Plan

Materials

Chalkboard

Chalk

Blackline Master

Types of STDs

Worksheet Master

STD FACT-O

Teaching the Lesson Plan

1 Explain to students that this lesson plan is called *STD FACT-O* and gives students facts about STDs. Define sexually transmitted disease. A **sexually transmitted disease (STD)** is a disease caused by germs that are spread from an infected person to an uninfected person during intimate sexual contact.

2 Give each student a copy of the Worksheet Master *Types of STDs*. Tell students that they will be responsible for learning the definitions, signs and symptoms, diagnosis and treatment, and health problems that can result from infection with certain STDs.

3 Give each student a copy of the Blackline Master *STD FACT-O*. Tell students to play *STD FACT-O*. Explain to students how to complete their gameboards.

The directions are as follows:

• Tell students to write the name of an STD in each of the 16 spaces on the *STD FACT-O* gameboard. Tell students that they are to write all of the STDs and repeat some.

• Tell students to write the definition beneath each STD that they wrote in one of the spaces on their *STD FACT-O* gameboard.

Write the following example on the chalkboard:

STD: Syphilis

Definition: An STD caused by spirochetes that produce a chancre and a skin rash

4 Play *STD FACT-O* as follows:

- State a symptom for one of the STDs. For example, you might state a symptom of pubic lice as follows: Little black spots on the skin near the pubic hair.

- Students should then look on their *STD FACT-O* gameboard and find the STD (pubic lice) that matches this symptom. Students should write an X through the word pubic lice. Students only should put one X on their cards per symptom.

- Continue playing by stating a symptom for another STD. Students should complete the same process.

- A student who completes a line of Xs across, down, or diagonally should say "FACT-O!" and he or she will be the winner.

5 Play *STD FACT-O* a second time.

- State another fact about one of the STDs. For example, you might state the diagnosis, the treatment, or health problems that can result.

- Students should then look on their *STD FACT-O* gameboard and find an STD that matches the facts you stated. If this STD appears on their gameboards, they should draw a circle around it.

- Continue by stating other facts about one of the STDs. Students will complete the same process.

- A student who completes a line of circles across, down, or diagonally should say "FACT-O!" and he or she will be the winner.

6 Explain that choosing abstinence from sex is the best way to prevent STDs. Define abstinence from sex. **Abstinence from sex** is choosing not to be sexually active. Explain that a drug-free lifestyle reduces the risk of STDs. Define drug-free lifestyle. A **drug-free lifestyle** is a lifestyle in which a person does not misuse or abuse drugs. Tell students that alcohol and other drugs affect the part of the brain that helps them think clearly. Tell students that a person stays in control when he or she chooses a drug-free lifestyle and does not make decisions that he or she will later regret.

Assessment

Give each student a copy of the Worksheet Master *STD FACT-O*. Name an STD. The students must write the STD in one of the spaces, spell it correctly, and write its definition. Repeat until all 16 squares are full. Then have students write the definitions for abstinence and drug-free lifestyle on the back of their sheet of paper. They also are to write a four line poem that encourages students their age to practice abstinence and a drug-free lifestyle.

Types of STDs

Types	Chlamydial infection (kluh·MI·dee·uhl) is an STD caused by bacteria that causes inflammation of reproductive organs.	Gonorrhea (gah·nuh·REE·uh) is an STD caused by bacteria that produces a discharge from the urethra and vagina.
Signs and Symptoms Males	• Painful urination • Clear discharge from penis • Inflammation of urethra • Pain or swelling in scrotum	• White, milky discharge from the urethra • Burning during urination
Signs and Symptoms Females	• Sometimes no symptoms are present • Burning during urination • Discharge from the vagina • Inflammation of vagina and cervix	• Sometimes no signs or symptoms present • Discharge from the vagina • Burning during urination
Diagnosis	• Cotton swab used to collect discharge • Discharge examined at lab	• Cotton swab used to collect discharge • Discharge examined at lab
Treatment	• Antibiotics for two to three weeks	• Antibiotics • Some strains are resistant to antibiotics.
Health Problems That Can Result	• Blindness or pneumonia in babies born to infected mothers	• Sterility • Blindness in babies born to infected mothers • Infected heart valves, joints, and brain

Types of STDs (continued)

Types	**Syphilis** (SI·fuh·luhs) is an STD caused by spirochetes that produce a chancre and a skin rash.	**Genital herpes** (HER·peez) is an STD caused by a virus that produces blisters on the reproductive organs or mouth.
Signs and Symptoms **Males**	• Painless sores called chancres on the penis or mouth • Skin rash • Fever, tiredness, headache, sore throat, swollen glands	• Blisters in the genital area or mouth • Swollen glands • Fever • Headache • Tiredness
Signs and Symptoms **Females**	• Painless sores called chancres in or near the vagina or mouth • Skin rash • Fever, tiredness, headache, sore throat, swollen glands	• Blisters in the genital area or mouth • Swollen glands • Fever • Headache • Tiredness
Diagnosis	• Blood test for spirochetes	• Fluid from blisters examined under a microscope
Treatment	• Antibiotics	*No known cure; once infected, a person will always be infected.* • A drug to relieve symptoms and help prevent blisters from appearing again
Health Problems That Can Result	• Heart disease • Death • Mental retardation and other birth defects in babies born to infected mothers	• Recurring blisters • Infect eyes if fingers touch sores and are used to rub eyes • Brain infection in babies born to infected mothers

Types of STDs (continued)

Types	Genital warts are dry wartlike growths caused by a virus.	Candidiasis (kan·duh·DY·uh·suhs) is an STD caused by fungi that produces itching and burning.
Signs and Symptoms Males	• Warts on the penis	• Burning during urination • Itching during urination • Discharge from the penis
Signs and Symptoms Females	• Warts in the vaginal area	• Itching • White, foul-smelling discharge
Diagnosis	• Visual inspection for presence of warts	• Observation by a physician
Treatment	*No treatment to completely get rid of the virus causing warts; once infected, a person will always have the virus.* • Laser surgery to remove the warts • Freezing of warts with liquid nitrogen	• Creams and tablets
Health Problems That Can Result	• Recurring warts • Increased risk of cancers of the cervix and penis	

Types of STDs (continued)

Types	Trichomoniasis (tri·kuh·muh·NY·uh·suhs) is an STD caused by protozoa that infect reproductive organs.	**Pubic lice** are tiny insects that attach to pubic hair and feed on blood.
Signs and Symptoms Males	• Usually no symptoms • If symptoms, pain and burning during urination	• Little black spots on the skin near the pubic hair • Itching and swelling in the pubic area
Signs and Symptoms Females	• No symptoms in half of females • If symptoms, greenish-yellow discharge that has an odor • Itching and burning during urination	• Little black spots on the skin near the pubic hair • Itching and swelling in the pubic area
Diagnosis	• Examination of a discharge under a microscope	• Visual inspection for presence of lice
Treatment	• Prescription drug	• Special shampoo containing a drug to kill lice
Health Problems That Can Result	• A low birth weight in babies born to infected mothers	• Blisters • Itching • Irritation

STD FACT-O

Name of the STD Definition	Name of the STD Definition	Name of the STD Definition	Name of the STD Definition
Name of the STD Definition	Name of the STD Definition	Name of the STD Definition	Name of the STD Definition
Name of the STD Definition	Name of the STD Definition	Name of the STD Definition	Name of the STD Definition
Name of the STD Definition	Name of the STD Definition	Name of the STD Definition	Name of the STD Definition

Did You Know?

The Curriculum

Life Skill

■ I will choose behaviors to reduce my risk of HIV infection.

Objective

■ Students will state ways to reduce their risk of HIV infection.

The National Health Education Standards

■ Students will demonstrate the ability to use goal-setting and decision-making skills that enhance health.

Preparing to Teach the Lesson Plan

Materials

Color index cards for one-half of the class

White index cards for one-half of the class

Twelve index cards marked with an X

Teaching the Lesson Plan

1 Tell students that you are going to make them aware of statistics pertaining to sexually transmitted diseases including HIV. Define sexually transmitted disease, HIV, and helper T cells. A **sexually transmitted disease (STD)** is a disease caused by germs that are spread from an infected person to an uninfected person during intimate sexual contact. **HIV** is a germ that destroys helper T cells in the body. **Helper T cells** are white blood cells that trigger the production of antibodies.

2 Give each student an index card. Students will receive either a colored index card or a white index card. Do not tell students why you are giving them the index cards. Randomly pass out an additional twelve index cards marked with an X. Students who receive an index card marked with an X now will have two cards.

3 Tell the twelve students who have index cards marked with an X to stand. Have them stand for three minutes. Then tell the students that in the three minutes that have just passed twelve more people in the world have become infected with HIV. Explain that more than one person becomes infected with HIV every fifteen seconds.

4 Tell the students who are holding a colored index card to stand. Ask the class to estimate the percentage of the students in the class who are standing. Students will say 50 percent of the class is standing. Tell the students that 50 percent of persons who reach 25 years of age have been infected by one or more STDs. Explain that practicing abstinence from sex is one way they can reduce their risk of being infected with an STD including HIV.

5 Tell students that they must avoid risk behaviors and risk situations for HIV infection. A **risk behavior** is an action that can be harmful to health. Risk behaviors for HIV infection include:

- having close sexual contact;
- sharing a needle for IV drug use;
- sharing a needle for ear-piercing or body piercing,
- sharing a needle to make a tattoo.

6 Define risk situation. A **risk situation** is a condition that can harm a person's health. Risk situations for HIV infection include:

- being born to a mother infected with HIV;
- having a transfusion with HIV-infected blood.

7 Tell students there are ways to prevent the risk of HIV infection.

- Choose abstinence from sex.
- Do not use illegal injecting drugs.
- Do not share a needle to pierce ears or other body parts.
- Do not share a needle to get a tattoo.

8 Explain to students that a person infected with HIV might not know that he or she is infected. This person might

- appear healthy;
- not know that he or she is infected;
- might know that he or she is infected and tell you that he or she is not.

Explain that a person who has exhibited risk behaviors or been in a risk situation for HIV must be tested. Define HIV positive. **HIV positive** is a term used to describe a person who has HIV antibodies in the blood.

Assessment

Have students play a game called "Do You Want to Be a Billionaire?" Ask for student volunteers to play. Use the following questions:

- How many people in the world become infected with HIV during a three-minute time period?
- How often does another person in the world become infected with HIV?
- What are four risk behaviors for HIV infection?
- What are two risk situations for HIV infection?
- What are four ways to reduce the risk of being infected with HIV?
- What is HIV positive?
- What is a helper T cell?
- What is an STD?

Compassion

The Curriculum

Life Skill

■ I will choose behaviors to reduce my risk of HIV infection.

Objectives

■ Students will give reasons why they want to keep from being infected with HIV.

■ Students will discuss treatment for HIV infection and AIDS.

The National Health Education Standards

■ Students will demonstrate the ability to use goal-setting and decision-making skills that enhance health.

Preparing to Teach the Lesson Plan

Materials

None

Blackline Master

AIDS Can Happen to You!

Teaching the Lesson Plan

1 Define the immune system. The **immune system** is made up of body organs, tissues, and cells that destroy pathogens. One kind of cells is helper T cells. Define helper T cells. **Helper T cells** are white blood cells that trigger the production of antibodies. Antibodies are protein substances in the blood that destroy pathogens. A large number of helper T cells are found in the lymph nodes. Define lymph nodes. **Lymph nodes** are glands located in the neck, armpits, and groin that filter wastes.

Helper T cells go to work when pathogens enter the body. They signal the lymph nodes to send antibodies to look for the pathogens. Antibodies find the pathogens, surround them, and destroy them. This is how the immune system works in a healthy person.

2 Define human immunodeficiency virus. **Human immunodeficiency virus (HIV)** is a germ that destroys helper T cells in the body. Define Acquired Immune Deficiency Syndrome. **Acquired Immune Deficiency Syndrome (AIDS)** is a condition that results when HIV infection causes a breakdown of the body's ability to fight other infections.

3 Explain that HIV is in the body fluids of people who are infected. The body fluids through which HIV can be spread are:

• blood,

• semen,

• vaginal secretions, and

• breast milk.

A small amount of HIV has been found in the saliva and tears of persons infected with HIV.

4 Explain ways HIV is spread. HIV is spread by:

• having close sexual contact with an infected person;

• sharing a needle for injecting drugs with an infected person:

• sharing a needle for body-piercing with an infected person;

• sharing a needle to make a tattoo with an infected person;

• being born to a mother infected with HIV;

• having a transfusion with HIV-infected blood.

5 Identify ways HIV is not spread. According to Centers for Disease Control and Prevention, HIV is not spread in the following ways:

• hugging;

• kissing with the mouth closed;

- touching, holding, or shaking hands;
- inhaling moist droplets from someone's cough or sneeze;
- sharing restroom facilities;
- using the same pencil;
- being a blood donor;
- attending school with someone who is infected.

6 Identify risk behaviors and risk situations for HIV infection. They are:

- Having close sexual contact (risk behavior)
- Sharing a needle for IV drug use (risk behavior)
- Sharing a needle for ear-piercing (risk behavior)
- Sharing a needle to make a tattoo (risk behavior)
- Being born to a mother infected with HIV (risk situation)
- Having a transfusion with HIV-infected blood (risk situation)

7 Define universal precautions. **Universal precautions** are steps taken to keep from having contact with pathogens in body fluids. They include:

- Wear disposable latex or polyurethane gloves.
- Do not wear disposable gloves more than once.
- Wash your hands well with soap and water after you remove gloves.
- Wear a face mask or shield if you give first aid for breathing.
- Do not use a face mask or shield more than once without disinfecting it.
- Cover any cuts, scrapes, and rashes on your body with plastic wrap or a sterile dressing.
- Do not eat or drink anything while giving first aid.
- Do not touch your mouth, eyes, or nose while caring for a victim.

8 Define HIV status, HIV negative, HIV positive, ELISA, and Western blot. **HIV status** is the result of testing for HIV antibodies in the blood. **HIV negative** is a term used to describe a person who does not have HIV antibodies in the blood. **HIV positive** is a term used to describe a person who has HIV antibodies in the blood. **ELISA** is a test used on body fluids

to check for HIV antibodies. **Western blot** is a test used to confirm ELISA. Explain that a person who tests HIV negative might still be infected with HIV. This is because it takes from two weeks to several months for the immune system to make enough antibodies to get an accurate test. Persons who choose risk behaviors and risk situations must be retested to get an accurate test. They can infect others even though they have tested HIV negative.

9 Identify opportunistic infections. **Opportunistic infections** are infections that develop when a person has a weak immune system. **Pneumocystis carinii pneumonia (PCP)** is a type of pneumonia found in people who have AIDS. **Kaposi's sarcoma** is a type of cancer in people who have AIDS. **AIDS dementia** is a loss of brain function caused by HIV infection. Identify treatments for HIV and AIDS. **DdI** is a drug that slows down the rate at which HIV multiplies. **AZT** is a drug that slows down the rate at which HIV multiplies. **Protease inhibitors** are antiviral drugs that decrease the amount of HIV in the blood and increase the helper T cell count.

10 Explain that many people are living with HIV and AIDS. Define compassion. **Compassion** is showing concern and a desire to be helpful. Give each student a copy of the Blackline Master *AIDS Can Happen to You*. Explain that the letter was written by the mother of Jim and appears in a book titled *Wrapped in Love* (copyright 1991 by Ruth Grove). The cover of the book is a color picture of an AIDS quilt made by Jim's family. Ask students why they think she chose the title for the book. Tell students to write a letter to Jim's mother expressing compassion. Ask students to read their letters to the class.

Assessment

Have students design a pamphlet on HIV. It should include an explanation of how HIV destroys the immune system, ways HIV is spread, ways HIV is not spread, risk behaviors and risk situations for HIV infection, HIV tests and HIV status, drugs used in treatment, ways to reduce the risk of infection, universal precautions, and compassion for persons living with HIV and AIDS.

AIDS Can Happen to You!

I'm the mother of a son who has died of AIDS.

Jim wasn't concerned about AIDS because he thought AIDS only hit druggies, and didn't do drugs.

Jim wasn't concerned about AIDS because he thought AIDS only hit those with several sexual partners, and he had only one.

Jim wasn't concerned about AIDS because he thought AIDS only hit the poor uneducated minorities, and he was white, educated, and had a good job.

Jim wasn't concerned about AIDS because he thought AIDS only hit people who were poorly nourished and had poor health habits, and he ate carefully, didn't smoke, and prided himself with regular workouts and running marathons.

Jim wasn't concerned about AIDS because he thought AIDS only hit the unhealthy, and he had regular physical and dental check-ups.

But, Jim tested positive for HIV. He still wasn't going to get AIDS because he was really taking care of himself—6'2" tall, 180 lb., and feeling great!

But, Jim did get AIDS. He missed three months of work because of pneumonia, but then again felt great, and was back to work and running marathons.

Jim was going to beat this disease. But no one beats AIDS, and after 18 months Jim was too ill to work.

After a year, Jim was too sick to take care of himself.

And, after another year, he had six major diseases, was taking 26 medications by mouth, and having constant intravenous drugs and several units of blood per week.

Jim died from AIDS-related causes as a young man, with a college education, a nice car and a good job, and a lot of living to do.

Jim was infected with HIV as a teenager.

He was my only son.

AIDS can happen to you!

Sincerely,

Ruth Grove

(Ruth Grove, M.S.Ed., is an HIV Education Specialist,
Comprehensive Health Unit, Arizona Department of Education.)

HIV and AIDS: The Facts

The Curriculum

Life Skill

■ I will choose behaviors to reduce my risk of HIV infection.

Objectives

■ Students will describe how HIV destroys the immune system.

■ Students will discuss risk behaviors and risk situations for HIV infection.

■ Students will explain why a person can spread HIV before testing positive for HIV.

■ Students will discuss treatment for HIV infection and AIDS.

■ Students will state ways to reduce their risk of HIV infection.

The National Health Education Standards

■ Students will demonstrate the ability to use goal-setting and decision-making skills that enhance health.

Preparing to Teach the Lesson Plan

Materials

Scissors

Photos

Pen

Blackline Master

Ways HIV Is Spread

Teaching the Lesson Plan

To prepare for this lesson, cut out ten photos of a variety of healthy-looking individuals from magazines. Do not use photos of people who are likely to be known to students, such as sports stars. The photos should be large enough for the class to see as you walk around and show them. Number each photo 1–10. Choose three photos at random. Put a plus sign (+) on the backs of these photos.

1 Ask students to name some body defenses against pathogens. Students might say skin, tears, stomach acids, white blood cells, and antibodies. Say white blood cells if students do not do so. Ask students what they think might happen if white blood cells were destroyed. Students might say the person would get sick or the body would not be able to fight pathogens.

2 Define human immunodeficiency virus. **Human immunodeficiency virus (HIV)** is a germ that destroys helper T cells in the body. Define helper T cells. **Helper T cells** are white blood cells that trigger the production of antibodies. Define Acquired Immune Deficiency Syndrome. **Acquired Immune Deficiency Syndrome (AIDS)** is a condition that results when HIV infection causes a breakdown of the body's ability to fight other infections. HIV gets into helper T cells and destroys them. There are fewer helper T cells to tell the body to make antibodies. As HIV destroys more helper T cells, the body is unable to keep making enough helper T cells to fight pathogens. The number of helper T cells gets lower. The person develops AIDS.

3 Define opportunistic disease. An **opportunistic disease** is a disease that would not occur if body defenses were working normally. Examples are a special kind of pneumonia and a type of skin cancer.

4 Give each student a copy of the Blackline Master *Ways HIV Is Spread.*

5 Discuss ways HIV is not spread. Tell students HIV is not spread by casual contact. Define casual contact. **Casual contact** is daily contact without touching body fluids. Examples of casual contact are shaking hands, using the same pencil, holding hands, and hugging.

6 Tell students to number 1–10 on a sheet of paper. Hold up each photo you prepared before class so that all students can see it. Students are to write a plus sign (+) next to the corresponding number on their paper if they think the person is HIV positive. They are to write a minus sign (–) next to the corresponding number if they think the person is HIV negative.

7 Tell students you put a plus sign (+) on the back of three of the photos. Turn the photos over and students will see which three have the plus sign (+) on them. Explain that you do not really know whether any of these people are infected with HIV. You chose these photos to make a point. Emphasize to students that it is impossible to identify a person who has HIV by appearance alone. Explain that people can have HIV and appear to be healthy. This is because a person might not have symptoms for years after being infected with HIV. However, the person can still spread HIV to another person.

8 Tell students it is important for them to choose behaviors to keep from getting infected with HIV. It is important for them to take these actions with anyone because they cannot tell by looking who is infected with HIV. Define universal precautions. **Universal precautions** are steps taken to keep from having contact with pathogens in body fluids.

Assessment

Ask students why it is important to choose behaviors to keep from getting infected with HIV. Have students explain why it is impossible to identify a person who has HIV by appearance alone. Have students explain how they can reduce their risk of HIV infection.

Ways HIV Is Spread

 Not sticking to your decision to avoid risk behaviors;

 Sharing a needle to inject drugs with a person who has HIV;

 Sharing a needle to pierce ears or other body parts with a person who has HIV;

 Sharing a needle for tattooing with a person who has HIV;

 Pricking your finger and rubbing blood together to become a blood brother or sister with a person who has HIV;

 Touching the blood from a nosebleed or cut of a person who has HIV.

Family Sculpture

The Curriculum

Life Skills

■ I will develop healthful family relationships.

■ I will work to improve difficult family relationships.

■ I will make healthful adjustments to family changes.

Objectives

■ Students will explain how they can be a loving family member.

■ Students will explain why they need to follow family guidelines.

■ Students will tell reasons to participate in The Family Round Table.

■ Students will discuss ways to cope with difficult family relationships.

■ Students will discuss ways families might change.

■ Students will discuss ways to make healthful adjustments to family changes.

The National Health Education Standards

■ Students will demonstrate the ability to use interpersonal communication skills to enhance health.

■ Students will demonstrate the ability to practice health-enhancing behaviors and reduce health risks.

Preparing to Teach the Lesson Plan

Materials

None

Teaching the Lesson Plan

1 Define healthful family relationships. **Healthful family relationships** are relationships in which family members relate well, show respect for each other, and behave in responsible ways. Tell students that healthy families are families that have healthful family relationships. Tell students that in order for a family to have healthful family relationships, the family members must be able to communicate effectively with each other. Define communication. **Communication** is the sharing of feelings, thoughts, and information with others. Tell students that one way for a family to communicate is by having The Family Round Table. Define The Family Round Table. **The Family Round Table** is a special time when family members meet as a group to talk. Explain to students that all families communicate in different ways. Tell students that some of these ways are more healthful than others.

2 Explain to students that they are going to form family sculptures. Tell students that these family sculptures help them understand the different ways that families communicate. Pick five student volunteers. Tell the class that these five student volunteers represent a family. The family could be a mother, stepfather, stepbrother, stepsister, and grandmother. Have the five students stand in a circle facing each other. Have each student place one hand inside of the circle. Have them stack their hands as if they were football players in a huddle. Explain to students that this family sculpture represents a family that has a healthful family relationship. Tell students that this family sculpture represents a family whose members are able to communicate effectively with each other. Explain to students that this family is healthful because each member of the family is separate but every member still feels connected to the family.

3 Tell students that they are going to form another family sculpture. Pick four different student volunteers. Tell students that these four student volunteers represent another family. This family is a mother, father, and two children. Have the student who is the mother and the student who is the father stand back to back. Have the students who are the children stand facing the mother. Explain to students that this sculpture represents a family that does not have a healthful family relationship. Show students that the father is not facing the rest of the family. Show students that the mother is standing in between the father and the children. Explain to students that members of this family sculpture might be dealing with a difficult situation. For example, the father in this family sculpture might have a drug dependence. Define drug dependence. **Drug dependence** is the compelling need to take a drug even though it harms the body, mind, and relationships. The mother in this family sculpture is protecting the children from the father. The children in this family sculpture are not able to share their feelings with their father. The children keep their feelings inside. This family does not communicate in effective ways.

4 Tell students that families might change in many ways. Separation, divorce, illness, or death are ways in which a family might change. Define separation. **Separation** is a situation in which a couple remains married but lives apart. Define divorce. **Divorce** is a legal way to end a marriage. Tell students that young people must talk to their parents during these changes in the family. Parents can answer questions and give support.

5 Divide the class into groups of four or five students. Tell students that each group is going to work together to make a family sculpture. Explain that the students in the group must decide which family members will be in their sculpture. Students then must decide how the family members will communicate with each other. For example, the mother and father might face each other and not face the children and grandmother. Finally, students must create a family sculpture that shows the way this family communicates.

6 Tell each group to make their family sculpture for the rest of the class. Have the rest of the class describe the way that the family members are communicating with each other. The group will then tell the class what they were trying to show with their family sculpture.

Assessment

Have students draw a continuum. They should write Difficult Family Relationships on one end of the continuum and Healthful Family Relationships on the other end. Then they can list words that describe these two kinds of relationships. For example, under Difficult Family Relationships they might write "drug dependence" and "lack of communication" while under Healthful Family Relationships they might write "loving" and "I-messages." Have students write a paragraph telling ways to adjust to family changes.

The Parenting Magazine

The Curriculum

Life Skills

■ I will develop healthful family relationships.

■ I will develop skills to prepare for marriage.

■ I will develop skills to prepare for parenthood.

Objectives

■ Students will explain how they can be a loving family member.

■ Students will explain why they need to follow family guidelines.

■ Students will tell reasons why monogamous marriage protects society.

■ Students will tell reasons why children need responsible parents.

■ Students will tell ways to help care for younger children.

■ Students will give reasons why they want to avoid teen marriage, teen pregnancy, and teen parenthood.

The National Health Education Standards

■ Students will demonstrate the ability to use interpersonal communication skills to enhance health.

■ Students will demonstrate the ability to use goal-setting and decision-making skills that enhance health.

Preparing to Teach the Lesson Plan

Materials

Old magazines

Scissors

Glue

Colored paper

Poster paper

Blackline Master

How to Be a Loving Family Member

Teaching the Lesson Plan

1 Ask students the meaning of the word *responsibility*. Define responsibility. **Responsibility** is being accountable for what you say and do. Ask students what a responsible parent is. Students might answer that a responsible parent is a parent who helps his or her child with the child's homework. Another answer might be that a responsible parent is one who spends time with his or her child. Another answer might be that a responsible parent is a parent who takes care of his or her child. Explain to students that there are many different ways that a parent can be a responsible parent. Give each student a copy of the Blackline Master *How to Be a Loving Family Member*.

2 Tell students that they are going to pretend to be magazine publishers. Tell students that they will publish a magazine for parents. The magazine will be called *The Parenting Magazine*. Tell students that their magazine will discuss the responsibilities of parenthood.

3 Divide the class into groups of five. Give each group several old magazines. These magazines should have a lot of pictures. Tell students to cut out pictures from the magazines that show responsible parents. Explain to students that these pictures will be the "art" for their magazine articles. Students will glue the pictures onto another piece of paper. On this sheet of paper, students will write the way the parent is being responsible. The students should write a guideline for responsible parenthood. For example, a student might find a picture of a parent having dinner with his or her child. A guideline for the picture might be, "A responsible parent spends time with his or her child. A responsible parent provides food for his or her child." Another example might be a photo of a parent giving a child a time-out. The guideline for the picture might be, "A responsible parent shows his or her child that the child has done something wrong without hurting him or her."

4 Have each group make a magazine that has about ten pictures and ten guidelines. If time permits, have each group make a cover for its magazine. Each group will then present its magazine to the class. Students should take turns showing the different pages and reading the guidelines. Tell students to explain why each of the guidelines is important for responsible parenthood.

Assessment

Tell each group to design a poster for its favorite page in the magazine. The posters should include a picture of a responsible parent and a guideline for responsible parenthood. Display student posters around the classroom.

How to Be a Loving Family Member

Communicate with family members in a healthful way.

- Share positive feelings with family members.
- Spend time with family members.
- Encourage family members in their projects and hobbies.
- Give family members emotional support.
- Use I-messages rather than you-messages.
- Work out disagreements in a calm way.

Be a responsible family member.

Define responsible. To be **responsible** is to be dependable.

Pay attention to family guidelines.

Define family guidelines. **Family guidelines** are rules set by your parents or guardians that help you know how to act.

It's a Boy! It's a Girl!

The Curriculum

Life Skill

■ I will learn facts about pregnancy and childbirth.

Objectives

■ Students will explain how the sex of a baby is determined.

■ Students will explain the difference between a dominant gene and a recessive gene.

■ Students will explain where and how fertilization takes place.

■ Students will explain how identical twins and fraternal twins are produced.

■ Students will tell what happens during labor and childbirth.

The National Health Education Standards

■ Students will comprehend concepts related to health promotion and disease prevention.

Preparing to Teach the Lesson Plan

Materials

Tennis ball

Table tennis ball

Construction paper of different colors

Scissors

Marker

Tape

Rubber band

Two matching soup dishes

Blackline Master

Sex Determination

Teaching the Lesson Plan

1 Explain to students they will be studying about heredity. Define heredity. **Heredity** is the sum of traits that have been passed, or transmitted, from your biological parents to you. Cut a tennis ball in half. Do the same with a table tennis ball. Explain to students that the tennis ball represents a cell. The table tennis ball represents a nucleus that contains DNA. Define nucleus and DNA. The **nucleus** is the center of a cell. The nucleus carries DNA. **DNA** is the material that makes up chromosomes. Using a marker, print DNA on the table tennis ball. Cut 46 small strips of colored construction paper to represent chromosomes. Define chromosome. A **chromosome** is a structure that carries genes. Define gene. A **gene** is a tiny piece of information that influences heredity. Define dominant gene. A **dominant gene** is a gene that produces a trait that is seen. Define recessive gene. A **recessive gene** is a gene that produces a trait that is seen only if the other gene in the pair is the same. Put these strips of colored paper inside the table tennis ball. Tape the table tennis ball back together and place it inside the tennis ball. Hold the tennis ball together with a rubber band.

2 Explain that there are many cells inside the body. Each cell has DNA. Open the tennis ball and show students the table tennis ball with DNA marked on it. Explain that DNA is controlling in that it determines what characteristics people have, such as what eye color they will have and how fast they will grow. Explain that DNA gets its knowledge from the 46 chromosomes. These chromosomes carry genes. The genes are tiny pieces of information that influence heredity. To clarify this, open the table tennis ball and pull out the strips of colored paper representing chromosomes. Tell students that each chromosome carries genes, or tiny pieces of information.

3 Define fertilization. **Fertilization** is the joining of an ovum and a sperm to make a single cell. Define fertilized ovum. The **fertilized ovum** is an egg that has been fertilized by a sperm. Show students how a fertilized ovum gets a total of 46 chromosomes. Take two soup dishes and place them rim to rim to represent an ovum. Now place 22 strips of colored paper plus one marked *X* inside the ovum. Make four halves of sperm out of construction paper. Tape two halves together at the bottom, leaving the top open so that you can slide 22 strips of colored paper plus a strip marked *X* inside the sperm. This represents the sperm to make a girl. Tape the other sperm halves together at the bottom, leaving the top open, so that you can slide the 22 strips plus a strip marked *Y* inside the sperm. This represents a sperm cell to make a boy. Place the sperm containing the *X* inside the egg.

4 Give each student a copy of the Blackline Master *Sex Determination*. You can explain that DNA gets half of its information from the biological mother and half from the biological father. The mother's ovum has 22 chromosomes plus an X chromosome for a total of 23 chromosomes. The father's sperm also contains a total of 23 chromosomes. Some of the father's sperm contain 22 chromosomes plus an X chromosome. Some of the father's sperm contain 22 chromosomes plus a Y chromosome.

5 Explain that during fertilization, the chromosomes from the ovum and sperm combine to make a total of 46 chromosomes. Place a sperm that has 22 chromosomes plus X into the soup bowl representing the ovum. Explain there are now 44 chromosomes plus XX for a total of 46 chromosomes. Tell the class that when there are 44 chromosomes plus XX, the baby will be a girl. Then repeat this demonstration a different way. Place a sperm that has 22 chromosomes plus Y into the soup bowl representing the ovum. Explain there are now 44 chromosomes plus XY for a total of 46 chromosomes. Tell the class that when there are 44 chromosomes plus XY, the baby will be a boy.

6 Explain to students how identical and fraternal twins are produced. Define labor. **Labor** is a series of changes that results in the birth of a baby. Define childbirth. **Childbirth** is the process by which the baby moves from the uterus to the outside of the mother's body.

Assessment

Have students use the materials and repeat the demonstration. A student can show the combination of chromosomes that produce a girl baby. Another student can show the combination of chromosomes that produce a boy baby. Have students define heredity, nucleus, DNA, chromosome, and gene. The mother's ovum has 22 chromosomes plus an X chromosome for a total of 23 chromosomes. The father's sperm also contains a total of 23 chromosomes. Some of the father's sperm contain 22 chromosomes plus an X chromosome, while others contain 22 chromosomes plus a Y chromosome.

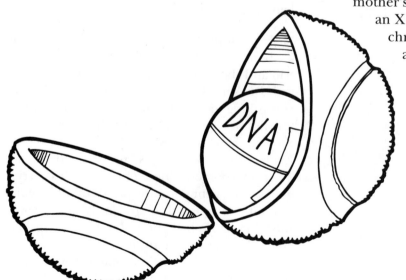

Sex Determination

Ovum

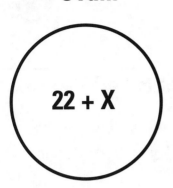

Ova always have 22 chromosomes
plus an X sex chromosome
(for a total of 23 chromosomes).

Sperm

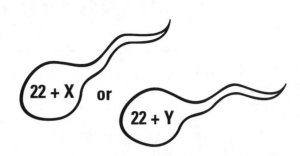

Sperm always have 22 chromosomes
plus either an X or a Y sex chromosome
(for a total of 23 chromosomes).

A fertilized ovum has 44 chromosomes plus 2 sex chromosomes
(for a total of 46 chromosomes).

It's a girl!

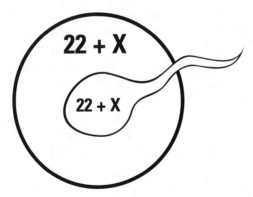

44 + XX
(for a total of
46 chromosomes)

A fertilized ovum with
44 chromosomes plus XX
will develop into a girl.

It's a boy!

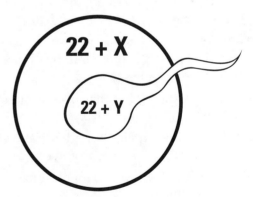

44 + XY
(for a total of
46 chromosomes)

A fertilized ovum with
44 chromosomes plus XY
will develop into a boy.

What's KNOT Good for an Unborn Baby

The Curriculum

Life Skill

■ I will learn facts about pregnancy and childbirth.

Objectives

■ Students will explain where and how fertilization takes place.

■ Students will explain how the sex of a baby is determined.

■ Students will explain the difference between a dominant gene and a recessive gene.

■ Students will explain how an unborn baby gets healthful substances from its mother.

■ Students will tell what is included in prenatal care.

■ Students will tell how a father-to-be who smokes can affect his unborn baby.

■ Students will name harmful substances that can pass from the mother-to-be's blood into her unborn baby's blood.

■ Students will tell how harmful substances can affect the unborn baby.

■ Students will explain how identical twins and fraternal twins are produced.

■ Students will tell what happens during labor and childbirth.

The National Health Education Standards

■ Students will comprehend concepts related to health promotion and disease prevention.

Preparing to Teach the Lesson Plan

Materials

Rope or clothesline that is three to four feet long

Blackline Masters

Protecting the Developing Baby

Practice Abstinence from Sex to Avoid Teen Marriage, Teen Pregnancy, and Teen Parenthood

---

Teaching the Lesson Plan

1 Tell students they will learn how a mother-to-be's health habits affect the health of her developing baby. Give each student a copy of the Blackline Master *Protecting the Developing Baby*. Ask students to name harmful substances. Students might say alcohol or caffeine. Tell students that nicotine from cigarette smoke, crack and cocaine, alcohol, chemicals in glues or pesticides, ingredients in secondhand smoke, caffeine, and HIV are harmful substances that a mother-to-be might pass to her baby. Ask students to name healthful substances. Students might say vitamins or water. Tell students that vitamins and minerals from healthful foods and from supplements and calcium from milk and other dairy products are healthful substances that a mother-to-be might pass to her baby. Tell students that healthful and harmful substances pass from the mother-to-be's blood into the baby's blood.

2 Give one end of the rope to a student. Tell the student to name a harmful substance a mother-to-be should avoid. The student might say nicotine. Tell the student to tie a loose knot in the rope. Explain to students that the rope represents the umbilical cord. Substances in the blood of the mother-to-be pass through the umbilical cord into the unborn baby's blood. Tell the class that the knot represents a substance that is not good for the unborn baby. Tell the student who has just tied the knot in the rope to give the rope to another student. The second student names a harmful substance. Then the second student ties a loose knot in the rope. Continue this activity until there are at least six knots in the rope.

3 After there are at least six knots in the rope, give the rope to another student. Tell the student to name a healthful substance that is good for a developing baby. The student might say calcium. Tell the student to untie one of the loose knots in the rope. Tell the student who has just untied the knot in the rope to give the rope to another student. The second student names a healthful substance. Then the second student unties one of the loose knots in the rope. Continue this activity until all of the loose knots have been untied.

4 Define marriage. A **marriage** is an emotional and legal commitment made by a couple. Explain to students that it is important to wait until they complete school, can earn a living, and marry before they have a baby. Explain to the class that children need responsible parents. A baby benefits from bonding with its mother and father. Define bonding. **Bonding** is a process in which people develop a feeling of closeness. Bonding between parents and a baby begins at birth. Soft touches, gentle words, and physical closeness help bonding. Tell the class that they might take care of a younger brother or sister. They might childsit for a younger child. Tell the class these three ways they can help care for younger children:

1. Allow the child to play only with toys or objects that are safe.

2. Know what the child is doing at all times.

3. Get your parents or guardians if an emergency happens.

5 Give each student a copy of the Blackline Master *Practice Abstinence from Sex to Avoid Teen Marriage, Teen Pregnancy, and Teen Parenthood.*

Tell students that teen marriage is risky. Teens are not yet self-sufficient. Define self-sufficient. To be **self-sufficient** is to have the skills and money to take care of yourself. Tell students that they need an education to be self-sufficient. They also need to wait until they are self-sufficient to get married. Teens who marry are less likely than other teens to complete their education, have money, and be comfortable with body changes.

Tell students that teen pregnancy also is risky. A teen is more likely than an adult to choose risk behaviors. She might smoke cigarettes or drink alcohol. She might stop these behaviors when she learns she is pregnant. But the fertilized egg has divided many times before pregnancy is confirmed. Any drug use harms the developing baby. Babies born to teen parents might be born prematurely. Define premature birth. **Premature birth** is the birth of a baby before the 37th week of pregnancy. They might have low birth weights. Define low birth weight. A **low birth weight** is a weight at birth that is less than 5.5 pounds (2.5 kilograms).

Tell students that teen parenthood is risky. They need to wait until they are self-sufficient, have an education, and are a married adult to become parents. Girls their age risk having many health problems if they get pregnant. They might drop out of school. They also might have financial problems. They have little if any time for social lives. Boys their age have problems if they become fathers. They must work to support a child. They might drop out of school. They might go to school and work long hours. This leaves little time for activities with friends.

435

Assessment

Tell students to design a certificate. Tell students to write on the certificate that they will avoid teen marriage, teen pregnancy, and teen parenthood. Have the students sign their certificates. Students should include reasons why they should avoid teen marriage, teen pregnancy, and teen parenthood. Tell students to refer to the Blackline Master *Practice Abstinence from Sex to Avoid Teen Marriage, Teen Pregnancy, and Teen Parenthood* when making their certificates.

Protecting the Developing Baby

A mother-to-be should avoid harmful behaviors to protect her developing baby.

A mother-to-be should:

■ **not smoke.** Nicotine from cigarette smoke is a harmful drug. It can make a baby's heart beat faster.

■ **stay away from secondhand smoke.** If a mother-to-be breathes secondhand smoke it can harm the baby.

■ **not use harmful drugs.** Harmful drugs can cause birth defects.

■ **not drink alcohol.** Alcohol is a drug that can harm the baby.

■ **not breathe chemicals.** Any chemicals that the mother breathes can get into the baby's blood.

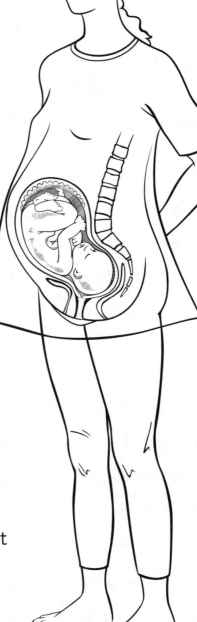

A mother-to-be should practice healthful behaviors to protect her developing baby.

A mother-to-be should:

■ **eat healthful foods.** Fruits and vegetables are good for a baby. Milk and milk products help a baby's bones and teeth grow strong.

■ **take vitamins and minerals.** A doctor might tell a mother-to-be to take vitamins and minerals to help a baby grow.

Practice Abstinence from Sex to Avoid Teen Marriage, Teen Pregnancy, and Teen Parenthood

Teen Marriage is risky.

- You need to wait until you are self-sufficient to get married. Being **self-sufficient** is to have the skills and money to take care of yourself.

- Teens who marry are less likely than other teens to complete their education, have money, and be comfortable with body changes.

- Most teens do not have the skills needed for successful marriage and parenthood.

Teen Pregnancy is risky.

- Babies born to teen parents might be born prematurely.

- Babies born to teen parents might have low birth weights.

- Teens often lack money for prenatal care.

Teen Parenthood is risky.

- Girls your age risk having many health problems if they get pregnant.

- Girls your age might drop out of school if they get pregnant.

- Girls your age might have financial problems if they get pregnant.

- Girls your age have little if any time for social lives if they get pregnant.

- Boys your age must work to support a child if they become fathers.

- Boys your age might drop out of school if they become fathers.

- Boys your age might go to school and work long hours if they become fathers. This leaves little time for activities with friends.

Section

6

Grades 7–8
Lesson Plans and Blackline Masters

Table of Contents

Hang On to Responsible Values

The Curriculum

Life Skill

■ I will show good character.

Objectives

■ Students will explain how they can develop good character.

■ Students will explain why it is important to have a good reputation.

■ Students will list and discuss ways to do a character checkup.

The National Health Education Standards

■ Students will demonstrate the ability to practice health-enhancing behaviors and reduce health risks.

Preparing to Teach the Lesson Plan

Materials

Ball of yarn

Blackline Masters

Ten Responsible Values That Show You Have Good Character™

Character Checkup

Teaching the Lesson Plan

1 Give each student a copy of the Blackline Master *Ten Responsible Values That Show You Have Good Character*. Define character. **Good character** is the use of self-control to act on responsible values. Define self-control and responsible value. **Self-control** is the effort a person makes to resist temptation. A **responsible value** is a belief that guides a person to act in responsible ways. Review each of the ten responsible values identified in the Blackline Master.

2 Explain that the ten responsible values guide a person to show good character. Tell students that their character will influence their reputation. Define reputation. **Reputation** is the quality of a person's character as judged by others. When a person has good character, his or her reputation remains favorable.

3 Tell students they are going to play "Hang On to a Good Reputation." Have your students sit in a circle. Take a ball of yarn. Wrap the end of the yarn around your index finger. Mention one responsible value that helps you hang on to a good reputation. Then roll the ball of yarn to a student sitting in the circle. This student wraps a piece of yarn around his or her index finger and states another responsible value. Continue until each student has wrapped the yarn around an index finger and stated a responsible value.

4 Explain to students that they are connected to the other students. They are connected to students who have stated a responsible value. Further explain that they need to be connected to friends who choose responsible values to hang on to a good reputation.

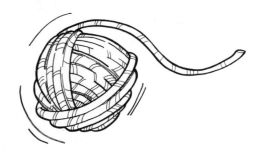

5 Give each student a copy of the Blackline Master *Character Checkup.* Explain to students that they can give themselves a character checkup by asking the twelve questions found on the Blackline Master.

Assessment

Have students write an essay explaining how they will hang on to a good reputation. Their essay must explain why having a good reputation is important to them. It must include a discussion of the responsible values they must practice. It must include how to do a character checkup.

Ten Responsible Values That Show You Have Good Character™

1 Honesty is refusing to lie, steal, or deceive anyone.

2 Self-discipline is the effort you make to follow through.

3 Fairness is following rules so everyone has the same chance.

4 Abstinence from sex is choosing not to be sexually active.

5 Determination is working hard to get what you want.

6 Courage is showing strength when you might otherwise be afraid.

7 Citizenship is following the laws of your community and nation.

8 Responsibility is being accountable for what you say and do.

9 Respect is having a high regard for someone.

10 Integrity is acting on responsible values regardless of the consequences.

Character Checkup

1. Do my parents or guardians think that I show good character?

2. Do I choose friends that show good character?

3. Do I act on responsible values?

4. Do I communicate in an open and honest way?

5. Do I treat myself and others with respect?

6. Am I nonviolent?

7. Do I make responsible decisions?

8. Do I resist temptation when pressured to choose wrong actions?

9. Do I take steps to correct wrong actions?

10. Do I practice abstinence from sex?

11. Do I lead a drug-free lifestyle?

12. Do I obey laws?

The CD Stuck on NO

The Curriculum

Life Skills

■ I will make responsible decisions.

■ I will use resistance skills when appropriate.

Objectives

■ Students will use *The Responsible Decision-Making Model*™ to make decisions.

■ Students will identify six questions to ask to evaluate the possible outcomes of a risk or dare before they take it.

■ Students will tell the difference between an unnecessary risk and a calculated risk.

■ Students will identify resistance skills they can use to say NO to negative peer pressure.

■ Students will demonstrate resistance skills if they are pressured to do something wrong.

■ Students will explain what to do if they give in to negative peer pressure.

The National Health Education Standards

■ Students will demonstrate the ability to use goal-setting and decision-making skills that enhance health.

Preparing to Teach the Lesson Plan

Materials

Cardboard

Colored construction paper

Markers

Scissors

Blackline Master

The Responsible Decision-Making Model™

Teaching the Lesson Plan

1 Discuss the importance of making responsible decisions. Define *The Responsible Decision-Making Model*™. **The Responsible Decision-Making Model**™ is a series of steps to follow to assure that the decisions a person makes result in actions that promote health, protect safety, follow laws, show respect for self and others, follow the guidelines of parents and of other responsible adults, and demonstrate good character. Give each student a copy of the Blackline Master *The Responsible Decision-Making Model*™. Explain that students can use the six steps of *The Responsible Decision-Making Model*™ to calculate whether or not a risk or dare is worth taking. Define calculated risk. A **calculated risk** is a chance that is worth taking after you consider the possible outcomes. Define unnecessary risk. An **unnecessary risk** is a chance that is not worth taking after you consider the possible outcomes.

2 Students who follow *The Responsible Decision-Making Model*™ should encourage others to do the same. This is known as positive peer pressure. Define peer pressure. **Peer pressure** is the effort other teens make to influence you. Students who do not follow *The Responsible Decision-Making Model*™ might want others to make those same harmful choices. This is known as negative peer pressure. Explain that it is important to say "no" when students use negative peer pressure. Explain that resistance skills are ways teens can say "no" to harmful choices. Define resistance skills. **Resistance skills** are skills that help you say NO to an action or to leave a situation. Explain that this is what a person should do:

• Say "no" with self-confidence.

• Give reasons for saying "no" using *The Responsible Decision-Making Model*™ .

- Repeat your reasons for saying "no" if you need to.
- Don't send a mixed message.
- Avoid situations in which there will be pressure to do something wrong.
- Avoid being with people who do not have good character.
- Influence others to have good character.

3 Explain that the CD-stuck-on-NO technique is a way of saying "no" to risks that are not worth taking. When a student uses the CD-stuck-on-NO technique, the student thinks of one reason he or she does not want to do something. Then, he or she repeats the reason for saying "no" like a skipping CD each time he or she is pressured to do something wrong. For example, suppose a student is being pressured to smoke a cigarette. That student could say, "I do not want to smoke cigarettes because I am on the track team and there is a rule against smoking." Then, when the student is pressured again and again, he or she keeps repeating his or her reason for saying "no," like a CD stuck on NO.

4 Tell students to get a partner. Have the partners stand in front of the class and ask one another to respond to the following situations using the CD-stuck-on-NO technique:

- A student offers a drink of alcohol.
- A student suggests hitchhiking.
- A student suggests copying homework.
- A student suggests smoking cigarettes.
- A student suggests watching a movie that shows sex and violence.
- A student wants to skip class and go to a restaurant.
- A student wants to make fun of another student because he or she is new or different.
- A student invites another student to his or her house for the weekend when his or her parents are not home.

- A student suggests smoking pot.
- A student suggests playing video games that show violence.

5 Have students make a CD using cardboard, colored construction paper, and markers. Where the CD title usually appears, have students write a pressure statement such as "Just one cigarette won't hurt you." Have students write on their CDs reasons to say "no" to smoking just one cigarette.

6 Tell students what to do if they make a wrong decision. Tell students to take responsibility for their actions, make restitution for wrong decisions, recognize that some wrong decisions can't be "fixed," and listen to the advice of responsible adults.

Assessment

Divide the class into two groups. Have one student make a pressure statement to the other group such as "Let's drink beer this weekend." Have a student from the second group respond by using the CD-stuck-on-NO technique. For example, the student might respond by saying, "No, we shouldn't drink beer because it is unhealthy and against the law." Have the first student repeat the pressure statement. Have each student in the group repeat the reason for saying "no."

The Responsible Decision-Making Model™

STEP 1 Describe the situation that requires a decision.

STEP 2 List possible decisions you might make.

STEP 3 Share the list of possible decisions with a parent, guardian, or other responsible adult.

STEP 4 Use six questions to evaluate the possible consequences of each decision.

Will this decision result in actions that:

1. promote health?

2. protect safety?

3. follow laws?

4. show respect for myself and others?

5. follow the guidelines of my parents and of other responsible adults?

6. demonstrate good character?

STEP 5 Decide which decision is most responsible and appropriate.

STEP 6 Act on your decision and evaluate the results.

Talk the Talk

The Curriculum

Life Skills

■ I will express feelings in healthful ways.

■ I will use conflict resolution skills.

Objectives

■ Students will use honest talk.

■ Students will use I-messages and active listening skills.

■ Students will avoid sending mixed messages.

■ Students will describe anger cues and signs of hidden anger.

■ Students will explain how to use anger management skills.

■ Students will discuss how nonverbal behavior and mixed messages affect communication.

■ Students will explain how to use conflict resolution skills.

■ Students will identify the six questions from *The Responsible Decision-Making Model*™ that you can use to evaluate possible solutions to conflict.

■ Students will explain how to deal with people who settle conflict in harmful ways.

■ Students will explain how an adult mediator can help teens resolve conflicts.

The National Health Education Standards

■ Students will demonstrate the ability to use interpersonal communication skills to enhance health.

Preparing to Teach the Lesson Plan

Materials

Index cards

Pen or pencil

Blackline Master

Conflict Resolution Skills

Teaching the Lesson Plan

Write these three harmful conflict styles on each of three index cards:

"Button Pusher." Under the title, write the following: "A button pusher is a person who pushes the 'hot button' of another person to cause trouble. The button pusher keeps referring to the sensitive issue. The button pusher wants a response from you. The button pusher wants you to lose control and say or do something foolish or wrong."

"Time Bomb." Under the title, write the following: "A time bomb is a person who has a quick temper and is ready to explode without warning. The slightest threat can set off a time bomb. A time bomb is at risk for harming you and others. A time bomb also can self-destruct."

"Sulker." Under the title, write the following: "A sulker is a person who uses the silent treatment. Sulkers want to get even. They usually are hurt by something that has happened or has been said. They want to respond by doing something hurtful. If you ask them what is wrong, they probably will mutter 'nothing.' They do not take responsibility for settling disagreements. They want you to figure out the problem. If you do not, they will continue to punish you with the silent treatment."

1 Tell students that they should express feelings in healthful ways. Tell students to use honest talk to let people know how they feel. Define honest talk. **Honest talk** is the straightforward sharing of thoughts and feelings. Tell students that using I-messages and active listening is a healthful way to express feelings. Explain to students that nonverbal behavior and mixed messages affect communication. The way a person uses his or her body language affects communication just as the words used and the tone of voice do. Define nonverbal communication. **Nonverbal communication** is the use of actions instead of words to express your thoughts and feelings. Define mixed message. A **mixed message** is a message that conveys two different meanings. Explain how to use anger management skills to students. Tell students that they should:

- Recognize anger cues. Define anger cue. An **anger cue** is a body change that occurs when a person is angry.

- Take a deep breath through their nose and blow it out through their mouth.

- Express their anger in a healthful way. Use I-messages to express their anger.

- Blow off steam with physical and creative activity.

- Talk with a responsible adult, such as their parents, their guardian, or a mentor.

2 Divide the class into three groups. Give each group an index card showing a harmful conflict style. Then tell the groups to write a script that demonstrates the use of their harmful conflict style. Groups should then act out their scripts. For example, the group with the index card titled "Sulker" would give his or her partner the silent treatment while the partner would try to work out the resolution. Groups should guess one another's harmful conflict style.

3 Tell students that there are at least three reasons why they need to learn to resolve conflict in healthful ways:

1. They will be less likely to develop diseases due to stress.

2. They will have better relationships.

3. They will decrease their risk of injury from violence.

Tell students how to use conflict resolution skills. Define conflict resolution skills. **Conflict resolution skills** are steps that can be taken to settle a disagreement in a responsible way. Give each student a copy of the Blackline Master *Conflict Resolution Skills*.

Assessment

Tell the class to role-play what is written on the piece of paper again. However, this time, the students acting out the script should try to resolve the conflict using conflict resolution skills. Students in the other groups should name which conflict resolution skills were used to resolve the conflict.

Conflict Resolution Skills

1. Remain calm.

2. Discuss the ground rules with the other person.

- Do not blame.
- Do not use put downs.
- Do not interrupt.
- Do not use threats.

3. Describe the conflict.

- Tell what you think happened.
- Be honest about what you have said or done to cause the conflict.
- Use I-messages to express your feelings about the conflict.
- Allow the other person to describe what he or she thinks happened.
- Listen without interrupting.
- Respond to the other person's feelings.

4. Brainstorm a list of possible solutions.

5. Use the six questions from *The Responsible Decision-Making Model*™ to evaluate each possible solution before agreeing to one.

- Will the solution lead to actions that are healthful?
- Will the solution lead to actions that are safe?
- Will the solution lead to actions that are legal?
- Will the solution lead to actions that show respect for you and others?
- Will the solution lead to actions that follow the guidelines of responsible adults, such as your parents or guardians?
- Will the solution lead to actions that demonstrate good character?

6. Agree on a solution.

- Keep your word and follow the solution on which you agreed.

7. Ask a trusted adult for help if you cannot agree on a solution.

Stop in the Name of Love

The Curriculum

Life Skills

■ I will practice protective factors to reduce the risk of violence.

■ I will practice self-protection strategies.

■ I will participate in victim recovery if I am harmed by violence.

Objectives

■ Students will explain how to recognize violence.

■ Students will discuss protective factors that reduce their risk of being involved in violence.

■ Students will identify self-protection strategies they can practice.

■ Students will discuss guidelines they can follow to reduce the risk of rape.

■ Students will explain the steps in victim recovery.

The National Health Education Standards

■ Students will demonstrate the ability to practice health-enhancing behaviors and reduce health risks.

Preparing to Teach the Lesson Plan

Materials

Index cards, enough for half of the class

Copy of the recording "Stop in the Name of Love" by Diana Ross and the Supremes

Blackline Master

Steps of Victim Recovery

Teaching the Lesson Plan

On index cards, write risk situations for rape or date rape. Some examples might be:

- *You have set a limit for expressing affection at closed-mouth kissing. A boy or girl tries to kiss you with an open mouth.*

- *A boy or girl is sexually aggressive, touching your body.*

- *A member of the opposite sex whom you have just met asks you to come home with him or her. No one will be at home.*

- *A boy or girl becomes rough or violent.*

- *You are invited to a party where teens are drinking alcohol.*

Make index cards for half of the class.

1 Explain to the class that teen violence has increased in recent years. Violence against teens and violence by teens is on the rise. Tell students that they will learn self-protection strategies to protect themselves from a form of violence. Explain to students that one form of violence is rape. Define rape. **Rape** is having sex with a person who has not given or is not capable of giving consent. Both males and females can be raped. Define acquaintance rape. **Acquaintance rape** is rape in which the rapist is known to the person who is raped. Define date rape. **Date rape** is rape that occurs in a dating situation. A person can practice self-protection strategies to reduce the risk of rape. Define self-protection strategies. **Self-protection strategies** are strategies that can be practiced to protect oneself and others from harm. Tell the class these self-protection strategies to follow to reduce the risk of rape:

- Do not spend time alone with a person you do not know or trust.

- Set clear limits for expressing affection and stick to them.

- Avoid a person who does not respect you or tries to control you.

2 Play the song "Stop in the Name of Love" by Diana Ross and the Supremes. Some of the words to the song are

> Stop, in the name of love,
>
> before you break my heart.
>
> Think it over.

Divide the class into pairs. Pass out the index cards. Tell one pair of students to come to the front of the class. A person in the pair will read what is on the index card. For example, the student might say, "A boy or girl starts becoming sexually aggressive, touching your body." Tell the class to sing, "Stop, in the name of love, before you break my heart. Think it over." The partner of the student who read the index card then would say a way to reduce the risk of rape. A student might say, "Think it over. Set clear limits for expressing affection and stick to them."

3 Repeat the activity until each pair has had a chance to state a line and respond with a way to reduce the risk of rape.

4 Tell the class that if any of them is a victim of violence, there are steps that can be taken to recover from violence. Define victim recovery. **Victim recovery** is a person's return to physical and emotional health after being harmed by violence. Give each student a copy of the Blackline Master *Steps of Victim Recovery*. Explain to students that it is important for a victim of violence to follow the steps for recovery. If a victim does not follow these steps, the victim is at increased risk for acting violently.

Assessment

Tell students to write "Stop in the Name of Love" at the top of a piece of paper. Tell students to name ten behaviors or situations they should avoid to reduce the risk of rape. For example, students might say, "I will avoid attending parties where alcohol might be served." Or students might say, "I will not date someone who will not respect the limits I place on expressing affection."

© 2001 Everyday Learning Corporation

Steps of Victim Recovery

1. Victims must receive treatment for any physical injuries.

2. Victims should receive treatment for emotional pain.

3. Victims will recover more completely if they have support from family and friends.

4. Victims should attempt to be repaid for money or property losses.

5. Victims should educate themselves about self-protection strategies.

Smash or Trash?

The Curriculum

Life Skills

■ I will choose healthful entertainment.

■ I will develop media literacy.

Objectives

■ Students will discuss reasons why they need to choose healthful entertainment.

■ Students will identify *Guidelines for Choosing Entertainment That Promotes Responsible Behavior.*

■ Students will give examples of TV programs, movies, and computer games that show healthful relationships.

■ Students will recognize and evaluate media messages.

■ Students will describe appeals used in advertisements.

The National Health Education Standards

■ Students will analyze the influence of culture, media, technology, and other factors on health.

Preparing to Teach the Lesson Plan

Materials

Pencil

Paper

Wastebasket

Blackline Masters

Guidelines for Choosing Entertainment That Promotes Responsible Behavior

Ten Tempting Advertising Appeals

Teaching the Lesson Plan

1 Explain that students can make healthful and responsible entertainment choices. Entertainment choices can affect students' relationships and can influence their character. Define healthful entertainment. **Healthful entertainment** is entertainment that promotes physical, mental, or social health. An example of a healthful entertainment choice is a movie showing a family working through a conflict. Healthful entertainment also promotes family values. Define family values. **Family values** are beliefs that strengthen family bonds. Give each student a copy of the Blackline Master *Guidelines for Choosing Entertainment That Promotes Responsible Behavior.* Movies and television shows should be approved by parents and guardians. Explain that healthful entertainment should not show drug-use or violence. It should not show sex outside of marriage.

2 Tell students that this activity will teach them how to evaluate entertainment as healthful or harmful entertainment. Divide the class into groups of five. Tell the class that they are going to play a game called "Smash or Trash." Tell each group to get out two sheets of paper. Tell each group to label one of the sheets "Smash" and the other sheet "Trash." Tell students to write the names of television programs that do not follow the *Guidelines for Choosing Entertainment That Promotes Responsible Behavior* on the paper labeled "Trash." Tell students also to write situations that might appear in a television show that do not follow these guidelines, such as a situation that includes violence or alcohol use.

3 Tell each group to write the names of television programs that follow the *Guidelines for Choosing Entertainment That Promotes Responsible Behavior* on the paper

© 2001 Everyday Learning Corporation

labeled "Smash." Tell students to write some of the situations that promote responsible behavior that appeared in the programs.

4 Tell each group to come to the front of the room with their "Smash" and "Trash" lists. Tell each group to read its list of "Trash" programs. Tell the groups to crumple up their "Trash" lists and throw them into the wastebasket. Tell students that "Trash" belongs in the garbage. Tell each group to read its list of "Smash" programs. Tell the groups to select one of the "Smash" programs and describe it for the class.

5 Tell students that they also can be wise consumers by learning how to evaluate media messages, such as advertisements. Give each student a copy of the Blackline Master

Ten Tempting Advertising Appeals. Tell students that these appeals are designed to persuade a person to buy a product and influence consumer choices. These appeals usually get an emotional response from consumers. Tell students that recognizing appeals is one way to lessen the effects ads and commercials have on a person.

Assessment

Divide the class into groups of four or five. Tell each group to write a short script for a television program that follows the *Guidelines for Choosing Entertainment That Promotes Responsible Behavior.* Tell each group to present its program to the class.

Guidelines for Choosing Entertainment That Promotes Responsible Behavior

1 Entertainment should be approved for your age group.

2 Entertainment should be approved by your parents or guardians.

3 Entertainment should **not** present harmful drug use as acceptable behavior.

4 Entertainment should **not** present violence as acceptable behavior.

5 Entertainment should **not** lead you to believe that sex outside of marriage is acceptable behavior.

Ten Tempting Advertising Appeals

1. Bandwagon appeal

is an advertising appeal that tries to convince you that everybody is using a particular product or service, and you should too.

2. Brand loyalty appeal

is an advertising appeal that tries to convince you that one brand is better than the rest.

3. False image appeal

is an advertising appeal that tries to convince you that you will have a certain image if you buy a specific product or service.

4. Glittering generality appeal

is an advertising appeal that includes a general statement that is exaggerated to appeal to the emotions.

5. Humor appeal

is an advertising appeal that contains a catchy slogan, jingle, or cartoon that grabs attention.

6. Progress appeal

is an advertising appeal that emphasizes that a product is "new and improved."

7. Reward appeal

is an advertising appeal that offers a special prize, gift, or coupon when a specific product or service is purchased.

8. Scientific evidence appeal

is an advertising appeal that includes the results of surveys and laboratory tests.

9. Testimonial appeal

is an advertising appeal that focuses on a person, often a celebrity, who gives a statement about the benefits of a specific product or service.

10. Sex appeal

is an advertising appeal that tries to convince you that others will find you irresistible if you use a specific product or service.

Web Wise

The Curriculum

Life Skills

■ I will choose healthful entertainment.

■ I will develop media literacy.

Objectives

■ Students will discuss reasons why they need to choose healthful entertainment.

■ Students will identify *Guidelines for Choosing Entertainment That Promotes Responsible Behavior.*

■ Students will give examples of TV programs, movies, and computer games that show healthful relationships.

■ Students will recognize and evaluate media messages.

■ Students will describe appeals used in advertisements.

The National Health Education Standards

■ Students will analyze the influence of culture, media, technology, and other factors on health.

■ Students will demonstrate the ability to use goal-setting and decision-making skills to enhance health.

Preparing to Teach the Lesson Plan

Materials

Construction paper

Art supplies

Teaching the Lesson Plan

1 Tell students that in this lesson they will learn how to choose wisely when choosing entertainment. Define entertainment. **Entertainment** is something that is designed to hold the interest of people. Explain that entertainment does not necessarily portray life in a realistic way. Ask students how many times they have seen a television show wherein a teen helps with household chores? How many shows have they seen in which two teens who care about each other make a responsible decision and practice abstinence from sex until marriage? Entertainment often includes situations and people who differ from real life. This approach to entertainment attempts to get people "hooked" on a glamorous-life-without-consequences. For example, television shows that depict teens who are sexually active rarely describe the consequences of the teens' actions. In real life, teens who are sexually active might get infected with STDs, including HIV, and/or have unwanted pregnancies. The danger to becoming too involved in this kind of entertainment is that a person loses perspective on real life.

2 Explain that students can make wise entertainment choices when they are choosing television shows, movies, computer games, or Internet sites. Teens should follow these guidelines when choosing entertainment:

• Entertainment should follow family guidelines.

• Entertainment should be approved for your age group.

• Entertainment should not show inappropriate content, such as violence or sex.

• Entertainment should not portray harmful drug use as acceptable behavior.

3 Explain that some teens spend large amounts of time using the computer. They play computer games for long periods of time. They form relationships on-line by e-mailing people and participating in discussion groups or "chat groups." They might "surf the Internet" for hours. These teens might find it easier to talk with others by computer than to have relationships in person. These teens do not have the opportunity to have healthful friendships and develop social skills.

4 Teens can use the Internet responsibly. Define the Internet. The **Internet** is an on-line telecommunications system that connects computer networks from around the world. Teens can choose healthful Internet Web sites that provide factual information. For example, students can learn health information on the World Wide Web. Define the World Wide Web. The **World Wide Web**, or **Web**, is a graphic system on the Internet made up of a huge connection of documents. Teens can use a program called a search engine to search for Web sites that contain information about health.

5 Give students construction paper and other art supplies. Tell students that they will design a home page for a Web site that contains health information. Tell students to come up with a name for their Web site. Students should have a Web address for their site. Students should put all the important information contained on the Web site on their home page. Students should write a paragraph explaining the purpose of the Web site. Students should include buttons and links to other Web sites. Students should design appealing sites that will be entertaining as well as informative.

Assessment

Tell students to design a pamphlet that includes the guidelines to follow when choosing entertainment. Tell students to target the pamphlet to people who use the Internet or World Wide Web. Get permission to allow students to leave the pamphlet in the school library.

Maintaining a Healthful Balance

The Curriculum

Life Skills

■ I will develop healthful relationships.

■ I will recognize harmful relationships.

Objectives

■ Students will explain why it is more important to be respected than it is to be popular.

■ Students will describe the balance of giving and taking in a healthful relationship.

■ Students will list the six criteria to use to evaluate decisions made with friends.

■ Students will give examples of "sick" relationships and tell what to do about them.

■ Students will explain when and how to end a friendship.

The National Health Education Standards

■ Students will demonstrate the ability to use interpersonal communication skills to enhance health.

Preparing to Teach the Lesson Plan

Materials

Paper

Pen or pencil

Journal or notebook, one for each student

Blackline Master

The Responsible Decision-Making Model™

Teaching the Lesson Plan

1 Ask students what they think is more important: to be respected or to be popular. Students will probably say to be respected. Explain to students the difference between being respected and being popular. Define to be respected. **To be respected** is to be held in high regard by others because one behaves in responsible ways. Define to be popular. **To be popular** is to be liked by others. Tell students that a person might:

• Be respected and be popular. For example, a straight-A student who also plays quarterback might be both respected and popular.

• Be respected and not be popular. A person who leaves a party where alcohol is served might lose some friends, but other teens who act in responsible ways would respect him or her.

• Not be respected and be popular. A star basketball player who smokes and drinks might be popular, but not respected.

• Not be respected and not be popular. A student who acts like a bully and does not work hard might not be respected or popular.

2 Tell students to fold a sheet of paper in half horizontally and then vertically to make four sections. They should write each of the following in one of the sections: respected and popular; respected, but not popular; not respected, but popular; not respected and not popular. Tell students to list traits for each kind of student in the sections. The students should list as many traits as possible. For example, in the square with the words not respected and not popular, students might write the following: poor grades, bully, smoker.

3 Tell students that they should use *The Responsible Decision-Making Model*™ when evaluating decisions that they make with friends. Define *The Responsible Decision-Making Model*™. ***The Responsible Decision-Making Model*™** is a series of steps to follow to assure that decisions lead to actions that promote health; protect safety; follow laws; show respect for self and others; follow guidelines set by responsible adults, such as a person's parents or guardians; and demonstrate good character.

4 Ask students to discuss the traits they wrote for each of the four sections. Tell students that they should concentrate on being liked and respected for having good character. Define character. **Character** is a person's use of self-control to act on responsible values. Define self-control. **Self-control** is the effort you make to resist temptation. Tell students that developing healthful relationships that involve mutual respect and that promote responsible behavior is part of having good character. Define healthful relationships. **Healthful relationships** are relationships that promote mutual respect and responsible behavior. In a healthful relationship, one person does not do all the giving while the other does the taking. One-sided relationships and abusive relationships are "sick" relationships.

5 Tell students that it is better to be respected than it is to be popular. Tell students that if a person is respected, others have high regard for him or her because he or she behaves in responsible ways. But if a person is popular, others might like him or her for the wrong reasons. They might like him or her because he or she goes along with their wrong actions. They might like him or her because he or she has material things, such as clothes or jewelry, that others do not have. Although he or she might want to be respected *and* be popular, this is not always possible.

6 Tell students that friendships change for many different reasons. A friend might move away and not keep in touch. A friend might break a confidence, and the friendship is never the same again. A friend might bring out the worst in a person. A friend might try to get a person to use illegal drugs. Tell students that it is not in their best interest to continue such friendships.

Tell students that when a friendship ends to avoid gossiping about the former friend. Tell students to keep the confidences that their former friend shared. Explain that if they do not, others might question whether or not they can be trusted.

Tell students not to try to get even if the friendship ended due to hurt feelings. Tell students that they might be sad for a period of time if a friendship ends. They might feel disappointed or let down. Tell students to remember why they ended the friendship. The friendship was ended to protect their health and reputation. Tell the students that their parents might have asked them to end the friendship, and that it is important to follow their parents' guidelines.

Tell students that they should discuss their feelings with their parents or guardians if a friendship ends. Parents can help students' deal with the feelings of loss. Tell students to put time and effort into new and healthful relationships.

Assessment

Tell students to keep a journal for one week. The journal should be a list of all of the activities in which they participated. Tell the students to divide the activities into two lists: the activities that would earn them respect, and the activities that would make them popular. Ask students to observe the differences. At the end of a week, have students write a paper about why it is more important to be respected than it is to be popular.

The Responsible Decision-Making Model™

Use the *Responsible Decision-Making Model™* when making decisions with friends.

STEP 1   Describe the situation that requires a decision.

STEP 2   List possible decisions you might make.

STEP 3   Share the list of possible decisions with a parent, guardian, or other responsible adult.

STEP 4   Use six questions to evaluate the possible consequences of each decision.

Will this decision result in actions that:

1. promote health?
2. protect safety?
3. follow laws?
4. show respect for myself and others?
5. follow the guidelines of my parents and of other responsible adults?
6. demonstrate good character?

STEP 5   Decide which decision is most responsible and appropriate.

STEP 6   Act on your decision and evaluate the results.

Do You Want to be Prepared for Dating?

The Curriculum

Life Skill

■ I will develop dating skills.

Objectives

■ Students will explain how to stick to limits for expressing affection.

■ Students will list their parents' or guardians' guidelines for dating.

■ Students will list and explain do's and don'ts of dating.

■ Students will list the questions in *The Respect Checklist™* that tell them whether someone of the opposite sex shows respect for them.

■ Students will discuss ways to reduce the risk of date rape.

The National Health Education Standards

■ Students will demonstrate the ability to use interpersonal communication skills to enhance health.

Preparing to Teach the Lesson Plan

Materials

Chalkboard and chalk

Transparency projector and screen

Blackline Masters

Information to Discuss with Parents or Guardians Before Going Out on a Date

Ways to Set Limits for Expressing Affection

The Respect Checklist™

Teaching the Lesson Plan

1 Define dating. **Dating** is having social plans with another person. Ask students to name other words that they use for dating. They might say that dating is referred to as "going out" or "hanging out." Explain that parents and guardians want their teens to have positive dating experiences. That is why they set standards and have specific expectations for their teens when they give them permission to date or to "go out" or "hang out." Give each student a copy of the Blackline Master *Information to Discuss with Parents or Guardians Before Going Out on a Date.* Review the Blackline Master and suggest that students review it with their parents or guardians. Suggest that they work together with their parents or guardians to make a list of family guidelines for dating.

2 Ask students to identify expectations they have for dating. List their expectations on the chalkboard. Tell students the do's and don'ts of dating:

• Do follow your parents' or guardians' guidelines for dating.

• Do respect the feelings of a person who asks you out on a date.

• Do call your parents or guardians if you are on a date and need help.

• Don't go on a date where teens will be drinking alcohol or using other drugs.

• Don't rush into a steady relationship.

• Don't consider yourself a success or failure based on your ability to get a date.

• Don't date someone who hits you, shoves you, hurts you, threatens you, or says cruel words to you.

3 Emphasize that teens who date, "go out" or "hang out" must have mutual respect for one another. Ask students to identify behaviors that indicate teens respect themselves and others. Review the following ways that a teen might know that another teen respects him or her. The teen who shows respect will:

- build you up;
- show interest in what you say and do;
- encourage you to do your best in school;
- make responsible decisions;
- practice a drug-free lifestyle;
- be nonviolent;
- obey laws;
- have a healthful attitude about members of both sexes; and
- practice abstinence from sex

4 Define abstinence from sex. **Abstinence from sex** is choosing not to be sexually active. Give each student a copy of the Blackline Master *Ways to Set Limits for Expressing Affection.* Define affection. **Affection** is a fond or tender feeling for another person. Tell students that when teens are sexually attracted to one another they must set limits for expressing affection so that they can stick to their decisions to practice abstinence from sex. Tell the class the five ways to set limits for expressing affection. The five ways are:

1. Limit your expressions of affection to hand-holding, hugging, and casual kissing to keep your brain in control of your decisions and actions.

2. Tell a person your limits before expressing affection.

3. Do not date someone who does not respect your limits.

4. Avoid drinking alcohol and using other drugs that dull your brain and interfere with wise judgment.

5. Do not date someone who drinks alcohol or uses other drugs that dull the brain and interfere with wise judgment. Tell students that by using resistance skills, setting limits for the expression of affection, and avoiding risk factors and risk situations, they can reduce the risk of being a victim of date rape. Define date rape. **Date rape** is rape that occurs in a dating situation.

5 Tell students that they are going to participate in a version of a popular television quiz show. On the show, the host asks a participant a series of questions. The host gives the participant four answers from which he or she can choose. Only one of the answers is correct. If the participant knows the correct answer, he or she responds right away. If the participant does not know the correct answer, he or she can use one of two helplines. The helplines are two persons that the participant has chosen who can be called to help him or her answer the question correctly. The participant continues playing "Do You Want to be Prepared for Dating?" until he or she has answered one of the questions incorrectly.

6 Divide the class into six groups to write questions and answers for the host to use in the quiz show. An example of a question and the four answers might be:

Before going out on a date, teens should:

a. discuss their plans with older teens who might advise them;

b. discuss their plans with their parents or guardians; (correct answer)

c. have a great outfit to wear in order to be extra attractive;

d. find out if the person they want to go out with is popular with other teens

7 Collect the questions and answers that the groups wrote. Select appropriate questions and answers and write them on overhead transparencies. Select a student to host the quiz show. Then select the first participant. The participant is permitted to select two other students to be his or her helplines. Begin the quiz show by having the host ask the questions. Have the other students in the class record the answers they would select on sheets of paper.

Assessment

Give each student a copy of the Worksheet Master *The Respect Checklist*™. Tell students to evaluate one of their relationships using *The Respect Checklist*™. Then ask each student to write a one-page paper on why it is important to limit expressions of affection. Have students include in their papers their own family's guidelines for dating.

Ways to Set Limits for Expressing Affection

Respect Yourself!   Respect Yourself!   Respect Yourself!   Respect Yourself!

Respect Yourself!

Respect Yourself!

1 Limit your expressions of affection to hand-holding, hugging, and casual kissing to keep your brain in control of your decisions and actions.

2 Tell a person your limits before expressing affection.

3 Do not date someone who does not respect your limits.

4 Avoid drinking alcohol and using other drugs that dull your brain and interfere with wise judgment.

5 Do not date someone who drinks alcohol or uses other drugs that dull the brain and interfere with wise judgment.

Respect Yourself!   Respect Yourself!   Respect Yourself!   Respect Yourself!

Information to Discuss with Parents or Guardians Before Going Out on a Date

- Your date's name

- Your date's age

- Where your date attends school

- The names and phone numbers of your date's parents or guardians

- The time you will go out

- The place(s) you will go

- The time you are expected home

- The transportation you will use

- Where you can reach your parents or guardians if there is a problem

- Who will pay for the date

The Respect Checklist™

Use *The Respect Checklist*™ to help you choose a friend. You know a friend respects you if you check all of the boxes in the left-hand column. You know a friend does not respect you if you check any of the boxes in the right-hand column.

RESPECT	DISRESPECT
☐ Builds me up	☐ Puts me down
☐ Shows interest in what I say and do	☐ Shows interest only in himself or herself
☐ Encourages me to do my best in school	☐ Does not encourage me to do my best in school
☐ Makes responsible decisions	☐ Makes wrong decisions
☐ Encourages me to make responsible decisions	☐ Encourages me to make wrong decisions
☐ Practices a drug-free lifestyle	☐ Misuses or abuses drugs
☐ Is nonviolent	☐ Is violent
☐ Obeys laws	☐ Breaks laws
☐ Has a healthful attitude about members of both sexes	☐ Has a negative attitude about members of one or both sexes
☐ Practices abstinence	☐ Pressures me to become sexually active

Resisting Temptation

The Curriculum

Life Skills

■ I will practice abstinence from sex.

■ I will use resistance skills when appropriate.

Objectives

■ Students will identify *The Top Ten List of Reasons to Practice Abstinence™*.

■ Students will use the *The Responsible Decision-Making Model™* to explain why abstinence is the expected standard for teens.

■ Students will outline resistance skills they can use if they are pressured to be sexually active.

The National Health Education Standards

■ Students will demonstrate the ability to practice health-enhancing behaviors and reduce health risks.

■ Students will demonstrate the ability to use goal-setting and decision-making skills that enhance health.

Preparing to Teach the Lesson Plan

Materials

Two pieces of soft candy in a wrapper for two-thirds of the students

Blackline Masters

Seven Ways to Resist Pressure to Be Sexually Active

The Top Ten List of Reasons to Practice Abstinence™

Teaching the Lesson Plan

1 Divide the class into three groups. The first group is the risk behavior group. Define risk behavior. A **risk behavior** is an action that threatens health and can cause disease, injury, and premature death. An example of a risk behavior is smoking. Smoking threatens health, increases the likelihood of illness and premature death, and harms the quality of the environment. Give each person in the risk behavior group a piece of candy. The second group is the risk situation group. Define risk situation. A **risk situation** is a circumstance that threatens health and can cause disease, injury, and premature death. An example of a risk situation is riding in a car with a driver who is intoxicated. Give each person in the risk situation group a piece of candy. The third group is the healthful behavior group. Define healthful behavior. A **healthful behavior** is an action that promotes health; prevents injury, illness, and premature death; and improves the quality of the environment. An example of a healthful behavior is eating fruits and vegetables. Eating fruits and vegetables promotes health and helps prevent illness, injury, and premature death. Do not give the students in this group any candy.

2 Define peer pressure. **Peer pressure** is the effort other teens make to influence you. Some peers might pressure a person to do something wrong, such as cheating on a test or stealing something from a store. Tell the students in the first group to eat the candy in front of the second group. Tell them to pressure the members of the second group to eat their candy, also. See whether anyone in the second group eats his or her candy. Ask the students for pressure statements the members of the first group used to try to encourage the members of the second group to eat their candy.

3 Tell the members of the second group to take a small bite out of their candy. Tell them to hold the rest in their hands near their mouths without eating it. Tell the members of the first group to pressure the members of the second group to eat the rest of the candy. Discuss the results of the activity. Ask students what techniques were used by members of the first group to pressure members of the second group. Ask students to discuss whether they were more tempted to eat the candy before they unwrapped it or after they had unwrapped it and taken a small bite. Students will probably say that they were more tempted to eat the candy after they had unwrapped it and taken a small bite. Tell students that this is why it is important to set limits on most behaviors to avoid participating in risk behaviors. For example, taking a sip of beer might lead to drinking. Tell students that the same is true for sexual intercourse. Open-mouth kissing and petting might lead to sexual intercourse.

4 Define resistance skills. **Resistance skills** are skills that help you say NO to an action or to leave a situation. Tell the class that there are seven ways to resist pressure to be sexually active. Give each student a copy of the Blackline Master *Seven Ways to Resist Pressure to Be Sexually Active.* The seven ways are:

1. Be confident and say, "No, I do not want to be sexually active."
2. Give reasons why you practice abstinence.
3. Repeat your reasons for practicing abstinence.
4. Do not send a mixed message.
5. Avoid situations in which there might be pressure to be sexually active.
6. Break off a relationship when someone does not respect your limits.
7. Influence others to practice abstinence.

Take the members of the third group aside. Tell them that they should not touch the candy. Tell them to use resistance skills each time they are pressured by a member of the first or second group to eat the candy. Tell them that after they are pressured three times by a member of the first or second group, they are to move away from the person offering them the candy. Give the first and second groups

more candy to offer to the members of the third group. Tell the first and second groups to pressure the members of the third group into eating the candy.

5 Ask students what happened when members of the third group avoided the risk behavior by using resistance skills. Emphasize to students the importance of resisting temptation. Tell students that if they are pressured to be sexually active, they can use resistance skills. Give each student a copy of the Blackline Master *The Top Ten List of Reasons to Practice Abstinence*™. Tell students that it is never too late to practice abstinence. Tell students that even teens who have been sexually active can take steps to change their behavior. They can:

- tell their parents or guardians;
- have a medical checkup; and
- choose behaviors that support their decision to practice abstinence.

Tell students they can use *The Responsible Decision-Making Model*™ to explain why abstinence is the expected standard for teens. They should ask themselves six questions:

1. Is it healthful for me to be sexually active? Why or why not?
2. Is it safe for me for me to be sexually active? Why or why not?
3. Do I follow rules and laws if I am sexually active? Why or why not?
4. Do I show respect for myself and others if I am sexually active? Why or why not?
5. Do I follow my family's guidelines if I am sexually active? Why or why not?
6. Do I show good character if I am sexually active? Why or why not?

Assessment

Tell students the following scenario: A classmate invites four of his or her friends to his or her home. His or her parents are not at home. One of the classmates suggests playing spin the bottle. Three of the students decide they want to play. They are trying to pressure the other classmate to join them. Tell students to identify resistance skills they would use to resist the pressure of playing spin the bottle.

Seven Ways to Resist Pressure to Be Sexually Active

1 Be confident and say, "No, I do not want to be sexually active."

2 Give reasons why you practice abstinence.

3 Repeat your reasons for practicing abstinence.

4 Do not send a mixed message.

5 Avoid situations in which there might be pressure to be sexually active.

6 Break off a relationship when someone does not respect your limits.

7 Influence others to practice abstinence.

The Top Ten List of Reasons to Practice Abstinence™

1 I want to follow family guidelines.

2 I want to respect myself.

3 I want to respect others.

4 I want to have a good reputation.

5 I do not want to feel guilty.

6 I am not ready for marriage.

7 I do not want to risk pregnancy.

8 I am not ready to be a parent.

9 I do not want to be infected with an STD.

10 I do not want to be infected with HIV.

Looking Ahead

The Curriculum

Life Skill

■ I will practice abstinence from sex.

Objectives

■ Students will discuss the benefits of a monogamous traditional marriage.

■ Students will identify the harmful consequences that can result from having babies outside of marriage.

The National Health Education Standards

■ Students will demonstrate the ability to practice health-enhancing behaviors and reduce health risks.

Preparing to Teach the Lesson Plan

Materials

Yardstick

Blackline Masters

Risks to Babies Born to Teen Parents

Risks to Teen Mothers

Risks to Teen Fathers

Benefits of a Traditional Monogamous Marriage

Teaching the Lesson Plan

1 Select a student to do a demonstration for the class. Have the student place the tip of a yardstick on his or her finger. Tell the student to try to balance the yardstick while looking down at where the yardstick rests on his or her finger.

2 Repeat the demonstration. This time, have the student look about two-thirds of the way toward the top of the yardstick while trying to balance it. The yardstick should stay balanced longer than before.

3 Explain to students that looking at the bottom of the yardstick is similar to making decisions without thinking about the consequences. For example, being sexually active can have harmful consequences. A female could become pregnant or become infected with an STD. A male could get someone pregnant or become infected with an STD. Tell students that harmful consequences, like becoming a teenage parent, might happen to a person if he or she does not think about what might happen later. Define abstinence from sex. **Abstinence from sex** is choosing not to be sexually active. Abstinence from sex is the expected standard for teens.

Tell students that there are risks associated with becoming teen parents. There are risks to babies born to teen parents. Give each student a copy of the Blackline Master *Risks to Babies Born to Teen Parents*.

Babies born to teen parents

• often do not receive adequate nourishment.

• often do not receive adequate prenatal care. **Prenatal care** is care that is given to a mother-to-be and her developing baby.

• risk being born prematurely and having low birth weights. **Premature birth** is the birth of a baby before it is fully developed or the birth of a baby less than 38 weeks from the time of conception. **Low birth weight** is a weight at birth that is less than 5.5 pounds (2.5 kilograms). Low birth weight is a major cause of infant death and mental retardation.

• are more likely to be abused by their parents.

• are less likely to have adequate medical and dental care as children.

Give each student a copy of the Blackline Master *Risks to Teen Mothers*.

Teen mothers

- risk anemia during pregnancy. **Anemia** is a condition in which the oxygen-carrying pigment in the blood is below normal.

- risk toxemia of pregnancy. **Toxemia of pregnancy** is a disorder of pregnancy characterized by high blood pressure, tissue swelling, and protein in the urine.

- risk premature birth.

- are more likely to drop out of school.

- are less likely to meet their career goals.

- have limited social opportunities.

- are more likely to have low incomes.

- are more likely to abuse their children.

Give each student a copy of the Blackline Master *Risks to Teen Fathers*.

Teen fathers

- have to pay child support and might be financially stressed.

- are more likely to drop out of school because they have to work.

- might have to change career plans.

- often lack contact with their children.

- are more likely to abuse their children.

- are less likely to meet their career goals.

4 Explain to students that looking about two-thirds of the way toward the top of the yardstick is similar to making decisions while thinking about what could happen later. Tell students that it is risky for a person to become a parent before he or she is in his or her 20s, married, and self-sufficient. Define self-sufficient. **Self-sufficient** is to have the skills and financial resources to care for oneself.

5 Define traditional monogamous marriage. A **traditional monogamous marriage** is a marriage in which a husband and wife have sex only with one another. Give each student a copy of the Blackline Master *Benefits of a Traditional Monogamous Marriage*.

Tell students these benefits of a traditional monogamous marriage:

- protects the marriage commitment;

- preserves the marriage tradition;

- helps prevent divorce;

- provides a loving relationship in which parents raise children together;

- provides emotional security and trust; and

- helps protect marriage partners from infection with HIV and other STDs.

Assessment

Ask students to discuss the goals they have for the future. Write the goals students share on the board. Some of these goals might be to attend college, to get a good job, to support themselves financially, or to graduate from high school. Ask for a student volunteer. Give the student volunteer an eraser. Ask the class to tell why each goal might not be reached if a person becomes a teen parent. For example, a student might say that a teen parent might not be able to attend college because they need to work a full-time job to support the baby and wouldn't have the time to attend classes. As a student names why future goals might not be reached, have the student volunteer erase that goal.

Risks to Babies Born to Teen Parents

Babies Born to Teen Parents:

1. **Often do not receive adequate nourishment.**

2. **Often do not receive adequate prenatal care.**
   Prenatal care is care that is given to a mother-to-be and her developing baby.

3. **Risk being born prematurely and having low birth weights.**
   Premature birth is the birth of a baby before it is fully developed or the birth of a baby less than 38 weeks from the time of conception. **Low birth weight** is a weight at birth that is less than 5.5 pounds (2.5 kilograms). Low birth weight is a major cause of infant death and mental retardation.

4. **Are more likely to be abused by their parents.**

5. **Are less likely to have adequate medical and dental care as children.**

Risks to Teen Mothers

Teen Mothers:

1. **Risk anemia during pregnancy.**
   Anemia is a condition in which the oxygen-carrying pigment in the blood is below normal.

2. **Risk toxemia of pregnancy.**
   Toxemia of pregnancy is a disorder of pregnancy characterized by high blood pressure, tissue swelling, and protein in the urine.

3. **Risk premature birth.**

4. **Are more likely to drop out of school.**

5. **Are less likely to meet their career goals.**

6. **Have limited social opportunities.**

7. **Are more likely to have low incomes.**

8. **Are more likely to abuse their children.**

Risks to Teen Fathers

Teen Fathers:

1. Have to pay child support and might be financially stressed.

2. Are more likely to drop out of school because they have to work.

3. Might have to change career plans.

4. Often lack contact with their children.

5. Are more likely to abuse their children.

6. Are less likely to meet their career goals.

Benefits of a Traditional Monogamous Marriage

A Traditional Monogamous Marriage:

1. Protects the marriage commitment.

2. Preserves the marriage tradition.

3. Helps prevent divorce.

4. Provides a loving relationship in which parents raise children together.

5. Provides emotional security and trust.

6. Helps protect marriage partners from infection with HIV and other STDs.

You Booze, You Lose

The Curriculum

Life Skill

■ I will practice abstinence from sex.

Objective

■ Students will explain how a drug-free lifestyle supports their decision to practice abstinence.

The National Health Education Standards

■ Students will demonstrate the ability to practice health-enhancing behaviors and reduce health risks.

Preparing to Teach the Lesson Plan

Materials

Sheet of paper

Pen or pencil

Blackline Master

Why It Is Risky to Drink Alcohol and Use Other Harmful Drugs

Teaching the Lesson Plan

1 Explain to students the effects of alcohol on responsible decision-making. Explain that alcohol is a depressant drug that slows down the part of the brain responsible for reasoning and judgment.

2 Tell students that they are going to demonstrate how a drug such as alcohol can affect their decision-making. Tell students to write their names on a sheet of paper. Tell students to hold one foot straight out in front of them as they write. They should use the foot that corresponds to the hand that they use for writing. For example, a right-handed person would hold out his or her right foot.

3 Tell students to make circles with their feet in a clockwise fashion. While they are making circles with their feet, students should write their names again under the first signature. Students will find that it is difficult to maintain a circular motion with the extended foot. Tell students to compare their two signatures.

4 Ask students to say what they experienced. Students will probably say that it was more difficult to write their names the second time. Tell students that this is because their minds could not fully concentrate on writing their signatures. Instead, their minds were under the influence of another factor—moving their feet. Tell students to use this information to discuss how being under the influence of alcohol might affect responsible decision-making regarding sexual behavior. Explain to students that when a person drinks alcohol, he is is she is not in control of his or her decisions. A person might not stick to his or her decision to practice abstinence. Explain to students that practicing abstinence from sex and using alcohol or other harmful drugs do not mix. Give each student a copy of the Blackline Master *Why It Is Risky to Drink Alcohol and Use Other Harmful Drugs*.

Assessment

Tell students to design a warning label for a bottle of alcohol. The warning label should make a specific statement about the effects of drinking alcohol on responsible decision-making and sexual behavior. It should refer to at least one way using alcohol or other harmful drugs is risky.

Why It Is Risky to Drink Alcohol and Use Other Harmful Drugs

1. You might not stick to your decision to practice abstinence.

2. You increase your risk of getting pregnant or getting someone pregnant.

3. You increase the risk of becoming infected with HIV and other STDs.

4. You increase the risk of being in situations in which rape occurs. **Rape** is having sex with a person who has not given or is not capable of giving consent.

5. You are around teens who use drugs, which puts you at risk for being slipped a drug. **Drug slipping** is placing a drug into someone's food or beverage without that person's knowledge.

6. You might become drug dependent and exchange sex for drugs or for money to buy drugs.

7. You might share a needle that has infected blood on it.

Unfriendly Persuasion

The Curriculum

Life Skills

■ I will practice abstinence from sex.

■ I will use resistance skills when appropriate.

Objectives

■ Students will outline resistance skills they can use if they are pressured to be sexually active.

■ Students will be able to explain how a drug-free lifestyle supports their decision to practice abstinence.

■ Students will explain how abstinence reduces their risk of becoming infected with HIV and other STDs.

The National Health Education Standards

■ Students will demonstrate the ability to practice health-enhancing behaviors and reduce health risks.

■ Students will demonstrate the ability to use goal-setting and decision-making skills that enhance health.

Preparing to Teach the Lesson Plan

Materials

Index cards

Blackline Master

The Model for Using Resistance Skills

Teaching the Lesson Plan

This activity is designed for students to work in groups of five. For each group, prepare one card that reads, "You are at a party with your friends, and they all are drinking alcohol. They want to convince you to drink alcohol also, but you do not want to join them." For each group, prepare four cards that say, "You are at a party drinking alcohol. You want to convince the one person at the party who is not drinking to join the others and drink."

1 Explain to students that alcohol and other harmful drugs affect the part of the brain that controls judgment. When a person drinks alcohol or uses another harmful drug, his or her ability to make responsible decisions is affected. When a person drinks alcohol or uses another harmful drug, he or she might not stand by his or her decision to practice abstinence. Give each student a copy of the Blackline Master *The Model for Using Resistance Skills*. Tell students the seven ways to resist pressure to be sexually active. The seven ways are:

1. Say "no" with confidence.

2. Give reasons why you practice abstinence.

3. Repeat your reasons for practicing abstinence.

4. Don't send a mixed message.

5. Avoid situations in which there will be pressure to be sexually active.

6. Break off a relationship when someone does not respect your limits.

7. Influence others to practice abstinence.

2 Divide the class into groups of five. Pass out the five cards for each group. Each student should have a card. Tell students to play the roles that are written on the cards. Tell the student holding the appropriate card to resist the pressure to drink alcohol by using the seven resistance skills. Give the groups about five minutes to role-play within their groups.

3 Tell the class to come together. Have students discuss what happened in each of the groups. Students will probably say that the four members of the group were unsuccessful in pressuring the one member of the group into drinking. Discuss the effects that drinking alcohol and using other drugs have on sexual decision-making. Review with students the seven reasons it is risky to drink alcohol and use other drugs. The seven reasons are:

1. You might not stick to your decision to practice abstinence.

2. You increase your risk of getting pregnant or getting someone pregnant.

3. You increase the risk of becoming infected with HIV and other STDs.

4. You increase the risk of being in situations in which rape occurs. Define rape. **Rape** is having sex with a person who has not given or is not capable of giving consent.

5. You are around teens who use drugs, which puts you at risk for being slipped a drug. Define drug slipping. **Drug slipping** is placing a drug into someone's food or beverage without that person's knowledge.

6. You might become drug dependent and exchange sex for drugs or for money to buy drugs.

7. You might share a needle that has infected blood on it.

Define drug-free lifestyle. A **drug-free lifestyle** is a lifestyle in which a person does not misuse or abuse drugs. A person who lives a drug-free lifestyle is in control of his or her decisions, reduces the risk of being slipped a drug, will not become dependent on drugs, and will not share a needle with infected blood on it.

Assessment

Tell students to answer the following letter to Dear Helper.

Dear Helper:

I have talked to my parents about guidelines to follow when I attend parties where there will be people of both sexes. My parents have said that it is very important that I not be tempted to drink alcohol when I am at these parties. Why are they so concerned about me drinking alcohol when I am at a party with people of the opposite sex? What are some ways I can resist peer pressure to drink alcohol?

Concerned

The Model for Using Resistance Skills

1. Say NO with self-confidence.

2. Give reasons for saying NO.

> NO. I want to promote my health.
>
> NO. I want to protect my safety.
>
> NO. I want to follow laws.
>
> NO. I want to show respect for myself and others.
>
> NO. I want to follow the guidelines of my parents and other responsible adults.
>
> NO. I want to demonstrate good character.

3. Use the CD-stuck-on-NO technique.

4. Use nonverbal behavior to match verbal behavior.

5. Avoid being in situations in which there will be pressure to make wrong decisions.

6. Avoid being with people who make wrong decisions.

7. Resist pressure to engage in illegal behavior.

8. Influence others to make responsible decisions.

Masculine/Feminine

The Curriculum

Life Skills

■ I will recognize habits that protect male reproductive health.

■ I will recognize habits that protect female reproductive health.

■ I will be well groomed.

Objective

■ Students will accept body changes that occur during puberty.

The National Health Education Standards

■ Students will comprehend concepts related to health promotion and disease prevention.

Preparing to Teach the Lesson Plan

Materials

Chalkboard
Chalk
Magazine pictures
Scissors
Tape

Blackline Masters

Male Secondary Sex Characteristics
Female Secondary Sex Characteristics

Teaching the Lesson Plan

1 Write the words *masculine* and *feminine* on two different areas of the chalkboard.

Explain that the word *masculine* means characteristics or behaviors usually associated with males. Explain that the word *feminine* means characteristics or behaviors usually associated with females. Define puberty. **Puberty** is the stage of growth and development when the body becomes capable of producing offspring. Have students share examples of characteristics that are associated with males and females going through puberty. Students might say that males begin to grow facial hair, or that females begin menstruation.

2 Define secondary sex characteristics. **Secondary sex characteristics** are physical and emotional changes that occur during puberty. Give each student a copy of the Blackline Master *Male Secondary Sex Characteristics*. Give each student a copy of the Blackline Master *Female Secondary Sex Characteristics*.

The male secondary sex characteristics are:
• increase in height;
• increase in perspiration;
• growth of underarm hair;
• growth of pubic hair;
• broadening of shoulders;
• deepening of voice;
• increase in size of reproductive organs;
• increase in muscle mass; and
• formation of sperm.

The female secondary sex characteristics are:
• increase in height;
• increase in perspiration;
• growth of underarm hair;
• growth of pubic hair;
• increase in breast size;
• widening of hips;
• increase in size of reproductive organs;
• beginning of menstruation; and
• formation of mature ova.

3 Pass out magazines. Tell students to cut out two different pictures from the magazines. The first picture should be a boy or girl before puberty. The second should be either a teenage or adult male or female.

Ask students how the two pictures show the maturing of the secondary sex characteristics through puberty. For example, a student might cut out a picture of a short girl and a tall woman to demonstrate the increase in height that females experience during puberty.

4 Tell students to tape their magazine pictures to the board either in the designated masculine area or the designated feminine area. Have students come up to the chalkboard and rearrange the pictures to show other secondary sex characteristics. For example, a student might come up and rearrange two pictures already on the board to show how a boy grows facial hair as he reaches adulthood. Ask students to discuss the similarities and differences of the male and female secondary sex characteristics. Students might say that both males and females grow taller during puberty. Students might say

that a male's skin gets thicker and tougher, but a female's skin gets softer and smoother during puberty.

Explain to students that they can stay well-groomed during puberty. Increased perspiration during puberty can cause body odor. Students can use grooming products to prevent body odor. Students should wash their skin with soap to reduce body odor. They can use deodorant or antiperspirant to reduce perspiration under the arms. Students should keep their feet clean and wear clean socks to reduce foot odor.

Assessment

Have students write an essay about how the male and female bodies change during puberty. Make sure that the students include both the similar changes and the different changes that occur in males and females during puberty. Have students include ways they can stay well-groomed during puberty.

© 2001 Everyday Learning Corporation

Male Secondary Sex Characteristics

1 Increase in height

2 Increase in perspiration

3 Growth of underarm hair

4 Growth of pubic hair

5 Broadening of shoulders

6 Deepening of voice

7 Increase in size of reproductive organs

8 Increase in muscle mass

9 Formation of sperm

Female Secondary Sex Characteristics

1 Increase in height

2 Increase in perspiration

3 Growth of underarm hair

4 Growth of pubic hair

5 Increase in breast size

6 Widening of hips

7 Increase in size of reproductive organs

8 Beginning of menstruation

9 Formation of mature ova

Reproductive Health: Media Literacy

The Curriculum

Life Skills

■ I will recognize habits that protect male reproductive health.

■ I will recognize habits that protect female reproductive health.

■ I will have regular examinations.

■ I will keep a personal health record.

Objectives

■ Students will practice habits that protect male reproductive health (if they are male).

■ Students will practice habits that protect female reproductive health (if they are female).

■ Students will explain what happens during the menstrual cycle.

■ Students will explain why smoking is NOT sexy.

■ Students will tell why they need regular medical checkups.

■ Students will tell why they need to keep a personal health record.

The National Health Education Standards

■ Students will comprehend concepts related to health promotion and disease prevention.

■ Students will demonstrate the ability to access valid health information and health-promoting products and services.

■ Students will demonstrate the ability to advocate for personal, family, and community health.

■ Students will demonstrate the ability to practice health-enhancing behaviors and reduce health risks.

Preparing to Teach the Lesson Plan

Materials

Posterboard

Markers

Construction paper

Pens and pencils

Magazines and newspapers

Scissors

Blackline Master

Questions to Evaluate Media Messages™

Teaching the Lesson Plan

1 Define media. **Media** are the various forms of mass communication. Ask students to name kinds of media. Students might say television or magazines. Define media literacy. **Media literacy** is the ability to recognize and evaluate the messages in media, recognize ways these messages can influence behavior, and produce accurate messages for media. Give each student a copy of the Blackline Master *Questions to Evaluate Media Messages*™. Explain to students that there is a difference in the kinds of messages provided by public service announcements (PSAs) and by commercial media advertisements. Commercial media advertisements are paid for by companies that are marketing commercial products, such as athletic equipment. PSAs are often paid for by non-profit organizations or civic groups. These advertisements often educate or inform the public about a certain issue.

2 Divide the class into six groups. Tell the class that each group will design part of a PSA media campaign on reproductive health. Tell students that the media campaign will include these six components:

1. *A radio advertisement on the importance of wearing an athletic supporter.*

2. *A television advertisement on the importance of practicing abstinence from sex.* Define abstinence from sex. **Abstinence from sex** is choosing not to be sexually active.

3. *A poster stating that smoking is not sexy.* The poster should give facts about the effects of smoking on reproductive health.

4. *Brochures on testicular self-examination (TSE) and breast self-examination (BSE).* Define testicular self-examination (TSE). **Testicular self-examination (TSE)** is a check for lumps and tenderness in the testes. Define breast self-examination (BSE). A **breast self-examination (BSE)** is a monthly check for lumps and changes in the breasts.

5. *A brochure on tampons and toxic shock syndrome (TSS).* Define toxic shock syndrome (TSS). **Toxic shock syndrome (TSS)** is a severe illness resulting from toxins secreted by *Staphylococcus* bacteria.

6. *A poster on the stages of the menstrual cycle.* Define menstrual cycle. The **menstrual cycle** is a monthly cycle that involves ovulation, changes in the uterine lining, and menstruation.

3 Tell students that there are other ways to take care of their reproductive health. Tell students that they also need regular medical checkups to help take care of their reproductive health. These checkups are an important part of personal health and hygiene. Explain to students that having regular checkups is important because checkups will let a health care provider run tests and watch out for the early symptoms of serious health problems.

Tell students that they should keep a personal health record. Define personal health record. A **personal health record** is documentation of information pertaining to a person's health, health care, and health care providers. A personal health record should include the students' health habits. It should include information about the students' family health history. A female might keep track of her menstrual cycle on a calendar as part of her personal health record. Tell students that this information is important and should be shared with a physician.

4 Give the groups time to complete their component of the media campaign. Groups might need additional time to research their topics. Tell each group to share its part of the media campaign with the rest of the class. Ask students to discuss the component of each group. Tell students to think about the following questions: Which parts of the campaign were effective and why? Which parts of the campaign were not effective and why? Would this campaign convince a person to practice habits that protect male and/or female reproductive health? Why or why not? Would the television advertisement convince teens to practice abstinence from sex? Why or why not?

Assessment

Pass out magazines and newspapers to the class. Tell students to find advertisements in the magazines and newspapers that portray active males and females. Tell students to change the messages in the advertisements to state ways in which males and females can protect their reproductive health. For example, a student might find an advertisement that shows football players wearing brand name logos on their uniforms. The student could change the media message to state why a male should wear an athletic supporter and protective cup for some sports.

Questions to Evaluate Media Messages™

1 What is the purpose of the message?

2 Who is the target audience for the message?

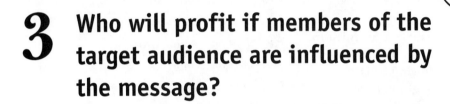

3 Who will profit if members of the target audience are influenced by the message?

4 Does the message encourage members of the target audience to choose responsible behavior? How?

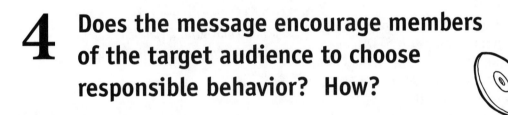

5 What techniques are used to make the message appealing to the target audience? Why?

6 What information is missing from the message?

7 Is this message consistent with messages found in other media on the same subject? How?

STDs: Questions and Answers

The Curriculum

Life Skills

■ I will choose behaviors to reduce my risk of infection with sexually transmitted diseases.

■ I will not misuse or abuse drugs.

Objectives

■ Students will identify the cause, transmission, symptoms, diagnosis, and treatment, and complications for the following STDs: chlamydia, genital herpes, genital warts, gonorrhea, pubic lice, syphilis, trichomoniasis, and viral hepatitis.

■ Students will discuss ways to reduce their risk of becoming infected with STDs.

■ Students will tell why they must change their behavior and be tested for STDs and HIV if they have been sexually active.

■ Students will tell why it is important to choose a drug-free lifestyle.

■ Students will explain why they should avoid the use of injection drugs.

■ Students will tell why they should change their behavior if they use drugs.

■ Students will explain why they should avoid sharing a needle to make tattoos or to pierce ears and other body parts.

■ Students will explain why they should follow universal precautions.

The National Health Education Standards

■ Students will demonstrate the ability to use goal-setting and decision-making skills that enhance health.

Preparing to Teach the Lesson Plan

Materials

None

Blackline Masters

Fact Sheet on Chlamydia

Fact Sheet on Genital Herpes

Fact Sheet on Genital Warts

Fact Sheet on Gonorrhea

Fact Sheet on Pubic Lice

Fact Sheet on Syphilis

Fact Sheet on Trichomoniasis

Fact Sheet on Viral Hepatitis

How Can I Reduce My Risk of Becoming Infected with STDs?

Teaching the Lesson Plan

1 Tell the class that they are going to learn about sexually transmitted diseases (STDs). Define sexually transmitted disease. A **sexually transmitted disease (STD)** is a disease caused by pathogens that are transmitted from an infected person to an uninfected person during intimate sexual contact. Some STDs also can be spread in other ways.

2 Explain to students how to use the fact sheets on STDs. Tell students that the fact sheets have five parts: the definition and cause of the STD, how the STD is transmitted, the symptoms of the STD, how the STD is diagnosed and treated, and the complications of the STD. Define transmit. To **transmit** is to cause something to spread. For example, pubic lice can be transmitted by sleeping on infested sheets. Define symptom. A **symptom**

© 2001 Everyday Learning Corporation

is a change in a body function from the normal pattern. For example, a symptom of genital herpes is cold sores in the mouth. Define diagnosis. The **diagnosis** is the determination of a person's condition after testing or control observation. Define treatment. **Treatment** is what is done to improve a condition or disease. For example, chlamydia is diagnosed by examining a discharge sample in a laboratory. Once diagnosed, chlamydia is then treated with antibiotics. Define complication. A **complication** is something serious that happens as a result of having had a condition or a disease. A complication from infection with syphilis can be organ damage.

3 Give each student a copy of the STD fact sheets. Review the STD fact sheets with students. Explain that some STDs have no cure. For example, genital herpes and genital warts cannot be cured. Genital herpes is caused by the herpes simplex virus (HSV). Genital warts is caused by the human papillomavirus (HPV). Symptoms of genital herpes and genital warts can be treated. However, once a person is infected with one of these viruses, a person will always be infected with the virus that caused the STD.

Explain to students that there are ways to reduce the risk of becoming infected with an STD. Give each student a copy of the Blackline Master *How Can I Reduce My Risk of Becoming Infected with STDs?* Discuss these nine ways to reduce the risk of becoming infected with an STD:

1. Abstain from sex until you are married.
2. Change your behavior and be tested for STDs and HIV if you have been sexually active.
3. Have a monogamous traditional marriage if you choose to marry in the future.
4. Choose a drug-free lifestyle.
5. Avoid the use of injection drugs.
6. Change your behavior if you use drugs.
7. Avoid sharing a needle to make tattoos or to pierce ears and other body parts.
8. Follow universal precautions.
9. Choose other responsible behaviors.

4 Have students assess one another's knowledge of STD facts. Tell students to write their names at the top of a sheet of paper. Have them write ten questions about STDs on the sheet of paper. Questions should cover the content from the STD fact sheets. Students should write the answers to the ten questions on another sheet of paper. Tell students to trade the papers on which they have written ten questions with another student. Have students write answers to each of the ten questions under each question. Tell students to return their papers to the person who wrote the questions. Students who wrote the ten questions should check the answers.

Assessment

Tell students that they are going to do further research on chlamydia, genital herpes, genital warts, gonorrhea, pubic lice, and syphilis. Tell students to conduct the research on the Internet, using a Web page of the National Institute of Allergy and Infectious Disease (NIAID)/National Institute of Health (NIH), (http://www.niaid.nih.gov/factsheets/stdinfo.htm). Ask students to research the following questions (answers are in italics):

- Why is syphilis called "the great imitator"? *Syphilis is called the "great imitator" because its early symptoms are similar to those of many other diseases.*

- While infected with pubic lice, why shouldn't a person touch the infected area? *It is important not to touch the infected area because scratching might spread the lice to other parts of the body.*

- What medication is prescribed to treat genital warts? *Several medications are prescribed to treat genital warts. These medications are imiquimod cream, 20 percent podophyllin solution, 0.5 percent podofilox solution, 5 percent 5-fluorouracil cream, or trichloroacetic acid (TCA).*

- According to the Institute of Medicine, how many new cases of gonorrhea occur each year in the United States? *According to the Institute of Medicine, 800,000 new cases of gonorrhea occur each year in the United States.*

- What new research is being done to prevent infection with chlamydia? *Researchers are working on two strategies to prevent infection: topical microbicides and a vaccine.*

- Can genital herpes increase the risk of acquiring HIV? Why or why not? *Yes. Genital herpes increases the risk of acquiring HIV. Open sores and broken blisters from genital herpes can provide a point of entry for HIV.*

Fact Sheet on Chlamydia

Chlamydia (kluh·MID·ee·uh) is an STD that produces inflammation of the reproductive organs. It is caused by the bacterium *Chlamydia trachomatis*.

■ How Is Chlamydia Transmitted?

- Through intimate sexual contact with an infected partner
- From an infected mother to her baby during vaginal delivery

■ What Are the Symptoms of Chlamydia?

Many people who have chlamydia have no symptoms.

In males:

- Painful urination
- Discharge from the penis
- Inflammation of the urethra
- Pain or swelling in the scrotum

In females:

- Inflammation of the vagina and cervix
- Burning sensation during urination
- Unusual discharge from the vagina

■ How Is Chlamydia Diagnosed and Treated?

A cotton swab is used to collect a discharge sample. The sample is then examined in a laboratory for the presence of *Chlamydia trachomatis* bacterium. Antibiotics are used to treat chlamydia. Those infected must take all the prescribed antibiotics, even after symptoms disappear. A follow-up visit to a physician is necessary.

■ What Are the Complications of Chlamydia?

- Pelvic inflammatory disease (PID), which can cause sterility and ectopic pregnancy
- Blindness or pneumonia in babies born to infected mothers

Fact Sheet on Genital Herpes

Genital herpes is an STD that produces cold sores or fever blisters in the genital area and mouth. It is caused by the herpes simplex virus (HSV).

■ How Is Genital Herpes Transmitted?

- Through intimate sexual contact with an infected partner
- By open-mouth kissing with a person who has broken blisters or open sores
- By touching broken blisters or open sores and then touching other parts of the body
- From an infected mother to her baby during vaginal delivery

■ What Are the Symptoms of Genital Herpes?
In males and females:

- Itching or burning sensation
- Pain in the legs, buttocks, or genital area
- Feeling of pressure in the abdominal area
- Clusters of small, painful blisters or open sores in the genital area
- Fever, headache, muscle aches, painful or difficult urination, swollen glands in the groin area
- Vaginal discharge (females)
- Cold sores or fever blisters in the mouth or on the lips

■ How Is Genital Herpes Diagnosed and Treated?

The sores or blisters of genital herpes usually are visible. Fluid from the blisters is examined under a microscope to diagnose genital herpes. Blood tests also can be given to diagnose genital herpes. There is no known cure for genital herpes. Drugs can be given to relieve symptoms and reduce the likelihood of recurrences.

■ What Are the Complications of Genital Herpes?

- Recurrence of symptoms because there is no cure
- Cancer of the cervix in females
- Other pathogens, such as HIV, can enter the body if blisters break
- Infection in babies born to infected mothers

Fact Sheet on Genital Warts

Genital warts is an STD that produces wart-like growths on the genitals. It is caused by certain types of the human papillomavirus (HPV).

■ How Are Genital Warts Transmitted?

- Through intimate sexual contact with an infected partner
- By direct contact with infected bed linens, towels, and clothing
- From an infected mother to her baby during vaginal delivery

■ What Are the Symptoms of Genital Warts?

In males and females:

- Soft, red or pink warts that look like cauliflower on moist skin areas
- Hard, yellow-gray warts that appear on dry skin areas

In males:

- Warts on the tip of the penis, on the shaft of the penis, on the scrotum, or around the anus

In females:

- Warts on the external genitals, inside the vagina, on the cervix, or around the anus

■ How Are Genital Warts Diagnosed and Treated?

A physician inspects the warts to make a diagnosis. Laboratory tests can identify specific types of HPV. Because of the increased risk of cervical cancer, a Pap smear might be taken from females. There is no treatment available to get rid of the virus completely. Once infected, a person will always have HPV in the body. Medication, laser surgery, and freezing using liquid nitrogen can be used to remove warts, but they might reappear.

■ What Are the Complications of Genital Warts?

- Recurrence of warts because there is no cure
- Cancers of the male and female genitals and anus
- Itching and irritation
- Difficulty urinating for pregnant females
- Warts in the throats of babies born to infected mothers

Fact Sheet on Gonorrhea

Gonorrhea (GAH·nuh·REE·uh) is an STD that infects the lining of the genital and urinary tracts. It is caused by the gonococcus bacterium *Neisseria gonorrhoeae*.

■ How Is Gonorrhea Transmitted?

- Through intimate sexual contact with an infected partner
- From an infected mother to her baby during vaginal delivery

■ What Are the Symptoms of Gonorrhea?

Many people who have gonorrhea have no symptoms.

In males:

- White, milky discharge from the penis
- Burning sensation during urination
- Pain and increased urination

In females:

- Burning sensation during urination
- Discharge from the vagina
- If not treated, abdominal pain, bleeding between menstrual periods, vomiting, or fever

■ How Is Gonorrhea Diagnosed and Treated?

Diagnosis is made by examining the discharge under a microscope. Antibiotics are used to treat gonorrhea. Some strains are resistant to some antibiotics, which makes treatment difficult. Those infected should take all of the prescribed medication, even if symptoms disappear. A follow-up visit to a physician is necessary. Most states require that medication be put in the eyes of newborn babies to prevent blindness in case the mother is infected.

■ What Are the Complications of Gonorrhea?

- Infections of joints, heart valves, and brain
- Permanent sterility
- Pelvic inflammatory disease (PID) (females)
- Blindness in newborns

Fact Sheet on Pubic Lice

Pubic lice is an infestation of the pubic hair by pubic or crab lice. To **infest** is to be present in large numbers. Lice are insects that attach to the skin and cause itching and swelling. They survive by feeding on human blood.

■ How Are Pubic Lice Transmitted?

- Through intimate sexual contact with an infected partner
- By sleeping on infested sheets, wearing infested clothing, sharing infested towels, or sitting on a toilet seat that has been used by a person who has pubic lice

■ What Are the Symptoms of Pubic Lice?

In males and females:

- Itching and swelling in the pubic area
- Little black spots on body parts that have dense hair growth

■ How Are Pubic Lice Diagnosed and Treated?

A physician examines the body to find the lice. A prescription shampoo is used to kill the lice. Over-the-counter shampoos also can be used. After the lice are killed, itching might continue until the skin has time to heal. Certain medications can stop the itching.

■ What Are the Complications of Pubic Lice?

- Itching
- Irritation

Fact Sheet on Syphilis

Syphilis (SI·fuh·luhs) is an STD that produces chancres in the genital area and damage to organs if untreated. A **chancre** (SHANG·kuhr) is a hard, round, painless sore. Syphilis is caused by the bacterium *Treponema pallidum*.

■ How Is Syphilis Transmitted?

- Through intimate sexual contact with an infected partner
- From a pregnant woman to her developing baby

■ What Are the Symptoms of Syphilis?

Many people who have syphilis have no symptoms.

In males and females:

During primary or the first stage of syphilis:

- Chancre on the genitals or in the mouth, appearing within ten days to three months after exposure to syphilis

During secondary or the second stage of syphilis:

- A skin rash on part or all of the body, appearing three to six weeks after the chancre appears
- Fever, tiredness, and headache
- Sore throat and swollen glands
- Loss of weight and hair

During late syphilis or the final stage of syphilis:

- Damage to body organs such as the heart, eyes, brain, nervous system, bones, joints, or other body parts

■ How Is Syphilis Diagnosed and Treated?

People with a skin rash or sore in the genital area should be checked by a physician. A blood test is used to diagnose syphilis. Syphilis is treated with antibiotics. Treatment in the later stages cannot reverse damage to body organs.

■ What Are the Complications of Syphilis?

- Irreversible damage to major organs and bones
- Mental illness, blindness, paralysis, and death
- Miscarriage, stillbirth, and fetal death
- Mental retardation and birth defects in babies born to infected mothers

Fact Sheet on Trichomoniasis

Trichomoniasis (TRI·kuh·muh·NY·uh·suhs) is an STD that infects the urethra in males and the vagina in females. It is caused by the protozoan *Trichomonas vaginalis*.

■ How Is Trichomoniasis Transmitted?

- Through intimate sexual contact with an infected partner
- By sharing infected, damp towels
- Through the frequent use of vaginal sprays and douches that allow existing protozoa to multiply in females

■ What Are the Symptoms of Trichomoniasis?

Many people who have trichomoniasis have no symptoms.

In males:

- Thin, white discharge from the penis
- Painful or difficult urination

In females:

- Yellow-green or gray vaginal discharge that has an odor
- Painful urination
- Itching in the genital area
- Pain in the abdomen

■ How Is Trichomoniasis Diagnosed and Treated?

The discharge is examined under a microscope to diagnose trichomoniasis. The drug Metronidazole is used to treat it.

■ What Are the Complications of Trichomoniasis?

- Low birth weight and premature birth in babies born to infected mothers.

Fact Sheet on Viral Hepatitis

Viral hepatitis (HE·puh·TY·tuhs) is a viral infection of the liver.

■ How Is Viral Hepatitis Transmitted?

- Through intimate sexual contact with an infected partner
- By sharing needles for injection drug use that contain infected blood
- From contaminated food and water
- From an infected mother to her baby during vaginal delivery

■ What Are the Symptoms of Viral Hepatitis?

Many people who have viral hepatitis have no symptoms.

In males and females:

- Mild fever, headache, muscle aches, tiredness, loss of appetite, nausea, vomiting, and diarrhea
- Later, dark and foamy urine, pale-colored feces, abdominal pain, and jaundice; jaundice (JAWN·duhs) is yellowing of the skin and whites of the eyes.

■ How Is Viral Hepatitis Diagnosed and Treated?

Blood tests are used to diagnose viral hepatitis. A physician also can observe symptoms. Treatment includes bed rest, a healthful diet, and avoidance of alcoholic beverages. Drugs might be prescribed to improve liver function.

■ What Are the Complications of Viral Hepatitis?

- Liver failure and possible death
- Liver cancer

How Can I Reduce My Risk of Becoming Infected with STDs?

1 Abstain from sex until you are married. The pathogens that cause STDs are transmitted during intimate sexual contact in which body fluids are exchanged. When you practice abstinence from sex, you avoid risk behaviors in which STDs are transmitted. You will not become infected with STDs for which there is no cure. You avoid legal complications that might arise should you infect another person.

2 Change your behavior and be tested for STDs and HIV if you have been sexually active. Begin to practice abstinence from sex right now. See a physician or go to a clinic and be tested for STDs. If you are infected, you need prompt treatment. Remember, you can be infected and not have symptoms. If you are infected with genital warts or genital herpes, you have an obligation to tell other people. If you choose to marry in the future, you must tell a potential partner that you are infected with genital warts or genital herpes because there is no cure. Discuss your past behavior with your parents or guardian and ask for their help and support.

3 Have a monogamous traditional marriage if you choose to marry in the future. A monogamous traditional marriage is a marriage in which partners have sex only with one another. It provides security and protects partners from infection with STDs, including HIV.

4 Choose a drug-free lifestyle. Drugs dull the part of your brain used for reasoning. You might not think clearly and stick to your decision to practice abstinence from sex until marriage. You might become infected with an STD.

5 Avoid the use of injection drugs. Sharing a needle, syringe, or injection equipment for drug use is a risk behavior for STDs.

6 Change your behavior if you use drugs. If you misuse or abuse drugs, see your physician or go to a clinic and get tested for STDs. If you are infected, you need prompt treatment. If you have drug dependence, you need treatment to stop. Ask your parents or guardian for their help and support.

7 Avoid sharing a needle to make tattoos or to pierce ears and other body parts. Sharing a needle to make a tattoo or to pierce ears and other body parts is a risk behavior. These procedures should only be performed by qualified people who use sterile equipment.

8 Follow universal precautions. **Universal precautions** are steps taken to keep from having contact with pathogens in body fluids. Always follow universal precautions when you have contact with a person's blood and other body fluids. Wear disposable latex gloves and wash your hands with waterless antiseptic hand cleanser after removing the gloves. Use a face mask or shield with a one-way valve if you perform first aid for breathing emergencies. Avoid touching objects that have had contact with a person's blood. Do not eat or drink anything or touch your mouth, eyes, or nose while performing first aid.

9 Choose other responsible behaviors. Do not engage in open-mouth kissing with someone who has blisters, lesions, ulcers, or chancres in the mouth. Avoid contact with infected objects, linens, and clothing or with another person's damp towels.

The Pressure Builds

The Curriculum

Life Skills

■ I will choose behaviors to reduce my risk of infection with sexually transmitted diseases.

■ I will use resistance skills when appropriate.

Objectives

■ Students will discuss ways to reduce their risk of becoming infected with STDs.

■ Students will explain why a person should abstain from sex until he or she is married.

■ Students will explain why they should have a monogamous traditional marriage if they choose to marry in the future.

■ Students will tell why it is important to choose a drug-free lifestyle.

■ Students will explain why they should avoid the use of injection drugs.

■ Students will tell why they should change their behavior if they use drugs.

■ Students will explain why they should avoid sharing a needle to make tattoos or to pierce ears and other body parts.

■ Students will explain why they should follow universal precautions.

The National Health Education Standards

■ Students will demonstrate the ability to practice health-enhancing behaviors and reduce health risks.

Preparing to Teach the Lesson Plan

Materials

Balloon

Baking soda

Vinegar

Long-neck bottle

Chalkboard

Chalk

Blackline Masters

Nine Ways to Reduce the Risk of STDs

How Can I Resist Pressure to Be Sexually Active?

Teaching the Lesson Plan

1 Explain to students that they face a variety of pressures every day. One of these pressures might be to become sexually active. For example, a person might be pressured to engage in sexual intercourse. Explain to students that abstinence from sex is the expected standard for teens. Define abstinence from sex. **Abstinence from sex** is choosing not to be sexually active. Tell the class that practicing abstinence from sex until marriage is healthful. Explain to students that practicing abstinence from sex reduces the risk of becoming infected with sexually transmitted diseases (STDs) including HIV. Tell the class that it is important to have a monogamous traditional marriage if they choose to marry. Define monogamous traditional marriage. A **monogamous traditional marriage** is a marriage in which a husband and wife have sex only with one another. Explain to students that a monogamous traditional marriage is healthful and reduces the risk of becoming infected with STDs including HIV.

502

Give each student a copy of the Blackline Master *Nine Ways to Reduce the Risk of STDs.* Tell students that being drug-free also reduces the risk of infection with STDs. Following universal precautions also reduces their risk. Define universal precautions. **Universal precautions** are steps taken to keep from having contact with pathogens in body fluids.

2 Statements made to convince a partner to engage in sexual intercourse are known as pressure statements. An example of a pressure statement is, "If you loved me, you would show it." Tell students in the class to brainstorm pressure statements they have heard from other students, in the movies, or on television. Write these pressure statements on the chalkboard.

3 Use a bottle that has an opening of between one-half inch and one inch for this activity. The bottle should have a neck that is about two inches long and is about the same diameter as the opening of the bottle. Add vinegar to the bottle to a depth of one inch. Using a balloon with a wide neck, place two teaspoons of baking soda inside the balloon.

4 Tell students to read the pressure statements on the chalkboard. As the class reads, tell them that the pressure to be sexually active is mounting. Stretch the neck of the balloon over the opening of the bottle and hold the balloon upright. Students will notice that the baking soda will drop into the bottom of the bottle where it reacts with the vinegar. This reaction will create a gas that will cause the balloon to expand as a result of the pressure. Hold the balloon around the rim of the bottle so that it does not slip off.

5 Explain that the pressure inside the balloon represents pressure to be sexually active. Tell students that this pressure needs to be relieved. Tell students that they can relieve the pressure to be sexually active by using resistance skills. Define resistance skills. **Resistance skills** are skills that help you say NO to an action or to leave a situation. Give each student a copy of the Blackline Master *How Can I Resist Pressure to Be Sexually Active?* Tell the class to think of counter statements to the pressure statements.

For example, a counter statement to "If you loved me, you would show it," might be, "If you loved me, you would show it by respecting my wishes to choose abstinence from sex until I am married." Allow the gas inside the balloon to leak out each time a student gives a counter statement. Tell students that the counter statements are helping to relieve the pressure to be sexually active.

Assessment

Divide the class into groups of six. Tell the students in each group to write down five pressure statements that might be used to pressure a person into becoming sexually active. Tell each group to swap their statements with another group. Tell the groups to use the nine ways to reduce the risk of STDs to come up with a counter statement for each pressure statement they receive.

Eight Ways to Reduce the Risk of STDs

 1 Abstain from sex until you are married.

 2 Have a monogamous marriage if you choose to marry in the future.

 3 Choose a drug-free lifestyle.

 4 Avoid the use of injection drugs.

 5 Change your behavior if you use drugs.

 6 Avoid sharing a needle to make tattoos or to pierce ears and other body parts.

 7 Follow universal precautions. Define universal precautions. Universal precautions are steps taken to keep from having contact with pathogens in body fluids.

 8 Take other precautions to prevent STDs.

How Can I Resist Pressure to Be Sexually Active?

Suppose you are pressured to be sexually active. Use resistance skills. **Resistance skills** are skills that help you say NO to an action or to leave a situation.

➡ **Say NO with confidence.**

➡ **Give reasons why you practice abstinence.**

➡ **Repeat your reasons for practicing abstinence.**

➡ **Don't send a mixed message.**

➡ **Avoid situations in which there will be pressure to be sexually active.**

➡ **Break off a relationship when someone does not respect your limits.**

➡ **Influence others to practice abstinence.**

HIV: You Have Entered

The Curriculum

Life Skill

■ I will choose behaviors to reduce my risk of HIV infection.

Objectives

■ Students will list ways HIV is and is not spread.

■ Students will explain why saying NO to injecting drugs, using alcohol and other drugs, and sharing a needle to make tattoos or to pierce ears or other body parts protects you from HIV infection.

■ Students will explain how HIV infection progresses to AIDS.

■ Students will explain why they need to follow universal precautions to protect themselves from HIV infection.

The National Health Education Standards

■ Students will demonstrate the ability to use goal-setting and decision-making skills that enhance health.

Preparing to Teach the Lesson Plan

Materials

Two clear, rigid glasses filled halfway with water

Plastic Food Wrap

Red Food Coloring

Blackline Masters

HIV Infection Progression to AIDS

Follow Universal Precautions to Protect Yourself from HIV Infection

Teaching the Lesson Plan

1 Ask students if they know what HIV stands for. HIV stands for human immunodeficiency virus. Define human immunodeficiency virus (HIV). **Human immunodeficiency virus (HIV)** is a pathogen that destroys infection-fighting T cells in the body. HIV is the pathogen that causes the disease AIDS. Define AIDS. **AIDS**, or **Acquired Immune Deficiency Syndrome**, is a condition that results when infection with HIV causes a breakdown of the body's ability to fight other infections.

2 Fill two glasses halfway with water. Put these glasses on your desk. Cover the top of each of the glasses with clear plastic wrap. Tell the class that the water inside the cups represents blood. Tell the class that the glass represents the blood vessel holding the blood. Tell the class that the plastic wrap represents the skin. Show the class the red food coloring. Tell the class that the red food coloring represents HIV.

3 Put red food coloring on the plastic cover on the top of one of the glasses. The red food coloring will remain on the top of the cover. Ask students to describe what happened to the water. Students might say that the water did not change color. Ask students to describe why the water did not change color. Students might say that there was no break in the plastic wrap, or skin, so the red food coloring, or HIV, could not enter the glass, or bloodstream.

4 Make a slit through the plastic wrap covering the other glass. Put several drops of red food coloring on the plastic wrap. The drops of red food coloring will go through the opening you made and into the water. Ask students to describe what happened to the water. Students will say that the water, or blood, turned red because red food coloring, or HIV, got into the bloodstream through a break in the skin.

© 2001 Everyday Learning Corporation

5 Swirl the glass containing the red food coloring. The red food coloring will appear as if it is widely spreading throughout the water. Ask students how they might remove the red food coloring from the water. Students will say that they cannot remove the red food coloring from the water. Tell students that it is impossible to remove the food coloring from the water. Explain to the class that once HIV gets into the bloodstream, it cannot be removed. Explain to students that HIV infection can progress to full-blown AIDS, which can lead to death. The signs of HIV infection might appear right away or they might take years to appear. Early signs include tiredness, fever, swollen glands, rashes, and headaches. Explain that a person infected with HIV has AIDS when he or she has 200 or fewer helper T cells per microliter of blood or an opportunistic infection.

6 Define helper T cell. A **helper T cell** is a white blood cell that signals B cells to make antibodies. Define opportunistic infections. **Opportunistic infections** are infections that develop when a person has a weak immune system. Give each student a copy of the Blackline Master *HIV Infection Progression to AIDS*. Explain to students that after HIV enters the body, it attaches to and takes control of helper T cells. HIV then reproduces itself and destroys helper T cells. HIV continues to destroy helper T cells until the body can no longer fight infection. Then a person who is HIV positive has an opportunistic infection. The person has AIDS.

7 Explain to students that there are certain behaviors that can lead to HIV infection, such as using injecting drugs and sharing a needle to make tattoos or to pierce ears or other body parts. Tell students that engaging in these risk behaviors increases the chances that HIV-infected fluids can enter the body through a break in the skin. Explain to students that using drugs a person does not inject, such as marijuana, is still dangerous and a risk behavior for HIV. Drugs affect the part of the brain used for clear thinking and reasoning. So, a person might not consider the risks of

being sexually active, such as HIV infection, STDs, and unwanted pregnancy, when the person is under the influence of harmful drugs. Tell students to always get permission from their parents or guardians if they consider getting a tattoo or piercing their ears or other body parts. Tell students that there are people who are licensed to make tattoos and to pierce ears who are required to use sterile equipment.

8 Explain to students that they can be infected with HIV if they have contact with the blood or other body fluids, mucous membranes, or broken skin of a person who is infected with HIV. Give each student a copy of the Blackline Master *Follow Universal Precautions to Protect Yourself from HIV Infection*. Define universal precautions. **Universal precautions** are steps taken to keep from having contact with pathogens in body fluids.

Assessment

Divide the class into groups of five. Each group is to prepare a five-minute special for the evening news. The purpose of the special is to educate the public about HIV infection and AIDS. Each group's news special should include ways HIV is and is not spread, ways to reduce the risk of being infected with HIV, how HIV infection progresses to AIDS, and how to follow universal precautions.

HIV Infection Progression to AIDS

HIV enters the body.

HIV attaches to and takes control of helper T cells.

HIV reproduces itself and destroys helper T cells.

HIV continues to reproduce and to attack and destroy helper T cells. This weakens the body's ability to fight infection.

According to the Centers for Disease Control and Prevention, a person infected with HIV has AIDS when he or she has 200 or fewer helper T cells per microliter of blood or has an opportunistic infection.

Follow Universal Precautions to Protect Yourself from HIV Infection

1 **Wear disposable latex or polyurethane gloves.**
Do not wear disposable gloves more than once.

2 **Wash your hands well with soap and water after you remove the gloves.**

3 **Wear a face mask or shield if you give first aid for breathing.**
Do not use a face mask or shield more than once without disinfecting it.

4 **Cover any cuts, scrapes, and rashes on your body with plastic wrap or a sterile dressing.**

5 **Do not eat or drink anything while giving first aid.**

6 **Do not touch your mouth, eyes, or nose while caring for a victim.**

Infected Needles

The Curriculum

Life Skills

■ I will choose behaviors to reduce my risk of HIV infection.

■ I will use resistance skills when appropriate.

Objectives

■ Students will explain why saying NO to injecting drugs, using alcohol and other drugs, and sharing a needle to make tattoos or to pierce ears or other body parts protects them from HIV infection.

■ Students will outline resistance skills they can use if they are pressured to choose risk behaviors for HIV infection.

■ Students will identify ways in which HIV and AIDS threaten society.

■ Students will discuss tests used to determine HIV status.

■ Students will discuss the latest treatments for HIV and AIDS.

The National Health Education Standards

■ Students will demonstrate the ability to use goal-setting and decision-making skills that enhance health.

Preparing to Teach the Lesson Plan

Materials

Apple

Eye dropper

Food coloring

Knife

Blackline Master

Resist Pressure to Choose Risk Behaviors for HIV Infection

Teaching the Lesson Plan

Insert the end of an eye dropper through the skin of an apple and inject the food coloring. Allow the apple to stand for one hour.

1 Explain to students that certain risk behaviors for HIV infection need to be avoided. Tell students that HIV can be transmitted if a person shares a needle to make a tattoo or to pierce ears or other body parts. Tell students to always get permission from their parents or guardians if they are considering getting a tattoo or piercing their ears or other body parts. Tell students that there are people who are licensed to make tattoos and pierce ears who are required to use sterile equipment. Tell students that tattooing and piercing ears and other body parts break the skin. HIV can enter the body through cuts or breaks in the skin. Tell students that a needle is used to place dye into the skin when a person gets a tattoo. If the equipment used to make the tattoo is not handled in a sanitary manner, HIV from an infected person can remain on it. If the contaminated equipment is used to tattoo someone else, HIV can enter through the skin of the other person and infect that person. Tell students that the same is true of equipment used for piercing ears and other body parts. Tell students they can use resistance skills if they are pressured to share a needle to get a tattoo or to have ears or other body parts pierced. Define resistance skills. **Resistance skills** are skills that help you say NO to an action or to leave a situation. Give each student a copy of the Blackline Master *Resist Pressure to Choose Risk Behaviors for HIV Infection*.

2 Tell students that drug use also can lead to HIV infection. Tell students that sharing needles to inject drugs is a common way HIV is spread. Define injecting drug user. An **injecting drug user** is a person who injects illegal drugs into the body with syringes, needles, or other injection equipment. If an injecting drug user has HIV, drops of blood with HIV can infect the injection equipment. If the injecting drug user shares the injection equipment with infected blood, the person with whom it is being shared will be infected with HIV. In addition, harmful drugs affect the part of the brain used for clear thinking and reasoning. People who use drugs might not consider the risks of being sexually active. They might engage in sexual risk behaviors for HIV infection.

3 Show the prepared apple to the class and have students observe that the outside of the apple does not appear unusual. Tell students that the apple represents a person who is an injecting drug user. This "injecting drug user" used another person's needle to inject drugs. The "injecting drug user" became infected with HIV. Tell students that there is no way of knowing this just by looking at the outside of the apple, or "injecting drug user."

4 Use a knife to cut through the apple where you injected the food coloring. Tell students to observe the inside of the apple. Students will notice that the food coloring has spread. Explain to students that the food coloring represents HIV. Tell students that only by examining the inside of the apple, or "injecting drug user," was the food coloring, or "HIV," able to be seen.

5 Tell students about tests used to determine HIV status. Define ELISA. **ELISA** is a test used on body fluids to check for HIV antibodies. Define Western blot. **Western blot** is a test used to confirm ELISA. Anyone who has been sexually active, uses injecting drugs, shares a needle, or has certain signs or symptoms of HIV infection should be tested. Tell students the latest treatments for HIV and AIDS. Define ddI. **DdI** is a drug that slows down the rate at which HIV multiplies. Define AZT. **AZT** is a drug that slows down the rate at which HIV multiplies. Define protease inhibitors. **Protease inhibitors** are antiviral drugs that decrease the amount of HIV in the blood and increase the T cell count. To date, there is no cure for HIV infection or AIDS.

Assessment

Select two students to role-play an ear piercing situation. Tell one student to ask the other if he or she can pierce his or her ear. The student should say, "There's nothing to worry about, I pierce ears all the time." Tell the other student to refuse to get his or her ear pierced. Tell the student to explain why ear piercing in circumstances other than those that are followed by qualified personnel in an appropriate setting is a risk factor for the transmission of HIV.

Resist Pressure to Choose
Risk Behaviors for HIV Infection

1. Be confident and say, "NO, I do not want to risk becoming infected with HIV."

2. Give reasons you will not choose risk behaviors for HIV infection.

3. Repeat your reasons for NOT choosing risk behaviors for HIV infection.

4. Do not send a mixed message.

5. Avoid situations in which there might be pressure to choose risk behaviors for HIV infection.

6. Break off a relationship when someone continues to pressure you to choose risk behaviors for HIV infection.

7. Influence others to AVOID risk behaviors for HIV infection.

Pass That Cookie

The Curriculum

Life Skill

■ I will choose behaviors to reduce my risk of HIV infection.

Objective

■ Students will explain why practicing abstinence protects them from HIV infection.

The National Health Education Standards

■ Students will demonstrate the ability to use goal-setting and decision-making skills that enhance health.

Preparing to Teach the Lesson Plan

Materials

Two large, hard cookies such as oatmeal cookies

Pictures from magazines

Scissors

Blackline Master

Ways in Which HIV and AIDS Threaten Society

Teaching the Lesson Plan

1 Ask a student volunteer to come to the front of the room. Tell the volunteer to pick a cookie and to hold it. Tell the volunteer not to eat the cookie. Tell him or her to remain standing in front of the room holding the cookie.

2 Beginning in one corner of the room, tell another student to pick a cookie. Tell this student and the class that this cookie is going to be passed around the room and that everyone should touch the cookie. After the cookie is passed around the room, take it. When you take the cookie, cough and cover your mouth with your hand. Hold the cookie with the hand that you used to cover your mouth.

3 Tell the volunteer at the front of the room that you wish to trade cookies with him or her. Tell the volunteer that he or she could eat the cookie that you are holding. The volunteer might say that he or she does not want to eat that cookie. The volunteer might say that the cookie you are holding has been touched by everyone in the class and that you coughed and put your hand on it. The volunteer might say that the cookie is full of germs. Ask these questions to the volunteer:

• How do you know this cookie is full of germs?

• Could you observe germs on the cookie?

• Are you basing your assumption that there are germs on the cookie on your observations of other people having physical contact with it?

• If you had not observed anyone having physical contact with this cookie and it were placed back in its package, would you have eaten it?

• Does the cookie I offered to you differ in appearance from the one you are holding?

4 Explain to students that had they not seen the cookie being passed around the room, they would not have known that the cookie was covered with germs. Explain to students that just like a person could not tell that the cookie was covered by germs, a person cannot tell by looking at another person whether or not that person has HIV.

5 Explain to students that HIV and AIDS threaten society in several ways. Give each student a copy of the Blackline Master *Ways in Which HIV and AIDS Threaten Society.* Tell students that they can help protect themselves and society. They can resist pressure to be sexually active. They can practice abstinence from sex. **Abstinence from sex** is choosing not to be sexually active. Tell students that they cannot ignore these facts:

• A person who is infected with HIV might appear healthy.

• A person who is infected with HIV might not know he or she is infected.

• A person who is infected with HIV might know he or she is infected and tell you he or she is not.

6 Have students make palm cards that list resistance skills they can use if they are pressured to be sexually active. Their palm cards should contain this list:

• Be confident and say, "NO, I do not want to risk becoming infected with HIV."

• Give reasons why I will not choose risk behaviors for HIV infection.

• Repeat my reasons for NOT choosing risk behaviors for HIV infection.

• Don't send a mixed message.

• Avoid situations in which there will be pressure to choose risk behaviors for HIV infection.

• Avoid being with people who continue to pressure me to choose risk behaviors for HIV infection.

• Influence others to avoid risk behaviors for HIV infection.

Assessment

Have students develop a public service announcement for radio in which they explain why teens who practice abstinence from sex protect themselves from HIV infection. Have students tape record their individual public service announcements. Play them back for the class.

Ways in Which HIV and AIDS Threaten Society

Increase in health care costs

Cause people to die at a young age

Cause families to grieve the loss of a loved one

Cause people who are infected to suffer from illness

Cause babies to be born with HIV or with AIDS

The Costs of Rearing a Child

The Curriculum

Life Skills

■ I will develop skills to prepare for marriage.

■ I will develop skills to prepare for parenthood.

Objectives

■ Students will discuss the benefits of monogamous marriage.

■ Students will outline responsibilities of married adults and parents.

■ Students will identify reasons why they should be adults before they marry or become parents.

■ Students will explain why teens who feel unloved are more at risk for teen marriage and teen parenthood.

The National Health Education Standards

■ Students will demonstrate the ability to use goal-setting and decision-making skills that enhance health.

Preparing to Teach the Lesson Plan

Materials

Five-pound bag of flour or sugar

Art supplies

Journal

Chalkboard

Chalk

Blackline Masters

Why Is Teen Parenthood Risky?

Developmental Tasks of Adolescence

Major Tasks of the Passages of Marriage

Teaching the Lesson Plan

Have each student bring a five-pound bag of flour or sugar to class the day before teaching the lesson plan.

1 Tell students that teenage pregnancy is a major health problem in the United States today. Give each student a copy of the Blackline Master *Why Is Teen Parenthood Risky?* Review the Blackline Master *Why Is Teen Parenthood Risky?* with students. Explain to students that teen parents are not capable of meeting the responsibilities of parenthood. Teen mothers and teen fathers face many more difficulties than do married adult parents. For example, teen mothers risk anemia during pregnancy. Define anemia. **Anemia** is a condition in which the oxygen-carrying pigment in the blood is below normal. Explain that teen fathers often lack contact with their children. Some teens might grow up feeling unloved and are at more risk for having a baby. These teens might think that having a baby will fill the loneliness in their lives. Explain to students that having a baby does not fill up empty feelings and creates additional, difficult life experiences for teens. Emphasize that students are not ready for parenthood. Students should practice abstinence from sex.

2 Tell students that this activity will help them understand the responsibilities of having a baby. Tell students that the bag of flour or sugar they brought to class will be their baby for the next week. Have students decorate their five-pound bag of flour or sugar to look like a baby. Students can draw clothes and faces on their bags. Tell students that they must take their baby with them wherever they go for a week. Students must take care of the baby during classes and outside of school. Explain to students that having a baby is a full-time job. As parents, they are responsible for their baby 24 hours a day. Emphasize that

© 2001 Everyday Learning Corporation

the babies should not be damaged at the end of the week. Tell students that they cannot replace their babies if they lose them. Explain to students that the reason for decorating the babies is so students cannot substitute another baby for their damaged or lost baby. Have students write in a journal the problems they have caring for their baby during the week. For example, what did students do with their baby when they needed to use the restroom? What happened when they went to soccer or basketball practice? What did their friends say when the baby had to come along with them on social outings?

3 Lead a discussion every day with students. Ask some of the following questions:

- How does having a baby affect your daily life?
- Are there people who will help you take care of your baby?
- What activities are you not able to do with a baby?
- How do you feel having a baby with you 24 hours a day?
- Would the baby be easier to take care of if there were two parents?

At the end of a week, ask students to share their journals. Ask them to discuss the problems they had with their babies.

4 Tell students that teen parents do not have the opportunity to complete the developmental tasks of adolescence. Give each student a copy of the Blackline Master *Developmental Tasks of Adolescence*. Teens need to develop healthful relationships with both sexes. They need to become comfortable with their maleness or femaleness. When teens become parents, they do not have the opportunities to socialize that allows them to develop healthful relationships with members of both sexes. Teen parents do not have the opportunities to develop other skills that might prepare them for a career or for marriage.

5 Explain to students the benefits of a traditional monogamous marriage. A traditional monogamous marriage:

- protects the marriage commitment;

- preserves the marriage tradition;
- helps prevent divorce;
- provides a love in which parents raise children together;
- provides emotional security and trust; and
- helps protect marriage partners from infection with HIV and other STDs.

Tell students that teens who marry are not prepared to tackle the major tasks of the passages of marriage. Give each student a copy of the Blackline Master *Major Tasks of the Passages of Marriage*. Tell students that it is important for married couples to complete these stages in order to develop intimacy in their marriage and to raise children in a healthful environment.

Assessment

Have students write a list of the responsibilities of parenthood. Ask students to share their answers with the class. List the responsibilities on the board. When the list is complete, ask students why a teen cannot fulfill each responsibility. Discuss the advantages of waiting to be a parent until one is a married adult. Some advantages are the following:

- Married adult parents are better able to provide a stable homelife for their children.
- Married adult parents are more likely to have the financial resources that are needed to raise a child.
- Married adult parents are more mature and capable of meeting the responsibilities of parenthood.

Why Is Teen Parenthood Risky?

Babies born to Teen Parents:
- Often do not receive adequate nourishment
- Often do not receive adequate prenatal care
- Risk being born prematurely and having low birth weights
- Are more likely to be abused by their parents
- Are less likely to have adequate medical and dental care as children

Teen Mothers:
- Risk anemia during pregnancy
- Risk toxemia during pregnancy
- Risk premature birth
- Are more likely to drop out of school
- Are less likely to meet their career goals
- Have limited social opportunities
- Are more likely to have low incomes
- Are more likely to abuse their children

Teen Fathers:
- Have to pay child support and may be financially stressed
- Are more likely to drop out of school because they have to work
- Might have to change career plans
- Often lack contact with their children
- Are more likely to abuse their children
- Are less likely to meet their career goals

- A **premature birth** is the birth of a baby before it is fully developed or the birth of a baby less than 38 weeks from the time of conception.

- A **low birth weight** is a weight at birth that is less than 5.5 pounds (2.5 kilograms).

- **Anemia** is a condition in which the oxygen-carrying pigment in the blood is below normal.

- **Toxemia of pregnancy** is a disorder of pregnancy characterized by high blood pressure, tissue swelling, and protein in the urine.

Developmental Tasks of Adolescence

1 Develop **healthful relationships** with members of both sexes.

2 Become **comfortable** with your maleness and femaleness.

3 Become **comfortable** with your body.

4 Become **emotionally independent** from adults.

5 **Learn skills** you will need later if you marry and become a parent.

6 Prepare for a **career.**

7 Have a clear set of **values** to guide your behavior.

8 Understand and achieve **socially responsible behavior.**

Major Tasks of the Passages of Marriage

The First Stage: **The First Two Years**	The Second Stage: **The Third Through the Tenth Years**	The Third Stage: **The Eleventh Through the Twenty-Fifth Years**	The Fourth Stage: **The Twenty-Sixth Through the Thirty-Fifth Years**	The Fifth Stage: **The Thirty-Sixth Year and On**
The newly married couple overcome their idealistic notions of marriage and begin to form a family. The partners strive to:	The couple gain a realistic view of their marriage and of one another and must settle into dealing with their individual weaknesses and make an effort to avoid dysfunctional behaviors. Their goals are to:	The couple establish and maintain individual identity and deal with issues of forgiveness, aging, adolescent children, and intimacy. They recognize the need to:	The couple must master tasks from the first three stages that were not previously mastered, confront changes in sexuality, and grieve over their losses. They determine to:	The couple find new reasons for existing after the major life tasks of achieving financial security and nurturing their family have been completed; partners confront their feelings about death. They agree to:
■ maintain individual identity at the same time as they form a family; ■ develop cooperation and reduce the need to control the other; ■ develop a sexual bond with the other that leads to deeper intimacy; ■ develop an effective decision-making style; ■ recognize the difficulties in their parents' marriages and anticipate how those difficulties might affect their marriage.	■ recognize and confront the weaknesses of both partners; ■ examine relationships and avoid dysfunctional behaviors; ■ reaffirm commitment to sexual intimacy, including sexual fidelity; ■ examine the influence of children on marriage and to agree upon child-raising methods.	■ reexamine and maintain individual identity and develop mutual dependence; ■ recognize that one another will not be perfect; ■ forgive one another for shortcomings and mistakes; ■ confront the crises of middle age, including aging, sexuality, and job and financial security; struggle for individuality; ■ reevaluate and make a plan for maintaining and developing intimacy.	■ reevaluate the tasks from the previous stages and determine if they have been successfully mastered; ■ recognize the physical changes that accompany aging and affect sexuality and to rekindle romance; ■ grieve over losses such as death of parents and children leaving home.	■ prepare for retirement; ■ renew intimacy and develop ways to continue sexual intimacy; ■ prepare for death and for the death of the marriage partner; ■ accept death as a stage of life.

(Adapted from Minirth, et al. *Passages of Marriage,* 1991)

Difficult Family Relationships

The Curriculum

Life Skills

■ I will develop healthful family relationships.

■ I will work to improve difficult family relationships.

■ I will make healthful adjustments to family changes.

Objectives

■ Students will identify different kinds of family patterns.

■ Students will discuss actions that can help them develop healthful family relationships.

■ Students will discuss reasons why they should follow family guidelines.

■ Students will identify three kinds of problems that can occur in dysfunctional families.

■ Students will explain steps that can be taken to improve dysfunctional family relationships.

■ Students will discuss changes that might occur in family relationships.

■ Students will describe ways they can adjust to changes in family relationships.

■ Students will discuss ways parents' divorce can affect a teen's future relationships.

The National Health Education Standards

■ Students will demonstrate the ability to use interpersonal communication skills to enhance health.

■ Students will demonstrate the ability to practice health-enhancing behaviors and reduce health risks.

Preparing to Teach the Lesson Plan

Materials

Two clear plastic cups

Distilled vinegar

Water

Blackline Master

Family Guidelines

Teaching the Lesson Plan

Fill one of the plastic cups with water. Fill the other cup half with water and half with distilled vinegar. Fill these glasses without allowing the class to see you.

1 Define healthful family relationships.
Healthful family relationships are relationships in which family members relate well, show respect for each other, and behave in responsible ways. Tell students that they need to spend time with their families in order to have healthful family relationships. These are reasons to spend time:

• To fulfill their need to belong

• To practice taking calculated risks in a safe setting. A **calculated risk** is a chance that is worth taking after you consider the possible outcomes.

• To learn and practice skills they can use in future relationships.

2 Explain that they must follow family guidelines to have healthful family relationships.
Family guidelines are rules set by your parents or guardian that help you know how to act. Give each student a copy of the Blackline Master *Family Guidelines*. There are good reasons to follow family guidelines:

- To protect your health and safety
- To follow rules and laws
- To show respect for yourself and others
- To show good character

3 Show the students the two plastic cups. Without allowing them to smell the contents, ask students if they notice any difference between the two cups. Students will respond that there is no visible difference that can be seen right away. Then have a student volunteer observe the contents of the two cups more closely. Allow the student volunteer to smell the two cups and he or she will note that there is a difference. Tell students that you added something to one cup—vinegar. When you added the vinegar, it permeated the entire cup of water. Adding vinegar changed all of the water.

4 Explain that this demonstration was done to illustrate how things might be changed if something is added. Explain that this is true of healthful family relationships. Some things will change the whole family and will disrupt healthful family relationships. Then family relationships will become difficult family relationships. The family might be described as a dysfunctional family. A **dysfunctional family** is a family that lacks the skills to be successful and to function in healthful ways.

5 Explain that drug use might develop drug dependence. **Drug dependence** is the compelling need to take a drug even though it harms the body, mind, and relationships. Explain that the lives of family members who are drug dependent become dominated by the need to obtain and use drugs. This poisons family relationships just as the vinegar changed the water. Family members might try to keep the problem a secret. They might try to protect the family member who is drug dependent by lying or making excuses. They might deny the problem and stop trusting their own feelings.

6 Explain that family members might develop codependence. Define codependence. **Codependence** is a mental disorder in which a person denies feelings and begins to

cope in harmful ways. Family members deny feelings by:

- pretending a problem does not exist;
- blaming someone else for what is happening;
- offering excuses;
- attacking others who talk about the problems.

Explain that teens with codependence might become enablers. Define enabler. An **enabler** is a person who supports the harmful behavior of others. Discuss the dangers of being an enabler. Teens who are enablers might pretend problems do not exist. They might make excuses for the wrong behaviors of others. They might get used to sick relationships and not expect others to treat them with respect. They might choose friends who are abusive or who use drugs. Teens who are enablers usually need help changing their behavior. Teens who live in families with drug dependence are at risk for using drugs and becoming drug dependent. Counseling can be very helpful.

7 Explain that abuse can cause difficult family relationships. Define abuse. **Abuse** is the harmful treatment of another person. Four kinds of abuse might occur in the family:

- **Physical abuse** is harmful treatment that results in physical injury.
- **Neglect** is failure to provide proper care and guidance.
- **Emotional abuse** is putting down another person and making that person feel worthless.
- **Sexual abuse** is sexual contact that is forced on a person.

Explain that teens who have been abused need help sorting out their feelings. An abused teen might be told "I love you" and at the same time be beaten, put down, or sexually abused. The words and actions of the abuser are inconsistent. Because teens want to feel loved, they might believe the words used. However, the words do not match the actions. To cope, teens begin to deny their feelings that something is wrong. They might begin to blame themselves for the way they are treated. Teens who have been sexually abused are at risk for being sexually active. They might act out and have harmful relationships. Teens who have been abused need to talk to a trusted adult who can get help for them.

8 Explain that violence can cause difficult family relationships. **Violence** is the use of threats and physical force with the purpose of causing harm. **Domestic violence** is violence that occurs within a family. Explain that the family member who begins the violence wants to control others. Violent outbursts become the way to gain control. Family members often respond by giving the violent family member even more control as a way to avoid disagreements. They change their behavior to avoid upsetting the violent family member. They look for reasons for the violent outbursts. They might even blame themselves. Teens who live in homes where there is domestic violence are at special risk. They might copy the behavior they have experienced and try to control others by force.

9 Discuss steps that can be taken by teens who live in families in which there is drug dependence, abuse, and/or violence. The following steps can be taken:

- Keep a journal. Write the date and time. Describe the difficult family situation. Tell how the situation affected you. Tell how you feel about it.

- Talk to a responsible adult family member. Talk to another adult if there is no family member with whom you can speak and be honest. Share your journal. Talk about the difficult family situation. Tell how it affects you. Tell how you feel about it.

- Join a recovery program. A **recovery program** is a group that provides support to members who want to change their behavior. Teens can get help for codependence or for being an enabler.

- Get a mentor. A **mentor** is a responsible person who guides another person.

10 Tell students that you are going to introduce a new topic. The topic is changes that might occur in families and ways to adjust to these changes. Identify the following ways that a family might change:

- Death of a family member

- Separation of parents. A **separation** is an agreement between a couple to live apart but remain married.

- Divorce of parents. A **divorce** is a legal way to end a marriage.

- Parental dating

- Remarriage. A **remarriage** is a marriage in which a person who was married before marries again.

- Formation of a stepfamily. A **stepfamily** is a family that consists of marriage partners, their children from their previous marriages, and children they have together.

- Birth of a baby

11 Talk about ways to adjust to family changes.

- Talk to parents or guardians and share feelings.

- To relieve anxiety ask questions about what will happen and when.

- Follow family guidelines.

- Spend time with family members.

Assessment

Have students develop a family magazine. They must give the magazine a title. Then they must develop a table of contents for the magazine. They need to list the articles that will appear in the magazine and provide a very short description of what will be in each article. They should give the articles clever names. There must be an article on each of the following topics:

- healthful family relationships

- family guidelines

- dysfunctional families

- ways families change

Family Guidelines

To protect your health and safety

Your parents or guardian make rules to protect your health and safety. Your parents or guardian do not allow you to smoke. They might have a no smoking rule for guests in your home. Their rules protect your health. They expect you to cross the street at an intersection. They expect you to stay away from gangs. They expect you to be home by your curfew. Their rules keep you safe.

To follow rules and laws

Rules and laws protect society. Your parents or guardian can teach you about rules and laws. For example, you might play on a sports team. Your parents or guardian will tell you to follow the rules for safe play. They know you can be injured if you do not follow the rules. They expect you to obey the coach and referee. Your parents or guardian expect you to follow laws. They expect you to wear a safety belt when you ride in an automobile. They expect you not to steal or destroy property. Rules and laws protect you and society.

To show respect for yourself and others

Your parents or guardian want you to have self-respect and respect for others. They expect you to show respect for them. They make rules to teach you self-respect. For example, they expect you to tell them if someone abuses you. They make rules to teach you how to respect others. For example, they do not allow you to interrupt other family members when they are talking. They expect you to stand if an older person, such as a grandparent, needs a chair.

To show good character

Your parents or guardian know the responsible values that make up good character. They set rules in order to teach you to act on responsible values. For example, they expect you not to swear. If you swear, they punish you in an appropriate way. They punish you because they want you to have good character. Your parents or guardian might not allow you to watch television programs or movies with sex, violence, and swearing. They have this rule to keep you from being influenced in wrong ways.

I Am a Responsible Parent

The Curriculum

Life Skill

■ I will learn facts about pregnancy and childbirth.

Objectives

■ Students will discuss the importance of prenatal care.

■ Students will explain ways a mother-to-be's behaviors can affect the health of her baby.

■ Students will explain ways a father-to-be's behaviors can affect the health of his baby.

■ Students will identify problems that can occur during pregnancy.

The National Health Education Standards

■ Students will comprehend concepts related to health promotion and disease prevention.

Preparing to Teach the Lesson Plan

Materials

Construction paper

Scissors

Pens or markers

Dice from a board game

Coins to use as playing pieces

Blackline Masters

The Parent Pledge to a Child

Parenthood Board Game

Parenthood Board Game Cards

Teaching the Lesson Plan

Using scissors, cut ten strips of construction paper. Write each of the ten statements from the Blackline Master The Parent Pledge to a Child *on each strip of construction paper.*

1 Do not tell students the content of this lesson plan in advance of teaching the lesson plan. Pass out the ten strips of construction paper to ten students. Tell each student to read aloud what is on his or her strip. After all students have read aloud their strips of paper, ask the class, "Who am I?" Students might guess that the answer is a responsible parent.

2 Tell students that responsible parents make raising their children a priority. Responsible parents bond with a newborn baby right away. Define bonding. **Bonding** is a process in which people develop a feeling of closeness. Give each student a copy of the Blackline Master *The Parent Pledge to a Child.*

3 Ask the class to give examples of how parents or guardians might fulfill each of the promises in *The Parent Pledge to a Child.* For example, a student might say that a parent might hug a child good-bye each day before the child goes to school. The student might say that this act is an example of a parent giving a child love and affection.

4 Tell students that both a father-to-be's and a mother-to-be's health habits can affect the developing baby. Tell students that a father-to-be might harm the developing baby if he is exposed to paints and pesticides; if he smokes, drinks, or uses drugs; or if he smokes around a pregnant female. Tell students that a mother-to-be might harm the developing baby if she smokes cigarettes, uses crack or cocaine, drinks alcohol, or inhales chemicals and secondhand smoke. Tell students that pregnant females who smoke have smaller babies. These babies are in poorer general health than babies of non-smoking females. Tell students that smoking and breathing smoke increase the risk of complications, miscarriage, and stillbirth during pregnancy. Define miscarriage. A **miscarriage** is a natural early ending of a pregnancy. Tell students that if there are drugs present in a female's bloodstream, they can pass into the developing baby's bloodstream. These drugs can harm the developing baby. Tell students that a female should not drink alcohol during pregnancy. Define fetal alcohol syndrome (FAS). **Fetal alcohol syndrome (FAS)** is birth defects in a baby born to a mother who drank alcohol during pregnancy. Tell students that it is important that a pregnant female get prenatal care as soon as possible after learning she is pregnant. Define prenatal care. **Prenatal care** is care that is given to a mother-to-be and her developing baby.

Assessment

Divide the class into groups of four or more. Give a copy of the Blackline Master *Parenthood Board Game* to each group. Give a copy of the Blackline Master *Parenthood Board Game Cards* to each group. Tell each group to cut out the cards. Each group will have a set of the *Parenthood Board Game Cards*. Tell the groups to place the cards in the space on the game board named "cards." Give each group two to three sheets of construction paper. Tell students to make a set of play money with the construction paper. The dollar bills should be in the following denominations: $10, $20, $50, and $100. The board game has spaces with the names of items a parent should buy for a baby, such as a high chair or a baby crib. The object of the game is to buy all of the items needed for a baby without going bankrupt. Tell students to write down the items they purchase on a sheet of paper. Each student should buy each item once. If a student lands on an item, he or she must buy that item if he or she does not already own it. If a student lands on an item he or she has already bought, the next

player takes a turn. If a student cannot afford an item, that student is bankrupt and is out of the game. The board game also has spaces that instruct players to pick a card. The cards show how a mother-to-be's and a father-to-be's behaviors can affect the health of a baby. For example, a student might pick a card that reads, "The mother-to-be smokes a cigarette, move back three spaces." Each student should have a total of $1000 at the start of the game. The bank should have a total of $1000 at the start of the game.

The Parent Pledge to a Child

1 I will set aside quality time to spend with you.

2 I will learn about your growth and development.

3 I will keep you healthy and safe.

4 I will give you love and affection.

5 I will speak to you in kind ways.

6 I will teach you how to have good character.

7 I will not abuse you in any way.

8 I will work to have the financial resources I need to raise you.

9 I will treat you with respect.

10 I will be a responsible parent who does not abuse drugs or participate in other addictive behaviors, such as gambling.

Parenthood Board Game

Diapers $100	Stroller $200	Draw a Card	Hospital Expenses $3000
Draw a Card			Medicine $150
Blankets $75	Parenthood Board Game Cards		Clothes $200
Baby Formula $50			Draw a Card
GO collect $100	Draw a Card	Baby Crib $500	Car Seat $250

Cut along line

Parenthood Board Game Cards

"The mother-to-be gets early prenatal care. Receive $200 from the bank."

"The father-to-be smokes around the mother. Move back three spaces."

"The father-to-be and mother-to-be take a tour of the hospital. Receive $200 from the bank."

"The father-to-be misses a childbirth class. Lose $50."

"The mother-to-be drinks. Lose $200."

"The father-to-be is exposed to pesticides before conception. Lose $100."

"The father-to-be and mother-to-be are teenagers. Lose $500."

"The mother-to-be does not take vitamin supplements from her doctor. Lose $200."

"The mother-to-be smokes a cigarette, move back three spaces."

"The father-to-be takes childbirth classes. Receive $200 from the bank."

"The father-to-be drinks alcohol around the time of conception. Go back three spaces."

"The female stops smoking before she tries to conceive. Go forward three spaces."

Teen Pregnancy Misfortune

The Curriculum

Life Skill

■ I will learn facts about pregnancy and childbirth.

Objectives

■ Students will explain the process of conception.

■ Students will explain what happens in the first week after conception.

■ Students will list the signs of pregnancy.

■ Students will describe the development of a baby from conception through birth.

■ Students will explain what happens during labor and childbirth.

The National Health Education Standards

■ Students will comprehend concepts related to health promotion and disease prevention.

Preparing to Teach the Lesson Plan

Materials

Chalkboard

Chalk

Index cards (10 for each student)

Blackline Masters

Fertilization

Development of the Baby—Conception Through Birth

Labor and Childbirth

Teaching the Lesson Plan

1 Define pregnancy. **Pregnancy** is the time between conception and birth. When a female becomes pregnant, hormones change how her body works. Tell students that these changes might include missed menstrual periods, enlarged or tender breasts, frequent urination, tiredness, and morning sickness. Define morning sickness. **Morning sickness** is nausea that can occur at any time of the day during pregnancy. Explain to students that a female who thinks she might be pregnant should have a pregnancy test. The test should be confirmed by a physician. Give each student a copy of the Blackline Master *Fertilization*.

2 Define fertilization. **Fertilization** is the union of a sperm and ovum. Tell students what happens in the first week after conception. The fertilized ovum begins to divide right away as it moves through a Fallopian tube to the uterus. The outer cells of the fertilized ovum form the placenta. Define placenta. The **placenta** is a structure that attaches the ovum to the inner wall of the uterus. Define umbilical cord. The **umbilical cord** is a rope-like cord that connects the developing baby to the placenta. Define amniotic sac. The **amniotic sac** is a pouch of fluid that surrounds a developing baby. Tell students that a baby's development is measured in trimesters. Define trimester. A **trimester** is one of three three-month periods during a human pregnancy. Give each student a copy of the Blackline Master *Development of the Baby—Conception Through Birth*. Discuss the different changes a baby goes through in each trimester.

3 Tell students that as a baby is about to be born, a pregnant woman might experience contractions. Define contractions. **Contractions** are severe cramps during childbirth. A woman might also have a discharge of blood from the

© 2001 Everyday Learning Corporation

cervix. Tell students that the amniotic sac will break and cause water to flow out of the woman's vagina. Define labor. **Labor** is a series of changes that result in the birth of a baby. Define childbirth. **Childbirth** is the process by which the baby moves from the uterus out of the mother's body. Give each student a copy of the Blackline Master *Labor and Childbirth*. Discuss the three stages of labor with students.

4 Tell students that teen parenthood is risky. Explain that teen parenthood is risky to babies born to teen parents and to teen mothers and fathers. Divide the class into three teams. Tell the groups that they are going to play a game called "Teen Pregnancy Misfortune." Tell the class that you are going to draw the correct number of spaces on the chalkboard for a puzzle to fit. The puzzle will be a vocabulary word. Draw the correct number of spaces on the chalkboard for the answer to the puzzle to fit. For example, the answer to the puzzle might be "Fertilization." Draw the following on the board:

— — — — — — — — — — — — —

5 Tell the class that the object of the game is to solve the puzzle. Each team will take turns guessing letters in the puzzle until one team guesses the correct answer. For example, the first team might guess the letter *A*. You would write the letter *A* in the appropriate spaces. The second team might guess the letter *N*. You would write the letter *N* in the appropriate spaces. Repeat the activity until one of the teams guesses the correct term.

6 Repeat the activity four more times. The answers to the four puzzles should be umbilical cord, pregnancy test, heartbeat, and birth canal.

Assessment

Divide the class into pairs. Give each pair 20 index cards. Tell students they will play "Pregnancy and Childbirth Concentration." Tell each pair of students to write 10 vocabulary words from the Lesson Plan on 10 index cards. Tell each pair of students to write 10 definitions on the other 10 index cards. Tell each pair of students to mix the index cards. Each pair of students should place each index card face down in rows. One student in each pair should turn over a card. Then the student should turn over a second card to match a vocabulary word with its definition. Tell students that if the card matches, then the student keeps the cards and takes another turn. If the cards do not match, the cards are turned face down again and the other student in the pair takes a turn. Tell students to repeat this until all of the cards have been matched. The student with the most cards wins.

P _ _ _ G N _ N _ _

Fertilization

Fertilization usually occurs in the Fallopian tube.
Fertilization is the union of a sperm and ovum.

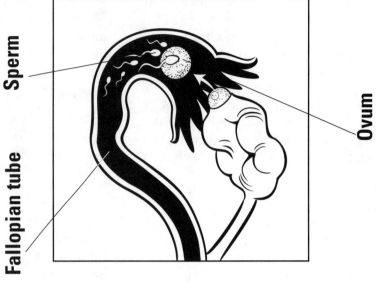

Sperm

Ovum

Fallopian tube

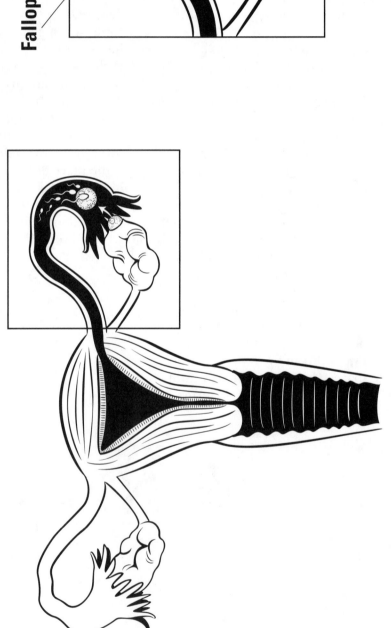

Development of the Baby—
Conception Through Birth

First Trimester

End of 1st month
- Heart, brain, nerves, and lungs form.
- Digestive system forms.
- Eyes and ears can be seen.
- Length is 1/3 inch (0.085 cm).
- The baby is called an embryo.

End of 2nd month
- Arms, fingers, legs, and toes form.
- Heart becomes four chambers.
- Head becomes larger.
- Facial characteristics appear.
- Length is 1 inch (2.54 cm).
- The baby is called a fetus.

End of 3rd month
- First external signs of sex appear.
- Some movement begins.
- Weight is about 1.5 ounces (42 g).
- Length is about 1.5 inches (3.81 cm).

Second Trimester

End of 4th month
- Skin is developing.
- Fetus kicks its legs and moves its arms.
- Weight is about 6–7 ounces (168–196 g).
- Length is about 4–5 inches (10.16–12.7 cm).

End of 5th month
- Fine hair develops.
- Eyelashes and nails appear.
- Rate of growth slows.
- Weight is about 1 pound (0.45 kg).
- Length is about 9–10 inches (22.86–25.4 cm).

End of 6th month
- Fetus responds to noise and pressure with movement.
- Heartbeat increases.
- Fetus moves vigorously.
- Weight is about 1.5 pounds (0.68 kg).
- Length is about 11.5–12.5 inches (29.21–31.75 cm).

Third Trimester

End of 7th month
- Eyes open.
- Legs and arms move often.
- Weight is about 3 pounds (1.35 kg).
- Length is about 15 inches (38.1 cm).

End of 8th month
- Almost all organs are complete.
- Weight is about 4 pounds (1.8 kg).
- Length is about 18 inches (45.72 cm).

End of 9th month
- Skin is smooth and polished.
- Eyes are slate-colored.
- Weight is about 6–9 pounds (2.7–4.05 kg).
- Length is about 19–21 inches (48.26–53.34 cm).

Labor and Childbirth

Stage 1

The lower part of the uterus—the cervix—dilates, or widens, enough for the baby to pass through. This stage can last from two hours to an entire day.

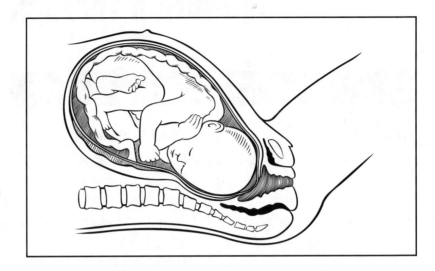

Stage 2

The baby passes into the birth canal, or vagina. The baby passes out of the birth canal and begins to breathe on its own. The umbilical cord is cut.

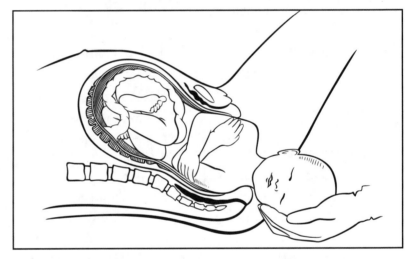

Stage 3

The placenta passes out of the birth canal. If this does not occur, the doctor removes the placenta.

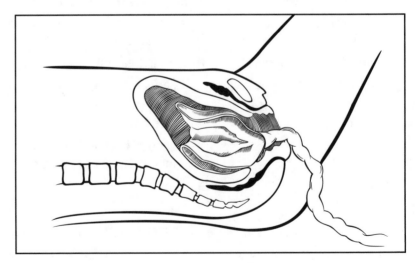

Grades 9–12
Lesson Plans and Blackline Masters

Table of Contents

A Me Advertisement

The Curriculum

Life Skill

■ I will use resistance skills when appropriate.

Objectives

■ Students will differentiate between positive peer pressure and negative peer pressure.

■ Students will demonstrate resistance skills that can be used to resist pressure to do something wrong.

■ Students will explain why it is important to show remorse for wrongful behavior.

■ Students will identify steps to take to correct wrong actions.

■ Students will give examples of restitution, including ways to pay back and pay forward.

The National Health Education Standards

■ Students will demonstrate the ability to use interpersonal communication skills to enhance health.

■ Students will demonstrate the ability to advocate for personal, family, and community health.

Preparing to Teach the Lesson Plan

Materials

Advertisements for health care products from old magazines or newspapers

Blackline Master

Questions to Evaluate Media Messages™

Teaching the Lesson Plan

1 Explain to students that they are going to learn steps to take if they make a wrong decision. Tell students that decisions are sometimes made based on peer pressure. Define positive peer pressure. **Positive peer pressure** is influence from peers to behave in a responsible way. Define negative peer pressure. **Negative peer pressure** is influence from peers to behave in a way that is not responsible. Define wrong decision. A **wrong decision** is a choice that leads to actions that harm health, are unsafe, are illegal, show disrespect for self and others, disregard the guidelines of parents and of other responsible adults, and lack good character. Tell students that it is important to show remorse for a wrong decision. Tell students that there are four steps to take to correct a wrong decision:

1. Take responsibility and admit you have made a wrong decision.

2. Do not continue actions based on wrong decisions.

3. Discuss the wrong decision with a parent, guardian, or other responsible adult.

4. Make restitution for harm done to others. Define restitution. **Restitution** is making good for loss or damage. Apologizing or replacing a lost jacket are examples of restitution. Tell students to use resistance skills if they are pressured to do something wrong.

2 Show advertisements for health care products from old magazines or newspapers to the class. You might want to make overhead transparencies of the advertisements you choose. Give each student a copy of the Blackline Master *Questions to Evaluate Media Messages*™. Have students analyze the advertisements. Discuss what advertisers try to do to sell their products. For example, the advertisements might emphasize the benefits the product can bring to a person who uses it, such as social acceptance. The advertisements might describe how the product is better than other similar products. Or the advertisements might indicate how a person will feel if he or she uses the product. Have students identify additional ways advertisers try to promote their products. Have students use the seven questions to evaluate media messages. For example, a student might find an advertisement for an athlete's foot product. The student could say that the target audience of the advertisement is athletes or other people with athlete's foot fungus.

3 Tell students that they are going to play the role of advertisers. Each student is going to design an advertising campaign. The ads will promote the importance of following the four steps to take to correct a wrong decision. Pass out old magazines and newspapers. The students will select an advertisement from an old magazine or newspaper. They are to adapt the theme of the advertisement to promote the importance of taking the four steps to correct a wrong decision. For example, a student might find a full-page advertisement for a specific brand of toothpaste. The student might cover up the name of the toothpaste and write "make restitution" on the advertisement. The student would then write other statements that highlight what a person should do if he or she makes a wrong decision. The student might write the following in the advertisement:

"Do you like to talk? Then discuss wrong decisions with a parent, guardian, or other responsible adult."

"Unlike her competitors, Susie does not continue actions based on wrong decisions."

4 You also might choose to have students do this activity at home and make packages for their products. Students could write promotional sayings on their products. You could have students share their products with the class.

Assessment

Have students pair with each other. Each student should try to remember the advertisement of his or her partner. Have students tell their partners what they remember about the advertisements. Each partner then should modify the advertising campaign to incorporate any of the steps that were not mentioned in the original advertisement. For example, Tom's advertisement might emphasize that a person should make restitution for harm done to others. Tom's partner should then modify the advertisement to incorporate taking responsibility and admitting you have made a wrong decision; not continuing actions based on wrong decisions; and discussing the wrong decision with a parent, guardian, or other responsible adult. The modified advertisements should mention all four of the steps to take when a person makes a wrong decision.

© 2001 Everyday Learning Corporation

Questions to Evaluate Media Messages™

1	What is the purpose of the message?
2	Who is the target audience for the message?
3	Who will profit if members of the target audience are influenced by the message?
4	Does the message encourage members of the target audience to choose responsible behavior? How?
5	What techniques are used to make the message appealing to the target audience?
6	What information is missing from the message?
7	Is this message consistent with messages found in other media on the same subject? How?

539

A Pat on the Back

The Curriculum

Life Skills
■ I will express emotions in healthful ways.
■ I will use conflict resolution skills.

Objectives
■ Students will construct sample I-messages to express different emotions.
■ Students will demonstrate ways to implement active listening.
■ Students will give examples of ways people relate using nonverbal communication.
■ Students will explain how sending mixed messages might affect the quality of their relationships.
■ Students will identify three conflict response styles and explain how each one might affect the quality of their relationships.
■ Students will demonstrate how to use conflict resolution skills.

The National Health Education Standards
■ Students will demonstrate the ability to use interpersonal communication skills to enhance health.
■ Students will demonstrate the ability to advocate for personal, family, and community health.
■ Students will demonstrate the ability to practice health-enhancing behaviors and reduce health risks.

Preparing to Teach the Lesson Plan

Materials
Paper
Pencil
Tape

Blackline Masters

I-Messages

Conflict Resolution Skills

Teaching the Lesson Plan

1 Tell students that this activity is intended to help them communicate with others in healthful ways. One way to develop good character is to have healthful relationships. Define healthful relationship. A **healthful relationship** is a relationship that promotes self-respect, encourages productivity and health, and is free of addictions and violence. Healthful relationships are the cornerstone of good character.

2 Have students write their names at the top of a sheet of paper. Have each student tape the sheet of paper to his or her back. Students will need help to do this. Have students select partners. When they have selected partners, they are to say an I-message or a you-message to their partner. The partner should say the opposite. For example, if a student says an I-message to his or her partner, then his or her partner should say a you-message to him or her. Give each student a copy of the Blackline Master *I-Messages*. Define I-message. An **I-message** is a statement describing a specific behavior or event, the effect that behavior or event has on a person, and the feelings that result. For example, one student in a pair could say "When I was interrupted on the phone, I couldn't talk with my friend, and that irritated me." Define you-message. A **you-message** is a statement that blames or shames another person. The other student in the pair could say "You were rude and selfish to pick up the phone when I was trying to have a conversation." Have each partner write his or her name on the partner's sheet of paper. Then have each partner select a new partner and repeat the process. Emphasize that each

© 2001 Everyday Learning Corporation

person should say an I-message or a you-message to at least five people.

3 Have students remove the sheets of paper from their backs. Ask students how they felt telling students I-messages and you-messages.

4 Discuss active listening skills. Define active listening. **Active listening** is a way of responding to show that a person hears and understands. For example, a student might show he or she is actively listening by asking for more information, repeating in his or her own words what the speaker said, summarizing the main ideas, or acknowledging and showing appreciation for the speaker's feelings. A person might also smile or frown, or shake his or her head "yes" or "no." Repeat the exercise with one student in a pair saying an I-message while the other student in the pair uses active listening. Discuss how students felt listening to an I-message.

5 Define balanced friendship. A **balanced friendship** is a friendship in which two people give and receive acts of kindness between each other. In balanced friendships, there generally is an equal exchange of giving and receiving. The giving and receiving might not be balanced at all times. For example, if a friend is sick or is going through difficult times, a person might need to do more giving than usual. But after a period of time, the friend is able to reciprocate. This shift back and forth is healthful. Students should avoid sending a mixed message. Define mixed message. A **mixed message** is a message that conveys two different or double meanings. For example, a student might tell his or her father that he or she would be happy to childsit for a younger brother or sister, but roll his or her eyes in disgust.

6 Define conflict. A **conflict** is a disagreement between people or between choices. Tell students the following three conflict response styles: conflict avoidance, conflict confrontation, and conflict resolution. Define conflict avoidance. **Conflict avoidance** is a conflict response style in which a person avoids disagreements at all costs. The person is so

concerned others will not like him or her that he or she does not challenge others' behavior. Define conflict confrontation. **Conflict confrontation** is a conflict response style that attempts to settle a disagreement in a hostile, defiant, and aggressive way. The person likes to confront others. Define conflict resolution. **Conflict resolution** is a conflict response style in which a person uses conflict resolution skills to resolve disagreements. Define conflict resolution skills. **Conflict resolution skills** are steps that can be taken to settle a disagreement in a responsible way. Give each student a copy of the Blackline Master *Conflict Resolution Skills.*

Assessment

Write the following scenario on the chalkboard:

Assume that you have an older brother. You are watching television and your brother enters the room and turns the channel so that he can watch his favorite television program. You are angry because you have a different program that you want to watch.

Answer the following questions:

1. How might you respond using conflict avoidance?

2. How might you respond using conflict confrontation?

3. How might you respond using conflict resolution?

4. What I message might you use to express your angry feelings?

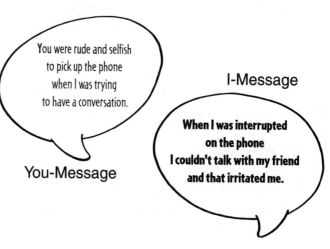

You were rude and selfish to pick up the phone when I was trying to have a conversation.

You-Message

I-Message

When I was interrupted on the phone I couldn't talk with my friend and that irritated me.

I-Messages

I-Messages are statements used to express feelings.

They Contain:

1	**2**	**3**
a specific behavior or event,	the effect that behavior or event has on a person,	the feelings that result.

Example:

1	**2**	**3**
When you didn't arrive to childsit on time,	we were late to the movie,	and I was upset.

Conflict Resolution Skills

1. Remain calm.

2. Set the tone.

3. Define the conflict.

4. Take responsibility for personal actions.

5. Use I-messages to express needs and feelings.

6. Listen to the needs and feelings of others.

7. List and evaluate possible solutions.

8. Agree on a solution.

9. Keep your word and follow the agreement.

10. Ask for the assistance of a trusted adult if the conflict cannot be resolved.

Brown Bag

The Curriculum

Life Skill

■ I will develop good character.

Objectives

■ Students will explain why it is important to practice moderation and be able to delay gratification.

■ Students will identify the responsible values that make up good character.

■ Students will explain why they must demonstrate each of the responsible values that make up good character to have healthful relationships.

■ Students will identify reasons they need good character.

The National Health Education Standards

■ Students will comprehend concepts related to health promotion and disease prevention.

■ Students will demonstrate the ability to use interpersonal communication skills to enhance health.

Preparing to Teach the Lesson Plan

Materials

Paper bag

Various items students will bring to class

Blackline Masters

Ten Responsible Values That Make Up Good Character™

Good Character Checklist

Teaching the Lesson Plan

1 *Tell students to bring a paper bag filled with five items to class the following day. The items should be objects that represent responsible values they have. Define value. A **value** is a standard or belief. These objects should be related to something positive about their character. The objects students bring to class should not be of monetary value. For example, a student might bring an apple to class. The student might say that the apple represents his or her respect for the teacher. Respect is a responsible value.*

2 Explain to students that you are going to discuss the importance of having good character. Define character. **Character** is a person's use of self-control to act on responsible values. Define self-control. **Self-control** is the effort a person makes to regulate his or her behavior. Give each student a copy of the Blackline Master *Ten Responsible Values That Make Up Good Character*™. Explain to students that the actions they choose demonstrate whether or not they have good character. Define responsible value. A **responsible value** is a belief that guides a person to act in responsible ways. There are ten responsible values that make up good character:

1. Honesty. Define honesty. **Honesty** is refusing to lie, steal, or deceive anyone.

2. Self-discipline. Define self-discipline. **Self-discipline** is the effort a person makes to follow through on what he or she says.

3. Fairness. Define fairness. **Fairness** is following the same rules so everyone has a fair chance.

4. Abstinence from sex. Define abstinence from sex. **Abstinence from sex** is choosing not to be sexually active.

5. Determination. Define determination. **Determination** is working hard to get what a person wants.

6. Courage. Define courage. **Courage** is showing strength when a person otherwise would be afraid.

7. Citizenship. Define citizenship. **Citizenship** is following the laws of a person's community and nation.

8. Responsibility. Define responsibility. **Responsibility** is being accountable for what a person says or does.

9. Respect. Define respect. **Respect** is liking that comes from having esteem for someone's admirable characteristics and responsible and caring actions.

10. RIntegrity. Define integrity. **Integrity** is acting on responsible values regardless of the consequences.

3 Tell students to take four items out of the paper bag, leaving one item in the paper bag. Each student should tell how each of the four items represents a good character trait he or she has.

4 Tell students to leave the bags with one item in it on the table. Tell students to pick up one bag from the table that is not their own. Ask students to guess whose bag they have. Tell students to give reasons why they chose the person. For example, Keenan might pick up a bag with a trophy in it. Keenan might say that he thinks the bag was brought by Joshua because the trophy represents determination and Joshua is always determined. Make sure that everyone has a chance to make a guess.

5 Give each student a copy of the Blackline Master *Good Character Checklist*. Ask students why a person needs good character. Students might say that good character builds trust and self-respect. Tell students that the *Good Character Checklist* can help them choose friends who have good character.

Assessment

Have students write a one-page paper entitled "Who Am I?" No names are to be written on the papers. In the papers, students are to write five responsible values that they practice. Select several papers at random and have the class guess which student is being described.

Ten Responsible Values That Make Up Good Character™

Honesty

is refusing to lie, steal, or deceive anyone. Being honest is a sign of good character.

Courage

is showing strength when a person otherwise would be afraid. Showing courage is a sign of good character.

Self-discipline

is the effort a person makes to follow through on what he or she says. Being self-disciplined is a sign of good character.

Citizenship

is following the laws of a person's community and nation. Being a good citizen is a sign of good character.

Fairness

is following the same rules so everyone has a fair chance. Being fair is a sign of good character.

Responsibility

is being accountable for what a person says or does. Taking responsibility is a sign of good character.

Abstinence from sex

is choosing not to be sexually active. Practicing abstinence is a sign of good character.

Respect

is liking that comes from having esteem for someone's admirable characteristics and responsible and caring actions. Showing respect is a sign of good character.

Determination

is working hard to get what a person wants. Having determination is a sign of good character.

Integrity

is acting on responsible values regardless of the consequences. Having integrity is a sign of good character.

Good Character Checklist

Yes   No

□ □ **1.** Do my parents or guardians think this person shows good character?

□ □ **2.** Does this person choose other friends who show good character?

□ □ **3.** Does this person act on responsible values?

□ □ **4.** Does this person communicate in an open and honest way?

□ □ **5.** Does this person treat me and others with respect?

□ □ **6.** Is this person nonviolent?

□ □ **7.** Does this person make responsible decisions?

□ □ **8.** Does this person resist temptation when pressured to choose wrong actions?

□ □ **9.** Does this person take steps to correct wrong actions?

□ □ **10.** Does this person practice abstinence from sex?

□ □ **11.** Does this person have a drug-free lifestyle?

□ □ **12.** Does this person obey laws?

Deep Thoughts, By Me

The Curriculum

Life Skill

■ I will make responsible decisions.

Objectives

■ Students will identify three decision-making styles and explain how each one might affect the quality of their relationships.

■ Students will use *The Responsible Decision-Making Model*™ to make decisions.

The National Health Education Standards

■ Students will demonstrate the ability to use goal-setting and decision-making skills that enhance health.

■ Students will demonstrate the ability to advocate for personal, family, and community health.

Preparing to Teach the Lesson Plan

Materials

Sheet of paper

Pen or pencil

Magazines

Scissors

Glue

Blackline Master

The Responsible Decision-Making Model™

Teaching the Lesson Plan

1 Ask students if they ever browse for birthday cards, anniversary cards, or other types of cards for a special occasion. Ask students to describe the different kinds of cards they have seen. Students might say some cards are very traditional and have lengthy poetry. Other cards are more contemporary and have only one- or two-line messages.

2 Tell students that they are going to create their own contemporary cards. The cards will have a one-line statement and a picture. Tell students to fold a sheet of paper in half to make the card. The students should write their names on the front of the card. Pass out magazines. Tell students to look for a picture in a magazine that shows a person who has self-respect. Define self-respect. **Self-respect** is a high regard for oneself because one behaves in responsible ways. Tell students that there are ten ways to improve their self-respect:

1. Pay attention to your appearance.

2. Make a list of your responsible actions and review the list often.

3. Be a friend to yourself by enjoying activities, such as hobbies, by yourself.

4. Write your feelings in a journal.

5. Make spending time with members of your family a priority.

6. Care for other people in the way you would like them to care for you.

7. Let other people know what helps you feel special.

8. Support the interests of family members and friends and ask them to support your interests.

9. Ask family members and friends to tell you examples of your actions that show you have good character.

© 2001 Everyday Learning Corporation

10. Get plenty of exercise to generate feelings of well-being. Define beta-endorphins. **Beta-endorphins** are substances produced in the brain that create a feeling of well-being.

3 Tell students to cut out the picture of the person who shows self-respect. Ask students to glue the magazine picture to the inside of the card. Tell students to write a way to improve their self-respect on the inside of the card. For example, a student could glue a picture of a well-groomed man who is walking on his card. The student could then write "Paying attention to your appearance puts your best foot forward." Have students share their cards with the class. Display students' cards on a bulletin board.

4 Explain to students that a person who has self-respect acts in responsible ways. Give each student a copy of the Blackline Master *The Responsible Decision-Making Model™*. Tell students they can use *The Responsible Decision-Making Model™* to make responsible decisions. Define *The Responsible Decision-Making Model™*. *The Responsible Decision-Making Model™* is a series of steps to follow to assure that the decisions a person makes result in actions that promote health, protect safety, follow laws, show respect for self and others, follow the guidelines of parents and of other responsible adults, and demonstrate good character.

5 Tell the class three decision-making styles. The three styles are:

1. Inactive decision-making style. Define inactive decision-making style. An **inactive decision-making style** is a habit in which a person fails to make choices, and this failure determines the outcome.

2. Reactive decision-making style. Define reactive decision-making style. A **reactive decision-making style** is a habit in which a person allows others to make his or her decisions.

3. Proactive decision-making style. Define proactive decision-making style. A **proactive decision-making style** is a habit in which a person takes responsibility for his or her decisions and uses *The Responsible Decision-Making Model™*.

Assessment

Have students write a ten-line poem titled "Give Yourself a Dose of Self-Respect." Each line should focus on one of the ten ways to improve self-respect. Have each student share his or her poem with the rest of the class.

Paying attention to your appearance puts your best foot forward

The Responsible Decision-Making Model™

STEP 1 **Describe the situation that requires a decision.** Describe the situation in writing if no immediate decision is necessary. Describe the situation out loud or to yourself in a few sentences if an immediate decision is necessary. Being able to describe the situation in your own words helps you see it more clearly.

STEP 2 **List possible decisions you might make.** List all the possible decisions you can think of in writing, if no immediate decision is necessary. If you must decide right away, review the possible decisions out loud or to yourself.

STEP 3 **Share the list of possible decisions with a parent, guardian, or other responsible adult.** Share possible decisions with a responsible adult when no immediate decision is necessary. If possible, delay making a decision. An adult might think of other possibilities. He or she might help you evaluate the possible consequences of each decision. Consider your options seriously.

STEP 4 **Use six questions to evaluate the possible consequences of each decision.**
Will this decision result in actions that:
1. promote health?
2. protect safety?
3. follow laws?
4. show respect for myself and others?
5. follow the guidelines of my parents and of other responsible adults?
6. demonstrate good character?

STEP 5 **Decide which decision is most responsible and appropriate.** Rely on the six questions in STEP 4 as you compare the decisions.

STEP 6 **Act on your decision and evaluate the results.** Follow through with your decision with confidence. You will be confident if you pay attention to the six questions in STEP 4.

A Dis-Heartening Experience

The Curriculum

Life Skills

■ I will practice protective factors to reduce the risk of violence.

■ I will practice self-protection strategies.

■ I will participate in victim recovery if I am harmed by violence.

Objectives

■ Students will identify and discuss risk factors for harmful and violent relationships.

■ Students will describe profiles of people who relate with others in harmful ways.

■ Students will explain why some people match-up to form harmful relationships.

■ Students will discuss steps to prevent and/or resolve harmful relationships.

■ Students will discuss four types of abusive relationships: physical, emotional, neglect, and sexual.

■ Students will identify and describe kinds of self-defense strategies.

■ Students will identify *Self-Protection Strategies for the Home.*

■ Students will identify *Self-Protection Strategies for the School.*

■ Students will identify *Self-Protection Strategies for Traveling.*

■ Students will discuss recovery strategies for victims and survivors of violence.

The National Health Education Standards

■ Students will demonstrate the ability to practice health-enhancing behaviors and reduce health risks.

■ Students will demonstrate the ability to use interpersonal communication skills to enhance health.

■ Students will demonstrate the ability to use goal-setting and decision-making skills that enhance health.

Preparing to Teach the Lesson Plan

Materials

Large sheet of red construction paper

Scissors

Pencil

Teaching the Lesson Plan

1 Ask students if they have ever heard of the saying, he or she "has a broken heart." Students will respond that they have. Tell students that having a broken heart usually refers to having had a relationship that was painful. Tell students that for this lesson a broken heart will refer to having had a harmful and/or violent relationship. Define harmful relationship and violent relationship. A **harmful relationship** is a relationship that destroys self-respect, interferes with productivity and health, and includes addictions and/or violence. A **violent relationship** is a relationship that harms another person physically, mentally, and/or emotionally.

2 List on the chalkboard and discuss the following risk factors for being involved in harmful and/or violent relationships:

• Lacking self-respect

• Being raised in a dysfunctional family

• Living in an adverse environment

• Lacking social skills

• Being unable to manage anger

• Resolving conflict in harmful ways

• Practicing discriminatory behavior

• Misusing or abusing alcohol and/or other drugs

• Being a consumer of entertainment that portrays harmful and violent relationships

• Being a victim of violence

3 Tell students that a profile is a very brief sketch or outline. Further explain that there are ten profiles of people who relate in harmful ways. The names and definitions are:

1. A **people pleaser** is a person who constantly seeks the approval of others.
2. An **enabler** is a person who supports the harmful behavior of others.
3. A **clinger** is a person who is needy and dependent.
4. A **fixer** is a person who tries to fix other people's problems.
5. A **distancer** is a person who is emotionally unavailable to others.
6. A **controller** is a person who is possessive, jealous, and domineering.
7. A **center** is a person who is self-centered.
8. An **abuser** is a person who is abusive.
9. A **liar** is a person who does not tell the truth.
10. A **promise breaker** is a person who is not reliable.

Have students role play these ten profiles.

4 Explain to students that they can take steps to keep from having harmful relationships.
- Evaluate their relationships regularly.
- Recognize the necessity to end a harmful relationship.
- Identify changes in behavior that must occur in a harmful relationship to promote healthful interaction.
- Seek the advice of a respected adult or a skilled professional about expected changes in a relationship.
- Have a frank discussion with the other person about concerns about expectations for a relationship.
- Set a future date to reevaluate the relationship.

5 Identify four kinds of abusive relationships. **Physical abuse** is harmful treatment that results in physical injury to the victim. **Emotional abuse** is "putting down" another person and making the person feel worthless. **Neglect** is failure to provide proper care and guidance. **Sexual abuse** is sexual contact that is forced on a person.

6 Differentiate between a perpetrator, victim, and survivor of violence. A **perpetrator of violence** is a person who commits a violent act. A **victim of violence** is a person who has been harmed by violence. A **survivor of violence** is a person who was harmed by violence, has participated in recovery to heal from its emotional effects, and has adopted self-protection strategies. **Self-protection strategies** are strategies that can be practiced to protect oneself and others from harm.

7 Cut a large sheet of red construction paper into the shape of a heart. Draw lines on the heart to divide the heart into four parts. Write one of the following on each of the four parts: self-respect, health, relationships with others, goals. Tell students that the heart represents a person who has been the victim of violence. Using the scissors, cut away the part of the heart with self-respect written on it. Tell students that victims of violence might lose their self-respect. They might feel worthless as a result of being harmed and/or abused. Cut away the part of the heart with health written on it. Ask students what might happen to a victim of violence's health. They might mention pregnancy, STDs, HIV infection, injury to body parts, etc. Cut away the part of the heart with relationships with others written on it. Ask students how a victim of violence's relationships might be affected. Explain that a victim of violence might be fearful and untrusting of others. A victim of violence also might be angry or withdrawn. Cut away the part of the heart with goals written on it. Ask students how a victim of violence's goals might be affected. There might be a variety of answers. A victim of violence might have difficulty accomplishing goals. He or she might begin to act in violent ways without help.

8 Explain that a victim of violence must get help. Then he or she might become a survivor of violence. Strategies for recovering and healing from violence include:
- a medical examination;
- management of STDs including HIV;
- issues resolving pregnancy;
- treatment for post traumatic stress disorder;
- treatment for injures;
- joining a recovery group;
- having counseling for emotional difficulties.

9 **OPTIONAL** Refer to Chapter 2 in this book and share with students *Self-Protection Strategies for the Home, Self-Protections Strategies for the School,* and *Self-Protection Strategies for Traveling.*

Assessment

Have students use red construction paper and cut out a large heart. Have them list steps to prevent and/or resolve harmful relationships on the heart.

I'm Harassed

The Curriculum

Life Skills

■ I will practice protective factors to reduce the risk of violence.

■ I will practice self-protection strategies.

■ I will participate in victim recovery if I am harmed by violence.

Objectives

■ Students will discuss *Guidelines to Follow to Reduce the Risk of Rape.*

■ Students will discuss *Guidelines to Follow When Sexual Harassment Occurs.*

■ Students will discuss *Steps to Take When Being Stalked.*

■ Students will discuss the health-related risks of prostitution.

■ Students will discuss the health-related risks of sexual addiction.

■ Students will explain why paraphilias are inappropriate.

■ Students will identify and describe kinds of self-defense strategies.

The National Health Education Standards

■ Students will demonstrate the ability to practice health-enhancing behaviors and reduce health risks.

■ Students will demonstrate the ability to use interpersonal communication skills to enhance health.

■ Students will demonstrate the ability to use goal-setting and decision-making skills to enhance health.

Preparing to Teach the Lesson Plan

Materials

Red, yellow, and green construction paper
Scissors

Blackline Masters

Guidelines to Follow When Sexual Harassment Occurs
Guidelines to Follow When Stalking Occurs
Guidelines to Follow to Reduce the Risk of Rape

Teaching the Lesson Plan

1 Define sexual harassment. **Sexual harassment** is unwanted sexual behavior that ranges from making sexual comments to forcing another person into unwanted sexual acts. Tell students that sexual harassment includes telling sexual jokes, making inappropriate gestures, staring someone up and down, and touching, grabbing, or pinching someone in sexual ways.

2 Cut enough red, yellow, and green circles with a diameter of four inches to give one to each student in the class. Tell students that you are going to present several scenarios. The scenarios will describe situations in which sexual harassment is occurring, sexual harassment might be occurring, or sexual harassment probably is not occurring. Tell students to hold up the appropriate circle for each scenario. Tell students that a red circle signals stop, a green circle signals go or OK, and a yellow circle signals caution. Tell students the following scenarios:

• Someone tells you that you look nice today. (green)

• Someone gives you a hug for what appears to be no reason. (yellow)

- Someone says that he or she wishes you were older so that he or she could go out with you. (yellow)

- Someone is upset at a business deal and uses inappropriate language around you. (red)

- Your boss tells you that he or she finds you sexually attractive and that you can use this attraction to get a promotion. (red)

- A classmate pinches you on your buttocks. (red)

- A classmate asks you on a date for the first time. (green)

Tell students that sometimes not enough information has been presented to indicate if a person is sexually harassing another person. Tell students that sometimes it depends on how a person makes a statement.

3 Explain to students that if they are sexually harassed, there are actions they can take to stop the harassment. Give each student a copy of the Blackline Master *Guidelines to Follow When Sexual Harassment Occurs.*

4 Define stalking. **Stalking** is harassing someone with the intent to threaten or harm that person. Give each student a copy of the Blackline Master *Guidelines to Follow When Stalking Occurs.* Define rape. **Rape** is the threatened or actual use of physical force to get someone to have sex without giving consent. Give each student a copy of the Blackline Master *Guidelines to Follow to Reduce the Risk of Rape.*

5 Explain to students other sexual behaviors that are harmful and inappropriate. Voyeurism is an example of a paraphilia. Define voyeurism. **Voyeurism** is the act of obtaining sexual gratification from looking at the bodies, sex organs, or sex acts of other people.

Assessment

Have students make palm cards with the guidelines to follow when sexual harassment, stalking, or rape occurs. A palm card is a small card that can fit in a wallet or a purse and that contains important information. Local emergency numbers are often provided on the cards. Tell students to write on the cards local emergency numbers that a victim of sexual harassment or of another violent crime could use to get help. Tell them to keep their palm card in their wallet, book bag, or purse.

Guidelines to Follow When Sexual Harassment Occurs

1. Ask the person who is harassing you to stop.

Be direct about what behavior is bothering you. Describe the situation and the behavior that made you uncomfortable.

2. Keep a record of what happened.

Write down the date and time, describe the situation and behavior, and explain how you handled the situation. Save any notes, letters, or pictures.

3. Check to see whether there are guidelines to follow for the specific situation.

For example, if the harassment was at school, check school guidelines; if at work, check work guidelines.

4. Report the harassment to the appropriate person in charge.

This may be a boss, teacher, or school counselor.

5. Determine if you want to take legal action.

Guidelines to Follow When Stalking Occurs

1. **Contact the police department** to report the stalking. Consider pressing charges against the person who is stalking you. This might be enough to frighten and stop the person.

2. **Keep a record** of each case of stalking. Write down the date, time, what was said, and what happened.

3. **Save any evidence,** including notes and letters that may have been written to you and answering machine tapes with messages left on them.

4. Try to **obtain a restraining order.** Define restraining order. A **restraining order** is an order by the court that forbids a person from doing a particular act.

5. **Tell your parents or guardians and school officials** what is happening. Tell them everything so they can do all they can to help protect you.

6. **Seek appropriate counseling** or join a support group for victims of stalking.

Guidelines to Follow to Reduce the Risk of Rape

1 Set clear limits for sexual behavior.

2 Communicate your limits to people whom you date.

3 Avoid sending mixed messages in which you say NO while continuing to encourage sexual advances.

4 Firmly tell a person to stop when you experience unwanted sexual advances.

5 Respond by yelling, screaming, or running away if the person does not stop unwanted sexual advances.

6 Avoid dating or being in the company of someone who is very controlling or demanding.

7 Avoid drinking alcohol and using other drugs that interfere with your judgment and ability to respond.

8 Avoid being in places where there is no one who will hear your call for help should unwanted sexual advances occur.

9 Report date rape to police should it occur.

10 Obtain prompt medical attention should date rape occur.

The Perfect Match

The Curriculum

Life Skills

■ I will develop healthful relationships.

■ I will recognize harmful relationships.

Objectives

■ Students will explain how to initiate friendships.

■ Students will discuss ways to handle rejection.

■ Students will explain how to maintain balanced friendships.

■ Students will identify behaviors that indicate respect in a relationship.

The National Health Education Standards

■ Students will demonstrate the ability to practice health-enhancing behaviors and reduce health risks.

■ Students will demonstrate the ability to use interpersonal communication skills to enhance health.

■ Students will comprehend concepts related to health promotion and disease prevention.

Preparing to Teach the Lesson Plan

Materials

Red and green construction paper

Black felt tip pen

Scissors

Blackline Masters

Patterns for Circles (Females)

Patterns for Circles (Males)

Teaching the Lesson Plan

1 *Cut eight circles from construction paper using the Blackline Masters* Patterns for Circles *as guides. Four circles should be green and four circles should be red. The green circles represent females. The red circles represent males. Each circle should have a diameter of eight inches. Copy the following sentences on each of the green circles. For example, sentences 1A and 1B should be copied on the green circles just as they appear on the circle #1 pattern for females.*

1A. *I am open, loyal, involved in school activities, and genuine.*

1B. *I am close to my family, honest, and reliable.*

2A. *I am the child of an alcoholic, overly responsible, and like to rescue others.*

2B. *I am angry and moody and drink too much.*

3A. *I am argumentative, critical, and abusive.*

3B. *I was physically abused and I am submissive.*

4A. *I will do anything not to lose my boyfriend. I feel unloved.*

4B. *I am promiscuous, possessive, and jealous.*

Copy the following sentences on each of the patterns for red circles:

1A. *I am sensitive, kind, trustworthy, and share feelings.*

1B. *I am respectful, self-confident, and have responsible values.*

2A. *I am angry and moody and drink too much.*

2B. *I am the child of an alcoholic, overly responsible, and like to rescue others.*

3A. *I have low self-esteem, am submissive, and was emotionally abused in a relationship.*

3B. *I have a violent temper, am dominant and controlling, and am physically abusive.*

4A. *If you love me, you will. I am self-centered and make false promises.*

4B. *I am not involved in school activities. I fear abandonment and am easily pressured.*

© 2001 Everyday Learning Corporation

*Place red circle #1 on top of green circle #1.
Match the cut lines and cut them into two parts as
indicated by the patterns. Repeat for red and green
circles #2, #3, and #4.*

2 Tell students that you are going to discuss
relationships. Define healthful relationship.
A **healthful relationship** is a relationship that
promotes self-respect, encourages productivity
and health, and is free of addictions and
violence. Tell students that they only should
initiate friendships with people who have good
character. They should determine an opening
move to initiate a friendship, such as calling
someone on the telephone. Making an
opening move involves taking a risk. But the
risk might be worth taking if a healthful relationship develops. However, sometimes a
person might experience rejection after
initiating a friendship. Define rejection.
Rejection is the feeling of being unwelcome
or unwanted. Tell students to express their
disappointments in a healthful way:

- Use I-messages to share your feelings with
the person who rejected you.

- Share your feelings with a trusted adult if you
cannot share them with the person who
rejected you.

- Remember that you are worthwhile even
when a person does not want to be your
friend or a when friend does not include you.

Define harmful relationship. A **harmful
relationship** is a relationship that destroys self-
respect, interferes with productivity and health,
and includes addictions and/or violence.

3 Tell students that this activity will help
them learn about harmful relationship
match-ups. People who relate in harmful ways
often are drawn together. This activity will
illustrate eight harmful match-ups. Give each
of eight male students half of a red circle.
Give each of eight female students half of a
green circle. Tell students to hold the halves
of their circles so that the blank side is facing
them. They should not read the side with
words printed on it.

4 Tell students to find their match. Their
match would be the opposite color that fits
into their half of a circle. For example, a male
student would look for a female student
holding half of a green circle that is cut to fit
his half of a red circle like pieces in a jigsaw
puzzle. Tell each student to find someone
whose circle fits theirs. Once students have
found their match, they can read what is on
their circles.

5 Tell the couple with circle halves labeled 1A
to come forward. Have each partner read
what is on his or her circle half. The female
will say, "I am open, loyal, involved in school
activities, and genuine." The male will say,
"I am sensitive, kind, trustworthy, and share
feelings." Tell students this is a match. These
behaviors show respect in the relationship.
This relationship is balanced. Define balanced
relationship. A balanced relationship is a
relationship in which two people give and
receive acts of kindness between each other.
Tell the couple to show the circle that their
combined halves made to the class. The pieces
will be equal, but not alike. Explain to the
class that in a balanced relationship, both
persons are equal although they are not alike.
Tell the couple with circle halves labeled 1B to
come forward. Have each partner read what is
on his or her circle half. The female will say,
"I am close to my family, honest, and reliable."
The male will say, "I am respectful, self-confident,
and have responsible values." Explain to the
class that this also is a healthful relationship.

6 Tell the couple with circle halves 2A to
come forward. The female will say, "I am
the child of an alcoholic, overly responsible,
and like to rescue others." The male will say "I
am angry and moody and I drink too much."
Define enabler. An **enabler** is a person who
supports the harmful behavior of others.
Define fixer. A **fixer** is a person who tries to fix
other people's problems. Tell the couple to
put their circle pieces together. Ask the class
why these two might have formed a match.
Students might say that these two formed a
match because the female is trying to rescue

the male from his drinking problem. Tell students that this is a harmful relationship. Tell the couple with circle halves 2B to come forward. The female will say, "I am angry and moody and I drink too much." The male will say, "I am the child of an alcoholic, overly responsible, and like to rescue others." Tell the class that in a relationship either the male or female might demonstrate the behaviors of an enabler or of a fixer.

7 Tell the couple with circle halves 3A to come forward. The female will say, "I am argumentative, critical, and abusive." The male will say, "I have low self-esteem, am submissive, and I was emotionally abused in a relationship." Define people pleaser. A **people pleaser** is a person who constantly seeks the approval of others. Define abuser. An **abuser** is a person who is abusive. Ask the class why these two might have formed a match. Students might say that a person who is an abuser often selects a partner who will allow the abuse to continue. Tell the couple with circle halves 3B to come forward. The female will say, "I was physically abused and I am submissive." The male will say, "I have a violent temper, am dominant and controlling, and am physically abusive." Define clinger. A **clinger** is a person who is needy and dependent. Define controller. A **controller** is a person who is possessive, jealous, and domineering. Tell students that both the male and the female can be abused or be abusive in a relationship.

8 Tell the couple with circle halves 4A to come forward. The female will say, "I will do anything not to lose my boyfriend." The male will say, "If you love me, you will. I am self-centered and make false promises." Define center. A **center** is a person who is self-centered. Define promise breaker. A **promise breaker** is a person who is not reliable. Tell the couple with circle halves 4B to come forward. The female will say, "I am promiscuous, possessive, and jealous." The male will say, "I am not involved in school activities. I fear abandonment and am easily pressured." Tell students that either a male or a female can fear abandonment and make compromises because of this feeling.

9 Tell students that people in harmful relationships often recognize that the relationship is not healthful. They might break off the relationship and look for a new relationship. But if they do not change what is written on half of the circle, then they will repeat the relationship pattern. Tell the students with the circle halves 1A and 1B to hold up their circle halves. Tell students that in order for a person to be in a healthful relationship, it is necessary to first work on their own circle half.

Assessment

Tell students to write a one-page paper in which they compare and contrast a healthful relationship and a harmful relationship. Tell them to write about how to maintain a balanced relationship and how to identify behaviors associated with the profiles of people who relate in harmful ways, such as the clinger and the distancer.

Patterns for Circles (Females)

Circle #1

1A
I am open, loyal, involved in school activities, and genuine.

1B
I am close to my family, honest, and reliable.

Circle #2

2A
I am the child of an alcoholic, overly responsible, and like to rescue others.

2B
I am angry and moody and drink too much.

Circle #3

3A
I am argumentative, critical, and abusive.

3B
I was physically abused and I am submissive.

Circle #4

4A
I will do anything not to lose my boyfriend. I feel unloved.

4B
I am promiscuous, possessive, and jealous.

Patterns for Circles (Males)

Circle #1

1A
I am sensitive, kind, trustworthy, and share feelings.

1B
I am respectful, self-confident, and have responsible values.

Circle #2

2A
I am angry and moody and drink too much.

2B
I am the child of an alcoholic, overly responsible, and like to rescue others.

Circle #3

3A
I have low self-esteem, am submissive, and I was emotionally abused.

3B
I have a violent temper, am dominant and controlling, and am physically abusive.

Circle #4

4A
If you love me, you will. I am self-centered and make false promises.

4B
I am not involved in school activities. I fear abandonment and am easily pressured.

Values Tug of War

The Curriculum

Life Skills

■ I will develop dating skills.

■ I will practice abstinence from sex.

Objectives

■ Students will list and discuss standards for dating.

■ Students will discuss each of the items on the *Dating Skills Checklist.*

■ Students will discuss *Guidelines to Follow to Reduce the Risk of Rape* (refer to Harmful and Violent Relationships).

■ Students will list and explain reasons to wait until marriage to have sex.

■ Students will identify the *Top Ten List of Reasons to Practice Abstinence™.*

■ Students will use *The Responsible Decision-Making Model™* to outline reasons why abstinence from sex is a responsible decision.

■ Students will explain how to set limits for expressing physical affection.

The National Health Education Standards

■ Students will demonstrate the ability to use interpersonal communication skills to enhance health.

■ Students will demonstrate the ability to use goal-setting and decision-making skills to enhance health.

■ Students will demonstrate the ability to practice health-enhancing behaviors and reduce health risks.

■ Students will demonstrate the ability to advocate for personal, family, and community health.

Preparing to Teach the Lesson Plan

Materials

Paper, 22 sheets

Markers

Masking tape

yarn

Blackline Masters

Top Ten List of Reasons to Practice Abstinence™

Dating Skills Checklist

Teaching the Lesson Plan

1 Define abstinence from sex. **Abstinence from sex** is choosing not to be sexually active. Give each student a copy of the Blackline Master *Top Ten List of Reasons to Practice Abstinence™*. Review reasons why abstinence from sex is a responsible choice. Tell students that *The Responsible Decision-Making Model™* can help them decide whether or not abstinence is a responsible choice. Define *The Responsible Decision-Making Model™*. ***The Responsible Decision-Making Model™*** is a series of steps to follow to assure that the decisions a person makes result in actions that promote health, protect safety, follow laws, show respect for self and others, follow the guidelines of parents and of other responsible adults, and demonstrate good character. Students can use *The Responsible Decision-Making Model™* when faced with a decision. Tell students that practicing abstinence from sex until marriage is a responsible decision.

2 Tell students that there are protective factors for sticking to a decision to practice abstinence from sex. Define protective factor. A **protective factor** is something that increases

563

the likelihood of a positive outcome. Tell students some protective factors will increase the likelihood that they will stick to a decision to practice abstinence. Tell students these protective factors for sticking to a decision to practice abstinence from sex:

- I will participate in activities that promote my self-concept.
- I will discuss family values with my parents.
- I will spend time with my family.
- I will spend time with friends who are not sexually active.
- I will avoid tempting situations.
- I will not use alcohol or other mood-altering drugs.
- I will set limits before I am in emotional situations.
- I will break off a relationship with someone who does not respect my limits.
- I will choose entertainment that promotes family values.
- I will change my behavior if I have been sexually active.

Ask a student to write each of these protective factors on a sheet of paper.

3 Define risk factor. A **risk factor** is something that increases the likelihood of a negative outcome. Some risk factors increase the likelihood that a person will not stick to a decision to practice abstinence from sex. Tell students these risk factors for not sticking to a decision to practice abstinence from sex:

- I will not participate in school activities.
- I will avoid discussing family values with my parents and significant others.
- I will not make time for family members.
- I will spend time with friends who are sexually active.
- I will participate in tempting situations.
- I will attend parties where there is alcohol and other mood-altering drugs.
- I will engage in heavy petting.
- I will be influenced by people who pressure me beyond my limits.
- I will choose entertainment that promotes permissive sex.
- If I am sexually active, I will continue to be.

Ask a student to write each of these risk factors on a sheet of paper.

Label the two remaining sheets of construction paper "Abstinence" and "Sexually Active." Tell each of 22 students to tape one of the labeled pieces of paper to the back of his or her shirt. (If there are fewer than 22 students, have students tape more than one sheet of paper to the back of their shirts). There must be an equal number of students who wear labeled sheets of paper with protective factors and risk factors.

4 Tell the class to form a tug of war with these 22 students divided into two sides. The student with the "Abstinence" label will hold one end of the yarn. The student with the "Sexually Active" label will hold the other end. The 11 students who are wearing protective factor labels will line up behind the student wearing the "Abstinence" label. The 10 students wearing risk factor labels will line up behind the student with the "Sexually Active" label. Tell students to hold the yarn and gently rock back and forth.

5 Tell five students representing protective factors to drop out of the tug of war. Tell students that if a young person decides not to practice these protective factors, he or she has changed his or her amount of support for abstinence.

6 Tell the five students who dropped out of the tug of war to return. Now, tell five students representing risk factors to drop out of the tug of war. Tell students that if a young person avoids risk factors, he or she has gained support for abstinence.

7 Tell every student representing a risk factor to join the abstinence side of the tug of war. As each student is joining the "Abstinence" team, tell him or her to say what he or she would do to turn his or her risk factor into a protective factor. Tell each student to use *The Responsible Decision-Making Model*™ when saying what he or she would do to turn his or her risk behavior into a healthful behavior. The students representing healthful behaviors will far outnumber the single student labeled "Sexually Active." Tell students that protective factors can help them to stick to their decision to practice abstinence.

8 Give each student a copy of the Blackline Master *Dating Skills Checklist*. Discuss the Blackline Master with students. Tell students that the checklist will help them rate their dating skills. Review the Blackline Master *Guidelines to Follow to Reduce the Risk of Rape* from the Lesson Plans on Harmful and Violent Relationships with the class.

Assessment

Tell students to write a response to the following letter. Students should use *The Responsible Decision-Making Model*™ in their replies.

Dear Helper:

I am very much attracted to another person in my class. Lately, we have been spending time alone and I have strong sexual feelings. I don't want to become sexually active. What should I do?

Emotionally Involved

Top Ten List of Reasons to Practice Abstinence™

1. I want to follow family guidelines.

2. I want to respect myself.

3. I want to respect others.

4. I want to have a good reputation.

5. I do not want to feel guilty.

6. I am not ready for marriage.

7. I do not want to risk pregnancy.

8. I am not ready to be a parent.

9. I do not want to be infected with an STD.

10. I do not want to be infected with HIV.

Dating Skills Checklist

Rate your dating skills. Pat yourself on the back for each of the following statements that describes your behavior.

1 I do not base my self-worth on my ability to get a date.

2 I ask a lot of questions and get the facts before I accept a date.

3 I decline a date when there will be pressure to drink or be sexually active.

4 I honor my dating commitments and do not change plans if someone better comes along.

5 I recognize the advantages of dating different people rather than going steady.

6 I would make a fast exit from a date instead of being or staying in a situation that is against my parents' or guardian's guidelines.

7 I would not hesitate to call my parents or guardian if I were on a date and needed help.

8 I am comfortable staying home when I do not want to date.

9 I am clear as to my expectations when I give or receive a gift in a dating situation.

10 I am honest and kind when I turn down someone for a date.

Unexpected Reaction

The Curriculum

Life Skills

■ I will practice abstinence from sex.

■ I will practice resistance skills when appropriate.

Objectives

■ Students will identify choices that reinforce their decision to practice abstinence from sex.

■ Students will outline resistance skills that can be used to say NO if they are pressured to be sexually active.

■ Students will list and discuss steps teens who have been sexually active can take to change their behavior.

The National Health Education Standards

■ Students will demonstrate the ability to practice health-enhancing behaviors and reduce health risks.

■ Students will demonstrate the ability to use goal-setting and decision-making skills to enhance health.

■ Students will demonstrate the ability to use interpersonal communication skills to enhance health.

■ Students will demonstrate the ability to advocate for personal, family, and community health.

Preparing to Teach the Lesson Plan

Materials

Two glasses of water

Distilled vinegar

Baking soda

Blackline Master

The Model for Using Resistance Skills

Teaching the Lesson Plan

1 Tell students the effects of alcohol on the brain. Alcohol has a depressant effect on the part of the brain responsible for reasoning and judgment. This may cause normal inhibitions to be removed and the intensity of sexual feelings to rise. Define sexual feelings. **Sexual feelings** are feelings that result from a strong physical and emotional attraction to another person. Tell students the following ways drinking affects thinking and decision-making:

• Drinking alcohol can cause you to make a wrong decision.

• Drinking alcohol can give you a false sense of self-confidence in social situations.

• Drinking alcohol can interfere with your judgment.

• Drinking alcohol can make you feel invincible.

• Drinking alcohol can increase the likelihood that you will give in to negative peer pressure.

• Drinking alcohol can dull your reasoning.

• Drinking alcohol slows your reaction time and affects your coordination.

• Drinking alcohol can cause you to have aggressive behavior.

• Drinking alcohol intensifies your emotions.

2 Add water to a glass until it is half full. Tell students that the half full glass represents normal sexual feelings. Add water to another glass until it is half full. Tell students that the two half full glasses represent a non-alcoholic drink, such as milk. Tell students that if you pour water from one glass into the other, you will have one full glass of water. Pour the two glasses together. Explain to students that when a non-alcoholic drink is added, normal sexual feelings are still able to be controlled.

3 Add distilled vinegar to a glass until it is half full. To another glass, add two tablespoons of baking soda and water until the glass is half full. Tell students that the half full glass of distilled vinegar represents strong sexual feelings. The half full glass of baking soda and water represents alcohol. Remind the class that when you poured the two half full glasses of water together in the first experiment, there was one full glass of water. Explain to students that according to the first experiment, if you add the contents of the glass containing baking soda and water to the glass containing distilled water, then you should have one full glass. (Make sure you have a bowl below the glass or do this activity over a sink.) Pour the baking soda and water into the glass containing distilled vinegar. The mixture will overflow. Explain to students that when a person adds alcohol to strong sexual feelings, he or she gets intense sexual feelings that are more difficult to control.

4 Ask students to give pressure statements a person might use to pressure someone to have sex. Students might answer, "If you loved me you would." Tell students they can use resistance skills is they are pressured to be sexually active. Define resistance skills. **Resistance skills** are skills that help a person say NO to an action or to leave a situation. Give each student a copy of the Blackline Master *The Model for Using Resistance Skills.*

5 Tell students that it is never too late to practice abstinence. Teens who have been sexually active can take steps to change their behavior. They can:

- tell their parents or guardians;
- have a medical checkup; and
- choose behaviors that support the decision to practice abstinence.

Assessment

Divide the students into groups of four. Tell the groups to write scripts for radio commercials about the effects of drinking alcohol on sexual decision-making. Ask students to perform or read from their scripts. Students should use at least three of the nine ways drinking affects thinking and decision-making.

The Model for Using Resistance Skills

1. **Say NO with self-confidence.** Look directly at the person or persons to whom you are speaking. Express yourself clearly.

2. **Give reasons for saying NO.** Use the six guidelines for making responsible decisions as your reasons for saying NO.
   NO. I want to promote my health.
   NO. I want to protect my safety.
   NO. I want to follow laws.
   NO. I want to show respect for myself and others.
   NO. I want to follow the guidelines of my parents and other responsible adults.
   NO. I want to demonstrate good character.

3. **Use the broken-record technique.** The **broken-record technique** is a way to strengthen a "no" response by repeating the same response several times. You will sound like a broken record, but each time you give the same "no" response it will be more convincing.

4. **Use nonverbal behavior to match verbal behavior.** **Nonverbal behavior** is the use of actions to express emotions and thoughts. Shaking your head "no" is an example of nonverbal behavior. Your verbal "no" should not be confused by a nonverbal behavior that is misleading.

5. **Avoid being in situations in which there will be pressure to make wrong decisions.** Think ahead. Avoid situations that might be tempting. For example, do not spend time at a peer's house when his or her parents or guardians are not home.

6. **Avoid being with people who make wrong decisions.** Remember that your reputation is the impression others have of you. Choose people to be with who have a reputation for making responsible decisions. Protect your good reputation.

7. **Resist pressure to engage in illegal behavior.** You have a responsibility to protect yourself and others and to obey the laws in your community.

8. **Influence others to make responsible decisions.** Remove yourself when a situation poses immediate risk or danger. If there is no immediate risk, try to turn a negative situation into a positive situation. Be a positive role model. Show others how to behave responsibly.

Reproduce My System

The Curriculum

Life Skill

■ I will recognize habits that protect male reproductive health.

Objectives

■ Students will discuss the physical and emotional changes males experience during puberty.

■ Students will name and give the function of the organs in the male reproductive system.

■ Students will discuss male reproductive physiology: erection, orgasm, and ejaculation.

The National Health Education Standards

■ Students will comprehend concepts related to health promotion and disease prevention.

Preparing to Teach the Lesson Plan

Materials

None

Blackline Masters

The Male Reproductive System Vocabulary
The Male Reproductive System
The Male Reproductive System Test

Teaching the Lesson Plan

1 Explain that the male reproductive system is a very important system in the body. Define male reproductive system. The **male reproductive system** consists of organs in the male body that are involved in producing offspring.

2 Tell students that they are going to learn about the male reproductive system. Give each student a copy of the Blackline Master *The Male Reproductive System Vocabulary*. Review the vocabulary words with students. Give each student a copy of the Blackline Master *The Male Reproductive System*. Explain that the external organs of the male reproductive system are the penis and the scrotum. The scrotum hangs from the body so that the testes have a lower temperature than the rest of the body. This lowered temperature allows the testes to produce sperm. Define sperm. **Sperm** are male reproductive cells.

3 Explain that the internal male reproductive organs include the testes, seminiferous tubules, epididymis, vas deferens, seminal vesicles, ejaculatory duct, prostate gland, Cowper's glands, and urethra. The testes are divided into several sections that are filled with seminiferous tubules. Sperm are produced in the seminiferous tubules. Define spermatogenesis. **Spermatogenesis** is sperm production, which takes place in the seminiferous tubules in the testes. After sperm are produced in the seminiferous tubules, they move to the epididymis. Some sperm are stored in the epididymis, but most move to the vas deferens after they mature. The vas deferens extend from the epididymis in the scrotum up into the abdomen. Sperm are then moved into the seminal vesicles where they are nourished and helped to move to the ejaculatory duct. The prostate gland keeps sperm alive with a special fluid.

4 Define erection. An **erection** is an involuntary process that occurs when the spongy layers inside the penis are engorged with blood and the penis elongates. Define orgasm. An **orgasm** is an explosive discharge of neuromuscular tensions at the peak of sexual response and is marked by rhythmic contractions and a sense of physiological and psychological release. Define ejaculation. **Ejaculation** is the sudden expulsion of seminal fluid from an erect penis.

Assessment

Collect the Blackline Masters *The Male Reproductive System* and *The Male Reproductive System Vocabulary*. Give each student a copy of the Blackline Master *The Male Reproductive System Test*. The copy should not have the parts of the male reproductive system identified. Tell students to write the correct names of the male reproductive organs on the appropriate lines. In addition, have students define the following terms on the Blackline Master: the penis, the scrotum, the vas deferens, and the prostate gland.

Read the answers. See how well students were able to label the different male reproductive organs. Write the number of correct answers from the students' papers on the board. For example, ask, "How many of you are holding papers with ten correct answers? Nine correct answers? Eight correct answers? and so on."

The Male Reproductive System Vocabulary

1. The **penis** is the male organ of sexual pleasure, reproduction, and urination.

2. The **scrotum** is a sac-like pouch in the groin that has two basic functions: to hold the testes and to regulate the temperature of the testes.

3. The **testes** are the two male reproductive glands inside the scrotum that secrete the male hormone testosterone and produce sperm.

4. The **seminiferous tubules** are a coiled network of tubes that fill the sections in each testis.

5. The **epididymis** is a comma-shaped structure found on the back and upper surface of each testis.

6. The **vas deferens** are two long, thin cords that extend from the epididymis in the scrotum, up through the inguinal canal, and into the abdomen.

7. The **seminal vesicles** are two small glands at the ends of each vas deferens that secrete an alkaline fluid rich in fructose, a sugar nutrient that is a source of energy for sperm.

8. The **prostate gland** is a gland that produces an alkaline fluid that aids sperm longevity.

9. The **Cowper's glands**, or **bulbourethral glands**, are two small pea-sized glands located on each side of the urethra and secrete a lubrication fluid.

The Male Reproductive System

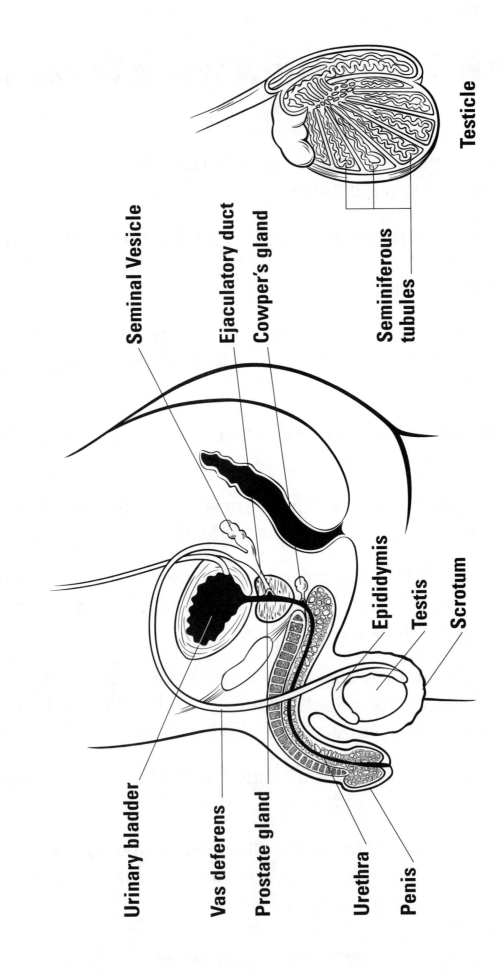

Urinary bladder

Vas deferens

Prostate gland

Urethra

Penis

Seminal Vesicle

Ejaculatory duct

Cowper's gland

Epididymis

Testis

Scrotum

Seminiferous tubules

Testicle

The Male Reproductive System Test

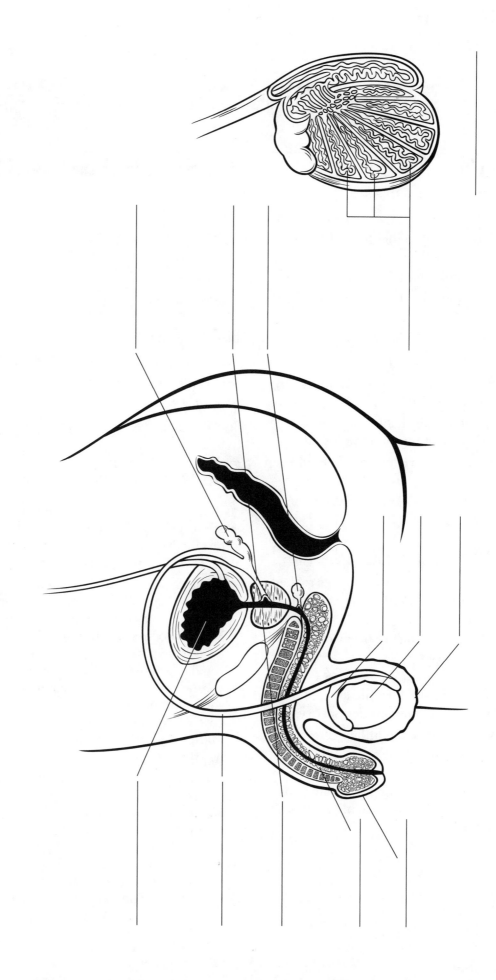

575

Balloon Blow Up

The Curriculum

Life Skills

■ I will recognize habits that protect male reproductive health.

■ I will have regular examinations.

■ I will keep a personal health record.

■ I will be well-groomed.

Objectives

■ Students will discuss information pertaining to male reproductive health.

■ Students will identify habits males must practice to protect reproductive health.

■ Students will explain why males should keep a personal health record.

■ Students will discuss ways for males to be well-groomed.

The National Health Education Standards

■ Students will comprehend concepts related to health promotion and disease prevention.

■ Students will demonstrate the ability to practice health-enhancing behaviors and reduce health risks.

■ Students will demonstrate the ability to access valid health information and health-promoting products and services.

■ Students will analyze the influence of culture, media, technology, and other factors on health.

■ Students will demonstrate the ability to use goal-setting and decision-making skills to enhance health.

Preparing to Teach the Lesson Plan

Materials

Two Balloons

Pin

Cellophane

Adhesive tape

Blackline Masters

Smegma, Circumcision/Non-Circumcision

Inguinal Hernia

Testicular Self-Examination

Rectal Examination of the Prostate

Teaching the Lesson Plan

1 Explain to the class that there are many things males can do to protect their reproductive health. Tell them these ways to protect male reproductive health:

• Bathe or shower daily. Keep the reproductive organs clean. Define smegma. **Smegma** is a cheesy substance that forms under the foreskin. Males who are not circumcised should pull the foreskin back and cleanse the penis regularly to prevent smegma from collecting. Define circumcision. **Circumcision** is the surgical removal of the foreskin from the penis. Give each student a copy of the Blackline Master *Smegma, Circumcision/Non-Circumcision.*

• Bend at the knees and keep the back straight when lifting heavy objects. Give each student a copy of the Blackline Master *Inguinal Hernia.* Define inguinal hernia. **Inguinal hernia** is a hernia in which some of the intestine pushes through the inguinal canal into the scrotum. Lifting heavy objects without bending correctly can stress the groin area. This can cause a hernia.

- Wear protective clothing and equipment when participating in sports and physical activities. Wearing protective equipment, such as a protective cup, provides extra support and helps prevent injury to the penis and testes.

- Perform testicular self-examinations. Define testicular self-examination (TSE). A **testicular self-examination (TSE)** is observation and palpation of the testicles to locate any mass or tenderness. Give each student a copy of the Blackline Master *Testicular Self-Examination.* Explain to students that testicular cancer is one of the most common cancers in young males.

- Have regular medical checkups. Define digital rectal examination. A **digital rectal examination** is an examination in which the physician inserts a gloved, lubricated finger into the rectum and examines the prostate and rectum for hard or lumpy areas. Give each student a copy of the Blackline Master *Rectal Examination of the Prostate.*

- Seek medical attention when you show signs of infection. Mumps is a viral infection that might cause sterility if contracted after puberty. Define sterility. **Sterility** is the inability to produce offspring.

- Practice abstinence from sex. Define abstinence from sex. **Abstinence from sex** is choosing not to be sexually active. Practicing abstinence from sex reduces the risk of infection with HIV and other STDS.

2 Use a balloon for the following demonstration. Have students identify excuses a male might use for not protecting reproductive health. For example, a student might say, "I forget to bend my knees when I lift heavy objects." Blow a puff of air into the balloon. Other examples of excuses:

- "It is uncomfortable to wear a protective cup for sports."

- "I don't know how to do a testicular self-examination."

- "I'm healthy and don't need regular medical checkups."

- "Practicing abstinence is not cool."

3 Prick the balloon with a pin so that it bursts (be cautious that the balloon will not strike a student). Explain that a male might have a surprise if he does not take care of his reproductive health. He might experience serious consequences. For example, if he is sexually active he might become infected with STDs, including HIV, or get someone pregnant. If he does not wear a protective cup, he could sustain injuries to his testicles. If he does not perform testicular self-examinations, he might miss a lump and not get early treatment for cancer.

4 Blow up a second balloon. Tell the class that the balloon represents a male who protects his reproductive health. Without students noticing, tape a piece of wide cellophane to the back of the balloon. Have students brainstorm more statements that a male makes to justify not protecting his reproductive health. For each statement, have another student make a counter statement that tells the importance of protecting male reproductive health. For example, one student might say, "It is uncomfortable to play basketball while wearing a protective cup." A second student could counter by saying, "Besides being safe, wearing a protective cup follows the rules of basketball." As a student makes a counter statement, stick the pin through the tape on the balloon. The balloon will not burst because only a slight amount of air will be let out. Students will wonder why the balloon is not bursting. Each prick of the balloon will release the pressure in the balloon.

Tell students this is like releasing the stress and pressure of not protecting male reproductive health. Continue to release the pressure in the balloon as students make counter statements that explain the importance of protecting male reproductive health.

5 Discuss penis size, nocturnal emissions, morning erection, anabolic steroids, prostatitis, and andropause with students. Define nocturnal emissions or wet dreams. **Nocturnal emissions**, or **wet dreams**, are spontaneous ejaculations that occur during sleep. Define morning erection. A **morning erection** is an erection that results from waking up during rapid eye movement (REM) or dreaming stage of sleep or from having a full bladder. Define anabolic steroids. **Anabolic steroids** are drugs produced from male sex hormones. Define prostatitis. **Prostatitis** is the inflammation of the prostate gland. Define andropause or the male climacteric. **Andropause**, or the **male climacteric**, is the decrease in male sexual function that results from diminished testosterone.

6 Tell students that they should keep a personal health record. Define personal health record. A **personal health record** is documentation of information pertaining to a person's health, health care, and health care providers. The personal health record should include the following information:

- vital statistics regarding your birth;
- detailed family health history;
- record of immunizations;
- personal health information;
- health habits;
- medical history;
- dental history;
- medications;
- health insurance information; and
- health care professionals.

Explain that a personal health record can be used to protect male reproductive health. For example, a male can record the dates he performed TSE. This information could be important to a male's physician.

Assessment

Have students design a one-page calendar. In each daily box on the calendar, they should write a reminder for males about reproductive health. Read the life skills for this lesson to students so that their reminders will be appropriate.

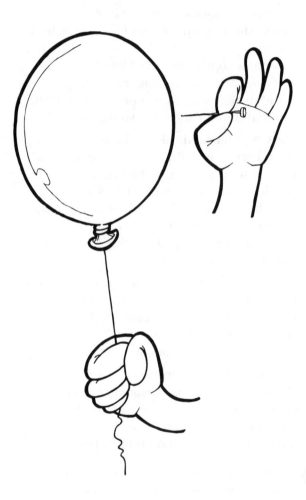

© 2001 Everyday Learning Corporation

Smegma, Circumcision/Non-Circumcision

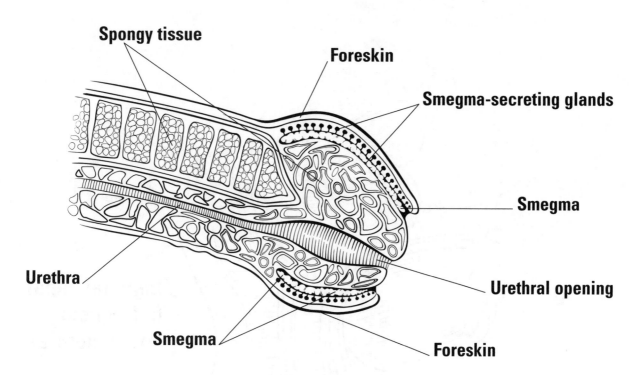

Spongy tissue

Foreskin

Smegma-secreting glands

Smegma

Urethra

Urethral opening

Smegma

Foreskin

Penis

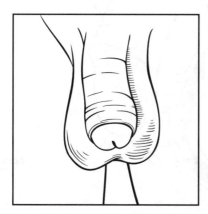

Uncircumcised penis

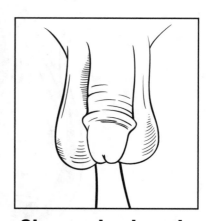

Circumcised penis

Males who are not circumcised might be at increased risk of infections. The risk of infection might be due to the presence of smegma. **Smegma** is a cheesy substance that forms under the foreskin.

Inguinal Hernia

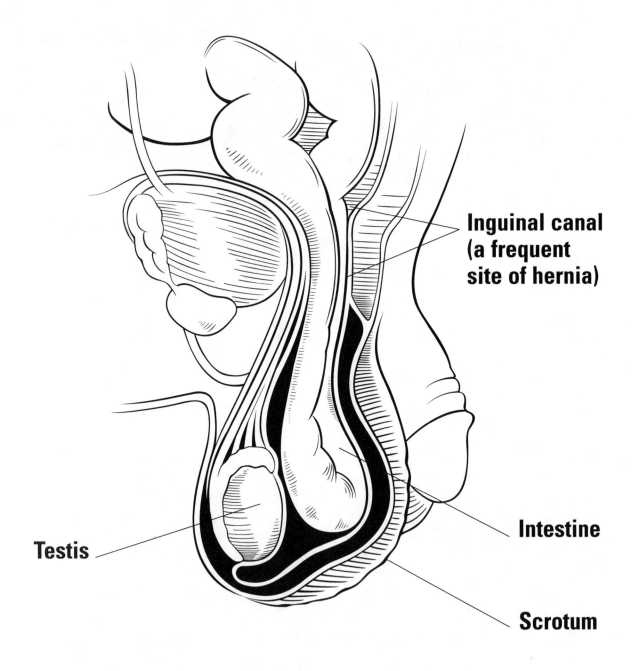

Inguinal canal (a frequent site of hernia)

Intestine

Testis

Scrotum

Testicular Self-Examination

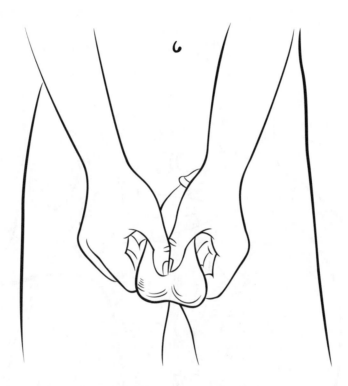

- Perform the testicular self-examination after a hot shower or bath as the heat causes the scrotal skin to relax and the testes to descend.

- Assume a comfortable sitting or standing position or lie on the back.

- Visually examine each testical for any changes.

- Place the thumbs of both hands on top of a testicle and the index and middle fingers on the underside of the testicles.

- Roll the testicle beneath the finger tips applying a small amount of pressure.

- Check to see that the surface of the testicle is firm and smooth.

Rectal Examination of the Prostate

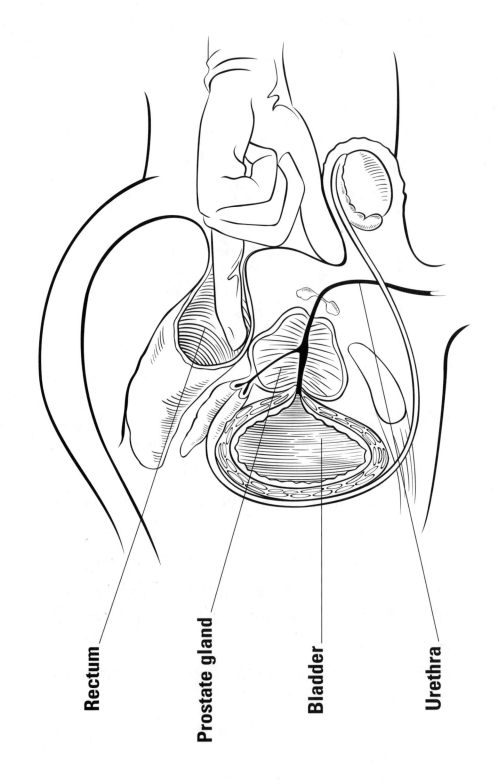

Rectum

Prostate gland

Bladder

Urethra

My Body, My System

The Curriculum

Life Skill

■ I will recognize habits that protect female reproductive health.

Objectives

■ Students will discuss the physical and emotional changes females experience during puberty.

■ Students will name and give the function of the organs in the female reproductive system.

■ Students will outline the physiological changes that occur in a menstrual cycle.

The National Health Education Standards

■ Students will comprehend concepts related to health promotion and disease prevention.

Preparing to Teach the Lesson Plan

Materials

None

Blackline Masters

The Female Reproductive System Vocabulary

The Female Reproductive System

The Menstrual Cycle

The Female Reproductive System Test

Teaching the Lesson Plan

1 Tell students that they are going to learn about the female reproductive system. Define female reproductive system. The **female reproductive system** consists of organs in the female body involved in producing offspring. Give each student a copy of the Blackline Master *The Female Reproductive System Vocabulary.* Review the vocabulary words with students. Explain that the external female reproductive organs are called the vulva. The vulva consist of the mons veneries, the labia majora, the labia minora, the clitoris, and the hymen. Tell students that during puberty, hair begins to cover both the mons veneries and the labia majora. Explain that the clitoris and the openings of the urethra and the vagina are located within the labia minora. Explain to students that the hymen has small openings in it. Some females do not have a hymen. Other females might break or tear the hymen when they ride bicycles or horses or exercise strenuously.

2 Give each student a copy of the Blackline Master *The Female Reproductive System.* Explain that the internal female reproductive organs are the ovaries, fallopian tubes, uterus, and vagina. Explain that a female is born with between 200,000 and 400,000 immature ova in her ovaries. About 375 of these ova will mature and be released in a female's lifetime. During puberty, the ova begin to develop. Each developing ova is enclosed in a small, hollow ball called a follicle. Each month during the menstrual cycle, an ovum matures and is released from its follicle. Define ovulation. **Ovulation** is the release of a mature ovum by an ovary and occurs on or about the fourteenth day before the expected beginning of the next menstrual period. When an ovum is released from an ovary it enters one of the fallopian tubes.

3 Give each student a copy of the Blackline Master *The Menstrual Cycle*. Define menstrual cycle. A **menstrual cycle** is a rhythmic cycle of approximately one month in which hormonal levels fluctuate to prepare a female's body for the possibility of pregnancy. Define menstruation. **Menstruation** is the process by which the lining of the uterus is expelled each month that an ovum is not fertilized. Females often describe menstruation as their period. Explain that on days 1 to 4 of the menstrual cycle the menstrual flow leaves the body. Follicle-stimulating hormone (FSH) causes follicles to grow. Define follicle-stimulating hormone. **Follicle-stimulating hormone (FSH)** is a hormone secreted by the pituitary gland that causes follicles to grow. On days 5 to 12 estrogen causes the lining of the uterus to thicken and ova in the follicles to mature. On days 13 to 14 ovulation occurs. The ovum travels down the fallopian tube toward the uterus. On days 15 to 20 the follicle that released the ovum becomes a corpus luteum and secretes progesterone. On days 21 to 28 the corpus luteum breaks down if the ovum is not fertilized. The bloody lining breaks away from the uterus.

Assessment

Collect the Blackline Masters *The Female Reproduction System* and *The Female Reproduction System Vocabulary*. Give each student a copy of the Blackline Master *The Female Reproductive System Test*. The copy should not have the parts of the female reproductive system identified. Tell students to write the correct names of the female reproductive organs on the appropriate lines. In addition, have students define the following terms on the Blackline Master: mons veneries, labia majora, labia minora, and hymen.

Read the answers. See how well students were able to label the female reproductive system with the different organs. Write the number of correct answers from the students' papers on the board. For example, ask, "How many of you are holding a paper with ten correct answers? Nine correct answers? Eight correct answers? and so on."

The Female Reproductive System Vocabulary

1. The **mons pubis** is a pad of fatty tissue that covers the front of the pubic bone and serves as a protective cushion for the female reproductive organs.

2. The **labia majora** are the outer lips, or heavy folds of skin, surrounding the opening of the vagina.

3. The **labia minora** are two smaller lips, or folds of skin, located between the labia majora.

4. The **clitoris** is a small, highly sensitive, cylindrical body about 3/4 inch (2.00 cm) long and about 3/16 inch (0.50 cm) in diameter projecting between the labia minora.

5. The **hymen** is a thin membrane that stretches across the vaginal introitus.

6. The **ovaries** are two almond-shaped female sex glands that produce ova and secrete hormones.

7. A **fallopian tube**, or **oviduct**, is a tube that extends from near the ovaries to the uterus.

8. The **uterus** is the organ that prepares each month to receive a fertilized ovum, to support the fertilized ovum during pregnancy, and to contract during childbirth to help with delivery.

9. The **cervix** is the lowest part of the uterus.

10. The **vagina** is a muscular passageway that lies between the bladder and the rectum, and it serves as the female organ of intercourse, the birth canal, and the passageway for the menstrual flow and the arriving sperm.

The Female Reproductive System

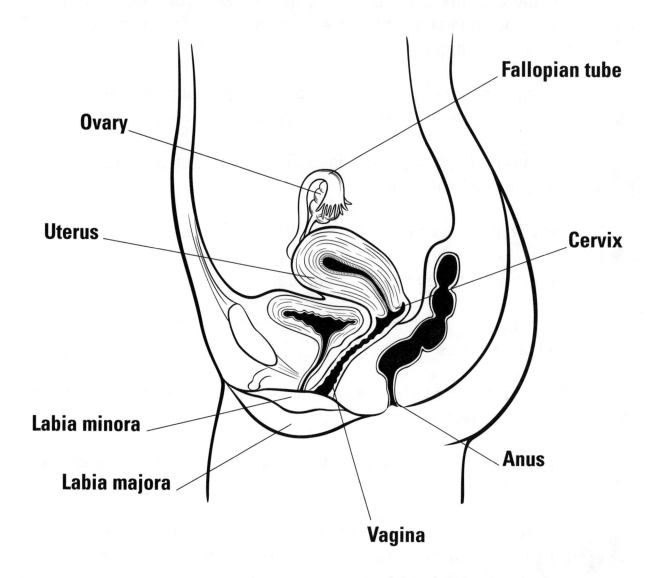

Ovary

Fallopian tube

Uterus

Cervix

Labia minora

Anus

Labia majora

Vagina

The Menstrual Cycle

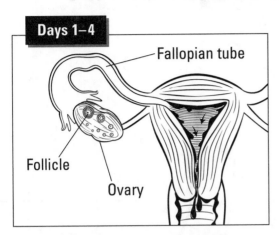

Days 1–4

Fallopian tube

Follicle

Ovary

Menstrual flow leaves the body. Follicle-stimulating hormone (FSH) causes follicles to grow.

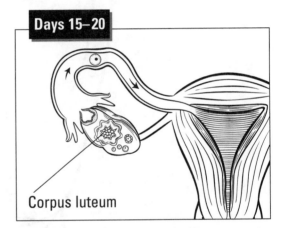

Days 5–12

Mature follicle on surface of ovary

Estrogen causes the lining of the uterus to thicken and ova in the follicles to mature.

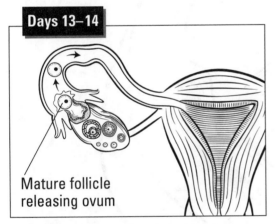

Days 13–14

Mature follicle releasing ovum

Ovulation occurs. The ovum travels down the fallopian tube toward the uterus.

Days 15–20

Corpus luteum

The follicle that released the ovum becomes a corpus luteum and secretes progesterone.

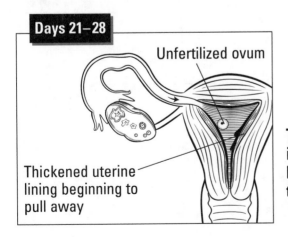

Days 21–28

Unfertilized ovum

Thickened uterine lining beginning to pull away

The corpus luteum breaks down if the ovum is not fertilized. The bloody lining breaks away from the uterus.

The Female Reproductive System Test

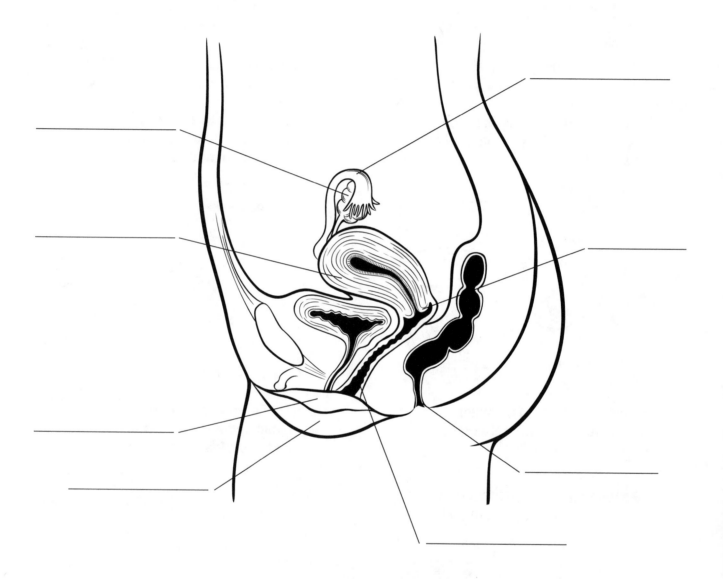

All Blown Up

The Curriculum

Life Skills

■ I will recognize habits that protect female reproductive health.

■ I will have regular examinations.

■ I will keep a personal health record.

■ I will be well-groomed.

Objectives

■ Students will discuss information pertaining to menstrual health: menarche, amenorrhea, oligomenorrhea, dysmenorrhea, menorrhagia, premenstrual syndrome, and toxic shock syndrome.

■ Students will discuss information pertaining to female reproductive health.

■ Students will discuss what is included in a pelvic examination.

■ Students will identify habits females must practice to protect female reproductive health.

■ Students will explain why females should keep a personal health record.

■ Students will discuss ways for females to be well-groomed.

The National Health Education Standards

■ Students will comprehend concepts related to health promotion and disease prevention.

■ Students will demonstrate the ability to practice health-enhancing behaviors and reduce health risks.

■ Students will demonstrate the ability to access valid health information and health-promoting products and services.

■ Students will analyze the influence of culture, media, technology, and other factors on health.

■ Students will demonstrate the ability to use goal-setting and decision-making skills to enhance health.

Preparing to Teach the Lesson Plan

Materials

Two balloons

Pin

Cellophane

Adhesive tape

Blackline Masters

Breast Self-Examination

Pap Smear

Female Reproductive Health

Teaching the Lesson Plan

1 Explain to the class that there are many things females can do to protect their reproductive health. Tell them these ways to protect female reproductive health:

• Keep a calendar in which you record information about your menstrual cycle. Many teens have irregular cycles. The length of their cycles might vary. The number of days of menstrual flow might vary. Define menarche. **Menarche** is the term used to describe the first menstrual bleeding. Define amenorrhea. **Amenorrhea** is the absence of menstruation. Define oligomenorrhea. **Oligomenorrhea** is scanty, irregular bleeding and/or a condition in which a female who is two years past menarche has one to six cycles a year. Define dysmenorrhea. **Dysmenorrhea** is very painful menstruation. Define menorrhagia. **Menorrhagia** is an abnormally heavy menstrual flow. Define premenstrual syndrome (PMS). **Premenstrual syndrome (PMS)** is a combination of severe physical and psychological symptoms during the four premenstrual and first four menstrual days of the menstrual cycle.

- Practice good menstrual hygiene habits. Pads, panty shields or liners, and tampons are products that can be used to absorb the menstrual flow. Wear a pad or panty shield at night instead of a tampon to reduce the risk of toxic shock syndrome. Define toxic shock syndrome (TSS). **Toxic shock syndrome (TSS)** is a rare, serious disease caused by certain toxin-producing strains of *Staphylococcus aureus* bacterium.

- Choose habits to prevent or lessen menstrual cramps. Regular exercise and a reduction in the amount of caffeine and salt in a female's diet might prevent or lessen menstrual cramps.

- Perform monthly breast self-examinations. Define breast self-examination (BSE). A **breast self-examination (BSE)** is a cancer screening procedure in which a female visually examines her breasts, palpates them to detect any lumps, and squeezes her nipples to check for any clear or bloody discharge. Give each student a copy of the Blackline Master *Breast Self-Examination.*

- Have regular medical checkups. Define pelvic examination. A **pelvic examination** includes the following: an inspection of the external genitalia, a speculum examination, a bimanual vaginal examination, and a recto-vaginal examination. Define Pap smear. A **Pap smear** is a screening test for cervical cancer in which cells are scraped from the cervix and examined for abnormalities. Give each student a copy of the Blackline Master *Pap Smear.* Explain that a speculum is used to hold open the vaginal walls. Define speculum. A **speculum** is an instrument inserted into the vagina to inspect the internal female reproductive organs. A spatula is inserted into the vagina and used to scrape cells from the cervix. The cells are then examined under a microscope for the presence of cancerous cells.

- Seek medical attention when you show signs of infection.

- Practice abstinence from sex. Define abstinence from sex. **Abstinence from sex** is choosing not to be sexually active.

2 Use a balloon for the following demonstration. Have students identify excuses a female might use for not protecting reproductive health. For example, a student might say, "I forget to write down information about my menstrual cycle." Blow a puff of air into the balloon. Other examples of excuses:

- "I don't want to take the time to change my tampon often."

- "I don't know how to do a breast self-examination."

- "I forgot to get a medical checkup."

- "I can't resist my boyfriend's pressure to be sexually active."

3 Prick the balloon with a pin so that it bursts (be cautious that the balloon will not strike a student). Explain that a female might have a surprise if she does not take care of her reproductive health. She might experience serious consequences. She might be sexually active and become pregnant or become infected with STDs, including HIV. She might develop toxic shock syndrome if she does not change her tampons frequently. She might have problems with reproductive organs if she skips medical checkups.

4 Blow up a second balloon. Tell the class that the balloon represents a female who protects her reproductive health. Without students noticing, tape a piece of wide cellophane tape to the back of the balloon. Have students brainstorm statements that a female makes to justify not protecting her reproductive health. For each statement, have another student make a counter statement that tells the importance of protecting female reproductive health. For example, one student might say, "I don't want to exercise and reduce the caffeine and salt in my diet." A second student could counter by saying, "Not only

© 2001 Everyday Learning Corporation

might getting exercise and consuming less caffeine and salt lessen your menstrual cramps, it also will make you feel better." As a student makes a counter statement, stick the pin through the tape on the balloon. The balloon will not burst because only a slight amount of air will be let out. Students will wonder why the balloon is not bursting. Each prick of the balloon will release the pressure in the balloon.

Tell students that this is like releasing the stress and pressure of not protecting female reproductive health. Continue to release the pressure in the balloon as students make counter statements that explain the importance of protecting female reproductive health.

5 Give each student a copy of the Blackline Master *Female Reproductive Health*. Discuss the following vocabulary words with students: mammography, fibrocystic breast condition, breast implants, uterine and cervical cancer, ovarian cancer, vaginal cancer, vaginitis, cystitis, endometriosis, endometritis, polyps, dilation and curettage.

6 Tell students that they should keep a personal health record. Define personal health record. A **personal health record** is documentation of information pertaining to a person's health, health care, and health care providers. The personal health record should include the following information:

- vital statistics regarding your birth;
- detailed family health history;
- record of immunizations;
- personal health information;
- health habits;
- medical history;
- medications;
- health insurance information; and
- health care professionals.

Assessment

Have students design a one-page calendar. In each daily box on the calendar, they should write a reminder for females about reproductive health. Read the life skills for this lesson to students so that their reminders will be appropriate.

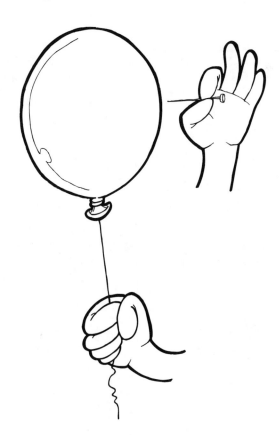

Breast Self-Examination

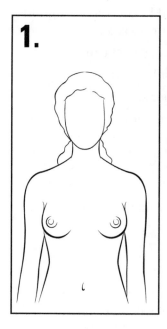

1. Stand in front of a mirror with arms at your sides. Examine breasts carefully for anything unusual—puckering, dimpling, changes in skin texture.

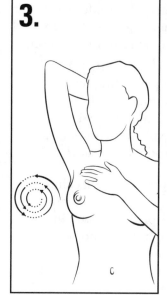

3. Raise your left arm. Use the fingers of the other hand to examine the left breast. Start at the outermost top edge of the breast. Go in circles toward the nipple. Fingers flat, press gently in small circles. Move the circles slowly around the breast. Include the area between the breast and the armpit and the armpit itself. Raise your right arm, and examine the right breast.

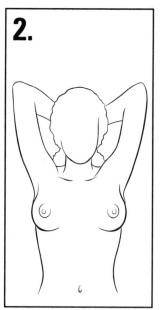

2. Clasp your hands behind your head. Press your hands forward. Look carefully for changes in size, shape, and contour of each breast.

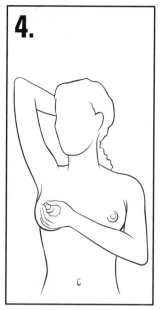

4. Gently squeeze each nipple between your thumb and index finger. Look for discharge.

Pap Smear

Spatula (used for scraping cells from cervix)

Speculum holds vaginal walls apart.

593

Female Reproductive Health

▶ A **mammography** is a highly sensitive X-ray screening test used to detect breast lumps and is a highly effective tool in the early detection of cancer.

▶ **Fibrocystic breast condition** is a condition in which the cysts and fibroadenomas cause lumpiness and breast tenderness and discomfort.

▶ **Breast implants** are materials that are surgically implanted into breast tissue to improve the size and shape of a breast.

▶ **Ovarian cancer** is a disease in which there are cancerous cells and/or malignant tumors in one or both of the ovaries.

▶ **Vaginal cancer** is a disease in which cancerous cells and/or malignant tumors are present in the vagina.

▶ **Vaginitis** is an irritation or inflammation of the vagina usually accompanied by a discharge.

▶ **Endometriosis** is a condition in which the endometrial tissue grows somewhere other than in the lining of the uterus.

Female Reproductive Health continued

▶ **Endometritis** is the inflammation of the uterine lining.

▶ **Polyps** are long tubelike protrusions that grow from mucous membranes inside the uterus or along the cervix.

▶ **Dilation and curettage (D and C)** is a surgical procedure in which the cervical opening is dilated by means of probes of increasingly larger sizes until a metal loop curette can be inserted to scrape the uterine lining.

▶ **Fibroids** are benign, slow-growing growths in the uterus.

All My Diseases

The Curriculum

Life Skill

■ I will choose behaviors to reduce my risk of infection with sexually transmitted diseases.

Objectives

■ Students will discuss the cause, transmission, symptoms, diagnosis, and treatment for common STDs: chlamydia, genital herpes, genital warts, gonorrhea, pubic lice, syphilis, trichomoniasis, viral hepatitis.

■ Students will discuss ways to reduce the risk of infection with STDs.

The National Health Education Standards

■ Students will demonstrate the ability to access valid health information and health-promoting products and services.

■ Students will demonstrate the ability to use goal-setting and decision-making skills that enhance health.

Preparing to Teach the Lesson Plan

Materials

Informational packets or brochures about STDs

Teaching the Lesson Plan

Get brochures about STDs from community health organizations. Local health departments, state health departments, and voluntary health agencies will have brochures or other health packets containing information about STDs.

1 Pass out the informational packets and brochures to students. Divide the class into 17 groups. Assign each group one STD.

Define sexually transmitted disease (STD). A **sexually transmitted disease (STD)** is a disease caused by pathogens that are transmitted from an infected person to an uninfected person during intimate sexual contact. Tell students that the 17 groups should be:

1. Bacterial vaginosis. **Bacterial vaginosis** is an STD caused by the *Gardnerella vaginalis* bacterium. Although these bacteria are normally found in the vagina at low levels, an increase in their growth produces typical symptoms of the disease.

2. Candidiasis. **Candidiasis** is an STD caused by the fungus, *Candida albicans*. It is commonly called a yeast infection.

3. Trichomoniasis. **Trichomoniasis** is an STD caused by the parasitic protozoan *Trichomonas*, which might infect the vagina, urethra, or prostate gland. This disease affects about 10 to 15 percent of persons who are sexually active.

4. Chlamydia infections. **Chlamydia infections** are STDs caused by the bacterium *Chlamydia trachomatis*, that might result in inflammation of the urethra and epididymis in males and inflammation of the vagina and cervix in females.

5. Gonorrhea. **Gonorrhea** is an STD caused by the bacterium *Neisseria gonorrhoeae*, which infects the epithelial surfaces of the genitourinary tract of males and females.

6. Nongonococcal urethritis (NGU). **Nongonococcal urethritis (NGU)** is an STD caused by pathogens other than *Neisseria gonorrhoeae*, which cause an infection and inflammation of the urethra.

7. Syphilis. **Syphilis** is an STD caused by the bacterium *Treponema pallidum*, which penetrates mucous membranes and abrasions in the skin and causes lesions that might involve any organ or tissue.

8. Genital herpes. **Genital herpes** is a highly contagious STD that is caused by two forms of the herpes simplex virus (HSV), HSV-1 and HSV-2. HSV-1 generally causes cold sores or fever blisters in the mouth or on the lips. HSV-2 is generally associated with sores or lesions in the genital area.

9. Genital warts. **Genital warts** are dry, wart-like growths that are caused by the human papillomavirus (HPV). The warts are painless and have a cauliflower shape.

10. Pediculosis pubis. **Pediculosis pubis** is infestation with *Phthirus pubis,* pubic or crab lice. Lice are parasitic insects that are yellowish-grey in color and about the size of a pinhead. The lice attach themselves to pubic hairs and burrow into the skin where they feed on blood. Female lice produce eggs called nits, that attach to body hair. The eggs hatch in sex to eight days and mature in 21 days. Since each female lays as many as 50 eggs, an infection can increase in a very short time.

11. Viral hepatitis. **Viral hepatitis** is an inflammatory infection of the liver caused by viruses. There are four types of viral hepatitis, all caused by different viruses. The four types are designated as hepatitis A (infectious hepatitis, hepatitis B (serum hepatitis), hepatitis C (sometimes called non-A/non-B hepatitis), and hepatitis D (delta hepatitis). The diseases caused by these viruses are very similar.

12. Molluscum contagiosum. **Molluscum contagiosum** is an STD caused by a large virus of the pox group.

13. Scabies. **Scabies** is a skin infestation by *Sarcoptes scabiei,* microscopic mites that are parasites. The female mite burrows under the skin and deposits eggs.

14. Shigellosis. **Shigellosis** is an STD caused by the *Shigella* bacterium.

15. Chancroid. **Chancroid** is an STD caused by the *Hemophilus ducreyi* bacterium. It is a common cause of genital ulcers. These ulcers are similar to the syphilis chancres but differ in that these are soft in comparison to the harder chancres associated with syphilis.

16. Lymphogranuloma venereum, or LGV. **Lymphogranuloma venereum,** or **LGV,** is an STD caused by the *Chlamydia trachomatis* bacterium.

17. Granuloma inguinale. **Granuloma inguinale** is an STD caused by the bacterium *Calymmatobacterium granulomatis.*

2 Tell each group it is to design a fact sheet that includes the following information about the STD it was assigned: cause, transmission, symptoms, diagnosis, and treatment. Collect the fact sheets designed by the students. Refer to Chapter 6 Sexually Transmitted Diseases to check the accuracy of the facts. Optional: duplicate the facts sheets and give a copy to each student.

3 Have each group write a portion of a mini-soap opera titled "All My Diseases." It should focus on the consequences of being infected with an STD. For example, a girl might be calling her boyfriend to tell him she has genital herpes. The mini-soap opera would include the boyfriend's reactions. The group should review its fact sheet for the class and then perform its mini-soap opera. After each mini-soap opera, review the ways that being infected with an HIV might affect a teen's life. Emphasize that there are reasons students should avoid infection with STDs. Review Table 6.11 Reasons to Avoid Infection with STDs on page 131.

4 Discuss ways to reduce the risk of being infected with STDS. Refer to Table 6.1 Risk Behaviors and Risk Situations for Transmission of STDs on page 113.

Assessment

Have students write an ad telling about the soap opera "All My Diseases." Their ad must promote a future program in which one STD is covered. Their ad must include five facts about the STD. It must include two consequences teens might experience from having this STD. It also must include at least three reasons to avoid infection with this STD.

Defend That Line

The Curriculum

Life Skill

■ I will choose behaviors to reduce my risk of HIV infection.

Objectives

■ Students will explain how the immune system responds to most pathogens.

■ Students will explain how the immune system responds when HIV enters the body.

■ Students will explain the progression of HIV infection and AIDS, including the opportunistic infections that might develop.

The National Health Education Standards

■ Students will comprehend concepts related to health promotion and disease prevention.

■ Students will demonstrate the ability to use goal-setting and decision-making skills that enhance health.

Preparing to Teach the Lesson Plan

Materials

Poster board

Marker

String

Scissors

Blackline Master

HIV Progression to AIDS

Teaching the Lesson Plan

On each of five sheets of poster board, outline a t-shirt with a marker. Punch two holes in the "t-shirt" on each side of the neck. Insert string through each hole so that a person could wear the t-shirt like a billboard. On the front of each t-shirt in large letters should be written one of these five terms: skin, helper T cell, B cell, antibody, and macrophage. Written on the back of each t-shirt should be information about or the definition of each term. For example, on the back of the B cell t-shirt you could write, "I'm the white blood cell that produces antibodies."

Cut three strips from the poster board. Write one of the following opportunistic infections on each of the strips: Pneumocystis carinii pneumonia, Kaposi's sarcoma, and AIDS dementia complex.

1 Tell five students each to wear one of the five "t-shirts." Introduce the five students as the t-shirt team. Tell the class the function of each member of the team. Define lymphocyte. **Lymphocytes** are white blood cells that circulate throughout the lymphatic system to help the body fight pathogens. When pathogens enter the body, lymphocytes multiply in the lymph tissue to fight infection. Define B cell. A **B cell** is the blood cell that produces antibodies. Define helper T cell or CD4+T cell. A **helper T cell**, or **CD4+T cell**, is a white blood cell that signals B cells to make antibodies. Define antibody. An **antibody** is a protein produced by B cells that helps destroy pathogens inside the body. B cells produce antibodies in the blood soon after a pathogen enters the body. B cells enter the lymph nodes and other lymph tissues. Antibodies then travel through the lymph vessels to destroy the pathogen. Antibodies make the pathogens ineffective and susceptible to macrophages. Define macrophage. **Macrophages** are white blood cells that surround and destroy pathogens.

2 Ask for a student volunteer. The volunteer will be a non-HIV pathogen. Tell the t-shirt team to line up in the following order: skin, helper T cell, B cell, antibody, and macrophage. Tell the volunteer that he or she should try "to get into the body" by breaking through the skin. The student representing the skin is to prevent the person from getting through. Tell the student representing the helper T cell to hug the volunteer representing the non-HIV pathogen in order to simulate that this type of cell will multiply and prevent the non-HIV pathogen from causing harm. Tell the student representing the B cell to arrive and bring the student representing the antibody. Tell the student representing the macrophage to kill and digest the non-HIV pathogen.

3 Give each student a copy of the Blackline Master *HIV Progression to AIDS*. Ask for another student volunteer. This volunteer will represent HIV. Tell the student representing HIV to "break through" the student representing the skin and to attack the student representing the helper T cell. Tell students that helper T cells signal to B cells to produce antibodies, but helper T cells are destroyed. Explain that HIV reproduces. HIV invades and destroys more helper T cells. This causes the body to produce fewer and fewer antibodies. Tell three other students in the class to pretend to be the HIV that has multiplied in the body. Tell the students that are representing HIV to give to three students the strips of poster board with the names of opportunistic infections written on them. Define opportunistic infections. An **opportunistic infection** is an infection that develops in a person with a weakened immune system. Define *Pneumocystis carinii* pneumonia or PCP. *Pneumocystis carinii* **pneumonia**, or **PCP**, is a form of pneumonia that results from a weakened immune system. PCP makes it very difficult to breathe. Define Kaposi's sarcoma or KS. **Kaposi's sarcoma**, or **KS**, is a type of cancer that is a common opportunistic infection in people who have AIDS. KS causes purple spots to develop on the skin. Define AIDS dementia complex. **AIDS dementia complex** is a loss of brain function caused by HIV infection. It causes changes in thinking, memory, and coordination. Explain to the class that HIV destroys helper T cells. The reduction in the number of helper T cells weakens the body's ability to fight infections. Eventually, these opportunistic infections can cause death.

Assessment

Have students divide a paper into two columns. In the first column, have them draw an illustration with labels to explain how the immune system responds to most pathogens. In the second column, have them draw an illustration with labels that explains how the immune system responds when HIV enters the body. Have students turn their papers over and explain the progression of HIV infection and AIDS, including the opportunistic infections that might develop.

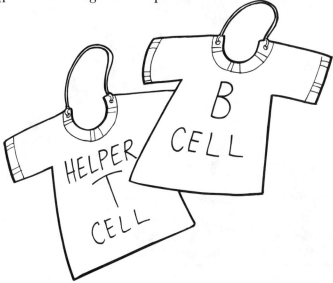

HIV Progression to AIDS

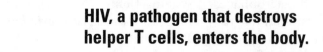

HIV, a pathogen that destroys helper T cells, enters the body.

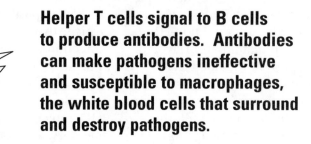

Helper T cells signal to B cells to produce antibodies. Antibodies can make pathogens ineffective and susceptible to macrophages, the white blood cells that surround and destroy pathogens.

HIV attaches to a molecule called CD4 on the helper T cells.

HIV takes control of the helper T cells and continues to reproduce more HIV.

HIV attaches to and takes control of more helper T cells. The body produces fewer and fewer antibodies. The body's ability to fight infection is weakened.

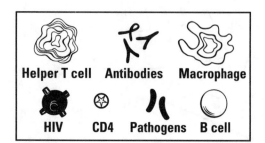

Helper T cell	Antibodies	Macrophage
HIV	CD4	Pathogens	B cell

According to the Centers for Disease Control and Prevention, a person infected with HIV has AIDS when he or she has 200 or fewer helper T cells per microliter of blood or has an opportunistic infection.

It Just Keeps on Spreading

The Curriculum

Life Skill

■ I will choose behaviors to reduce my risk of HIV infection.

Objectives

■ Students will identify and discuss risk behaviors and risk situations for transmission of HIV.

■ Students will identify and discuss ways HIV is not transmitted.

The National Health Education Standards

■ Students will comprehend concepts related to health promotion and disease prevention.

■ Students will demonstrate the ability to use goal-setting and decision-making skills that enhance health.

Preparing to Teach the Lesson Plan

Materials

Index cards, one for each student

Blackline Masters

Ways HIV Can Be Transmitted

Ways HIV Cannot Be Transmitted

Teaching the Lesson Plan

1 *Number the index cards. There should be one card for each student in the class. In addition, write "Shake hands with anyone" on all of the odd numbered cards. Label the even numbered cards as follows:*

Card #2 will say, "I am HIV-positive."

Card #4 will say, "Shake hands only with Card #6."

Card #6 will say, "Shake hands only with Card #4."

Card #8 will say, "Do not shake hands with anyone."

2 Distribute the cards. Tell students not to reveal what is on their cards. Tell students that there will be three rounds of exchanging hand shakes. Tell students to write "Round One" on their cards. Tell students to shake the hand of any other person (unless their card indicates otherwise). Tell students to write down the number written on the card of the person with whom a handshake was exchanged.

3 Tell students to write "Round Two" on their cards. Tell students to shake the hand of any other person (unless their card indicates otherwise). Tell students to write down the number written on the card of the person with whom a handshake was exchanged.

4 Tell students to write "Round Three" on their cards. Tell students to repeat the same steps as in the first two rounds. Tell students that the handshakes symbolized sexual intercourse. Tell the student with Card #2 to read the number of the person on his or her card listed under Round One. Tell the student whose number was just called to stand. Tell the student with Card #2 to tell this person what is written on Card #2. Explain to students that another person in the class now has a risk of being HIV-infected. Tell the student with Card #2 and the student identified from Round One to read the number of the person on their cards listed under Round Two. Tell the students whose numbers were just called to stand. Tell the class that these two students now have a risk of being HIV-infected. Repeat the same procedure for Round Three. Eight people in the class now are possibly HIV-infected. Explain to students that only one person in the class was HIV-infected when Round One began.

5 Explain that a person who has sexual intercourse with a partner does not know what other sexual partners that person has had. The greater the number of partners, the greater the risk that the person will be infected with HIV. Ask students how the previous activity demonstrated this risk. Students might say that some of their classmates became infected with HIV from a partner who had become infected from another person.

6 Discuss the significance of the statements that were written on the other cards. Tell the students with Cards #4 and #6 to stand. These cards were written for a couple that has a monogamous marriage. Define monogamous marriage. A **monogamous marriage** is a marriage in which both people remain sexually faithful to one another. This couple also entered marriage without either partner having been infected with HIV. Emphasize that abstinence from sex until marriage and monogamous marriage protects a couple from HIV infection. Of course the couple also must abstain from injecting drug use.

7 Tell the student with Card #8 to stand and read his or her card to the class. Tell the class that this student did not shake hands with anyone. This student practiced abstinence from sex. Define abstinence from sex. **Abstinence from sex** is choosing not to be sexually active. Explain that abstinence from sex eliminates the risk of sexual transmission of HIV. This is one reason why family guidelines emphasize that abstinence from sex is the expected standard for teens.

8 Give each student a copy of the Blackline Master *Ways HIV Can Be Transmitted* and *Ways HIV Cannot Be Transmitted*. Review Table 7.3 Risk Behaviors and Risk Situations for Transmission of HIV on page 135.

Assessment

Write the life skill for the lesson on the chalkboard, "I will choose behaviors to reduce my risk of HIV infection." Have students write a one-page paper in which they identify behaviors they will choose and explain why.

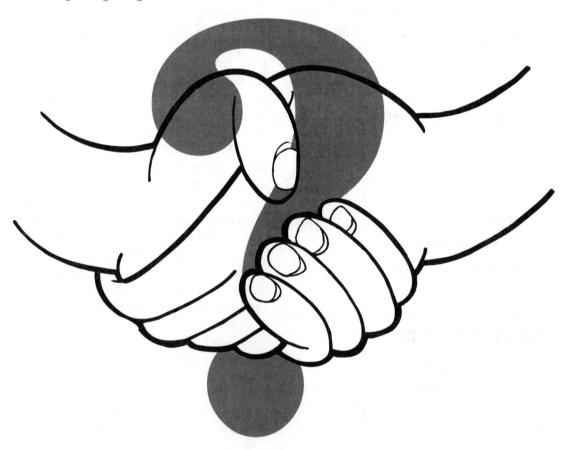

Ways HIV Can Be Transmitted

1 Having sexual contact with an infected person.

2 Open-mouth kissing with an infected person.

3 Sharing needles, syringes, or other injection equipment for injecting drugs. An **injecting drug user** is a person who injects illegal drugs into the body with syringes, needles, and other injection equipment.

4 Sharing needles to make tattoos and to pierce ears and other body parts.

5 Having contact with the blood or other body fluids, mucous membranes, or broken skin of an infected person.

6 Having a blood transfusion with infected blood or blood products.

7 Having a tissue transplant (organ donation).

8 Being born to a mother infected with HIV. A **perinatal transmission** is the transfer of an infection to a baby during pregnancy, delivery, or breastfeeding.

Ways HIV Cannot Be Transmitted

HIV is **NOT** transmitted through casual contact, such as the following:

1. Closed-mouth kissing

2. Hugging

3. Touching, holding, or shaking hands

4. Coughing or sneezing

5. Sharing food or eating utensils

6. Sharing towels or combs

7. Having casual contact with friends

8. Sharing bathroom facilities or water fountains

9. Sharing a pen or pencil

10. Being bitten by insects

11. Donating blood

12. Eating food prepared or served by someone else

13. Attending school

14. Using a telephone or computer used by someone else

15. Swimming in a pool

16. Using sports and gym equipment

HIV Conference

The Curriculum

Life Skill

■ I will choose behaviors to reduce my risk of HIV infection.

Objectives

■ Students will discuss tests used to determine HIV status.

■ Students will discuss treatment for HIV infection and AIDS.

The National Health Education Standards

■ Students will comprehend concepts related to health promotion and disease prevention.

■ Students will demonstrate the ability to practice health-enhancing behaviors and reduce health risks.

■ Students will demonstrate the ability to use goal-setting and decision-making skills that enhance health.

Preparing to Teach the Lesson Plan

Materials

None

Teaching the Lesson Plan

1 Explain to students that they are going to review information about HIV tests. An antibody test is the only way to tell whether or not a person is infected with HIV. Define ELISA or enzyme-linked immunosorbent assay. **ELISA**, or **enzyme-linked immunosorbent assay**, is a blood test used to check for antibodies for

HIV. If two or more ELISA tests are positive, a Western blot test is given. Define Western blot. **Western blot** is a blood test used to check for antibodies for HIV and to confirm an ELISA test. Used together, ELISA and Western blot are correct more than 99.9 percent of the time. Two home collection kits for HIV antibody testing were approved by the FDA in 1996. Define Orasure Western blot. **Orasure Western blot** is a test for HIV in which a tissue sample is collected using a cotton swab between the gum and cheek. Define Amplicor HIV-1 monitor test. **Amplicor HIV-1 monitor test** is a test that measures the level of HIV in the blood. Define home collection kit for HIV antibody testing. A **home collection kit for HIV antibody testing** is a kit that allows a person to take a blood test sample at home, place drops of blood on a test card, mail the card to a lab, and call a toll-free number for the results of the test. Define HIV positive. **HIV positive** is a term used to describe a person whose test results indicate the presence of HIV antibodies in the blood. Define HIV negative. **HIV negative** is a term used to describe a person whose test results do not indicate the presence of HIV antibodies in the blood.

2 Explain to students that they are going to review information about treatments for HIV infection and AIDS. The FDA has approved drugs for treating HIV and AIDS-related conditions. Define ddI. **DdI** is a drug that slows the rate at which HIV multiplies. Define AZT or zidovudine. **AZT**, or **zidovudine**, is a drug that slows down the rate at which HIV multiplies. Define aerosolized pentamidine isethionate. **Aerosolized pentamidine isethionate** is a drug to prevent *Pneumocystis carinii* pneumonia (PCP). Define Interferon alfa-2a and Interferon alfa-2b. **Interferon alfa-2a** and **Interferon alfa-2b** are drugs to treat Kaposi's sarcoma (KS). Protease inhibitors are newer and more effective against HIV than some other drugs. However, researchers aren't sure how long protease inhibitors will work in people infected with HIV or how well they work in different people. Define Protease inhibitors. **Protease inhibitors** are antiviral drugs that decrease the amount of HIV in the blood and increase the helper T cell count.

3 Divide the class into 5 groups. Tell the groups to pretend that they are at a convention on HIV and AIDS. Each group is going to give a lecture on either HIV tests or HIV treatments. Tell the groups to get information from local and state health agencies and the library. Tell students that other places from which to get information are reliable sources on the Internet, such as the Centers for Disease Control and Prevention. Give students time to research their lecture topics.

4 After each group has presented its lecture, tell the students to ask questions about the topic covered. For example, a student might ask, "Is it true that while taking protease inhibitors some people have had the amount of HIV in the blood drop to a level where it cannot be detected?" Then, a member of the group giving the lecture on protease inhibitors might respond, "That is true; however, physicians believe HIV is still in their bodies and that it will reproduce quickly if they stop taking the protease inhibitors."

Assessment

Give students a matching test. They must match the following vocabulary words with their correct definitions: ELISA, Western blot, Orasure Western blot, Amplicor HIV-1 monitor test, home collection kit for HIV antibody testing, HIV positive, HIV negative, ddI, AZT, aerosolized pentamidine isethionate, interferon alfa-2a, interferon alfa-2b, and protease inhibitors.

The Odds Aren't Great

The Curriculum

Life Skills

■ I will choose behaviors to reduce my risk of HIV infection.

■ I will not misuse or abuse drugs.

■ I will practice abstinence from sex.

Objective

■ Students will discuss ways to reduce the risk of HIV infection.

The National Health Education Standards

■ Students will comprehend concepts related to health promotion and disease prevention.

■ Students will demonstrate the ability to use goal-setting and decision-making skills that enhance health.

Preparing to Teach the Lesson Plan

Materials

Construction paper

Markers and pens

Blackline Master

How to Reduce the Risk of HIV Infection

Teaching the Lesson Plan

1 Tell students the following scenario:

You have been offered a trip to anywhere you would like to visit. You can go anywhere you desire around the world. You will travel by airplane. Ask students to share where they would like to visit. Students might say London or Tokyo. Tell students that they will receive free airline tickets. Ask students how they would feel about receiving free airline tickets. Students will probably respond that they would accept the tickets.

2 Explain to students that there is one fact you have not told them about the airline upon which they will travel if they accept the tickets. Flying on this airline is risky. The planes often crash. Ask students if, knowing this information, they still would want the free airline tickets? Would they take the chance and make only one round-trip on this airline?

3 Review Table 7.3, page 135, Risk Behaviors and Risk Situations for Transmission of HIV. Explain to students that most of them said they would not make even one round-trip on the airline because of the facts pertaining to its safety record. Further explain that you have just identified risk behaviors and risk situations for HIV infection. Engaging in these just one time also puts them at risk. Give each student a copy of the Blackline Master *How to Reduce the Risk of HIV Infection*.

Assessment

Tell students that they are going to design airline tickets that encourage others to "Fly the Safety Skies." Using construction paper and other art supplies, design an airline ticket that describes a way to reduce the risk of HIV Infection.

How to Reduce the Risk of HIV Infection

1. Abstain from sex until you are married.

2. Do not engage in open-mouth kissing with a person who is infected with HIV.

3. Change your behavior if you have been sexually active.

4. Have a monogamous marriage if you choose to marry in the future. A **monogamous marriage** is a marriage in which both people remain sexually faithful to one another.

5. Do not inject illegal drugs.

6. Change your behavior if you have injected illegal drugs.

7. Do not share a needle to make tattoos or to pierce ears and other body parts.

8. Follow universal precautions. **Universal precautions** are steps taken to prevent the spread of disease by treating all human blood and certain body fluids as if they contained HIV, hepatitis B virus (HBV), and other pathogens.

9. Ask your dentist if he or she autoclaves dental pieces and accessories between patients. To **autoclave** is to sterilize with steam under pressure.

10. Inquire about the safety of having a transfusion or tissue transplant.

The AIDS News of the Day

The Curriculum

Life Skills

■ I will choose behaviors to reduce my risk of HIV infection.

■ I will use resistance skills when appropriate.

Objectives

■ Students will discuss ways to reduce the risk of HIV infection.

■ Students will outline resistance skills that can be used to resist pressure to engage in risk behaviors and risk situations for transmission of HIV.

The National Health Education Standards

■ Students will comprehend concepts related to health promotion and disease prevention.

■ Students will demonstrate the ability to practice health-enhancing behaviors and reduce health risks.

■ Students will demonstrate the ability to use goal-setting and decision-making skills to enhance health.

Preparing to Teach the Lesson Plan

Materials

None

Teaching the Lesson Plan

1 Tell students that any person, regardless of gender, age, race, or sexual orientation, can become infected with HIV by engaging in specific risk behaviors.

2 Divide the class into groups of five students. Tell each group that it will put on a news show for the rest of the class. The news show will have five segments: local news, national news, international news, sports, and health. Tell the class that each of the segments should focus on one of the ten ways to reduce the risk of HIV infection (see the Lesson Plan "The Odds Aren't Great"). For example, the local news might be about dentists who sterilize their equipment, using high pressure steam. Tell the class that each member of the group will be responsible for one segment.

3 Tell students to arrange special ways to present their news shows. For example, students might use an interview format. Tell each group to make a plan for you to review that describes how they will present their news show.

4 Have students create a public service announcement (PSA) about using resistance skills to resist pressure to choose risk behaviors for HIV infection. The seven resistance skills are

1. Be confident and say, "No, I do not want to risk becoming infected with HIV."
2. Give reasons why you will not choose risk behaviors for HIV infection.
3. Repeat your reasons for NOT choosing risk behaviors for HIV infection.
4. Don't send a mixed message.
5. Avoid situations in which there will be pressure to choose risk behaviors for HIV infection.
6. Avoid being with people who continue to choose risk behaviors for HIV infection.
7. Influence others to avoid risk behaviors for HIV infection.

Assessment

Select one newscaster from each group. The newscasters you select will become an expert panel. Tell other students to each write five questions and answers about ways to reduce the risk of HIV infection. Then have them quiz the panel.

Stressors of Teen Marriage

The Curriculum

Life Skill

■ I will develop skills to prepare for marriage.

Objectives

■ Students will identify factors used to predict success in marriage.

■ Students will explain four kinds of intimacy in marriage.

■ Students will explain two important ways marriage partners can ensure that their marriage will last.

■ Students will discuss the risks associated with teen marriage.

■ Students will discuss ways teen marriage interferes with mastery of the eight developmental tasks of adolescence.

The National Health Education Standards

■ Students will demonstrate the ability to practice health-enhancing behaviors and reduce health risks.

■ Students will demonstrate the ability to use interpersonal communication skills to enhance health.

■ Students will demonstrate the ability to advocate for personal, family, and community health.

Preparing to Teach the Lesson Plan

Materials

Pitcher of water

Sponge

Large bowl or trash can

Blackline Masters

Developmental Tasks of Adolescence

Major Tasks of the Passages of Marriage

Teaching the Lesson Plan

1 Give each student a copy of the Blackline Master *Developmental Tasks of Adolescence.* Define developmental task. A **developmental task** is an achievement that needs to be mastered to reach the next level of maturity. Tell students that they are responsible for achieving these developmental tasks before adulthood:

• develop healthful friendships with members of both sexes;

• become comfortable with their maleness or femaleness;

• become comfortable with their body;

• become emotionally independent from adults;

• learn skills they will need later if they marry and become a parent;

• prepare for a career;

• have a clear set of values to guide their behavior;

• understand and achieve socially responsible behavior.

Ask students why it is important for them to achieve these tasks now.

2 Tell students that in the future they might choose to get married. Tell students they are not prepared for marriage now. Explain to students that marriage is a serious commitment. Tell students two ways marriage partners can ensure that their marriage will last:

1. Marriage partners must be committed to actions that honor their wedding vows.

2. Marriage partners must work together to master the developmental stages of marriage.

Tell students factors that can be used to predict success in a marriage such as similar age and interests. Give each student a copy of the Blackline *Master Major Tasks of the Passages of Marriage.* Focus on the first two years of marriage. Ask students why each of these tasks is important for a married couple to master. Marriage partners must:

- maintain individual identity at the same time as they form a family;

- develop cooperation and reduce the need to control the other;

- develop a sexual bond with the other that leads to deeper intimacy;

- develop an effective decision-making style; and

- recognize the difficulties in their parents' marriages and anticipate how those difficulties might affect their marriage.

3 Tell students that there are four kinds of intimacy in a marriage: philosophical intimacy, psychological intimacy, creative intimacy, and physical intimacy. Explain that achieving the four kinds of intimacy in a marriage is important for a lasting marriage. Define philosophical intimacy. **Philosophical intimacy** is the sharing of beliefs and values. Marriage partners share the values that determine their day-to-day priorities. Define psychological intimacy. **Psychological intimacy** is the sharing of needs, emotions, weaknesses, and strengths. Marriage partners share their needs and their weaknesses. Psychological intimacy deepens with time. Define creative intimacy. **Creative intimacy** is the sharing of efforts to accomplish tasks and projects. Creative intimacy goes beyond sharing feelings

or discussing goals. This kind of intimacy involves cooperation in a joint effort, such as planting a garden. Define physical intimacy. **Physical intimacy** is the sharing of physical affection. This can include touching, caressing, holding hands, kissing, and sexual intercourse.

4 Ask students why they think it is important for teens to learn the developmental tasks of adolescence before they tackle the tasks for a healthy marriage. Students might answer that if they get married before they master the adolescent tasks, they might miss out on important steps in their emotional growth such as becoming emotionally independent from adults. Emphasize that students are not ready for marriage at this time in their lives. Explain that abstinence from sex is the expected standard for teens.

5 Select two student volunteers. Tell the class that one of the students will represent a teen who is married. The other student will represent a teen that waits to be married until he or she has mastered the developmental tasks of adolescence and is an adult. Have the student who represents the married teen hold a pitcher of water. Have the student who represents a teen waiting until adulthood to be married hold a sponge in one hand. The sponge should be held over a large bowl or a trash can. Tell students that married teens have not mastered the developmental tasks of adolescence. Thus, married teens experience many stressors. Define stressor. A **stressor** is a source or cause of stress. Have the student representing a married teen identify one of the stressors of teen marriage. For example, a stressor of teen marriage could be not having any time for friends. Another stressor could be not having money to go out. Tell the student representing a married teen to pour some water on the sponge each time he or she names a stressor of teen marriage. Students will notice that the sponge is soon soaked with water. Explain that married teens absorb a lot of stress. Without mastering the developmental tasks of adolescence, married teens do not have the ability to deal with stress well. Tell students that this is one of the reasons that the divorce rate is very high for teens who marry.

6 Explain to students that you are going to repeat the demonstration with one difference. Again, have the student that represents the married teen identify stressors of teen marriage and pour water on the sponge. Tell the student representing the teen that is waiting until adulthood to get married that every time a stressor is named, he or she is to name one reason he or she is waiting until adulthood to get married. Each time the student names a reason for waiting until adulthood to get married, he or she should squeeze the water out of the sponge. For example, the married teen might say, "I have no time for school," and pour water into the sponge. The student representing the teen that is waiting until adulthood to get married might respond, "I will wait to get married until I have finished my education," and squeeze the water from the sponge. Explain that teens who wait until adulthood to get married master the developmental tasks of adolescence. Mastering these tasks helps teens who wait until adulthood to get married to not absorb the stress that married teens absorb. Tell students that these teens are better able to manage stress and problems. Explain to students that waiting until adulthood to get married will make them better prepared for the stressors of marriage.

Assessment

Ask students to write an essay explaining why marriages during the teenage years often end in divorce. Tell students to include a discussion of the developmental tasks of adolescence and the tasks of the first two years of marriage.

© 2001 Everyday Learning Corporation

Developmental Tasks of Adolescence

1 Develop healthful relationships with members of both sexes.

- Initiate a new friendship with a responsible person.
- Evaluate the friendships you already have to make sure they are healthful.
- Make an effort to be a good friend to others.

2 Become comfortable with your maleness or femaleness.

- Participate in a variety of social activities.
- Consider what you expect males to be like.
- Consider what you expect females to be like.
- Discuss unrealistic, uncertain, or uncomfortable expectations about sex roles with a responsible adult, such as a parent or guardian.

3 Become comfortable with your body.

- Discuss any concerns you have about your body with a responsible adult.
- Maintain a healthful appearance.
- Practice habits that will keep your body in top condition.
- Perform regular breast self-examinations or testicular self-examinations.

4 Become emotionally independent from adults.

- Use *The Responsible Decision-Making Model*™ when you make a decision.
- Keep a journal. Note decisions that did not turn out as you expected. Analyze what you might have done differently.
- Stay close to your parents or guardian by sharing your decisions and emotions with them.

5 Learn skills you will need later if you marry and become a parent.

- Analyze whether you make wise choices about the people with whom you share your thoughts and feelings.
- Review your relationships that have not been healthful and supportive.
- Discontinue all relationships that have been destructive.
- Practice relating to infants and children.

6 Prepare for a career.

- Work with your high school guidance counselor to select the right courses to prepare for the career in which you are interested.
- Study hard.
- Get your high school diploma.
- Speak with adults who have careers of interest.
- Participate in volunteer opportunities.
- Get a part-time job.

7 Have a set of values to guide your behavior.

- Examine how the values you have learned from your parents or guardian have guided your behavior.
- Identify what you stand for.
- Examine whether your behavior is consistent with the values you say are important to you.

8 Understand and achieve socially responsible behavior.

- Participate in volunteer activities that benefit others, such as collecting food for the needy.
- Join clubs at school that volunteer in the community.
- Look for ways to help out at home.

Major Tasks of the Passages of Marriage

The First Stage: **The First Two Years**	The Second Stage: **The Third Through the Tenth Years**	The Third Stage: **The Eleventh Through the Twenty-Fifth Years**	The Fourth Stage: **The Twenty-Sixth Through the Thirty-Fifth Years**	The Fifth Stage: **The Thirty-Sixth Year and On**
The newly married couple overcome their idealistic notions of marriage and begin to form a family. The partners strive to:	The couple gain a realistic view of their marriage and of one another and must settle into dealing with their individual weaknesses and make an effort to avoid dysfunctional behaviors. Their goals are to:	The couple establish and maintain individual identity and deal with issues of forgiveness, aging, adolescent children, and intimacy. They recognize the need to:	The couple must master tasks from the first three stages that were not previously mastered, confront changes in sexuality, and grieve over their losses. They determine to:	The couple find new reasons for existing after the major life tasks of achieving financial security and nurturing their family have been completed; partners confront their feelings about death. They agree to:
■ maintain individual identity at the same time as they form a family; ■ develop cooperation and reduce the need to control the other; ■ develop a sexual bond with the other that leads to deeper intimacy; ■ develop an effective decision-making style; ■ recognize the difficulties in their parents' marriages and anticipate how those difficulties might affect their marriage.	■ recognize and confront the weaknesses of both partners; ■ examine relationships and avoid dysfunctional behaviors; ■ reaffirm commitment to sexual intimacy, including sexual fidelity; ■ examine the influence of children on marriage and to agree upon child-raising methods.	■ reexamine and maintain individual identity and develop mutual dependence; ■ recognize that one another will not be perfect; ■ forgive one another for shortcomings and mistakes; ■ confront the crises of middle age, including aging, sexuality, and job and financial security; struggle for individuality; ■ reevaluate and make a plan for maintaining and developing intimacy.	■ reevaluate the tasks from the previous stages and determine if they have been successfully mastered; ■ recognize the physical changes that accompany aging and affect sexuality and rekindle romance; ■ grieve over losses such as death of parents and children leaving home.	■ prepare for retirement; ■ renew intimacy and develop ways to continue sexual intimacy; ■ prepare for death and for the death of the marriage partner; ■ accept death as a stage of life.

(Adapted from Minirth, et al. *Passages of Marriage*, 1991)

Handle That Crying

The Curriculum

Life Skill

■ I will discuss skills to prepare for parenthood.

Objectives

■ Students will explain the three "Rs" (reasons, resources, responsibilities) to consider before becoming a parent.

■ Students will explain four kinds of intimacy in the parent-child relationship.

■ Students will outline the growth and development of a child: from birth to six months, six months to twelve months, twelve months to eighteen months, eighteen months to two years, two years to two and one-half years, two and one-half years to three years, three years to four years, four years to five years, and five years to six years.

■ Students will explain ways parents and guardians help their children develop self-discipline and self-control.

■ Students will identify skills that must be developed by teens who plan to childsit.

The National Health Education Standards

■ Students will demonstrate the ability to practice health-enhancing behaviors and reduce health risks.

■ Students will demonstrate the ability to use interpersonal communication skills to enhance health.

■ Students will demonstrate the ability to advocate for personal, family, and community health.

Preparing to Teach the Lesson Plan

Materials

Cassette recorder
Cassette tape of baby crying
School book

Teaching the Lesson Plan

Before teaching the lesson, record the sounds of a baby crying. You may know someone who has a newborn baby whose crying you can record for this activity. You will need about ten minutes of crying for this lesson.

1 Tell students to copy a paragraph on a sheet of paper as you read it aloud to them. Before students start writing, play the cassette tape of the baby crying. Keep the tape playing while you are reading the paragraph to students. Observe students' reactions. Do not tell students why you are playing the tape of the baby crying.

2 After you read the paragraph, tell students you are going to say ten words. After saying the words, students are to write down in order as many of the ten words as they can. Meanwhile turn up the volume on the cassette recorder. Ten words you can use are typewriter, licorice, mallard, popcorn, principal, luggage, mousepad, telephone, forest, and lightbulb.

3 Ask students to share their lists of words with the class. Most of the students will not be able to list all ten words. They will say the crying affected their concentration. Discuss ways that hearing a baby cry might affect activities in the teen years. What might it be like to study for an exam while a baby was crying? Watch a sporting event on television?

Get a good night's sleep? Have students discuss ways in which being a teen parent might affect them. Remind them that abstinence from sex is the expected standard for them. Tell them that teen pregnancy is a serious problem for society. More than 3 out of 10 teen females become pregnant before age 20. Of those who become pregnant before 15, 60 percent will become pregnant again. Teens are more likely to have a baby with a low birth weight. Pregnant teens are more likely to drop out of school. Teen fathers also are more likely to drop out of school. Babies born to teen parents are at risk for having parents with inadequate parenting skills.

4 Explain that adults are more equipped to handle the three "Rs" associated with parenthood: reasons, resources, responsibilities. They choose to have a baby for the correct reason. They have the resources to provide for a baby. They can handle the responsibilities of parenthood. Review Table 8.3, page 157, The Parent Pledge to a Child.

5 Discuss the parent-child relationship. Explain that parents must develop intimacy with a child. Philosophical intimacy involves teaching their child beliefs and values. Psychological intimacy involves teaching their child trust. Creative intimacy involves teaching their child teamwork. Physical intimacy involves teaching their child appropriate ways to express love and affection.

6 Review how a child grows and develops from birth to age six. Refer to pages 158 through 162. Explain that responsible parents teach their children self-discipline and self-control. Responsible parents:

- set limits for their children,

- are consistent in their actions,

- are neither too strict nor too permissive,

- discuss acceptable behavior with their children,

- listen to their children and pay attention to their feelings.

7 Discuss childsitting. Define childsitter. A **childsitter** is a person who provides care for infants and children with the permission of a parent or guardian. Have students design a form that they might use if they childsit. The form should include the following:

- The parents' name, home address, and telephone number.

- The telephone numbers of the family doctor, the police department, and the fire department.

- The name, address, and telephone number where the parents can be reached.

- The name and telephone number of nearby neighbors to be contacted in an emergency.

- The telephone number and name of a relative or close friend to be used as a back-up.

- The time they expect to return.

8 **OPTIONAL** Review the Childsitter's Check Sheet (page 165), The Childsitter's List of Skills for the Care of Infants and Toddlers (page 166), and The Childsitter's List of Skills for the Care of Young Children (page 167).

Assessment

Have students pretend that they are teaching a high school course on how to prepare for parenthood. The class will meet five times. Have them outline what will be included in each meeting. The five topics: the three "Rs" of parenthood; parent-child intimacy; the growth and development of a child from birth to age six, ways parents teach their children self-discipline and self-control, and skills for childsitting.

Family Circles

The Curriculum

Life Skills

■ I will develop healthful family relationships.

■ I will work to improve difficult family relationships.

■ I will make healthful adjustments to family changes.

Objectives

■ Students will contrast the ideal family relationships with dysfunctional family relationships, using *The Family Continuum.*

■ Students will list and explain skills children who have ideal family relationships learn from their parents or guardians.

■ Students will discuss the causes of dysfunctional family relationships.

■ Students will discuss feelings and behaviors that describe family members who are codependent.

■ Students will outline ways to improve dysfunctional family relationships.

■ Students will discuss adjustments children might make if their parents divorce.

■ Students will discuss adjustments children might make if they live in a single-custody family.

■ Students will discuss adjustments children might make if a parent or parents remarry.

■ Students will discuss adjustments children might make if a parent(s) loses a job.

■ Students will discuss adjustments children might make if a parent goes to jail.

The National Health Education Standards

■ Students will demonstrate the ability to use interpersonal communication skills to enhance health.

■ Students will demonstrate the ability to use goal-setting and decision-making skills that enhance health.

■ Students will demonstrate the ability to practice health-enhancing behaviors and reduce health risks.

Preparing to Teach the Lesson Plan

Materials

Chalkboard

Chalk

Blackline Masters

The Family Continuum

Roots and Characteristics of Codependence

Codependence Self-Check

Teaching the Lesson Plan

1 Define a family. A **family** is a group of people who are related by blood, adoption, or marriage. Tell students that there are two extremes of family life: an ideal family and a dysfunctional family. Define the ideal family. An **ideal family** is a family that has all the skills needed for loving, responsible relationships. In an ideal family, parents teach their children:

• self-respecting behavior;

• healthful attitudes towards sexuality;

• effective communication;

• a clear sense of values;

• responsible decision-making;

• ways to resolve conflict;

• effective coping skills;

• ways to delay gratification;

- ways to express affection and integrate love and sexuality;
- how to give and receive acts of kindness;
- a work ethic; and
- respect for authority.

Define dysfunctional family. A **dysfunctional family** is a family that lacks the skills to be successful and to function in healthful ways. Tell students these causes of dysfunctional family relationships:

- chemical dependence;
- other addictions;
- perfectionism;
- violence;
- physical abuse;
- emotional abuse;
- neglect;
- sexual abuse;
- abandonment; and
- mental disorders.

2 Explain to students that studying these two extremes of family life is a way to learn about relationships within a family. Give each student a copy of the Blackline Master *The Family Continuum.* Explain to students that *The Family Continuum* shows two extremes of family life—the ideal family and the dysfunctional family. Tell students the majority of families rank in the middle of the continuum. These families are not ideal, but neither are they completely dysfunctional. Explain that families do not always stay in the same place on the continuum.

3 Explain that in an ideal family, family members learn skills to make responsible decisions and to remain interdependent. Define interdependence. **Interdependence** is a condition in which two people depend upon one another, yet each has a separate identity. Draw four circles on the chalkboard (see illustration 1). Show students that although the circles are touching, each circle has an

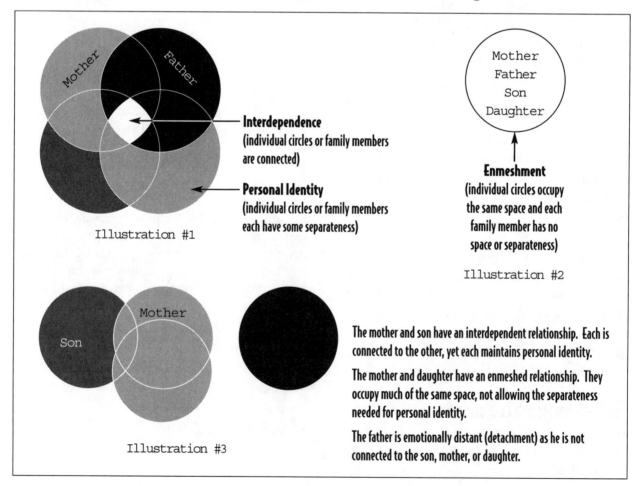

Interdependence
(individual circles or family members are connected)

Personal Identity
(individual circles or family members each have some separateness)

Illustration #1

Enmeshment
(individual circles occupy the same space and each family member has no space or separateness)

Illustration #2

Illustration #3

The mother and son have an interdependent relationship. Each is connected to the other, yet each maintains personal identity.

The mother and daughter have an enmeshed relationship. They occupy much of the same space, not allowing the separateness needed for personal identity.

The father is emotionally distant (detachment) as he is not connected to the son, mother, or daughter.

area that is separate. Explain that each circle represents a member of an ideal family. In an ideal family, members are connected to each other but still remain independent.

4 Tell students that in a dysfunctional family, family members do not learn skills to make responsible decisions. Family members become enmeshed. Define enmeshment. **Enmeshment** is a condition in which a person becomes obsessed with the needs of another person and no longer can recognize his or her own needs. Draw four more circles on the board. Draw these four circles directly on top of one another (see illustration 2). Explain that each circle represents a member of a dysfunctionally enmeshed family. In a dysfunctionally enmeshed family, members become entirely dependent upon other family members.

5 Give each student a copy of the Blackline Master *Roots and Characteristics of Codependence*. Explain that family members who become enmeshed suffer from codependence. Define codependence. **Codependence** is a mental disorder in which a person denies feelings and begins to cope in harmful ways.

6 Draw four more circles on the chalkboard (illustration 3). Explain to students that there are varying degrees of interdependence and enmeshment in all families. Tell students that the four circles represent another dysfunctional family. In this family, the father is removed from the rest of the family. The mother and the son have a healthy interdependent relationship. The mother and the daughter are strongly enmeshed. Ask students to describe what might be going on in this family. Students might suggest that the adult son is independent of parents, but that the adult daughter is dependent on parents. They might suggest that the parents are divorcing, and that the mother has been trying to fill new emotional needs with her daughter.

7 Ask for several student volunteers. Ask the student volunteers to draw different family circles on the chalkboard. Tell them they are not to draw their own family. Ask students to describe the family they have drawn.

8 Give each student a copy of the Blackline Master *Codependence Self-Check*. Ask students to complete the *Codependence Self-Check* at home. Tell them they can discuss this self-check with their parents or guardians. Tell them you will not collect it.

9 Ask students what adjustments a person must make if his or her parents divorce. Students might say that a person would have to adjust to less or no contact with one parent. Ask students what adjustments a person must make if he or she lives in a single parent family. Students might say that a person must look for a mentor to serve as a role model. Ask students what adjustments a person must make if his or her parent remarries. Students might say that a person must respect the new guidelines for his or her behavior. Ask students what adjustments a person must make if a parent loses a job. Students might say that a person must discuss with his or her parents what changes will occur in the family budget. Ask students what adjustments a person must make if a parent goes to jail. Students might say that a person must discuss his or her feelings with a trusted adult.

Assessment

On a sheet of paper, have students define family, ideal family, dysfunctional family, enmeshment, and interdependence. Have them discuss what parents teach children in an ideal family. Have students draw family circles describing an ideal family and a dysfunctional family.

The Family Continuum

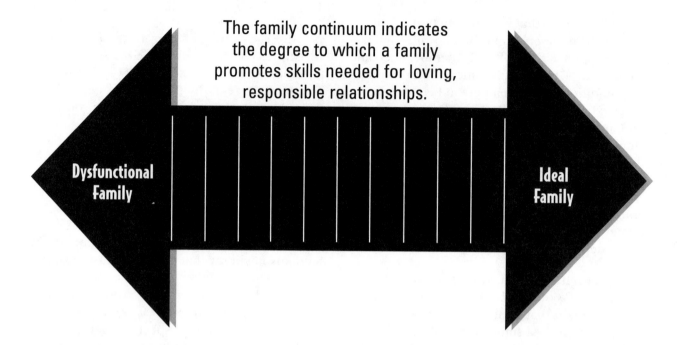

The family continuum indicates the degree to which a family promotes skills needed for loving, responsible relationships.

Dysfunctional Family

Ideal Family

In ideal families, family members have:

1. Self-respecting behavior
2. Healthful attitudes toward sexuality
3. Effective communication skills
4. Good character
5. Responsible decision-making skills
6. Conflict resolution skills
7. Effective coping skills
8. The ability to delay gratification
9. The ability to integrate love and sex
10. The ability to give and receive acts of kindness
11. A work ethic
12. Respect for authority

In dysfunctional families, family members have:

1. Self-centered behavior
2. Unhealthful attitudes toward sexuality
3. Ineffective communication skills
4. Poor character
5. Poor decision-making skills
6. Inadequate conflict resolution skills
7. Inadequate coping skills
8. An inability to delay gratification
9. An inability to integrate love and sex
10. An inability to give and receive acts of kindness
11. A sloppy work ethic
12. Disrespect for authority

Roots and Characteristics of Codependence

People who are codependent struggle in their relationships. They cannot develop intimacy. Intimacy is a deep and meaningful kind of sharing between two people. People with codependence avoid intimacy by choosing one extreme or another.

1. They focus on trying to please another person or people and deny their own needs.

or

2. They avoid being close to another person or people to keep from being hurt.

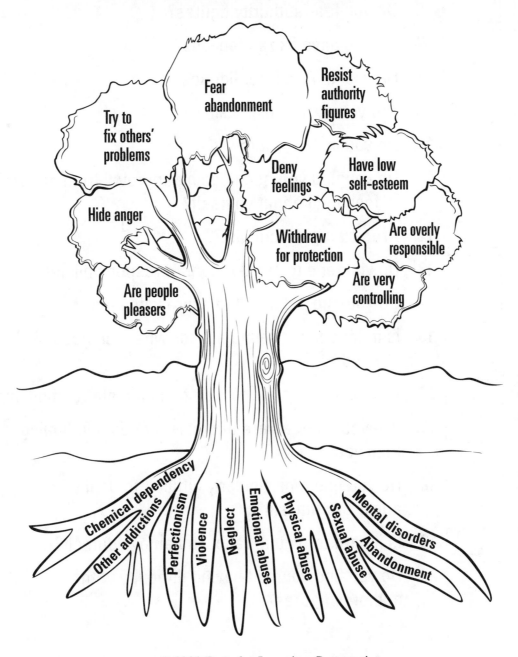

Codependence Self-Check

Yes	No	
☐	☐	**1.** Do you try to hide your anger?
☐	☐	**2.** Are you a people pleaser?
☐	☐	**3.** Are you a caretaker?
☐	☐	**4.** Are you a controlling person?
☐	☐	**5.** Do you fear abandonment?
☐	☐	**6.** Do you fear authority figures?
☐	☐	**7.** Do you have frozen feelings?
☐	☐	**8.** Do you lack self-confidence?
☐	☐	**9.** Are you overly responsible?
☐	☐	**10.** Do you isolate yourself?
☐	☐	**11.** Do you find yourself needing approval from others to feel good about yourself?
☐	☐	**12.** Are you a perfectionist?
☐	☐	**13.** Do you tend to avoid or ignore responsibilities?
☐	☐	**14.** Do you find it difficult to express feelings?
☐	☐	**15.** Is it difficult for you to ask for what you need from others?
☐	☐	**16.** Is it difficult for you to maintain intimate relationships?
☐	☐	**17.** Are you more aware of others' needs and feelings than your own?
☐	☐	**18.** Do you find it particularly difficult to deal with anger or criticism?
☐	☐	**19.** Is it hard for you to relax and enjoy yourself?
☐	☐	**20.** Do you find yourself having difficulty with authority figures?

Pregnancy and Childbirth

■ Grades 9–12

Pregnancy Test

The Curriculum

Life Skill

■ I will learn about pregnancy and childbirth.

Objectives

■ Students will explain how a baby's sex and inherited traits are determined.

■ Students will discuss lifestyle habits that a couple should adopt before the couple plans to have a baby.

■ Students will explain fertilization.

■ Students will discuss male and female infertility.

■ Students will discuss ways to increase fertility and the probability of conception.

■ Students will identify assisted reproduction technologies.

■ Students will explain how pregnancy and the estimated delivery date are determined.

■ Students will discuss the importance of prenatal care.

■ Students will identify atypical conditions that might occur during pregnancy.

■ Students will discuss ways birth defects are detected.

The National Health Education Standards

■ Students will comprehend concepts related to health promotion and disease prevention.

■ Students will demonstrate the ability to access valid health information and health-promoting products and services.

Preparing to Teach the Lesson Plan

Materials

None

Blackline Masters

Conception

Sex Determination

Amniocentesis

Ultrasound

Artificial Insemination

Teaching the Lesson Plan

1 Explain that teens are not ready to marry and have a baby right now. However, teens can learn about marriage, pregnancy, and childbirth right now. This lesson is about pregnancy. Explain that a married couple should adopt certain lifestyle habits before planning to have a baby. These include:

• healthful diet

• responsible use of medicine

• drug-free lifestyle

• physical activity and fitness

These habits get the female in the best condition she can be. A male who has these habits supports his partner. In addition, by not smoking he protects the health of the sperm he produces. By not smoking, he also protects the health of his partner. By not drinking alcohol and using other harmful drugs, he protects the quality and quantity of the sperm he produces.

2 Give students a copy of the Blackline Master *Conception.* Define conception or fertilization. **Conception**, or **fertilization**, is the union of a sperm and ovum. Explain that one ovum matures and is released from an ovary each month. Define ovulation. **Ovulation** is the release of a mature ovum by an ovary and occurs on or about the fourteenth day before the expected beginning of the next menstrual period. The ovum enters a fallopian tube. Conception, or fertilization, can occur if sperm are present. Conception usually takes place in the upper third of the fallopian tube.

3 Tell students that heredity is determined at conception. Define heredity. **Heredity** is the passing of characteristics from biological parents to their children. Explain that all body cells, except sperm and ova, contain 23 pairs of chromosomes. Define chromosome. A **chromosome** is a threadlike structure that carries genes. Define gene. A **gene** is a unit of hereditary matter. Give students a copy of the Blackline Master *Sex Determination.* Explain that sex is determined at conception. In a female, the 23 pairs of chromosomes are identical. In a male, one pair of chromosomes is not made up of identical chromosomes. In both males and females, one pair is called the sex chromosomes. In females, the pair of sex chromosomes is identical and is called XX. Every ovum produced by a female contains an X chromosome. Sperm produced by a male contain either an X or a Y chromosome. The presence of a Y chromosome is essential for the development of male characteristics.

4 Explain that some diseases are inherited. Define genetic counseling. **Genetic counseling** is a process in which a trained professional interprets medical information concerning genetics to prospective parents. This helps prospective parents plan for the care of their baby before it is born. Sickle cell disease is an example of a disorder linked to genes. Define sickle cell disease. **Sickle cell disease** is a genetic disorder caused by an abnormal type of hemoglobin. A person's red blood cells are sickle-shaped, fragile, and do not carry oxygen as they should. Symptoms are fatigue, headache, and shortness of breath.

Give each student a copy of the Blackline Master *Amniocentesis.* Define amniocentesis. **Amniocentesis** is a simple diagnostic procedure in which a needle is inserted through the uterus to extract fluid from the amniotic sac. Define amniotic sac. The **amniotic sac** is a pouch of fluid that surrounds a fetus. Cells are extracted from the amniotic fluid and analyzed. They provide information about genetics. This also helps prospective parents plan for the care of their baby before it is born.

5 Give each student a copy of the Blackline Master *Ultrasound.* Define ultrasound. An **ultrasound** is a diagnostic technique that uses sound waves to create pictures of internal body structures. An ultrasound is used in different ways. During pregnancy, it is used to create a picture of the developing baby shown on a monitor. An ultrasound has made it possible to visualize the embryo as early as six to eight weeks after a female has missed her last menstrual period. A physician can monitor its growth. A physician can use it before delivery to see if the mother-to-be will have multiple births and to see the position of the baby or babies.

6 Explain that a female needs a pregnancy test if she misses a menstrual period. A missed menstrual period can indicate pregnancy. However, a female also might miss a menstrual period for other reasons, such as stress, poor diet, too much physical activity, an eating disorder, and illness. Blood and urine tests and a pelvic examination are used to confirm pregnancy. The estimated delivery date is 40 weeks from the beginning of the last menstrual period or a total of 280 days. A pregnant female needs prenatal care. This includes regular medical examinations, healthful diet, screening for gestational diabetes, screening for STDs, and monitored use of prescription drugs.

7 Have students use two pieces of notebook paper. One one piece, they are to write YES. On the other piece of paper, they are to write NO WAY. Then explain that each student will stand and state either a healthful or harmful habit practiced by a couple expecting its first child. If the habit is healthful, they are to hold up the YES. If the habit is harmful,

624 © 2001 Everyday Learning Corporation

they are to hold up the NO WAY. For example, a student might say, "The father-to-be smokes cigars to celebrate the pregnancy." The other students in class should hold up NO WAY.

8 Discuss atypical conditions that might occur in pregnancy: pseudocyesis, ectopic pregnancy, Rh factor, rubella, multiple births, miscarriage, and preterm birth.

9 Define infertility. **Infertility** is the inability to conceive a child after a year of unprotected sexual intercourse. A male might be infertile because he has a low sperm count or his sperm do not move. He might be infertile because he had an STD or mumps. A female might be infertile because she does not ovulate. She also might be infertile because she has had an STD. Habits, such as smoking, drinking, and other drug use, can produce infertility in both males and females. Fertility might be increased by timing of sexual intercourse, frequency of sexual intercourse, position during sexual intercourse, fertility drugs, surgical procedures, and reduced stress.

10 **OPTIONAL** Have students research the following assisted reproductive technologies: intrauterine insemination (IUI), male factor infertility treatments, in vitro fertilization (IVF), gamete intrafallopian transfer (GIFT), zygote intrafallopian transfer (ZIFT), donor egg IVF, embryo freezing, and surrogate mothers. Check their findings against pages 191–193.

Assessment

Have students write The Top Ten Wish List for a Developing Baby. Their list might include habits a couple should adopt before the pregnancy, prenatal care the mother-to-be should receive, tests the mother-to-be might have, etc. Have students present The Top Ten Wish Lists for a Developing Baby they have prepared.

Conception

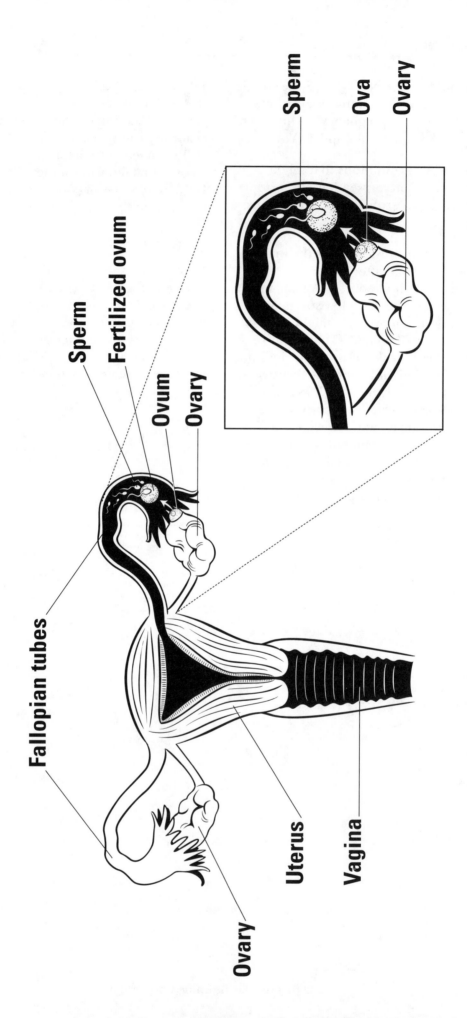

Fallopian tubes

Sperm

Fertilized ovum

Ovum

Ovary

Ovary

Uterus

Vagina

Sperm

Ova

Ovary

Sex Determination

Ovum

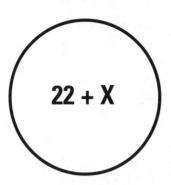

Sperm

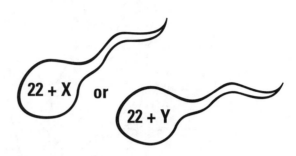

Ova always have 22 chromosomes plus an X sex chromosome (for a total of 23 chromosomes).

Sperm always have 22 chromosomes plus either an X or a Y sex chromosome (for a total of 23 chromosomes).

A fertilized ovum has 44 chromosomes plus 2 sex chromosomes (for a total of 46 chromosomes).

It's a girl!

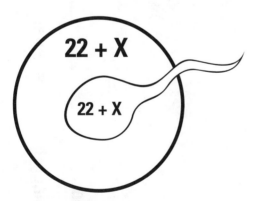

44 + XX
(for a total of
46 chromosomes)

A fertilized ovum with 44 chromosomes plus XX will develop into a girl.

It's a boy!

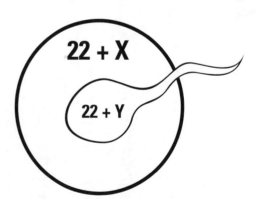

44 + XY
(for a total of
46 chromosomes)

A fertilized ovum with 44 chromosomes plus XY will develop into a boy.

Amniocentesis

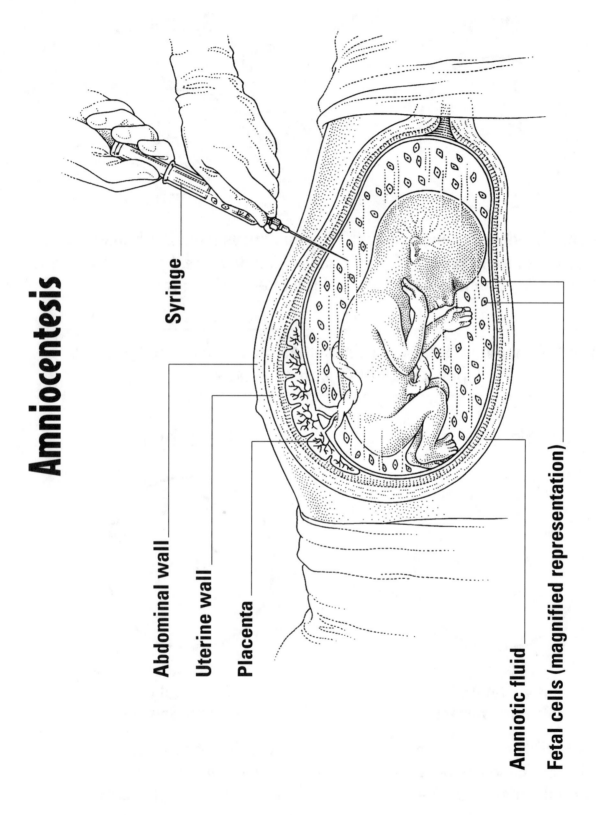

Syringe

Abdominal wall

Uterine wall

Placenta

Amniotic fluid

Fetal cells (magnified representation)

Ultrasound

Ultrasound is a diagnostic technique that uses sound waves to create pictures of internal body structures.

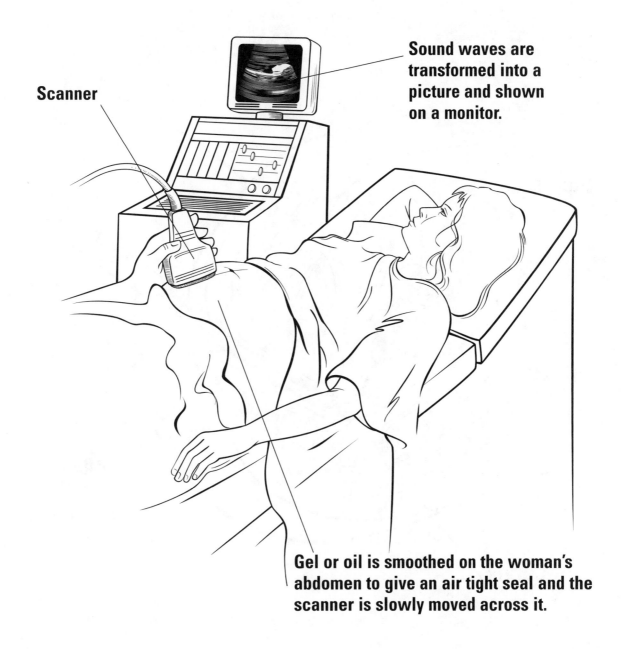

Scanner

Sound waves are transformed into a picture and shown on a monitor.

Gel or oil is smoothed on the woman's abdomen to give an air tight seal and the scanner is slowly moved across it.

Artificial Insemination

Artificial insemination is introducing semen into the vagina or uterus by artificial means so that conception can occur.

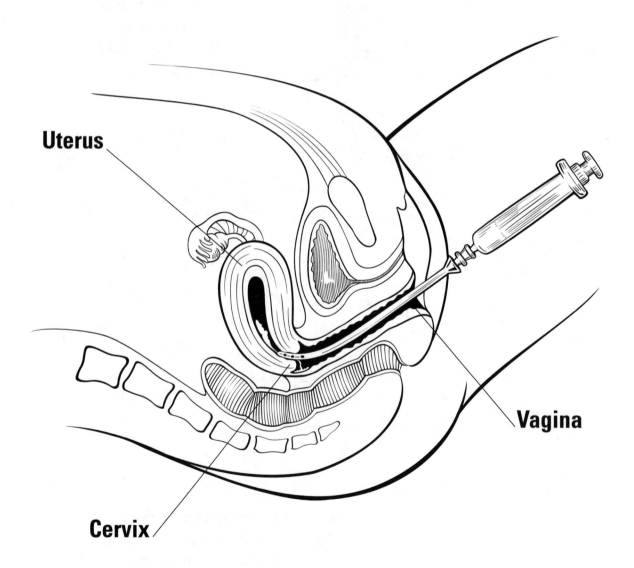

Uterus

Vagina

Cervix

Bonding with Baby

The Curriculum

Life Skill

■ I will learn about pregnancy and childbirth.

Objectives

■ Students will describe the development of the embryo and fetus during three trimesters of pregnancy.

■ Students will describe the effects of pregnancy on the mother-to-be and father-to-be.

■ Students will discuss the risks associated with teen pregnancy.

■ Students will discuss birth place alternatives and childbirth preparation.

■ Students will discuss pain management alternatives for childbirth.

■ Students will discuss what happens during each of the three stages of labor.

■ Students will discuss the postpartum period, including breastfeeding and parental bonding.

The National Health Education Standards

■ Students will comprehend concepts related to health promotion and disease prevention.

■ Students will demonstrate the ability to access valid health information and health-promoting products and services.

Preparing to Teach the Lesson Plan

Materials

Paper

Paper clips

Scissors

Blackline Masters

Fraternal Twins and Identical Twins

Ectopic Pregnancy

Childbirth

Cesarean Section

Birth Positions

Teaching the Lesson Plan

1 Tell students that in this lesson they will learn about pregnancy and childbirth. Explain to students that they are not ready for marriage or parenthood. Teens must concentrate on completing the developmental tasks of adolescence right now. They must gain financial and emotional independence from adults.

Explain that even though students are not ready to marry and become parents, they need to know some facts now. They can learn facts about pregnancy and childbirth. After conception, a fertilized egg continues to divide and move through the fallopian tube. The fertilized egg divides to become two cells. The two cells then divide to become four cells. The four cells divide to become eight cells, and so on. This cluster of cells attaches to the endometrium, or lining of the uterus. Define embryo. Embryo is the name given a developing baby through the second month of growth after conception. Give each student a copy of the Blackline Masters *Fraternal Twins and Identical Twins* and *Ectopic Pregnancy*.

2 Explain that there are three stages of pregnancy: the first, second, and third trimesters. Explain that the first trimester is the first three months after conception. By the end of the second month of pregnancy, an embryo is called a fetus. Define fetus. A **fetus** is the name given a developing baby from the ninth week until birth. During the first trimester the embryo starts to form arms, legs, fingers, toes, ears, eyes, and facial features. At the end of the third month, the major internal organs have begun to form and function. At the end of the first trimester, the fetus is about four inches long and weighs one ounce.

During the second trimester, the fingernails, toenails, eyebrows, and eyelashes develop. Teeth begin to form, lips appear, and head hair might start to grow. The mother-to-be might feel the developing baby moving during the second trimester. At the end of the second trimester, the fetus is about 12 inches long and weighs approximately 1.5 pounds.

Explain that if a baby is born prematurely at the beginning of the third trimester (the seventh month), it has a 20 percent chance of surviving. A baby born between 38 and 40 weeks of pregnancy is considered to be full-term. At the end of the third trimester when a baby is full-term, it is between 19 and 21 inches long and usually weighs between six and nine pounds.

3 Tell students that a married couple has many options regarding the place of birth of the baby. Explain that besides the hospital setting, a married couple might choose to have a baby in a birthing room within a hospital, at a birth center, or at home. Define labor. **Labor** is the process of childbirth. There are signs that indicate the beginning of labor. Muscular contractions of the uterus start, become more intense, last longer, and become more frequent. The amniotic sac might rupture before or shortly after labor begins. A discharge or gushing of water from the vagina indicates the

sac has broken. There might be a bloody show. The bloody show is the discharge of the mucous plug that sealed the cervix during pregnancy.

4 Explain that several pain management techniques are available for the mother-to-be. The couple might have taken childbirth preparation classes to help the mother-to-be manage labor pains. The couple might have taken Lamaze classes. The Lamaze Method is a childbirth preparation method based on relaxation and controlled breathing. These methods help the mother-to-be focus on something other than labor pains.

5 Give each student a copy of the Blackline Master *Childbirth*. Tell students that there are three distinct stages of labor. The first stage of labor, dilation of the cervix, is the longest stage. It can last from two hours to an entire day. Dilation or widening of the cervix occurs. The cervical opening enlarges eight to ten centimeters, wide enough for the baby to move through. The second stage, delivery of the baby, begins when the cervix is completely dilated and ends with the delivery of the baby. The baby moves farther down into the birth canal, usually head first. The mother-to-be pushes and the muscles in the uterus contract to push the baby out. The third stage, delivery of the placenta, is the expulsion of the afterbirth. Define afterbirth. The **afterbirth** is the placenta that is expelled in the final stage of labor. If this does not occur naturally, the physician removes it.

6 Give each student a copy of the Blackline Master *Birth Positions*. Explain that some babies are in the breech or transverse position before birth. Define breech birth position. A **breech birth position** is a position in which the baby's buttocks is presented first. Define transverse birth position. A **transverse birth position** is a position in which the baby's shoulder, arm, or hand is presented first. When a baby cannot be delivered vaginally, a cesarean section might need to be performed. Define cesarean section or c-section. A **cesarean section**, or **c-section**, is the surgical removal of the fetus through an incision made in the mother's abdomen and uterus. Give each student a copy of the Blackline Master *Cesarean Section.*

7 Define postpartum period. The **postpartum period** is the first several weeks after delivery. Define bonding. **Bonding** is a process in which people develop a feeling of closeness. Bonding between a baby and its parents begins with soft touches, words, and physical closeness. A mother might bond with her baby when she breastfeeds the baby. A father might bond with his baby when he gives the baby a bottle. Both parents might sing to the baby, rock the baby, and change its diaper.

8 Have students cut strips of paper. Have them write words that describe ways a mother or father might bond with a baby. For example, a student might write, "Change the baby's diaper" or "Rock the baby to sleep" or "Smile at the baby." Have students attach a paper clip to each of the strips of paper they prepare. Place all of the strips of paper on the floor. Have students stand in a circle around the strips of paper. Have one student take a magnet and place it by one of the strips of paper. The magnet will attach to the strip of paper. Have the student read what is on the strip of paper. Explain that a parent can become attached or bond with a baby in this way. Further explain that this attachment influences the rest of the baby's life.

Assessment

Have students design a flyer that might be distributed by physicians or hospitals. The purpose of the flyer is to encourage prospective parents to sign up for childbirth classes. The flyer should provide a brief description of:

- the three trimesters of pregnancy,
- birthplace alternatives,
- stages of childbirth,
- importance of bonding.

Fraternal Twins and Identical Twins

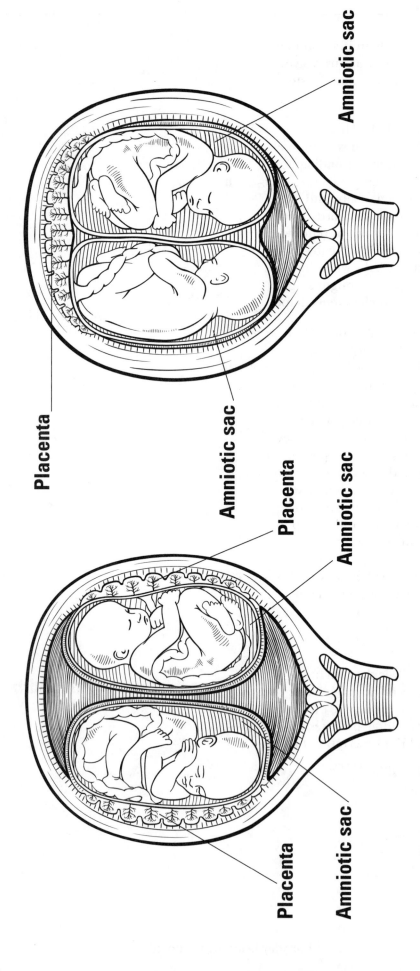

Amniotic sac

Placenta

Amniotic sac

Placenta

Amniotic sac

Placenta

Amniotic sac

Fraternal twins are twins that develop from two separate ova that are fertilized by two different sperm.

Identical twins are twins that develop from a single ovum fertilized by a single sperm.

Ectopic Pregnancy

An ectopic pregnancy is a condition wherein a fertilized ovum implants itself in any place other than in the lining of the uterus.

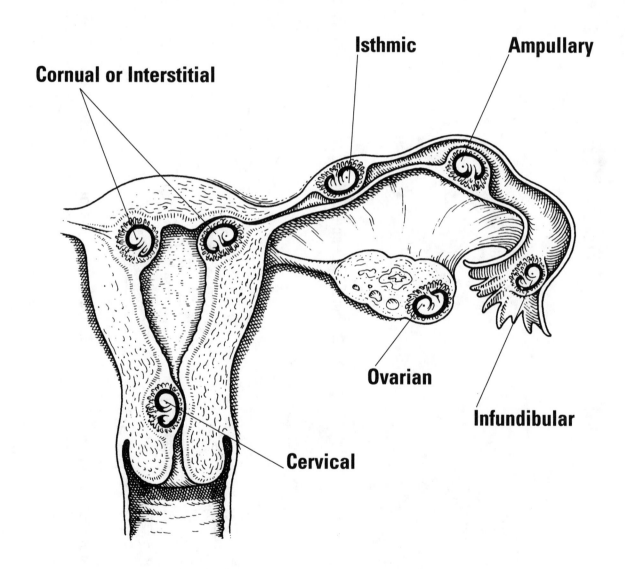

Childbirth

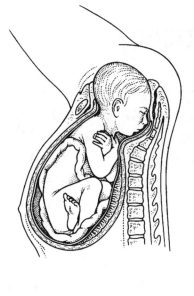

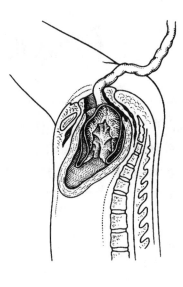

1. Beginning descent

3. Extension—emergence begins

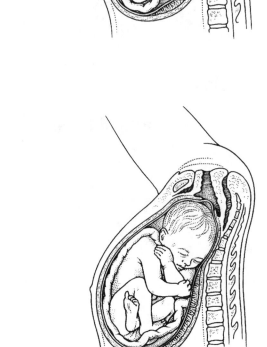

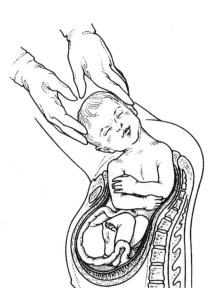

2. Further descent, rotation

5. Delivery of the posterior shoulder

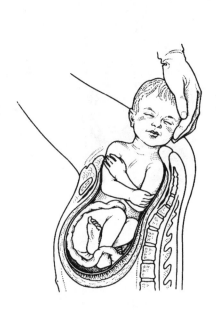

4. Anterior shoulder delivered

6. Placenta separates from uterine wall

636

Cesarean Section

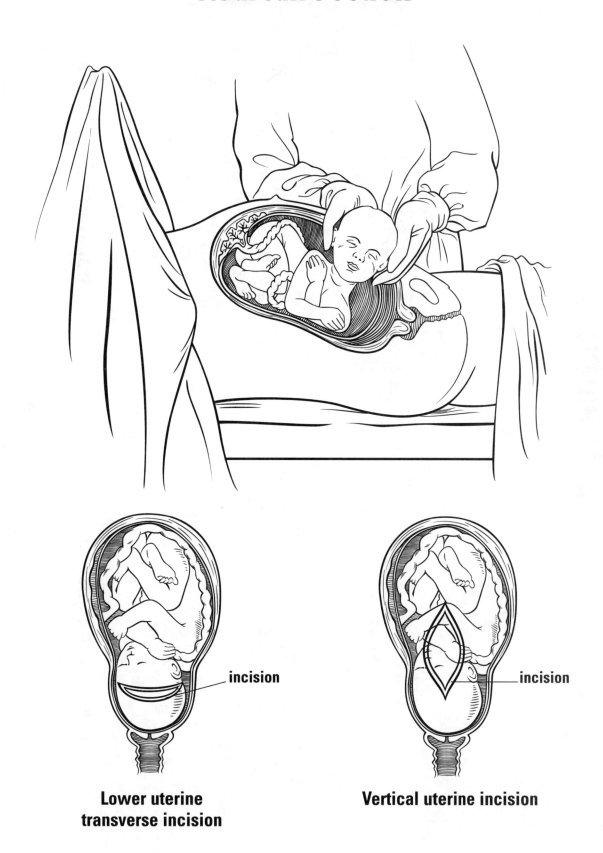

incision

incision

Lower uterine transverse incision

Vertical uterine incision

Birth Positions

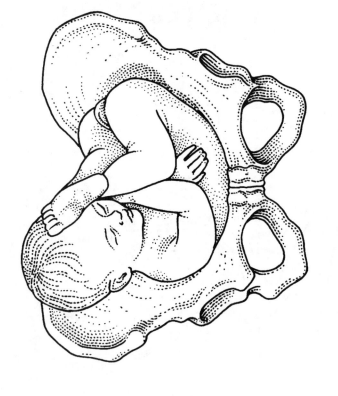

Transverse Birth Position

Breech Birth Position

Glossary

a

abandonment: removing oneself from those whose care is one's responsibility.

abstinence from sex: choosing not to be sexually active.

abuse: the harmful treatment of another person.

abuser: a person who is abusive.

acquaintance rape: rape in which the rapist is known to the person who is raped.

Acquired Immune Deficiency Syndrome (AIDS): a condition that results when infection with HIV causes a breakdown of the body's ability to fight other infections.

active listening: a way of responding to show that a person hears and understands.

addiction: a compelling need to take a drug or engage in a specific behavior.

adverse environment: a set of conditions and surroundings that interferes with a person's growth, development, and success.

aerosolized pentamidine isethionate: a drug to prevent *Pneumocystis carinii* pneumonia (PCP).

affection: a fond or tender feeling that a person has toward another person.

afterbirth: the placenta that is expelled in the final stage of labor.

AIDS dementia complex: a loss of brain function caused by HIV infection.

Al-Anon: a recovery program for people who have friends or family members with alcoholism.

Alateen: a recovery program for adolescents who have friends or family members with alcoholism.

alcohol: a drug that depresses the central nervous system and often changes behavior.

Alcoholics Anonymous (AA): a recovery program for people who have alcoholism.

alienation: the feeling that one is apart from others.

amenorrhea: the absence of menstruation.

amniocentesis: a simple diagnostic procedure in which a needle is inserted through the uterus to extract fluid from the amniotic sac.

amphetamines: drugs that "speed up" the central nervous system.

Amplicor HIV-1 monitor test: a test that measures the level of HIV in the blood.

anabolic steroids: drugs produced from male sex hormones.

andropause or the **male climacteric:** the decrease in male sexual function that results from diminished testosterone.

anemia: a condition in which the oxygen-carrying pigment in the blood is below normal.

anger: the feeling of being irritated, annoyed, and/or furious.

anger triggers: thoughts or events that cause a person to become angry.

annulment: a legal way to end a marriage in which it is decided that what was thought to be a legally binding marriage was not.

antibodies: proteins produced by B cells that help destroy pathogens inside the body.

areola: the darkened area in the center of each breast, and it contains oil-producing sebaceous glands.

asymptomatic: being without signs and symptoms.

authority: the power and right to apply laws and rules.

autoclave: to sterilize with steam under pressure.

AZT or **zidovudine:** a drug that slows down the rate at which HIV multiplies.

b

B cells: the blood cells that produce antibodies.

bacterial vaginosis: an STD caused by the *Gardnerella vaginalis* bacterium.

balanced friendship: a friendship in which two people give and receive acts of kindness between each other.

Bartholin's glands: a pair of bean-shaped glands that are located near the labia minora and that secrete a few drops of fluid during sexual excitement.

basal body temperature method: a birth control method in which a female uses her basal body temperature to predict ovulation.

behavior modification: a disciplinary technique in which positive rewards are used to encourage desirable behavior and negative consequences are used to stop undesirable behavior.

benign prostatic hyperplasia: a condition in which the prostate gland increases in size and puts pressure on the urethra, causing a decrease in urine flow.

bimanual pelvic examination: a procedure in which a physician or nurse practitioner inserts the index and middle finger of one hand into the vagina and puts the other hand on the abdomen to check reproductive organs.

biopsy: the removal of tissue from a lump to determine if cancerous cells are present.

blended family or **stepfamily:** a family consisting of the marriage partners, children one or both of them had previously, and the children whom they have by their marriage to one another.

blood pressure: the force exerted by the flowing blood against the walls of arteries.

body or **shaft:** the main part of the penis.

bonding: a process in which people develop a feeling of closeness.

Braxton Hicks contractions: irregular, painless contractions of the uterine muscles.

breast cancer: a disease in which malignant tumors grow in the breast tissue.

breast implants: materials that are surgically implanted into breast tissue to improve the size and shape of a breast.

breasts: organs consisting of fatty tissue and mammary gland tissue.

breast self-examination (BSE): a cancer screening procedure in which a female visually examines her breasts, palpates them to detect any lumps, and squeezes her nipples to check for any clear or bloody discharge.

breech birth position: a position in which the baby's buttocks is presented first.

C

candidiasis: an STD caused by the fungus, *Candida albicans.*

cells: highly organized units that are microscopic and make up all living things.

center: a person who is self-centered.

cervical biopsy: the surgical removal of cervical tissue for the purpose of laboratory examination.

cervix: the lowest part of the uterus.

cesarean section or **c-section:** the surgical removal of the fetus through an incision made in the mother's abdomen and uterus.

chancres: hard, round, painless sores with raised edges resulting from syphilis.

chancroid: an STD caused by the *Hemophilus ducreyi* bacterium.

character: a person's use of self-control to act on responsible values.

chemical dependence: the compelling need to take a drug even though it harms the body, mind, or relationships.

child abuse: the harmful treatment of a minor.

childsitter: a person who provides care for infants and children with the permission of a parent or guardian.

chlamydial infections: STDs caused by the bacterium *Chlamydia trachomatis*, that might result in inflammation of the urethra and epididymis in males and inflammation of the vagina and cervix in females.

cholesterol: a saturated fat that is normally found in the brain, nerves, and skin and is associated with a risk of cardiovascular disease.

chromosome: a threadlike structure that carries genes.

cilia: hairlike projections on the inner surface of the oviducts.

circumcision: the surgical removal of the foreskin from the penis.

citizenship: following the laws of a person's community and nation.

clinger: a person who is needy and dependent.

clitoris: a small, highly sensitive, cylindrical body about 3/4 inch (2.00 cm) long and about 3/16 inch (0.50 cm) in diameter projecting between the labia minora.

cocaine: a drug that stimulates the central nervous system and its use frequently results in drug dependence.

codependence: a mental disorder in which a person denies feelings and begins to cope in harmful ways.

codependent: a person who wants to rescue and control another person.

codominance: a condition that occurs when two different variations of a gene, called alleles, are inherited from the mother and the father.

colostrum: a yellowish fluid that is secreted by the mammary glands in preparation of milk production.

colposcopy: a screening exam in which a microscope is used to detect abnormal and cancerous cells.

commitment: a pledge or promise that is made.

communication: the sharing of emotions, thoughts, and information with another person.

computer addiction: the compelling need to use the computer beyond required use, such as for work.

conception: the union of a sperm and ovum.

conflict: a disagreement between people or between choices.

conflict avoidance: a conflict response style in which a person avoids disagreements at all costs.

conflict confrontation: a conflict response style that attempts to settle a disagreement in a hostile, defiant, and aggressive way.

conflict resolution: a conflict response style in which a person uses conflict resolution skills to resolve disagreements.

conflict resolution skills: steps that can be taken to settle a disagreement in a responsible way.

conflict response style: a pattern of behavior that a person demonstrates when a conflict arises.

congenital syphilis: the transmission of syphilis to a fetus from an infected pregnant female.

conjoined twins or **Siamese twins:** twins who are physically joined at birth.

conscience: a person's inner sense of right and wrong.

consumer: a person who chooses sources of information and buys or uses products and services.

controller: a person who is possessive, jealous, and domineering.

conversation: a verbal exchange of feelings, thoughts, ideas, and opinions.

coping: a person's ability to confront negative feelings such as hurt or anger that can result from life changes and to make appropriate readjustments.

corona: the rim or crown where the glans rises slightly over the shaft.

corpus or **body:** the upper muscular division of the uterus.

corpus cavernosum: the two upper cylinders containing erectile tissue on the top of the penis.

corpus luteum: the yellow glandular body that is formed in the ovary from the follicular remains.

corpus spongiosum: the single cylinder containing erectile tissue beneath the penis.

courage: showing strength when a person otherwise would be afraid.

couvade: a condition in which a male experiences the same physical and psychological symptoms of pregnancy that the expectant mother experiences, including depression, nausea, vomiting, and labor pains.

Cowper's glands or **bulbourethral glands:** two small pea-sized glands located on each side of the urethra and secrete a lubrication fluid.

crack: a drug that is pure cocaine and produces rapid ups and downs.

creative intimacy: the sharing of efforts to accomplish tasks and projects.

cremaster muscles: muscles that contract to pull the testes closer to the body to warm them and relax to lower the testes away from the body to cool them.

crowning: the beginning of the head emerging during birth.

cryosurgery: a procedure in which the tissue is frozen in order to remove small numbers of cancerous cells from the surface of the cervix.

cryptorchidism: a condition in which one or both testes do not descend through the inguinal canal into the scrotum before birth.

curfew: a fixed time when a person is to be at home.

custodial parent: the parent with whom a child or children live and the parent who has the legal right to make decisions about the health and well-being of the child or children.

cycle of abuse: the repeating of abuse from one generation to the next.

cyst: a sac that is formed when fluid becomes trapped in a lymph duct.

cystitis: the inflammation of the urinary bladder.

cytomegalovirus or **CMV:** a virus in the herpes group.

d

date rape: rape that occurs in a dating situation.

dating: having social plans with another person.

dating skills: competencies that help a person when he or she has a date.

ddI: a drug that slows the rate at which HIV multiplies.

decision: a choice that a person makes.

delay gratification: to postpone satisfaction until an issue has been confronted and resolved.

delayed gratification: voluntarily postponing an immediate reward in order to complete a task before enjoying a reward.

denial: a condition in which a person refuses to recognize what he or she is feeling because it is extremely painful.

deoxyribonucleic acid (DNA): a large molecule that contains all the genetic information needed to form and sustain life.

desensitization: the effect of reacting less and less to the exposure to something.

determination: working hard to get what a person wants.

developmental stages of marriage: five stages of marriage during which couples must master certain tasks in order to develop and maintain intimacy.

developmental task: an achievement that needs to be mastered to reach the next level of maturity.

diabetes: a disease in which the body is unable to process sugar in food in normal ways.

diethylstilbestrol (DES): a drug that was used to prevent miscarriage.

differentiation: the process by which cells become more complex and assume adult forms.

digital rectal examination: an examination in which the physician inserts a gloved, lubricated finger into the rectum and examines the prostate and rectum for hard or lumpy areas.

dilation: the widening of the cervix.

dilation and curettage (D and C): a surgical procedure in which the cervical opening is dilated by means of probes of increasingly larger sizes until a metal loop curette can be inserted to scrape the uterine lining.

discipline: training that develops self-control.

discriminatory behavior: to make distinctions in treatment or to show behavior in favor of or prejudiced against an individual or group of people.

dispiriting relationships: relationships that depress the spirit and contribute to a lack of well-being.

displacement: the releasing of anger on someone or something other than the cause of the anger.

dissolution: a legal way to end a marriage in which the marriage partners decide the terms with respect to property, custody, and support.

distancer: a person who is emotionally unavailable to others.

divorce: a legal way to end a marriage in which a judge or court decides the terms with respect to property, custody, and support.

domestic violence: violence that occurs within a family.

dominant gene: a gene that overrides the expression of the other gene.

doula: an assistant to the new mother during birth and in the first few days after giving birth.

downsize the workforce: to reduce the number of employees in a company.

drug abuse: the use of drugs that lessen the user's ability to function normally or that are harmful to the user or others.

drug dependence: the continued use of a drug even though it harms the body, mind, and relationships.

drug misuse: the incorrect use of a prescription or over-the-counter (OTC) drug.

drugs: substances that change the way the body and/or mind work.

dysfunctional family: a family that lacks the skills to be successful and to function in healthful ways.

dysmenorrhea: very painful menstruation.

e

ectopic pregnancy: a condition wherein a fertilized ovum implants itself in any place other than in the lining of the uterus.

effacement: the thinning out of the cervix.

ejaculation: the sudden expulsion of seminal fluid from an erect penis.

ejaculatory duct: a short, straight tube that passes into the prostate gland and opens into the urethra.

elder abuse: the harmful treatment of an aged family member.

ELISA or **enzyme-linked immunosorbent assay:** a blood test used to check for antibodies for HIV.

emotional abuse: "putting down" another person and making the person feel worthless.

empowered: to be energized because a person has some control over his or her decisions and behavior.

enabler: a person who supports the harmful behavior of others.

endometriosis: a condition in which the endometrial tissue grows somewhere other than in the lining of the uterus.

endometritis: the inflammation of the uterine lining.

endometrium: the inner lining of the uterus.

entertainment: something that is designed to hold the interest of people.

entertainment rating systems: ratings to assist people in determining the suitability of content for certain age groups.

environment: everything that is around a person and the place in which a person lives.

epididymis: a comma-shaped structure found on the back and upper surface of each testis.

epididymitis: an inflammation of the epididymis.

epidural: an injection of an anesthetic into the back that eliminates pain below the waist.

episiotomy: a cut made in the perineum to facilitate easier passage of the baby's head through the vagina and to prevent the vaginal tissues from tearing.

erectile dysfunction: the inability to sustain an erection sufficient for sexual intercourse.

erection: an involuntary process that occurs when the spongy layers inside the penis are engorged with blood and the penis elongates.

estrogen: a female sex hormone that produces female secondary sex characteristics and affects the menstrual cycle.

exhibitionism: the exposure of the sexual organs to other people in situations in which exposure is socially defined as inappropriate and when exposure, at least in part, is for the purpose of obtaining personal sexual arousal and gratification.

extended family members: the members of a family in addition to parents, brothers, and sisters.

f

fairness: following the same rules so everyone has a fair chance.

fallopian tubes or **oviducts:** tubes that extend from near the ovaries to the uterus.

false pregnancy or **pseudocyesis:** a condition wherein a female believes that she is pregnant and shows some of the signs and symptoms of pregnancy, even though she is not pregnant.

family: a group of people who are related by blood, adoption, or marriage.

family relationships: the connections a person has with family members, including extended family members.

Family Round Table, The: a special time when family members meet to discuss important topics of interest or concern, share feelings, discuss opinions and decisions, and encourage responsible behaviors that are associated with good character.

faulty thinking: a thought process in which a person denies facts or believes erroneous facts.

fertile: to be capable of producing offspring.

fertile period: the days in a female's menstrual cycle during which sexual intercourse can lead to conception.

fertilization: the union of a sperm and ovum.

fetal alcohol syndrome (FAS): a birth defect characterized by growth retardation, facial abnormalities, and central nervous system dysfunction.

fibroadenoma: a lump that is formed when fluid becomes trapped in a lymph duct.

fibrocystic breast condition: a condition in which the cysts and fibroadenomas cause lumpiness and breast tenderness and discomfort.

fibroids: benign, slow-growing growths in the uterus.

fimbria: the fingerlike projections at the end of each oviduct.

first trimester: the first three months after conception.

fixer: a person who tries to fix other people's problems.

flunitrazepam (floo·nuh·TRAZ·I·pam) or **Rohypnol:** an odorless, colorless sedative drug.

follicle-stimulating hormone (FSH): a hormone secreted by the pituitary gland that causes follicles to grow.

foreskin or **prepuce:** a circular fold of loose skin that covers the glans of the penis in males who are not circumcised.

foster care: an arrangement in which another unrelated adult or adults assume temporary responsibility for a child or children.

fragile X syndrome: a genetic disorder caused by breakage or weakness at the end of the X chromosome and is associated with mental retardation.

fraternal twins: twins that develop from two separate ova that are fertilized by two different sperm.

frenulum: the underside of the penis where the glans is attached to the foreskin.

fusion inhibitors: a class of drugs that reduce the presence of HIV in persons with viral strains that are resistant to combination therapy.

g

gamete intrafallopian transfer (GIFT): a procedure in which sperm and ova are placed directly in a fallopian tube where fertilization takes place naturally.

gene: a unit of hereditary matter.

general anesthetic: an anesthetic used to eliminate pain in the whole body, creating temporary but complete unconsciousness.

genital herpes: a highly contagious STD that is caused by two forms of the herpes simplex virus (HSV), HSV-1 and HSV-2.

genital warts: dry, wart-like growths that are caused by the human papillomavirus (HPV).

glans: the tip of the clitoris or penis.

gonads: reproductive glands.

gonorrhea: an STD caused by the bacterium *Neisseria gonorrhoeae,* which infects the epithelial surfaces of the genitourinary tract of males and females.

good character: the use of self-control to act on responsible values.

Graafian follicle: an immature primary follicle that balloons into full maturity in the middle of a female's menstrual cycle.

grandparents' rights: the visitation rights with grandchildren courts have awarded grandparents when their son's or daughter's marriage ends.

granuloma inguinale: an STD caused by the bacterium *Calymmatobacterium granulomatis.*

h

hairy leukoplakia: an opportunistic infection characterized by the presence of white patches on the surface of the tongue.

harmful relationships: relationships that destroy self-respect, interfere with productivity and health, and include addictions and/or violence.

health history: a detailed description of a person's health status that includes information about diseases, disorders, and conditions as well as about healthful behaviors and risk behaviors in which a person engages.

health literacy: competence in critical thinking and problem-solving, responsible and productive citizenship, self-directed learning, and effective communication.

health literate person: a person who is skilled in critical thinking, responsible citizenship, self-directed learning, and effective communication.

healthful behaviors: actions a person chooses that promote health; prevent injury, illness, and premature death; and improve the quality of the environment.

healthful friendship: a balanced relationship that promotes mutual respect and healthful behavior.

healthful relationships: relationships that promote self-respect, encourage productivity and health, and are free of addictions and violence.

helper T cells or **CD4+T cells:** white blood cells that signal B cells to make antibodies.

hemoglobin: a substance that combines with oxygen in the blood.

herniation: the protrusion of the contents of one of the body's cavities through an abnormal opening in the cavity wall.

heroin: a drug that slows body functions such as heart rate and breathing and produces drowsiness and mood swings.

hidden anger: anger that is not recognized or is expressed in a harmful way and might result in inappropriate behavior and poor health.

highly active antirectroviral therapy or **HAART:** a combination of protease inhibitors and two reverse transcriptase inhibitors, such as AZT and ddI.

HIV negative: a term used to describe a person whose test results do not indicate the presence of HIV antibodies in the blood.

HIV positive: a term used to describe a person whose test results indicate the presence of HIV antibodies in the blood.

HIV status: a term used to describe whether or not a person has antibodies for HIV present in the blood.

home collection kit for HIV antibody testing: a kit that allows a person to take a blood test sample at home, place drops of blood on a test card, mail the card to a lab, and call a toll-free number for the results of the test.

homologous cells: cells that are identical.

honest talk: the straightforward sharing of feelings.

honesty: refusing to lie, steal, or deceive anyone.

hormone replacement therapy (HRT): the use of supplemental estrogen and progesterone to supplement or replace the decreasing amounts of hormones produced during menopause.

human immunodeficiency virus (HIV): a pathogen that destroys infection-fighting helper T cells in the body.

hymen: a thin membrane that stretches across the vaginal introitus.

hysterectomy: the surgical removal of the entire uterus and cervix, but not the ovaries.

i

ideal family: a family that has all the skills needed for loving, responsible relationships.

identical twins: twins that develop from a single ovum fertilized by a single sperm that divides after fertilization to form two zygotes.

I-message: a statement describing a specific behavior or event, the effect that behavior or event has on a person, and the feelings that result.

immune system: the body system that removes harmful substances from the blood and combats pathogens.

imperforate hymen: a condition in which there is no central perforation in the hymen.

inactive decision-making style: a habit in which a person fails to make choices, and this failure determines the outcome.

incest: the practice of sexual intercourse with a family member.

induced labor: a procedure that involves dilating the cervix and administering a hormone intravenously to initiate rhythmic uterine contractions and thus initiate labor.

infertile: to be incapable of producing offspring.

infertility: the inability to conceive a child after a year of unprotected sexual intercourse.

inguinal hernia: a hernia in which some of the intestine pushes through the inguinal canal into the scrotum.

injectable progestin: a shot of synthetic progesterone that is given every three months to change the natural menstrual cycle and to prevent ovulation.

injecting drug user: a person who injects illegal drugs into the body with syringes, needles, and other injection equipment.

inspiriting relationships: relationships that lift the spirit and contribute to a sense of well-being.

instant gratification: choosing an immediate reward regardless of potentially harmful effects.

integrity: acting on responsible values regardless of the consequences.

interception: a chemical or physical method of preventing implantation of the fertilized ovum in the uterine lining.

Interferon alfa-2a and **Interferon alfa-2b:** drugs to treat Kaposi's sarcoma (KS).

intimacy: a deep and meaningful kind of sharing between two people.

intracytoplasmic sperm injection: a technique for fertilizing an ovum through surgical means, in which an ovum is injected with one sperm to produce an embryo that can implant and grow in the uterus.

intrauterine insemination (IUI): the process of introducing semen into the vagina or uterus by sperm preparation techniques so that conception can occur.

in vitro fertilization (IVF): a procedure in which mature ova are removed from a female's hormone-stimulated ovary and placed in a lab dish to be fertilized by sperm.

isthmus: the constricted area of the uterus below the corpus.

j

joint custody: an arrangement in which both parents keep legal custody of a child or children.

juvenile delinquent: a young person who has antisocial behavior or refuses to follow the law.

k

Kaposi's sarcoma or **KS:** a type of cancer that is a common opportunistic infection in people who have AIDS.

l

labia majora: the outer lips, or heavy folds of skin, surrounding the opening of the vagina.

labia minora: two smaller lips, or folds of skin, located between the labia majora.

lactation: the production of milk in the mother's breasts following childbirth.

legal age of consent: the age when a person is legally able to give permission to have sex.

liar: a person who does not tell the truth.

life change: an event or situation that requires a person to make a readjustment.

life skills: healthful actions students learn and practice for the rest of their lives.

liking: affection and respect for another person.

local anesthetics: drugs used to eliminate pain in small specific areas for short periods of time.

lochia: a thick, dark red fluid consisting of blood, mucous, and tissue.

logical consequences discipline: a disciplinary technique in which the child is allowed the opportunity to experience the results of undesirable behavior so that he or she will want to change the undesirable behavior.

loneliness: an anxious, unpleasant, and painful feeling that results from having few friends or from being alienated.

low birth weight (LBW): a weight at birth that is less than 5.5 pounds (2.5 kilograms).

lumpectomy: the surgical removal of the lump itself and a small bit of surrounding tissue.

luteinizing hormone (LH): a hormone that stimulates a special group of testicular cells, the interstitial cells (cells of Leydig), to produce testosterone.

lymphadenopathy: the presence of swollen lymph glands.

lymphatic system: the part of the immune system that includes lymph vessels, lymphocytes, lymph nodes, the thymus gland, tonsils, and the spleen.

lymphocytes: white blood cells that circulate throughout the lymphatic system to help the body fight pathogens.

lymphogranuloma venereum or **LGV:** an STD caused by the *Chlamydia trachomatis* bacterium.

m

macrophages: white blood cells that surround and destroy pathogens.

mammogram: the image of the breast tissue created by mammography and is read by a qualified physician to detect breast lumps.

mammography: a highly sensitive X-ray screening test used to detect breast lumps and is a highly effective tool in the early detection of cancer.

manners: rules of conduct and behavior.

marijuana: a drug containing THC that impairs short term memory and causes mood changes.

marital conflict resolution: a process in which married partners identify their problems, agree upon solutions, and reestablish intimacy.

marital separation: the living apart of marriage partners.

mastodynia: the term used for the swelling and painful tenderness of the breasts accompanying the menstrual cycle.

media: the means of communication including television, radio, the movies, and newspapers that influence a consumer's information and decisions.

meiosis: a form of cell division that results in cells that have half the number of chromosomes that other body cells have.

menarche: the term used to describe the first menstrual bleeding.

menopause: the cessation of the monthly menstrual cycle pattern as part of the natural process accompanying aging.

menorrhagia: an abnormally heavy menstrual flow.

menstrual cycle: a rhythmic cycle of approximately one month in which hormonal levels fluctuate to prepare a female's body for the possibility of pregnancy.

menstrual phase: the third phase of the menstrual cycle, and during this phase the corpus luteum degenerates, the secretion of estrogen and progesterone sharply decreases, and the menstrual flow occurs.

menstruation: the process by which the lining of the uterus is expelled each month that an ovum is not fertilized.

mental disorder: a mental or emotional condition that makes it difficult for a person to live in a normal way.

microinsemination: the use of a micromanipulator to fertilize an ovum.

micromanipulation: the use of tiny instruments attached to a microscope to examine or work with minute objects.

miscarriage or **spontaneous abortion:** a natural expulsion of the embryo or fetus before it has reached a point of development at which it can survive outside the mother's body.

mitosis: the process of cell division in which a cell divides to form two "daughter" cells that have the same number of chromosomes as the "parent" cell.

mixed message: a message that conveys two different or double meanings.

Model for Using Resistance Skills, The: a list of suggested ways to resist negative peer pressure.

moderation: placing limits to avoid excess.

modified radical mastectomy: the surgical removal of the breast, some lymph nodes under the arm, the lining over the chest muscles, and sometimes part of the chest wall muscles.

molluscum contagiosum: an STD caused by a large virus of the pox group.

monogamous marriage: a marriage in which both people remain sexually faithful to one another.

mons pubis: a pad of fatty tissue that cover the front of the pubic bone and serve as a protective cushion for the female reproductive organs.

morning erection: an erection that results from waking up during rapid eye movement (REM) or dreaming stage of sleep or from having a full bladder.

motility: the ability of sperm to propel themselves to reach an ovum.

mucus method: a birth control method in which a female records changes in the mucous discharge from her vagina to predict her fertile period.

myometrium: the muscular layer of the uterus.

n

National Health Education Standards, The: standards that specify what students should know and be able to do regarding health.

needle aspiration: a procedure in which a needle is inserted into the lump to determine if it contains fluid.

negative peer pressure: influence from peers to behave in a way that is not responsible.

neglect: failure to provide proper care and guidance.

neutrophils: white blood cells produced in the tissue that lies in the hollow part of the bone known as bone marrow.

nipple: the tip of a female's breast.

nocturnal emissions or **wet dreams:** spontaneous ejaculations that occur during sleep.

nongonococcal urethritis (NGU): an STD caused by pathogens other than *Neisseria gonorrhoeae*, which cause an infection and inflammation of the urethra.

nonverbal communication: the use of actions instead of words to express a person's thoughts and feelings.

o

oligomenorrhea: scanty, irregular bleeding and/or a condition in which a female who is two years past menarche has one to six cycles a year.

one-sided friendship: a friendship in which one person does most of the giving and the other person does most of the receiving.

oophorectomy: the surgical removal of the ovaries.

opportunistic infection: an infection that develops in a person with a weakened immune system.

Orasure Western blot: a test for HIV in which a tissue sample is collected using a cotton swab between the gum and cheek.

orchitis: a condition that causes the seminiferous tubules to swell and lose their function, resulting in sterility.

orgasm: an explosive discharge of neuromuscular tensions at the peak of sexual response and is marked by rhythmic contractions and a sense of physiological and psychological release.

ovarian cancer: a disease in which there are cancerous cells and/or malignant tumors in one or both of the ovaries.

ovaries: two almond-shaped female sex glands that produce ova and secrete hormones.

ovulation: the release of a mature ovum by an ovary and occurs on or about the fourteenth day before the expected beginning of the next menstrual period.

p

Pap smear: a screening test for cervical cancer in which cells are scraped from the cervix and examined for abnormalities.

paracervical block: an injection of an anesthetic around the cervix in order to numb the cervix and uterus before delivery.

parent: to guide a child to responsible adulthood.

parent abuse: the harmful treatment of a parent.

partial mastectomy or **segmental mastectomy:** the surgical removal of the lump, some breast tissue, the lining over the chest muscles beneath the tumor, and some lymph nodes.

parturition: the technical name for the process of childbirth.

pathogen: a germ that causes disease.

pay back: to make restitution for harm to a person.

pay forward: to make restitution to society.

PCP or **angel dust:** a drug that changes the way people see things.

pediculosis pubis: infestation with *Phthirus pubis,* pubic or crab lice.

peer: a person of similar age or status.

peer pressure: the influence that people of similar age or status apply to effect certain behaviors.

pelvic examination: includes the following: an inspection of the external genitalia, a speculum examination, a bimanual vaginal examination, and a rectovaginal examination.

penis: the male organ of sexual pleasure, reproduction, and urination.

people pleaser: a person who constantly seeks the approval of others.

perfectionism: the compelling need to be accurate.

perimetrium: the outermost layer of the uterus.

perinatal transmission: the transfer of an infection to a baby during pregnancy, delivery, or breastfeeding.

perineum: the area between the vaginal opening and the anal opening.

perpetrator of violence: a person who commits a violent act.

philosophical intimacy: the sharing of beliefs and values.

physical abuse: harmful treatment that results in physical injury to the victim.

physical intimacy: the sharing of physical affection.

physical punishment: a disciplinary technique in which an act is used to teach a child not to repeat undesirable behavior.

Pneumocystis carinii **pneumonia** or **PCP:** a form of pneumonia that results from a weakened immune system.

polyps: long tubelike protrusions that grow from mucous membranes inside the uterus or along the cervix.

pornography: sexually explicit material that is sexually arousing and obscene.

positive peer pressure: influence from peers to behave in a responsible way.

postpartum period: the first several weeks after delivery.

poverty: a condition in which a person does not have the financial resources or other assistance to sustain a healthful life.

preejaculatory fluid: fluid that is secreted on the tip of the penis when a male becomes sexually aroused.

prejudice: suspicion, intolerance, or irrational hatred directed at an individual or group of people.

premenstrual syndrome (PMS): a combination of severe physical and psychological symptoms during the four premenstrual and first four menstrual days of the menstrual cycle.

preputial glands: a number of small glands located in the foreskin that secrete an oily, lubricating substance.

preterm baby or **premature baby:** a baby that is born before 37 weeks of pregnancy.

preterm birth or **premature birth:** birth before the 37th week of gestation.

preventive discipline: a disciplinary technique in which a parent explains correct behavior and the consequences of wrong behavior.

preventive mastectomy or **prophylactic mastectomy:** the surgical removal of one or both breasts.

primary amenorrhea: the absence of menarche more than four years after the female's body shows signs of pubertal development (usually age 15).

primary dysmenorrhea: caused by uterine contractions and usually starts within three years of menarche and lasts 1 to 2 days each month.

primary follicles: podlike structures that contain immature, or unripened, ova.

proactive decision-making style: a habit in which a person takes responsibility for his or her decisions and uses *The Responsible Decision-Making Model*™.

procrastinate: to postpone something until a future time.

progesterone: a hormone secreted by the corpus luteum to initiate the nourishing secretions for the ovum in the fallopian tube, to inhibit the contraction of the muscular layer of the uterus, to stimulate the breasts' ducts, and to thicken the uterine lining to receive the ovum.

progestin-only pill or **mini-pill:** a pill that contains progesterone, which changes the natural menstrual cycle and prevents ovulation.

projection: blaming others for actions or events for which they are not responsible.

proliferative phase or **estrogen phase:** the first phase of the menstrual cycle when FSH causes 15 to 20 primary follicles to grow in the ovaries and when ovulation occurs.

promise breaker: a person who is not reliable.

prostaglandins: hormonelike substances produced by the uterus and other body tissues.

prostate gland: a gland that produces an alkaline fluid that aids sperm longevity.

prostatitis: the inflammation of the prostate gland.

protease inhibitors: antiviral drugs that decrease the amount of HIV in the blood and increase the helper T cell count.

psychological intimacy: the sharing of needs, emotions, weaknesses, and strengths.

puberty: the stage of growth and development when both the male and female body become capable of producing offspring.

pudendal block: an injection of an anesthetic around the nerves on each side of the vagina in order to numb the perineum and vulva.

punishment: a penalty for wrongdoing.

q

quickening: the awareness of feeling the fetus move for the first time.

r

radical mastectomy: the surgical removal of the entire breast, the underlying pectoral muscle, and the lymph nodes.

radical prostatectomy: the surgical removal of the entire prostate gland.

rape: the threatened or actual use of physical force to get someone to have sex without giving consent.

Rape-Related Post-Traumatic Stress Disorder or **RR-PTSD:** a condition in which a rape survivor experiences emotional responses and physical symptoms over a period of time.

reactive decision-making style: a habit in which a person allows others to make his or her decisions.

receptive partner: the partner into whose rectum the penis is inserted during penile-anal intercourse.

recessive gene: a gene whose expression is overridden by the other gene.

recovery program: a group that supports members as they change their behavior to be responsible.

rectovaginal examination: a procedure in which a physician or nurse practitioner places one finger in the vagina and another finger in the rectum and presses together to check for rectal lesions.

regional anesthetics: drugs used to affect a larger area of the body, and although they are temporary, they might be longer lasting than local anesthetics.

rejection: the feeling of being unwelcome or unwanted.

relationships: the connections that people have with each other.

remarriage: a marriage in which a previously married person marries again.

remorse: the expression of regret for having caused harm.

reputation: the quality of a person's life as judged by others.

resiliency: the ability to adjust, recover, bounce back, and learn from difficult times.

resistance skills: skills that help a person say NO to an action or to leave a situation.

respect: liking that comes from having esteem for someone's admirable characteristics and responsible and caring actions.

responsibility: being accountable for what a person says or does.

responsible decision: a choice that leads to actions that promote health, protect safety, follow laws, show respect for self and others, follow the guidelines of parents and other responsible adults, and demonstrate good character.

Responsible Decision-Making Model™, *The:* a series of steps to follow to assure that the decisions a person makes result in actions that promote health, protect safety, follow laws, show respect for self and others, follow the guidelines of parents and of other responsible adults, and demonstrate good character.

responsible value: a belief that guides a person to act in responsible ways.

restitution: making good for loss or damage.

retrograde ejaculation: an ejaculation in which semen is expelled into the bladder instead of out of the penis.

Rh factor: an inherited protein substance in red blood cells.

Rh negative (Rh–): a lack of Rh in a person's blood.

Rh positive (Rh+): the presence of Rh in a person's blood.

risk behavior: an action a person chooses that threatens health and can cause disease, injury, and premature death.

risk factor: something that increases the likelihood of a negative outcome.

risk situation: a circumstance that threatens health and can cause disease, injury, and premature death.

root or **base:** the part of the penis that is attached to the pelvic area.

S

saddle block: an injection of an anesthetic into the spinal fluid that numbs only those parts of the body that would touch a horse's saddle.

scabies: a skin infestation by *Sarcoptes scabiei*, microscopic mites that are parasites.

scrotum: a sac-like pouch in the groin that has two basic functions: to hold the testes and to regulate the temperature of the testes.

second generation of STD pathogens: those pathogens that cause STDs that have mutated and are more difficult to treat and control.

second trimester: the fourth, fifth, and sixth months after conception.

secondary amenorrhea: the prolonged cessation (for 6 months or more) of menstrual bleeding after menarche has been established.

secondary dysmenorrhea: associated with pelvic inflammatory disease, endometriosis, or uterine fibroids and usually starts later in life.

secretory phase or **progestational phase:** the second phase of the menstrual cycle, and during this phase the corpus luteum secretes progesterone and estrogen to prepare a female's body for the implantation of a fertilized ovum.

sedative-hypnotic drugs: drugs that depress the central nervous system and are called "downers."

self-centered behavior: actions that fulfill personal needs with little regard for the needs of others.

self-control: the effort a person makes to regulate his or her behavior.

self-defense classes: classes that provide training in techniques to protect people from bodily harm.

self-defense devices: protective devices such as chemical sprays, whistles, personal sirens, cellular telephones, and reflective material that can be worn while jogging at dawn or at night.

self-defense posturing: the exhibiting of verbal and nonverbal behavior that indicates self-confidence and self-protection.

self-destructive behavior: behavior in which a person harms himself or herself.

self-discipline: the effort a person makes to follow through on what he or she says.

self-protection strategies: strategies that can be practiced to protect oneself and others from harm.

self-protections strategies for social situations: ways that people might reduce the risk of harm in social relationships.

self-respect: a high regard for oneself because one behaves in responsible ways.

self-respecting behavior: treating oneself in healthful and responsible ways.

seminal vesicles: two small glands at the ends of each vas deferens that secrete an alkaline fluid rich in fructose, a sugar nutrient that is a source of energy for sperm.

seminiferous tubules: a coiled network of tubes that fill the sections in each testis.

sex role: the way a person acts and the feelings and attitudes he or she has about being male or female.

sex-linked characteristics: genetic conditions that affect either the X or the Y chromosome, and therefore will only be expressed in one gender.

sexual abuse: sexual contact that is forced on a person.

sexual assault: a violent sexual attack on another person.

sexual feelings: feelings that result from a strong physical and emotional attraction to another person.

sexual fidelity or **sexual faithfulness:** a promise in a marriage to have sex only with one's marriage partner.

sexual harassment: unwanted sexual behavior that ranges from making sexual comments to forcing another person into unwanted sexual acts.

sexuality: the feelings and attitudes a person has about his or her body, sex role, and relationships.

Sexuality and Character Education Curriculum: a curriculum that teaches knowledge, behaviors, attitudes, and skills that promote committed family relationships, healthful relationships, good character, healthful sexuality, and reproductive health.

sexually transmitted diseases (STDs): diseases caused by pathogens that are transmitted from an infected person to an uninfected person during intimate sexual contact.

shigellosis: an STD caused by the *Shigella* bacterium.

shingles: an infection that produces a severely painful skin eruption of fluid-filled blisters.

sickle cell disease: a genetic disorder caused by an abnormal type of hemoglobin.

single custody: an arrangement in which one parent keeps legal custody of a child or children.

single-custody family: a family in which a child or children live with one parent who has custody.

smegma: a cheesy substance that forms under the foreskin.

social skills: the abilities that a person uses to interact effectively with other people.

spermatogenesis: sperm production, which takes place in the seminiferous tubules in the testes.

spermatogonium: the earliest form in the development of mature sperm cells.

spermicide: a foam, cream, jelly, film, or suppository that forms a barrier and contains a chemical that might kill some sperm.

spinal anesthetic: an injection of an anesthetic administered into the spinal fluid surrounding the lower spinal cord.

spirit-relationship continuum: a continuum that shows the range of relationships with dispiriting relationships at one end and inspiriting relationships at the other end.

spouse abuse: the harmful treatment of a husband or wife.

stalking: harassing someone with the intent to threaten or harm that person.

sterility: the inability to produce offspring.

stigma: a small dot or nipplelike protrusion that develops on the surface of the Graafian follicle.

subdermal implants: flexible plastic tubes that are inserted under the skin in the upper arm and that release progestin.

survivor of violence: a person who was harmed by violence, has participated in recovery to heal from its emotional effects, and has adopted self-protection strategies.

syphilis: an STD caused by the bacterium *Treponema pallidum*, which penetrates mucous membranes and abrasions in the skin and causes lesions that might involve any organ or tissue.

t

television addiction: the compelling need to watch television.

testes: the two male reproductive glands inside the scrotum that secrete the male hormone testosterone and produce sperm.

testicular self-examination (TSE): observation and palpation of the testicles to locate any mass or tenderness.

testosterone: the male hormone that is released into the bloodstream from the testes and causes male secondary sex characteristics to develop during puberty.

theoretical effectiveness: the percentage that tells how well the birth control method works for adult users if it is used every time, always used in the correct way, and used by adults who have no preexisting conditions that reduce how well it works.

third trimester: the seventh, eighth, and ninth months after conception.

thrush: an overgrowth of the yeast *Candida* in the mouth, esophagus, and vagina.

thyroid gland: an endocrine gland located just below the larynx (voice box) and in front and to the side of the trachea (windpipe).

total mastectomy or **simple mastectomy:** the surgical removal of the entire breast and possibly a few lymph nodes.

toxemia or **preeclampsia:** a condition characterized by high blood pressure, edema, the presence of protein in the urine, and rapid weight gain during pregnancy.

toxemia of pregnancy: a disorder of pregnancy characterized by high blood pressure, tissue swelling, and protein in the urine.

toxic shock syndrome (TSS): a rare, serious disease caused by certain toxin-producing strains of *Staphylococcus aureus* bacterium.

traditional marriage: an emotional, spiritual, and legal commitment a male and a female make to one another.

transition: the end of Stage 1.

transrectal ultrasonography: a test in which a probe inserted into the rectum sends sound waves that create a picture or sonogram on a screen.

transverse birth position: a position in which the baby's shoulder, arm, or hand is presented first.

trichomoniasis: an STD caused by the parasitic protozoan *Trichomonas*, which might infect the vagina, urethra, or prostate gland.

triglycerides: substances stored in fat tissue and are associated with a risk of cardiovascular diseases.

trimester: one of three three-month periods during a human pregnancy.

tubal ligation: a surgical procedure in which the fallopian tubes are closed off, cauterized, or cut.

tuberculosis: a contagious, potentially fatal, bacterial infection of the lungs.

Turner's syndrome: a genetic disorder caused by the lack of or defectiveness of the X chromosome in one or more cells and affects females only.

U

ultrasound: a diagnostic technique that uses sound waves to create pictures of internal body structures.

universal precautions: steps taken to prevent the spread of disease by treating all human blood and certain body fluids as if they contained HIV, hepatitis B virus (HBV), and other pathogens.

unnecessary risk: a chance that is not worth taking after the possible outcomes are considered.

urethra: a tubelike passageway that extends from the urinary bladder to the outside tip of the penis in the male or the vaginal opening in the female and serves as a passageway for semen in the male and urine in the male and the female.

urinalysis: a chemical or microscopic examination of the urine collected under special conditions.

uterus: the organ that prepares each month to receive a fertilized ovum, to support the fertilized ovum during pregnancy, and to contract during childbirth to help with delivery.

V

vagina: a muscular passageway that lies between the bladder and the rectum, and it serves as the female organ of intercourse, the birth canal, and the passageway for the menstrual flow and the arriving sperm.

vaginal cancer: a disease in which cancerous cells and/or malignant tumors are present in the vagina.

vaginal opening: the opening from the vagina to the outside of the body.

vaginitis: an irritation or inflammation of the vagina usually accompanied by a discharge.

value: a standard or belief.

vas deferens: two long, thin cords that extend from the epididymis in the scrotum, up through the inguinal canal, and into the abdomen.

vasectomy: a surgical procedure in which the vas deferens are cut, tied, or cauterized.

V-Chip: a small electronic device that can be installed in a television set to block transmission of television programs.

vestibule: the space between the labia minora into which open the urethra, the vagina, and the ducts of the Bartholin's glands.

victim of violence: a person who has been harmed by violence.

violence: the use of physical force to injure, damage, or destroy oneself, others, or property.

violent relationship: a relationship that harms another person physically, mentally, and/or emotionally.

viral hepatitis: an inflammatory infection of the liver caused by viruses.

visitation rights: guidelines set for the visitation of children by the parent who does not have custody.

vulva: the external organs of the female reproductive system.

W

wasting syndrome: an unexplained loss in body weight of more than ten percent of the total body weight.

Western blot: a blood test used to check for antibodies for HIV and to confirm an ELISA test.

wisdom: good judgment and intelligence in knowing what is responsible and appropriate.

withdrawal: the removal of the penis from the vagina before ejaculation of semen occurs.

work ethic: an attitude of discipline, motivation, and commitment toward tasks.

Y

you-message: a statement that blames or shames another person.

Z

zygote: the cell that forms from the fertilized ovum.

zygote intrafallopian transfer (ZIFT): a combination of IVF and GIFT.

Index

　　　　© 2001 Everyday Learning Corporation

660